9E

TRANSPORTATION
A GLOBAL SUPPLY CHAIN PERSPECTIVE

NOVACK/GIBSON/SUZUKI/COYLE

CENGAGE

Australia • Brazil • Mexico • Singapore • United Kingdom • United States

Transportation: A Global Supply Chain Perspective, Ninth Edition
Robert A. Novack, Brian J. Gibson, Yoshinori Suzuki and John J. Coyle

Senior Vice President, Higher Ed Product, Content, and Market Development: Mike Schenk

Product Director: To provide

Product Manager: Aaron Arnsparger

Content Developer: Tara Slagle, MPS

Product Assistant: Renee Schnee

Sr. Marketing Manager: Nate Anderson

Manufacturing Planner: Ron Montgomery

Intellectual Property
   Analyst: Terina Bradley
   Project Manager: Nick Barrow

Project Management and Compostion: SPi Global

Senior Art Director: Michelle Kunkler

Cover Designer: Laura Brown

Cover Image Credit: Travel mania/ Shutterstock.com

For product information and technology assistance, contact us at **Cengage Customer & Sales Support, 1-800-354-9706.**

For permission to use material from this text or product, submit all requests online at **www.cengage.com/permissions.** Further permissions questions can be emailed to **permissionrequest@cengage.com.**

Library of Congress Control Number: 2017962612
ISBN: 978-1-337-40664-2

Cengage
20 Channel Center Street
Boston, MA 02210
USA

Cengage is a leading provider of customized learning solutions with employees residing in nearly 40 different countries and sales in more than 125 countries around the world. Find your local representative at **www.cengage.com.**

Cengage products are represented in Canada by Nelson Education, Ltd.

To learn more about Cengage platforms and services, visit **www.cengage.com.**

To register or access your online learning solution or purchase materials for your course, visit **www.cengagebrain.com.**

Printed in the United States of America
Print Number: 03   Print Year: 2018

A very special note of thanks and appreciation is due to our families. Bob Novack would like to thank his wife Judith and their children Tom and his wife Meghan, Elizabeth and her husband Paul, and Alex. Brian Gibson would like to recognize his wife Marcia and son Andy. Yoshi Suzuki would like to thank his wife Kazuko and their children Takeshi and Mia. John Coyle would like to thank his wife Barbara, their children John and Susan, and their grandchildren Lauren, Matthew, Elizabeth Kate, Emily, Ben, Cathryn, and Zachary. Special mention should be made in reference to Dr. Edward J. Bardi to express our deep appreciation of his many contributions not only to the continuing development of this text but also to the supply chain management text.

Brief Contents

Contents

Part II

Preface

Transportation is the critical link in successful supply chains. It is a key facilitator of global economic development, quality of life improvement, and enterprise success. Effective transportation processes ensure the rapid flow of essential goods across complex global supply chains. Efficient transportation operations keep delivery costs in check to ensure that products are affordable in multiple markets.

Transportation professionals are tasked with balancing these effectiveness and efficiency goals. They must also manage complex transportation networks and minimize disruptions of cross-border product flows to meet the ever-increasing service demands of the 21st century customer. While these are not easy tasks, high-quality work by dedicated transportation professionals is essential for global trade to thrive.

In this book, *Transportation: A Global Supply Chain Perspective*, Ninth Edition, we continue to focus on the widespread impact of commercial transportation on worldwide commerce. We believe that the contents of this book will help future transportation professionals prepare for successful careers in this dynamic field. Our text follows the format of the previous edition with three sections and thirteen chapters. Substantive additions and revisions have been made to enhance the content and organization. In particular, the critical role of technology in global transportation receives special attention in this edition.

Part I provides the foundation for the overall text. Chapter 1 explores the nature, importance, and critical issues in the global economy, which are important to understand for the current and future transportation systems. Chapter 2 provides the economic foundation and rationale for the role of transportation as well as its political and social importance. Chapter 3 highlights the expanding role of technology in transportation, addressing both software and equipment innovations that drive greater service and lower costs. Chapter 4 offers a discussion of transportation costing and pricing in a market-based economy.

Part II provides an overview of the major transportation alternatives available to individual and organizational users. Chapters 5 through 8 discuss and examine the key features and issues of the five basic modes of transportation, namely, motor (5), rail (6), airline (7), water and pipeline (8). Each of the basic modes offers inherent advantages for shippers of particular commodities or locations that need to be appreciated and understood to gain the economic benefits they offer. The dynamic market environment that exists in many economies demands continuous improvement of modal capabilities if they are to remain relevant.

The chapters in Part III cover a variety of important issues related to the successful management of transportation flows. Each of the five chapters in this section have been updated and revised to further improve their value to the readers. Chapter 9 supplements the information provided in Part II with a detailed discussion of logistics service providers that support the transportation industry. These organizations improve the efficiency, effectiveness, and execution of global supply chain flows. Chapter 10 discusses the topic of risk management, a key concern for many organizations because of the increasing threat of supply chain disruptions in the global economy. Strategies, methods, and outcomes for risk management are explored as well as overall security enhancement. Chapter 11 provides an in-depth discussion of the planning and execution of global transportation with emphasis on trade facilitation, product flows, and information sharing. Chapter 12

APICS

This textbook is recommended by APICS® as a valuable study resource for the Certified in Logistics, Transportation, and Distribution professional certification program. For details go to http://www.apics.org/credentials-education/credentials/cltd.

covers the all-important role of government policy, regulation, and promotion in fostering a strong transportation network. Finally, Chapter 13 explores some of the major challenges for transportation in the 21st century, namely, infrastructure funding needs, talent management gaps, environmental sustainability, and fuel management. Each issue threatens to disrupt transportation flows, reduce competitiveness, and increase costs if not managed proactively.

Overall, we are convinced that transportation is a critical engine for business growth and societal advancement, but is often taken for granted until a crisis arises. As stated previously, it may be the most important industry for all economies regardless of their stage of development. Such recognition needs to be accorded to transportation in the future.

Features

1. Learning objectives in the beginning of each chapter provide students with an overall perspective of chapter material and serve to establish a baseline for a working knowledge of the topics that follow.
2. Transportation Profile boxes are the opening vignettes at the beginning of each chapter that introduce students to the chapter's topics through familiar, real-world examples.
3. On the Line features are applied, concrete examples that provide students with hands-on managerial experience of the chapter topics.
4. Transportation Technology boxes help students relate technological developments to transportation management concepts.
5. Global Perspectives boxes highlight the activities and importance of transportation outside of the United States.
6. End-of-chapter Summaries and Study Questions reinforce material presented in each chapter.
7. Short cases at the end of each chapter build on what students have learned. Questions that follow the cases sharpen critical thinking skills.

Ancillaries

1. The *Instructor's Manual* includes chapter outlines, answers to end-of-chapter study questions, commentary on end-of-chapter short cases, and teaching tips.
2. A convenient *Test Bank* offers a variety of multiple-choice, short-answer, and essay questions for each chapter.
3. *PowerPoint slides* cover the main chapter topics and contain figures from the main text.
4. The book companion site (www.cengagebrain.com) provides additional resources for students and instructors. Appendix A, Selected Transportation Publications, and Appendix B, Transportation-Related Associations, can be found on the companion site. The Instructor's Manual and PowerPoint files are downloadable from the site for instructors.

Acknowledgments

The authors are indebted to many individuals at our respective academic institutions as well as other individuals with whom we have had contact in a variety of venues. Our university students and our executive program students have provided an important sounding board for the many concepts, techniques, metrics, and strategies presented in the book. Our faculty and corporate colleagues have provided invaluable insights and appropriate criticism of our ideas. Some individuals deserve special consideration: Ryan Wilson (Penn State), Ms. Tracie Shannon (Penn State), and Kusumal Ruamsook (Penn State). The authors would also like to thank the following fellow faculty members for their insightful contributions to several chapters in this text: John C. Spychalski, Professor Emeritus of Supply Chain Management (Penn State); and Joe Hanna, Associate Dean and Professor of Supply Chain Management (Auburn). Finally, we would like to thank Michael Levans, Group Editorial Director of Logistics Management magazine for his support in allowing us to use material from his publication in this text.

Robert A. Novack is currently an Associate Professor of Supply Chain Management and Associate Director in the Center for Supply Chain Research at Penn State. Dr. Novack worked in operations management and planning for the Yellow Freight Corporation and in planning and operations for the Drackett Company. He received his bachelor's and MBA degrees from Penn State and a PhD from the University of Tennessee in Knoxville. Dr. Novack has numerous articles published in the *Journal of Business Logistics*, the *Transportation Journal*, and the *International Journal of Physical Distribution and Logistics Management*. He is also the coauthor of three textbooks: *Creating Logistics Value: Themes for the Future*, *Supply Chain Management: A Logistics Perspective* (8e), and *Transportation*. He is on the editorial review board for the *Journal of Business Logistics* and is an area editor for the *Journal of Supply Chain Management*. Dr. Novack is very active in the Council for Supply Chain Management Professionals, having served as overall program chair for the annual conference, as a track chair, and as a session speaker. In addition, he has served on numerous committees with this organization. Dr. Novack holds the CTL designation from the American Society of Transportation and Logistics. His current research interest is on the development and use of metrics in managing supply chains. In 2009, he received the Atherton Teaching Award from Penn State, the highest award given for teaching at that university.

Brian J. Gibson is the Wilson Family Professor of Supply Chain Management and Executive Director of the Center for Supply Chain Innovation at Auburn University. Previously, he served on the faculty of Georgia Southern University and as director of the Southern Center for Logistics and Intermodal Transportation. Dr. Gibson also served as a logistics manager for two major retailers. He is an accomplished faculty member who has received multiple awards for outstanding teaching, research, and outreach. Dr. Gibson has coauthored numerous articles in the *Journal of Business Logistics*, *Supply Chain Management Review*, *International Journal of Logistics Management*, and other leading industry publications. He is also the coauthor of three textbooks: *Supply Chain Management: A Logistics Perspective* (10e), *The Definitive Guide to Integrated Supply Chain Management*, and *Transportation*. He is actively engaged in executive education, seminar development, and consulting with leading organizations. Dr. Gibson currently serves as Secretary and Treasurer for the Council for Supply Chain Management Professionals, Education Advisor for the National Shippers Strategic Transportation Council, and Supply Chain Steering Committee Member for the Retail Industry Leaders Association. Dr. Gibson earned a BSBA from Central Michigan University, an MBA from Wayne State University, and a PhD in logistics and transportation from the University of Tennessee.

Yoshinori Suzuki is Dean's Professor of Supply Chain Management and associate chair of the Department of Supply Chain and Information Systems at the College of Business, Iowa State University. He holds a BS degree in Business and Economics from Sophia University (Tokyo Japan), an MBA degree in Marketing from New York University Stern School of Business, and a PhD degree in Business Logistics from The Pennsylvania State University Smeal College of Business. His research interest is in mathematical modeling of logistics and transportation problems. During his 20-year academic career, he has conducted numerous research projects with both private and public organizations, which include Ruan Transportation Management Systems, GROWMARK Inc., C.H. Robinson, Renewable Energy Group (REG), Des Moines International Airport, and

National Aeronautics and Space Administration (NASA). His recent research work has appeared in journals such as *Computers & Industrial Engineering, Transportation Research* (various parts), *Journal of Transportation Engineering, Naval Research Logistics, Decision Sciences, Decision Support Systems, Journal of Business Logistics, International Journal of Production Economics, Transportation Journal, Journal of the Transportation Research Forum,* and *International Journal of Physical Distribution and Logistics Management.* He has several years of industry experience. His work experience includes sales, logistics management, and transportation management duties. Dr. Suzuki is currently serving as the co-editor-in-chief of *Transportation Journal.*

John J. Coyle is director of corporate relations for the Center for Supply Chain Research (CSCR) and professor emeritus of Logistics and Supply Chain Management in the Smeal College of Business at Penn State University. He holds a BS and an MS from Penn State and earned his doctorate from Indiana University in Bloomington, Indiana, where he was a U.S. Steel Fellow. He joined the Penn State faculty in 1961 and attained the rank of full professor in 1967. In addition to his teaching responsibilities, he served in a number of administrative positions, including chairman of the Department of Business Logistics, faculty director and assistant dean for Undergraduate Programs, senior associate dean, and executive director of the CSCR. He also played a major role in the development of Smeal's Executive Education Programs. At the university level, he served as chairman of the Faculty Senate, Special Assistant for Strategic Planning to two university presidents (Jordan and Thomas). He also served as Penn State's faculty representative to the NCAA for 30 years and to the Big Ten for 10 years.

Dr. Coyle was the editor of the *Journal of Business Logistics* from 1990 to 1996. He has authored or coauthored 23 books or monographs and 38 articles in reputable professional journals. He has received 14 awards at Penn State for teaching excellence and/or advising. Former students and friends have endowed a scholarship fund and two Smeal Professorships in his honor. He received the Council of Logistics Management's Distinguished Service Award in 1991; Penn State's Continuing/Distance Education Award for Academic Excellence in 1994; the Eccles Medal for his contributions to the U.S. Department of Defense and the Lion's Paw Medal from Penn State for Distinguished Service, both in 2004. Dr. Coyle currently serves on the board of three logistics and supply chain companies.

PART I

The major driving forces of change for supply chains during the first two decades of the 21st century have been globalization and technology. That is not to say that there are not additional exogenous factors impacting supply chains and necessitating changes in managerial tactics and/or strategies because there have been. However, none have been of the magnitude of globalization and technology. Interestingly, they were major forces in the last two decades of the 20th century as was cited in previous editions of this text. The fact that they continue to have such an impact is certainly worth noting, but one must also appreciate the depth and scope of these two external forces not only on supply chains but also upon consumer and organizational behavior.

Transportation is an important part of supply chain management that has been described figuratively previously as the "glue" that holds the supply chain together and is a key enabler for important customer-oriented strategies such as overnight or same-day delivery. Transportation is often the final phase or process to touch the customer and may have a lasting impact on the success of the transaction. This is the micro dimension, but on a macro level transportation can be viewed as the "life blood" of global supply chains, and it has been argued that efficient and effective transportation is the most important business for a country or region and the cornerstone of a modern economy.

Global transportation systems have been seriously challenged in the 21st century by high fuel costs, changing capacity, and regulation. In addition, the transportation infrastructure, namely seaports, airports, highways, and so on, is not sufficient to accommodate the flow of global commerce in many countries thus stymying the economic progress of the region. Many parts of the infrastructure require government or public funding because of the different users. The public coffers are frequently financially strained because of the many alternative demands for these somewhat limited resources. Transportation infrastructure has to "compete" for an allocation of public funds, and the benefits, while real, are more long run in terms of outcome and value. Consequently, such needed resources might not be allocated in a timely manner. This is the dilemma of the 21st century. Transportation and the related logistics systems are a necessary requirement for all economies, developed and underdeveloped, but the public investment in social capital necessary to not only improve but also sustain the infrastructure has not been forthcoming in many countries. Hopefully, one of the outcomes of this text will be a better understanding and appreciation for the criticality of efficient and effective transportation systems for economic development and social welfare.

Part I will provide an overview and foundation for the role and importance of improved transportation from a micro and macro perspective in global supply chains. The discussion will cover economic and managerial dimensions of transportation in the global economy. Part I is designed to provide the framework for the analysis and discussion in the following sections of the book.

Chapter 1 examines the nature, importance, and critical issues in the global economy, which are important to understand for the current and future transportation systems, that will provide the needed service for the diverse requirements of the various regions and countries. This chapter will also discuss the special nature of transportation demand and how transportation adds value to products. There is also an overview of the concept of supply chain management and the important role of transportation in supply chains of various organizations.

Chapter 2 examines the role of transportation from a macro and micro perspective. The chapter adds to the discussion in Chapter 1 but explores more broadly the special significance of improved transportation systems. The analysis includes not only the economic impact but also the political and social impact of transportation. Current and historical perspectives are provided in the discussion to help the reader appreciate and better understand the contribution of improved transportation in an economy. The discussion also examines the impact of improved transportation upon land values and prices of products and services.

Chapter 3 is new and provides an overview of the technology and systems currently in use and planned for execution in the transportation sector. Special attention is given to the technology used in the various modes, including On-Board Recorders (OBRs) and driverless vehicles in the motor carrier industry and Positive Train Control (PTC) in the railroad industry. The discussion also emphasizes the impact the various technologies have had on transportation efficiency.

Chapter 4 extends the discussion of costing and pricing introduced in Chapters 1 and 2. Given the importance of transportation on a micro and macro level to the cost and value of products and services, costing and pricing deserves a more detailed examination. There are unique dimensions to transportation services in general and between the basic modes that need to be understood by managers and public officials. Chapter 4 provides an analysis of the differences and unique dimensions of transportation services.

1

GLOBAL SUPPLY CHAINS: THE ROLE AND IMPORTANCE OF TRANSPORTATION

Learning Objectives

After reading this chapter, you should be able to do the following:

> Appreciate why efficient transportation systems are so critical to advance the growth and development of regions and countries, and how they contribute to social and political systems as well as national defense

> Discuss the importance of transportation to globalization and how it contributes to the effective flow of commerce among close and distant regions

> Understand how global supply chains can contribute to the competitive position of countries and allow them to penetrate global markets

> Appreciate the dynamic nature of the global economy, which can impact and change the competitive position of a region or country in a relatively short period of time

> Explain the underlying economic basis for international exchange of goods and services for the overall benefit of two or more countries or regions and gain some perspective on the volume and overall importance of the more advanced countries of the world

> Discuss the size and age distribution of the population and the growth rate of the major countries of the world and understand how the size of the population can impact a country positively or negatively

> Understand the challenges and opportunities associated with the worldwide growth in urbanization and why there has been such a major shift from rural to urban areas

> Appreciate the importance and impact of land and resources to the economic advancement and development of the various countries of the world and how they can be exploited to their advantage

> Explain why technology has become such an important ingredient for the economic progress of companies and countries in today's global economy and understand the need for and types of technology

> Discuss the overall characteristics and importance of globalization and supply chains in the highly competitive world economies of the 21st century

TRANSPORTATION **PROFILE**

Critical Role of Transportation in Global Economy

Transportation is one of the most important tools or methods that developing societies or countries use to advance economically, politically, and socially. It impacts every phase and facet of our existence. Transportation is probably the most important industry in any country or in the global economy. Without it, we could not operate a grocery store or run a factory. The more complex or developed a country is, the more indispensable an efficient and effective transportation system is for continued survival and growth.

In advanced societies, transportation systems are so well developed that most citizens do not think about or realize the many benefits that accrue from good transportation systems. They use transportation everyday directly or indirectly. It provides the thoroughfare for commerce, the means of travel locally or for longer distances, and the assistance for many other important aspects of their lives. People seldom stop to think how restricted their lives would be without good transportation. However, if one travels to an underdeveloped country, it is obvious that the lack of good transportation is inhibiting their economic prosperity and personal convenience. The current physical decay of the highway infrastructure in the United States and the lack of investment for improvement is a critical concern to many private and public organizations because of its importance to continued economic growth and global expansion.

The development of the global economy has increased the criticality of transportation for economic, political, and national defense purposes. Globalization has brought many benefits to countries throughout the world, but we are much more interdependent and at risk when some calamity occurs in another part of the world that can interrupt supply of raw materials or finished products and/or shut down a market for domestic products. Efficient and effective transportation can help to mitigate the impact, for example, of a natural disaster such as a hurricane, typhoon, or flood by providing products and services from alternate sources and access to other markets quickly and efficiently.

The importance of transportation cannot be overemphasized. It is a necessary ingredient for the progress and well-being of all citizens. An appreciation and understanding of its historical and economic role and significance, as well its political and social significance, is a requisite for managers in any organization and other interested parties. An appreciation of this tenet will be an important part of the discussion in this text.

Introduction

In previous editions of this text, transportation was referred to as the "glue" that holds the supply chain together and an enabler of the underlying tactics and strategies that have catapulted supply chain management to the level of acceptance, which it now enjoys in many organizations, both private and public. For example, transportation management systems technology along with complimentary software is used by many organizations to improve logistics and supply chain efficiency, effectiveness, and execution. Transportation has moved from playing a reactive or supporting role to a role that is more proactive and enabling. In other words, transportation has become much more strategic for organizations in determining their ability to compete in the growing and complex global marketplace.

The global marketplace is also changing on a continuing basis, that is, it has become very dynamic, and is buffeted by economic, political, social, and natural forces, which can impact a country or region negatively or positively in the short or long run. For example, the high cost of fuel has impacted the rates charged by transportation service providers, which in turn impacts the distance that it is economically feasible to transport goods. The cost of labor can change over time to the disadvantage of some geographic areas and benefit others. For example, the labor cost advantage that China enjoyed, along with low rates for ocean carrier movement, had a positive impact on their ability to sell products on a global basis. These advantages have diminished somewhat allowing other countries to develop an improved competitive position because of market proximity, labor costs, or other factors. These changes in turn impact global supply chains and their associated flow of goods.

In this chapter, the initial focus will be upon developing an overview of the flow of global commerce and trade overtime on a worldwide basis not only to understand the importance and magnitude of global supply chain flows but also to gain some perspective on important changes that have occurred. A variety of economic data will be used to illustrate the impact of the overall changes that have occurred. The next section will examine the underlying rationale and economics of global flows of goods and services. In other words, the "why" of global flows will be discussed to understand the advantages of international trade to countries and consumers in contrast to the "what" of the first section of this chapter. The third section will provide additional insights into the factors that can contribute to the economic advancement and development of countries. The final section of the chapter will provide an overview of the supply chain concept including its development, key characteristics, and major activities.

Global Supply Chain Flows

Early in the 21st century, frequent reference was made to acronyms such as the BRIC (Brazil, Russia, India, and China) or VISTA (Vietnam, Indonesia, South Africa, Turkey, and Argentina) countries. The former were identified as the top emerging economies and the latter as those developing at a fast pace. The development of the BRIC and VISTA countries was seen an indication of opportunities for "sourcing" of materials, products, and services and the identification of potential markets for the more developed economies such as the United States, the European Union (EU), and Japan. Also, they were a sign of a more economic balance in the world and continued growth. Consequently, one noted author[1] declared that the world was really flat because of the developing economies. Interestingly, there have been some economic shifts already with respect to these countries, and the future importance of some of the VISTA countries is not clear. For example, South Africa has been added to the first group, BRICS, by some economic pundits. Nevertheless, all of this supports the observation made earlier about the dynamic and competitive nature of world markets. An important caveat is the potential for disruption caused by political instability, associated acts of terrorism, and military actions, which can cause a major disruption in global trade flows.

Figure 1-1 and Table 1-1 indicate export trade flows of merchandise from various country or region origins. In Figure 1-1, the size of the circle indicates the importance and volume of exports on a worldwide basis. It is interesting to note the large number of exporting countries and the big differences in the volume. Table 1-1 shows the value of world exports in U.S. dollars. China is clearly number one for exports of merchandise and the United States is second, but what may be surprising is Germany being third. They are relatively close to the United States in terms of the value of their exports. If we added up the value of exports for all the EU countries, it would by far exceed the United States (about double). The EU also compares favorably to the Asian block of countries in terms of exports.

Figure 1-2 and Table 1-2 show the import trade flows of merchandise into various countries and regions. Figure 1-2 is interesting because it is a visual representation of the magnitude of the value of imports and provides some perspective of the differences in the world markets. In terms of regions, Exhibit 1-2 indicates that Asia is the largest importing region and is followed by the EU. North America is third in terms of the value of imports. Among individual countries, the United States is the largest importer, followed by China and then Germany.

A comparison of relative shares of imports and exports provides some additional perspectives. China's share of global exports in terms of value is 13.8 percent and their share of imports is 10.1 percent making them a net exporter, whereas the United States by comparison is a net importer with 9.1 percent of merchandise exports and 13.8 percent of the global imports. Germany is also a net exporter with exports representing 8.1 percent of the global

FIGURE 1-1 Export–Trade Flows of Merchandise

Economy	Million US Dollars
China	2,209,626.00
United States	1,578,971.70
Germany	1,452,795.40
Japan	715,097.20
Netherlands	663,524.30
France	579,646.90
Korea, Republic of	559,632.00
United Kingdom	541,348.00
Hong Kong, China	535,546.00
Russian Federation	523,327.00
Italy	517,673.30
Belgium	468,817.80

FIGURE 1-2   Import–Trade Flows of Merchandise

Economy	Million US Dollars
United States	2,329,059.80
China	1,949,992.00
Germany	1,188,883.80
Japan	833,166.10
France	681,016.00
United Kingdom	655,318.60
Hong Kong, China	622,276.40
Netherlands	589,768.10
Korea, Republic of	515,586.00
Italy	477,391.50
Canada	474,270.00
India	466,042.10
Belgium	450,706.00

total with imports of 6.3 percent of the total. There are economic implications associated with these differences, but the merchandise flows do not provide a complete economic picture because the value of services imported and exported are also important for the balance of payments of individual countries. However, the focus of this text is obviously upon merchandise flows.

The importance of the so-called developed countries/economies is evident from the information presented earlier, but additional insight can be gained by summarizing the impact of the top countries in each category (see Tables 1-1 and 1-2). In 2015, the top 30 exporting countries accounted for 84 percent of the world's exports, but the top three (China, United States, and Germany) accounted for about 31 percent of the total exports. The top 30 importing countries accounted for 82.1 percent of the total imports, but the top three (United States, China, and Germany) accounted for 30.1 percent of the total imports. The data presented in Tables 1-1 and 1-2 substantiate the observation about the important role of developed economies made earlier.

Additional insight can be gained by examining the growth in the volume of global trade over the course of the last 47 years (see Table 1-3). The 30-year growth from 1970 to 1999 was steady. In recent years, especially the period from 2000 to the present, the growth has been spectacular, except for a decline in export growth in 2001 and the global recession in 2009. The total volume of trade more than doubled, led by China, Japan, the United States, and the EU. A number of factors came into play to explain the increased growth rate including trade agreements among countries along with a reduction in tariffs, which promoted global trade and its associated benefits. There was also greater acceptance of importing finished products that were manufactured in foreign countries.

Traditionally, many countries imported raw materials that were scarce or not available in the importing country, and they then produced finished products mostly for domestic consumption. The raw materials were much lower in value than the finished products that contributed to the imbalance of trade among developing and developed economies.

Table 1-1	Top 30 Exporters, 2015			
RANK	**EXPORTERS**	**VALUE**	**SHARE**	**ANNUAL % CHANGE**
1	China	2,275	13.8	−3
2	United States	1,505	9.1	−7
3	Germany	1,329	8.1	−11
4	Japan	625	3.8	−9
5	Netherlands	567	3.4	−16
6	Korea, Republic of	527	3.2	−8
7	Hong Kong, China	511	3.1	−3
8	France	506	3.1	−13
9	United Kingdom	460	2.8	−9
10	Italy	459	2.8	−13
11	Canada	408	2.5	−14
12	Belgium	398	2.4	−16
13	Mexico	381	2.3	−4
14	Singapore	351	2.1	−14
15	Russian Federation	340	2.1	−32
16	Switzerland	290	1.8	−7
17	Chinese Taipei	285	1.7	−11
18	Spain	282	1.7	−13
19	India	267	1.6	−17
20	United Arab Emirates	265	1.6	−29
21	Thailand	214	1.3	−6
22	Saudi Arabia, Kingdom of	202	1.2	−41
23	Malaysia	200	1.2	−15
24	Poland	198	1.2	−10
25	Brazil	191	1.2	−15
26	Australia	188	1.1	−22
27	Vietnam	162	1.0	8
28	Czech Republic	158	1.0	−10
29	Austria	152	0.9	−15
30	Indonesia	150	0.9	−15
	World	16,482	100.0	−

Source: World Trade Organization.

However, that situation has changed, countries that previously imported materials for domestic production and consumption are exporting more finished products while so-called underdeveloped countries are participating more in manufacturing, especially of parts of a finished product. A very good example is the automobile industry. The typical automobile of today has over 10,000 parts, which can be manufactured in many different countries. Furthermore, the individual parts may be exported and put together into subassemblies that are frequently shipped to an assembly plant in another location. So a Ford assembled in Detroit

Table 1-2	Top 30 Importers, 2015			
RANK	IMPORTERS	VALUE	SHARE	ANNUAL % CHANGE
1	United States	2,308	13.8	−4
2	China	1,682	10.1	−14
3	Germany	1,050	6.3	−13
4	Japan	648	3.9	−20
5	United Kingdom	626	3.7	−9
6	France	573	3.4	−15
7	Hong Kong, China	559	3.3	−7
8	Netherlands	506	3.0	−14
9	Korea, Republic of	436	2.6	−17
10	Canada	436	2.6	−9
11	Italy	409	2.4	−14
12	Mexico	405	2.4	−2
13	India	392	2.3	−15
14	Belgium	375	2.2	−17
15	Spain	309	1.8	−14
16	Singapore	297	1.8	−19
17	Switzerland	252	1.5	−9
18	Chinese Taipei	238	1.4	−16
19	United Arab Emirates	230	1.4	−8
20	Australia	208	1.2	−12
21	Turkey	207	1.2	−14
22	Thailand	203	1.2	−11
23	Russian Federation	194	1.2	−37
24	Poland	193	1.2	−14
25	Brazil	179	1.1	−25
26	Malaysia	176	1.1	−16
27	Saudi Arabia, Kingdom of	172	1.0	−1
28	Vietnam	166	1.0	12
29	Austria	155	0.9	−15
30	Indonesia	143	0.9	−20
	World	16,725	100.0	−

Source: World Trade Organization.

may have less U.S.-made parts than a Toyota assembled in Mexico. The efficiency of global supply chains and especially the transportation systems afford these more complex operations as compared to an earlier era when the auto parts were produced in locations which were more contiguous to the assembly plants. This is also an excellent example of companies using logistics systems analysis to evaluate the trade-offs among production costs, transportation services, and inventory carrying costs to arrive at the overall best location for efficiency and effectiveness.

TABLE 1-3	Volume of World Merchandise Exports and Gross Domestic Product, 1950–2010 (Annual Percentage Change)

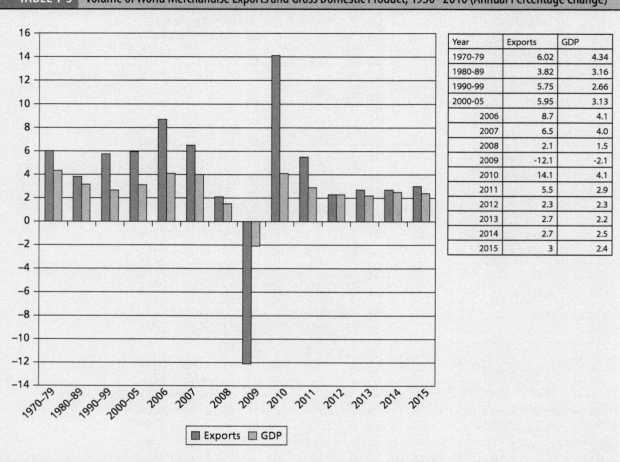

Year	Exports	GDP
1970-79	6.02	4.34
1980-89	3.82	3.16
1990-99	5.75	2.66
2000-05	5.95	3.13
2006	8.7	4.1
2007	6.5	4.0
2008	2.1	1.5
2009	-12.1	-2.1
2010	14.1	4.1
2011	5.5	2.9
2012	2.3	2.3
2013	2.7	2.2
2014	2.7	2.5
2015	3	2.4

Source: World Trade Organization.

As indicated earlier, the global supply chains of today allow production of products with parts being produced in several countries before the final finished product is assembled. A major contributing factor to the global supply chains and the economics of production is the efficiency and effectiveness of global transportation and associated services. The improved global supply chains with faster transit times and lower rates help to promote global trade. Consumers received not only lower prices but also in many instances better quality food and manufactured products. In the next section, we will examine the economic basis and complimentary logic for global trade.

The Economic Basis and Logic of Improved Global Trade

International trade is not a post–World War II phenomenon. During the Middle Ages, it was not uncommon for "traders" to cross regional and country borders by land or sea to buy, sell, or trade selected commodities. The Bible even references traders from other regions.

The exploits of European explorers studied in high school and college history books were often rationalized upon finding high value or exotic products to bring back to their home country in exchange for their domestic products or valued items. The discovery of foreign lands for future settlement was also a motive but with the recognition of the potential trade opportunities. Obviously, the trading was inefficient and slow because of the bartering required and the transportation.

Absolute and Comparative Advantage

As the European countries advanced economically in the 18th century, there was a growing recognition of the value and potential of international trade. Adam Smith in his 1776 book, *The Wealth of Nations*,[2] not only provided a rational basis for a market economy based upon open or free competition, but also advanced the so-called Theory of Absolute Advantage that provided an economic basis for "free trade" among countries. Essentially, he stated that if two regions or countries produced and consumed the same two products—for example, eggs and butter—but had different costs of production, trade could be beneficial. For example, if Country A had an advantage with producing eggs (50 cents versus $1 per dozen) and Country B had the advantage with butter (75 cents versus $1.25 per pound), Smith concluded that A should produce eggs and buy butter from B, while B should produce butter and buy eggs from A. Both would benefit by being able to buy more of each product at lower prices than if they each continued to produce both products. This example is somewhat simplistic because it does not consider transportation costs for delivery or other costs that could be incurred. If the additional costs were added to the production costs, the subsequent "landed cost" would have to be lower than the importing country's cost of production. In other words, in the example earlier, the eggs produced in A would have to have a landed cost in B (50 cents plus transportation costs) less than $1.00.

This same logic was used by Smith to advance the rationale for specialization or division of labor that supported the concept of mass or assembly line production, which will be discussed more fully in the next chapter. The important point is that global or regional trade could be based upon the lack of certain materials or products in an area, but also upon differences in the cost of producing two or more products in two or more different countries.

The Theory of Comparative Advantage was advanced about 40 years after the publication of Smith's *Wealth of Nations* by several economists.[3] They maintained that even if two countries produced and consumed the same two products and one country could produce both products at a lower cost (absolute advantage in both products) than the other country, it could possibly be beneficial for both countries to specialize and trade. It would require the country with the advantages to specialize in the product that it had the greatest comparative advantage over the other country. For example, if Country A could produce butter for 75 cents less than Country B and Country B could produce eggs for 25 cents more than Country A, A should produce butter while B should produce eggs. Again, transportation cost and other costs would have to be considered to develop a landed cost.

The concepts of absolute and comparative advantage are logical but relatively simple for the more complex economic environment of the 21st century. As one would expect, there have been economists who have enhanced or modified these earlier concepts. For example, one such enhancement is the so-called Factor Endowment Theory advanced by Heckscher and Ohlin that enhances Ricardo's Theory of Comparative Advantage.[4] Ricardo's theory was based upon a difference in efficiency associated with better technology, whereas the Factor Endowment Theory postulates that when a country has more of one of the four factors of production (land, labor, capital, or entrepreneurship), they can have a comparative advantage in producing one or more products. Therefore, a country with an abundance of capital and an educated workforce can produce high-tech products and import agriculture products from other countries.

In today's more complex, global economy, there are more variables than the traditional factors of production (land, labor, capital, and entrepreneurship) that can give advantages to countries and provide a basis for global trade flows. Some of these factors help to explain the development of the so-called BRIC and VISTA countries that were previously discussed. For example, two of the BRIC countries, India and China, have developed and prospered during the last 20 years because of factors such as improved global transportation, faster communication with lower costs, population growth, and technology advancement. China, for example, has taken advantage of their low labor costs, including skilled workers, ample raw materials, and capital to invest in production facilities. India's expanding population and growth in technology expertise contributed to their economic advancement. In a later section of this chapter, China and India's advancing economies and leadership positions in the world economy will be discussed in more detail.

Contributing Factors for Global Flows and Trade

Important factors that are frequently cited for greater economic development may include population growth and age distribution, urbanization, land and resources, economic integration, knowledge dissemination, labor mobility, financial flows, and investment in infrastructure by public and/or private agencies to promote improved transportation, faster communication systems, improved financial services, and increased flow of goods and services. These same factors also become the driving forces for overall globalization. At this juncture, it would be worthwhile to examine some of these factors in terms of the global economic growth and development of selected countries.[5]

Population Size and Distribution

Table 1-4 shows the population of the 10 largest countries and the total world population, which can be used as a basis for understanding current and future economic growth and development potential. The table includes totals for 2000, 2010, and 2017 and a projection for 2050. The top 10 countries account for about 58 percent of the total world population and China plus India account for over 36 percent of the total. Additionally, China has over a billion more people than the United States. By 2050, it is projected that India will have over a billion more people than the United States, and India will have a larger population than China unless there is some change in their respective birth rates. The sheer size of their respective populations is an important advantage in terms of one of the previously noted factors of production, that is, labor. The size of their labor forces along with their education and skills will continue to be a strategic advantage, especially in light of the "aging" populations of other countries, which will be discussed later in this chapter.

Table 1-5 depicts the total world population and indicates a decrease in the birth rate percentage from 1950 to 2100. Experts point out that the worldwide rate of population growth has already peaked and is now declining, which is important in terms of global resource base.[6] Additionally, the population growth rate is greatest in some areas that can probably least afford it. Unless there is some change in their economic development, the population explosion in certain underdeveloped economies could lead to dire levels of poverty and other health-related problems and potential political unrest.

While the total population of a country is an indicator of economic growth potential in terms of workforce and consumers, it has some limits. We need additional information about the population to draw meaningful conclusions such as age distribution and education levels.

TABLE 1-4	Top Ten Countries with the Highest Population			
	COUNTRY	2000 POPULATION	2010 POPULATION	2017 POPULATION	2050 EXPECTED POPULATION
1	China	1,268,301,605	1,330,141,295	1,388,232,693	1,301,627,048
2	India	1,006,300,297	1,173,108,018	1,342,512,706	1,656,553,632
3	United States	282,162,411	310,232,863	326,474,013	398,328,349
4	Indonesia	214,090,575	242,968,342	263,510,146	300,183,166
5	Brazil	174,315,386	201,103,330	211,243,220	232,304,177
6	Pakistan	152,429,036	184,404,791	196,744,376	290,847,790
7	Nigeria	123,945,463	152,217,341	191,835,936	391,296,754
8	Bangladesh	128,734,672	156,118,464	164,827,718	193,092,763
9	Russia	147,053,966	139,390,205	143,375,006	129,908,086
10	Mexico	99,775,434	118,600,000	130,222,815	150,567,503
	Top Ten	3,597,108,845	4,008,284,649	4,176,380,247	4,950,140,178
	Rest of the world	2,487,798,751	2,829,120,878	3,005,478,372	4,329,774,957
	Total	6,084,484,918	6,837,405,527	7,181,858,619	9,374,484,225

Source: Internet World Stats, Usage and Population Statistics, Miniwatts Marketing Group.

TABLE 1-5	Population by Major Age Group and Percentage Distribution by Age Group for the World and the Development Groups, 1950, 1980, 2005, 2050, and 2100									
	POPULATION (MILLIONS)					PERCENTAGE				
AGE GROUP	1950	1980	2005	2050	2100	1950	1980	2005	2050	2100
WORLD										
0–14	867	1,572	1,828	2,073	1,985	34.3	35.4	28.0	21.3	17.7
15–64	1,529	2,609	4,217	6,093	6,680	60.6	58.8	64.7	62.7	59.6
65+	129	259	475	1,559	2,548	5.1	5.8	7.3	16.0	22.7
Total	2,525	4,440	6,520	9,725	11,213	100.0	100.0	100.0	100.0	100.0
MORE DEVELOPED REGIONS										
0–14	223	243	204	202	197	27.4	22.5	16.9	15.7	15.4
15–64	527	712	819	744	710	64.8	65.8	67.8	57.8	55.6
65+	63	126	185	341	371	7.7	11.7	15.3	26.5	29.0
Total	813	1,081	1,208	1,287	1,278	100.0	100.0	100.0	100.0	100.0

(continued)

TABLE 1-5	Continued									
	POPULATION (MILLIONS)					**PERCENTAGE**				
AGE GROUP	**1950**	**1980**	**2005**	**2050**	**2100**	**1950**	**1980**	**2005**	**2050**	**2100**
LESS DEVELOPED REGIONS										
0–14	644	1,329	1,624	1,871	1,789	37.6	33.8	30.6	22.2	18.0
15–64	1,002	2,474	3,397	5,349	5,970	58.5	62.9	64.0	63.4	60.1
65+	66	133	290	1,218	2,178	3.9	3.3	5.4	14.4	21.9
Total	1,712	3,936	5,311	8,438	9,937	100.0	100.0	100.0	100.0	100.0

Source: *World Population Prospects: The 2015 Revision, Volume I*, United Nations, 2016.

If we examine population age distribution on a macro level, the young-age balance is shifting throughout the world. In the more developed regions in 2005, the proportion of older people (over age 65) is almost the same as children (under age 15), 15.3 percent versus 16.9 percent, but by 2050, the numbers are predicted to be 29 percent versus 15.4 percent, respectively. Europe will have the greatest disparity followed by North America. The longer life spans in developed countries is exacerbating the young-age disparity ratio and has important implications for the labor force in various countries and the needs of consumers for food, housing, and medical care. Figure 1-3 shows the number of persons aged 65 or older per 100 children under age 15 for 2000 and a projection for 2050. The difference between 2000 and 2050 is quite evident. Figure 1-4 shows the median ages for 1950 and 2000 and the projection for 2050—the total world, less developed, more developed, and least developed regions. The median age has and will change for all four regions, but the differences among the regions are important, especially between the more developed and the least developed.

FIGURE 1-3	Number of Persons 65 or Over per Hundred Children Under 15: World and Development Regions, 1950–2050

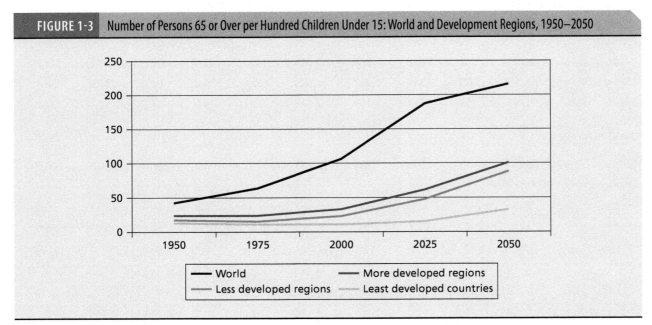

Source: United Nations, Department of Economic and Social Affairs, Population Division, World Ageing Population: 1950–2050, Chapter 3.

FIGURE 1-4 Median Age of the Population: World and Development Regions, 1950–2050

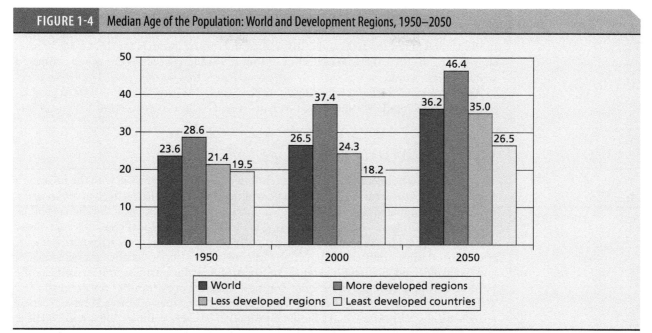

Source: United Nations, Department of Economic and Social Affairs, Population Division, World Ageing Population: 1950–2050, Chapter 3.

The private sector and the public sector will be challenged by these changes in terms of the size of the workforce, medical care, and even retirement benefits, but some opportunities are likely for certain types of businesses including health care, housing, transportation, food products, and so on. Much depends upon immigration policies, technology, retirement ages, and educational opportunities. However, there could be benefits but challenges also will persist. An interesting opportunity could occur with more mobile migration among countries. The European countries with their "graying" populations could probably benefit with a migration of younger individuals from less developed countries not only to help care for

TABLE 1-6 Breakdown of the United States by Age, 2000–10

	2000		2010		CHANGE	
	NUMBER	PERCENT	NUMBER	PERCENT	NUMBER	PERCENT
Total population	281,421,906	100	308,745,538	100	27,323,632	9.7
Sex						
Male	138,053,563	49.1	151,781,326	49.2	13,727,763	9.9
Female	143,368,343	50.9	156,964,212	50.8	13,595,869	9.5
Selected Age Groups						
<18 Years	72,293,812	25.7	74,181,467	24	1,887,655	2.6
18 to 24 Years	27,143,454	9.6	30,672,088	9.9	3,528,634	13
25 to 44 Years	85,040,251	30.2	82,134,554	26.6	−2,905,697	−3.4
45 to 64 Years	61,952,636	22	81,489,445	26.4	19,536,809	31.5
> = 65 Years	34,991,753	12.4	40,267,984	13	5,276,231	15.1

Sources: U.S. Census Bureau, Census 2000 Summary File 1 and 2010 Census Summary File 1.

the older citizens but also to provide a younger workforce for the developed economies. Even in the United States, this could be a possible benefit. Table 1-6 compares selected age groups in the United States for 2000 and 2010, and an interesting group is the 25–44-age bracket showing that in 2010, there was a decline of almost 3 million people in this group compared to 2000. Furthermore, it was the only age group where that was the case. The ripple effect in future years may turn out to be important for population growth and workforce productivity. We could join Japan and Russia with an overall decline in population at some point.

Urbanization

There has been a noticeable demographic shift in a number of countries with the migration from rural to urban areas. In 2000, 47 percent of the world's population lived in urban areas. By 2030, it is estimated that the number will increase to 60 percent, and the change will be most rapid in underdeveloped countries. This will cause additional challenges for those countries to provide the housing, infrastructure, health care, and security necessary for effective and prosperous expansion. The rural areas will also face challenges with smaller and likely older populations. There will be opportunities for business to help alleviate the burdens for the public sector and develop new business opportunities for domestic and global economic expansion. The challenges will be daunting in some cases. A relatively new term is the *megacity* (more than 10 million people). It has been estimated that Asia will have 18 megacities, the United States will have five, but there will be none in Europe.[7] This will be an interesting demographic change with important implications for global trade. The megacities in some countries, especially Africa, will be faced with inadequate infrastructure, especially transportation and utilities, to support the population growth.

One of the interesting megacities or a so-called metropolis is Lagos in West Africa, which is being referred to as Africa's Big Apple by some economists and demographers. Lagos has new tech hubs, a new wealthy class, and an exploding population, but with many in poverty status. The estimated population based on UN data is 15 million although local officials claim a population of 18 million. In the 1970s, the population was estimated to be about 2 million. Lagos has developed into a powerful economic engine based upon an oil boom and a growing economy. The average Nigerian woman gives birth to more than five children in her lifetime, and the population of Lagos expands by about 600,000 a year. The growth has pluses and minuses and has many challenges with its limited infrastructure. However, there are those who maintain that Lagos is Africa's future, which you can interpret in different ways, good or bad. One of the critical ingredients needed for improvement is local and inter-regional transportation systems. As pointed out previously, the lack of adequate transportation will hinder and restrain economic development.

Land and Resources

The availability of land and critical resources such as energy, food, and water are of paramount importance for economic viability and future development. Technology will play a critical role in mitigating the scarcity of key resources from desalinization of ocean water, to fracking for increased oil and gas production, to biotechnology for improving crop yield and food production. Fracking for oil and gas has already changed the global dynamics for energy with the United States likely to become a net exporter and the changes in transportation requirements, which will be discussed in later chapters. All three are keys to stable economic growth and development, but the geographic disparity among areas of the world could be daunting and lead to political conflicts. The public and private sectors can both be instrumental in alleviating the challenges and potential crises. Our success in this area will be of immeasurable importance for peace and prosperity. Transportation can play an important role in resolving the disparity by moving these resources efficiently and effectively among regions and countries, but governments and businesses have to provide the stable and economic basis for this to happen. The expansion of oil and gas pipelines in recent years and improvements in rail tank cars and water vessels are based upon such growth.

Technology and Information

Technology has two important dimensions. It can be viewed as an internal change agent that can enhance the efficiency and effectiveness of an organization and its ability to compete in the global marketplace. However, technology can also be viewed as an external driver of change similar to globalization. In many organizations, the rapid development of new technology by technology companies whether it was hardware or software changed the "rules of engagement" and enabled new forms of competition or new business models. The new technology and new companies changed the nature of the competition, which meant that existing companies had to change or perish. There are many examples of established organizations that were blindsided by the technology. The Internet alone was the biggest "culprit" or agent of change because it made information available in real time to large segments of the population via their personal computers, telephones, or other devices.

The development and sharing of so much information is a major force for changing business models and for the obsolescence of some businesses. Travel agents, for example, became passé. Amazon without stores can compete with Walmart's store network, as can Zappos with more traditional shoe sales organizations. Technology and transportation services have been major factors supporting these changes. For example, companies have been able to outsource selected internal functions like customer service centers or personnel services. One of the most significant impacts has probably been more efficient and effective supply chains and related services such as high-tech warehousing and overnight delivery via Federal Express or UPS. From the specially designed supply chains of Amazon and Zappos to the realigned supply chains of companies like Macy's or Kimberly Clark, supply chains have become a critical ingredient for profitability and customer service. In other words, supply chains are a staple for the success of overall corporate strategy, and transportation is an integral part of these new supply chains.

While information technology has become an important dynamic for external and internal change, there is another important dimension of technology, especially for supply chains, and that is industrial robotics. They have been around for over 50 years and do not resemble R2D2, as depicted in the *Star Wars* film. The first generation of industrial robots was "one-armed" and installed in a permanent position to carry out simple and routine tasks usually on an assembly line. It has been estimated by the International Federation of Robotics that there are over 1.1 million working robots around the world.[8] The largest users are in the automotive industry, and they operate about 80 percent of the total. There is a new wave of less expensive and more flexible robots becoming available for a wider array of manufacturing and distribution tasks. In distribution, these robots will store, retrieve, and pack goods for efficient and effective delivery.

As businesses and other logistics organizations invest in robotic development, the robots will have a positive impact on global trade flows. The newer robots will be used in an environment where humans will be working with them side by side combining the skills of humans with the precision and efficiency of robots. This may allow for smaller-scale operations not only for manufacturing but also for distribution, for example, warehouses and transportation terminals with logistics and supply chain networks being changed accordingly.[9]

Another technology with the potential of having a major impact upon supply chains, logistics, and transportation systems is digitization of manufacturing with facilities being run with smarter software using inputs from product development, historical production data, and advanced computational methods to model and change the entire manufacturing process for individual orders quickly and efficiently. This will also reduce the required scale of operations and allow faster responses to change in the short run as well as the long run.

A related technology is additive manufacturing or so-called 3-D printing, which has been creating a real buzz in business circles, and even President Obama mentioned it in one of his speeches as being a potential force for positive change in the future to make the United States more competitive on a global basis. Essentially, a 3-D printer would allow organizations to make a physical 3-D copy of a product or a part. Despite the buzz, 3-D printing is a long way from producing a car or making assembly lines obsolete. Material costs are extremely high for a number of reasons including higher purity standards and the "middlemen" in the material supply chains. However, 3-D printing is already being used to produce some customized, smaller products such as the covers for iPhones and some specialized parts for automobiles. The latter use will probably continue to be the leader for 3-D printing in the short run, but the long-run development of more, smaller, and better machines will have a major impact on logistics and supply chains. For example, if repair technicians who travel about in vans with inventory can have a 3-D printer in the van with one of each part, they could reduce inventory costs and never be out of stock. Many smaller-scale operations could also benefit with major implications as indicated earlier for supply chains including producers of products. It would probably be comparable to the impact that the improved printers for personal and business computers and related software have had upon commercial printing operations. Some organizations or parts of supply chains will become obsolete or redundant. Like globalization, to be discussed next, technology will continue to be an agent for change up and down supply chains making them and the transportation system more efficient.[10]

Globalization

Globalization has become a very frequently used term or concept not only in business-related conversations but also in more casual settings. Individuals probably have many interpretations and use the word differently in different settings. However, in this particular context, globalization can be used synonymously with economic integration and development across country and regional borders. The integration will increase the flow of goods and services globally based upon the logic of comparative advantage discussed previously. Also the efforts to eliminate and/or reduce tariff and non tariff barriers will promote greater interregional flows. However, military and terroristic interruption pose a real threat to increased global economic progress as demonstrated in the Middle East and the Gaza Strip in 2014.

The global interdependence can be good or bad news. On the good side, the lower prices, wider availability of goods and services, land and resource development, and new employment opportunities have benefited many countries and regions of the world, both developed and developing areas. However, the benefits and advantages have not been equal for all, that is, some have benefited more than others, but on a macro level, and one could argue that the wins have outnumbered the losses. The BRIC and VISTA countries mentioned previously are an indication of some positive outcomes of globalization. On the negative side, the interdependence can lead to global recessions as was the case in 2009 with serious repercussions felt throughout the world. The economic recovery has been very painful and has required government intervention. There are still lingering economic problems from this recession in some areas of the world. However, there have been strong recoveries in other regions such as North America and some countries in Europe.

On a micro level, the global interdependence has increased the level of complexity and competition with shorter product life cycles, new forms of competition, and new business models. Outsourcing, offshoring, and insourcing have become part of the lexicon of businesses. The information technology previously discussed has allowed supply chains to be reexamined and redesigned for more efficiency and effectiveness and even better execution. The fast or even real-time information flows globally have allowed companies to connect in sharing information and to collaborate much more expeditiously than in the past. This has placed a premium on flexibility of planning and operations to respond and adjust to changes in the competitive environment. Also, visibility of inventory and other assets has become an important dimension for efficiency and effectiveness. Successful and well-established business enterprises have felt the impact of the new competitive environment and changing consumer tastes and needs. Again, it is important to recognize the importance and need for good transportation for the success of global supply chains—their efficiency and effectiveness depend on good transportation.

Supply Chain Concept

References to supply chain management can be traced to the 1980s, but it was not until the 1990s that supply chains captured the attention of senior level management in many organizations. They began to recognize the potential of effective supply chain management to improve global competitiveness and to increase market share with consequent improvement in shareholder value.

Development of the Concept

Supply chain management is not a new concept. Rather, supply chain management represents the third phase of an evolution that started in the 1960s with the development of the physical distribution concept, which focused on finished goods or the outbound side of a firm's logistics system—in other words, the distribution-related activities that occurred after a product was produced. In the 1980s, the concept of business logistics or integrated logistics was developed and added the inbound side to the outbound side. Logistics management was the second phase of development for the supply chain concept. As indicated previously, the supply chain management concept was developed primarily in the 1990s and represented the third phase of development.

GLOBAL **PROFILE**

EU: Be a Player, Not a Follower

According to Dr. Riamund Klinker, president and chairman of BVL in Germany, Europe's largest logistics association, foreign trade and the international division of labor are just as important for American economic development as they are for Europe.

Klinker is convinced that, as an experienced entrepreneur, Donald Trump is aware that pure protectionism cannot be the road to economic success. "Realism and sound judgment are required if Trump is to deliver what he promised the people during his campaign: jobs and prosperity," says Klinker, who added that he's optimistic that Europe will once again build on its strengths and get back to being an active player instead of a "follower" of the United States.

"To achieve that, European unity is more important than ever, in economic policy as well as in questions of security," says Klinker. "Of course, it's harder to take proactive, cooperative action than to play the role of follower—but it offers more potential for success."

Klinker's American colleague Moe Ergin, BVL's representative in Chicago, fears that a breakdown in U.S./EU trade could have other effects than just the free flow of clients' goods. "Our biggest fear as a German company in the United States that strives to have a multinational workflow is the proposed restriction on migrant workers wishing to work in the country and concentrating on giving jobs to Americans," he said.

German businesses, including many logistics service companies, provide many jobs in the United States and contribute to the country's growth. According to statistics from the U.S. Department of State, U.S. affiliates of German companies employed over 670,000 American workers in 2015. Deutsche Post DHL is one of them and has been strongly committed to the U.S. market for many years.

For example, DHL Express recently announced that it would be opening up around 900 new positions as it completes the latest $108 million expansion of its Americas Hub at the Cincinnati/Northern Kentucky Airport. Additional sorting capacity and projected growth in shipments are expected to boost the hub's workforce to more than 3,300 employees.

Source: Adapted from Dagmar Trepins, "The Glass Is Half Full," *Logistics Management*, April 2017, pp. 39–40. Reprinted with permission of Peerless Media, LLC.

The focus of **physical distribution management** was on system costs and analyzing trade-off scenarios to arrive at the best or lowest physical distribution system cost. The system relationships that exist among transportation, inventory levels, warehousing, protective packaging, materials handling, and customer service were analyzed and evaluated. For example, rail and motor carrier service impact inventory, warehousing, packaging, customer service, and materials handling costs, but motor carriers would have a different impact on the same cost centers. Rail service would usually have the lowest transportation rate, but there could be higher costs for inventory, warehousing, and packaging that would result in higher total costs than motor carrier service. The type of product, volume, distance, and other factors would influence which mode of transportation would have the lower total cost. Managers in certain industries, such as consumer package or grocery products, high-tech companies, and other consumer product companies, as well as some academicians, became very interested in physical distribution management. A national organization called the National Council of Physical Distribution Management (NCPDM) was organized to focus the leadership, education, research, and interest in the area of physical distribution management.

The 1980s were a decade of change with the deregulation of transportation, financial institutions, and the communication industry. The technology revolution was also underway. During the 1980s, the **business logistics** or **integrated logistics management** concept developed in a growing number of organizations (see Figures 1-5 and 1-6). The deregulation of transportation provided an opportunity to coordinate the inbound and outbound

FIGURE 1-5   Typical Logistics Network—Physical Distribution

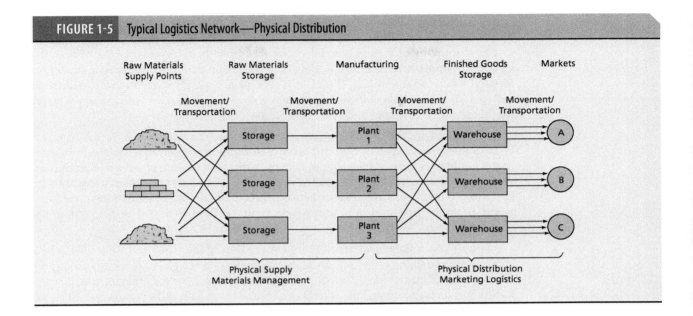

FIGURE 1-6   Typical Logistics Network—Materials Management

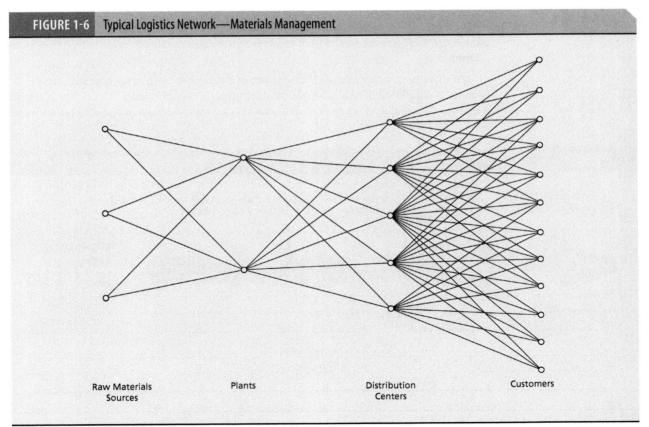

Source: Center for Supply Chain Research, Penn State University, 2004.

transportation movements of large shippers, which could impact a carrier's outbound costs by minimizing empty backhauls, and lead to lower rates for the shipper. Also, international or global sourcing of materials and supplies was growing in importance. As will be discussed subsequently in more detail, global transportation presents some special challenges for production and scheduling. Therefore, it became increasingly apparent that coordination between the outbound and the inbound sides of logistics systems provided an opportunity for the increased efficiency and also better levels of customer service.

The underlying logic of the systems concept was also the rationale for the development of the logistics management concept, because in addition to analyzing trade-offs for total cost it could also include the value of demand aspects of customer service effectiveness. Also, procurement was usually included as an element in a logistics system because of the opportunity for a trade-off analysis between procurement quantity discounts, transportation discounts, inventory, and warehousing costs, and other related costs to obtain the lowest cost.

Supply chain management came into vogue during the 1990s and continues to be a focal point for making organizations more competitive in the global marketplace. Supply chain management can be viewed as a pipeline or a conduit for the efficient and effective flow of products and materials, services, information, and financials (usually cash) from the supplier's supplier through the various intermediate organizations out to the customer's customer (see Figure 1-7). In essence, it is a system of connected networks between the original vendor and the ultimate final consumer. The extended enterprise or boundary spanning perspective of supply chain management represents a logical extension of the logistics concept, providing an opportunity to view the total system of interrelated companies and their impact on the final product in the marketplace in terms of its price–value relationship.

At this point, a more detailed discussion of the supply chain is appropriate. Figure 1-7 presents a simplified, linear example of a hypothetical supply chain. A real-world supply chain would usually be more complex than this example because supply chains are often

FIGURE 1-7 Integrated Supply Chain

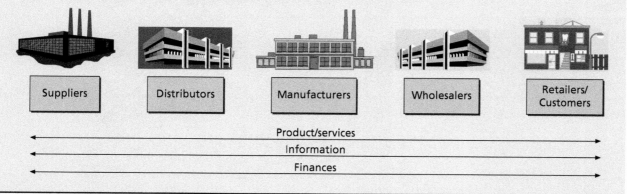

Source: Center for Supply Chain Research, Penn State University.

nonlinear and have more supply chain participants. Also, Figure 1-7 does not adequately portray the importance of transportation in the supply chain. As indicated previously, transportation can be viewed as the glue that holds the supply chain together to allow the member organizations to operate efficiently and effectively as a system. It should be noted that some companies may be a part of several supply chains. For example, chemical companies may provide ingredients for manufacturers of different products that will be distributed by many different retail and wholesale establishments.

Figure 1-7 does illustrate the basic characteristics of a supply chain that are important to this discussion. The definition, which is a part of the illustration, indicates several important points. A supply chain is an **extended enterprise** that crosses the boundaries of the individual firms to span their related activities involved in the supply chain. This extended enterprise should attempt to execute a coordinated or integrated two-way flow of goods, information, and financials (especially cash). The three flows illustrated in the figure are very important to the competitive success of the organizations. Integration across the boundaries of the several organizations in the essence means that the supply chain needs to function like one organization in satisfying the ultimate customer by delivering an appropriate price–value relationship for products in the marketplace.

The top flow, products and related services, has traditionally been an important focus of logistics and transportation and is an important element in supply chain management. This particular flow is directly dependent upon effective transportation, which is the focus of this text. Customers expect their orders to be delivered in a timely, reliable, and damage-free manner, and transportation is critical to this outcome. Figure 1-7 also indicates that product flow is a two-way flow in the environment of the 21st century because a growing number of organizations are involved in **reverse logistics systems** for returning products that were unacceptable to the buyer for some reason—damage, maintenance, obsolescence, and so forth. Note also that networks for reverse systems usually have to be designed somewhat differently than for forward systems. The location, size, and layout of facilities are frequently different. The transportation carriers that need to be utilized may be different. Consequently, there are a growing number of logistics companies (including transportation companies) that specialize in managing reverse flow systems for retailers and manufacturers. They can provide a valuable service in appropriate situations.

The second flow indicated is the **information flow**, which has become a very important factor for success in supply chain management. Figuratively, information is the trigger or signal for the logistics or supply chain system to respond to a customer order. Traditionally, we have viewed information as flowing back from the marketplace as customers purchased products and wholesalers and retailers replenished their inventory. The information was primarily demand or sales data, which triggered replenishment and was also the basis for forecasting future sales or orders. Note that in addition to the retailer or final seller, the other members of the supply chain traditionally reacted to replenishment orders. If there were long time intervals between orders, the members of the supply chain were faced with uncertainty about the level and the potential pattern of demand, which usually resulted in higher inventory (safety stock) or stock out costs. The uncertainty contributed to a phenomenon known as the **bull whip effect** in the supply chain. One of the objectives of supply chain management is to mitigate the bull whip effect by reducing the level of uncertainty. In traditional supply chains with independent organizations, the level or magnitude of uncertainty increased with the "distance" from the market or customer. Therefore, the level of safety stock increased to cover the degree of uncertainty as you moved back through the supply chain.

ON THE **LINE**

Port Tracker Calls for Strong Annual Growth in First Half of 2017

While U.S.-bound retail container volumes trended down in December, the overall outlook for 2017 volumes appears to be solid, according to the most recent edition of the "Port Tracker" report issued by the National Retail Federation (NRF) and maritime consultancy Hackett Associates.

For the first half of 2017, the report authors expect import volumes to be up 4.6 percent annually at 9.4 million twenty-foot equivalent units (TEU). They attributed the projected growth to ongoing economic improvement and growing retail sales. Should this forecast hold true, the report said that it would nearly triple the 1.6 percent growth rate that occurred in the first half of 2016 compared to 2015.

"This is very much in line with what we're forecasting for retail sales and consumer spending this year," said Jonathan Gold, vice president for supply chain and customs policy at NRF. "Retailers try to balance inventories very carefully with demand. So, when retailers import more merchandise, that's a pretty good indicator of what they're expecting with sales."

For the month of December, the most recent month for which data is available, total volume dropped 3.8 percent compared to November and was up 10.2 percent annually at 1.58 million TEU. January was pegged at 1.59 million TEU for a 6.6 percent annual gain, and February is expected to hit 1.53 million TEU, which would mark a slight 0.6 percent drop off. March is forecasted to see a significant 7.8 percent annual gain.

In the report, Hackett Associates founder Ben Hackett wrote that while the global economy over the last six years has seen very slow growth "bordering on stagnation," the driver for what little growth was seen was due to consumer activity.

"Despite the global outlook, the United States is well placed in 2017 and is likely to outperform most of the rest of the developed economies," wrote Hackett. "If the infrastructure investments promised by the new administration come about, we can expect stronger growth than in 2016, but that assumes good relationships with U.S. trading partners. If a protectionist agenda is enforced, however, then there is a strong likelihood that growth could be in danger of declining, but that is unlikely to happen before late in the year."

Source: Jeff Berman, *Logistics Management*, March 2017, p. 15. Reprinted with permission of Peerless Media, LLC.

One of the realizable outcomes of supply chain management is the sharing of sales information on a more real-time basis to reduce uncertainty, which reduces the need for safety stock. In this sense, the supply chain is compressed through timely information flows from the marketplace. In other words, inventory can be reduced in the supply chain by timely, accurate information about demand. If point of sale (POS) data were available from the retail level on a real-time basis, it would help to mitigate the bull whip effect associated with supply chain inventories and would reduce costs. It should also be noted that transportation plays an important role in the level of supply chain inventory. One of the components of transportation service as discussed was reliability of delivery. It was noted that if service was unreliable, companies carried more inventory or safety stock, which would be true along the whole supply chain. It was also noted that transit time had an effect upon inventory, namely, longer transit times could contribute to higher inventory levels. Longer transit times combined with unreliable service exacerbate the need for safety stock in the supply chain.

Consequently, transportation is an important cog in the whole supply chain in terms of efficiency and effectiveness.

Note the illustration also indicates a two-way flow of information. In a supply chain environment, information flowing forward in the supply chain has taken on increased significance and importance. Forward information can take many forms, such as **advanced shipment notices** (ASNs), order status information, and inventory availability information. The overall impact of good forward information has been to reduce uncertainty with respect to order replenishment. A related aspect of forward information flow has been the increased utilization of bar codes and radio frequency tags, which can increase inventory visibility and help reduce uncertainty in the safety stock. The improved visibility of pipeline inventory, including transportation equipment, also makes possible many opportunities for improved efficiency such as transportation consolidation and merging in transit strategies. These latter two have contributed to some shift in modal selection because of the opportunity for consolidation of larger shipments and the opportunity to use merging in transit strategies to eliminate warehousing. The combined two-way flow of timely, accurate information lowers supply chain–related costs (including transportation), which also improves effectiveness or customer service.

The third and final flow indicated is financials, or usually and more specifically, cash. Traditionally, financial flows have been viewed as one-directional—backward in the supply chain. In other words, this flow is payment for goods, services, and orders received. A major impact of supply chain compression and faster cycle times has been faster cash flow. Customers receive orders faster, they are billed sooner, and companies can collect sooner. The faster cash-to-cash or order-to-cash cycle has been very important for companies because it reduces the amount of working capital they need in their system. If cash flow is slow, a company needs more working capital to finance the processes until they collect from the customers. There are some companies that have negative working capital or what financial organizations refer to as **"free" cash flow**. They collect from their customers before they have to pay their vendors or suppliers. In such companies as Dell and Hewlett Packard, the period between collection and payment may be as much as 30 or more days. This cash can be used for financial investment purposes or another source of funding for product development or other improvements. Cash flow measures have become an important metric of the financial community to gauge the viability of companies. Slower cash flows increase the need for working capital and may require loans from time to time to pay suppliers, service providers, or even employees. Frequently, one will see in the financial analysis of an organization references to their cash flow situation. Supply chain management provides organizations with an opportunity to improve customer service and cash flow, and transportation service is an important part of this equation.

As indicated previously, it is important to be aware of the significant role that transportation provides in the supply chain framework. At the "end of the day," the customer expects to have the right product, delivered at the right place, at the right time, in the right quantity, in the right condition, and at the right cost. Transportation plays a critical role in these attributes for an efficient and effective logistics and supply chain system.

SUMMARY

- Transportation is one of the most critical and important ingredients for the economic and social advancement of geographic regions. From the corner grocery stores to large complex factories, efficient and effective transportation is the lifeblood of their ability to operate and compete. Globalization has made transportation even more important with the increased distances and the importance of reliability for today's organizations.

- Transportation was often viewed as the "glue" to hold complex global supply together to make good on the potential, competitive advantages that were frequently extolled for effective supply chain management. Globalization has elevated transportation to a more strategic role in many organizational supply chains.

- There have been some notable changes in the global economic landscape in the last 20 years or so. The emergence of the so-called BRIC (Brazil, Russia, India, and China) and VISTA (Vietnam, Indonesia, South Africa, Turkey, and Argentina) countries are examples of that change. The first group is the more advanced of the two groups, especially China and India who are challenging the more advanced economies. The second group are more appropriately labeled emerging economies, but some faster than others.

- The global flow between countries of imports and exports continues to expand, which is a clear indication of the theories of absolute and comparative advantage at work. While many countries participate in these flows, the more developed countries in Asia, the EU, and the United States dominate the volume. China, the United States, Germany, and Japan are the world leaders.

- An important contributing factor to the growth in trade flows among countries is the more sophisticated supply chains and transportation services, which permit the production and assembly of parts for finished products to be produced in several countries with appropriate sequencing. Overall growth of global trade more than doubled between 2000 and the present with help from trade agreements and increased acceptance of foreign products.

- Population growth, age distribution, and urbanization will play important roles in fostering economic development and associated global trade flows. The populations of China and India exceed a billion in each country and represent an important advantage for these two countries in terms of labor and potential consumers as their economies have grown and developed in the last 25 years.

- Land and resources are also important elements for increased economic development, especially energy, food, and water. Energy has provided the basis for improved economies in a number of countries in the Middle East and Africa, but even developed countries in Europe, and the Unites States and Canada have added growth because of energy growth associated with new technology for recovering oil and natural gas. Advancements in crop production have helped to alleviate food shortages, but there is much more that can and should be done in this area.

- Technology has played a major role on a macro and micro level to influence the growth of global trade flows. Information technology and knowledge dissemination have promoted economic growth and development by allowing more countries to participate in the production of goods and services while separated by distance but connected through information technology.

- Technology is broader than information and consideration has to be given to the "hard side" of technology. Industrial robots are making inroads into the production and distribution phases of global supply chains making them more efficient as well as more effective. In some cases, technology is replacing humans, while in other instances, complementing human effort. Industrial robotics can play an increased and important role in the future.

- Increased globalization by crossing country borders through economic integration has the potential to improve the economies of many countries of the world with consequent economic advantage of their respective citizenry, but the political tensions and actual combat will thwart these efforts and protectionism may rear its "ugly head" again to the detriment of all.

STUDY QUESTIONS

1. Transportation has sometimes been described as the glue that holds global supply chains together. What is the meaning of this statement and do you agree? Why or why not?

2. During the last 20 to 30 years, there have been a number of countries whose economies have experienced important economic expansion and development. One group of countries has been labeled the BRIC and the other the VISTA. Identify each of the nine countries and provide some insights about their economies and economic importance.

3. The theories of absolute and comparative advantage have been offered as economic rationale for trade between and among regions and countries. Compare and contrast the two concepts. Which of the two do you think is more important for explaining the growth in global trade during the last 25 years? Why?

4. The overall growth of global trade has more than doubled since 2000. Why? What has been the most important factor prompting this growth. Is this rate of growth likely to continue in the future? Why or why not?

5. The size of a country's population and the associated age distribution can be causal factors for economic growth. Why is the size of the population important to economic development? Can size be a disadvantage? Why is age distribution important?

6. Energy, food, and water are frequently cited resources that are critical for economic development. Explain the importance of each one to economic development. What disparities exist among countries with respect to these three resources? How can these challenges be resolved?

7. Technology can impact economic development on both a macro and a micro level. What types of technology do we need to have such impacts on a macro basis? On a micro basis?

8. Robotics have attracted more attention in recent years. Why? How are robots being used in supply chains?

9. The economic integration associated with globalization can provide an opportunity for more widely dispersed development. Why is this possible? What are the major stumbling blocks to such integration?

10. Supply chain management has enabled some companies to operate more efficiently and compete more effectively on a global basis. What inherent characteristics of supply chain management contribute to these outcomes?

CASE 1-1

Clearfield Cheese Company Case: A Sequel

Background

The Clearfield Cheese Company was established by two brothers, Terry and Ted Edwards, in 1931, in Clearfield, Pennsylvania. This section of Central Pennsylvania's economy was based largely upon coal and agriculture at this point in time. The U.S. economy was in the throes of what is usually referred to as the Great Depression, and coal production and agriculture were both experiencing the effects of the slumping economy. The farms in the area were mostly small- to medium-size dairy operations. The farmers were under financial duress because they could not sell their milk in the local area for a price to cover their cost of production. There were better market opportunities in Pittsburgh and Harrisburg, Pennsylvania, but their transportation costs put their "landed cost" at a disadvantage with dairy farmers in Erie, Pennsylvania, and Eastern Ohio. The Edwards brothers were not farmers but rather entrepreneurs and owned several tanker trucks, which could be used for hauling milk. They decided that instead of using their equipment to haul milk to potential markets for very meager profits they would start a cheese processing operation in Clearfield. They had some savings and were able to borrow money from The First National Bank of Clearfield, which was still solvent. Their grandfather who had emigrated from Switzerland was knowledgeable about cheese production and processing and helped them get started. They purchased milk from local farmers with lenient payment terms and started a successful venture. World War II presented some challenges in terms of labor supply and fuel rationing, but they survived and prospered by hiring more women and utilizing more rail service.

The next major hurdle was the government-subsidized cheese producers in Canada selling into the Pennsylvania market in the 1980s. Tom Powers, CEO of the Clearfield Cheese Company, with the assistance of two of his key executives, Andy Reisinger (CIO) and Sandy Knight (CSCO), developed a plan, which included improving their supply chain operation efficiency by lowering inventory levels with better forecasting and procurement practices. They expanded their product offerings by adding cottage cheese, sour cream, and yogurt. They also purchased a Canadian company in 1995 because their Canadian sales were growing. This lowered their costs to serve the growing Canadian market and made them much more competitive in Canada. This was an important step to make them a global company.

Current Situation

Their board of directors in 2017 was delighted with their cash flow and profits. However, they were concerned about future growth because of changing diets of many consumers who had become more concerned about consuming milk-based products. The company had already added low-fat versions of the major products, but the board members were concerned that this would not be sufficient to sustain their growth and profits. Some possibilities that were suggested for consideration included (1) setting up a new company to produce non dairy-based products such as almond milk and other alternatives to cow milk. All the new products would have a healthy "spin" such as the White Wave company; (2) market expansion of their existing product lines into Mexico and Central America; (3) expanding their current product offerings by adding ice cream, high-end cheeses made from goat and sheep milk, and high-end milk-based candy; and (4) a combination of one or more of these alternatives.

1. Evaluate all three alternatives offering pros and cons of each.
2. What would you recommend? Why?

CASE 1-2
TEA Logistics Services, Inc.

Company Overview

TEA Logistics Services, Inc. (TEA) was started in 2005 by three siblings in a family that had a long history of involvement in logistics. TEA began operations primarily as a freight brokerage in the United States, matching shipper loads with carrier capacity. While this operation was profitable, it did not give TEA the opportunity to develop deeper partnerships with its clients. So, in 2010, TEA decided to become an asset-based third party logistics (3PL) company that focused on three verticals: electronics, automotive, and pharmaceutical in the United States. Their assets included temperature-controlled and dry van trailers with over-the-road tractors, delivery vans, and leased distribution center capacity. TEA continued its brokerage operation until 2012 and then decided to cease that operation and focus on 3PL activities.

Current Situation

The success of the brokerage operation gave TEA numerous contacts in the shipper community. One of them, Systa Technologies, was a major U.S.-based assembler of high-end computer servers and storage units. Systa, based in Houston, Texas, had assembly facilities in California, Alabama, and Minnesota. Systa relied on 3PL transportation and warehousing companies to provide their logistics services. TEA proposed that it act as a 3PL and 4PL (non asset-based provider) to manage Systa's transportation and distribution needs. In 2014, the contract was signed and TEA became Systa's sole provider of logistics services in the United States.

Expansion Opportunity

While Systa was a world leader in the quality of its products, it was being pressured to increase margins because of global competition. One of its major costs of assembling servers and storage capacity in the United States was labor. Systa made a strategic decision to open a new assembly facility in South Africa. It chose South Africa for three reasons. First, South Africa has abundant and low cost labor. Second, the Chinese have been investing billions of dollars in building infrastructure in South Africa to accommodate the eventual relocation of assembly plants from China to South Africa. Third, China was not selected for the facility because its labor rates are on par with those in the United States. Systa has proposed to TEA that it expand into South Africa as well so it can handle all of Systa's logistics needs in that country. TEA has never operated outside of the United States.

1. What opportunities do you see for TEA to expand globally, specifically to South Africa?
2. What challenges do you see facing TEA in making this operating expansion?
3. If TEA were to accept the offer, how would you suggest that TEA enter the South African market when establishing its operations?

NOTES

1. Thomas Friedman, *The World Is Flat: A Brief History of the Twenty-First Century*, New York: Farrar, Strauss, and Giroux, 2005.

2. Pierre David, *International Logistics: The Management of International Trade Operations*, 4th ed., 2013, Berea, OH: Cicero Books, pp. 21–22.

3. Ibid., pp. 26–27.

4. Fariborz Ghadar and Erik Peterson, *Global Tectonics*, University Park, PA: Center for Global Business Studies, Smeal College of Business, Penn State University, 2008, pp. 13–18.

5. Ibid.

6. Ibid.

7. Vienne Walt, "Africa's Big Apple," Fortune.com, June 30, 2014.

8. Kusumal Roansook, "Supply Chain Technology," Working Paper, Center for Supply Chain Research, Smeal College of Business, Penn State University, University Park, PA, 2014.

9. Ibid.

10. Ibid.

2

TRANSPORTATION AND THE ECONOMY

Learning Objectives

After reading this chapter, you should be able to do the following:

> Understand the importance of transportation to the economic vitality of the United States and other countries and regions and why it is probably our most important industry

> Appreciate the role and contributions of transportation systems to the economic development of countries or regions

> Understand how transportation of goods and people impacts the social and political dimensions of an economy or region

> Appreciate the historical role of transportation from an economic, social, and political perspective

> Discuss the impact that improved transportation has upon land values and economic development

> Understand how transportation affects the price of goods, services, and market areas

> Appreciate the function and scope of transportation in advanced and developed economies

Introduction

Transportation is a pervasive and extremely vital function in all industrialized economies. Transportation systems provide the necessary critical links between producers and consumers both domestically and globally. The citizens of industrialized countries are dependent upon transportation systems to move products from distant locations where they are produced to markets where they are needed and where they can be sold and consumed. An efficient and effective transportation system is essential for businesses to produce and sell products and services. It has long been recognized that one of the critical ingredients for underdeveloped countries to improve economically is the need to invest in transportation infrastructure. This investment is frequently referred to as social capital, that is, society as a whole is the beneficiary of such investment because of the economic benefits associated with new businesses, higher wages, more jobs, and social benefits associated with mobility, improved educational systems, and communication. Even developed countries like the United States need to continually evaluate the adequacy of their transportation infrastructure to insure that the system needs of the economy.

Transportation is one of the requirements of a developed economy because it can bring order out of chaos. It reaches and touches every phase and facet of our well-being. Viewed in totality from a historical, economic, social, and political perspective, it is the most important industry in the world. Without transportation, you could not operate a retail store or win a war. The more complex society becomes and the more developed the economy, the more indispensable is the transportation system.

Unfortunately, the transportation system is frequently taken for granted, and the benefits that accrue to the economy from the transportation system are not fully appreciated. Therefore, it would be appropriate at this point to discuss the many benefits of improved transportation. This chapter will investigate the historical, economic, environmental, social, and political impact of a well-designed and improved transportation system.

Up and Down with the Big Muddy

The Mississippi River has been an important avenue of commerce for several centuries in the United States. It has been referred to as the "Big Muddy" by many individuals because of the color of the water and the amount of soil that washes down the river from northern states, especially during the spring, and is deposited in the so-called deltas near the Gulf of Mexico. That dimension of the river may be important for agricultural and other important reasons, but from the perspective of the economy, it indicates a challenge to utilizing the river as a major transportation artery because flooding and droughts change the channel depths. The Big Muddy is an important component of our transportation system and especially for the Inland River System since the volume of traffic (599.4 million tons in 2014) is very significant.

Like many parts of the transportation system, there is a tendency to take the Mississippi River for granted and not recognize its impact on the economy until there is an obstacle to navigation on the river. Some potential obstacles are probably obvious to many people such as flooding or freezing, but one that is not as obvious to many is a long-term drought, which lowers the depth of the river. The newer, larger vessels to be discussed in Chapter 8 require deeper channels. In normal times, these larger vessels are an important dimension of the efficiency of river transportation, but when the river is low, they are stymied. Also, the solution is basically in the "hands of Mother Nature." Flooding is frequently a problem for a shorter duration, but a serious drought is usually more long term and requires seeking alternative means of transportation.

The recent major variation in weather patterns (flooding in 2011 and drought in 2012) have been a growing problem for shippers and the barge lines. Shippers of harvested agricultural products like corn and wheat do not want to be caught without service to bring their product to market. Low water levels will halt barge service and/or mandate reduction in the loads that the barges can carry. The higher costs by alternate types of carriers, rail or motor carrier, can reduce farm profits significantly. The lesson here is that efficient and reliable transportation service is a critical ingredient for all segments of our economy. Shippers that use the Mississippi River System regularly need to have alternative shipping plans in place to protect their businesses from the vagaries of the river.

Historical Significance

The importance of transportation becomes more apparent when one understands its historical role. The growth of civilizations is associated with the development of transportation systems. For example, the strengths of ancient Egypt demonstrated how one form of transportation, water, could become the foundation for a great society. The Nile River helped to integrate Egypt. It provided a means to transport Egyptian goods, a way to communicate, and a method for Egyptian soldiers to move to defend their country. The Nile River, like all transportation systems, also affected the society's political and cultural development as people traveled and communicated.

A transportation system can help create a social structure because people traveling or living within the bounds of a particular transportation network will tend to share ideas and experiences. Eventually a society develops, with somewhat unified political opinions, cultural ideals, and educational methods. However, methods of transportation also can disrupt societies. People may become alienated from a distant central government system. For example, America's secession from Great Britain is partly attributable to localized transportation systems developing in the 13 colonies. Transportation to and from Britain was slow and inefficient, and American families could lead better lives trading among themselves without having to pay duties (taxes) to the government of King George III. As the colonies developed into a separate economic system, political and cultural attitudes that were unique to America prevailed, which led to alienation with Great Britain and eventually to the Revolutionary War.

The United States continued to grow in tandem with its transportation networks in the 19th century. Few families thought to move West without first knowing that explorers had blazed trails and found rivers suitable for travel. The **Erie Canal**, steamboats, early turnpikes, and the early rail system were developed to meet the economic and social needs of the growing nation. Table 2-1 provides an overview of transport developments in the United States.[1]

Transportation also plays a major role in **national defense**, which has been recognized by governments. The Roman Empire built its great system of roads primarily for military purposes, but they had an overall positive economic impact. Sir Winston Churchill pointed out that transport was the underlying basis for all that could be accomplished in effectively fighting a war. In other words, transportation was a critical ingredient for success on the battlefield. United States requirements for national defense have been a major reason for a number of important transportation projects. As indicated previously, under the Eisenhower administration, enabling legislation was passed for a National System of Interstate and Defense Highways. This highway system was envisioned as being a system of superhighways connecting the states and their major centers within the states, which could enhance our ability to defend against enemy attack. The economic and social benefits of the Interstate Highway System have far exceeded the defense contribution. Generally, the expenditures on air transport infrastructure are based primarily on military and political consideration

TABLE 2-1	U.S. Transport Developments		
YEAR	**DEVELOPMENT**	**YEAR**	**DEVELOPMENT**
1774	Lancaster Turnpike: first toll road—Pennsylvania	1940	National Transportation Policy Statement
1804	Fulton's steamboat—Hudson River, New York	1961	Manned space flights begin
1825	Erie Canal: first canal—New York	1970	Amtrak established
1830	Baltimore and Ohio Railroad begins service	1976	Conrail established
1838	Steamship service—Atlantic Ocean	1978	Act to deregulate airlines passed
1865	First pipeline—Pennsylvania	1980	Act to deregulate motor carriers and Staggers Rail Act
1866	Completion of transcontinental rail link	1982	Double Stack Rail container service initiated
1869	Bicycles introduced—United States	1986	Conrail profitable and sold by government
1887	First daily rail service coast to coast	1990	Amended National Transportation Policy Statement
1887	Federal regulation of transportation begins	1995	ICC succeeded by Surface Transportation Board
1903	First successful airplane flight—Wright Brothers	1998	Internet applications widely used in transportation
1904	Panama Canal opens	1999	Norfolk Southern and CSX acquire Conrail
1919	Transcontinental airmail service by U.S. Post Office begins	2002	Protective action against Terrorist attacks after 9/11
1925	Kelly Act: airmail contract to private companies	2002	Airline industry enters decade of restructuring
1927	Lindbergh solo flight—New York to Paris	2014	Political disputes of infrastructure funding

as opposed to economic benefits, but the economic benefits usually outweigh the political and military benefits over the longer run.[2]

In the 21st century, transportation systems will face significant challenges and problems because of global competition, government budget constraints, increasing demand from special interest groups such as senior citizens, infrastructure challenges, sustainability issues, and energy costs. The pattern of trade that helps to drive transportation requirements is changing more quickly and becoming more complex because of the dynamic global environment and the changing economic base in the United States.

Economics of Transportation

Transportation touches the lives of all U.S. citizens and citizens in other areas of the world. It affects their economic well-being, their safety, their access to other people and places, and the quality of their environment. When the transportation system does not function well, it is a source of great personal frustration and perhaps economic loss. But when the transportation system performs well it provides opportunity and rewards for everyone. Understanding the basic fundamentals of transportation economics will provide important insights into the role of transportation in the economic viability of a country, and also the businesses and other organizations that provide the output, revenue, and income that really drives an economy.

Demand for Transportation

The economic growth of the U.S. economy, as well as the economies of most industrialized countries, is attributable, in part, to the benefits derived from mass production and the associated division or specialization of labor, which enables mass production to occur.

Specialization of labor and production can result in an oversupply of goods at one location and unmet demand for these goods in another area. For example, a large food processing plant in Hanover, Pennsylvania, can produce far more product than can be consumed in the immediate market area and will need to sell its output in distant markets to take advantage of the scale of their plant operations. Transportation plays an important role in helping to bridge the supply and demand gap inherent in the mass-production–oriented approach.

The interrelationship between transportation and mass production points out the dependency of our global economy upon transportation. As geographical areas begin to specialize in the production of particular goods and/or services, they are relying more upon the other regions to produce the additional goods and services that they need or desire. We depend upon transportation to move these goods and provide these services in an efficient and effective manner. Like the citizens of most industrialized countries, U.S. citizens, as individuals, are not self-sufficient. On a global scale, countries recognize their international interdependencies. United States supplies many countries with a variety of agricultural products, manufactured products, and other types of services. While other countries provide the United States with raw materials, other agricultural products and additional manufactured products. For example, the United States is dependent upon the Middle East, South America, and Canada for energy production. Even though the United States produces energy, the amount produced is not sufficient to provide what is needed. Other countries usually rely on the United States to provide a variety of manufactured goods such as aircraft, clothing, and computers to meet their needs. Again, transportation plays a key role in this international or global dependency by providing the ability to match supply and demand requirements on a global basis. The ability of countries to trade among themselves and to efficiently move goods is a key element in the success of global development.

Passenger Demand

Similarly, people move from areas where they are currently situated to areas where they desire to be on a daily, weekly, or permanent basis. Transportation also provides the bridging function between supply and demand for people to move from their current places of residence to new locations. As with freight, people depend on transportation for mobility. The more developed a society, the more critical an efficient economical passenger system is to its citizens. With today's technology, an executive in Chicago can leave home early on a Monday morning and catch a flight to Los Angeles to attend an early afternoon meeting. At the end of the afternoon that same executive can board a flight to Australia with a continuation to London later in the week. This global workweek is possible because of the speed and effectiveness of air transportation, and such travel has become more commonplace in the global economy.

The automobile has been a form of transportation that affects most people's lifestyle, particularly in the United States. The convenience, flexibility, and relatively low cost of automobile travel allow individuals to live in locations distant from where they work. The growth of suburban areas is usually attributable largely to the automobile and the appropriate roadway infrastructure. Although in some areas, efficient mass transportation or passenger transportation is also important. It is not unusual in some areas of the United States for people to travel 20-plus miles one way to go to work. The automobile also enables people to seek medical, dental, and recreational services at various locations throughout their region or even their country.

Rising costs of automobile and air travel occurring as a result of escalating energy, labor, and equipment costs is beginning to cause some change in lifestyles. Instead of traveling longer distances for vacation, some people may stay closer to home or not travel at all. Areas of a country that are highly dependent on tourists have experienced some economic difficulties and a need for changing their economic base. This same set of factors is impacting the movement of freight and causing companies to source or purchase for their supply chains in more contiguous locations. The combination of low labor costs in some global locations and relatively low transportation costs made some distant sources of supply more attractive, but this has been changing with the rising costs of energy and labor mentioned above. Consequently, some companies are reevaluating their logistics and transportation networks to determine more optimum, usually closer, locations.

Transport Measurement Units

Transportation demand is essentially a request to move a given weight or amount of cargo a specific distance between two specific points. The demand for transportation is usually measured in weight-distance units for freight and passenger-distance units for people. For freight, the usual demand metric is the **ton-mile**, and for people, the unit is the **passenger-mile**. Both measurements are two dimensional, which can present some challenges for modal comparisons. The ton-mile, for example, is not homogeneous for comparison purposes. The demand for 200 ton-miles of freight transportation could be a movement of 200 tons for one mile, 100 tons for two miles, or 1 ton for 200 miles. In fact, any combination of weight and distance that equals 200 ton-miles would be regarded as the same or equal. In addition, the unique transportation requirements for transportation, equipment, and service may vary among customers for a 200 ton-mile movement. The same unit of demand could have different costs for producing it and different user requirements. However, measuring only the miles moved or the weight moved does not adequately reflect the components of freight transport demand for comparison purposes. The relative importance of transportation movements can best be measured using the ton-mile concept.

Similarly, the passenger-mile is a heterogeneous unit. Five hundred passenger-miles could be one passenger moving 500 miles or 500 passengers moving 1 mile. The demand for 500 passenger-miles could be automobile, railroad, or airplane. The demand attributes of the passenger-mile vary from passenger to passenger. However, the passenger-mile is still the single best measure of the relative importance of transportation alternatives. While

ON THE **LINE**

Cass Freight Index Paints Optimistic Future

Freight transportation shipments and expenditures finished the first quarter on an upswing, according to the March edition of the "Cass Freight Index" from Cass Information Systems. March shipments at 1.080 were up 0.9 percent annually and up 0.5 percent sequentially. As for the latter, expenditures at 2.355 rose 3 percent annually and dropped 1.2 percent compared to February. This marks the third month in a row—or the entire first quarter—in which both metrics have been positive. The report's author, Donald Broughton, transportation analyst at Avondale Partners, wrote that this is in tandem with a growing number of increasingly positive U.S. economic data. What's more, last October marked the first time in 20 months that shipments turned positive, which Broughton said was "one of the first indications that a recovery in freight had begun in earnest."

Source: *Logistics Management*, May 2017, page 1. Reprinted with permission of Peerless Media, LLC.

neither the ton-mile nor the passenger-mile is perfect, they are still the best metric available. As long as we recognize, the challenges inherent in the units when comparisons are made both are useful.

The demand for transportation can be examined at different levels of aggregation. Aggregate demand for transportation is the sum of the individual demands for freight or for passengers. In addition, aggregate demand is the sum of the demand for transportation via different modes or the aggregate demand for a particular mode. Table 2-2 shows the allocation of aggregate passenger-miles, and Table 2-3 shows the allocation of aggregate tons via different modes of transportation for 2007, 2013, and 2040. Table 2-3 shows that motor carriers move a majority of the freight tons in the United States. However, if current data were available, it would show that railroads move the most ton-miles in the United States. Rail and pipeline are very competitive when comparing the number of tons moved. This is not surprising since oil and oil-related products are moved by both modes. Overall, the tons and passenger-mile metrics are useful modal comparisons or modal splits.

Modal split is a useful analytical tool for the study of transportation because it divides the total transportation market for passenger and freight movements according to use or volume by the major modes of transportation. Highway transportation (public and private) dominates the movement of people in the United States and represents more than 82 percent of passenger-miles traveled in the United States in 2014. The proportion of highway travel decreased slightly over the past three decades due to growth in airline travel and higher fuel prices. Deregulation of airline service in the late 1970s brought about an increase in travel options and services for the traveling public. During this period, the relative level of airfares did not keep pace with the overall inflation level. As a result, air travel became more convenient and relatively cheaper for long-distance travel.

The freight intercity modal split is dominated by trucks, with about 77 percent of the tons moved in 2013. Railroads declined in relative share after World War II but have

TABLE 2-2	Passenger Miles: 2011–2014 (millions)			
	AIR	RAIL	BUS	LIGHT DUTY VEHICLES
2011	575,613	37,562	292,716	3,650,223
2012	580,501	37,878	313,357	3,669,278
2013	589,692	39,116	321,539	3,688,161
2014	607,772	39,288	339,177	3,731,888

Source: U.S. Department of Transportation, Bureau of Transportation Statistics, 2017, Washington, DC.

TABLE 2-3	U.S. Tons of Freight (millions)				
YEAR	AIR	TRUCK	RAIL	WATER	PIPELINE
2007	13	12,778	1,900	950	1,493
2013	15	13,955	1,858	808	1,539
2040	53	18,786	2,770	1,070	1,740

Source: U.S. Department of Transportation, Bureau of Transportation Statistics, *Freight Facts and Figures 2015*, Table 2-3.

increased in share since 1990 because of fuel prices and other factors. Motor carriers have also increased their relative share of the total ton-mile market after 1980, but their share has remained relatively stable since 2000. Railroads typically move bulk, low-value commodities such as grain, coal, ore, and chemicals for longer distances, which impacts their ton-miles share. In recent years, rail traffic by container, which transports relatively higher-value finished goods, has increased. The air mode, while more visible, still handles less than 1 percent of the total ton-miles in the United States. Each of these modes will be accorded more detailed analysis in subsequent chapters (Chapters 5 through 8).

In recent years, the economy has expanded at a faster rate than the demand for freight transportation. The increase in global trade is one of the reasons for this phenomenon. For example, in the past, a domestic steel firm usually purchased transportation service for inbound raw materials (ore, lime, coal) and the movement of the outbound finished goods to the customer domestically. At the very minimum, this involved four different movements. Today the steel may be imported, requiring one domestic movement between the port and the customer. Even if the steel is being used in the economy, fewer transportation moves are involved in making it available to the customer.

As stated previously, good transportation spurs economic development by giving mobility and lower **landed cost** to production factors, which permits scale economies and increased efficiency. Good transportation enlarges the area that consumers and industries can draw on for resources and products. Good transportation expands the area to which a given plant or warehouse can distribute its products economically, and the resulting specialization and scale economies provide a wider choice of products for consumers at a lower cost. The overall economic importance and significance of improved transportation systems need to be understood and appreciated.

Demand Elasticity

Demand elasticity refers to the sensitivity of customers to changes in price. If customers are sensitive to price, a price reduction should increase the demand for the item and the total revenue should also usually increase. An increase in price will have the opposite effect—less revenue and a reduction in sales. If customers are not sensitive to a change in price, we consider that demand to be inelastic because a price reduction will result in a small relative increase in the quantity demanded, and the total revenues will decrease. In mathematical terms, demand elasticity is the ratio of the percentage change in the quantity demanded to the percentage change in price or elasticity equals percentage change in quantity divided by percentage change in price. If demand is elastic, the quantity demanded changes more than the change in price, and the elasticity coefficient is greater than one. Conversely, a product or service said to be price inelastic or insensitive to price changes, if the quantity demanded changes less than the change in price or in other words, the coefficient is less than one.

Elasticity = % change in quantity /% change in price

In general, aggregate demand for transportation is **inelastic**. Freight rate reductions will not dramatically increase the demand for freight transportation because transportation costs generally represent, in the aggregate, less than 4 percent of a product's landed cost, and the demand is a derived demand (to be discussed subsequently). Substantial rate reductions would be required for a meaningful increase in the demand for the product and consequently, the demand for transportation of that product. On the other hand, if we consider specific modes of transportation or specific carriers, the demand is generally elastic or price sensitive. The modal share of the aggregate demand is, in part, determined by the rates charged. Reductions in rates charged by a particular mode will usually result in increases in the volume of freight by that mode, other things being equal. This assumes that the mode that reduced the rate is physically capable of transporting the freight.

For example, long-haul transportation of new automobiles was dominated by motor carriers in the 1960s and 1970s. The railroads developed a new railcar specifically designed to transport new automobiles. This new railcar enabled the railroads to improve efficiency and reduce the rates that they charged for hauling automobiles while also improving some of the service characteristics of the movements. The percentage of new automobiles hauled by railroads increased with the introduction of the new railcar and the lower rates, and the share of intercity ton-miles of new automobiles transported by motor carriers decreased. Today, motor carriers are usually used primarily to transport new automobiles shorter distances from rail yards to dealerships. In addition, when plant locations are close to the points where new cars are needed or where dealers are located, motor transportation is frequently used.

For modal shipments or for a specific carrier within that mode, demand may also have service elasticity. Assuming no price changes, the mode or specific carrier demand is often sensitive to changes in service levels provided by competing carriers. For example, many air passengers monitor the on time service levels of the various air carriers and when possible will select the air carrier that provides the best on time transportation service. Transit time and service reliability have become much more important to freight movement during the last several decades, as shippers have become increasingly aware of the impact of carrier service on inventory levels and customer service. Consequently, higher cost service providers such as UPS and Federal Express now move larger-sized shipments because of their superior direct service and some of the ancillary logistics services that they provide.

Freight Transportation Demand

The demand for freight transportation is usually dependent upon the demand for a product in another location. As indicated previously, specialization and mass production create a need for market expansion at more distant locations, which gives rise to increased demand for freight transportation. In this section, attention is given to the characteristics of freight transportation demand.

Derived Demand The demand to transport a product in a given location usually depends on the existence of demand to consume or use that product in the distant location. Freight is not usually transported to another location unless there is a need for the product. Thus, the demand for freight transportation is generally referred to as a **derived demand**. Sometimes it is also referred to as a secondary as opposed to a primary demand. Derived demand is not unique to transportation since the demand for many raw materials is dependent upon the demand for the finished products, which are produced from these raw materials. Figure 2-1 illustrates the derived demand nature of freight transportation. If a supply of widgets is available at the production site, City A, widgets will not be moved or transported to City C because there is no demand for widgets at City C. However, there is a demand for widgets at City B. Because of the demand for 100 widgets in City B, there is a demand for transportation of 100 widgets from City A to City B.

The derived demand characteristics implied that freight transportation would not be affected by transport carrier actions. As noted above, this assumption is true for the demand for transportation at the aggregate level. For example, if a freight carrier lowers the rate to zero for moving high-tech personal computers from the United States to a developing nation,

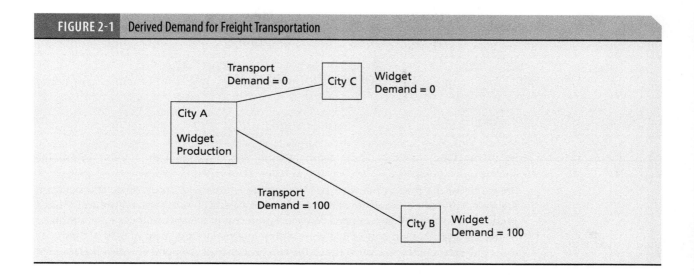

FIGURE 2-1   Derived Demand for Freight Transportation

this free transportation may not materially change the demand for personal computers in a developing nation since it is a derived demand. The demand for personal computers is dependent on the educational level of the citizens, electrical availability, and the price of the computer itself. However, at the disaggregate level (modal carrier or specific traffic lane) the rates charged for the service level provided usually influence the demand for the product and the demand to transport the product. The impact on product demand considers the value of the service provided to the user of the product, which is discussed in the next section.

Value of Service   **Value of service** considers the impact of transportation costs and service on the demand for the product. Lower transportation costs can cause a shift in demand for transportation among the modes and the specific carriers. It can also affect the demand to transport freight over a specific traffic lane where several carriers are competing for the traffic. The impact of transportation costs on the demand for a product at a given location usually focuses on the landed cost of the product. The landed cost includes the cost of the product at the source, the cost to transport the product to its destination, plus any ancillary expenses such as insurance or loading costs. If the landed cost of the product is lower than that of other sources, there usually will be a demand for that product and also for the transportation of that product from its origin point.

For example, in Figure 2-2, a manufacturer of bicycle tires located in Chicago is competing in Boston with local producers. For the Chicago bicycle tire manufacturer to be competitive, the landed costs of the tire must be lower than the cost of the local manufacturer's tire prices. Assume that the Boston manufacturers have a cost of $4.00 per tire, whereas, the Chicago manufacturer can produce the same tire for $3.00 because of its inherent advantages in labor productivity. As long as the transportation costs per tire from Chicago to Boston are less than $1, the Chicago tire maker will have a landed cost advantage and a demand for the Chicago tire will probably exist in Boston (assuming the quality is equal to that of the locally produced tires). Conversely, if transportation costs exceed $1 per tire, Boston consumers will not likely purchase tires from Chicago.

The **landed cost** also determines the extent of the market for business. The greater the distance the product is shipped, usually the higher the landed cost. At some distance from the product's source, the landed cost usually becomes prohibitive to the buyer, and there will be no demand for that product at that point. In addition, the landed cost usually determines

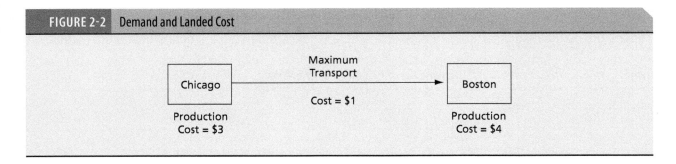

FIGURE 2-2 Demand and Landed Cost

the extent of the market between two competing companies. To illustrate this concept, Figure 2-3 presents an example of two producers located 200 miles apart. Producer P has a production cost of $50 per unit and transportation cost of $.60 per unit per mile. Producer S also has a production cost of $50 per unit but a transportation cost of $.50 per unit per mile. The extent of the market between the two producers is the point at which their landed costs of P is equal to the landed cost of S:

$$LC(P) = LC(S)$$
$$\text{Production Cost (P)} + \text{Transportation Cost (P)} = \text{Production Cost (S)}$$
$$+ \text{Transportation Cost (S)}$$

$$\$50 + \$0.60(x) = \$50 + \$0.50(200 - x)$$
$$\$0.60(x) + \$0.50(x) = \$50 + \$100 - \$50$$
$$\$1.10(x) = \$100$$
$$x = 90.9 \text{ miles from P}$$

Solving the equation for x, P's market area will extend 90.9 miles from its plant and x will have a market area that extends about 109 miles from its facility. Just examining the numbers, one would conclude that the company located at S with the transportation costs of $.50 per unit would have an advantage, but this formula will allow a precise calculation of the distance of the market areas between the two companies.

Service Components of Freight Demand

Shippers of freight have varying service requirements for their transportation providers, as indicated previously. These service requirements range from specific pickup times to communication requirements. The service demands affect the cost of the service provided. The transportation service characteristics to be discussed include transit time, reliability, accessibility, capability, and security.

Service Characteristics of Freight Demand[3] **Transit time** can affect the level of inventory held by the shipper and the receiver as well as the associated carrying cost of holding that

FIGURE 2-3 Extent of Market Area

inventory. The longer the transit time, the higher the inventory levels required and the higher the carrying costs. In addition, transit times impact the inventory costs in the overall supply chain. For example, the supply of clothing produced in the Pacific Rim might require 45 days of transit time from manufacturer's shipping point to a specific retail store. While the clothes are in transit for 45 days, either a buyer or a seller incurs the cost of financing the inventory for the 45 days. If the transit time is reduced to 15 days by use of air transportation, the in-transit inventory financing costs will be reduced by two-thirds. Also, as the transit time increases the potential cost for stock outs increases as well. Using the Pacific Rim example above, a stock out of clothing at the retail store could mean a maximum of 45 days without inventory with sales and the related profits lost during this period. Shorter transit times reduce the potential losses from stock outs.

Reliability refers to the consistency of transit times. Meeting pickup and delivery schedules enables shippers and receivers to optimize service levels and minimize stock out costs. Unreliable transit time requires the freight receiver to either increase inventory levels to guard against stock out conditions or incur stock out related costs. Reliable service directly affects the level of modal and specific carrier demand, that is, a shipper may shift from an unreliable carrier to one that is more reliable and service is more consistent. The customer may switch from a supplier that provides unreliable delivery service to one that is reliable thereby impacting the transportation demand for specific carriers or specific traffic lanes.

Accessibility is the ability of the transportation provider to move freight between a specific origin and destination. The inability of a carrier to provide direct service between an origin and destination results in added costs and transit time for the shipper. For example, an air carrier does not move freight from Toledo, Ohio, directly to Angers, France. First the freight is moved by motor carrier from Toledo to Detroit, Michigan, and then flown to Paris where it will be moved to Angers by either motor or rail. When a carrier cannot provide direct service between the shipping and receiving points, it usually requires additional transportation service by motor carrier, which adds to the transit time and the total cost. Motor carriers have a distinct advantage over other carriers in terms of accessibility in most countries.

The ability of the carrier to provide special service requirements is the essence of **capability**. Based on the physical and marketing characteristics of the freight, shippers might have unique demands for the transportation, facilities, and communication—for example, products requiring controlled temperature would necessitate the use of a refrigerated vehicle; time sensitive shipments would need state-of-the-art communications systems to monitor their exact location and arrival times; or even the cubic capacity for a large piece of equipment. Marketing considerations might dictate that the carriers provide freight consolidation and break-bulk facilities to lower freight costs and transit time. These are just a few of the many and varied demands placed on the transportation service providers. Their capability to provide these required services are often instrumental in getting the business.

Finally, **security** is concerned with the safety of the goods in transit. Shipments that are damaged or lost in transit can cause increased cost in the areas of inventory and/or stock outs. A damaged shipment will usually not be accepted and the buyer faces the possibility of losing a sale or stopping the production process. Increasing inventory levels to protect against stock out costs relating from a damaged shipment causes increased inventory carrying costs. Table 2-4 provides a summary to the transportation service components of freight demand. As indicated previously, the focus upon supply chain management has raised the awareness of shippers to the importance of carrier service characteristics to total cost and to customer service.

TABLE 2-4	Service Components of Freight Demand
SERVICE COMPONENT	**USER IMPLICATION**
Transit Time	Inventory, Stock Out Costs
Reliability	Inventory, Stock Out Costs
Accessibility	Transit Time, Transportation Cost
Capability	Meets Products' Unique Physical and Marketing Requirements
Security	Inventory, Stock Out Costs

TRANSPORTATION **PROFILE**

Uber Freight Makes Official Entrance into Trucking Market

While anticipated for some time, ubiquitous ride-sharing service Uber said last month it has officially entered the freight transportation arena, specifically truckload brokerage, with the introduction of Uber Freight. In a blog posting, Eric Berdinis, Uber Freight product manager, wrote that Uber Freight is an app that matches trucking companies with loads to haul—taking the guesswork out of finding and booking freight, a stressor for drivers.

"What used to take several hours and multiple phone calls can now be achieved with the touch of a button," Berdinis explained. Vetted users download the Uber Freight app, search for a load and tap to book it. Rate confirmation comes within seconds, eliminating the common anxiety about confirmation. And, Berdinis said that rather than the common practice of a trucker waiting 30 days or more to get paid, Uber Freight is "committed to paying within a few days , fee-free, for every single load," and "when things don't go as planned or drivers have to wait longer than expected, we pay for that, too," with accessorial rates published on the Uber Freight blog and website.

Uber has had its sights on the truckload brokerage market for some time, with a September 2016 Reuters report noting that it was keen on becoming a freight hauler through its acquisition of Otto, a self-driving truck startup for $680 million in August 2016, and a technology partner for trucking. Uber is now pitching its services to shippers, truck fleets, and independent drivers, not just to outfit trucks with self-driving technology, but also to be a player in the highly competitive $700 billion truckload brokerage arena—which is replete with major players such as C.H. Robinson Worldwide, XPO Logistics, Echo Global Logistics, among others.

Uber's Berdinis said in an interview that the company has been testing its freight platform for several months. "We firmly believe we can make a significant impact in the future of trucking with a new way of booking freight and a new way of connecting small fleets and owner-operators with a large tail of capacity out there to the community of shippers that don't traditionally have the resources to go out and find capacity," he said.

Prior to this launch, Uber had been piloting a program with a handful of U.S.-based shippers as well as a number of small carriers based in the triangle between Dallas, Houston, and San Antonio.

Going forward, Berdinis said that Uber Freight will focus on independent drivers and small fleets, noting that owner-operators may be viewed as a dying breed these days due to the challenges in finding consistent freight.

Uber Freight's initial focus is on the two most common freight types in the United States, dry van and refrigerated (reefer), which offers a lot of space to route and optimize movements of these small fleets using the app. "Going into this space and doubling down on small fleets and creating a top-quality service for a shipper base offers room for growth," he said.

According to Morgan Stanley analyst Ravi Shanker, the move marks an escalation in the truck brokerage disruption wars. "Thus far, we've seen several startups vying to be the 'Uber of freight' achieve scale in the past two years, but Uber's launch marks the entry of the first tech giant into this space ahead of Amazon's impending launch this summer."

In the long-term, Shanker says his firm is seeing secular margin compression at all of the 3PLs. "This is due to the threat of increased competition from startups vying to crowd-source freight, and they continue to raise meaningful amounts of private capital; insourcing at e-commerce and other logistics giants; and vertical integration into the asset-light business by asset-heavy players including, eventually, OEMs."

Source: Jeff Berman, *Logistics Management*, June 2017, p. 12. Reprinted with permission of Peerless Media, LLC.

Value of Goods

Transportation systems help determine the economic value of products. A simple model will serve to illustrate this point. Consider a certain commodity that is desired in one location, provided it is offered below a certain price. In Figure 2-4, this commodity is produced at point A and costs OC at the point of production. The community that needs the commodity, located at point B, is the distance AB from A. The maximum price that people will pay for the commodity is shown on the vertical axis as OE, at community B.

If the original, inefficient transport system is used, moving the commodity from A to B will cost CH. The CD portion of the cost line is known as the fixed cost, and the DH portion of the line is the cost per mile (a variable cost) or slope of the line. With the inefficient system, the total cost at B is OH, a price greater than the maximum cost or price limit (OE) in community B.

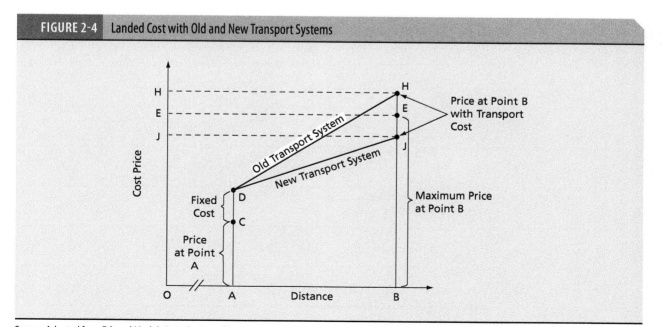

FIGURE 2-4 Landed Cost with Old and New Transport Systems

Source: Adapted from Edward Morlok, *Introduction to Transportation, Engineering, and Planning*, New York: McGraw-Hill, 1978, p. 33.

Assume the transport system is improved, and the cost per mile or slope is reduced, and the transportation variable cost line becomes DJ. Now, the cost at community B becomes OJ, which is below the maximum cost or price limit of OE. The market for the commodity produced at A will be expanded to community B. The efficiency of the new system enables the producer located at Point A to expand their market area to include B, which is a value-added service.

Place Utility The reduction in transportation costs, illustrated above, between points A and B gives the commodity **place utility** or **place value**. In the less efficient system, the goods will have no value at B because they could not be sold at the market price. The more efficient method of transportation creates place utility; since the goods can now be sold at point B for a competitive price.

Reductions in transportation costs permit market areas to purchase products from more distant suppliers that might otherwise only be produced locally at a higher price. The reduction in transportation cost is actually greater for longer distances than for short ones because of the fixed charges. If a supplier can cover the transportation cost in their price range, an increase in the distance over which this given amount will cover the transport of goods will increase the market area of the product in an even greater ratio.

Dionysius Lardner, an early transportation economist, referred to this phenomenon as the **Law of Squares** in Transportation and Trade (also known as **Lardner's Law**). As shown in Figure 2-5, a producer at Point A can afford to transport a product 100 miles and meet competitive landed costs. The boundary of the relevant market area is shown by the circumference of the smaller circle. If transportation cost is cut in half, the same sum will now transport the supplier goods for twice the distance, that is, 200 miles. Now the market boundary is shown by the circumference of the larger circle. The relevant market area increased four times in size when the radius doubled from 100 to 200 miles.

Time Utility The concept of **time utility** is closely aligned to that of place utility. The demand for a particular commodity may only exist during certain periods of time. If a product arrives

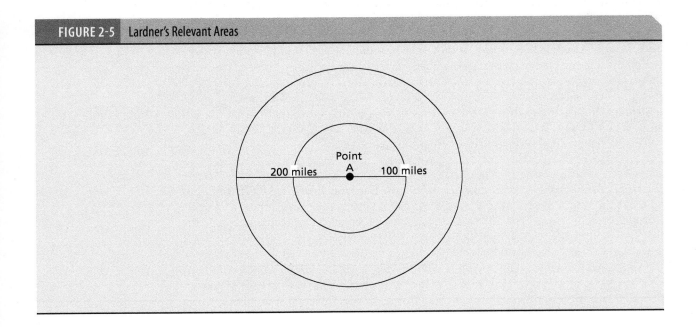

FIGURE 2-5   Lardner's Relevant Areas

in a market at a time when there is no demand for it, then it possesses no value. For example, the demand for Halloween costumes exists during a specific time of the year. After Halloween passes, these goods cannot be sold because they have little or no value in the market. Effective transportation can create time utility by ensuring that products arrive at the proper locations when needed. For example, raw materials for production, fruit, and Christmas toys all need to be at certain locations during specific times, or their value will be diminished. The increased emphasis upon just-in-time and scheduled deliveries as well as lean inventories has heightened the importance of time utility, especially for high-value products and emergency shipments. Air freight shipments are an indication of the importance of time utility.

Lardner's Law can also be related to time utility. For example, the speed of transportation might be a governing factor for the transportation of certain perishable products that have a limited shelf life. Assume the small circle in Figure 2-5 represents the current market area based on a specific transportation speed. If the speed were doubled, the potential service area would quadruple.

Quantity Utility In addition, transportation provides **quantity utility** through the assurance that the goods demanded will arrive without damage in the right quantity. Quantity utility has increased in importance in recent years with the increased emphasis placed on minimizing safety stock inventories for both shippers and receivers. Shippers might alter the form of the product to ensure safe transportation or change carriers with repeated failures. Carriers can use special bracing, blocking, and/or strapping, along with temperature control, to help ensure damage-free delivery. Time and quantity utility generally increase in importance as the value of goods increase because of related inventory carrying cost and stock out costs. For example, if the sale of a product is dependent upon its delivery on Tuesday afternoon and it arrives on Wednesday, the potential buyer may reject delivery. If the product had a profit margin of $100.00, the late delivery would cost the seller $100.00 in lost sales or more if additional charges were incurred.

Large-Scale Production Geographic specialization is complemented by large-scale production or **economies of scale**, which are the result of more efficient operations. However, without the use of efficient transportation networks, the advantages of scale economies, production efficiencies, and specialization could be lost. The raw materials for production need to be transported to a manufacturing facility, and the finished products must be transported out of an area at reasonable costs to markets and consumers at acceptable prices. Otherwise, the goods have no value. Geographic specialization assumes that the large-scale production of goods is demanded at different locations. Therefore, an area cannot rely upon its comparative advantage and large-scale production without the use of efficient transportation systems. The more efficient the transportation, the larger the potential market area and the possibility of increased scale economies. Time value can also be important in these situations, especially with perishable and/or seasonal products.

Land Values Transportation improvements that enhance an area's economy also can increase the value of land that is adjacent to or served by the transport improvements because the land becomes more accessible and potentially more useful. Today, the suburban centers provide excellent examples of land areas that have increased in value due to the accessibility that results from efficient transportation systems or infrastructure. Suburbanites can take advantage of nearby city life for work and pleasure and then retire to rural areas via public transportation networks or highways to avoid crowded living conditions. Commuters from Greenwich, Connecticut, to New York City and from Cherry Hill, New Jersey, to Philadelphia all reap both city and suburban benefits as the result of reliable transportation systems.

Consequently, the value of the land in the suburban areas has increased to reflect the advantageous lifestyles that the new or improved transportation systems have made possible. The land values within the city are obviously also enhanced by the economic development.

It is important to note that transportation may not always have a positive impact on land values. Noise and air pollution accompanying some networks can decrease adjacent land values. The homeowners who have to bear the burden of pollution can also suffer from overaccessibility. Like most system changes, there are always advantages and disadvantages when transportation improvements are made. Consequently, it is important that a thorough analysis be made of costs, including social costs, and potential benefits before an investment in transportation infrastructure is made. Such cost-benefit analysis is not an exact science, but careful analysis can help preclude a bad investment decision.

Gross Domestic Product (GDP)

Transportation plays a major role in the overall economy of the United States (see Table 2-5). On average, transportation accounts for about 9.0 percent of gross domestic product in the United States compared to housing (19.0%), health care (16.0%), food (10.0%), and education (7.0%). It is safe to say, that transportation is a major component of total expenditures in the U.S. economy. If we examine transportation as a component of household expenditures (Table 2-6), it accounts for 17 percent of household expenditures. Transportation expenditures are only exceeded by housing (33.0%). This is another indication of its importance not only in the economy but also to individual households.

TABLE 2-5	U.S. Gross Domestic Product by Major Societal Function 2015
FUNCTION	**PERCENT OF GDP**
Housing	19.0%
Health Care	16.0%
Transportation-related	9.0%
Food	10.0%
Education	7.0%
Other	39.0%

Source: U.S. Department of Transportation, Bureau of Transportation Statistics, *Pocket Guide to Transportation—2017*, Washington, DC, p. 49.

TABLE 2-6	Average Household Expenditures, 2015
CATEGORY	**PERCENT OF HOUSEHOLD EXPENDITURES**
Housing	33.0%
Transportation	17.0%
Personal Insurance and pensions	11.0%
Food	13.0%
Health Care	8.0%
Apparel and Services	3.0%
Other	15.0%

Source: U.S. Department of Transportation, Bureau of Transportation Statistics, *Pocket Guide to Transportation—2017*, Washington, DC, p. 52.

Passenger transportation has been growing in relation to the GDP until recently. Much of this increase was due to the greater use of automobiles and the energy costs associated with operating them. Air travel also accounted for a major part of transportation expenditures in the economy. The U.S. Department of Transportation (DOT) reports that in 2014 airlines accounted for about 16.4 percent of the total passenger-miles. Travel for business, personal, and vacation purposes are an important activity in the economy. With fuel prices fluctuating, it is anticipated that private vehicle travel will decrease with a move to public transportation and increased joint ridership.

Environmental Significance

Although transportation provides the economy with numerous benefits, these positive aspects are not without some associated social costs. As indicated previously, transportation sometimes pollutes the environment and exploits natural resources, although many citizens feel that the overall benefits provided by transportation exceed these costs. The environmental challenge of the future will be to accurately assess the relationship between industrial and consumer benefits compared to their construction and external, societal costs associated with transportation improvements.

The Environment

There has been growing concern over the impact of transportation on the environment in recent years, with particular emphasis on air quality (pollution), noise, and water quality. The synergy between the transportation system and the environment is increasingly being investigated by both environmentalists and by transportation planners at all governmental levels. In fact, increasing pressure from the environmentalists has resulted in legal restrictions that help govern the balance between a sound and efficient transportation system and a safe and clean environment. The term, **sustainability**, has become a part of our vocabulary. Transportation is an important part of all supply chains and will receive increasing attention in environmental analyses and discussions. The major change that has occurred is the acceptance by businesses and other organizations that they have an important role to play in helping to make improvements in this area. Perhaps, even more important is a growing recognition that it does not have to be a "zero sum game." In other words, reductions in an organization's carbon footprint, for example, can be accomplished along with reductions in the cost of transportation operations with careful planning. Many companies are looking at their transportation operations from this "win-win" perspective.

There is already a growing challenge in the 21st century to ensure efficient transportation facilities and mobility by maintaining the present system and developing alternatives to meet the growing needs of individuals and organizations. There will probably be even more trade-offs between competing objectives. Highway and air planners will be particularly challenged to develop innovative design solutions because of the large number of federal statutes and executive orders governing the environment. From a user perspective, these constraints may be viewed as burdensome bureaucracy that slows down the completion of the project, but they are, for the most part, a necessary "filter" to screen and mitigate negative changes in our transportation infrastructure.

Maritime Water Quality   The protection of the marine environment from the adverse effects of oil spills, garbage dumping from ships, hazardous material losses, and so on is a growing concern shared by many federal and state agencies. One of the largest oil spills occurred in 1989 near Valdez, Alaska, from a tanker ship carrying crude oil from Alaska for the Exxon

Oil Company. Almost 11 million gallons of crude oil were spilled; this environmental disaster raised awareness for controls and better contingency preparedness to respond to such accidents. But there have been a continuing number of spills on various waterways and in the oceans. The increased size of vessels has heightened the concern and increased the potential for significant damage.

In recent years, there has been a growing concern about the damage that plastic items and other ship-generated garbage can cause to the marine environment. Birds, marine mammals, and sea turtles are susceptible to this type of refuse because they can ingest the materials and die as a result. It is estimated that more than one million birds die each year from ingesting these materials. It is very difficult to control and/or regulate this form of pollution.

Water quality, both for surface water and drinking water sources, is an area of risk and concern. Both surface water and drinking water sources are highly susceptible to many types of potential pollutants. Again, there will be continuing pressure to protect water quality by governmental controls and standards.

Noise Another type of pollution is noise, which can emit from many sources, including transportation. There is an annoyance factor, but also a health concern involved. Airplanes and motor vehicles are the major causes of noise. The U.S. DOT and the Federal Aviation Administration have been particularly active in this area, helping to guide land use planning for compatibility with transportation facilities and conducting research to help solve the problem. Noise emissions are governed by the Noise Control Act of 1972, which allows the setting of operational standards for aircraft and trucks and even rail equipment operated by interstate carriers.

Safety

One of the more disturbing by-products of transportation is injury and loss of life. In 2014, a total of 34,641 persons lost their lives in the United States while engaged in transport. Approximately 78 percent of those fatalities occurred in highway vehicles. However, the number of deaths has remained relatively stable in relation to the ever-growing demand for transportation. This positive statistic is the result of increased licensing regulations and more reliable vehicle designs. Unfortunately, trends in the area of safety for freight transportation are not as promising. Train accidents, oil spills, and the threat of gaseous explosions while in transit have increased. With an increasing variety of products being shipped and an increasing volume of transportation, these problems require greater attention. We can hope that safety in freight transportation will soon parallel the progress made in passenger transportation; however, much work remains to be done.

Social Significance

A good transportation system also can enhance the health and welfare of a population. One of the major problems that has faced the famine relief efforts in the various regions of Africa is the lack of sufficient and effective transportation networks to move needed food and farm supplies from the ports inland to the population centers. Insufficient railroads, roads, vehicles, storage, and related distribution facilities hampered effective delivery of the needed food and supplies. In addition, one of the problems facing the region in normal times is insufficient transportation, which hinders inbound and outbound product flows.

A well-developed transportation system also contributes improved health and education delivery systems and effective communications among regions of a country. Overall, transportation plays a major social role in our economy that is not always fully appreciated nor understood by the citizenry.

Political Significance

The origin and maintenance of transportation systems are dependent on the government. Government intervention is needed to design feasible routes, cover the expense of building public highways, and develop harbors and waterways. Adequate transportation is needed to create national unity; the transportation network permits the leaders of government to travel rapidly to and communicate with the people they govern.

Closely connected with transportation's political role is its function as a provider for national defense. Today our transportation system enhances our lifestyles and protects us from foreign enemies. The ability to transport troops acts as both a weapon and a deterrent in this age of energy shortages and global conflicts. The conflicts in Central America, Africa, and the Middle East place even greater emphasis on the importance of transportation in protecting our distant vital interests.

Although it is accurate to say that the American transportation system has been shaped by economic factors, political and military developments have also played important roles. Transportation policy incorporates more than economics—the expected benefits of the system extend beyond the economic realm.

SUMMARY

- Transportation is a pervasive and very important part of all developed economies and is a key ingredient for underdeveloped countries to progress to economic development and independence.
- The history of the United States is replete with evidence of the close correlation of advances in transportation technology with our advancing economic development from the Erie Canal to our modern highways and air systems.
- Transportation systems are the lifelines of cities and the surrounding suburbs. Tons of products are moved into cities every day to promote the health and welfare of its citizens. In addition, products which are produced in the cities are moved out for shipment elsewhere.
- Transportation contributes to the value of goods by providing time and place utility. That is, effective and efficient transportation moves products to points where there is a demand for the product and at a time when it is needed.
- Geographic and labor specialization are important cornerstones of industrialized countries and transportation provides one of the necessary ingredients for this to occur.
- The more efficient the transportation system, the greater the possibility of scale economies and increased market areas.
- Improved transportation in an area will usually increase land values because of the improved accessibility to raw materials and markets.
- The flow and patterns for commerce influence transportation infrastructure patterns of developing countries.

- Transportation expenditures for freight and passengers are an important part of the gross domestic product in the United States.
- While transportation provides many benefits, it can also contribute to environmental problems including pollution, poor air quality, acid rain, and global climate changes.

STUDY QUESTIONS

1. There is much discussion on the local, state, and federal levels about the need to repair and improve the Interstate Highway System. Provide a rationale for this need.

2. "Transportation is the most important economic factor for economic development." Do you agree or disagree with this statement? Why or why not?

3. The opening of the Erie Canal and the building of the transcontinental railroads in the 19th century were described as significant milestones for the economic development in the United States. Explain their importance individually and collectively.

4. The highways and other transportation networks that serve major metropolitan areas are frequently described as the lifelines of the metropolitan area. Do you agree with this statement? Why or why not?

5. Compare and contrast time and place utility, and explain how they contribute to the value of products. What is the importance of time and place utility in our global economy?

6. Adam Smith stated that specialization of labor was limited by the extent of the market and that transportation helps to expand the market. Explain the meaning and importance of this statement.

7. Economists often point to the impact of improved transportation on land values and related economic development. What is the nature and significance of the transportation impact?

8. While improved transportation systems provide economic benefits, there may be some associated environmental costs. What are the major environmental costs associated with transportation and what are their potential negative impacts?

9. "Improved transportation systems can also have social and political significance." Why are these important considerations for evaluating existing and/or proposed additions to the transportation system?

10. The service characteristics of freight movements are considered by some shippers to be as important as or more important than the freight rate. Discuss the various service characteristics for freight demand. Do you agree with the statement that they may be as important as or even more important than the freight rate? Why or why not?

NOTES

1. D. Philip Locklin, *Economics of Transportation*, 7th ed., Homewood, Illinois: Richard D. Irwin, Inc., 1972, pp. 28–33.

2. Ibid., pp. 34–37.

3. Ibid., pp. 38–40.

CASE 2-1
Highways Galore

Kelly Edwards, the recently appointed vice president of development for HOG, Inc., a highway construction company in central Pennsylvania, had just returned from meeting with the senior management team of the company. At the meeting, Harry O. Growbaker, president of HOG, Inc., had reported on his most recent meetings with the Pennsylvania Department of Transportation in Harrisburg. The focus of the presentation and discussion was a new state funding initiative that would support regional highway projects throughout the state. The highways, bridges, and overall infrastructure throughout the state needed improvements and expansion. The development of significant shale gas and oil drilling had strained the existing network but had provided additional tax funds for needed public projects. Harry O. Growbaker was convinced that HOG, Inc. was in a unique position to participate, but that they needed to be proactive to demonstrate the economic benefit and impact of such stimulus spending in central Pennsylvania. Harry asked Kelly to provide some discussion points for the next meeting of the senior management team.

Kelly decided to meet with two of her senior staff members, Shaun Knight and Barb Collins, to help with this assignment. During the course of their discussion, Kelly pointed out the lack of efficient and effective highway connections throughout the center of the state. Interstate 80 was a major east–west corridor for interstate traffic between the Midwest and major East Coast cities, but with limited impact overall in much of central Pennsylvania, particularly for north–south flows. The potential economic growth in central Pennsylvania was creating a need for a more effective north–south link and also more efficient local roadways. Barb Collins felt that a proposed highway link would be attractive to the state and also the federal government.

Shaun, who had participated in many economic impact studies, pointed out the possible synergism with the University Park campus of Penn State and perhaps some of their satellite locations throughout the state. He noted the development of the research park at Penn State's University Park Campus and the new University president's interest in helping the state with economic development and playing a more active role in encouraging new companies based upon applied research at the university. Shaun felt that there was much opportunity to encourage and enhance such development with improved transportation.

Kelly Edwards became excited as she listened to this discussion and was convinced that they could develop a list of discussion points for the next senior management meeting that could then be developed into a white paper for the state and Federal Departments of Transportation.

You have recently been hired by HOG, Inc., and Ms. Edwards has asked you to develop an initial set of discussion points that would indicate the economic and, perhaps, social benefits from new highway links in central Pennsylvania.

CASE 2-2

Transportation and Economic Activity

The oldest and most economically, socially, and politically developed cities in the world are located on the coasts of the major continents. This is no surprise since water transportation is the oldest form of established transportation in the world. In the United States, cities like Philadelphia and New York were established centuries ago because of access to the Atlantic Ocean.

However, a similar pattern can be found in the United States with inland cities, such as Pittsburgh, Pennsylvania, and Detroit, Michigan. While these cities do not have access to coastal waters, they are situated near inland waterways. Also unique to these two cities was their manufacturing specialization: steel in Pittsburgh and automobiles in Detroit. Using the information contained in this chapter:

1. Explain what role transportation played in the development of these two cities.
2. Discuss what factors would lead to their manufacturing specialization.
3. Identify any other benefits to a city or geography that manufacturing specialization would create.

CHAPTER

3

TRANSPORTATION TECHNOLOGY AND SYSTEMS

Learning Objectives

After reading this chapter, you should be able to do the following:

› Appreciate the critical role of information in transportation management

› Explain transportation information requirements

› Understand the capabilities of transportation software

› Describe and differentiate between planning, execution, and performance management tools

› Articulate the benefits of transportation management systems

› Discuss the critical issues in technology selection and implementation

› Recognize the important role of equipment technology in transportation sustainability, safety, and cargo security

› Identify the disruptive technologies that will spur transportation service innovation

TRANSPORTATION **PROFILE**

Cold Chain Pharma Logistics Is Heating Up

Most of us have seen the ads where millions are ordering fresh food delivered as ready-to-prepare ingredients to their homes—products that require control of exposure to extreme temperatures and extended last-mile transit times.

This consumer-focused "cold chain"—temperature-controlled supply chain—is only a recent example of a decades-long push to perfect a global system of item-level tracking in supply chain management. While the food industry has been dealing with this issue for hundreds of years, the pharmaceutical (pharma) industry is, by comparison, just getting warmed up.

Two major factors are driving the change in the pharma supply chain. First is the critical need to eliminate counterfeit drugs. The World Health Organization (WHO) is estimating that 10 percent of the drugs that reach consumers are fake—that is to say "useless" or even containing harmful substitutes. To solve this challenge, the industry is adopting technology to maintain a "pedigree," or a chain of ownership from manufacturing through retail distribution.

The second factor is the increasing variety of drugs that require temperature control while in transit. "The storage and distribution of controlled room temperature life science products are a costly and complex process, and requires attention at every level from packaging to logistics and monitoring to data," Lisa Forian, senior director of product quality management at Johnson & Johnson recently wrote. "As we enter an age of biologically based medicines, the need to monitor and control temperature sensitivity is increasing."

To summarize Forian's comments, reaching patients in remote areas, perhaps by drone, with a prescription that is 2 degrees to 8 degrees centigrade is a challenge worthy of our best supply chain engineers.

Indeed, the temperature challenge is more difficult for pharma shippers, and requires both a monitoring tool and a symphony of coordinated actions all along the supply chain. The solution for shippers and service providers in both areas is LCP—learn, collaborate, and pilot.

Under "learn," I recommend becoming familiar with international efforts in safe pharma logistics. The WHO has issued good distribution practices (GDP) for pharmaceutical products standards, and I would consider becoming a temperature assurance packaging (TAP) professional through courses offered by industry professionals.

Mastery of the subject means one can understand the fundamentals of temperature assurance packaging and be able to evaluate different solutions that best meet the needs of one's company; guide the implementation of temperature assurance packaging solutions within your organization; and grasp the key processes, protocols, and techniques involved in designing temperature-controlled packaging.

Under "collaborate," shippers need to be become even more transparent with their partners and work jointly to model and build end-to-end supply chains with tracking. In fact, I recently had the honor of leading a joint industry team of shippers, third-party logistics providers and carriers in testing tracking capabilities using RFID hardware combined with tracking software shared by the participants.

This was one of several labs developed to successfully demonstrate pedigree logistics feasibility to the U.S. Food and Drug Administration. The parties openly shared internal processes and technologies in order to achieve remarkable visibility to possession and handling of the product.

"Pilot" is the step where the parties actually move products through the supply chain, monitoring each step and critically evaluating their own and their partners' performance. When you boil it all down, digital communication and data collection are the true enablers for cold chain.

While technologies are becoming available, the processes and people skills needed are still in development. Shippers and carriers in the cold chain stream need to step up and learn, collaborate, and pilot for safe, efficient service to customers.

Source: Peter Moore, "Cold Chain Pharma Logistics Is Heating Up," *Logistics Management*, August 28, 2017. Retrieved October 5, 2017, from http://www.logisticsmgmt.com/article/cold_chain_pharma_logistics_is_heating_up/transportation.

Introduction

Transportation is the critical linking mechanism in the supply chain. It ensures that food, fuel, and medical supplies are readily available at the point of demand. Also critical is information about the in-transit freight. Transportation professionals need up-to-date knowledge about freight location, quantity, status, and expected arrival for planning, quality control, and customer service. Awareness of the product pedigree and in-transit temperature also are essential, according to the Transportation Profile feature. This type of knowledge ensures that food and pharmaceutical products are kept safe as they move across the cold chain.

Monitoring temperatures, managing flows, and meeting delivery deadlines cannot be accomplished manually. With so much product in motion between worldwide origin and destination points, technology is needed to maintain control and promote safe, timely, and cost-efficient transportation. Correctly used, these tools provide remote data collection, rapid digital communication, and decision support for transportation of products across cold chains and every other type of supply chain.

Recognizing the value and potential of transportation technology to provide greater visibility and supply chain optimization, organizations have invested vast sums of money to capture, analyze, and share critical information about their freight flows. The global market for transportation management system (TMS) software was $9.6 billion in 2016. An industry report projects that TMS sales will reach $30 billion by the end of 2025, driven by the rise of mobile computing platforms, intermodal transportation, and cloud-based solutions.[1]

Robust spending on transportation technology extends beyond software. Companies are investing in technologies to make their transportation equipment safer and more fuel efficient. Innovators are rapidly developing and testing drone technology and autonomous vehicles for freight movement. And, everyone is looking to harness emerging technologies like the Internet of Things (IoT) for transportation visibility, control, and decision making.

This chapter focuses on the role of information and technology in transportation. It is intended to highlight the key information issues and tools that facilitate perfect delivery processes. The chapter is divided into five sections that address the following topics: (1) information requirements, (2) transportation software solutions, (3) transportation software selection and implementation, (4) transportation equipment technology, and (5) emerging technologies. Throughout the chapter, you will learn that technology drives transportation in successful 21st century supply chains.

Information Requirements[2]

Supply chains rely upon three flows—product, money, and information. Nowhere is the information aspect more relevant than in transportation. With so many transportation activities occurring after a shipment leaves your facility—intermodal transfers, border crossings, re-routing, and final delivery, to name a few possibilities—it can be very difficult to maintain control. You need accurate, timely information to stay connected to the freight. That information-based visibility is key to maintaining cross-chain knowledge, assessing situations, and taking appropriate corrective actions when a vehicle breaks down, port congestion becomes severe, or a driver goes off-route.

Effective transportation management and decision making depends on three fundamental information requirements. First, the information available to transportation professionals must meet quality standards to support fact-based analysis. Second, the information must readily flow within and between organizations. Third, the information must be actionable to support transportation decision making.

These three elements are essential to maintaining a virtual line of sight to freight at all points across the supply chain. Otherwise, blind spots will result and opportunities for collaboration will be lost. Transportation professionals will be relegated to making educated guesses based on individual assumptions rather than shared truths. That is not an effective way to manage transportation processes.

Quality Standards

Information quality is a critical characteristic of the vast amounts of data flowing across a transportation network. Value trumps volume and transportation professionals must be sure that they are basing decisions on correct information. A twist on the seven rights of logistics definition provides clarity about what transportation information must achieve—getting the right information to the right partners, in the right quantity, in the right format, at the right place, at the right time, and at the right cost. Change any "right" to "wrong" and transportation decision makers will find the information to be of limited quality and value.

To ensure that actionable knowledge readily flows between shippers, carriers, and customers, information must display a variety of key characteristics. Chief among these attributes are accuracy, accessibility, relevancy, timeliness, and transferability. Also important are issues of usability, reliability, and value.

Accuracy Transportation information must depict reality. A true picture of freight status and location that is free of errors facilitates logical decision making. In contrast, decisions based on inaccurate information can lead to delivery delays, inventory shortages, and unhappy customers. For example, Toyota and other lean manufacturers depend on timely delivery of materials. If a transportation planner schedules a delivery appointment at the Toyota factory but has miscalculated the transit time by six hours, the appointment will be missed and the assembly line may shut down due to a parts shortage.

Accessibility Accurate transportation information must be available to supply chain professionals who have a legitimate need for it, regardless of their role, location, or employer. For example, UPS needs insight to Amazon's order volume to stage an adequate number of trailers at Amazon's shipping docks each day. Gaining accessibility to needed information can be difficult because transportation data often are dispersed among multiple companies, locations, and information systems. Technical barriers must be overcome to ensure systems connectivity and good information flows.

Relevancy Transportation professionals must have access to pertinent information for analysis and decision making. Irrelevant data and unnecessary details must be avoided as they hide important details, waste time, and distract decision makers. When an Apple expeditor logs on to the FedEx website to track a critical delivery, he doesn't need to know about every Apple shipment handled by FedEx that day. He wants quick access to the status of the one shipment in question, allowing him to respond accordingly.

Timeliness To be relevant, transportation information must be up-to-date and available in a reasonable time frame. Timely data flows from a highly synchronized information system allow you to monitor network conditions and respond quickly with corrective actions to avoid additional problems. For example, rapid discovery of a major accident on a highway would allow transportation dispatchers to re-route trucks away from the bottleneck until the congestion has dissipated. That will avoid lost productivity and delivery delays.

Transferability Information also needs to be transferred quickly between locations and systems in the transportation network to facilitate accessibility and timeliness. A paper-based transportation system cannot support these requirements. Hence, information must reside in electronic formats that can be readily transmitted and converted. Fortunately, digitalization of transportation information makes electronic transfers relatively easy, inexpensive, and safe, though organizations must protect against security breaches.

Usability Information is useful only if it can drive effective decision making. Up-front efforts must be made to define information requirements and capture appropriate data. This will avoid the time and costs of capturing extraneous data that will not be used by transportation decision makers. Also, information is only usable if it can be seamlessly shared and translated from one format to another with no discernible loss of data.

Reliability The information contained in transportation reports and transaction data sets must come from trustworthy internal and external sources. The data must be accurate, unaltered, and reasonably complete to support the intended uses. When incomplete or estimated data is provided, a clear explanation of the missing values and assumptions is needed so that a decision maker's analysis can be adjusted accordingly.

Value Achieving these seven quality standards is neither an easy nor a cost-free proposition. The hardware and software needed to capture and disseminate transportation data can be expensive, though costs are coming down thanks to innovations like cloud computing. Transportation professionals must target information technology investments that enhance knowledge and generate tangible benefits.

Multidirectional Flow

The engagement of multiple stakeholders in transportation planning and decision making drives a need for multidirectional information flows across the network. Internal information sharing supports cross-functional collaboration and organization-wide performance optimization. Transportation planners must be privy to demand forecasts, order fulfillment schedules, and customer service commitments to secure adequate capacity with quality carriers.

Information must flow seamlessly between a company, its suppliers, and its customers. Information sharing promotes integrated decision making and process synchronization. For example, shared insights regarding suppliers' production schedules facilitates alignment and efficient execution of inbound transportation. A steady stream of timely and accurate customer demand data is needed to drive effective scheduling for outbound deliveries. Being able to coordinate inbound and outbound requirements will support continuous routes and high equipment utilization.

Transportation providers must also be kept in the information loop regarding upstream and downstream customer requirements. This knowledge allows the service providers to marshal needed labor and equipment resources. A failure to communicate with service providers can lead to fulfillment delays and customer dissatisfaction.

Likewise, the transportation providers must support customers' information requirements. Visibility and analytics provide timely insights that assist customers with decision making. The On the Line feature reveals that technology can provide insights that differentiate a transportation provider from its competition.

Information flows must also be established with groups that indirectly impact transportation processes. Financial institutions participate in the movement of relevant information regarding payments and transactions. Government agencies require ongoing communication regarding trade data and regulatory compliance. Financial consequences can result from a failure to properly establish information flows with these organizations.

ON THE LINE

Maersk Makes Bold Bid at Differentiation by Teaming with CRM Giant

There was much talk at IANA this week about the ocean carrier's failure to differentiate their services amid ever greater consolidation and alliances. Some of that apprehension may have been addressed by Maersk today when it announced that it has teamed with Salesforce, the San Francisco-based leader in CRM.

Maersk Line—a worldwide leader in transportation and logistics, with a fleet of more than 600 vessels that move in excess of 12 million shipping containers each year—is expanding its use of Salesforce, adding Salesforce Marketing Cloud, Einstein Analytics, and Community Cloud to its current deployment of Sales Cloud and Service Cloud.

Steen Erik Larsen, senior director IT at Maersk Line A/S notes that success in the complex and high-stakes world of global transport and logistics relies on meeting customer expectations every step of the way. With Salesforce, he says, Maersk is bringing the entire shipper "journey," on one platform and adding analytics to get deeper insights that will allow the carrier to prepare for evolving needs.

Maritime industry analysts have been challenging the idea that carriers are adequately prepared for today's dynamic and fluid marketplace. But Cindy Bolt, SVP, Salesforce Industries, Manufacturing and Consumer Goods, maintains that this partnership is a sign that one major player is shipper-focused.

"Shipping line operations are immensely complex," she says. "Equally complex is the ability to provide seamless customer experiences on a global scale. Maersk Line is addressing this challenge by unifying its sales, service and marketing on Salesforce, which will lead to more personalized, 1-to-1 experiences across the customer lifecycle."

Source: Patrick Burnson, "Maersk Makes Bold Bid at Differentiation by Teaming with CRM Giant," *Logistics Management*, September 21, 2017. Retrieved October 12, 2017, from http://www.logisticsmgmt.com/article/maersk_makes_bold_bid_at_differentiation_by_teaming_with_crm_giant/transportation. Reprinted with permission.

Decision Support

With rapid delivery service becoming the norm in many supply chains, access to transportation information must expand. Managers at every location connected to the transportation network require information to excel in their roles. This intelligence is needed for strategic decision making, tactical planning, routing decision making, and execution and transaction processing.[3]

Strategic decision-making focuses on the creation of long-range transportation plans that are aligned with the organization's mission and strategies. The required information is often unstructured and may differ from one project to the next. For example, a decision to expand from domestic to global markets will require a great deal of supporting data regarding transportation service availability, modal options and prices, and infrastructure quality in the proposed markets. The transportation data is used to evaluate market entry alternatives, facility locations, and economic viability of the proposal.

Tactical planning focuses on cross-organization linkages and transportation activity coordination. Information must be readily available, support mid-range planning processes, and be in a flexible format that can be modified by the participants for use in their systems. For example, transportation contract negotiations require information sharing by the customer about freight volume and timing, origin and destination points, service level requirements, and related data to facilitate effective analysis and proposal development by the transportation provider.

Routine decision-making leverages operational level information for rules-based decision making. The input data needs to be standardized so that the information system can generate appropriate solutions. For example, an automated transportation routing guide uses a shipment's origin, destination, product characteristics, weight, dimensions, rates, and service-level requirements data to recommend an appropriate mode and carrier. Decision makers retain the ability to review and adjust the recommended solution as needed.

Execution and transaction processing uses fundamental information from supply chain databases, customer profiles, transportation routing guides, and related sources to complete fulfillment and delivery activities. As discussed earlier in this section, the information must be accurate, readily retrievable, and useable so that it can be processed automatically in a timely fashion. For example, selection of a transportation provider for an omnichannel order should be made without human intervention. The TMS system should optimize the decision based on customer location, speed of service requested, and the contract price established with each carrier.

Ultimately, all three information requirements must be met to drive efficient and effective transportation decisions. Quality information must readily flow to essential stakeholders across the transportation network so that they can take appropriate short-, mid-, and long-range actions in support of supply chain excellence.

Transportation Software

The importance of information in transportation cannot be understated. Transportation professionals need easy access to data in a usable format, accurately analyze the data, and properly apply the output to their decisions. That is an arduous task, given the volume and variety of transportation data that is constantly being created.

Also creating complexity is the variety of issues that must be considered and decisions that must be made. Before a shipment is scheduled for delivery, it must be evaluated by both transportation providers and freight shippers in terms of the various lane/mode/carrier/ service level/price combinations available. After the parties agree upon a price for the chosen service level, pickup must be arranged, routing planned, equipment selected, and an operator assigned. During transit, the shipment must be monitored and tracked. Upon arrival, the delivery must be confirmed and the freight inspected. After customer acceptance, the freight bill must be paid and the operator and equipment need to be reassigned.

Fortunately, transportation professionals no longer need to manage these tasks with pencil, paper, landline telephones, expert intuition, and hope. Powerful software is readily available to help both transportation providers and freight shippers make key decisions, proactively manage freight flows, and simultaneously achieve optimal cost control and excellent service performance.

These software tools cover a wide range of capabilities. Point solutions address a single need such as load configuration or route planning. Highly integrated systems with multiple capabilities combine many of the crucial point solutions and provide decision support for all aspects of the delivery process. This section presents an overview of the most widely used integrated system.

Transportation Management Systems

The planning and flow of materials across the supply chain are handled by a Transportation Management System (TMS). The core set of business needs handled by a TMS include: routing and rating, executing the shipment across multiple modes, tracking and tracing loads, and freight settlement.[4] This simple booking, execution, and payment perspective focuses on freight management, but a TMS can be much more than a transaction-focused tool. Leading edge TMS suites provide hybrid planning–execution–evaluation capabilities and a wide array of functionality to generate numerous benefits across the entire shipping process.

TMS Decision Support Capabilities[5] As the capabilities and scope of a TMS expand, the software moves from being a routine decision support tool to a much more integrative system. It provides greater decision support for transportation strategic, tactical, and operational planning, as well as delivery execution, in-transit visibility, and performance evaluation.

The planning capabilities of TMS assist supply chain managers with preshipment decisions related to network design, fleet planning, rate analysis and contracting, mode and carrier selection, and routing and scheduling. The optimization capabilities of TMS allow managers to rapidly assess all possible delivery options versus the hours that it would take to manually develop a transportation plan that considers only a finite number of options. Up-to-date information from the organization's warehouse management system (WMS), demand forecasts, and customer orders can be used to make more effective transportation decisions.

TMS execution capabilities help transportation professionals improve decisions about transit-related activities. The TMS should enable managers to seamlessly interface with order management and WMS applications to quickly identify transportation needs based on order size, origin, destination, and service requirements. By automating many of these execution activities, a TMS helps an organization reduce errors and delays, improve accountability and visibility, and limit deviation from standard operation procedures. The result will be lower cost, higher quality delivery processes.

A TMS makes it easier to have freight visibility across the transportation network so that everyone involved, including the customer knows exactly where the shipments are at any time. Transportation professionals can use TMS-driven visibility to monitor freight movement progress, environmental conditions inside the container, and estimated arrival time versus the commitment made to a customer. If alerted to a potential problem or delay, the transportation professional can use this knowledge to take corrective actions.

TMS evaluation tools give organizations the postshipment ability to rapidly analyze delivery metrics related to timeliness, cost, safety, and customer satisfaction. Much of the needed information is captured directly by the TMS while other data comes from other systems and delivery documents. A strong TMS can coalesce and present the data in performance reports and scorecards that can be used for carrier benchmarking, invoice auditing, performance improvement planning, and future purchase decisions.

TMS Functionality[6] As described above, a comprehensive TMS can assist transportation professionals in nearly every aspect of freight movement. From strategic planning that focuses on complex multimodal and multileg route planning for international shipments to straightforward load configuration analysis for greater trailer utilization, the functionality is quite powerful. Figure 3-1 highlights the broad array of TMS capabilities in each decision area.

From a planning perspective, TMS functionality focuses on the up-front effort to create optimal deliveries that balance cost and service. Key planning support capabilities include:

- **Routing and scheduling**—Proper planning of delivery routes has a major impact on customer satisfaction, supply chain performance, and organizational success. TMS software uses mathematical models and optimization routines to identify feasible routes that meet service constraints. Typical TMS output includes a detailed schedule of the routes, cost analysis, and route maps.

- **Mode and carrier selection**—A TMS identifies the most appropriate mode and carrier in terms of efficiency and timing. Using the organization's contracts and routing guide criteria, the system can pinpoint the best choices based on shipment

FIGURE 3-1 TMS Capabilities

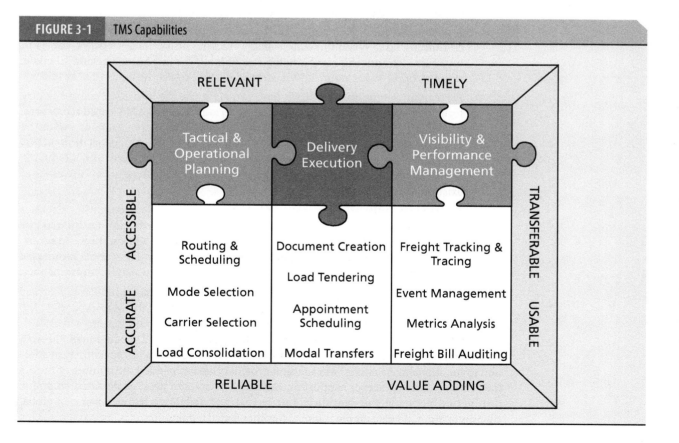

characteristics, previous carrier performance and price, and service requirements. This improves contract compliance, service, and freight spending.

- **Load planning**—Effective preparation of safe, efficient deliveries can be accomplished via TMS load optimization programs. Based on product dimensions, loading requirements, and equipment capacity, the TMS software determines how shipments should be arranged in the container or on a pallet. The result is reduced damage risk and improved cargo space utilization.

In the execution area, a TMS can automate a variety of activities to save time, avoid errors, and reduce cost. Typical TMS execution functionality includes:

- **Document creation**—Freight movement requires a significant amount of documentation, particularly for international shipments. An effective TMS automates document production and customs reporting, helping to ensure that all of the paperwork required to complete a shipment is prepared correctly and presented to the right people at the right time, and in the right format.

- **Load tendering**—For a given origin–destination pair and shipment size, multiple carriers may be available, though at slightly different rates. When the WMS indicates that an order is ready for shipping, the TMS will tender the load to the appropriate carrier.

- **Appointment scheduling**—To avoid facility congestion, equipment delays, and operator inefficiency, organizations use TMS capabilities to automate the scheduling function. Many systems support Internet-based access to the scheduling system where carriers can schedule pickup and delivery times at specific dock locations.

Importantly, a TMS provides valuable intelligence during and after the delivery process. Necessary visibility and performance management functionality include:

- **Track and trace**—Maintaining shipment visibility across the network is a time-consuming task. When linked to satellite tracking or a cellular network, the TMS monitors in-transit shipment location and status. If the shipment is behind schedule, stopped, or off-route, notifications are made so that corrective action can be taken.

- **Performance monitoring**—TMS tools can automate the measurement of key performance indicators and dissemination of periodic reports. TMS-based scorecards, dashboards, and reports provide information on overall performance as well as the results in specific segments of the transportation operation. Transportation professionals can use this output resourcefully for making effective decisions, identifying needs and key areas of functional enhancement, and evaluating the effectiveness of existing strategies.

- **Freight bill auditing**—Payments made to carriers must reflect the contractual rates and the services promised. To ensure that they are neither being overcharged nor undercharged for freight services, many organizations use TMS software to reconcile invoices with their contracts prior to making payments. These tools automate a manual process that did not always catch discrepancies in a timely, accurate manner.

Each year, Gartner evaluates TMS software vendors on a variety of criteria to identify the key players in the marketplace. Gartner notes that the functionality continues to expand: "TMS suites have been extended to include all transportation management functions across multiple modes—from strategic planning, strategic freight sourcing and procurement, through visibility and performance management, to freight payment and audit capabilities. In addition to functional expansion, TMS solution providers have expanded the number of modes they support, adding deeper support for modes such as small package or parcel shipping, private fleet planning and execution, intermodal, and rail. With the expansion of global supply chains, TMS also embrace global logistics functions and features."[7]

TABLE 3-1	Benefits of a TMS
CATEGORY	**DETAIL**
Reduce expedited order costs	Many firms report a reduction in high-cost, expedited shipments due to better planning and system-directed exception handling.
Increase load consolidation	By using the TMS to consolidate loads from parcel to LTL and from LTL to TL, firms report significant savings.
Optimize carrier and mode selection	Reduced costs due to automating the selection of lowest-rate carrier, mode, and accessorial combination.
Identify transportation invoice discrepancies	Discrepancies can be identified by automating the audit of freight invoice against the original contract.
Track carrier performance	Firms report using the carrier performance information to help negotiate better rates.
Lower administrative costs	With the automation of the tendering, shipment creation, and consolidation processes, firms report being able to re-deploy staff.
More accurate "available to promise"	Some firms report an increase in sales as a direct result of being able to quote response time more quickly.
Contract savings	By improving demand estimates, firms can procure materials in advance and save by negotiating long-term contracts.
Utilize assets more effectively	Increasingly, TMS solutions are taking on asset-based fleet management functions to better leverage drivers and equipment.

Source: Forrester Research, Inc. Retrieved from http://www.scdigest.com/assets/newsViews/08-04-03-1.php?cid=1588&gt.

TMS Benefits An investment in a TMS can generate a variety of cost and operational benefits. Table 3-1 summarizes the value proposition of a TMS.

A widely cited and highly desirable advantage offered by a TMS is cost savings that increase return on investment (ROI). Various studies indicate that use of a TMS helps an organization reduce freight costs by 6 percent to 10 percent. Users have attributed the savings to more effective mode selection, better routing, and better procurement negotiations.

By providing transportation professionals with desktop and mobile access to carrier rates and service information, a TMS also provides the ability to make better, faster carrier selection decisions that optimize costs, flows, and delivery. With this access, the freight buyer can quickly choose the best available option.

Another important reason to use TMS is the dramatic increase in end-to-end transportation network visibility. The TMS organizes relevant information into precise and easy-to-read lists, which equips the transportation professional to make impactful business decisions during critical moments that improve customers' experiences.

Increased paperwork accuracy results from automated documentation processes. Key documents are produced using the TMS database of international, regulatory, and multilingual documentation and creating electronic and nonelectronic customs filing. This capability helps the transportation professional avoid delays due to missing or incorrect documentation.

Other notable TMS benefits include improved customer delivery performance, greater compliance with regulatory requirements, and stronger data security. Effective TMS suites also integrate effectively with WMS and order management systems to seamlessly share information and support end-to-end fulfillment processes.

Additional Applications

A TMS is not the only software resource available to transportation professionals. Most TMS functions, such as routing and scheduling tools and freight costing tools, can be purchased as stand-alone applications. Users may find that these individual tools offer more features, greater customization and power than found in a TMS suite.

Transportation providers and private fleets may use mode-specific software to plan and execute their operations. These for-hire or internal service providers must be concerned with issues regarding transportation equipment maintenance, fuel cost and management, driver communication, fleet optimization, and regulatory compliance for drivers and equipment. Many of these functions are found in enterprise-wide solutions like McLeod LoadMaster and MercuryGate Fleet that support asset-based carriers.

Specialized carriers often rely upon hazardous materials transportation software to ensure safety and compliance. Shipping dangerous goods is a complicated, time-consuming process and keeping up in the rapidly changing regulatory world requires the use of technology. Most hazmat shipping software functions as an add-on solution to a TMS and provides alerts and messages necessary to assist the user in making correct decisions. The software generates all necessary documents and labels that are required to comply with government and carrier regulations. Some solutions also include (and regularly update) electronic copies of hazmat publications to keep the organization properly informed.

International companies will find global trade management (GTM) software to be helpful with cross-border business. GTM systems focus on helping organizations comply with the myriad regulations governing how components and products cross borders. From a transportation standpoint, some GTM systems are adding tools that can help coordinate the physical flow of goods, provide visibility to inventory and products, check whether certain materials qualify for preferential treatment under a trade agreement, and help with transaction payments and settlement processes.[8]

Transportation Software Selection and Implementation[9]

As the preceding section indicates, numerous software tools support transportation planning, execution, visibility, and evaluation. Companies spend billions of dollars on technology with the goal of making their transportation networks more productive. However, the mere purchase of point solutions or software suites does not guarantee quick success. Systems integration complexities and training requirements translate into implementation times that can exceed six months at costs that may be twice the software price. Thus, gaining a rapid ROI on technology is challenging.

The key to harnessing the capabilities of transportation software within a reasonable time frame is informed decision making. Transportation professionals take the time to develop a clear vision regarding how technology spending will facilitate freight movement strategy and satisfy specific goals. It is possible to achieve a 12- to 18-month ROI if the transportation experts properly assess their needs, understand the options for software application delivery, and address the technical issues before making a purchase decision.

Needs Assessment

The crucial first step in software selection and implementation is to understand the transportation requirements that the technology is intended to support. Too often, technology buyers don't thoroughly understand their transportation processes or they apply software to outdated processes. This leads to deployments that are poorly matched to needs, unable to link stakeholders, and/or too narrowly focused to support cross-network visibility.

Knowledgeable transportation professionals, rather than information technology experts, must properly diagnose the situation. The needs assessment must address the links between effective business processes, appropriate technology, and transportation performance. They should benchmark their delivery process capabilities against the needs of their customers. If the current capabilities are deemed inadequate, improvements must be made prior to technology evaluation.

Companies can create a competitive advantage in their respective industries because they support innovative supply chain practices with effective transportation technology. They properly view transportation software as an enabler of rapid, reliable, and efficient delivery services. This ultimately leads to realistic expectations, effective implementation, and greater ROI for transportation software purchases.

Software Selection

Software selection is a multifaceted decision. First, transportation professionals must determine which type of software—planning, execution, and/or performance management—is needed. Additionally, transportation professionals must compare the advantages of commercial software to in-house solutions, choose between single vendor suites and applications from multiple vendors, and consider licensing versus on-demand purchases, among other issues.

Development Alternatives Software can be created in-house by the organization or it can be purchased from an external vendor. Walmart and Amazon.com have information technology departments to build some internal transportation applications. Some transportation providers create in-house solutions as well. While this requires significant resources and development time, the resulting tools are tailored to the company's supply chain requirements. Internal developers can achieve a level of customization that is not possible with off-the-shelf software.

Most organizations do not undertake development due to cost, capability, and priority challenges. They rely on external software vendors to develop and implement transportation technology. These tools effectively support transportation networks that are not overly unique or complex. Because they can be implemented faster than what could be accomplished in-house, are built with interoperability as a key focus, and have some ability to be tailored, vendor-developed tools are the proper choice for most organizations.

Solutions Packages If an organization chooses to purchase transportation software, it should determine what types of applications are needed and how they should be purchased. One option is to purchase individual applications from leading providers in each software category, commonly called "best-of-breed" solutions. Another option is to buy an integrated TMS suite from a single vendor. The middle ground option is to purchase the main applications from a single software vendor and selectively add other solutions as needed.

Each strategy has its merits. Single-vendor suites require less implementation time and cost versus a variety of tools from different vendors since there are fewer compatibility and connectivity issues. Also, there is only one vendor involved. This reduces complexity and coordination effort. Single-vendor suites also require less training time as users only need to learn one package. However, some suites do not contain the advanced functionality or industry-specific capabilities found in best-of-breed applications. They can also be tailored to an individual company's transportation requirements.

The challenge for the technology buyer is to understand the implementation issues; their organization's need for tailored, advanced capabilities; and the constantly changing vendor landscape.

Purchase Options Historically, transportation software buyers had one option—license software from vendors and install it on the buyer's system. This is a logical method for transportation processes with intense computational activity requirements. The downside of licensing is the capital investment and complex deployment. The buyer must pay for the software up front; address implementation issues; and manage software upgrades, fixes, and maintenance costs.

Another purchase option is hosted software. In this model, the customer purchases and owns the software, but it is installed at a data center or "hosting center" where either physical or virtualized servers that the company owns, leases, or finances are set up. The transportation software is implemented much like it would be done on-premise at the buyer's own facilities. This model offers the services of a highly secure data center with multisite backup. On the downside, hosted solutions can be expensive and access is lost when Internet service is unavailable.[10]

Cloud computing has changed the purchase landscape. Buyers can now use applications that are not permanently installed on the company's network. In the software as a service (SaaS) distribution model, software access is provided via the Internet. It is a pay-as-you-go method that allows the customer to use software as needed, without having to install it or purchase a license. SaaS applications can be accessed securely by multiple customers, each of whom typically pays a monthly usage fee.[11]

The SaaS model has grown in popularity as more TMS options have become available. The cloud platform supports a network that is multitenant, allowing many business partners to integrate using the same technology. This promotes accessibility to more data, partner collaboration, operational scalability, and visibility. The variable cost structure of a SaaS-based TMS generally produces faster ROI.[12]

Importantly, cloud-based solutions make the use of TMS more affordable for smaller organizations and that is leading to greater adoption. "Historically, if a company did not have over $20 million in freight spend, purchasing a TMS was out of the question," says Chris Cunnane, senior analyst with ARC Advisory Group. He notes that even the shipper with just $1 million in freight spend can now afford a TMS. "The emergence of SaaS solutions, and less-sophisticated, on-premise applications, has reduced that number significantly."[13]

Implementation Issues

Transportation professionals tend to focus on functionality when considering software, but they also must consider the implementation and operational issue. Potentially useful software will become "shelfware" if it is difficult to install, poorly linked to other tools, or too cumbersome to use. Hence, up-front effort must be expended to assess the implementation challenges before making software purchase decisions. Proper training, cultural change, systems interoperability, and data synchronization are keys to success. Two additional SCIS implementation issues are discussed as follows.

Data Standardization Given the variety of software vendors, proprietary tools, and legacy systems, coordinating and sharing information across the supply chain can be a significant challenge. Just as different languages, dialects, and alphabets hamper human communication, the variety of systems and programming languages used in transportation software make it difficult to bring data together in an efficient, useful manner.

The procurement of software with data standardization capabilities will ensure that information is quickly transferrable in a format that is usable across the transportation network. This will help buyers avoid costly, time-consuming translation efforts and improve transportation systems interoperability. Enhanced communication and visibility will also be achieved.

Application Integration Another prominent issue is seamless integration of transportation software. This can be readily accomplished within a self-contained TMS suite, but supply chain partners often rely on different vendors, applications, or software versions. The greater the variety of applications, the more challenging the connectivity and information-sharing issues become.

Extensive efforts have been made to improve application integration and foster supply chain information synchronization. Application programming interfaces (APIs) are sets of requirements that govern how one application can talk to another. By sharing some of a program's internal functions, it becomes possible to build compatible applications and readily share data.

Transportation technology buyers need to understand the challenges of application integration while pursuing improved delivery network connectivity. They must assess and compare integration methods, and then choose those that best fit current needs while providing the flexibility to meet future functionality requirements.

Ultimately, these standardization and integration issues must be addressed as they have the potential to derail a transportation technology implementation initiative.

Additionally, some fundamental issues must not be overlooked. Transportation professionals must diligently guide the software selection and implementation process and plan for possible disruptions. They would do well to follow these 10 golden rules for success:

1. Secure the commitment of senior management.
2. Remember that it is not just an information technology project.
3. Align the project with business goals.
4. Understand the software capabilities.
5. Select partners carefully.
6. Follow a proven implementation methodology.
7. Take a step-by-step approach for incremental value gains.
8. Be prepared to change business processes.
9. Keep end users informed and involved.
10. Measure success with key performance indicators.[14]

If a company intelligently selects capable software, understands the challenges of implementation, and follows the "golden rules for success," then the process should not be overly daunting. When done correctly, getting TMS base functionality up and running can take less than three months, according to industry observers.[15]

Transportation Equipment Technology

The exciting and beneficial technological innovations in transportation are not limited to software. Transportation providers, freight shippers, government agencies, and other stakeholders are on a continuous quest to improve the functionality, cost efficiency, and reliability of transportation equipment. Ongoing development, testing, and investment in new equipment features are being made to make transportation more sustainable, improve safety in the transportation network, and reduce the potential for freight loss and damage.

Sustainability Initiatives

Transportation is a major consumer of fuel and produces significant greenhouse gas emissions. Based on 2015 data, the U.S. trucking industry consumed 36.3 billion gallons of diesel fuel and 4.4 billion gallons of gasoline and U.S. airlines used 12.5 billion gallons of jet fuel. As a whole, the transportation industry created 27 percent of greenhouse gas emissions in 2015 with the clear majority coming from trucks.[16] Without question, the transportation industry has a financial and societal need to focus on sustainable operations.

The trucking industry has been on a quest to improve its fuel efficiency. Fuel is the second highest cost of trucking operations and can be as much as 20 percent of operating costs. Improvements in fuel economy have a positive impact on company profits and reduce emissions.

One set of trucking equipment innovation focuses on making tractors and trailers more aerodynamic. Efforts to reduce wind resistance and drag can yield valuable fuel efficiency improvements. Aerodynamic devices such as trailer skirts, trailer tails, and gap reducers can lead to fuel savings of 9 percent or more, according to SmartWay. Additionally, the use of low rolling resistance tires can add another 1 percent of savings for a net fuel savings of 10 percent or more.[17] Figure 3-2 highlights some of these cost-effective equipment modifications.

Another technology strategy is to upgrade fleets through the purchase of power units with technologically advanced engines. In the trucking industry, new technologies such as electronic controls, common rail fuel injection, variable injection timing, improved combustion chamber configuration, and turbocharging have made diesel engines cleaner, quieter, and more powerful than past vehicles.[18] And, the industry is looking to renewable energy sources for future equipment. The Transportation Technology feature focuses on the race to commercialize heavy duty electric trucks.

FIGURE 3-2   Fuel Saving Equipment Modifications

Technology innovations are also driving sustainability initiatives in other modes:

- Airline industry—commercial aircraft turbofans are getting bigger. Larger fans and higher bypass ratios mean greater propulsive efficiency and lower fuel consumption.[19]

- Railroad industry—General Electric's Evolution Series Tier 4 locomotive engine has 50 sensors to measure valve control, fuel air mix, engine speed, manifold temperature, and load, and it manipulates fuel and air throughout the combustion process accordingly. That level of precision improves efficiency, ensuring the engine meets both the emissions and performance requirements for the train.[20]

- Ocean shipping industry—The longtime user of oil-fueled engines is responding to tougher international and environmental standards with engines that use liquified natural gas (LNG). It is a much less expensive fuel and LNG-fueled ships emit almost zero sulphur oxide emissions and 25 percent less carbon dioxide gas than existing oil-run engines.[21]

TRANSPORTATION **TECHNOLOGY**

The Electric Truck Race

Heavy-duty trucking is a difficult sector to electrify because trucks generally need to be capable of high speeds and must have the ability to haul a lot of weight. However, the race is on with the August 29, 2017, Cummins Inc. introduction of its first zero-emissions engine that runs entirely on electricity. Cummins estimates that production will begin in 2019.

The prototype vehicle is an 18,000-pound tractor cab, dubbed AEOS after one of the four-winged horses driving the chariot of the Greek sun god, Helios. The Class 7 urban hauler tractor is fully operational and capable of hauling a 22-ton trailer up to 100 miles. Today, the Cummins engine can be recharged in about an hour at a 140 kWh charging station. The company's goal is to reduce charge time to 20 minutes by 2020.

An extended range version, which uses an efficient diesel engine as an on-board generator, will be available a year later, offering up to 300 miles between charges and 50 percent fuel savings compared to today's diesel hybrids, with zero emissions. Besides the fuel saving and environmental impact benefits, electric trucks could reduce maintenance needs by 35 percent to 65 percent, according to ARK Invest's research.

The target market for the Cummins electric power train is urban delivery vehicles that make short-haul trips such as beer trucks and food delivery trucks. Another potential market is intermodal drayage vehicles at ports and railheads. And, the technology can be used for buses in municipal transit systems.

Cummins will have to move quickly to fend off competition. Several well-established companies, like Wrightspeed and Proterra, are already making electric and hybrid–electric buses and garbage trucks. Tesla, Ford, and other vehicle manufacturers are racing to produce the first commercially viable all-electric engine for daily use in heavy trucks. Tesla is reported to be developing truck engines with a 200- to 300-mile battery range.

Sources: James Briggs, "Tesla Gets Electric Truck Competition from Engine Maker Cummins," *USA Today*, August 29, 2017; retrieved October 7, 2017, from https://www.usatoday.com/story/money/cars/2017/08/29/tesla-gets-electric-truck-competition-engine-maker-cummins/612888001/. Megan Geuss, Engine Maker Cummins Shows Off All-Electric Truck, High-Efficiency Diesels, *ARS Technica*, August 31, 2017; retrieved October 7, 2017, from https://arstechnica.com/cars/2017/08/ahead-of-tesla-semis-cummins-shows-off-all-electric-powertrain-concept/. Joann Muller, "Cummins Beats Tesla to the Punch, Unveiling Heavy Duty Electric Truck," *Forbes*, August 29, 2017; retrieved October 7, 2017, from https://www.forbes.com/sites/joannmuller/2017/08/29/take-that-tesla-diesel-engine-giant-cummins-unveils-heavy-duty-truck-powered-by-electricity/\#14965d078f1b.

Safety Efforts

Safety is an ongoing concern in freight transportation. The size of commercial equipment, the distances traveled, and the shared access with passenger equipment on public thoroughfares makes it difficult to achieve total safety. In 2015, there were over 415,000 crashes involving large trucks with 116,000 injuries and 667 fatalities. In addition, the cost of large truck and bus crashes exceeded $118 billion.[22] Comparatively, fewer than 300 fatalities involved rail freight carriers, airlines, and water cargo transporters.[23]

Given these costs, it is no surprise that significant efforts are being made to improve both operator and equipment safety. Technology plays an important role in both. Among the variety of efforts being made to improve safety are enhanced safety features, electronic logging devices (ELDs), and fatigue reduction research.

Improving the safety of commercial trucks has long been a priority for equipment manufacturers and transportation providers. Continuous improvements are being made to stability control systems, collision warning and avoidance systems, and automatic emergency braking systems. Newer forward-looking radar and collision mitigation systems are improving due to rapid advances in computing and sensor systems and their active linkage to braking and powertrain controls. These safety features are becoming standard equipment on trucks and costs are coming down. This has led companies like UPS and Penske to include them in their new equipment orders.[24]

ELDs have been mandated by the U.S. Congress as of December 2017. In its simplest form, an ELD is used to electronically record a driver's Record of Duty Status, replacing the paper log book drivers have traditionally used to record their compliance with hours of service (HOS) requirements. The technology is intended to help create a safer work environment for drivers, and make it easier and faster to accurately track, manage, and share records of duty status data. An ELD synchronizes with a vehicle engine to automatically record driving time, for easier, more accurate hours of service recording.[25] The goal is to ensure that drivers do not exceed the legal limits for driving as excessive HOS can lead to fatigue and greater risk of crashes.

In an attempt to battle driver-fatigue-related crashes, the University of Liège in Belgium has developed technology to monitor eye images. The technology relies on cameras mounted on vehicle dashboards or airplane instrument panels. The camera takes 30 to 120 images of the eye per second and analyzes the images. Equipment operators and/or dispatchers can be alerted to fatigue risks. This technology can help prevent transportation accidents due to the operator falling asleep while driving a car, truck, or train, steering a boat, or flying an airplane.[26]

Cargo Security Innovations

Cargo theft is a multi-billion-dollar criminal industry and a growing threat to the economy and national security of the United States, according to the Federal Bureau of Investigation (FBI). Often cargo theft offenses are part of larger criminal schemes and have been found to be elements of organized crime rings, drug trafficking, and funding for terrorism. Cargo is stolen from tractor–trailers, railcars, ships, planes, and even directly from warehouses and the goods are sometimes sold on the Internet. To combat the problem, the FBI has established seven cargo task forces across the country.[27]

Transportation providers and freight shippers must also take a proactive role in cargo security. To secure cargo, transportation professionals employ a multilayered approach that incorporates the latest technology and fine-tuned basic practices, such as preemployment background checks, extensive staff training, and validation of driver credentials when tendering loads. Global positioning satellite (GPS) tracking systems, onboard sensors and analytics, and intelligence information sharing are three technology-based cargo security initiatives that can be used to combat criminals.

Maintaining visibility and control of in-transit cargo is an excellent way to prevent theft. Tractors, trailers, containers, and other transportation equipment can be outfitted with GPS systems to achieve cargo-tracking capabilities. Geofencing technology, which allows users to define geographical boundaries, can be used to enhance freight control. If the equipment goes outside the defined boundaries, an alarm sounds, and the dispatcher or security personnel try to reach the operator to determine why the equipment left its route. If the operator cannot be contacted, the vehicle engine can be shut down remotely to prevent a hijacking.

Internet of Things (IoT) sensors can be integrated into asset tracking solutions for an additional layer of cargo security. The sensors can be used to detect when:

- container locks and seals have been tampered with,
- container doors have been opened,
- cargo is present or absent inside the container,
- temperature readings inside a container exceed acceptable ranges.

These unexcepted conditions are captured in real-time. Text messages and email alerts are sent to key stakeholders. Rapid response by the stakeholders is the key to thwarting thieves. This information can also be used to quickly adjust climate conditions inside the container that may harm temperature- and humidity-sensitive products.

IoT sensors also provide a great deal of data that can be used as both an audit trail to verify chain-of-custody and as the basis for predictive modeling of security issues. Reviewing loss rates by shipment and product makes it possible to forecast expected losses for cargo. This helps transportation providers and customers deploy the right amount of security technology and other resources by shipment category, geographic region, and mode of transportation.[28]

Data from individual companies can be combined into industry-wide initiatives to understand and thwart theft. Given the high value of pharmaceutical products and the risk of another incident like the $90 million theft from an Eli Lilly warehouse, prescription drug manufacturers are collaborating to reduce their exposure to theft. The Pharmaceutical Cargo Security Coalition brings together pharmaceutical industry professionals, law enforcement, transportation providers, and insurance companies to share security alerts, cargo theft intelligence, and training on technologies used to secure the supply chain.[29] Similar cargo theft prevention coalitions, such as the Transportation Asset Protection Association and the National Cargo Theft Task Force, work across industry sectors and transportation modes to thwart criminal activity.

Emerging Technologies

It is an exciting time in the transportation world with technological innovation emerging at a rapid pace. Transportation companies and their clients must clarify needs, evaluate options wisely, and select technologies that have excellent prospects for long-term use. Venturing too far toward the cutting-edge can be costly as these technologies may not achieve widespread adoption and may not live up to their initial promise. Avoiding these flash-in-the-pan "solutions" will do little to promote operational efficiency, customer service excellence, or provide cargo security enhancement.

Technology spending is on the rise. Gartner forecasts that global spending on transportation systems and resources will increase to $130 billion in 2017.[30] Much of the investment will be in TMS implementation and upgrades, but a growing portion will go toward disruptive technologies that will usher in new delivery methods and better ways to use big data. Three of these promising disruptors are briefly discussed to conclude the chapter.

Autonomous Transportation

Transportation is a labor-intensive business, and operator roles like driving a truck, piloting a ship, or operating a train can be a difficult job with odd hours, time away from home, and stressful deadlines. That combination can lead to fatigue, poor decision making, and accidents. Also, turnover can be high, particularly among the ranks of truck drivers.

Efforts are under way to take many of the routine operator tasks in trucks, ships, and trains, and turn them over to computers, similar to what is done in the commercial airline industry with autopilot capabilities. Larger, more sophisticated aircraft have multiple autopilot systems that can control almost all aspects of the airplane's movement and an auto-throttle system that is able to fully control the speed of the airplane. On a Boeing 737, the autopilot can be turned on at 1,000 feet above the ground on takeoff. The second autopilot is engaged with the first one to add a layer of redundancy to the autopilot.[31]

Big name companies are racing to revolutionize the trucking industry with self-driving trucks. Mercedes has its "Future Truck 2025" already on the highways. Apple and Microsoft are involved. There is another combined effort by Waymo/Google/Alphabet that is working out kinks in technology. Lyft and General Motors are combining efforts. Tesla and its innovative CEO Elon Musk, the business magnate, investor, engineer, and inventor is bullish. In addition, Uber's entry (formerly called Otto) successfully produced a self-driving truck that hauled a load of Budweiser beer without incident on a 120-mile trek through Colorado.[32]

These autonomous vehicles are being developed and operated on test tracks and remote highways, usually with a driver onboard to handle complex tasks like parking or driving on city streets and to provide a backup safety system should the system not work properly. That's comparable to the role of airline pilots in the cockpit of a large jet.

Thanks to heavy investment, rapid improvements capability and cost are being achieved. For example, Uber has installed its fast-evolving technology on Volvo tractors. Unlike the bolted-on, unattractive hardware that has been on test vehicles, newer versions of the company's sensor and processing arrays are more seamlessly integrated throughout the Volvo cab. The equipment includes four forward-facing video cameras, radar, and a box of accelerometers for more effective guidance. A lidar system uses a pulsed laser to amass detailed data about the truck's surroundings and support the software system's decision making. While Uber spends close to $100,000 per lidar system, the company has a team designing a proprietary version that could cost less than $10,000.[33]

Another autonomous concept involves truck platooning. The startup Peloton is working on platooning trucks, or groups of vehicles that communicate via a wireless connection that helps them time their movements. Soon, the system will allow the lead driver to take over the steering, while the drivers at the wheels in the other vehicles could snooze, catch up on paperwork, or take a break.[34] Platooning tests are already approved in the United Kingdom where up to three wirelessly connected vehicles will travel in a convoy, with acceleration, braking and steering controlled by the lead vehicle. Each truck will have a driver in the cab ready to retake control at any time.[35]

The future is quite promising for autonomous transportation, though there are both technological and political barriers to overcome. The technology is not flawless and it struggles in bad weather. There is no federal legislation regarding autonomous vehicles, meaning that developers must deal with a patchwork of inconsistent state rules and regulations. Also, pushback is being received from safety groups and the Teamsters.

Though it will be a bumpy road forward, it is widely predicted that autonomous trucks will be on highways within 10 to 15 years. As the Global Perspectives feature reveals, autonomous operations are expected to come much sooner to the ocean shipping industry.

Blockchain for Freight

Initially developed to enable the existence of cryptocurrency like Bitcoin, blockchain is a way to structure data. Blockchain is a digital, decentralized ledger that keeps a record of all transactions that take place across a peer-to-peer network. The major innovation is that the technology allows market participants to transfer assets across the Internet without the need for a centralized third party.[36] No single party has the power to tamper with the records; the math keeps everyone honest.

GLOBAL **PERSPECTIVES**

Shipping Without Sailors

The autonomous transportation concept is not limited to the trucking industry. Major initiatives led by Norway-based Kongsberg in partnership with Yara, a Norwegian chemical company; Rolls-Royce; and the Japanese shipping industry, have each revealed plans to develop all-electric and autonomous container ships by 2020.

The two Norwegian companies are rapidly developing a $25 million crewless ship that will transport fertilizer between a production facility and a port 37 miles away. The autonomous ship will be able to navigate itself around other ship traffic and dock on its own. The developers estimate that annual operating costs can be cut by up to 90 percent and emissions reduced thanks to fewer fertilizer-filled trucks on the roadways.

The ship will become autonomous in stages. At first, a single container will be used as a manned bridge on board. Then the bridge will be moved to shore and become a remote-operation center. The ship will eventually run fully on its own, under supervision from shore, in 2020.

Rolls-Royce has mounted a joint industry project in Finland called Advanced Autonomous Waterborne Applications. The participants hope to create the technology for a remotely controlled or fully autonomous ship that will operate in coastal waters before the end of the decade. The company also plans to make a self-piloting navy ship, powered by artificial intelligence, sophisticated sensors, and advanced propulsion, for sale to military forces around the world. The 60-meter-long autonomous craft will have a range of 3,500 nautical miles and would be able to operate on its own without human intervention for more than 100 days.

Japan's ship-builders and maritime shippers are teaming up to make self-navigating ships a reality by 2025. The artificial-intelligence-driven steering system would use IoT technologies to instantaneously gather and analyze data about weather at sea and dangerous obstacles, as well as shipping information. The artificial intelligence would use this data to plot the most fuel-efficient, safest, and shortest route.

The smart ships would also predict onboard malfunctions and other troubles, to avoid maritime accidents. In addition, the parties aim to implement fully unmanned shipping at some point down the road, hoping to halve the present count of roughly 2,000 maritime accidents per year.

Similar to the autonomous truck initiatives, a number of technological, engineering, regulatory, and legal issues will need to be resolved. However, it won't be long before these short voyage tests of small ships lead to international voyages of large, crewless containerships.

Sources: Nathan Borney, "Rolls-Royce Reveals Self-Piloted Navy Ship Powered by Artificial Intelligence," *USA Today*, September 12, 2017; retrieved October 8, 2017, from https://www.usatoday.com/story/money/2017/09/12/rolls-royce-autonomous-naval-ship-artificial-intelligence/656642001/. Nikkei Asian Review, *Japan Aims to Lauch Self-Piloting Ships by 2025*, June 8, 2017; retrieved October 8, 2017, from https://asia.nikkei.com/Tech-Science/Tech/Japan-aims-to-launch-self-piloting-ships-by-2025. Costas Paris, "Norway Takes Lead in Race to Build Autonomous Cargo Ships," *The Wall Street Journal*, July 22, 2017; retrieved October 8, 2017, from https://www.wsj.com/articles/norway-takes-lead-in-race-to-build-autonomous-cargo-ships-1500721202. The Maritime Executive, *Autonomous Ships before Autonomous Cars?* September 12, 2017; retrieved October 8, 2017, from https://www.maritime-executive.com/article/autonomous-ships-before-autonomous-cars.

Information held on a blockchain exists as a shared—and continually reconciled—database. This is a way of using the network that has obvious benefits. The blockchain database isn't stored in any single location, meaning the records it keeps are truly public and easily verifiable. No centralized version of this information exists for a hacker to corrupt. Hosted by millions of computers simultaneously, its data is accessible to anyone on the Internet.[37]

While currency exchange is the genesis of blockchain, it is being studied by other industries for appropriate applications. It is seen as a tool to streamline financial systems with reduced fees and delays, less paperwork, and fewer opportunities for fraud and crime. Equipment manufacturers of long lifecycle assets with replacement parts such as aircraft can use blockchain technology to reduce the potential for counterfeit parts to enter the supply chain. In addition, the food industry can use the tool to track and trace the true source of ingredients. Should an ingredient recall be needed, the problematic source could be pinpointed and its inventory removed rather than all suppliers' inventories.

Where does blockchain intersect with transportation? There are tremendous opportunities to drive efficiencies and safety in global trade and transportation. Global supply chains are slowed by the complexity and sheer volume of point-to-point communication across a loosely coupled web of land transportation, freight forwarders, customs brokers, governments, ports, and ocean carriers. Major problems include poor documentation workflows and limited in-transit visibility.

A major source of the documentation problems stem from the transportation paperwork that facilitates goods transfers across international borders. A simple shipment of refrigerated goods from East Africa to Europe can go through nearly 30 people and organizations, including more than 200 different interactions and communications among them, according to Maersk. That leads to high costs, inefficient processing, and security risks.

With a single containership carrying thousands of shipments, the need for change is obvious. International trading partners and transportation providers need a faster, security rich, and more efficient way to handle the documentation.

IBM and Maersk are addressing these problems using blockchains to exchange event data and handle document workflows. By enabling the real time exchange of original supply chain events and documents through a digital infrastructure, or data pipeline that connects the participants in a supply chain ecosystem, blockchain promotes sustainable transport by integrating shipping processes and partners, and establishing evaluation frameworks through increased transparency and trusted access.

The solution helps to manage and track the paper trail of tens of millions of shipping containers across the world. Supply chain processes will be digitized from end-to-end to enhance transparency and sharing of information among trading partners will be more secure. Fraud and error will be reduced, transit delays avoided, and inventory management improved. With widespread adoption, the blockchain solution will have the potential to save the industry billions of dollars.[38]

Next Generation TMS

As discussed earlier in the chapter, current TMS software helps organizations plan, execute, and measure their transportation operations. Most systems will support the analysis of key performance indicators and help transportation professionals create scorecards for decision-making purposes. That is very beneficial, but still requires a great deal of human intervention.

Over the past year, the level of visibility provided by a TMS has greatly improved. Better visibility means new opportunities to streamline transportation networks while achieving greater cost- and time-efficiency. TMS vendors have also expanded options for tendering

TABLE 3.2	Sources of Additional Information: Transportation Technology
SOURCE	**WEBSITE**
DC Velocity	www.dcvelocity.com/channels/technology
Eye For Transport	www.eft.com/technology
Gartner	www.gartner.com
IndustryWeek	www.industryweek.com/supply-chain
Logistics Viewpoints	www.logisticsviewpoints.com
Supply Chain 24/7	www.supplychain247.com/topic/category/technology
TechCrunch	www.techcrunch.com/transportation
USDOT Volpe Center	www.volpe.dot.gov

Source: Brian J. Gibson, PhD. Used with permission.

and delivering loads, making the process more efficient. In addition, greater connectivity with enterprise solutions will be possible as large ERP vendors refine their TMS offerings.[39]

Going forward, TMS software will harness the power of business analytics tools, machine learning, and ultra-fast processers to quickly evaluate the vast number of options in a transportation network, monitor the terabytes of data that companies have amassed, and make decisions with little or no human intervention. This type of next-generation TMS will analyze far more variables than a human could handle, refresh its records with real-time data, quickly calculate the optimal shipping method, and even act on its findings, according to industry experts. Adding these embedded analytics to a TMS platform will allow transportation providers, brokers, and customers to base decisions on current data being collected rather than on human interpretations of partial data and perceived trends.[40]

The advanced capabilities are needed to keep up with the growing demands for faster delivery of small shipments. Both are expensive outcomes of the shift to e-commerce and omnichannel retailing. Transportation providers and retailers must figure out ways to reduce delivery costs, improve on-time, in-full deliveries, and better manage capacity. Next-generation TMS capabilities will help them reduce empty miles, build more effective multi-stop routes, and develop more creative solutions.

These three innovations are just a sampling of the disruptive technologies that are changing the transportation industry for the better. These potential game-changers have the potential to drive greater transportation visibility, control, and performance. To stay in tune with these issues you need to continuously scour the Internet for new developments. Table 3.2 provides a list of websites that will help you stay current on transportation technology innovations and issues.

SUMMARY

- Transportation technology is needed to maintain cargo control and promote safe, timely, and cost-efficient delivery of goods.
- To produce actionable knowledge, transportation information must be high quality, readily flow between organizations, and support a variety of decision types.
- Transportation information must be accurate, accessible, relevant, timely, and transferable to be of value.
- A well-designed TMS provides excellent decision support for strategic, tactical, and operational planning, as well as delivery execution, in-transit visibility, and performance evaluation.
- Primary TMS functionality includes routing and scheduling, mode and carrier selection, and load planning, document creation, load tendering, appointment scheduling, track and trace, metrics monitoring, and freight bill auditing.

- Savvy transportation professionals know that a TMS can provide cost savings and generate service improvements.

- To maximize transportation software investment success, efforts must be made to assess internal requirements, understand software capabilities and purchase options, and address the technical implementation issues.

- Opportunities exist to leverage the latest transportation equipment technology for more sustainable operations, enhanced safety, and greater freight protection.

- The technology landscape is ever changing and transportation professionals must evaluate how innovations such as autonomous vehicles, blockchain, and next-generation TMS capabilities will drive improvements in delivery efficiency and effectiveness.

STUDY QUESTIONS

1. Discuss the role of transportation information and how it supports network visibility, control, and service consistency.
2. Describe the attributes of information quality and how they impact transportation decision making.
3. Explain how a TMS enables delivery process planning, execution, and control.
4. What are some of the most valuable TMS functionalities? How do they contribute to both cost reduction and service improvement?
5. How can a company facilitate a smooth and timely implementation of a TMS?
6. What options are available for procuring transportation software? Why would a company pursue each option?
7. How is new equipment technology contributing to transportation sustainability initiatives?
8. How can technology promote transportation safety?
9. Discuss how transportation professionals are deploying technology in their quest to minimize freight theft.
10. Why are technology and transportation equipment companies investing so much time, money, and effort into autonomous transportation research?
11. Why should transportation professionals pay attention to the emerging area of blockchain?
12. What capabilities and benefits will result from the development of next generation TMS tools?

NOTES

1. DC Velocity Staff, "TMS Market to Reach $30 Billion by 2025, Report Says," *DC Velocity*, May 22, 2017. Retrieved October 5, 2017, from http://www.dcvelocity.com/articles/20170522-tms-market-to-reach-30-billion-by-2025-report-says/.

2. This section is adapted from John J. Coyle, C. John Langley, Jr., Robert A Novack , and Brian J. Gibson, *Supply Chain Management: A Logistics Perspective*, *11e*, Boston, MA: Cengage Learning, 2017, pp. 551–558.

3. Cecil B. Bozarth and Robert B. Handfield, *Introduction to Operations and Supply Chain Management*, *4th ed.*, Upper Saddle River, NJ: Pearson Education Inc., 2015.

4. Adrian Gonzalez, "The Industry's Struggle to Define TMS," *Supply Chain 247*, December 20, 2016. Retrieved October 6, 2017, from http://www.supplychain247.com/article/the_industrys_struggle_to_define_tms/3gtms.

5. This section is adapted from Brian J. Gibson, Joe B. Hanna, C. Clifford Defee, and Haozhe Chen, *The Definitive Guide to Integrated Supply Chain Management*, Upper Saddle River, NJ: Pearson Education, 2015, pp. 113–132.

6. This section is adapted from J. J. Coyle, C. J. Langley, R. A. Novack, and B. J. Gibson, *Supply Chain Management: A Logistics Perspective, 11e*, Boston, MA: Cengage Learning, 2017, pp. 453–454.

7. Bart De Muynck, *Magic Quadrant for Transportation Management System*, Stamford, CT: Gartner, Inc., March 30, 2016, p. 1.

8. Karen M. Kroll, "Global Trade Management Systems: You've Got the Whole World in Your Hands," *Inbound Logistics*, March 15, 2016. Retrieved October 6, 2017, from http://www.inboundlogistics.com/cms/article/global-trade-management-systems-youve-got-the-whole-world-in-your-hands/.

9. This section is adapted from J. J., Coyle, C. J. Langley, R. A. Novack, and B. J. Gibson, *Supply Chain Management: A Logistics Perspective, 11e*, Boston, MA: Cengage Learning, 2017, pp. 566–570.

10. Clients First Business Solutions, Cloud, SaaS, and Hosted…What's the Difference?", May 23, 2011. Retrieved October 6, 2017, from http://www.erpsoftwareblog.com/2011/05/cloud-saas-and-hosted-whats-the-difference/.

11. Andrea Joseph, What's the Difference Between Software-As-A-Service (SAAS) vs. Hosted?, September 18, 2015. Retrieved October 6, 2017, from https://www.verticalrail.com/kb/saas-hosted-difference/.

12. Adam Robinson, *The 5 Benefits of Hybrid SaaS TMS*, April 8, 2015. Retrieved October 6, 2017, from http://cerasis.com/2015/04/08/saas-tms/.

13. "State of TMS 2016: ROI Is in the Cloud," *Logistics Management*, January 1, 2016. Retrieved October 6, 2017, from http://www.logisticsmgmt.com/article/state_of_tms_2016_roi_is_in_the_cloud.

14. Jose Favilla and Andrew Fearne, "Supply Chain Software Implementation: Get it Right," *Supply Chain Management*, October 2005, pp. 241–243.

15. Tony Wayda, *Debunked: The 3 Myths of TMS Implementation*, July 7, 2016. Retrieved October 8, 2017, from http://scapath.com/2016/07/tims-bs--debunked-the-3-myths-of-implementation/.

16. Office of Transportation and Air Quality, *Fast Facts: U.S. Greenhouse Gas Emissions 1990–2015*, Washington, DC: United States Environmental Protection Agency, July 2017.

17. United States Environmental Protection Agency, *SmartWay Designated Tractors and Trailers*?. Retrieved October 7, 2017, from https://www.epa.gov/verified-diesel-tech/smartway-designated-tractors-and-trailers.

18. Diesel Technology Forum, *What Is Clean Diesel?* Retrieved October 7, 2017, from https://www.dieselforum.org/about-clean-diesel/what-is-clean-diesel.

19. Graham Warwick, "Future Technology Innovations on the Horizon," *Aviation Week*, July 29, 2016. Retrieved October 7, 2017, from http://aviationweek.com/awst/future-technology-innovations-horizon.

20. Jordan Golson, "The Tech That Makes GE's New Locomotive Its Cleanest Ever," *Wired*, May 12, 2015. Retrieved October 7, 2017, from https://www.wired.com/2015/05/tech-makes-ges-new-locomotive-cleanest-ever/.

21. Bikram Singh, "Liquified Natural Gas (LNG) as Fuel for the Shipping Industry," *Marine Insight*, July 26, 2016. Retrieved October 7, 2017, from https://www.marineinsight.com/green-shipping/liquified-natural-gas-lng-as-fuel-for-the-shipping-industry/.

22. Federal Motor Carrier Safety Administration, *Pocket Guide to Large Truck and Bus Statistics 2017*. Retrieved October 7, 2017, from https://www.fmcsa.dot.gov/safety/data-and-statistics/commercial-motor-vehicle-facts.

23. Bureau of Transportation Statistics, Table 2-1: Transportation Fatalities by Mode. Retrieved October 7, 2017, from https://www.rita.dot.gov/bts/sites/rita.dot.gov.bts/files/publications/national_transportation_statistics/html/table_02_01.html_mfd.

24. Carly Shaffner, "Trucking Fleets Get Closer to Automation, Add Advanced Safety Features," Trucks. com, January 20, 2017. Retrieved October 7, 2017, from https://www.trucks.com/2017/01/20/ trucking-companies-automated-safety-features/.

25. Federal Motor Carrier Safety Administration, *Electronic Logging Devices*. Retrieved October 7, 2017, from https://www.fmcsa.dot.gov/hours-service/elds/electronic-logging-devices.

26. Phys.org, *New Transportation Safety Technology for Preventing Accidents Due to Falling Asleep at the Wheel*, March 20, 2017. Retrieved October 7, 2017, from https://phys.org/news/2017-03-safety-technology-accidents-due-falling.html\#jCp.

27. Federal Bureau of Investigation, Cargo Theft, January 26, 2012. Retrieved October 8, 2017, from https://www.fbi.gov/audio-repository/news-podcasts-thisweek-cargo-theft.mp3/view.

28. OpticalLock, *Freight Protection of High Value Goods in Transit*. Retrieved October 8, 2017, from http://www.opticallock.com/freight-protection-high-value-goods/.

29. Suzanne Heyn, "Cargo Security: Protecting the Supply Chain," *Inbound Logistics*, January 20, 2014. Retrieved October 8, 2017, from http://www.inboundlogistics.com/cms/article/cargo-security-protecting-the-supply-chain/

30. Venecia K. Liu and Rika Narisawa, *Forecast: Enterprise IT Spending for the Transportation Market, Worldwide, 2015–2021, 1Q17 Update*, April 27, 2017. Retrieved October 8, 2017, from https://www.gartner.com/doc/3696617/forecast-enterprise-it-spending-transportation.

31. Paul Templeton, *How Much Do Airline Pilots Actually Fly an Airliner by Hand?*, July 27, 2016. Retrieved October 8, 2017, from https://pilotjobs.atpflightschool.com/2016/07/27/how-much-do-airline-pilots-actually-fly-an-airliner-by-hand/.

32. John D. Schulz, Truckers Prepare for Era of Driverless Trucks—Coming Sooner Rather than Later, *Logistics Management*, March 13, 2017. Retrieved October 8, 2017, from http://www.logisticsmgmt.com/article/truckers_prepare_for_era_of_driverless_trucks_coming_sooner_rather_than_lat.

33. David H. Freedman, "10 Breakthrough Technologies: Self-Driving Trucks" *MIT Technology Review*. Retrieved October 8, 2017, from https://www.technologyreview.com/s/603493/10-breakthrough-technologies-2017-self-driving-trucks/.

34. Aarian Marshall, "The Human–Robocar War for Jobs Is Finally On," *Wired*, September 29, 2017. Retrieved October 8, 2017, from https://www.wired.com/story/trucks-robocar-senate-war/.

35. Gwyn Topham, "Semi-Automated Truck Convoys Get Green Light for UK Trials," *The Guardian*, August 24, 2017. Retrieved October 8, 2017, from https://www.theguardian.com/politics/2017/aug/25/semi-automated-truck-convoy-trials-get-uk-go-ahead-platooning.

36. Alan Morrison and Subhankar Sinha, "A Primer on Blockchain (Infographic)," *pwc blog*, December 6, 2016. Retrieved October 8, 2017, from http://usblogs.pwc.com/emerging-technology/a-primer-on-blockchain-infographic/.

37. Block Geeks, *What Is Blockchain Technology? A Step-by-Step Guide for Beginners*. Retrieved October 8, 2017, from https://blockgeeks.com/guides/what-is-blockchain-technology/.

38. Karen Lewis, "Blockchain: Four Use Cases Transforming Business," IBM Internet of Things Blog, May 25, 2017. Retrieved October 8, 2017, from https://www.ibm.com/blogs/internet-of-things/iot-blockchain-use-cases/.

39. Bridget McCrea, "State of Transportation Management Systems: Six Trends to Track in 2017," *Modern Materials Handling*, January 13, 2017. Retrieved October 8, 2017, from http://www.mmh.com/article/state_of_transportation_management_systems_six_trends_to_track_in_2017.

40. Ben Ames, "Keep Calm and Let the TMS Decide," *DC Velocity*, June 13, 2017. Retrieved October 8, 2017, from http://www.dcvelocity.com/articles/20170613-keep-calm-and-let-the-tms-decide/.

CASE 3-1

myIoT Inc.

myIoT Inc. is a mid-sized technology company that was early to market with Internet of Things (IoT) devices for the home. They make security cameras, thermostats, and lighting products that have Internet functionality for home automation. myIoT products have done well selling to specialty lighting retailers and the company is preparing to sell its award-winning products through major chains like Best Buy and The Home Depot. The company is also planning to expand its website from an information portal to an e-commerce website for direct sales.

Despite being a technology product company, myIoT is not particularly sophisticated in terms of transportation management technology. Since the inception of the company, spreadsheets, a simple database, and basic shipping software provided by a trucking company have served as the transportation information backbone of the company. With the growth in sales and larger orders rolling in, this homegrown "transportation management system" is starting to fail. An audit by an external consultant revealed that shipments are being routed inefficiently, the optimal carriers are not being selected, documents are incomplete, and deliveries are arriving late. Furthermore, myIoT has very limited visibility of in-transit freight and can't answer customer questions effectively.

Danny Updike, CEO of myIoT, grew increasingly frustrated as he read the auditor's report aloud to his leadership team. He concluded by saying: "How the heck can a technology products company be so inept at using technology to run its business? We need to get this issue resolved ASAP. Those holiday orders from the huge retailers will start to ship out in three months. We will lose their business with these types of basic transportation problems. Fix it now." Updike slammed the report on the table and stormed out of the conference room.

After the outburst, the remaining executives turned to Victor Michel for a solution. The transportation vice president responded by saying: "I have been telling you folks for a year that this was a growing problem and have been doing some research on technology options. Give me a reasonable budget and two months. We will replace our patchwork 'systems' with a transportation solution that really works."

CASE QUESTIONS

1. What types of software does myIoT need to support its business growth? What features and capabilities are needed?

2. To obtain the necessary transportation capabilities in a short timeframe, what type of software purchase option should myIoT pursue? Explain.

3. What types of technology implementation challenges might myIoT face? How can these risks be minimized?

4. How can myIoT benefit from the features that will soon be available in next-generation TMS?

Source: Brian J. Gibson, PhD. Used with permission.

CASE 3-2

Vital-E Nutrition

Sammy Killebrew is struggling to clear his head after a lengthy and unpleasant meeting with the CEO at Vital-E Nutrition (VEN). The company, a manufacturer of temperature-sensitive liquid and powder nutritional supplements, has had some high profile transportation disruptions and customer service failures over the past month.

The CEO was quite distressed about a spoiled product incident due to refrigeration unit failure on a company trailer, a number of missed pickups that resulted in late deliveries, and a lack of in-transit product visibility. The spoiled product incident led to $250,000 worth of product being destroyed. The late deliveries nearly cost VEN a major client. And, the visibility problem prevented VEN from rerouting a delivery away from a retailer that entered bankruptcy the day prior to delivery.

No matter how Sammy tried to explain that the problems were neither his fault nor things that VEN could have predicted, the CEO wasn't interested. She didn't care to hear about equipment failures, driver shortages, or weak technology. "Customers don't blame the trucking companies in these situations. They blame us for picking the wrong carriers," the CEO emphatically stated.

"Stop focusing on getting the lowest transportation rate," the CEO continued. "Sammy, saving $100 per truckload delivery doesn't do us a bit of good if we lose a shipment or a customer. Instead, hire carriers who have the expertise and technology to avoid these problems. Can you find those types of carriers?"

Sammy assured the CEO that the problems would be solved. His job at VEN was on the line and Sammy needed to quickly find some innovative solutions to these transportation woes.

CASE QUESTIONS

1. What types of track and trace capabilities could help VEN detect temperature problems and respond before the product is ruined?

2. Are autonomous trucks a potential answer to driver shortage problems that plague VEN's transportation providers? Why or why not?

3. What value could VEN derive from the analytics capabilities being embedded in a state-of-the-art TMS?

4

COSTING AND PRICING FOR TRANSPORTATION

Learning Objectives

After reading this chapter, you should be able to do the following:

> Understand the relationship between a rate and a price

> Be familiar with the various types of market structures found in the transportation industry

> Gain knowledge of the impact of transportation prices on the relevant market area for a product

> Be able to explain the differences between cost-of-service and value-of-service pricing

> Understand the different forms of rates used in transportation

> Appreciate how transportation rates have changed under deregulation

> Determine the strategic role of pricing for transportation firms

> Calculate the costs of both truckload and less-than-truckload freight moves

TRANSPORTATION **PROFILE**

Disintermediation to Hit Freight Brokerage

Years ago and before broadband, a domestic brokerage company we considered buying had a clever gimmick going where they offered a free PC and dial-up modem to small companies where the shipping clerk could enter data on a simple shipping questionnaire and then the PC would dial up the brokerage.

The broker would book the load and send back a filled-out Bill of Lading. Thus, the shipper needed very little transportation knowledge. Does this sound like an early version of Uber to you? Like Uber, the shipper was locked into the brokerage as the program was exclusive.

The shipper would just list "500 lbs. of toys to Chicago," and the carrier would be scheduled to pick up the load. Of course, the broker would make the selection and collect a very high margin. In the end, we ended up not buying the firm, but it was an education on how the freight brokerage business worked.

The tools today are different, but the model is the same. Small shippers with little or no transportation knowledge rely on third parties to guide them through complex pricing models and a variety of possible carriers.

However, the problem with the high margin end of almost all business is that innovation—especially that which continuously emerges from the Internet—is disrupting more and more specialist businesses where there are premium earnings.

Shippers and third-party logistics providers (3PLs) are absorbing brokerage functionality with help of software and instant connectivity, perhaps without realizing it. As the less-than-truckload (LTL) business gets "Uberized" through new non-NMFC pricing and Internet-based bookings apps, the need for a broker middleman is diminished.

My broker friends tell me that the death of the transport intermediary has been predicted before; however, they are still here. I, like others before me, say that this time it's different. I forecast that brokerage margins will be squeezed to the point that they become untenable as stand-alone companies and instead become functions of 3PLs or a part of a shipper's interactive transportation management system (TMS).

The last decade's improvements in TMS capability have provided load consolidation for individual shippers and sometimes with other 3PL clients. Until new pricing models came along, brokers still had better discounts than many small shippers—and thus could promise these shippers a break in LTL while collecting double-digit markups. Now, shippers can work with apps and network connections to collaborate with carriers to take advantage of operational savings opportunities on a daily basis.

With recently developed dimensional pricing models that do not require NMFC classifications, combined with apps that can tender and confirm loads, the need for intermediaries connecting the parties is reduced. The shippers or a 3PL's TMS that has been tweaked for dynamic interaction with carriers with Uber-style apps will connect directly.

However, this is not changing overnight, so shippers have time to re-engineer their transport contracting and operations practices. But, as previously reported in *Logistics Management*, there are numerous Silicon Valley players jumping in to capture the margins traditionally enjoyed by brokers. With all this unfolding before our eyes, there are four things shippers can do now.

First: Investigate the new technologies that enable dynamic pricing and contracting. They are available on a subscription basis.

Second: Know your freight characteristics, network, and best service providers.

Third: Understand the cost factors for carriers and where the pricing levers are.

> **Fourth:** Learn and practice collaborative contracting with emphasis on being a good customer with high ratings from service providers.
>
> Technology provides opportunity, but shippers need to stay on top of their game to improve cost and service while eliminating the middleman.
>
> Source: *Logistics Management*, July 2016, p. 20. Reprinted with permission of Peerless Media, LLC.

Introduction

Federal regulation of transportation business practices was initiated in the United States in 1887 when Congress passed the Act to Regulate Commerce (later named the Interstate Commerce Act). This legislation established a framework of control over interstate rail transportation and created the Interstate Commerce Commission (ICC) to administer it. Between 1906 and 1940, oil pipelines, motor carriers, and domestic water carriers were also subjected to ICC control. Air transportation came under federal economic regulation in 1938, with the passage of the Civil Aeronautics Act.

Reduction of federal economic regulation of the various modes began with partial curtailment of rail regulation in 1976 (Railroad Revitalization and Regulatory Reform Act), air cargo in 1977, and air passenger transportation in 1978 (Airline Deregulation Act). Two years later, interstate motor carriage was almost completely deregulated (Motor Carrier Act of 1980), and extensive additional reductions in railroad regulation were enacted (Staggers Rail Act of 1980). In the 1980s, legislative moves to further curtail transportation regulation continued. Intercity bus service was deregulated in 1982, followed by surface domestic freight forwarders in 1986.

A federal political climate favorable to deregulation continued in the 1990s. Passage of the Trucking Industry Regulatory Reform Act of 1992 removed the power of the states to regulate intrastate motor freight transportation. Three years later, passage of the ICC Termination Act of 1995 (ICCTA) eliminated almost all remaining elements of motor carrier regulation, further reduced rail regulation, and replaced the 108-year-old ICC with the Surface Transportation Board (STB). The STB holds responsibility for administering the remnants of economic rail regulation that remain law within the ICCTA.

A prime objective of deregulation was market-driven pricing of transportation services free from regulatory intervention. Thus, motor carriers are free to charge whatever rates they can to generate revenue. Deregulation also freed motor carriers to operate wherever they choose, geographically. Rail carriers are also free to charge rates based exclusively on market conditions, except in situations where the STB might find a rail firm's market power strong enough to subject rail customers to economic abuse or injury.

Before deregulation, all interstate rail freight traffic and much motor freight traffic was moved on published (tariff) rates. Both motor and rail carriers still offer tariff rates. However, under freedom from economic regulation, the use of rates set in confidential contracts between carriers and shippers has become prominent, particularly for traffic tendered by large-volume shippers.

The use of contracts, if managed well, ensures that both the carrier and the shipper have a clear understanding of each other's requirements (for instance, profitability of service rendered for the carrier and value derived from freight movement for the shipper) when they enter into a binding agreement. However, if a shipper or carrier negotiates terms that are unwise, no federal agency will be available to offer a remedy.

Individuals studying transportation should understand the theoretical underpinnings of the rates and prices of transportation agencies. A key point to master at the outset is the idea that a difference exists between the terms *rate* and *price*.

In the past, when transportation regulation was at its peak, it was more appropriate to use the term *rate* than *price*. A rate is an amount that can be found in a rate tariff book, as payment to a carrier for performing a given transportation service. This rate is the *lawful* charge that a carrier can impose on a given commodity movement; therefore, a rate has the full force of the law behind it for its timely payment. A rate is determined primarily by considering a carrier's costs only and not by assessing the overall market situation at that moment in time and how these market forces influence supply and demand. A discussion of cost concepts can be found in Appendix 4A.

A price, however, involves a much clearer notion of how postderegulation transportation firms determine and impose charges for their services. A price implies a value or level that is determined based on prevailing market forces. Clearly, the notion of *price* implies a dynamic economic environment, one that is receptive to changes in customer demand and carrier supply.

Although the transportation industry is not completely unique compared to other industries, there are enough differences to justify a thorough discussion of transportation pricing. The first part of this chapter on transport prices will explore the market structure of the transportation industry. The section on market structure will be followed by an analysis of cost-of-service pricing. This analysis will provide the basis for a discussion on value-of-service pricing. The final part of the chapter will address rate systems and pricing in transportation.

Market Considerations

Before discussing the characteristics of the transportation market, a brief review of basic market structure models is appropriate. Such a discussion will provide some insights into the unique nature of transportation market situations.

Market Structure Models

The necessary conditions for **pure competition** are generally stated as follows:

- There are a large number of sellers.
- All sellers and buyers are of such a small size that no one can influence prices or supply.
- There is a homogeneous product or service.
- There is unrestricted entry.

The demand curve facing the individual firm is one of perfect elasticity, which means the producer can sell all output at the one market price, but none above that price. Although pure competition is not a predominant market structure, it is frequently used as a standard to judge optimal allocation of resources.

If pure competition is one type of market structure, the other extreme is a perfectly **monopolistic** market with only one seller of a product or service for which there is no close competitor or substitute. In such a situation, the single seller is able to set the price for the service offered and should adjust the price to its advantage, given the demand curve. To remain in this situation, the single seller must be able to restrict entry. The single seller maximizes profits by equating marginal cost (MC) and marginal revenue (MR) and might make excess profit.

A third type of market structure is **oligopoly**. Oligopoly can be defined as competition between a few large sellers of a relatively homogeneous product that has enough cross-elasticity of demand (substitutability) that each seller must take into account competitors' reactions in making pricing decisions. In other words, oligopoly is characterized by mutual interdependence among the various sellers. The individual seller is aware that in changing price, output, sales promotion activities, or the quality of the product, the reactions of competitors must be taken into account. All modes encounter some form of oligopolistic competition.

The fourth type of market structure is **monopolistic competition**. In this type of market structure there are many small sellers but there is some differentiation of products. The number of sellers is great enough and the largest seller small enough that no one controls a significant portion of the market. No recognized interdependence of the related sellers' prices or price policies is usually present. Therefore, any seller can lower price to increase sales volume without necessarily eliciting a retaliatory reaction from competitors.

This brief description of the four basic market models is by no means complete. The interested student can obtain additional perspectives from any standard microeconomics text. For our purposes, the earlier discussion provides enough background to focus more closely on transportation markets.

Theory of Contestable Markets[1]

The relevant market structure faced by each mode of transportation provided the basis for arguments made by proponents of deregulation. This was especially the case with airline deregulation. For deregulation to work for a mode, its market structure must closely resemble pure competition. On the surface, it appeared that the passenger airline industry was oligopolistic, and therefore, would prevent the free entry of competitors. However, there was some consensus that the airline industry could perform in a competitive manner. That is, although there are only a limited number of players in the market, the market can actually behave like a competitive one. Note that if it is easy to enter and exit a market, potential entrants can use a hit-and-run strategy in which they can enter the market, make profits, and then run away quickly. This means that such a market should have enough threats of potential entries at any time, so that its behavior should resemble a highly competitive market. This type of market is called *contestable market*, and the rationale behind it is called the *theory of contestable markets*.[2]

For this theory to work, several conditions had to be met. First, barriers to entry could not exist. Such barriers could include physical barriers, informational barriers, and capital barriers.[3] Second, economies of scale could not be present. In the airline industry, this meant that operating many aircraft could not have a cost advantage over operating a single aircraft. Third, consumers had to be willing and able to switch quickly among carriers.[4] Finally, existing carriers had to be prevented from responding to new entrants' lower prices, assuming that the entrant possessed a lower cost structure than the incumbent.[5]

Although the theory of contestable markets proved to be correct in the early days of deregulation, incumbent airlines have been able to remove the potential threat of new entrants in today's operating environment, thus weakening the theory's application.[6] This conclusion points to the importance of understanding the market structures of the modes and how they will behave in a deregulated environment. It also leads to the conclusion that the passenger airline industry is indeed an oligopoly, and thus is subject to the potential abuses of this type of market.

Relevant Market Areas

A general statement classifying the market structure of the entire transportation industry cannot be made because it is necessary to view structures in particular market areas. In the railroad industry, for example, there exists a variety of different services, involving the transportation of thousands of different commodities between tens of thousands of different stations or geographic points, via a multiplicity of different routes and under various conditions of carriage.[7] The market structure in transportation must describe the situation at any one point, and even then the situation will differ between commodities. Therefore, to determine pricing in transportation, we must describe the situation between two points, for one commodity, in one shipment size, moving in one direction.[8]

For example, a particular railroad that provides service between Pittsburgh and Cincinnati might find that the movement of ordinary steel approximates what we have described as monopolistic competition. There is likely to be a large number of other carriers, especially motor carriers, that provide essentially the same service.

However, for the movement of a very large, sophisticated generator, the railroad might face an oligopolistic market on the move between Pittsburgh and Cincinnati because none of the motor carriers might be able to haul such a large piece of equipment and the railroad might be competing with only a few water carriers. It is possible to find some commodity where the railroad would be operating in a monopolistic position because of restrictions on operating authorities. Finally, there might even be a product for which the situation approaches pure competition. In fact, this might be true for certain steel products, given the availability of rail, motor, water, and private carrier. In summary, the relevant market situation for transportation consists of one commodity, moving between two points, in one shipment size, in one direction.

The market structure for a particular mode of transportation in one market could be described in more detail. This is especially true with respect to the railroad industry, the water carrier industry, and the pipeline industry. A typical situation in each of these industries could be described and made to fit one of the economic models previously mentioned. For example, it could be stated that between two particular cities the water carriers are faced with oligopolistic conditions. From this, the general pricing behavior of the industry could be discussed.[9] However, there is intermodal competition present in transportation, and it is necessary to take this fact into consideration to adequately describe market situations. Also, as has been stated, the situation varies by commodity.

The complexity of the situation does not eliminate the validity of the economic models described earlier. It only means that in order to make use of these models knowledge of the situation that exists in a particular market must be obtained. Although this might seem to be too much to expect at first, it can be accomplished. The elaborate classification system for rates (discussed later in this chapter) distorts the situation somewhat, but in our economy commodity rates are the most important in terms of total intercity ton-miles. Commodity rates are competitive on commodities between specific points. In setting prices, a carrier must have knowledge of the relevant market area. With this knowledge, it is possible to use one of the economic models described. Although there will be instances when carriers might find it expedient to generalize in adjusting prices, a much narrower focus is customary in the day-to-day negotiation and analysis of these prices.

The deregulation that has occurred in transportation between 1978 and 1996 has made these conclusions even more appropriate. Although it is true that there has been a general increase in competition, the competition has been uneven among market areas, commodities, and shipment sizes. The new competitive environment has made carriers and shippers more sensitive to the importance of the relevant market area concept. More prices are being negotiated by shippers and carriers and are taking into account the particular demand-and-supply situations for the movements affected.

The important point about this analysis is that, although transportation competition has indeed become more intense in the last four decades, the intensity is uneven. Therefore, all four types of markets can be found in transportation industries. This makes pricing very challenging. In addition, the derived nature of transportation demand further complicates the pricing situation.

Cost-of-Service Pricing[10]

There are two alternative concepts for **cost-of-service pricing**: basing prices on marginal cost or basing prices on average cost. To give adequate treatment to each alternative, some simplifying assumptions will be made and exhibited using Figure 4-1. The assumptions are that (1) the firm's product or service (such as transportation) is homogeneous, (2) only one group of customers is involved, (3) this group of customers is responsible for all costs, and (4) the firm possesses some degree of monopoly power, as indicated by a downward sloping demand curve as seen in Figure 4-1.

If the firm desires to maximize its profits (see Figure 4-1), it will produce quantity /it Q_m and charge price /it P_m (because this is where MR is equal to MC). By doing so, the firm would be making excess profits in the economic sense (that is, earning a rate of return on its invested assets in excess of that needed to attract and retain financial capital from investors). This result is good for the firm's investors (shareholders). However, it is not good from the standpoint of optimal allocation of resources for the economy at large, because the price is above **average cost** (AC) and the firm is not producing and selling as much as it would (Q_a) if its selling price was set equal to the average cost (P_a). This is a basic result of the firm's exercise of monopoly power.

FIGURE 4-1	Cost-of-Service Pricing

This result might induce government regulation of the firm's pricing. If regulation is imposed, the regulatory agency has two alternatives for attempting to improve economic efficiency in the economy at large and to increase the economic well-being of existing and prospective buyers of the firm's output. By ordering the firm to set its price at /it P_z, the firm's output and sales would increase from /it Q_m to /it Q_z, the firm's **marginal cost** would equal its average revenue (price), and the firm would neither earn excess profit nor incur a loss in the short run on any of the additional (marginal) units of output that it sells. Conceptually, this is identical to the outcome that would result under pure competition, where the forces of the market would cause a firm to sell its output at the going market price and where (assuming the firm is in a state of perfect equilibrium) the market price would be equal to the firm's marginal cost.

It should be noted here that some advocates of regulation have argued that ordering a firm to set price equal to average cost is more socially desirable, because the firm's customers would be obtaining more output (Q_a) at an even lower price (P_a). However, critics of this approach point out that the units of output between /it Q_z and /it Q_a are being sold at a price (P_a) that is less than the marginal cost of producing them and hence that buyers of these units are receiving a subsidy from investors in the firm.

In Adam Smith's terminology, the value in use is not as great as the cost of producing the additional output. Therefore, there are alternate uses in which the resources used to produce this additional output are valued more highly by consumers. When stated in this manner, the argument is based upon logic usually advanced under a label of "welfare economics."[11] Under the marginal-cost solution presented in Figure 4-1, there would be excess profits because price is above the average cost. However, this need not be a problem because the excess profits can be used to pay taxes.

One of the arguments frequently raised against a strict marginal-cost approach to pricing is that, under decreasing cost conditions (that is, AC is a decreasing function of Q within the entire range of Q in which a firm can operate, which implies that MC curve always lies beneath AC curve—see Figure 4-2), if the firm equates marginal cost with demand, then it will necessitate the firm's operating at a loss. However, the advocates of a strict marginal-cost approach would still present the argument that individuals are willing to pay the marginal cost of the additional output between /it Q_m and /it Q_r and therefore, it should be produced. There is one obvious solution and that is to allow the government to make up the deficit through a subsidy.[12] These subsidies could be offset by the taxes collected in the previous example. These are also additional ways to offset governmental subsidies.

Thus far in this discussion, no attempt has been made to substantiate one approach or the other. The arguments advanced by advocates of each approach have been presented. Before any critique can be presented of these alternate approaches, the assumptions that were made at the outset should be examined.

The assumption that only one group of customers is served is not the typical situation, except in very special cases among transportation companies. Likewise, costs are not usually separable according to the classes of customers receiving the same type of service, but rather, common costs are quite typical, particularly with respect to railroads. Already mentioned is that output is not homogeneous in many instances; rather, what exists are heterogeneous or multiple services. Transportation firms are not peculiar in this respect because so many firms have common costs.

The presence of **common costs** raises some problems for cost-of-service pricing, particularly the average-cost approach. If rates are based upon average or fully allocated costs, it becomes necessary to apportion these costs by some arbitrary means. Average cost pricing with fixed or common costs or both makes these costs price–determining when

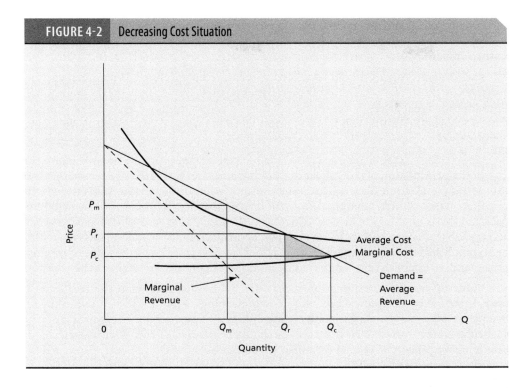

FIGURE 4-2 Decreasing Cost Situation

they should be price-determined. In other words, fixed costs per unit depend on the volume of traffic, and the volume of traffic depends on the rate charged. To some extent then, cost is a function of the prices; the prices are not a function of the cost.[13] In fact, it could be argued that not only do costs determine prices, but also that prices determine cost; in other words, the situation is analogous to the chicken and the egg argument.

The presence of common costs does not raise the same theoretical problem for marginal-cost pricing because no arbitrary allocation of these costs is technically necessary. Note that marginal cost can only be determined with large blocks of output such as a trainload or even a truckload, and that marginal costs could fluctuate widely depending on the volume of traffic offered. But the requirement of published rates (which applies to some transportation modes) would necessitate the averaging of these marginal costs to stabilize them, which would make them unequal with theoretical marginal costs.

Some theoretical and practical problems with cost-of-service pricing have been raised. An obvious question is whether cost-of-service pricing has any relevance for establishing prices. Prices charged by transportation companies are actually one of the criteria that guide intelligent shippers in selecting the mode of transportation or carrier that is most appropriate for their shipment. When the modal choice or carrier decision is made properly, the shipper will balance the carrier's price against the carrier's service characteristics such as transit time, reliability, and loss and damage record.

For the transportation decision to be properly made, the price charged should reflect the cost of providing the service to ensure carrier and economic system efficiency. The price(s) of carriers should be related to cost, but not to some arbitrary allocation of cost.

Railroads and pipelines require large, indivisible capital inputs because of their rights-of-way, terminals, and so on. The associated high fixed costs that are common costs to most of the traffic, if averaged over the units of traffic, will have to be allocated on an arbitrary basis, which will in turn lead to unwise and uneconomical pricing decisions. Adherence to an average cost or fully allocated cost approach does not make any sense in such situations.

Cost-oriented prices should be related to what we have defined as marginal cost or variable cost. Such costs, measured as precisely as possible, should serve as the conceptual floor for individual prices. Some traffic will move if prices are above marginal or variable cost, whereas other traffic will move at prices close to marginal cost, particularly under competitive circumstances. In other words, differential pricing seems to make sense in most instances, but the rationale needs further explanation.

In the presentation of cost-of-service pricing, mention was made of **decreasing cost industries** (recall from Figure 4-2). Some transportation firms fall into this category. If prices are based on strict marginal cost, the firm experiences a loss. A subsidy could be paid, but this is not likely to be done. Therefore, the firm has to recover its fixed costs. To accomplish this on the basis of an average-cost approach is not acceptable. However, it can be accomplished by using marginal cost as a floor for prices and using the value of service, or demand, to establish how far above this minimum the rate or price should be set.

Value-of-service pricing is sometimes defined as **charging what the traffic will bear**. In actuality, this phrase can assume two meanings. First, it can be used to mean that prices are set so that on each unit the maximum revenue is obtained regardless of the particular costs involved. That is, no service should be charged a lower price when it could bear a higher price. The second meaning, which can be more conveniently expressed in a negative form and which is germane to this discussion, is that no service should be charged a price that it will not bear when, at a lower price, the service could be purchased. This lower price will always cover the marginal cost incurred by the company in providing the service.

The differences in the elasticities of demand for the different services will determine the actual level of the prices. The presence of indivisibilities in the cost structure necessitates the dissimilar pricing. Therefore, the greater the amount of the indivisibilities in the cost structure, the greater the need for dissimilar pricing and the consequent practice of segregating services according to demand elasticity.

One final point should be discussed, and that is the desirability of dissimilar pricing. Dissimilar pricing allows common and fixed costs to be spread out over large volumes of traffic. In other words, dissimilar pricing might render economical benefits because prices might be lower than they otherwise would be. It is not unusual to hear statements in the railroad industry that the prices on captive traffic subsidize competitive traffic; coal, for example, will not move unless the rates are relatively low. It could be argued that, as long as the coal rates cover more than the marginal cost of the movement, they allow the railroad to charge lower rates on other traffic.

As previously mentioned, the variable or marginal cost of providing the service should serve as the floor for carriers when setting prices. This relies entirely on how marginal or variable cost is defined, as we will see later. With this mentality, a carrier will be able to recover related costs of providing a service, at least in the short run. This relationship can be seen in Figure 4-3. In this example, a carrier's variable cost for a particular move is $90, its average cost (also called *fully allocated cost*) is $100, and its potential price is $110 (which could result in a $10 profit). This example assumes that (1) the carrier knows its costs and (2) it is able to charge a price that will result in a profit. This second assumption can be called *value-of-service pricing*, which will be discussed in the next section.

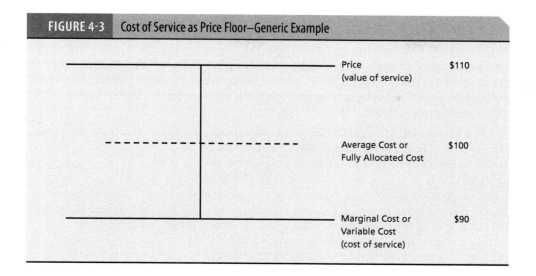

FIGURE 4-3 Cost of Service as Price Floor—Generic Example

Price (value of service)	$110
Average Cost or Fully Allocated Cost	$100
Marginal Cost or Variable Cost (cost of service)	$90

It can be said that dissimilar pricing is the logical approach for pricing in regulated industries. Cost indivisibilities necessitate the practice of discriminatory pricing, but this was approached within what might be called a cost framework. Marginal cost sets the minimum basis for prices, whereas fixed or common costs are, in effect, allocated on the basis of demand elasticity.

Value-of-Service Pricing

Value-of-service pricing is a frequently mentioned and often criticized approach to pricing that has generally been associated with the railroad industry. Part of the problem associated with value-of-service pricing is that a number of different definitions of it are offered by various sources. Therefore, a workable definition of the term will be developed.

One rather common definition of value-of-service pricing in transportation is pricing according to the value of the product; for example, high-valued products are assessed high prices for their movement, and low-valued commodities are assessed low prices. Evidence can be found to substantiate this definition by examining the class rate structure of railroads (class rates are discussed later in this chapter).

Several points are in order here. First, even if a cost-based approach is taken to setting prices, high-valued commodities would usually be charged higher prices because they are typically more expensive to transport. There is generally more risk involved in moving high-valued commodities and more expensive equipment is necessary. Second, the value of the commodity is a legitimate indicator of elasticity of demand; for example, high-valued commodities can usually bear higher prices because transportation cost is such a small percentage of the final selling price.

This concept can be seen in Figure 4-4. The demand curves of two different types of commodities for transportation services are shown. The high-value item has a steeply sloping demand curve implying price inelasticity. On the other hand, the low-value item has a gradual slope, implying price elasticity. To see how these elasticities relate to how a transportation firm can set prices based on product value, consider a price increase from price P_1 to price P_2. When the price of the transportation service increases for the high-value product, a small quantity-demanded decrease is observed from quantity Q_1 to quantity Q_2. For the same price increase, the low-value product cannot absorb the increased price. This inability to support the added price of the service is seen as a drop in the quantity demanded from Q_1 to Q_2. Clearly the decrease in quantity demanded for the low-value product is of a larger magnitude than the decrease for the higher-value product for the same price increase.

In a situation where a carrier has a complete monopoly, to consider value-of-service pricing only in terms of the commodity's value would not lead to serious traffic losses. It would be analogous to the idea behind progressive income taxes; that is, setting prices upon the ability or willingness to pay.[14] But where alternatives are present at a lower price, shippers are not willing to pay higher prices based upon the value of the product alone. This is one of the reasons why the motor carriers were able to make serious inroads in rail traffic during their early development. They undercut the prices on high-valued commodities when the railroads were the most susceptible to competition. In essence, the value of the commodity gives some indication of demand or the ability to bear a charge, but competition also will affect the demand for the service, that is, the height and slope of the demand curve.

Value-of-service pricing also has been defined as **third-degree price discrimination** or a situation in which a seller sets two or more different market prices for two or more separate groups of buyers of essentially the same commodity or service.[15] Three necessary conditions must exist before a seller can practice third-degree price discrimination. First, the seller must be able to separate buyers into groups or submarkets according to their different elasticities of demand; this separation enables the seller to charge different prices in the various markets. The second condition is that the seller must be able to prevent the transfer of sales between the submarkets. That is, the buyer must not buy in the lower-priced market and sell in the higher-priced markets. Third, the seller must possess some degree of monopoly power.

FIGURE 4-4   Influence of Value and Demand Elasticity on Price

Another name given to value-of-service pricing is **differential** pricing. Differential pricing can be done based on several methods of segregating the buyers into distinct groups. It can be done by commodity (such as coal versus computers), by time (seasonal discounts or premium rates), by place (as Figure 4-5 demonstrates), or by individual person. It should be noted, however, that discrimination based on an individual person is illegal per se on traffic that remains economically regulated by the STB.[16]

These conditions for third-degree price discrimination can be fulfilled in the transportation industry, as well as in other regulated industries. For example, in transportation shippers are separated according to commodities transported and between points of movement. The previous discussion of the relevant market area in transportation implied that there were different or separable customer-related markets—for example, one commodity between each pair of shipping points, each with a separate elasticity.

Another relevant point is the nature of "essentially the same commodity or service."[17] Actually, many transportation companies sell multiple or heterogeneous services that are technically similar. For example, rail movements of television sets or glassware are very different in terms of time, equipment, terminal facilities, and so on.

Value-of-service or differential pricing makes sense from the perspective of the railroads, considering their high level of fixed costs and need to attract traffic. Remember that railroads will experience declining average costs with increases in volume. If shipments are priced properly, this could mean increased revenues from higher volumes with more profit.

The key to success lies in being able to determine the appropriate costs and to estimate demand elasticity in the various markets. This essentially means determining what the shipper is willing to pay for the service given the competition in the market from other carriers, the demand for the product itself, and any other factors affecting demand.

Assume that a particular railroad is establishing prices on three different commodities.[18] One of the commodities is large computer systems, which have a very high value and for which there is limited substitutability. The second commodity is flat-screen television sets, which are of medium value and have some substitutes. The third commodity is coal, which is low in value and has substitutes.

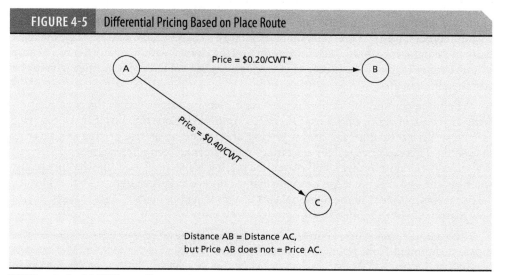

FIGURE 4-5   Differential Pricing Based on Place Route

Price = $0.20/CWT*

Price = $0.40/CWT

Distance AB = Distance AC,
but Price AB does not = Price AC.

*CWT "hundred weight:" 100-pound increments.

Assume further that the value of a particular computer system is $200,000 and that it weighs one ton. If the rate charged for movement was $1,000 per ton, it would still only be one-half percent (0.005) of the value of the product. The flat-screen television might have a value of $10,000 per ton. Therefore, a rate of $1,000 between the same points would represent 10 percent of the value. Finally, the coal might be worth $50 per ton. A rate of $1,000 would represent 2,000 percent of its value. Therefore, charging a common price would discourage some shippers, particularly of low-value products.

This example is obviously simplified. However, it does point out some of the underlying logic behind value-of-service or differential pricing. In theory, if all shippers are charged based on proper differential pricing, each particular commodity should be paying more than its variable cost and making a contribution to average cost, without discouraging any shipper from using the transportation service.

An argument can be made that the coal shippers are not paying their full share and the computer shippers are paying too much. However, another argument that is frequently advanced in such instances is that, if the coal did not move (remember it is paying more than the associated variable cost), then the other traffic (computers and televisions) would have to pay an even higher price to help cover the costs of running the railroad. The same analogy applies to the supersaver fares charged by airlines. Full-fare passengers complain sometimes that they are subsidizing discount-fare passengers. Actually, full fares might be higher if the special fares were not offered (further details on airline pricing will be discussed later in Appendix 4C).

The essential ingredient in the value-of-service analysis is the notion that each commodity movement has its own unique demand characteristics. If the railroad placed the same price on all commodities shipped, it would discourage some shippers from moving their goods at that price. Consider what would happen if the meat counter at the local supermarket priced all the various cuts and types of meats at the same level. Obviously, it would sell the T-bone steaks quickly and have only chopped steaks left.

Several points about this example need to be emphasized. First, the example is simplified. The determination of cost is a difficult task. Second, most railroads and many other carriers would be considering more than three commodities between two points. Third, the example applies to the railroad industry because it is more attractive in situations with high fixed costs, yet other carriers, even motor carriers, might find differential pricing attractive. Fourth, some difference would exist in rates among commodities because of cost differences; for instance, televisions cost more to handle than coal. Finally, the elasticity of demand for a particular commodity might change with competition or because of some other factors. Therefore, high rates on higher-valued commodities have to be continually evaluated.

The three commodity examples presented here are extensions of the example presented for cost-of-service pricing as shown in Figure 4-3. Conceptually, if cost-of-service pricing serves as the floor for carrier pricing, then value-of-service pricing can serve as the ceiling. This can be especially seen in the television and computer examples. However, if we accept the notion that value-of-service pricing is pricing based on what the traffic will bear, then an argument can be made that value-of-service pricing is also the floor for carrier prices, rather than the marginal cost of providing the service. This will depend on how marginal cost is defined in the context of the move.

An example might best represent this hypothesis. Assume that a truckload carrier moves a shipment from point A to point B with a variable cost of $90, an average cost of $100, and a price of $110. This relationship can be seen in Figure 4-6. This is called the carrier's **headhaul** because it is this demand that initiated the original movement of the carrier's equipment and the shipper's goods. As such, the carrier might be able to use value-of-service pricing, charging $110 (profit maximization) because of commodity and competitive circumstances. With the carrier's equipment at point B, it is necessary to bring the equipment and driver back to point A. This is called a **backhaul** because it is the result of the original move (headhaul). The carrier now faces a totally different market in this backhaul lane. Assume that marginal cost in this backhaul lane is defined as the variable cost of fuel and driver wages, or $90. If the carrier decides to price based on its marginal cost of $90 (cost-of-service pricing), it is very possible that the market from point B to point A will not bear this price and the carrier will be forced to return empty. This will result in a loss to the carrier of $90. Now suppose that the carrier prices this backhaul in accordance with market demands at a level of $80. Although this results in a price below marginal cost, the carrier has minimized its losses by losing only $10 on the move instead of $90. Pricing in this manner can be called *loss minimization*. So it can be argued that value-of-service pricing can be used as the price ceiling (profit maximization) and as the price floor (loss minimization). Both situations can be seen in Figure 4-6, and both assume that the carrier knows its costs and the market environment.

Now assume that the marginal cost in this backhaul lane is defined as those costs that would be avoided if the carrier, in fact, returned empty; that is, because the vehicle and driver are going to return anyway, the $90 for fuel and wages now becomes the fixed cost, which will now be included in the average-cost figure. Marginal cost now becomes the added cost of loading the shipment and the reduced fuel efficiency, which will be assumed to be $20. Figure 4-7 shows these relationships. On the headhaul, the price of $110 covers both the average cost of $100 and the marginal cost of $90. On the backhaul, the $90 is allocated as a fixed cost over the units of output to result in an average cost of $50. Now the $80 price charged covers both the average cost and marginal cost and results in a profit, just as the price produced a profit in the headhaul example. In this example,

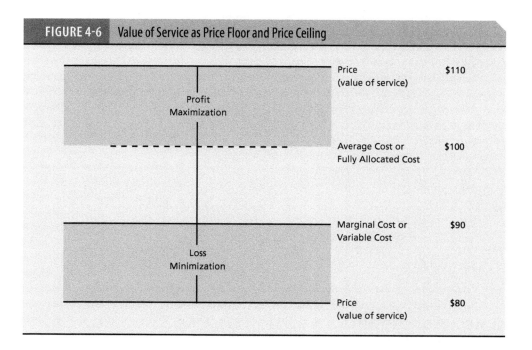

FIGURE 4-6   Value of Service as Price Floor and Price Ceiling

Profit Maximization

Price (value of service) — $110

Average Cost or Fully Allocated Cost — $100

Marginal Cost or Variable Cost — $90

Loss Minimization

Price (value of service) — $80

value of service provided the price ceiling and cost of service provided the price floor, as shown in Figure 4-3. The point of showing how different price floors can be justified is that prices will be set depending on how costs are defined. In Figure 4-6, backhaul variable costs were defined from an accounting perspective, that is, those costs directly related to the return move. In Figure 4-7, backhaul variable costs were defined from an economic perspective, that is, those costs that would be avoided if the carrier, in fact, returned empty. These two definitions result in two distinct perspectives on the profitability of the move for the carrier and would probably affect pricing and operations decisions of the carrier. Thus, when using costs as a basis for price, care must be taken to identify the proper role and definition of those costs in the pricing decision.

FIGURE 4-7 Cost of Service as Price, Floor, and Value of Service as Price Ceiling—Headhaul/Backhaul Example

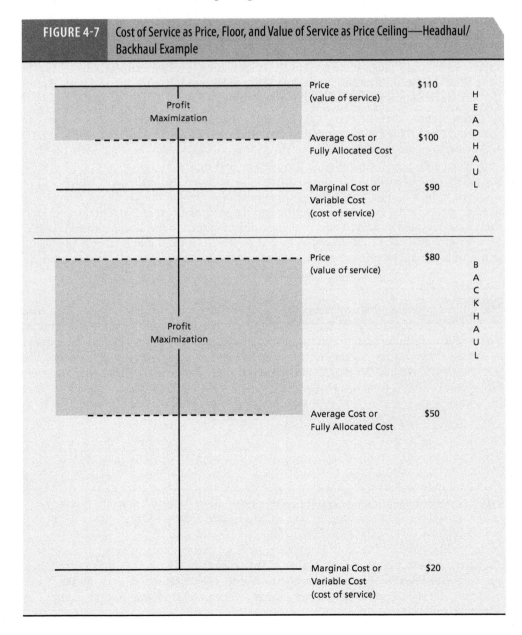

Rate Making in Practice

A complete understanding of carrier cost economics and behavior is a necessary prerequisite to effective management of carrier pricing. This section presents an overview of the general forms of pricing that are employed by carriers of all types. The form of each rate is discussed and analyzed, along with the primary inducements for the carrier and its users.

The overall carrier pricing function revolves around costing, rates, and tariffs. Carriers employ costing personnel who are responsible for determining the overall cost and productivity of the carrier operations as well as the specific routes, customer services, and equipment needs. The work of cost analysts should serve as a pricing input to rate personnel who are responsible for establishing specific rates and general rate levels for the carrier. Tariffs are the actual publications in which most rates are printed or are found on carrier websites. Some firms print their own tariffs, which are often referred to as *individual tariffs*, or they use a rate bureau that is common to many carriers to establish and publish rates. These tariffs are referred to as *bureau tariffs*. Carriers are no longer required to file individual tariffs with the STB. With the repeal of antitrust immunity for collective rate making, carriers today are more cautious with their efforts involving bureau tariffs.

Carriers today move a high percent of their volume under contracts with specific shippers. The form the rates take (for example, per mile, per container) in the contract is based on the preferences of the carrier and the shipper. So, the concepts of class, exception, and commodity rates would not apply under these contracts but will be contained in tariffs. However, the methodology used to determine these three rate forms underlies the construction of all rates, regardless of how they are quoted or where they are published. All rates are based on distance, weight, and commodity. As such, the discussion of class, exception, and commodity rates is still relevant today. These will be discussed in the following sections.

General Rates

There are class, exception, and commodity rate structures in the United States. The **class rate** system provides a rate for any commodity between any two points. It is constructed from uniform distance and product systems. **Exception rates** are designed so that carriers in particular regions can depart from the product scale system for any one of many possible reasons, which will be discussed later. **Commodity rates**, on the other hand, are employed for specific origin–destination shipping patterns of specific commodities. Each one of these three systems has a particular purpose.

It would be simple if all transportation services were sold on the basis of ton-miles; that is, we would have to pay x dollars to move one ton for one mile. But, in fact, transportation services are not sold in ton-miles; they are sold for moving a specific commodity in a specific shipment size between two specific points—for example, moving 10,000 pounds of glass from Toledo to New York City. This fact gives some insight into the enormous magnitude of the transportation pricing problem. There are thousands of important shipping and receiving points in the United States. Theoretically, the number of different possible routes would be all the combinations of these points. The result is in the trillions of possible rates. In addition, it is necessary to consider the thousands of different commodities and products that might be shipped over any of these routes. There are also different modes to consider and different companies within each mode. It also might be necessary to consider the specific supply–demand situation for each commodity over each route.

FIGURE 4-8 Class Rate Simplification

Simplification Objective → Simplification Result

Minimize number of shipping points → Table of rate basis points and number

Simplify rate structure → National scale of rates

Minimize number of commodities to be rated → Classification system

Class Rates Because it is obviously impossible to quote trillions and trillions of rates, the transportation industry has taken three major steps toward simplification. Figure 4-8 summarizes this class rate simplification.

The first step consolidates the thousands of shipping points into groups by dividing the nation into geographic squares. The most important shipping point (based on tonnage) in each square serves as the **rate base point** for all other shipping points in the square. These grouped points are found in a groupings tariff. This reduces the potential number of distance variations for rate-making purposes. The distance from each base point to each other base point was determined by the railroads and placed on file with the STB and published in the National Rate Basis Tariff. The distance between any two base points is referred to as the **rate basis number**. The first simplifying step reduced the number of possible origins and destinations for pricing purposes. (See Table 4-1 and 4-2 for examples of grouping and rate basis number tariffs.)

TABLE 4-1	Groupings Tariff Example[a]	
STATE	**POINT**	**APPLY RATES FROM OR TO**
Michigan	Climax	Battle Creek
	Coleman	Clare
	Comstock	Kalamazoo
	Columbiaville	Flint
	Cross Village	Cheboygan
Ohio	Clay Center	Toledo
	Clifford	Chillicothe
	Clement	Dayton
	Cleves	Cincinnati
	Climax	Marion

[a]Alphabetical listing of points by states from and to which rates apply.

TABLE 4-2	Rate Basis Numbers Tariff Example

And Points Taking the Following Basing Points	Between Points Taking the Following Basing Points			
	Chilicothe, OH	Cincinnati, OH	Columbus, OH	Dayton, OH
	Rate Basis Numbers			
Cheboygan, MI	550	570	490	510
Clare, MI	400	420	360	380
Flint, MI	275	300	227	214

The second step deals with the thousands of different items that might be shipped between any two base points. The railroads have established a national scale of rates that has been placed on file with the STB and gives a rate in dollars per hundredweight (cwt), which is dollars per cwt for each rate basis number. (The motor carriers established a similar rate structure.) The actual rate to move a commodity considered the commodity's transportation characteristic by means of the classification, the third simplification step.

The third step simply groups together products with similar transportation characteristics so that one rating can be applied to the whole group. Now one rate is quoted for the group into which a number of different commodities have been placed, thereby reducing the number of rates quoted by the carriers. Items that are placed into class 125 will be charged 125 percent of the first-class rate found in the uniform scales of rates. This percentage number is called a *class rating*, and it is the group into which the commodity is placed for rate-making purposes. Table 4-3 is a classification example similar to that used in the National Motor Freight Classification.

Classification Factors The factors that are used to determine the rating of a specific commodity are the product characteristics that impact the carrier's costs. In particular, the ICC has ruled and the STB has maintained that four factors are to be considered: product density, storability, handling, and liability. Although no specific formulas are used to assign a commodity to a particular class, the four factors are considered in conjunction by a carrier classification committee. This committee resides in the National Motor Freight Traffic Association and determines the characteristics of each of the 18 product classes. An individual carrier can establish a commodity classification that differs from the national classification; this individual carrier classification is termed an exception and takes precedence over the national classification.

Product density directly impacts the use of the carrier's vehicle and the cost per hundredweight. The higher the product density (ratio of weight to volume), the greater the amount of weight that can be hauled and the lower the cost per hundredweight. Conversely, the lower the product density, the lower the amount of weight that can be hauled and the higher the cost per hundredweight hauled.

As shown in Table 4-4 , only 6,000 pounds of a product that has a density of 2 pounds per cubic foot can be loaded into the trailer, which means the cost per hundredweight shipped is $6.67. However, 48,000 pounds of a product with a density of 16 pounds per

TABLE 4-3	Freight Classification Example			
			CLASSES	
ITEM	**ARTICLES**	**LTL**	**TL**	**MW**
156300	PLASTIC MATERIALS, OTHER THAN EXPANDED, GROUP: subject to Item 156100 Sheet or Plate, NOI. Self-supporting (rigid), see Note, Item 156302, other than in rolls or coils, in boxes, crates or Packages 248, 384, 930, 1029, 2187, 2207, or 2310			
Sub 1	Exceeding 9 feet, 6 inches in two dimensions or 20 feet in one dimension	85	45	30
Sub 2	Not exceeding 9 feet, 6 inches in more than one dimension nor 20 feet in one dimension	60	35	30
156500	PLASTIC OR RUBBER ARTICLES, OTHER THAN EXPANDED, GROUP: Articles consist of Plastic or Rubber Articles, other than foam, cellular, expanded or sponge articles, see Item 110, Sec. 15 and Note, Item 156502, as described in items subject to this grouping			
156600	Articles, NOI, in barrels, boxes or crates, see Note, Item 156602, also in Packages 870, 1078, 1170, 1241, 1273, 1409, 1456, 2195, 2212, 2213, or 2230			
Sub 1	LTL, having a density of, subject to Item 170			
Sub 2	Less than one pound per cubic foot, see Note, Item 156608	400		
Sub 3	One pound per cubic foot, but less than two pounds, see Note, Item 156608	300		
Sub 4	Two pounds per cubic foot, but less than four pounds, see Note, Item 156608	250		
Sub 5	Four pounds per cubic foot, but less than five pounds, see Note, Item 156608	150		
Sub 6	Six pounds per cubic foot, but less than 12 pounds, see Note, Item 156608	100		
Sub 7	12 pounds per cubic foot, but less than 15 pounds, see Note, Item 156608	85		
Sub 8	15 pounds or greater per cubic foot	70		
Sub 9	TL		100	10
			70	16
			60	21
			45	30
155000	Personal effects, other than household effects or furnishings, of commissioned or enlisted personnel of the U.S. Army, Air Force, Navy, or Marine Corps, or deceased veterans, moving on government bills of lading, see Note, Item 155024, in bags, traveling bags, boxes, or army trunk lockers or navy cruise boxes or foot lockers securely locked or sealed			
Sub 1	Each article in value in accordance with the following, see Note, Item 155022			
Sub 2	Released value not exceeding 10 cents per pound	100	70	16
Sub 3	Released to value exceeding 10 cents per pound, but not exceeding 20 cents per pound	125	77½	16
Sub 4	Released to value exceeding 20 cents per pound, but not exceeding 50 cents per pound	150	85	16
Sub 5	Released to value exceeding 50 cents per pound, but not exceeding $2.00 per pound	200	110	16
Sub 6	Released to value exceeding $2.00 per pound, but not exceeding $5.00 per pound	300	150	16

cubic foot can be hauled at a cost of $0.83 per hundredweight. Therefore, the higher the product density, the lower the carrier's cost per weight unit and the lower the classification rating assigned to the product.

Stowability and handling reflect the cost the carrier will incur in securing and handling the product in the vehicle. Product characteristics such as excessive weight, length, and height result in higher stowage costs for the carrier and a corresponding higher classification rating. Likewise, products that require manual handling or special handling equipment increase the carrier's costs and are given a higher rating.

TABLE 4-4	Product Density and Carrier Cost per Hundredweight (cwt) Hauled		
	PRODUCT DENSITY		
	16 LB/FT³	**10 LB/FT³**	**2 LB/FT³**
Shipment weight (lb)[1]	48,000	30,000	6,000
Carrier cost[2]	$400.00	$400.00	$400.00
Cost/cwt[3]	$0.83	$1.33	$6.67

[1]Shipment weight = product density × 3,000 ft³ (assumed capacity of 48-ft trailer).
[2]Carrier cost assumed for a given distance to be the same for each shipment weight.
[3]Carrier cost/shipment weight/100.

The final classification factor, **liability**, considers the value of the product. When a product is damaged in transit, the common carrier is liable for the value of the product. Because higher-valued products pose a greater liability risk (potential cost), higher-valued products are classified higher than lower-valued products. In addition, products that are more susceptible to damage or are likely to damage other freight increase the potential liability cost and are placed into a higher classification rating.

In Table 4-3, the stowability and handling factors are evidenced in the classification of Item 156300. Plastic sheets or plates that exceed 9 feet, 6 inches (Sub 1) have a higher rating than the same product that does not exceed 9 feet, 6 inches (Sub 2). The density factor is embodied in the classification of Item 156600, Subs 1 through 8; the higher the density, the lower the rating. Finally, product liability is a primary factor in the classification of Item 155000, personal effects of military personnel; the higher the declared value of the shipment, the higher the rating.

Determining a Class Rate The procedure for determining a class rate for moving a specific commodity between two points is outlined in Figure 4-9. The first step is to determine the

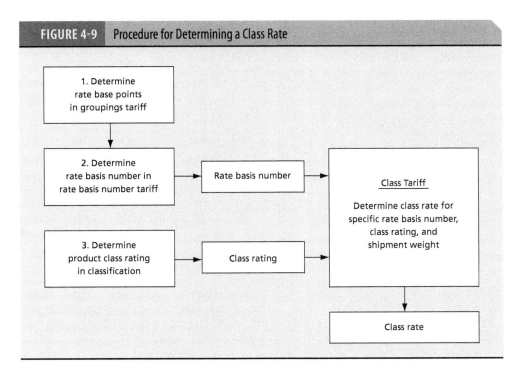

FIGURE 4-9   Procedure for Determining a Class Rate

rate base points for the specific origin and destination from the groupings tariff. Next, from the rate basis number tariff, determine the rate basis number for the relevant rate basis points. The class rating for the particular commodity being shipped is found in the classification. Finally, the rate is found in the class rate tariff for the appropriate rate basis number and class rating. The shipping charge for moving a product between a specific origin and destination is determined by multiplying the class rate, which is in cents per hundredweight, by the total shipment weight in hundredweight. Although actual rate determination may vary from one carrier to another, most carriers follow a procedure similar to this.

As an example, the total shipping charges for moving 11,000 pounds of plastic sheets, exceeding 9 feet, 6 inches, from Cross Village, Michigan, to Clifford, Ohio, will be determined. From the groupings tariff (Table 4-1), it can be seen that the rate basis point for Cross Village is Cheboygan, Michigan, and that for Clifford it is Chillicothe, Ohio. Next, the rate basis numbers tariff (Table 4-2) indicates that the rate basis number for rate basis points Cheboygan and Chillicothe is 550. From the classification (Table 4-3), it can be seen that the class rating for plastic sheets (Item 156300, Sub 1) is 85. Consulting the class tariff (Table 4-5) for a rate basis number of 550 and a class rating of 85, the resulting class rate is 846 cents per hundredweight for the weight group M10M (minimum of 10,000 pounds).

The computation of total shipping charges is as follows:

Shipment weight in cwt = 11,000/100cwt
Shipping charges at class rate = $8 46/cwt × 110cwt = $93.06

TABLE 4-5	**Sample Class Rate Tariff**				
			CLASSES (CENTS/100 LB)		
RATE BASIS NUMBER	**MINIMUM CHARGE**	**WEIGHT GROUP**	**200**	**100**	**85**
201 to 250		L5C	3,850	1,860	1,650
	4,500	M5C	3,105	1,500	1,325
		M1M	2,231	1,078	957
		M2M	1,825	882	781
		M5M	1,370	662	582
		M10M	1,264	611	540
		M20M	813	393	319
		M30M	650	314	255
		M40M	586	283	229
501 to 550		L5C	4,556	2,201	1,957
		M5C	3,775	1,824	1,633
	4,500	M1M	2,900	1,401	1,264
		M2M	2,488	1,202	1,092
		M5M	2,035	983	888
		M10M	1,933	934	846
		M20M	1,459	705	640
		M30M	1,292	624	572
		M40M	1,223	591	547

TABLE 4-6	Example of Commodity Rate				
ITEM	**COMMODITY**	**FROM**	**TO**	**RATE (CENTS PER 100 LB)**	**MINIMUM WEIGHT (LB)**
2315	Rubber (reclaimed, dispersed, liquid, or paste)	Akron, OH Barberton, OH Ravenna, OH Cleveland, OH	Warren, MI	726 518 496	2,000 5,000 10,000

Today, most carriers provide web portals that can compute their freight rates for their customers by using the logics described above. This means that customers can conveniently enter the necessary load-tender information online (such as origin, destination, weight and volume of load, and the shipping date), and receive freight rates instantaneously without having to understand the rate-determination procedures.

The term *tariff* is commonly used to mean almost any publication put out by a carrier or publishing agency that concerns itself with the pricing of services performed by the carrier. All the information needed to determine the cost of a move is in one or more tariffs.

Exception Rates An exception rate is a modification (change in rating, minimum weight, density group, and so on) to the national classification instituted by an individual carrier. Exception ratings are published when the transportation characteristics of an item in a particular area differ from those of the same article in other areas. For example, large-volume movements or intensive competition in one area might require the publication of a lower exception rating; in this case the exception rating applies, rather than the classification rating. There does not have to be an exception rate for every class rate.

Commodity Rates A commodity rate can be constructed on a variety of bases, but the most common is a specific rate published on a specific commodity or group of related commodities between specific points and generally via specific routes in specific directions. Commodity rates are complete in themselves and are not part of the classification system. If the commodity being shipped is not specifically stated, or if the origin–destination is not specifically spelled out in the commodity rate, then the commodity rate for the particular movement is not applicable.

When the commodity rate is published, it takes precedence over the class rate or exception rate on the same article between the specific points. A sample is shown in Table 4-6. The commodity rate in the table applies only to reclaimed, dispersed, liquid, or paste rubber. In addition, the commodity is direction-specific and applies from Akron, Barberton, Ravenna, and Cleveland, Ohio, to Warren, Michigan. This commodity rate is not applicable from Warren to Akron, for example.

This type of rate is offered for those commodities that are moved regularly in large quantities. Such a pricing system, however, completely undermines the attempts to simplify transportation pricing through the class rate structure. It has caused transportation pricing to revert to the publication of a multiplicity of rates and adds to the complexity of the pricing system.

Rate Systems Under Deregulation

General rate structures were the basis of tariffs published by rate bureaus. These rate-making bodies consisted of carriers that collectively met, established rates, published them in tariff form, and sold them on a subscription basis. Deregulation changes in both rail and motor modes have prohibited rate bureaus from discussing or voting on rates that involve only a single carrier. Similarly, joint rate making is limited to only those carriers involved in a movement and not all carriers in the bureau.

The diminished role of the rate bureau in carrier rate making has resulted in a plethora of individual carrier tariffs. In addition, the greater reliance upon the marketplace to control carrier rates has enabled the shippers to greatly increase negotiations, resulting in rate reductions, discounts, and contract rates. Although deregulation has somewhat diminished the use and application of the class, exception, and commodity tariff systems, various features of these tariff systems are widely used today for the pricing of small LTL freight.

The product classification feature of the former class rate system will no doubt survive for some time to come. This system of describing and classifying products simplifies the entire product description processes for all carriers. Carriers that are not even a part of the classification process often refer to these groupings to simplify their rate-making processes.

The class rate system also serves as a benchmark against which specific carrier rates and contract rates are created. Discount plans for specific shippers often are published as a percentage from the published class or exceptions-based rate.

Commodity rates published by individual carriers are similar in form to those published by the former rate bureaus. Most individual carriers publish commodity rates in a form similar to the one shown in Table 4-6.

Many innovative carriers have simplified their own class and commodity rate structures further. One way of accomplishing this is by providing shippers with small tariffs for moves from one or a few shipper points to any points within three-digit zip codes throughout the country. Thus, instead of describing the thousands of points in the United States, as in the rate base-point system, a maximum of 1,000 groupings is used (there are roughly 1,000 three-digit zip codes in the United States).

As briefly discussed earlier, many large motor carriers have computerized and/or created web-based zip code tariffs. The shipper enters into the computer the three-digit zip code for the origin, destination, and class rating of the commodity being shipped. The computer program searches for the appropriate rate and determines the freight charges with any applicable discounts. These computerized zip code tariffs are simply a variation of the class rate structure, relying on the classification rating and zip codes to delineate the product being shipped and the origin and destination (rate basis points) of the shipment.

Another variation on the commodity tariff system is the **mileage rate**. The mileage rate is quoted in cents per mile and not in cents per hundredweight. For example, the shipper pays $1.25 per mile times the number of miles the shipment moves, regardless of the shipment weight, which is limited by the physical or legal operating constraints.

In summary, the innovative rate structures being used in today's deregulated environment are variations of the class and commodity rate structures. The next section discusses the special rates used by carriers.

Special Rates

A myriad of special rate forms have evolved over the years either as a result of special cost factors or to induce certain shipment patterns. In their basic form, these special rates appear as class, exception, or commodity rates.

Character-of-Shipment Rates

One set of special rates relates to the size or character of the shipment. Carriers generally have certain fixed costs for each shipment. Many rate forms have been developed that take advantage of the fact that additional units or weight in each shipment do not incur additional amounts of these fixed costs.

LTL/TL Rates   Less-than-truckload (LTL) shipments require several handlings. Each one of these handlings requires dock personnel, materials-handling equipment, terminal investment, and additional communications and tracking effort. A truckload (TL) shipment, on the other hand, is generally loaded by the shipper and moved intact to the destination, where the consignee unloads it. No intermediate handlings are required, nor does it have to be loaded or unloaded by carrier personnel. The direct movement also avoids intermediate terminals. As a result of these factors, larger TL shipments have lower rates than LTL shipments.

Multiple-Car Rates   Railroads offer volume discounts for moves of more than one carload that are shipped as a single string of cars from one point to another. The cost of moving several cars in a single shipment is proportionally less than the cost of each car moved singly. For example, the multiple-car movement of 10 cars can be handled by the same effort (empty car drop-off, pickup, intermediate and delivery efforts, and documentation) as a single-car shipment. The only basic difference is the additional weight moved in the larger string of cars. Because of this economy of movement, railroads offer such rates in coal, grain, fertilizer, chemical, oil, and many other basic commodity moves.

Incentive Rates   The term **incentive rates** generally applies to a rate designed to induce the shipper to load existing movements and equipment more fully. These special rates usually apply only to weight or units loaded over and above the normally shipped quantities. For example, suppose an appliance manufacturer typically ships in carload quantities that only fill a car to 80 percent of its actual capacity. That is, the manufacturer typically ships 48,000 pounds of appliances in a car that can physically take up to 60,000 pounds of appliances. The carrier would prefer to have this car more fully loaded. In an incentive rate situation, the carrier would offer a rate lower than the carload rate that would only apply to the weight above the 48,000-pound norm in this example. It is more economical for the carrier to handle more weight in existing moves than to handle additional moves. By inducing the shipper to load each car more fully, fewer cars and moves would be required over the course of a year, and the same actual volume would be shipped.

Unit-Train Rates   A unit train service moves all cars (which typically contain the same commodity) from the same origin to the same destination seamlessly without having the cars split out or stopped while in transit. In many situations, the shipper or consignee provides the car investment. The railroad experiences economies through reduced assembling and disassembling of trains at rail yards, and through increased transit speed. This service also allows railroads to compete more effectively with other modes, such as road transportation, because of the increased service speed. Often, rail carriers use this type of rate for trailer on flatcar (TOFC) or container on flatcar (COFC) movements.

Per-Car and Per-Truckload Rates   Per-car or per-truckload rates are single-charge rates for specific origin–destination moves regardless of shipment commodity or weight. These rates also apply to container movements where the carriers' costs of movement are dominated by moving the equipment and not specifically by the weight of the shipment.

Any-Quantity Rates Any-quantity (AQ) rates provide no discount or rate break for larger movements. That is, there exists an LTL rate but no TL rate for large shipments. The AQ rates apply to any weight in a shipment. They are usually found with large, bulky commodities such as boats, suitcases, and cages where no economies are realized by the carrier for larger shipments.

Density Rates Some rates are published according to density and shipment weight, rather than by commodity or weight alone. These rates are common in air container shipments. For example, a density rate is published as, say, $10 per hundredweight for shipments up to 10 pounds per cubic foot, $9 per hundredweight for 11 to 20 pounds per cubic foot, and $8 per hundredweight for 21 pounds per cubic foot and up. These are applied when the carrier assesses rates on the basis of weight but does not experience lower costs for lighter-weight containers. Here, in fact, the carrier would experience a loss of revenue (due to a low weight) when moving a given amount of cubic footage.

A motor carrier variation on the density rate is the linear foot rule. The generalized linear foot rule applies on shipments that weigh more than 2,000 pounds and occupy more than one linear foot of space for every 350 pounds. If the shipment meets these criteria, the carrier reconstructs the weight of the shipment based on 350 pounds times the number of linear feet of space occupied and eliminates any discounts the shipper has negotiated. Air carriers use a similar approach to handling low-density articles.

ON THE **LINE**

Werner CEO: Truckload Rates Getting Back to "Equilibrium" After Slump

The brief period of bargain truckload (TL) rates that shippers enjoyed earlier this year is ending, as carriers have reduced capacity to adapt to the slight drop in freight demand that occurred in the first half of 2016.

"We're getting back to equilibrium on rates," said Derek Leathers, president and CEO of Werner Enterprises, the nation's fourth-largest TL carrier, in his address at the annual meeting of North American Transportation Employee Relations (NATERA) in New Orleans. "It's a simple reaction that when freight demand slumps, people park trucks.

"According to industry reports, the Great Recession reduced truckload capacity by 18 percent. And since that time, TL carriers have slowly rebuilt that capacity, but the bad news is that we did it a little too much," said Leathers.

He added that Werner is committing $400 million in capital expenditures this year to take advantage of the slump in heavy truck sales. Sales of Class 8 trucks fell 50 percent in July, and by the end of this year, Werner will have an average fleet age of just 1.5 years, compared to the 4- to 5-year industry average.

Werner is a 60-year-old, $2 billion company that earned a $124 million net income last year with 7,300 power units and 22,000 trailers. According to Leathers, correctly managing fluctuating freight demand for such a large organization is becoming more difficult due to the reduction of the so-called "peak season," which used to occur between October and early December.

Leathers said that when he broke into trucking 26 years ago as a dispatcher for Schneider, he was prohibited from taking vacation in October and November. "I don't know whether we will even see a fall peak," he said. "Today that peak season is compressed, and with e-commerce, people do a peak season in two days."

Werner was founded as an irregular route TL carrier. But increasingly, Leathers said, shippers are asking for other solutions, including dedicated trucks on fixed routes, logistics solutions, intermodal, and other customized services.

"In the end, we're a trucking company, but we're evolving," said Leathers. "Those Chicago-to-LA dry van truckload requests don't just happen as much anymore, and increasingly, we're being asked to solve problems. Today, we have to take on not just issues affecting trucking, but global issues as well in the 120 countries where Werner operates. We all have to evolve as organizations."

Source: *Logistics Management*, October 2016, p. 18. Reprinted with permission of Peerless Media, LLC.

Area, Location, or Route Rates

A number of rates relate to area, location, or route. These special rates deserve consideration and discussion.

Local Rates Local rates apply to any rate between two points served by the same carrier. These rates include full-cost factors for pickup, documentation, rating, billing, and delivery.

Joint Rates Joint rates are single rates published from a point on one carrier's route to another carrier's destination. They are usually lower in total charges than the combination of the local rates because of through-movement economy.

Proportional Rates Many carriers experience a competitive disadvantage when their line is part of a through line that competes with another, more direct line. If a combination of local rates were charged, the through-movement cost might still be higher than the charges over the direct route. In this situation, the carrier might publish a proportional rate (lower than the regular local rate) that applies only to through moves to certain destination points beyond its line.

Differential Rates The term *differential rates* generally applies to a rate published by a carrier that faces a service time disadvantage compared to a faster carrier or mode. For example, water carriers often publish differential rates that are below those of railroads. In this way, the lower rate somewhat overcomes the longer transit time disadvantage inherent to the water carriers. The term *differential* is also found in situations where an extra charge is assessed for high-cost services such as branch lines. With all the recent mergers, this type of rate making has fallen from widespread use.

Per-Mile Rates Some rail, motor, and air carriers provide rates that are based purely upon the mileage involved. This is a common practice in bulk chemical truck moves and air charter movements. Railroads also use these rates in special train movements (high, wide, and heavy). Similarly, special moves, such as the movement of circus trains and some postal moves, are based on these rates.

Terminal-to-Terminal Rates Terminal-to-terminal rates, often referred to as *ramp-to-ramp rates*, apply between terminal points on the carrier's lines. These rates require the shipper and consignee to perform the traditional pickup and delivery functions. Many air freight rates and some piggyback rates are found in this form.

Blanket or Group Rates These rates apply to or from whole regions, rather than points. For example, all shippers of lumber from an area in Oregon and Washington are generally treated as having the same origin. Destinations eastward are grouped into zones in which all receivers in an entire state pay the same rates regardless of the special origin point in the Pacific Northwest. Blanket systems are found in food shipments from California and Florida. These rates equalize shippers and consignees because plant location is not a factor in determining the rate charged.

Time/Service Rate Structures

The Staggers Rail Act of 1980 specifically sanctioned rail contract rates, many of which can be classified as time/service rate structures. These rates are generally dependent on the transit time performance of the railroad in a particular service. One such contract provides a standard rate for a transit time service norm. The shipper pays a higher rate for faster service and a lower rate for slower service. Another contract calls for additional shipper payments to the carrier for the fast return of empty backhaul shipper-leased cars. These rate forms either place incentives or penalties in areas where they tend to create desired results, or they reduce undesirable performance.

Contract Rates   Contract services are commonplace in motor carriage and rail moves, as well as in water and some air moves. These services are governed by contracts negotiated between the shipper and carrier, not by generally published tariffs. Some specific contract service features that are typically found are described here.

One basic contract service feature calls for a reduced rate in exchange for a guarantee of a certain minimum tonnage to be shipped over a specified period. Another contract service feature calls for a reduced rate in exchange for the shipper tendering a certain percentage of all tonnage over to the contracting carrier. In both these instances, a penalty clause requires the shipper to pay up to the regular rate if the minimum tonnage is not shipped.

Another type of rail contract service feature calls for the rate to be higher or lower depending on the specific type of car supplied for loading and shipment, called a **car-supply charge**. The higher rates apply on cars whose contents have not been braced or blocked by the shipper; the higher charge is used to compensate the carrier for a potentially higher level of damage to the contents and ultimately to the higher liability level of the carrier.

A few contract service features require the shipper to pay a monthly charge to the railroad that supplies certain special equipment for the shipper's exclusive use. This charge tends to increase the shipper's use of the cars; the shipper no longer views them as free capital goods that can be used for temporary storage or loosely routed and controlled. Here the shipper firm has the incentive to use these cars in a way that benefits the firm and the carrier.

Many different rate and service configurations are found in motor carriage. These contract rates call for such services as scheduled service, special equipment movements, storage service in addition to movement, services beyond the vehicle (such as retail store shelf stocking by the driver), small package pickup and movement, bulk commodity movement, or hauling a shipper-owned trailer.

A great degree of flexibility surrounds the contracts of both rail and motor carriage. Carriers and shippers are relatively free to specifically tailor contract services to particular movements, equipment, and time-related services. The key in any contract service is to identify the service and cost factors important to each party and to construct inducements and penalties for each.

Deferred Delivery   The deferred delivery rate is common in air transportation. In general, the carrier charges a lower rate in return for the privilege of deferring the arrival time of the shipment. For example, express parcel delivery companies offer a discount of 25 percent or more for second- or third-day delivery, as opposed to the standard next-day (overnight) delivery. The deferred delivery rate gives the carrier operating flexibility to achieve greater vehicle utilization and lower costs.

Other Rate Structures

Several other rate forms serve particular cost or service purposes.

Corporate Volume Rates A rate form called the *corporate volume rate* came into existence in 1981. It is a discounted rate for each LTL shipment that is related to the total volume of LTL shipments that a firm ships via a specific carrier from all shipping points. Generally, the more volume a shipper tenders to a particular carrier, the greater the discount.

The corporate volume rate is not widely used today, but the principle of gaining lower rates for shipping larger volumes via a carrier is the basis of many negotiated rates. The corporate volume concept brings the full market power of the shipper (total dollars spent on moving all inbound and outbound company freight) to bear on negotiations. Also, the practice of placing blocks of freight up for bid, such as all the freight moving into and out of the southeastern United States, uses the corporate volume approach to gain special rates from the accepted bidder (further details on transportation bidding or auction are discussed in Chapter 9, "Logistics Services").

Discounts In the motor carrier industry, a discount is a common pricing practice for LTL shipments moving under class rates. The typical discount ranges from 25 to 50 percent, with some discounts as high as 60 to 65 percent, off the published class rate. The discounts might apply to specific classes of LTL traffic moving between given origins and destinations, or all LTL commodities moving between any origin and destination. For the smaller shipper that does not have the corporate volume to effectively negotiate lower rates, the discount is a viable alternative to achieving reduced rates.

Loading Allowances A loading (unloading) allowance is a reduced rate or discount granted to the shipper that loads LTL shipments into the carrier's vehicle. Motor carriers are required to load and unload LTL shipments and their LTL rate structures include this loading and unloading cost. The shipper/receiver that performs this function is incurring a cost that would have been incurred by the carrier. Thus, the carrier agrees to reimburse the shipper for this expense in the form of a lower rate.

Aggregate Tender Rates This reflects a reduced rate or discount given to the shipper that tenders two or more class-rated shipments to the carrier at one time. Usually, the aggregate shipment weight must equal 5,000 pounds or some other minimum established by the carrier. By tendering two or more shipments to the carrier at one time, the shipper reduces the carrier's pickup costs by reducing the number of times the carrier goes to the shipper's facility to pick up freight. With the aggregate tender rate, the shipper reaps part of the cost-reduction benefit that the carrier realizes from the multiple shipment pickup.

FAK Rates FAK rates, also known as *all-commodity rates* or *freight-all-kinds rates*, are rates expressed in cents per hundredweight or total cost per shipment. The specific commodity being shipped is not important, which means the carrier is basing the rate on the cost of service, not the value of service. The FAK rate is most valuable to shippers that ship mixed commodity shipments to a single destination, such as a grocery distributor shipping a wide variety of canned goods, paper products, and so on, to a local warehouse.

Released Value Rates Released value rates are lower than the regular full-value rates because of the reduced carrier liabilities. Unlike the regular rates where shippers get up-to-total-value carrier compensation in the event of loss or damage, the released value rates impose the carriers only a limited obligation up to certain upper-bound dollar amounts per pound shipped. They traditionally are found in air freight, household goods, and a small number of motor- and rail-hauled commodities. The 1980 and 1995 regulatory changes allowed flexible use of this rate form in most types of service and commodities.

Empty-Haul Rates An empty-haul rate is a charge for moving empty rail or motor equipment that is owned or leased by, or assigned to, a particular shipper. The existence of this type of rate tends to induce the shipper to fully load all miles of the equipment movements.

Two-Way or Three-Way Rates The terms *two-way rates* and *three-way rates* apply to rates that are constructed and charged when backhaul or triangular moves can be made. The intent here is to tie a headhaul move with what would have been another firm's backhaul move. In this way, neither firm incurs the penalty for empty backhauls. Some bulk chemical motor carriers offer these rates. They reduce total transportation charges for the shippers, and the carrier's equipment is more fully utilized than it would be otherwise. The concept of maximizing truck capacity utilizations by matching headhaul and backhaul, or moving trucks in triangular patterns, is discussed in more depth in Chapter 9, "Logistics Services."

Spot-Market Rates "Spot-market" rates are different from the contractual rates in that they are negotiated on a load-by-load basis (contractual rates are usually negotiated based on the expected total shipment volume per specified time period, as discussed earlier). In the United States, most freights move on contractual rates, but some freights move on spot rates, which are often tendered to carriers through brokers and 3PLs (third-party logistics companies). Spot markets are often used by shippers to tender loads that need to be shipped immediately, or outside of the normal contractual agreements. Usually spot-market rates are more expensive than contractual rates, but this is not always the case. The spot market rates are determined by the supply and demand of equipment; that is, the spot rate will be high when demand is higher than supply, but it will be low when demand is less than supply.

Menu Pricing Carriers are beginning to provide more and more value-added services for shippers, such as loading/unloading, packaging, merge-in-transit, and sorting, along with traditional transportation services. Menu pricing allows the shipper to pick and choose those services the carrier should perform, and the shipper is charged accordingly. This concept is the same as that used in a la carte menus in restaurants. This type of pricing also requires the carrier to understand and know its costs in providing these services.

The regulatory standards legislated in 1980 and 1995, as well as altered administrative STB policies, have created a realm of flexibility and creativity in rate forms. Carriers are relatively free to develop rate systems to benefit them and shippers in ways that were neither common in the past, nor even existent. Any pricing system, however, should induce the buyer to buy in ways beneficial to the seller, be simple to understand and apply, and maximize the financial resources of the seller.

TRANSPORTATION **TECHNOLOGY**

Freight Payment Versus Freight Settlement

The shippers locked into classic procurement and freight payment processes need to pay attention to the changes that are coming in transportation operations. One example of the major changes coming is the evolution of "freight payment" to "freight settlement."

For many years, the function of freight payment has been a labor-intensive function involving accounts payable and transportation dealing with a form of "match-pay." Match-pay involves a physical comparison of a carrier invoice with a shipper rate file or accrual amount based on the shipper's rate file—this is a process that involves several people handling and rehandling documents or files.

However, there's a new approach involving a paradigm shift in payment that has three stages. In stage one, both the shipper and carrier agree on contract rates and, most importantly, agree on a single system of record to hold those rates. If the shipper system is chosen, then the carrier is paid upon completion of service automatically without invoicing.

If the carrier system is selected, then invoices are paid without review and sometimes by a debit to a shipper accrual account. Either of these "autopay" processes reduces costs for processing; and with billing and collections representing up to 7 percent of carrier costs, there are certainly savings to be had with autopay.

In the second stage, payment processing is replaced by settlement. Settlement implies multiple required actions being simultaneously closed with each freight transaction. In addition to a "proof of delivery" triggering the payment, the carrier provides detailed data electronically on service milestones such as pickup, transit time, and delivery time. This service information is a required part of the transaction—no data, no payment.

The value of detailed logistics data on service and cost improvements has been well documented. It reveals information about customer demands, network patterns, capacity utilization and backhaul opportunities among other business factors.

In stage three, parties step it up with disaggregation of the transaction elements to allow for pricing variations based upon factors such as time of day, risk, speed of loading and unloading, along with other agreed upon factors.

In this stage, the shipper is using predetermined contract factors to optimize cost and service. The carrier system has to be able to dynamically rate the shipment based upon real-time factors that the shipper can influence, because the shipper can directly impact the carrier's operating costs. Planning then becomes more dynamic, as shippers select from a menu of costs and service levels provided for under a collaborative contract.

This third stage mimics the process by which we select airline passenger tickets.

The carrier hosts the rate system and the shipper selects from a menu of cost and service selections that have a range of prices. Last minute moves cost more and flexibility in service allows the carrier to maximize capacity and optimize resources. This selection can be done automatically as shippers plan and tender to carriers.

For shippers, third-party logistics providers and their carrier partners, as well as freight audit and payment services, the change is coming. The exchange of funds for service is rapidly becoming the exchange of funds for information and dynamically planned service transactions. Smart companies are collaborating to win.

Source: *Logistics Management*, September 2016, p. 24. Reprinted with permission of Peerless Media, LLC.

Pricing in Transportation Management

For many years, carriers relied on tariffs as their price lists for their services. Under traditional economic regulation, little incentive was present for carriers to differentiate themselves through either service enhancements or pricing strategies. Today, however, both of these differentiating tactics are critical to carriers in all modes, regardless of market structure. Unfortunately, however, many carriers still rely on the tariff mentality when setting prices as a competitive weapon. This way of thinking normally uses cost as a base and pays little or no attention to price as a part of the marketing mix. Many carriers will admit that they know their costs but do not know how to price.

This section will present a basic discussion on pricing for transportation management. Its intent is to introduce some common pricing strategies and techniques that are commonly used in such industries as retailing. Further, in-depth discussions on these topics can be found in any basic marketing textbook.[19]

Factors Affecting Pricing Decisions

Many carrier pricing decisions are based on some reaction to a stimulus from the business environment. In transportation, the environment comprises many constituencies, four of which include customers (market), government, other channel members, and competition.

The discussion presented on value-of-service pricing in this chapter focused on the role of the market to determine prices. Obviously, a profit-maximization–oriented carrier will not set a price in the long run that prohibits the movement of freight or passengers. The carrier's price will be set at the level that maximizes its return. This, however, is dependent on what the market perceives to be a reasonable price and/or what the market is forced to pay (in monopolistic situations). The concept of price elasticity also plays an important role in the market's impact on carrier prices. For example, business travelers might be willing to absorb increases in airfares in exchange for the convenience of short-notice reservations, whereas leisure travelers might not. Customers then have a formidable impact on carrier prices.

Transportation was economically regulated by the federal government for well over 100 years because of potentially monopolistic abuses. Part of this regulation dealt with carrier prices in the forms of how they are constructed and how they are quoted. All of the economic transportation regulation falls under the responsibility of the STB. After the deregulatory efforts of the late 1970s through the 1990s, however, the Justice Department also entered the carrier pricing arena to monitor for antitrust violations. In some respects, these government agencies help mitigate the imperfections in the marketplace to control carrier pricing. As such, governmental controls affect how carriers price their services. (Government impact on carrier pricing is discussed at length in Chapter 3, "Transportation Regulation and Public Policy.")

In the case of carriers, other **channel members** can include other carriers in the same mode and in different modes. For example, interline movements between different carriers that involve revenue splits will certainly impact how each carrier prices its services. If one carrier decides to raise its price, the other carrier either has to reduce its price or risk losing business, given that the market has a high price elasticity. Such a case can be found in intermodal transportation in which different modes, for example, truck and railroad, are involved. Another case can be found in interline agreements between railroads for track usage. Because there is no single transcontinental railroad, it is quite likely that a shipment will have to use the tracks of more than one railroad in a cross-country move. If costs increase, rail carriers might have to increase their prices to customers (at the risk of losing tonnage on that move), or reduce their operating margins (if they wish not to lose tonnage).

Finally, competitors will impact carrier pricing strategies. History has shown that even in transportation oligopolies (such as airlines and LTL motor carriers), price leaders that offer discounts to customers will find that competitors will match those discounts, even at the risk of reducing industry profits. This could be a symptom of the continual pressure on carrier customers to reduce transportation costs in their firms. Across-the-board price increases are also usually matched by all the major competitors in a particular mode. However, occasions do occur when competitors do not follow price leader actions. An attempt by one airline to simplify its pricing structure by reducing the number of special fares was not matched by its competitors. Because of this, that airline was forced to abandon its original simplification strategy and return to normal airline pricing tactics.

Carriers then must respond to changes and directions from their operating environment. Sometimes these changes might not favor the carriers, such as when government regulations force carriers to make a change that reduces efficiency (for example, the change in Hours-of-Service rule in the motor carrier industry). However, these environmental forces do exert pressure on carrier pricing strategies and price levels.

Major Pricing Decisions

Every firm involved in delivering either a product or service faces major pricing decisions. These decisions can range from the very simple to the extremely complex. However, pricing decisions can be grouped into three categories. First, a carrier faces a decision when setting prices on a new service. For example, Federal Express had no precedent when setting prices on its first overnight delivery service. Today, same-day delivery is gaining in popularity with many Internet companies. Setting prices for these services could be difficult because it is based on little knowledge concerning the elasticity of the market to prices and the actual cost of providing the service. Also, if the price is set high enough to generate substantial profits, competitors will be enticed to enter the market at perhaps a lower price. On the other hand, if the price is set too low, although significant traffic might be generated, the carrier will not be maximizing its profits.

Second, a carrier must make decisions to modify prices over time. Market changes, carrier network changes (which can be caused by additions or removals of clients) operational changes, and service changes will require prices to be adjusted.

An important aspect of this decision is how and when to announce the changes to the market. For example, a major price increase by a carrier after announcing record company profits might get negative reactions in the market. In a manufacturing or retailing environment, price increases are sometimes announced in advance so customers can increase purchases to help offset the higher price. However, in transportation, services cannot be inventoried, so prior notification of a price increase does not accomplish the same objective, yet prior notification does allow for customers to seek alternative sources of supply.

Finally, carriers will make decisions initiating and responding to price changes. The concept of a *price leader* within an industry is not new. If a carrier is the price leader, then that carrier initiates the change; if not, then the carrier responds to the change. In transportation, where many of the markets are oligopolistic, downward price changes can be dangerous because of their potential to decrease industry revenues. Upward price changes can make a carrier the sole high-price service provider if competition does not follow the change, so how this decision is made can have a substantial impact on market share and profits.

Although there might be other types of price decisions, these represent the major ones that carriers will make. These can be considered strategic decisions because of the importance they have on carrier market position within the industry. For example, People's Express once offered a low-price, no-frills airline service and did not expect other carriers to match the low fares. However, some of the major trunk lines actually offered fares below People's, even though it meant a loss. With a high debt and stiff competition, People's Express eventually went out of business (after which the major trunk lines raised fares). Pricing, then, is a major marketing decision for every carrier.

Establishing the Pricing Objective

Pricing objectives for a carrier should reflect overall company objectives and reflect, in many ways, how the carrier will compete in its markets. Pricing objectives might also change for a particular service offering as it progresses through its product life cycle. Carriers with multiple markets might also establish various pricing objectives for these markets. For example, passenger airlines have separate pricing objectives for first-class and coach markets as well as for business and leisure travelers. This section will present several different pricing objectives that can be utilized in the transportation industry.

Especially in the case of ailing passenger airlines, **survival-based pricing** is aimed at increasing cash flow through the use of low prices. With this price level, the carrier attempts to increase volume and also encourage the higher utilization of equipment. Because an empty airline seat cannot be inventoried and is lost at takeoff, the marginal cost of filling that seat is small. Survival pricing then tries to take advantage of the marginal-cost concept. Closely related is a **unit volume pricing** objective. This attempts to utilize a carrier's existing capacity to the fullest, so the price is set to encourage the market to fill that capacity. Multiple pickup allowances in the LTL industry, space-available prices in the freight airline industry, and multiple-car prices in the railroad industry are examples of this type of pricing objective.

Another price objective is called **profit maximization**, which can occur in the short run or in the long run. Carriers using this type of pricing usually are concerned with measures such as return on investment. This type of objective also can utilize what is called a **skimming price**. A skimming price is a high price intended to attract a market that is more concerned with quality, uniqueness, or status and is insensitive to price.[20] For example, pricing for the ticket to space by Virgin Galactic ($250,000) was certainly aimed at those who would be willing to pay a high price because of the limited number of seats. This strategy works if competition can be kept out of a market through high investment costs or firm loyalty.

Many times a skimming price strategy is followed by a **penetration price** strategy. This can lead to a sales-based pricing objective, which can be an effective strategy because (1) a high price can be charged until competition starts to enter; (2) a higher price can help offset initial outlays for advertising and development; (3) a high price portrays a high-quality service; (4) if price changes need to be made, it is more favorable to reduce a price than to raise it; and (5) after market saturation is achieved, a lower price can appeal to a mass market with the objective of increasing sales.[21] A sales-based pricing objective also follows the life cycle approach of using skimming during the introduction and growth stages and penetration during the maturation stage. In transportation, this strategy would more likely be successful with passenger movements because of the reliance it places on the price–value relationship.

A **market share pricing** objective can be used in an industry whose revenues are stagnant or declining. This objective tries to take market share from competitors through the use of lower prices. This strategy is used frequently in passenger airlines and the LTL motor carrier industries. In some cases, this strategy assumes that competitors' offerings are substitutes and that competitors are not in a position to match the lower prices; if the services were not substitutes, a lower price would not provide a competitive advantage. For example, an airline that lowers its fares for business travelers to gain more of this market but does not offer the same number of departures and arrivals as a competitor might not succeed at gaining any market share.

Finally, a **social responsibility pricing** objective forgoes sales and profits and puts the welfare of society and customers first.[22] For example, after the tragic incident in New York City on September 11, 2001, many carriers offered to carry such items as food, clothing, building supplies, and medical supplies into the devastated area at greatly reduced prices or for free.

Because carriers in the various transportation industries service multiple markets, it is quite possible for them to employ several pricing objectives at one time. A carrier must be careful when setting an overall company pricing strategy to assure that these multiple pricing objectives are complementary, not conflicting.

Estimating Demand

Probably one of the most difficult tasks associated with pricing is estimating demand. In a perfectly competitive market, unit demand will decrease as price increases. This is reflected in the traditional demand-and-supply curve offered in basic economic theory. However, transportation carriers do not function in perfectly competitive markets. Demand estimation can become very tedious and difficult. However, certain concepts and procedures can be used in this process. One of these is the concept of *price elasticity*. Price elasticity refers to the change in demand because of a change in price. In an established market for a carrier, this relationship should be well developed to the point where demand implications from a price change should be easy to estimate. The example of business versus leisure travelers in the airline industry can be used to explain this concept. Business travelers are relatively price inelastic because demand for business travel by air does not fluctuate widely with increases in price. However, leisure travelers are very price elastic and might tend to delay travel or seek travel by an alternative mode if there is an increase in airfares. In a new market, estimations of price elasticity can be made by comparing the new market with a similar existing market.

A direct attitude survey might also be used in determining demand under a new pricing structure. For example, asking customers and/or potential customers how much business they would provide at certain price levels might produce some feel of how sensitive demand is to price. Caution has to be used in this method in how this question is asked because customers will usually tend to favor the lowest price.

Finally, a market test is a possible way to determine potential demand when market testing is feasible. This might involve a carrier introducing a new service at a high price in one area and at a higher price in another area to see how sensitive demand is to price. Important in this method is choosing test market areas that resemble the entire market for which the service is applicable.

Although not a science, demand estimation is a critical part of pricing strategy. Demand estimation results in potential revenue estimation. (Some of the theory behind demand estimation was presented earlier in this chapter, under the topic "Value-of-Service Pricing.") With revenue estimated, costs should next be established.

Estimating Costs

As mentioned previously, knowing cost is an important prerequisite for making proper pricing decisions. Thus, it is essential that carriers understand how costs behave at different levels of output or capacity. Here we introduce three concepts that are helpful for carriers to understand the cost behavior; namely, economies of scale, economies of density, and economies of scope. In the paragraphs that follow, we describe each concept briefly. Further discussion of these concepts, in particular, how they apply to each mode of transportation, are found in later chapters.

Economies of Scale It is said that economies of scale exists if the average cost (cost per unit of output) is a decreasing function of the firm output; that is, the more the firm output the lower the average cost. Economies of scale can be found in all modes of transportation, but it is particularly evident in those modes in which the fixed costs are high. This is because when the fixed costs are high, carriers can lower the average cost considerably by spreading out the high fixed cost to a large number of outputs. Notice that, since the average cost is given by the sum of unit variable cost (which is unaffected by output) and unit fixed cost (fixed cost divided by output—which is obviously a decreasing function of output), the average cost is always a decreasing function of the output. However, the extent to which the average cost decreases with output is dependent on the value of fixed cost, because the rate at which the cost decreases with output is positively affected by the value of fixed cost (that is, the larger the fixed cost the faster the rate of decrease caused by a unit increase in output—if you are familiar with differential calculus you can easily verify this claim). For example, the average cost of a motor carrier that operates many terminals can be reduced notably by increasing the number of loads that the carrier handles through the terminals, because by doing so the fixed cost of operating the terminals (which is high) can be distributed to a large number of loads. On the other hand, the average cost of a carrier that operates one terminal can be reduced only to a limited extent by increasing output, because the fixed cost is small.

Economies of Density This concept is similar to economies of scale, but it is lane specific. It is said that economies of density exists in a given lane (origin–destination pair) if the cost (average cost) of a carrier decreases with the increase of the carrier's shipment volume in the lane.

Economies of density is typically the result of increased capacity utilization in a given lane; that is, the higher the volume in a given lane the higher the capacity utilization of the equipment used in the lane. Economies of density may naturally exist in a given lane (for example, busy lanes in which substantial shipping demands exist), or can be created by carriers intentionally.

A good example of the intentional creation of economies of density can be found in the airline industry, where many carriers adopt the "hub-and-spoke" network systems. Without the hub-and-spoke system there are a large number of lanes in a network (for example, an airline with 10 serving airports would have $(10 \times 9)/2 = 45$ lanes), making the density of each lane to be very light. But if the airline decides to use one of its serving airports as a hub, the number of lanes in its network reduces dramatically (to nine lanes, which connect the hub to the remaining nine airports), so that within each lane the airline can enjoy significantly higher degrees of traffic density, which results in cost reduction.

Economies of Scope It is said that economies of scope exists if the cost (average cost) of a carrier decreases with the increase of the number of products or services which the carrier provides. Economies of scope can be found in all modes of transportation, but many good applications of this concept can be found in the trucking industry. For example, it has been shown that the operating cost of a motor carrier becomes lower if the carrier requires each vehicle to haul multiple types of products rather than a single type.[23] The basic logic here is that, when a vehicle is hauling multiple (rather than single) items, a number of distinct nonhomogeneous outputs are being produced from the same vehicle, so that joint and common costs arise, and the presence of this joint cost gives rise to economies of scope, as these costs can be shared by multiple outputs. It has also been shown that a carrier's cost becomes lower if the carrier is allowed to service a larger number of lanes in a given network[24] (primarily because of the reduced carrier uncertainties with respect to the backhaul movements—this issue will be discussed in more detail in Chapter 9).

To make proper pricing decisions carriers should consider all of these economies. Specifically, in every business opportunity, carriers should: (1) carefully assess the expected output from the potential business and understand its impact on reducing fixed costs (to assess economies of scale), (2) examine whether or not the potential business will enhance or reduce the traffic density of their networks (to assess economies of density), and (3) investigate whether or not the potential business would create joint and common costs with existing businesses (to assess economies of scope).

Price Levels and Price Adjustments

With demand and cost estimates generated, it is possible to set the actual price. Many methods for doing this exist, including demand-based methods, cost-based methods, profit-based methods, and competition-based methods. Lengthy discussions of these can be found in any basic marketing-text chapter on pricing.[25] However, a discussion of price adjustments is warranted because of the federal government regulations on such concepts as rebates.

Discounts are a reduction from a published price that rewards a buyer for doing something that is beneficial for the supplier.[26] In transportation, LTL versus TL prices reflect carrier savings from larger shipments, a portion of which is passed on to the customer in the form of a lower price. This could be called a quantity discount. Airlines use a form of seasonal discounts to encourage vacation passengers to travel during carrier off-peak periods. Cash discounts, relatively new to the transportation industry, reward customers who pay their bills within a stated period of time. A common form of a cash discount is "2/10, net 30," which means that the customer can take a 2 percent discount if the bill is paid within 10 days, or else pay the full amount within 30 days. This helps speed the cash flow for carriers, which is important for their financial stability.

Geographic adjustments are common in the transportation industry. Although not directly used by carriers, geographic adjustments are used by shippers and receivers to compensate for transportation costs in the final price to the customer. One common type of geographic price is FOB origin or FOB destination pricing. In FOB origin pricing, the buyer is responsible for transportation costs; in destination pricing, the shipper is responsible (see Figure 4-10).

Uniform-delivered pricing, a form of FOB destination pricing, offers a final price to customers for a product that includes all transportation costs. Related to this is **zone pricing**, in which every customer within a certain zone pays exactly the same price for a product based on average transportation costs within the zone.

When using discounts and allowances in the transportation industry, an important rule to remember is that a discount or allowance passed on to a customer must be the result of a reduction in carrier costs because of an action by the customer. Also, the discount or allowance given to the customer may not exceed the cost savings to the carrier.

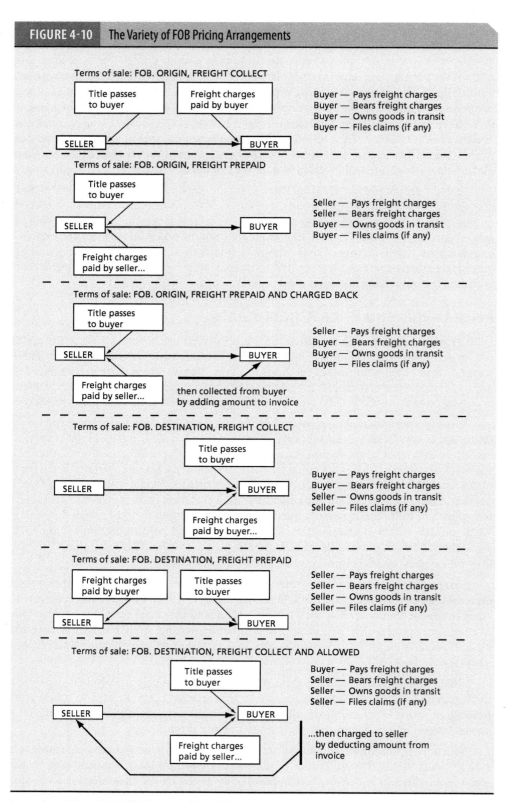

FIGURE 4-10   The Variety of FOB Pricing Arrangements

Terms of sale: FOB. ORIGIN, FREIGHT COLLECT

Title passes to buyer   Freight charges paid by buyer

SELLER   BUYER

Buyer — Pays freight charges
Buyer — Bears freight charges
Buyer — Owns goods in transit
Buyer — Files claims (if any)

Terms of sale: FOB. ORIGIN, FREIGHT PREPAID

Title passes to buyer

SELLER   BUYER

Freight charges paid by seller...

Seller — Pays freight charges
Seller — Bears freight charges
Buyer — Owns goods in transit
Buyer — Files claims (if any)

Terms of sale: FOB. ORIGIN, FREIGHT PREPAID AND CHARGED BACK

Title passes to buyer

SELLER   BUYER

Freight charges paid by seller...   then collected from buyer by adding amount to invoice

Seller — Pays freight charges
Buyer — Bears freight charges
Buyer — Owns goods in transit
Buyer — Files claims (if any)

Terms of sale: FOB. DESTINATION, FREIGHT COLLECT

Title passes to buyer

SELLER   BUYER

Freight charges paid by buyer...

Buyer — Pays freight charges
Buyer — Bears freight charges
Seller — Owns goods in transit
Seller — Files claims (if any)

Terms of sale: FOB. DESTINATION, FREIGHT PREPAID

Freight charges paid by buyer   Title passes to buyer

SELLER   BUYER

Seller — Pays freight charges
Seller — Bears freight charges
Seller — Owns goods in transit
Seller — Files claims (if any)

Terms of sale: FOB. DESTINATION, FREIGHT COLLECT AND ALLOWED

Title passes to buyer

SELLER   BUYER

Freight charges paid by seller...   ...then charged to seller by deducting amount from invoice

Buyer — Pays freight charges
Seller — Bears freight charges
Seller — Owns goods in transit
Seller — Files claims (if any)

Source: Bruce J. Riggs, "The Traffic Manager in Physical Distribution Management." *Transportation & Distribution Management*, June 1968, p. 45. Penton Media Inc.

Violating either of these rules of thumb exposes the carrier to the jurisdiction of the STB (rebates) and the Justice Department (antitrust and rebates).

Most Common Mistakes in Pricing

As previously mentioned, carriers have not had many years of experience in setting and managing prices on a strategic level. However, just like firms in any other industry, they are prone to certain mistakes. The first common mistake is to make pricing too reliant on costs. Although it is important to know the costs of providing a service, many other factors play a role in setting the appropriate price for a market. Competitive factors, customer preferences and values, and government regulations will affect the level at which the price will be most beneficial to the carrier.

The second common mistake is that prices are not revised frequently enough to capitalize on market changes. Under the previous regulatory environment, it was difficult for carriers to change prices because of the requirement of public notice and the burden of proof on the carrier. However, today's environment has allowed tremendous freedom and the flexibility for carriers to change prices. Unfortunately, for some carriers, the traditional mentality remains and can prevent a carrier from entering a market or, in some cases, creating a new market.

Setting the price independently of the marketing mix is a third common mistake. The **marketing mix**, also known as the "4 Ps," consists of product, price, promotion, and place. A carrier's product or output is transportation; its promotion is how it creates demand or advertises itself to customers; price is what it charges for its product or output; place is how it delivers its service to customers. All of these interact within a carrier's organization to provide access to and, it is hoped, success in current and potential markets. Managing one of these areas independently of the others will result in a suboptimization of the carrier's resources and its profits.

Finally, price is sometimes not varied enough for different service offerings and market segments. A "one price for all" mentality does not work in the transportation industry. As previously stated, carriers service multiple markets with differing service/ price requirements. Airlines use a concept called *yield management pricing* (also called *revenue management pricing*), a form of value-of-service pricing, which relates price to the availability of capacity and the willingness of passengers to pay, or to address this situation. Charging one price for all services is not going to maximize the profits for the carrier. Selected discussions on how yield management pricing is performed by airlines are provided in Appendix 4C.[27]

Pricing is a complex and challenging process that applies to all business entities. Pricing is also critical to a business's competitive advantage, position within its markets, and overall profitability. It must be managed within the context of the carrier's overall strategic plan, not independently of it.

SUMMARY

- The market structure for a carrier will be related to its cost structure; having a knowledge of this cost structure is necessary for the development of carrier prices.
- Cost-of-service pricing relies on the marginal cost of providing a service.
- Value-of-service pricing relies on the average cost of providing the service or on what the market will bear.
- Because of the high number of possible freight rates for commodities, tariffs were constructed to simplify them into class, exception, or commodity rates.
- Various types of special rates exist that allow carriers and shippers the flexibility to tailor rate structures to meet market needs.
- Pricing in transportation can be a strategic advantage if managed within the context of corporate strategy.
- Setting and managing prices in transportation are affected by actions of government, customers, competition, and other channel members.

STUDY QUESTIONS

1. Compare and contrast pure competition with monopoly from a pricing perspective. If you were a shipper, which would you prefer? Which would a carrier prefer?
2. Describe an oligopolistic market structure. What alternatives to price competition exist in such markets? Why would these alternatives be important to shippers?
3. What is value-of-service pricing? Is this approach to pricing valid today?
4. What is cost-of-service pricing? What is the relationship between value-of-service pricing and cost-of-service pricing?
5. What is a released value rate and how does its use affect a shipper's transportation costs?
6. What are the major forces that affect carrier pricing strategies?
7. How might pricing strategies differ among carriers in competitive markets, oligopolistic markets, and monopolistic markets?
8. What are the various factors used in classifying commodities for tariff purposes?
9. What are the differences among class, exception, and commodity rates?
10. Why were tariffs created? Are they still useful in today's transportation environment?
11. What are economies of scale, density, and scope in transportation? How do they affect the cost of carriers?

NOTES

1. For a more thorough discussion of contestable market theory, see W. J. Baumol, J. C. Panzar, and R. D. Willig, *Contestable Markets and the Theory of Industry Structure*, New York: Harcourt, Brace, Jovanovich, 1982.

2. Stanley E. Fawcett and Martin T. Farris, "Contestable Markets and Airline Adaptability Under Deregulation," *Transportation Journal*, Vol. 29, No. 1, 1989, pp. 12–24.

3. Ibid., p. 17.

4. Ibid., p. 14.

5. Ibid.

6. For a more detailed discussion of this conclusion, see ibid.

7. Winthrop M. Daniels, *The Price of Transportation Service*, New York: Harper and Brothers, 1942, p. 1.

8. John R. Meyer et al., *The Economics of Competition in the Transportation Industries*, Cambridge, MA: Harvard University Press, 1959, p. 205.

9. For an excellent analysis of industry pricing behavior, see ibid., pp. 203–211.

10. This section is based on the discussion in J. J. Coyle, "Cost-of-Service Pricing in Transportation," *Quarterly Review of Economics and Business*, Vol. 57, 1964, pp. 69–74.

11. Harold Hotelling, "The General Welfare in Relation to Problems of Taxation and of Railway and Utility Rates," *Econometrics*, Vol. 6, No. 3, 1938, p. 242.

12. R. W. Harbeson, "The Cost Concept and Economic Control," *Harvard Business Review*, Vol. 17, 1939, pp. 257–263.

13. Ibid.

14. George W. Wilson, "Freight Rates and Transportation Costs," *The Business Quarterly*, Summer 1960, pp. 161–162.

15. John J. Coyle, "A Reconsideration of Value of Service Pricing," *Land Economics*, Winter 1964, pp. 193–199.

16. George W. Wilson, *Theory of Transportation Pricing*, Bloomington, IN: Indiana University, 1985, p. 160.

17. For an extended discussion, see Coyle, "A Reconsideration of Value of Service Pricing," pp. 195–198.

18. This example is adapted from George W. Wilson and George W. Smerk, "Rate Theory," in *Physical Distribution Management*, Bloomington, IN: Indiana University, 1963, pp. 7–10.

19. See, for example, Eric N. Berkowitz, Roger A. Kerin, Steven W. Hartley, and William Rudelius, *Marketing*, 3rd ed., Homewood, IL: Richard D. Irwin, 1992.

20. Joel R. Evans and Barry Berman, *Marketing*, New York: Macmillan, 1982, p. 532.

21. Ibid.

22. Berkowitz et al., *Marketing*, p. 321.

23. Y. Suzuki and S. Lu, "Economies of Product Diversity in Collaborative Logistics," *Journal of Business Logistics*, Vol. 38, No. 2, 2017, pp. 145–157.

24. C. Caplice and Y. Sheffi, "Optimization-Based Procurement for Transportation Services,". *Journal of Business Logistics*, Vol. 34, No. 3, 2003, pp. 109–128.

25. Ibid., pp. 339–352.

26. Ibid., p. 354.

27. For further discussions of yield management pricing, see Sheryl Kimes, "The Basics of Yield Management," *The Cornell H.R.A. Quarterly*, November 1989, pp. 14–19; Walter J. Relihan III, "The Yield Management Approach to Hotel Room Pricing," *The Cornell H.R.A. Quarterly*, May 1989, pp. 40–45; Jefferey I. McGill and Garrett J. Van Ryzin, "Revenue Management: Research Overview and Prospects," *Transportation Science*, Vol. 33, No. 2, 1999, pp. 233–256.

CASE 4-1
Mid-West Trucking

Mid-West Trucking is a medium-sized TL carrier based in Des Moines, Iowa. Like many other carriers based in Iowa and surrounding states, Mid-West Trucking faces much demand for eastbound shipments (because in most cases productions of goods take place in Midwest areas and consumptions take place in large cities in East Coast regions). But since not much demand exists for westbound shipments (from East Coast cites to midwestern areas), the carrier had struggled with finding backhaul customers for many years. For this reason, Mid-West Trucking now provides a large price discount for the westbound shipments to capture the customer demands that would otherwise not exist (needless to say, generating a little money on backhaul is better than generating no money on backhaul).

The actual cost of moving a truck from a Midwest city to an East Coast city (and vice versa) is typically around $1,000. But because of the uncertainty the company faces for finding backhaul customers at East Coast cities, Mid-West Trucking typically charges $2,000 for an eastbound shipment. The extra $1,000 (beyond the cost) reflects the cost of backhaul (which is less than $1,000 in the long run, as the company can sometimes find backhaul customers), as well as the profit for the company. On the other hand, Mid-West Trucking charges roughly $700 for a westbound shipment. This means that, for westbound shipments, the company does not even charge enough to cover the cost (but once again, generating $700 is better than nothing, so the company is willing to do this). By using this strategy, Mid-West Trucking has been making a fair, but small, amount of profit over the past several years. The management has been happy with what they have been doing so far.

One day, James Black, the marketing manager of Mid-West Trucking, was meeting with David White, one of his clients who tenders many eastbound shipments to Mid-West Trucking. During this meeting, David expressed concerns about the large difference in pricing between eastbound and westbound shipments. Specifically, David said the following to James:

> "I am not happy with what you are doing for westbound shipments. I know what you charge does not even cover the cost. This means that you are making money from shippers like me, who tender eastbound shipments, and losing money from westbound shipments. This is not fair, because it is like we are subsidizing the cost of shipments for your westbound clients. I don't want to subsidize anyone whom I don't even know. You will have to stop doing this immediately. You must charge the same price for both eastbound and westbound shipments. Otherwise it is not fair."

James ponders how he should respond to this complaint made by David. James wants to make sure that all of his clients are happy, but at the same time, he also wants to make sure that Mid-West Trucking minimizes the cost of backhauling by finding westbound customers via large price discounts.

CASE QUESTIONS

1. Do you agree with David White? Why or why not?

2. If Mid-West Trucking follows the request by David White and stops providing discounts on westbound freights (charge both eastbound and westbound freights equally), what is the consequence for Mid-West Trucking and for its clients?

3. Should Mid-West Trucking stop providing discounts to westbound shipments immediately, as requested by David White?

CASE 4-2

Hardee Transportation

One of Jim O'Brien's customers has presented him with an opportunity for a significant amount of freight moving into a new market for Hardee. Hardee is a truckload carrier primarily moving freight in the East/West market in the United States. Although it has some movements in and out of Canada and Mexico, Hardee has focused on moving freight in eastward and westward directions. Hardee has dispatch centers located throughout the United States, which have some dock capacity.

The new move would be between Pittsburgh and Miami. Hardee has avoided this market because of the lack of backhaul opportunities that exist outbound from Florida. However, this new move offers a significant increase in volume for Hardee. A complicating factor in this move is the request that Hardee perform sorting and segregation at its dispatch centers. Each shipment will consist of straight (one product) pallet loads of various types of consumer goods freight destined for a retailer's distribution center in Miami. Sorting and segregation at Hardee's locations would consist of breaking the pallets and sorting the freight by the retailer's store locations, then repalletizing into rainbow (mixed products) pallets for each store.

Hardee has never experienced this type of request before. Jim knows that he needs to put some type of costs to this move to make sure that the moves are profitable. Because of the large volume involved, not covering Hardee's costs in pricing could result in large losses for Hardee. The relevant information for costing this move is as follows:

Equipment Cost Data

Equipment Purchase Price

1. Line-haul tractors = $120,000
2. Line-haul trailers = $40,000

Depreciation

1. Tractors = 5-year straight line
2. Trailers = 8-year straight line

Interest

1. Tractors = 6 percent APR for 5 years
2. Trailers = 6 percent APR for 8 years

Fuel

1. $3.83 per gallon for diesel
2. Line-haul tractors = 6.0 miles per gallon

Labor

1. Line-haul drivers = $0.45 per mile
2. Pickup and delivery (PUD) drivers = $30 (fully loaded) per hour
3. Dock workers = $25 (fully loaded) per hour

Miscellaneous

1. Insurance cost = $0.067 per mile
2. Maintenance cost = $0.152 per mile
3. Billing cost = $1.95 per freight bill
4. Tractors and trailers are available for use 24 hours per day, 365 days per year
5. Administrative overhead cost = 10 percent of total cost of move
6. Dock facility cost = $15 per hour
7. Line-haul vehicle averages 45 mph between origin and destination

Route and Time of Move

The shipment (45,000 pounds) originates at a customer location in Pittsburgh, located 20 miles from Hardee's dispatch center. A PUD driver is dispatched from the Hardee location at 8:30 a.m. on January 12, 2015, and arrives at the destination at 9:00 a.m. the same day. The shipment is loaded from 9:00 a.m. to 12:00 p.m. The PUD driver departs the customer location at 12:00 p.m. and arrives back at the Hardee dispatch center at 12:30 p.m.

The sort process starts at 12:30 p.m. and ends at 8:30 p.m. on January 12. It requires unloading the trailer, sorting, and repalletizing the load. This operation requires two dock workers, each working the same trailer for 8 hours in the dispatch center.

The line-haul portion begins with the vehicle being dispatched from the Pittsburgh location at 8:30 p.m. on January 12 and traveling to Charlotte, North Carolina, a distance of 481 miles, and arriving at Charlotte at 7:12 a.m. on January 13. The driver rests from 7:12 a.m. until 3:12 p.m. The trip continues with the vehicle departing Charlotte at 3:12 p.m. on January 13 and traveling to Jacksonville, Florida, a distance of 399 miles, arriving at Jacksonville at 12:06 a.m. on January 14. The driver rests from 12:06 a.m. until 10:06 a.m. The line-haul portion concludes with the vehicle departing Jacksonville at 10:06 a.m. and traveling to the customer's location in Miami, a distance of 369 miles, and arriving at the distribution center at 6:18 p.m. on January 14.

The line-haul driver stays with the vehicle while it is being unloaded (2 hours unload time). The driver then deadheads at 8:18 p.m. from the customer's distribution center and arrives at a Hardee dispatch center located in Miami at 8:48 p.m., a distance of 15 miles from the distribution center.

CASE QUESTIONS

1. What are the pickup, sort, line-haul, and delivery costs to Hardee for this move?
2. What is the total cost of this move? Cost per cwt? Cost per revenue mile?
3. If Hardee would put two drivers in the tractor for the line-haul move, there would be no rest required for drivers during the line-haul move. What would happen to total costs?
4. Assume that Hardee has no loaded backhaul to return the vehicle and driver to Pittsburgh. How would you account for the empty backhaul costs associated with this move? Would you include those in the headhaul move? How would this impact your pricing strategy?

APPENDIX 4A
Cost Concepts

Accounting Cost

The simplest concept or measure of cost is what has sometimes been labeled accounting cost, or even more simply as money cost. These are the so-called bookkeeping costs of a company and include all cash outlays of the firm. This particular concept of cost is not difficult to grasp. The most difficult problem with accounting costs is their allocation among the various products or services of a company.

If the owner of a motor carrier, for example, was interested in determining the cost associated with moving a particular truckload of traffic, then all the cost of fuel, oil, and the driver's wages associated with the movement could be quickly determined via the accounting cost concept. It might also be possible to determine how much wear and tear would occur on the vehicle during the trip. However, the portion of the president's salary, the terminal expenses, and the advertising expense should be included in the price. These costs should be included in part, but how much should be included is frequently a perplexing question. The computation becomes even more complex when a small shipment is combined with other small shipments in one truckload. In this case, some allocation would be necessary for the fuel expense and the driver's wages. Details of cost allocation methods are discussed later.

Economic Cost

A second concept of cost is economic cost, which is different from accounting cost. The economic definition of cost is associated with the alternative cost doctrine or the opportunity cost doctrine. Costs of production, as defined by economists, are futuristic and are the values of the alternative products that could have been produced with the resources used in production.

Therefore, the costs of resources are their values in their best alternative uses. To secure the service or use of resources, such as labor or capital, a company must pay an amount at least equal to what the resource could obtain in its best alternative use. Implicit in this definition of cost is the principle that if a resource has no alternative use, then its cost in economic terms is zero.

The futuristic aspect of economic costs has special relevance in transportation because, once investment has been made, one should not be concerned with recovering what are sometimes referred to as **sunk costs**.[1] Resources in some industries are so durable that they can be regarded as virtually everlasting. Therefore, if no replacement is anticipated, and there is no alternative use, then the use of the resource is costless in an economic sense. This is of special importance in the railroad industry.

Railroads have long been regarded as having durable, and therefore, costless resources. That is, some of the resources of railroads, such as concrete ties, some signaling equipment, and even some rolling stock, are so durable and so highly specialized that they have no alternative production or use potential. So the use of such resources, apart from maintenance, is costless in an economic sense. Consequently, in a competitive pricing situation, such resources could be excluded from the calculation of fixed costs. Also, such specialized resources can be eliminated in comparing cost structures.[2]

Although the economic logic of the earlier argument on the use of durable, specialized resources is impeccable, it is frequently disregarded by pricing analysts and regulators. In a sense, the elimination of such costs from pricing calculations defies common sense. From the money or accounting cost perspective, these costs usually should be included.

The conclusion that must be drawn is that economic costs differ from money or accounting costs. Money costs are by their very nature a measure of past costs. This does not mean that money costs do not have any relevance in the economic sense. Past costs do perform a very important function because they provide a guide to future cost estimates. However, complete reliance should not be put upon historical costs for pricing in the transportation industry.

Social Cost

A third category of costs—social costs—might also be considered. Some businesses might not concern themselves with social costs unless required to do so by law. These costs take into consideration the cost to society of some particular operation and, in fact, might outweigh money cost. For example, what is the cost to society when a company releases its waste materials into a stream? Today many regulations and controls are administered by various regulatory agencies to protect society from such costs. These agencies make the business organizations responsible for social costs. (For example, strip-mine operators are customarily required to backfill and plant.) In spite of such controls, however, there are still instances when chemicals or other hazardous materials are discharged or leak out, and society has to bear the cost of the cleanup operations as well as the health hazards.

This discussion is not trying to castigate business organizations or suggest that all investment decisions result in negative social costs because, in fact, there can be social benefits from business investments. However, to ensure that the discussion is complete, social costs must be considered.

Analysis of Cost Structures

There are two general approaches to an analysis of a particular cost structure. In the first approach, the distinction between common and separable costs is made with the idea that costs can be traced to specific accounts or products of the business. In the second approach, the distinction between fixed and variable is made to study variations in business as a whole over a period of time and the effect of these variations upon expenses.

Under the first approach, costs are classified as those that are directly assignable to particular segments of the business (such as products or services) and those that are incurred for the business as a whole. These two types of cost are generally designated as separable and common costs, respectively. **Separable costs** are used in a situation where costs can be directly attributed to the production of a specific unit of output. The classic example is that of a TL haul, where many costs such as fuel, driver wage, and highway tolls, can be directly attributed to a specific TL shipment. **Common costs** are used in a situation where costs cannot be directly attributed to a specific unit of output. It is generally accepted that large transportation companies, especially railroads, have a significant element of common costs because they have roadbed, terminals, freight yards, and so on, the cost of which is common to all traffic. Usually, common costs are further classified as joint common costs or nonjoint common costs.

In terms of transportation, **joint costs** occur when two or more services are *necessarily* produced together in fixed proportions. One of these services is said to be a by-product of the other. The most obvious illustration is that of the backhaul situation; the return capacity is the by-product of the loaded trip to the destination.[3,4] **Nonjoint common costs** are those that do not require the production of fixed proportions of products or services. Nonjoint common costs are more customary in transportation. For example, on a typical train journey on which hundreds of items are carried, the expenses of the crew and fuel are common costs incurred for all the items hauled (see Figure 4A-1).

Under the second approach to analyzing a particular cost structure, costs are divided into those that do not fluctuate with the volume of business in the short term and those that do. The time period here is assumed to be that in which the plant or physical capacity of the business remains unchanged. The two types of costs described above are usually referred to as *fixed* and *variable* costs, respectively. In other words, with fixed and variable costs the focus is on the fact that some costs increase and decrease with expansion and contraction of business volume, whereas other costs do not vary as business levels change.

Because there exist two different approaches to studying costs, it is possible that a certain cost might be classified as common on one hand and variable on the other, or common under one approach and fixed under the other, and so on, for all the possible combinations. Therefore, the only costs directly traceable or separable are the variable costs, which are also separable. For example, fuel expense is generally regarded as a variable cost, but it would be a common cost with a vehicle loaded with LTL traffic.

The second approach of cost analysis—namely, fixed and variable costs—is important and should be discussed further. As indicated previously, **total fixed costs** are constant regardless of the enterprise's volume of business. These fixed costs can include maintenance

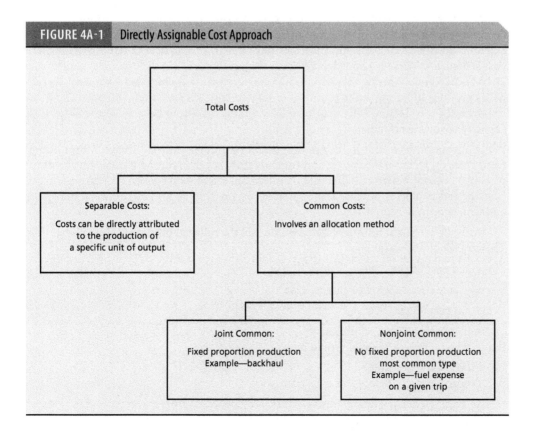

FIGURE 4A-1 Directly Assignable Cost Approach

expenses on equipment or right-of-way (track) caused by time and weather (not use), property taxes, certain management salaries, interest on bonds, and payments on long-term leases. **Fixed costs per unit** of output decline as more volume is allocated to a fixed-cost asset.

A business has a commitment to its fixed costs even with a zero level of output. Fixed costs might, in certain instances, be delayed, or to use the more common term, deferred. The railroads frequently delay or defer costs. For example, maintenance of railroad rights-of-way should probably be done each spring or summer, particularly, in the northern states. Freezing and thawing, along with spring rains, wash away gravel and stone (ballast) and may do other damage. Although this maintenance can be postponed, just as, for example, house painting might be postponed for a year or two, sooner or later, it has to be done if the business wants to continue to operate. There is a fixed commitment or necessity that requires the corrective action and associated expense.[6] The important point is that total fixed expenses occur independently of the volume of business experienced by the organization.

Variable costs, on the other hand, are closely related to the volume of business. In other words, firms do not experience any variable costs unless they are operating. The fuel expense for trains or tractor–trailers is an excellent example of a variable cost. If a locomotive or vehicle does not make a run or trip, there is no fuel cost. Additional examples of variable costs include the wear and tear on tractor–trailers (due to use) and the cost for tires and engine parts. Thus, variable cost per unit remains constant regardless of the level of output, while total variable costs are directly related to the level of output.

Another related point is that railroads and pipelines, like many public utility companies, are frequently labeled as decreasing cost industries. The relevance of this phenomenon to pricing was discussed earlier in this chapter, but it also deserves some additional explanation now. Railroads and pipelines have a high proportion of fixed costs in their cost structures. There is some debate about the percentage, but the estimates range from 20 to 50 percent. Contrast this with motor carriers whose average is 10 percent. As railroads produce more units, the proportion of fixed costs on each item will be lower. More importantly, this decline will occur over a long range of output because of the large-scale capacity of most railroads.

An example is useful here. Assume that a particular railroad incurs $5 million of fixed costs on an annual basis. In addition, assume that the railroad is analyzing costs for pricing purposes between Bellefonte, Pennsylvania, and Chicago. In its examination of cost, the railroad determines that the variable cost on a carload is $250 between Bellefonte and Chicago.

Although it might be unrealistic, assume that the railroad only moves 10 cars per year. The cost would be as follows:

Fixed cost $5,000,000

Variable cost $2,500 (10 cars × $250)

Total cost $5,002,500

Average cost $500,250 per car

If it moves 1,000 cars, the cost would be:

Fixed cost $5,000,000

Variable cost $250,000 (1,000 cars × $250)

Total cost $5,250,000

Average cost $5,250 per car

If it moves 100,000 cars, the cost would be:

Fixed cost $5,000,000

Variable cost $25,000,000 (100,000 × $250)

Total cost $30,000,000

Average cost $300 per car

The relationship is easy to see. If the number of cars increased in our example, the average cost would continue to decline. Theoretically, average cost would have to level out and eventually increase due to decreasing returns, but the important point is that the high proportion of fixed costs and the large capacity cause the average cost to decline over a great range of output (see Figure 4A-2). There would be a point, however, at which additional cars would require another investment in fixed cost, thus shifting the average-cost curve.

The significance of the declining cost phenomenon to a railroad is that volume is a very important determinant of cost and efficiency. Furthermore, pricing the service to attract traffic is a critical factor in determining profitability, particularly, where there is competition from alternate modes of transportation.

Another cost concept that is of major importance in this analysis is marginal cost, because of its key role in understanding pricing decisions. Marginal cost can be defined as the change in total cost resulting from a one-unit change in output, or as additions to aggregate cost for given additions to output. This latter definition probably makes more sense in transportation because of the difficulties of defining the output unit. Marginal cost also can be defined as the change in total variable cost resulting from a one-unit change in output, because a change in output changes total variable cost and total cost by exactly the same amounts. Marginal cost is sometimes referred to as *incremental cost*, especially in the transportation industry.

There is one other type of cost that should be mentioned because of its importance in price decision—**out-of-pocket costs**. Out-of-pocket costs are usually defined as those costs that are directly assignable to a particular unit of traffic and that would not have been incurred if the service or movement had not been performed. Within the framework of this definition, out-of-pocket costs could also be either separable costs or variable costs. Although the earlier definition states that out-of-pocket costs are specifically assignable to a certain movement, which implies separable costs, they can definitely be considered

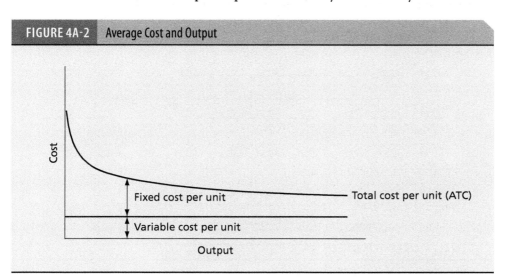

FIGURE 4A-2   Average Cost and Output

as variable costs because they would not have occurred if a particular shipment had not been moved. The definition also encompasses marginal cost because marginal cost can be associated with a unit increase in cost.

The vagueness of the out-of-pocket costs definition has left the door open to the types of cost included as a part of the total cost calculation. The difficulty lies in the fact that from a narrow viewpoint, out-of-pocket costs could be classified as only those expenses incurred because a particular unit was moved. For example, the loading and unloading expense attributable to moving a particular shipment, plus the extra fuel and wear and tear on equipment (relatively low for railroads) could be classified as out-of-pocket costs. On the other hand, a broad approach might be used in defining out-of-pocket costs in regard to a particular shipment, thereby including a share of all of the common variable expenses attributable to a particular movement between two points.

The confusion surrounding the concept of out-of-pocket costs would seem to justify elimination of its use. However, the continued use of the term would be acceptable if its definition was made synonymous with the definition of one of the particular economic costs that its definition implies—marginal costs—because this term is important in price and output decisions and evaluations of pricing economics. Typically, out-of-pocket costs are most important to the firm's accounting system because they are payments that must be made almost immediately as an operating expense. The out-of-pocket cost concept is useful in that it is used as a way to estimate the amount of liquid funds that a transportation firm must keep on hand for daily operations.[7]

Figure 4A-3 gives a good breakdown of the methods of cost analysis. It illustrates the close relationship between the three cost concepts of variable, marginal, and out-of-pocket costs.

It is to be noted that, in the last two decades, a new technique for allocating costs directly to activity centers has been implemented in both the carrier and shipper communities. This technique, called **activity-based costing (ABC)** identifies costs specifically generated by performing a service or producing a product. ABC does not allocate direct and indirect costs based on volume alone; it determines which activities are responsible

FIGURE 4A-3 Short-Run Cost/Volume Output Approach

for these costs and burdens these activities with their respective portion of overhead costs. One application for ABC today by both carriers and shippers is the calculation of customer profitability. Further details on ABC can be found in selected articles.[8]

In the rest of this appendix, we will discuss the cost structures of selected transportation modes. Although attention is devoted to cost structure in the separate chapters dealing with each of the modes of transportation, some consideration will be given in this appendix to an analysis of modal cost structures, as such discussion is useful and necessary background to the analysis of the approaches to pricing.

Rail Cost Structure

One of the characteristics of railroads, as previously noted, is the level of fixed costs present in their cost structures. It is a commonly accepted fact that a relatively large proportion of railway costs are fixed in the short run. At one time, it was believed that more than half of rail costs were fixed, and some individuals estimated that these costs ran as high as 70 percent of total cost. The exact proportion of fixed expenses is subject to some debate; however, it is generally accepted that fixed expenses constitute a significant portion of railroad total costs. The high proportion of fixed costs can be explained by railroad investment (in things such as track, terminals, and freight yards), which is much larger than the investment of motor carriers, for example. For this reason, railroads are generally regarded as having increasing returns, or decreasing costs per unit of output.[9]

As has been indicated, a significant amount of railroad costs also include common expenses because replacement costs of a stretch of track are shared by all traffic moving over it. This is also true with respect to other items of cost, including officers' salaries. Some of these common costs are also fixed costs, while others are variable costs (refer to Chapter 6, "Railroads").

Motor Carrier Cost Structure

The motor carrier industry is exemplified by a high proportion of variable costs. It has been estimated that variable costs in the motor carrier industry are 90 percent or more of total costs.[10] This is typical in the truckload sector while the less-than-truckload sector will usually have lower variable cost and higher fixed cost percentages because of their terminal network. But both sectors of the motor carrier industry are dominated by variable costs. This high degree of variability is explained to a large extent by the fact that motor carriers do not have to provide their own right-of-way because roads are publicly provided. It is true that motor carriers do pay fuel taxes and other taxes to defray the cost of providing the highways, but these expenses are variable because they depend on the use made of the highway.

The economic concept of the "long run" is a shorter period in the motor carrier industry than in the railroad industry. The operating unit, the motor carrier vehicle, has a shorter life span than the rail operating unit. It is smaller, and therefore, more adaptable to fluctuating business conditions. The capital investment required is smaller too, and fleets can be expanded and contracted more easily.

The motor carrier situation varies greatly with respect to common costs. Companies that specialize in LTL traffic will have a significant proportion of common cost, whereas contract carriers with only two or three customers who move only TL traffic will have a high proportion of separable costs. Other companies that carry a mixture of TL and LTL traffic will be in the middle of the two extremes (refer to Chapter 5, "Motor Carriers").

Other Carriers' Cost Structures

Information on water carrier cost structure is less prevalent because many companies are privately owned or exempt from economic regulation. The cost structure is probably very similar to that of motor carriers because their right-of-way is also publicly provided. There are some differences, however, because the investment per unit of output is greater, and a large volume of traffic is necessary to realize mass movement potentialities.[11] (See Chapter 8, "Water Carriers and Pipelines.")

The pipeline companies have a cost structure similar to that of railroads. The fact that they have to provide their own right-of-way and the fact that their terminal facilities are very specialized mean that they have a large element of fixed and usually sunk costs. They also usually have significant common costs because they move a variety of oil products through the pipeline (see Chapter 8, "Water Carriers and Pipelines").

The airline companies have a cost structure similar to that of water carriers and motor carriers because of the public provision of their right-of-way. Also, terminal facilities are publicly provided to a large extent, and the airlines pay landing fees based upon use. Airlines tend to have a significant element of common cost because of small freight shipments and the individual nature of passenger movements; for example, airlines very seldom sell a planeload to one customer (see Chapter 7, "Airlines").

The differences in the cost structures of the modes of transportation and their differing service characteristics make pricing of their services very important. If motor carrier service is better than rail service, motor carrier prices can exceed rail prices. The cost structure of the motor carrier might dictate that their prices can exceed rail prices. The cost structure of the motor carrier might dictate that their prices have to be higher than the rail prices. The critical question is what the relationship between demand and cost (supply) is in such cases.

NOTES

1. William J. Baumol et al., "The Role of Cost in the Minimum Pricing of Railroad Services," *Journal of Business*, Vol. 35, October 1962, pp. 5–6. This article succinctly presents the essence of sunk versus prospective costs.

2. A. M. Milne, *The Economics of Inland Transport*, London: Pitman and Sons, 1955, p. 146.

3. Robert C. Lieb, *Transportation, the Domestic System*, 2nd ed., Reston, VA: Reston Publishing, p. 138.

4. This problem was argued in the economic journals at an early date by two notable economists. See F. W. Taussig, "Railway Rates and Joint Cost Once More," *Quarterly Journal of Economics*, Vol. 27, May 1913, p. 378; F. W. Taussig and A. C. Pigou, "Railway Rates and Joint Costs," *Quarterly Journal of Economics*, Vol. 27, August 1913, pp. 535, 687; A. C. Pigou, *The Economics of Welfare*, 4th ed., London: Macmillan, 1950, Chapters 17 and 18. An excellent discussion of this debate is contained in D. P. Locklin, "A Review of the Literature on Railway Rate Theory," *Quarterly Journal of Economics*, Vol. 47, 1933, p. 174.

5. See, for example, Terrance L. Pohlen and Bernard J. LaLonde, "Implementing Activity-Based Costing (ABC) in Logistics," *Journal of Business Logistics*, Vol. 15, No. 2, 1994, pp. 1–23.

6. For an excellent discussion, see George W. Wilson and George W. Smerk, "Rate Theory," in *Physical Distribution Management*, Bloomington, IN: Indiana University, 1963, pp. 2–4.

7. Wayne K. Talley, *Introduction to Transportation*, Cincinnati, OH: Southwestern, 1983, p. 27.

8. George W. Wilson, *Essays on Some Unsettled Questions in the Economics of Transportation*, Bloomington, IN: Foundation for Economic and Business Studies, 1962, pp. 32–33.

9. Interstate Commerce Commission, Bureau of Accounts and Cost Finding, *Explanation of Rail Cost Finding Principles and Procedures*, Washington, DC: Government Printing Office, 1948, p. 88.

10. John R. Meyer et al., *The Economics of Competition in the Transportation Industries*, Cambridge, MA: Harvard University Press, pp. 112–113.

11. See, for example, Paul Davis, "Airline Ties Profitability Yield to Management," *SIAM News*, Vol. 27, No. 5, May/June 1994.

APPENDIX 4B
LTL and TL Costing Models

As mentioned in this chapter, understanding costs for costing purposes is critical to a carrier's ability to price in order to maximize profits. Costing and pricing can be extremely complex exercises, depending on the amount and complexity of inputs. The purpose of this appendix is to offer basic and simplistic costing models for LTL and TL that can be used to get a feel for the costs associated with a particular move. Obviously, these are not complex models and would need to be adjusted for actual costing purposes.

Operational Activities

The examination of LTL and TL operations might result in the conclusion that they are significantly different in how they operate. Actually, they are very similar. The major difference between the two is in the dock rehandling (or cross-docking) that is associated with the LTL operations, not the TL. However, to move a shipment, both operations provide a pickup service, a line-haul service, and a delivery service. These three activities, along with dock rehandling for LTL, can be used to begin to break out the appropriate costs associated with a move.

Cost/Service Elements

Within each operational activity, those cost/service elements that will actually be responsible for shipment costs need to be identified. These cost/service elements can be defined as time, distance, and support. The time it takes a carrier to pick up, cross-dock, line-haul, and deliver a shipment will impact its fixed costs, such as depreciation and interest, because these costs are allocated and determined by units of time. The distance a carrier has to move a shipment during these operational activities will affect its variable costs, such as fuel and wages. Support costs, such as equipment insurance and maintenance, are considered semi-fixed and semi-variable because they will exist if no activity takes place but will increase as activity increases. Finally, shipment billing can be considered a fixed cost because normally the cost to generate a freight bill is not related to shipment size or distance.

Having identified four operational activities (pickup, cross-dock, line-haul, and delivery) and three cost/service elements (time, distance, and support), it is possible to develop a costing methodology that will allow the approximation of costs that a carrier could incur for moving a shipment.

TL Costing

This section will present a simplified TL costing model that can be used to approximate the costs of moving a shipment between two points. This model can be used for calculating headhaul costs but does not include an adjustment for a possible empty return trip. However, as will be seen, headhaul costs could be adjusted to compensate for variable costs of an empty backhaul.

The following scenario is used:

Shipment and Equipment Characteristics The shipment consists of 400 cartons at 110 pounds each with each carton measuring 5 cubic feet. Carriers' trailers have a weight capacity of 45,000 pounds and 3,500 cubic feet. The shipment weighs 44,000 pounds (98 percent of weight capacity) and occupies 2,000 cubic feet (almost 57 percent of trailer cubic capacity).

Equipment Cost Data

Equipment Purchase Price

1. Line-haul tractors = $120,000
2. Trailers = $40,000 (53-foot dry van)

Depreciation

1. Tractors = 5-year straight line
2. Trailers = 8-year straight line

Interest

1. Tractors = 6 percent APR for 5 years
2. Trailers = 6 percent APR for 8 years

Fuel

1. $3.83 per gallon for diesel
2. Line-haul tractors = 6.0 miles per gallon

Labor Cost

1. Line-haul drivers = $0.45 per mile
2. PUD operation drivers = $22.00 per hour

Miscellaneous

1. Insurance cost = $0.067 per mile
2. Maintenance cost = $0.152 per mile
3. Billing cost = $1.95 per freight bill
4. Tractors and trailers are available for use 365 days, 24 hours per day
5. Administrative overhead cost = 10 percent of total cost of move

Route and Time of Move The shipment originates on June 2, 2017, from The Pennsylvania State University (located 35 miles from the carrier's dispatch/maintenance facility). A line-haul tractor and trailer are dispatched from the terminal at 7:30 a.m. (all times are Eastern Standard Time) and arrive at the shipper's dock at 8:30 a.m. The shipment is loaded from 8:30 a.m. to 12:00 p.m. Driver and tractor remain at Penn State during loading to visit the famous Nittany Lion statue. Driver and vehicle return to the carrier's terminal at 1:00 p.m. to pick up paperwork.

> **Total time for pickup = 5.5 hours**
>
> **Total distance for pickup = 70 miles**

The vehicle and the driver depart from the terminal at 1:00 p.m. on the same day for Dallas, Texas. The driver operates from 1:00 p.m. to 11:00 p.m. and travels 450 miles. The driver rests from 11:00 p.m. to 7:00 a.m. (on June 3) in Knoxville, Tennessee, and then operates another 8 hours (7:00 a.m. to 3:00 p.m.) and 375 miles. The driver rests again from 3:00 p.m. to 11:00 p.m. in Memphis, Tennessee. The driver concludes the trip by traveling 450 miles from 11:00 p.m. to 9:00 a.m. (June 4) to the consignee in Dallas, the Dallas Cowboys' training facility.

> **Total time for line-haul = 44 hours or 1.83 days**
>
> **Total distance for line-haul = 1,275 miles**

The trailer is unloaded from 9:00 a.m. to 12:00 p.m. with the driver and tractor remaining at the home to tour the museum dedicated to former Dallas Cowboys. The driver and vehicle then go to the carrier's Dallas terminal, located 45 miles from the Cowboys' facility, arriving at 1:00 p.m. to wait for further dispatch instructions.

Total time for delivery = 4 hours

Total distance for delivery = 45 miles

Cost Analysis Using the equipment cost data and the distance traveled and time elapsed for the shipment, an approximate cost for this move can be calculated. This analysis can be seen in Table 4B-1. In a real costing situation, certain changes might need to be made to the cost data included in this example. Tractor fuel economy, for example, might need to be increased or maintenance cost per mile might need to be decreased. The cost analyst would need to determine the appropriate levels for each cost element, depending on the type of equipment and nature of the move.

Pickup As can be seen in Table 4B-1, the pickup operation generated seven types of costs. *Depreciation expense* per hour is calculated by:

> *equipment cost/years depreciation/365/24*

This formula gives the hourly cost for depreciation for both the tractor and the trailer. *Interest expense (includes both principal plus interest)* per hour can be calculated using any interest payment calculator. The appropriate formulas can be found in tables in any introductory finance text.

Fuel cost per gallon and tractor fuel economy determine *fuel cost per mile.* This formula is:

> *fuel cost per gallon/miles per gallon*

Labor, maintenance, insurance, and billing costs are given and are relatively easy to calculate. *Total pickup costs for this move are $222.74.*

Line-haul Notice that the line-haul costs categories for this move are the same as for the pickup operation, except for the billing expense. This is simply because only one freight bill needs to be generated for this move. This will also be seen by the absence of a billing cost in the delivery section.

Also, during the pickup operation, the driver was paid by the hour because waiting time was involved. In the line-haul section, the driver was paid by the mile. Obviously, pay scales for drivers will be determined by company or union policies. *Other costs in the line-haul section are calculated in the same manner as they were in the pickup section.* Obviously, however, the time and distance generated by the line-haul activity are used. *Total line-haul costs for this move are $1,986.22.*

Delivery The delivery activity generates the same type of costs as did the pickup activity, except for billing. Again, the time and distance associated with delivery need to be used in calculating costs. *Costs for delivery are calculated in the same manner as they were in the pickup section. Total costs for delivery for this move are $155.50.*

Total Cost Adding the costs associated with pickup, line-haul, and delivery generates the total cost for this move of $2,364.46. Remember, however, that a 10 percent additional cost is added to make a contribution to the carrier's administration and overhead, so the *total cost for this move is $2,600.91.*

TABLE 4B-1 Costing Example

I. PICKUP

1. Depreciation	Tractor	5.5 hr @ $2.74/hr =	$15.07
	Trailer	5.5 hr @ $0.57/hr =	$3.14
2. Interest	Tractor	5.5 hr @ $3.18/hr =	$17.49
	Trailer	5.5 hr @ $0.72/hr =	$3.96
3. Fuel		70 miles @ $0.64/mile =	$44.80
4. Labor		5.5 hr @ $22/hr =	$121.00
5. Maintenance		70 miles @ $0.152/mile =	$10.64
6. Insurance		70 miles @ $0.067/mile =	$4.69
7. Billing			$1.95
		TOTAL PICKUP COST	$222.74

II. Line-haul

1. Depreciation	Tractor	44 hr @ $2.74/hr =	$120.56
	Trailer	44 hr @ $0.57/hr =	$25.08
2. Interest	Tractor	44 hr @ $3.18/hr =	$139.92
	Trailer	44 hr @ $0.72/hr =	$31.68
3. Fuel		1,275 miles @ $0.64/mile =	$816.00
4. Labor		1,275 miles @ $0.45/mile =	$573.75
5. Maintenance		1,275 miles @ $0.152/mile =	$193.80
6. Insurance		1,275 miles @ $0.067/mile =	$85.43
		TOTAL LINE-HAUL COST	$1,986.22

III. Delivery

1. Depreciation	Tractor	4 hr @ $2.74/hr =	$10.96
	Trailer	4 hr @ $0.57/hr =	$2.28
2. Interest	Tractor	4 hr @ $3.18/hr =	$12.72
	Trailer	4 hr @ $0.72/hr =	$2.88
3. Fuel		45 miles @ $0.64/mile =	$28.80
4. Labor		4 hr @ $22/hr =	$88.00
5. Maintenance		45 miles @ $0.152/mile =	$6.84
6. Insurance		45 miles @ $.067/mile =	$3.02
		TOTAL DELIVERY COST	$155.50

IV. Total Cost

1. Pickup, line-haul, delivery			$2,364.46
2. Administrative/overhead (10%)			$236.45
		TOTAL TL COST	$2,600.91

V. Revenue Needs

1. Per cwt ($2,600.91/440) = $5.91

2. Per revenue mile ($2,600.91/1,310 miles) = $1.99 miles)

Revenue Needs Carriers quote prices in many forms. Two of the more common methods are price per hundredweight (cwt) and price per revenue, or loaded, mile. In this example, although profit has not yet been added, to recover the fully allocated or average cost for this move, the carrier would quote a *price per cwt of $5.91 ($2,600.91/440 cwt)* or a *price per revenue mile of $1.99 ($2,600.91/1310 miles)*. Note that the loaded miles for this example (1,310 miles) is given by the sum of 35 miles (half of pickup miles from the shipper's dock to the carrier's terminal in Pennsylvania) and 1,275 miles (line-haul distance from the carrier's terminal in Pennsylvania to the consignee's facility in Dallas).

Once again, this model is a simplified version of those used by carriers. Certain adjustments and additions would need to be made to this model to make it more reflective of an actual move. For example, the cost of equipment depreciation and interests need to be adjusted in order for the carrier to fully recover these costs, because the method used in the above example simply calculates the equipment and interest costs per hour or per mile and determines the cost for a given shipment by multiplying these per-unit costs with hours used or miles driven. This means that this method cannot recover the full cost of depreciation or interest unless the equipment is used 24 hours per day, 7 days a week. Also, as mentioned previously, the above example ignores the cost of backhaul. Unless the carrier is 100 percent certain that it can find a backhaul customer, it should consider charging at least a portion of the backhaul cost to the headhaul cost (this practice of including the cost of backhaul in the headhaul price is called "hedging," and its implications for shippers and carriers are discussed in detail in Chapter 9, "Logistics Services"). However, it does give the analyst some idea of the approximate costs associated with a shipment.

LTL Costing

This section will present a simplified version of an LTL costing model. LTL costing is more difficult than TL costing because it requires arbitrary allocations of common and fixed costs to individual shipments. Although this does not make costing an LTL shipment impossible, it does require that the individual using the costs understand that averages and allocations were used. Thus, the resulting costs might not be as accurate as would be desired. However, this model will produce ballpark estimates for the cost of moving an individual shipment. *All* of the formulas for calculating depreciation costs, interest costs, and fuel costs are the same as those used in the TL costing example.

Shipment and Equipment Characteristics The shipment to be costed consists of 15 cartons, each weighing 40 pounds and measuring 16 cubic feet. The carrier's pickup and delivery trailers have a weight capacity of 40,000 pounds and a cubic capacity of 2,972 cubic feet, and the line-haul (LH) trailers have a weight capacity of 45,000 pounds and a cubic capacity of 3,500 cubic feet. This shipment then occupies 1.3 percent of the trailer's weight capacity and 6.85 percent of its cubic capacity. Because the cubic feet requirement is greater, it will be used to allocate costs in the line-haul move.

Equipment Cost Data

Equipment Purchase Price

1. PUD tractor = $65,000
2. LH tractor = $120,000
3. PUD trailer = $30,000 (45-foot)
4. LH trailer = $40,000 (53-foot)

Depreciation

1. Tractors = 5-year straight line
2. Trailers = 8-year straight line

Interest

1. Tractors = 6 percent APR for 5 years
2. Trailers = 6 percent APR for 8 years

Fuel

1. $3.83 per gallon for diesel
2. PUD tractors = 6.5 miles per gallon
3. LH tractors = 6.0 miles per gallon

Labor Cost

1. PUD drivers = $22.00 per hour
2. Dock handlers = $20.00 per hour
3. LH drivers = $22.00 per hour

Miscellaneous

1. Terminal variable cost per shipment at both origin and destination = $1.00
2. Terminal fixed cost per shipment at both origin and destination = $1.50
3. PUD equipment maintenance cost = $0.152 per mile
4. LH equipment maintenance cost = $0.152 per mile
5. PUD equipment insurance cost = $0.067 per mile
6. LH equipment insurance cost = $0.067 per mile
7. Billing cost = $1.95 per bill
8. Equipment is available 365 days, 24 hours per day
9. Administrative/overhead cost = 10 percent of total cost of move

Route and Time of Movement The shipment is picked up by the carrier's driver in a PUD city tractor/trailer unit on June 2, 2017, as one of 23 stops made by the driver that day from 7:30 a.m. to 6:30 p.m. The stops covered a total of 60 miles within the Altoona, Pennsylvania, satellite terminal service area. The shipment was one of four handled by the carrier at this particular shipper's location. Once the pickup vehicle returns to the Altoona terminal, it takes 15 minutes to move the shipment from the city unit across the dock to the line-haul trailer.

> **Total time for pickup = 11 hours**
>
> **Total distance for pickup = 60 miles**
>
> **Total dock time = 15 minutes**

The line-haul tractor/trailer departs from the Altoona terminal at 11:00 p.m. on June 2 and arrives at the Cleveland break-bulk terminal, which is approximately 200 miles from the Altoona satellite, at 4:00 a.m. on June 3. The shipment moves from the line-haul trailer across the dock to a PUD city tractor/trailer unit in 15 minutes.

> **Total time of line-haul = 5 hours**
>
> **Total distance for line-haul = 200 miles**
>
> **Total dock time = 15 minutes**

The shipment is delivered to the Cleveland consignee by the PUD driver in a PUD city tractor/trailer unit on June 2 as one of 16 stops made by the driver over the period from 7:30 a.m. to 6:00 p.m. The stops covered a total of 45 miles in the Cleveland area. This shipment is one of the three delivered to this particular consignee by the driver.

Total time for delivery = 10.5 hours

Total distance for delivery = 45 miles

Cost Analysis With the equipment cost data and route and time of movement, an individual LTL shipment can be costed. This analysis can be seen in Table 4B-2. Once again, *the calculations for depreciation, interest, and fuel costs are the same as they were in the TL example.*

TABLE 4B-2	LTL Costing Example		
I. PICKUP			
A. Route Costs			
1. Depreciation	PUD tractor	1 day @ $35.62/day =	$35.62
	PUD trailer	1 day @ $10.27/day =	$10.27
2. Interest	PUD tractor	1 day @ $41.31/day =	$41.31
	PUD trailer	1 day @ $12.96/day =	$12.96
3. Fuel		60 miles @ $0.59/mile =	$35.40
4. Labor		11 hr @ $22/hr =	$242.00
5. Maintenance		60 miles @ $0.152/mile =	$9.12
6. Insurance		60 miles @ $0.067/mile =	$4.02
	SUBTOTAL		$390.70
	\# Stops		23
	COST PER STOP		$16.99
	\# Shipments at stop		4
	ROUTE COST PER SHIPMENT		$4.25
B. Shipment Costs			
1. Billing			$1.95
2. Terminal variable cost			$1.00
3. Terminal fixed cost			$1.50
4. Dock		0.25 hr @ $20/hr =	$5.00
	INDIVIDUAL SHIPMENT COST		$9.45
C. Total Pickup Cost per Shipment			$13.70
II. Line-haul			
1. Depreciation	LH tractor	5 hr @ $2.74/hr =	$13.70
	LH trailer	5 hr @ $0.57/hr =	$2.85
2. Interest	LH tractor	5 hr @ $3.18/hr =	$15.90
	LH trailer	5 hr @ $0.72/hr =	$3.60
3. Fuel		200 miles @ $0.64/mile =	$128.00
4. Labor		5 hr @ $22/hr =	$110.00
5. Maintenance		200 miles @ $0.152/mile =	$30.40

(continued)

TABLE 4B-2	LTL Costing Example			
6. Insurance		200 miles @ $0.067/mile =		$13.40
	TOTAL LINE-HAUL FULL TRAILER			$317.85
	% capacity occupied by shipment			6.85%
	SHIPMENT LINE-HAUL COST			$21.77
III. Delivery				
A. Route Costs				
1. Depreciation	PUD tractor	1 day @ $35.62/day =		$35.62
	PUD trailer	1 day @ $10.27/day =		$10.27
2. Interest	PUD tractor	1 day @ $41.31/day =		$41.31
	PUD trailer	1 day @ $12.96/day =		$12.96
3. Fuel		45 miles @ $0.59/mile =		$26.65
4. Labor		10.5 hr @ $22/hr =		$231.00
5. Maintenance		45 miles @ $0.152/mile =		$6.84
6. Insurance		45 miles @ $0.067/mile =		$3.02
	SUBTOTAL			$367.67
	\# Stops			16
	COST PER STOP			$22.98
	\# Shipments at stop			3
	ROUTE COST PER SHIPMENT			$7.66
B. Shipment Costs				
1. Terminal variable cost				$1.00
2. Terminal fixed cost				$1.50
3. Dock		0.25 hr @ $20/hr =		$5.00
	INDIVIDUAL SHIPMENT COST			$7.50
C. Total Delivery Cost per Shipment				$15.16
IV. Total Cost per Shipment				
1. Pickup, dock, line-haul, delivery				$50.63
2. Administrative/overhead (10 percent)				$5.06
	TOTAL COST PER SHIPMENT			$55.69
V. Revenue Needs				
1. Per cwt ($55.69/6)				$9.28

Pickup In this example, a PUD tractor and trailer were used in the pickup operation. This is specialized equipment that really has no alternative uses in the line-haul operation. As such, when this equipment is done with the PUD operation during the day, it will normally sit idle at the satellite terminal. This explains why a full day's depreciation and interest are charged to both the PUD tractor and PUD trailer, even though they were only utilized for 11 hours during this particular day. Some arguments might exist that this places an excessive cost burden on these shipments through fixed-cost allocation. This might be true. However, the cost analyst must make the decision as to where fixed costs will be recovered. If not through this allocation, then fixed costs must be covered by some other method so debt can be serviced and plans for equipment replacement can be implemented.

The fuel, labor, maintenance, and insurance cost calculations are relatively straightforward. *Total route costs for this move are $390.70.* Remember, however, that this cost is for all shipments picked up and delivered by the driver during the day. This calculation is for the cost of only one shipment. To do this, first divide the total route cost by the number of stops made by the driver. *This results in a route cost per stop of $16.99.* Second, divide the per stop cost by the number of shipments at the shipper's location. *This results in a route cost per shipment of $4.25.* Both the stop cost and the shipment cost are averages that assume that each stop is basically the same and each shipment is the same. Adjustments could be made to these figures to more accurately reflect the time and distance actually used for the individual shipment. Remember, however, the per-shipment-route costs used in this example are averages.

Shipment costs are those assigned to each individual shipment that are not generated by the PUD operation. Billing, terminal variable cost, and terminal fixed cost are not dependent on shipment size but are allocated to each shipment. The shipment took 15 minutes for its cross-dock operation resulting in the dock charge of $5.00.

Total shipment cost for this move is $9.45. Combining the route cost per shipment and the shipment cost results in a total pickup cost per shipment of $13.70.

Line-haul Depreciation and interest for the line-haul equipment is charged only for the actual time the shipment is on this equipment. This is the same as in the TL example. Unlike the PUD equipment, this assumes that the line-haul equipment has alternative uses and is 100 percent utilized. Again, actual utilization rates can be used to adjust the allocation of depreciation and interest charges.

As previously mentioned, the shipment occupied 6.85 percent of the cubic capacity of the line-haul trailer. This is the basis used for allocating line-haul costs in a *line-haul cost per shipment of $21.77.* This allocation method assumes that all shipments in the line-haul trailer have approximately the same pounds per cubic foot requirement, and that the trailer would be cubed out before it would be weighted out. The analyst might want to make adjustments for this based on the known average weight and cube per shipment in the carrier's system.

Delivery The calculations for delivery cost are the same as those used for pickup costs. For route shipment cost, 16 stops and 3 stops per shipment are used to determine the *average route cost per shipment of $7.66.* Shipment costs are also the same, except that billing cost is not included, resulting in a *shipment cost of $7.50 and a total delivery cost per shipment of $15.16.*

Total Shipment Cost Combining the pickup cost of $13.70, the line-haul cost of $21.77, and the delivery cost of $15.16 results in a total cost per shipment of $50.63. Remember, like the TL example, a 10 percent cost is added to cover administrative and other overhead expenses, resulting in a *total cost for the shipment of $55.69.*

Revenue Needs Although prices are quoted in many different forms in the LTL industry, one popular form is in price per cwt. Taking the total shipment charge of $55.69 and dividing it by 6 cwt (15 cartons × 40 lbs. each = 600 lbs.) results in a *price per cwt of $9.28.* Remember this price does not yet include an allowance for profit for the carrier.

Conclusion

Determining the cost for a particular shipment can be a very complex and time-consuming task.

Detailed data requirements and knowledge of a carrier's operations are necessary inputs to developing accurate costs. However, a simplified approach can be taken to shipment costing that does not need these complex requirements and it results in approximate shipment costs. Thus, the advantage of these costing models is their simplicity and ease of calculation. Their disadvantage is that they use general data, allocations, and averages to determine shipment costs. The analyst must trade off these characteristics to determine the level of complexity needed for costing and whether these models will provide a sufficient level of cost detail.

APPENDIX 4C
Yield Management Pricing

Yield management pricing involves several elements, such as overbooking, seat allocation, and traffic management. The element that is most relevant to pricing is seat allocation, followed by overbooking and traffic management. This appendix describes seat allocation and overbooking, and how they affect ticket pricing and revenues achieved by airlines. For discussions on traffic management, the interested readers are referred to articles that focuses on discussing airline revenue management[11]

Seat Allocation

Airlines have different fare classes (such as First, Business, and Economy). Even within each class, especially within Economy class, there exist several different fare classes. The most expensive Economy fare is "full fare," and there are several other "discount fare" classes. When you book airline seat either via a travel agent or online, you often see several different Economy fares for the same origin-destination trip, and you may sometimes notice that for some fares it says "only three seats left at this price." Although this sounds like the number of available seats for each fare class is fixed (predetermined by airlines), this is not true. The allocation of seats to, say, full fare and discount fare is only virtual, meaning that airlines can change the number of seats allocated to each class conveniently at any time to increase the expected revenue generated by the seats. Let us explain how the virtual seat allocation works for airlines to maximize their revenue per seat, or equivalently, maximize the amount of money they can extract from the passengers' pocket. The goal of seat allocation, or any other element of airline yield management, is similar to the concept of "auction" in which the sellers (airlines) will attempt to make buyers (passengers) pay as much as possible up to "what they are willing to pay."

Consider a situation where you are trying to book a flight via a travel agent (or online—they both work exactly the same). You need to fly from Chicago to Atlanta three days from now to attend a wedding, and you are trying to buy a discount fare ticket to save your money. For this example, assume that there are only two types of fare classes—full fare and discount fare. The full fare is $100 per seat and the discount fare is $50 per seat. You saw an advertisement saying "Special fare from Chicago to Atlanta—only $50 round trip—but available seats are limited so hurry up." You called the travel agent and asked if this ticket is still available for your trip. The travel agent enters your trip details into the computer system, which is connected to the airline reservation system, to answer your question. The agent finds that there is only one seat left for the flight you want. This final seat may be sold either as a full-fare seat or as a discount-fare seat, depending on several factors.

When the travel agent inputs your trip details, the airline's computer reservation system uses a very sophisticated mathematical technique to determine the probability that this last seat can be sold at full fare before departure, if the agent declines your request to buy the seat at discount fare. This calculation of probability takes into account many factors such as the day of the week of the flight, time of departure, time left until actual departure, seasonality (summer vacation time, spring break season, Christmas season, etc.), and whether or not the trip involves Saturday night stay at destination. If the airline reservation system calculates this probability to be, say, 70 percent, which means that even if the agent does not sell the ticket to you the airline still has 70 percent chance of selling the seat at full fare before the flight departure. Given this probability, we can calculate two numbers, namely the expected seat revenue when selling the seat to you at discount fare (ESR_1) and that when not selling the seat to you (ESR_2). These two numbers can be obtained as followings:

$$ESR_1 = \$50.$$

$$ESR_2 = \$100 \times 70\% + \$0 \times 30\% = \$70.$$

Notice that there is no uncertainly involved in computing ESR_1 because when the seat is sold to you (satisfy the demand that already exists), the airline is guaranteed to make $50 from this seat. In contrast, computing ESR_2 involves uncertainties, because if the seat is not sold to you (miss the demand that already exists), there is no guarantee that the airline can sell the seat at full fare (that is, there is 30 percent chance, or risk, that the seat cannot be sold before departure—for simplicity, we ignore the possibility that the seat can be sold at discount fare in the future). As such, ESR_2 must be obtained by first multiplying the possible future outcomes ($100 for selling the seat at full fare and $0 for not being able to sell the seat before departure) with their respective probabilities (70 percent and 30 percent), and then adding the resulting figures (which results in expected revenue of $70). This means that the airline is better off (makes more revenue) by declining your request to buy the ticket at discount fare. Note that if the calculation of the above probability turns out to be less than 50 percent, the value of ESR_2 will be less than ESR_1 so that the airline would be better off by selling the ticket to you at discount fare price.

Based on the result of computing ESR_1 and ESR_2, the airline reservation system can give two different responses to the travel agent. First, if ESR_1 is higher than (or equal to) ESR_2, the system would tell the agent to say "Yes we have one last discount fare ticket available for you" (note that if ESR_1 is equal to ESR_2, the airline should prefer to sell the ticket to you rather than to decline your request because, while ESR_1 and ESR_2 are equal, the latter involves uncertainties, but the former does not). Second, if ESR_2 is higher than ESR_1 (as in the above example), the airline reservation system would tell the agent to say "I am sorry, but all the discount tickets are gone," but the system would also tell the agent to say "However, one full-fare ticket is still available for the flight. Would you be interested in that?" Maybe your answer to this question is "Well, I need to fly to Atlanta on that day, and if that is the only seat available, then yes I am interested." In this case, the airline has successfully extracted an additional $50 from your pocket by making the seat allocation to be "virtual" between the full fare and the discount fare. Note that even if your answer to the above question is "No, I am not willing to pay that much," the airline would still have 70 percent chance of selling the seat for $100, meaning that the expected revenue of the seat ($70) is still higher than ESR_1.

In practice, the seat allocation process involves allocating seats among a multitude of fare classes, not just a trade-off between two classes. But the basic procedure remains the same—that is, the marginal value of a request for a seat at a particular fare is compared against the marginal revenue from all other fare classes to make a final decision. You can see from this example that airlines are playing games with you when you are shopping airline seats. It is very difficult for you to win the game because airlines are the ones who created the game, and they are very good at playing the game. Many airlines have a separate department that specializes in developing algorithms and computer systems to play this game well, so that they can pull extra money out of your pocket. The idea of this seat allocation logic was first invented by the predecessor of British Air (British Overseas Airways). The algorithm was later refined by American Airlines by incorporating many additional factors.

Overbooking

Overbooking may not seem like it is part of the pricing scheme used by airlines, but it has considerable impacts on their pricing strategy. You may have had an experience of showing up to the airport with confirmed reservation on a flight, but denied a seat; that is, you were told that you had to give up your seat, either voluntarily or involuntarily, because the flight is overbooked. This does not mean that airline people cannot do the simple math of counting the number of passengers having reservations on a given flight. Indeed, they are smart people who can do much more than that.

It is known that a certain percentage of passengers who have reservations in a given flight do not show up to the gate (these passengers are called "no shows"). There are several reasons for no shows. Passengers, for example, may have simply forgotten about the flight, or they may have been involved in an accident or unexpected heavy traffic congestion on the way to the airport. Other passengers may simply have decided not to fly on that day (some of these passengers have refundable tickets and they may be able to get their money refunded). Since airline seats are "perishable" goods that cannot be inventoried for future uses (once an airplane departs the gate, the airline cannot sell the vacant seat any more), existence of no shows means that, if the number of tickets sold by airlines are upper-bounded by the seat capacity, many airline flights must depart with some vacant seats, even though the flight may be completely sold out (closed). This means that there are certain waste (unused capacity) observed in many flights, and that such waste can be eliminated by overbooking flights to a certain degree.

But overbooking is not an easy task because there are both advantages and disadvantages associated with it. The advantage is the additional revenue the airlines can realize by selling airplane seats beyond the physical capacity. There are several disadvantages, but the major ones include the monetary compensation that the airlines must offer to the passengers who are denied seats (bumped), and the loss of airline "goodwill." The monetary compensation varies from one airline to another, but in many cases, the bumped passengers are entitled to receive more than $1,000 (which may be given in cash or check, or in the form of free future air travel by the denying airline). When making overbooking decisions, therefore, airlines must consider the trade-off between these advantages and disadvantages. Let us consider a simple example below to illustrate how the overbooking works for most airlines.

An airline is accepting reservations for a flight from Chicago to Atlanta on a weekday. Since this is a very busy lane, especially during weekdays, the airline is considering overbooking the flight to enhance its unit revenue (flight revenue). For simplicity, assume that the airplane used for this flight has 100 seats, and that there is only one fare class for this flight ($100 per seat for all seats). The flight has just sold out, meaning that there are no more seats available. At this point, the airline has two options; either close the flight (stop selling any more seats), or continue to sell the seats beyond the physical capacity (overbooking). To decide whether the airline should overbook or not, they must first determine the *marginal revenue* and *marginal cost* of overbooking the flight by one additional passenger. The marginal revenue (extra revenue generated by selling one more ticket beyond the seat capacity—that is, the revenue obtained by booking the 101th passenger) is $100. Calculation of the marginal cost (extra cost incurred by accepting one more reservation beyond the seat capacity) is a bit more complicated, as it involves evaluating two possible outcomes (consequences of overbooking), along with their probabilities of occurrence.

One possible outcome is that the total number of show-up passengers is 100 or less (that is, one or more passengers do not show up to the gate), so that the airline would not have to bump any passenger. In this case, the monetary cost is $0, as it does not require the airline to pay any compensation. The other possible outcome is that all 101 passengers show up to the gate so that one passenger must be bumped. In this case, the monetary cost is the amount of compensation the airline must offer to the bumped passenger. The marginal cost is given by first multiplying the monetary cost of these two possible outcomes with their respective probabilities, and then adding the resulting figures (expected value). Let us assume that the compensation amount is $500, and that (based on the statistical analyses of historical no-show records, which is done by the airline computer reservation system), the probability that there is at least one no-show for the flight (that is, the probability that no passenger needs to be bumped) is 95 percent. The marginal cost can then be calculated as follows:

$$MC_1 = \$0 \times 95\% + \$500 \times 5\% = \$25.$$

Given this marginal cost, the airline would overbook the flight by one additional passenger because the marginal revenue ($100) is higher than the marginal cost ($25).

Now let us consider the problem of whether the airline should overbook the flight by one more passenger (that is, a total of two overbooked passengers). The marginal cost of overbooking the second (102nd) passenger is still $100, but the marginal cost is now higher than $25. Notice that, with two overbooked passengers, there are now three possible outcomes; namely, no bumped passenger, one bumped passenger, and two bumped passengers. Let us assume that the airline's computer reservation system indicates that, with two overbooked passengers, the probabilities that no passenger, one passenger, and two passengers need to be bumped for this flight are 75 percent, 20 percent, and 5 percent, respectively. In this case, the cost of overbooking the flight by two additional passengers (booking the flight with a total of 102 passengers) can be calculated as:

$$\$0 \times 75\% + \$500 \times 20\% + \$1,000 \times 5\% = \$150.$$

This, however, is not the marginal cost of overbooking an additional (102nd) passenger; instead, it represents the expected cost of overbooking the flight with a total of 102 passengers (denoted EC_{102}). The marginal cost of overbooking the flight by the second (102nd) passenger (MC_2) is obtained by subtracting MC_1 from EC_{102}:

$$MC_2 = \$150 - \$25 = \$125.$$

Observe that this marginal cost of overbooking the second passenger is higher than the marginal revenue. This means that the benefit of overbooking the second passenger is less than the cost of doing so, so that the airline would be better off not overbooking the flight by two passengers. Notice that if the airline decides to overbook the flight by two additional passengers, the airline would still make additional revenue (relative to no-overbooking scenario), which is given by $\$100 \times 2 - \$150 = \$50$. But this amount ($50) is less than that expected from overbooking the flight by only one additional passenger ($75), so that the airline should prefer overbooking the flight by one, not two, additional passengers. In essence, airlines are using something similar to this process to answer the question "To what extent should we overbook a given flight to maximize revenue?" The basic logic is to overbook as long as the marginal revenue is higher than the marginal cost, or equivalently, stop overbooking once the marginal cost exceeds the marginal revenue (see Figure 4C-1).

Overbooking has impacts on airline pricing. To see this, consider asking the following question to yourself: "Do I want the airlines to practice overbooking or not?" Many people answer immediately (and intuitively) that "I don't like overbooking, as I do not want to be bumped." This makes sense, but we need to understand the consequence of

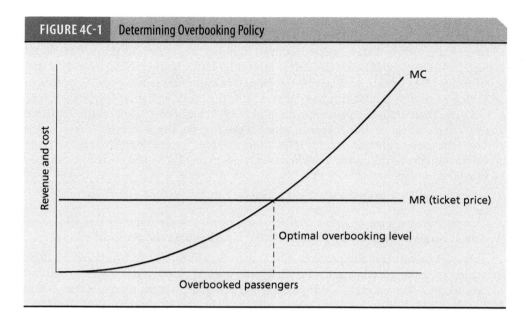

FIGURE 4C-1 Determining Overbooking Policy

forcing airlines to stop overbooking. If airlines are asked to stop overbooking, they will lose certain amounts of revenue that they were making via overbooking. This means that, to maintain the same level of profitability without overbooking, airlines must raise the ticket price per seat. This can result in a notable increase in price, because it is known that the money the airlines generate by practicing yield management (such as overbooking) sometimes accounts for more than half of their net profits. So, the more appropriate question you should ask to yourself would be: "Do I want to pay possibly double the price for an airline seat to guarantee my seat on every flight, or do I want to pay half of that price in every flight in exchange for a slight chance, perhaps less than 0.01 percent, of giving up my seat with compensation of, say, $1,000?" You can see from this example, how overbooking is affecting airline pricing, and how both you and airlines are getting benefits from this yield management technique.

Suggested Readings

Chapter 1   Global Supply Chains: The Role and Importance of Transportation

Bonney, Joseph, and William B. Cassidy, "Pain in the Dray." *Journal of Commerce* (March 31, 2014): 10–15.

Berman, Jeff, "UPS Expands Global Offerings with New China–Europe Rail Service." *Logistics Management* (July 2014): website.

Holdman, Jessica, "New N.D. Plan Looks to Identify Transport Bottlenecks." *Transport Topics* (July 14, 2014): 23.

O'Reilly, Joseph, "U.S. Welcomes European Invasion." *Inbound Logistics* (May 2014): 23–27.

Lapide, Larry, "Global Supply Chains: When Uncertainty Is a Certain Factor."*Supply Chain Management Review* (March/April 2014): 40–44.

Chapter 2   Transportation and the Economy

Pocket Guide to Transportation, *Bureau of Transportation Statistics* (2014).

Watson, Rip, "Broad-Based Growth Lifts All Trucking Sectors," *Transport Topics* (June 23, 2014): 1.

Krizner, Ken, "The Midwest Works," *World Trade* (May 2012): 39–41.

Fuetsch, Michele, "DOT to Slow Payments if Congress Doesn't Act," *Transport Topics* (July 7, 2014): 1.

McMahon, Jim, "Smart Robotics Meet E-Commerce," *World Trade 100* (July 2014): website.

Chapter 3   Transportation Regulation and Public Policy

Cassidy, William B., "Safety First." *Journal of Commerce* (March 31, 2014): 16–18.

Fuetsch, Michele, "States Slow Highway Projects as U.S. Funding Crisis Looms." *Transport Topics* (June 23, 2014): 1.

O'Reilly, Joseph, "U.S. Creates a 'Single-Window' for Import/Export Data Transmission." *Inbound Logistics* (April 2014): 25–28.

Terry, Lisa, "Protecting High-Value Cargo: A Sense of Security." *Inbound Logistics* (April 2014): 89–93.

Chapter 4   Costing and Pricing for Transportation

Watson, Rip, "UPS Prepares to Use Dimensional Pricing for Ground Shipment Rates." *Transport Topics* (June 23, 2014): 31.

Moore, Peter, "Moore on Pricing: Your 2014 Pricing Checklist." *Logistics Management* (January 2014): 18.

Everett, Brian, "Successful Shippers Focus on Long-Term Partnerships." *World Trade* (May 2012): 12.

Schultz, John D., "25th Annual State of Logistics: It's Complicated." *Logistics Management* (July 2014): 28–31.

PART II

The first four chapters of this text provided a background of the environment faced by the transportation industry. Chapters 1 and 2 discussed the role of transportation in the economy and in the firm, respectively. Chapter 3 discussed the transportation technology and systems, and how they affect the industry. Chapter 4 provided a basic discussion of the economics of costs and pricing for transportation providers.

Part II of this text focuses on each of the five modes of transportation. Each modal chapter contains an industry overview, operating and service characteristics, cost structure, and current challenges and issues.

Chapter 5 focuses on the motor carrier industry and differentiates between truckload (TL) and less-than-truckload (LTL) carrier operations. Fuel management issues in the motor carrier industry are presented in depth. A detailed discussion of LTL network structures and network decisions is also offered in this chapter. Finally, truck driver turnover and carrier safety issues are discussed.

Chapter 6 examines the railroad industry and its current operations. Special attention is given to recent attempts by the federal government to reregulate the railroad industry. A detailed discussion of new service innovations, including TOFC and COFC, is given focusing on the growth of intermodal car-loadings in the railroad industry. Because volatile fuel prices have substantial impacts on all transportation modes, a comparison is made in this chapter between railroad fuel efficiency and the other modes of transportation.

The airline industry is the topic of **Chapter 7**. As with the other modal chapters, a discussion of the impact of volatile fuel prices on the airline industry is offered. Along with this cost impact, labor costs in the airline industry are also discussed. This chapter offers a comprehensive view of aircraft operating characteristics as well as a listing of the top airlines in the United States. Because safety is critical in passenger air travel, a comparison of passenger fatalities between airlines and other passenger modes is offered.

Finally, **Chapter 8** presents a discussion of bulk carriers (water and pipeline). The historical development and significance of these modes are presented along with a discussion of the current status of each mode. The cost structures of each mode are presented along with their impacts on carrier operations and competitive advantage. Special attention has been given to the growing infrastructure issues faced by both water and pipeline carriers. Finally, the basics of intramodal and intermodal competition for each mode are examined.

5

MOTOR CARRIERS

Learning Objectives

After reading this chapter, you should be able to do the following:

> Understand the development of motor carriers and their contributions to the U.S. economy

> Be familiar with the different types of firms in the motor carrier industry

> Appreciate the market forces shaping the motor carrier industry

> Gain knowledge of the service characteristics of motor carriers

> Identify the different types of vehicles and terminals used in the motor carrier industry

> Understand the impact of fuel and labor on the motor carrier cost structure

> Be aware of current issues facing the motor carrier industry

TRANSPORTATION **PROFILE**

Increasing Complexity in Parcel

The major parcel carriers continue to experience growth supported by upward trends in consumer online shopping as well as B2B online catalog buying. In the meantime, service promises of two-day and even same-day fulfillment for shippers and buyers is proving to be addictive. And if past practice holds, we're about to get simultaneous "independent" price increase announcements this spring by the parcel carrier oligarchy.

It's important for buyers of these services to step up their game in four key areas in order to ring out as much value as possible from the premium highway and air charges the few providers insist upon.

First, shippers need to understand their parcel profile with respect to package "dimensional" rate scales. It's best to get on the same page with manufacturing and make any necessary/possible packaging adjustments to minimize cube before tendering to the carrier. Keep the following at the top of your mind.

- Know the dimensions and weight (density) of your packages before they get to the carrier.
- Understand dimensional/weight breaks of each carrier's contract so that you can optimize the splitting of shipments, timing, and consolidation of shipments for the lowest total cost.
- Shippers should have teams working to reduce the cube below the carrier's threshold if possible.

Remember that the charges for excess dimensional weight will come back to you after the shipment as a part of your invoice, and you will have a dilemma if you have already charged your customer for a shipment based upon an incorrect dimension.

Second, use technology to store and analyze your contract parcel freight rates so you can do some advanced planning and budgeting. When reviewing proposals, anticipate carrier rules and rates for oversized parcels or secure a time-phased rate change to give you time to modify packaging or make other changes.

If your distances are limited, try smaller regional carriers that may have different scales for dimensional/weight of your freight. It's important to know your various package densities in order to get discounts in the areas most important to you. The carrier will be using sophisticated analytics to study your freight spend so you need to ramp up the analysis.

Third, auditing services for parcel freight moves have proven to be cost justified for many companies, particularly as parcel spend and complexity rise. Auditing of freight bills in all modes is a common practice and has been done for many years with good results.

Arrange to have digital transaction records from parcel shipments sent to your auditing firm and have them check both rates and delivery performance for the requested service type.

And fourth, once you have the tactical things done, it's time to think more strategically. For starters, get an understanding if you're in a great location for service by the selected carriers because experience has shown that companies with good shipping locations and a well-designed routing guide for every parcel ship point can expect better service. In fact, the only way to ensure that the right service levels are being selected to serve your customer is to enforce the use of a routing guide.

Remember that other options may be available. For example, you may want to consider less-than-truckload and truckload shipments, zone skipping, cooperative shipping, or the use of a third-party logistics provider that might enjoy better discounts or perhaps freight consolidation opportunities in your area.

> In summary, it's time to understand your parcel characteristics as well as how the carriers will view your business. If you can position yourself and partners to be a shipper that parcel carriers can serve profitably, you will be rewarded with better discounts and have stronger negotiating leverage.
>
> Source: Peter Moore, *Logistics Management*, March 2017, p. 18. Reprinted with permission of Peerless Media, LLC.

Introduction

The motor carrier industry played an important role in the development of the U.S. economy during the 20th century, and it continues this role in the 21st century. The growth of this industry is noteworthy considering it did not get started until World War I, when converted automobiles were utilized for pickup and delivery in local areas. The railroad industry, which traditionally had difficulty with small shipments that had to be moved short distances, encouraged the early motor carrier entrepreneurs. It was not until after World War II that the railroad industry began to seriously attempt to compete with the motor carrier industry, and by that time it was too late.

The United States has spent more than $128.9 billion to construct its interstate highway system and the process has become increasingly dependent on this system for the movement of freight. The major portion of this network evolved as the result of a bill signed into law in 1956 by President Dwight D. Eisenhower to establish the National System of Interstate and Defense Highways, which was to be funded 90 percent by the federal government through fuel taxes.

As the interstate system of highways developed from the 1950s to 1991, motor carriers steadily replaced railroads as the mode of choice for transporting finished and unfinished manufactured products. Today, motor carriers have the largest share of U.S. freight movements among all the modes of transportation.

Industry Overview

Significance

In 2015, motor carriers moved 10.5 billion tons of freight in the United States, which represents roughly 70 percent of the total U.S. freight tonnage, and generated $726.4 billion in freight revenues, which represents about 81.5 percent of the U.S. freight bills.[1] This means that, on average, 82 cents of every dollar spent on transportation in the United States goes to the trucking industry. In 2014, the U.S. trucking industry operated roughly 31.4 million trucks (registered trucks), which collectively traveled 279.1 billion miles (excluding the government and farm sectors); burned 54.3 billion gallons of fuel; and employed 7.3 million people (including all jobs that relate to trucking activity)—3.4 million of whom are truck drivers.[2] Figures 5-1 and 5-2 show that, with one exception observed during the recession in 2009, the motor carrier industry is increasing its business volume steadily over many years (as measured by total tonnage and revenue). These figures clearly demonstrate the significant role that motor carriers play in our society and the dependence of U.S. companies on motor carrier service.

Types of Carriers

The U.S. motor carrier industry can be broken down into several segments. The first major division of motor carriers is between for-hire and private carriers. The **for-hire** carrier provides services to the public and charges a fee for the service. The **private** carrier provides a

FIGURE 5-1   For-Hire Truck Tonnage Index

Source: *American Trucking Trends 2016*, American Trucking Associations.

service to the industry or company that owns or leases the vehicles, and thus does not charge a fee, but obviously the service provider incurs cost. Private carriers might transport commodities for-hire. This is a strategy often used by private carriers to reduce empty backhaul miles (because in many cases they cannot fill backhaul truck capacities—if, for example, a private truck of a grocery chain store ships goods from warehouses to individual stores, the truck may not be able to fill its trailer on the way back to warehouses). When private carriers are operating in such a capacity, they are essentially for-hire carriers. Shippers must choose

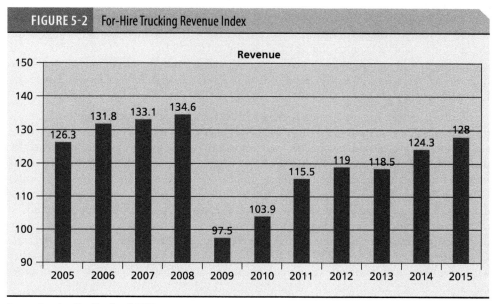

FIGURE 5-2   For-Hire Trucking Revenue Index

Source: *American Trucking Trends 2016*.

whether to use a for-hire carrier or to operate their own private fleet. The decision is based on what is best for their business. Trade-offs exist for both options, but the decision will ultimately be determined by the needs of the shipper.

For-hire carriers can be either local or intercity operators, or both. The local carriers pick up and deliver freight within the commercial zone of a city. The intercity carriers operate between specifically defined commercial zones to include the corporate limits of a municipality plus adjacent areas beyond the corporate limits determined by the municipal population. Local carriers frequently work in conjunction with intercity carriers to pick up or deliver freight in the commercial zone.

The for-hire carriers may be common, contract, and/or exempt operators. The common carriers are required to serve the general public upon demand, at reasonable rates, and without discrimination. The contract carriers serve specific shippers with whom the carriers have a continuing contract; thus, the contract carrier is not available for general public use. Contract carriers also typically adapt their equipment and service to meet shipper needs. Exempt carriers are those that transport exempt (unregulated) property owned by others for compensation.[3] The exempt commodities usually include unprocessed or unmanufactured goods, fruits and vegetables, and other items of little or no value.[4]

Another important distinction is between the truckload (**TL**) and less-than-truckload (**LTL**) carriers. The truckload carriers provide service to shippers who tender sufficient volume to meet the minimum weights required for a truckload shipment and truckload rate, or who are willing to pay the truckload rate even though their shipment sizes are less than the minimum weights. Less-than-truckload carriers provide service to shippers who tender shipments lower than the minimum truckload quantities, such as 50 to 10,000 pounds. Consequently, the LTL carrier must consolidate the numerous smaller shipments into truckload quantities for the line-haul (intercity) movement and disaggregate the full truckloads at the destination city for delivery in smaller quantities. In contrast, the TL carrier picks up a truckload and delivers the same truckload at the destination.

A hybrid type of carrier that has developed can best be characterized as a "heavy LTL" motor carrier. Shipment sizes carried by this type of carrier are in the upper end of what can be considered LTL shipments (that is, 12,000 to 25,000 pounds). This carrier utilizes consolidation terminals (like LTL carriers) to fully load trailers but does not utilize break-bulk facilities for deliveries. Rather, it delivers from the trailer, much like a "pool" carrier, charging line-haul rates plus a charge for each stop-off (like TL carriers). This type of carrier specializes in shipment sizes less than the TL carriers haul and more than LTL carriers haul. It has some fixed costs (because of the consolidation terminals), but not as much as in the LTL industry.

Motor carriers can also be categorized into two types based on the kind of drivers they use. The first carrier type is one that mostly uses company drivers. Company drivers are those who are hired by a specific carrier, and the trucks they operate are owned by the employer. For company drivers, the carrier (employer) provides the equipment (tractor and trailer), fueling, cards, and all the supporting systems (such as routing software, GPS systems, etc.) necessary to operate trucks. In other words, company drivers simply drive the trucks owned by the employer, and all the vehicle operating costs (including maintenance and fuel cost) are paid by the employer. As such the company drivers are paid only for their labor. The second carrier type is one that mostly uses owner-operators. Owner-operators are those who own their trucks; that is, the drivers are entrepreneurs who have their own companies and equipment. But since it is often difficult for an individual owner-operator to receive freight demands (load tenders), they normally work with larger carriers as contractors so that they can haul the freights of the contracting carriers.

Because owner-operators own their equipment, the contracting carriers will pay higher rates to owner-operators than to company drivers because owner-operators pay their own maintenance and fuel bills (that is, the rate the contracting carriers pay includes the cost of fuel, maintenance, etc., as the carriers do not have to pay these costs). Owner-operators, however, often receive some supporting service from contracting carriers, which may include the routing service (they can use the routing software that the carriers use), and the fuel optimization service (software that instructs where to buy fuel to minimize refueling cost—this will be discussed in detail later). In the United States, most motor carriers belong to the first type, where roughly 80 to 90 percent of drivers are company drivers (10 to 20 percent are owner-operators). There are some carriers that exclusively use owner-operators, such as Dart Transit in Minnesota. An advantage of using company drivers is that carriers have control over many things (such as the type of equipment to use), whereas an advantage of using owner-operators is that carriers can adjust its capacity (fleet size) flexibly at any time (for example, quickly reduce the number of contractors when the economy becomes soft).

Finally, the trucking industry can also be broken down into two segments based on the nature of the freight being transported, namely, general freight trucking and specialized freight trucking. General freight trucking provides transportation of general commodities, while specialized freight trucking provides transportation of freight that requires specialized equipment because of the nature of freight, such as size, weight, and shape.[5] Specialized freight may include petroleum products, refrigerated goods, forest products, and hazardous materials, and specialized equipment includes flatbeds, tankers, and refrigerated trailers.[6] The specialized freight trucking also includes furniture-moving companies.

Number of Carriers

Historically, motor carriers were required to have operating authority issued by either federal or state authorities. Since 1996, with the repeal of the Interstate Commerce Act and the elimination of the Interstate Commerce Commission (ICC), such authority is no longer required. The ICC Termination Act of 1995 removed virtually all motor carrier regulations and preempted the states from exercising any economic control over the motor carrier industry. Carriers are now only required to register with the Federal Motor Carrier Safety Administration and provide proof of insurance. They can then transport any commodity they wish, with only household goods and related items being subject to economic oversight. Because of this change, the motor carrier industry today consists of a large number of small carriers, particularly in the TL (truckload) segment of the industry. As of 2015, a total of 586,014 interstate motor carriers were on file with the Department of Transportation. Of these carriers, 90.8 percent operate with six or fewer trucks, and 97.3 percent operate fewer than 20 trucks.[7] This figure supports the small firm composition of the for-hire carrier industry. Keep in mind that many businesses do use their own private fleet (in 2015 there were 747,781 private carriers in the United States[8]).

A further explanation of the large number of small carriers is the limited capital needed to enter the TL industry. A motor carrier can be formed with as little as $5,000 to $10,000 equity, and the balance can be financed with the vehicle serving as collateral for the loan. However, LTL carriers have terminals that increase the capital requirements and thus add a constraint to entry.

There is a significant difference between TL and LTL carriers, both in terms of number and start-up costs. The great growth that occurred in the 1980s, when regulated carriers more than doubled, happened primarily in small TL carriers because of the low start-up costs indicated earlier.

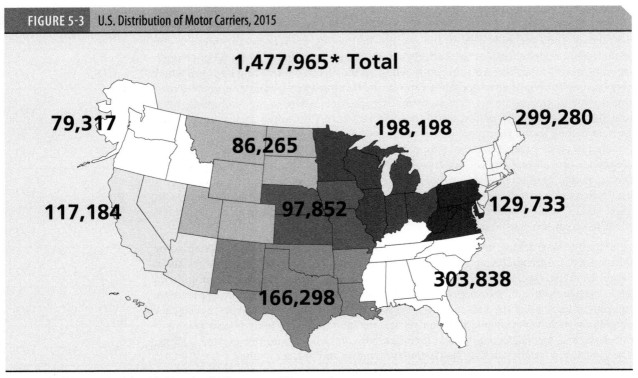

FIGURE 5-3 | U.S. Distribution of Motor Carriers, 2015

1,477,965* Total

79,317

86,265

198,198

299,280

117,184

97,852

129,733

166,298

303,838

Source: Federal Motor Carrier Safety Administration, U.S. Department of Transportation.

The LTL segment of the motor carrier industry requires a network of terminals to consolidate and distribute freight, called a "hub-and-spoke" system. The large LTL carriers moved to expand their geographic coverage after 1980, and many of them eliminated their TL service. Because of this relatively high level of fixed costs, the LTL industry has continued to consolidate. In August 2003, Yellow Corporation announced that it would buy Roadway Corporation for $1.1 billion. After it was approved by the appropriate government agencies, this consolidation created a company (whose name was changed to YRC Freight in 2012) that controls approximately 29 percent of the national LTL carrier market.[9]

Perhaps a brief description of an LTL operation would be helpful here. Shippers that have small shipping requirements use LTL carriers (for example, the cubic capacity of a 53-foot trailer is not needed for the shipment). Also, the LTL shipper typically has shipments headed for more than one destination. The LTL carrier collects the shipments at the shipper's dock with a **pickup and delivery (PUD)** vehicle. This vehicle, as its name implies, does the collection and delivery of all shipments. After a PUD vehicle has finished collecting and delivering shipments, it returns to a consolidation or break-bulk facility. Once at the consolidation facility, the packages collected are sorted by their final destination. The next part of the trip is called the **line-haul** segment. For this portion of the trip, the shipments are loaded into 28-foot, 48-foot, or 53-foot trailers. If 28-foot trailers are used, they are hooked together in combinations of twos and threes, depending on the state's trailer configuration permitted over the route of travel. Although small, the 28-foot trailer is often used because it is easier to unload two 28-foot trailers at separate bays than to unload one 48-foot or 53-foot trailer at one bay. Another reason for using the 28-foot trailer is because LTL carriers find that it is easier to utilize the capacity of a 28-foot trailer. After the line-haul portion of the trip, the trailers are unloaded at another break-bulk facility and are then sorted and reloaded into a PUD vehicle to be delivered to the receiver.

The TL segment of the industry has been experiencing some limited concentration. Carriers such as J.B. Hunt and Schneider National have become increasingly larger. The ability of the larger TL carriers to compete effectively with small TL companies with their value-added services might change the structure of the TL segment. This may be exemplified by the recent mega-merger of Swift and Knight in 2017, which created a new TL giant with $5 billion annual revenue, 23,000 power units (tractors), 77,000 trailers, and 28,000 employees.[10]

With the repeal of the Interstate Commerce Act, combined with changes in distribution patterns, a climate was created in which new TL carriers could easily enter the business. The "trucking recession" of 1994, 1995, and 2009, during which capacity greatly exceeded demand, removed many of the weaker firms through either bankruptcy or merger. However, low start-up costs in this sector still enabled new entrants to attempt success in this area.

Market Structure

When discussing the motor carrier industry, consideration must be given to the commodities hauled. Motor carrier vehicles, both for-hire and private, primarily transport manufactured, high-value products. These vehicles carry more than a majority of the various manufactured commodity categories. The commodity list includes food and manufactured products, consumer goods, and industrial goods. In addition, these vehicles transport almost all of the sheep, lambs, cattle, calves, and hogs moving to stockyards.[11]

Motor carriers transport less of commodities such as grain, primary nonferrous metal products, motor vehicles and equipment, and paper and allied products. Because such commodities generally must move long distances and in large volumes, shipping them by rail and water is usually less expensive.

From a market structure perspective, the TL market can be considered as monopolistic competition. With the low entrance to market requirements (that is, capital), individuals can easily obtain equipment and begin operation within a specific geographic region. The LTL market, on the other hand, is oligopolistic in nature. This is the result of the significant investment needed by these carriers in break-bulk and other facilities. As such, barriers to entry exist in the LTL industry.

Competition

Motor carriers compete vigorously with one another for freight. With the large number of for-hire motor carriers, rivalry between firms can be intense. However, the most severe competition for for-hire carriers often comes from the private carrier.

As indicated earlier, the TL motor carrier industry offers few capital constraints to entry. With a relatively small investment, an individual can start a motor carrier business and compete with an existing carrier. Thus, freedom of entry, discounting, and lack of regulatory constraints appear to dominate the industry and suggest that competition between firms can control the industry. Such a conclusion has been the basis for greater reliance on the marketplace and less reliance on regulation. Even though the LTL segment is more concentrated, there is still intense competition between the top carriers. Other competitors include United Parcel Service, FedEx, and FedEx Ground.

Certain segments of motor carriers have higher capital requirements than others, as indicated, and therefore have some degree of capital constraint for entry. The major segment that has extensive capital requirements for entry is the LTL carrier. The LTL carrier must invest in terminals and freight-handling equipment that are simply not needed by the TL carrier. Special equipment carriers—carriers of liquefied gases or frozen products—usually have larger investments in equipment and terminals than those involved with general freight. The large TL carriers like J.B. Hunt and Schneider National also have significant capital investment.

On the whole, the motor carrier industry, especially for contract carriers, has been market oriented. Meeting customer requirements has been a common trait of motor carriers. The small size of the majority of for-hire carriers allows them to give individualized attention to customers. As carriers have grown in size, this close carrier–customer relationship has been strained. However, the responsiveness to customer demands for service still dominates all motor carrier organizations, and shippers expect carriers to respond to their needs.

Operating and Service Characteristics

General Service Characteristics

The growth and widespread use of motor carrier transportation can be traced to the inherent service characteristics of this mode. In particular, the motor carrier possesses a distinct advantage over other modes in the area of accessibility. The motor carrier can provide service to virtually any location as operating authority of the for-hire carrier no longer places restrictions on the areas served and commodities transported. Motor carrier access is not constrained by waterways, rail tracks, or airport locations. The U.S. system of highways is so pervasive that virtually every shipping and receiving location is accessible via highways. Therefore, motor carriers have potential access to almost every origin and destination.

The accessibility advantage of motor carriers is evident in the pickup or delivery of freight in an urban area. It is very rare to find urban areas not served by a pickup–delivery network. In fact, motor carriers provide the bridge between the pickup and delivery point and the facilities of other modes; that is, the motor carrier is referred to as the universal coordinator.

Another service advantage of the motor carrier is speed. For shipments going under 800 miles, the motor carrier vehicle can usually deliver the goods in less time than other modes. Although the airplane travels at a higher speed, the problem of getting freight to and from the airport via motor carrier adds to the air carrier's total transit time. In fact, the limited, fixed schedules of the air carriers might make motor carriers the faster mode even for longer distances. For example, a delivery to a destination 800 miles away might take 17.8 hours by motor carrier (800 miles at 45 mph). Although the flying time between airports is 1.5 hours, 3 hours might be needed for pickup and 3 hours for delivery, plus time for moving the freight from one vehicle to another. If the airline has scheduled only one flight per day, the shipment could wait up to 24 hours before being dispatched. The motor carrier, however, proceeds directly from the shipper's door to the consignee's door. This service advantage became evident in the wake of September 11, 2001, when U.S. air traffic was shut down. The U.S. Post Office issued a statement alerting customers of delays for any package or letter traveling more than 800 miles because any Post Office shipment moving over 800 miles travels by air and under 800 miles travels by motor carrier.

When compared to the railcar and barge, the smaller **carrying capacity** of the motor carrier vehicle enables the shipper to use the TL rate, or volume discount, with a lower volume. Many TL minimum weights are established at 20,000 to 30,000 pounds. Rail carload minimum weights are often set at 40,000 to 60,000 pounds, and barge minimums are set in terms of hundreds of tons. The smaller shipping size of the motor carrier provides the buyer and seller with the benefits of lower inventory levels, lower inventory-carrying costs, and more frequent services.

Another positive service characteristic is the smoothness of transport. Given the suspension system and the pneumatic tires used on their vehicles, the motor carrier ride is smoother than rail and water transport and less likely to result in damage to the cargo (although there can still be some cargo damage with motor carrier transportation). This relatively damage-free service reduces the packaging requirements and thus packaging costs.

Lastly, the for-hire segment of the motor carrier industry is customer or market oriented. The small size of most carriers has enabled or even forced the carriers to respond to customer equipment and service needs.

Equipment

Many of the motor carrier service advantages emanate from the technical features of the transportation vehicle. The high degree of flexibility, the relatively smooth ride, and the small carrying capacity of the vehicle are the unique characteristics that result in greater accessibility, capability, frequency of delivery and pickup, cargo safety, and lower transit time.

The motor carrier vehicle can also be loaded quickly. A railroad operation needs to collect a number of freight cars to be pulled by one power unit; the motor carrier has just one or two. The ability to operate one cargo unit eliminates the time needed to collect several cargo units.

The other dimension of motor carrier equipment flexibility is the lack of highway constraint. Unlike the railroad and water carriers, the motor carrier is not constrained to providing service over a fixed railway or waterway. The motor carrier can travel over the highway, paved or unpaved, servicing virtually every conceivable consignee in the United States.[12] There are, however, gross vehicle weight and axle weight restrictions on vehicles while traveling the highway system.

In most cases, equipment represents the largest operating asset that a carrier maintains. With all of the different types and locations of equipment, positioning becomes critical to successful operations. Seasonal influences such as holidays or harvest times must also be considered, as they can drastically alter demand.

TL and LTL carriers need to make two types of equipment decisions: type of tractor (power unit) and type of trailer. In a TL operation, equipment positioning at terminals is not as important as in an LTL operation. However, power must be specified to be able to handle the size and length of the load, along with the terrain over which it travels. Many different specifications for tractors can be used, including single axle and twin axle, with different engine and drive train combinations. Decisions regarding trailers include length (28 feet, 45 feet, 48 feet, 53 feet, and so on) and trailer type (dry van, refrigerated, ragtop, container, flatbed, and so forth). These decisions will be made in light of market demands and the type of carrier operation.

LTL carriers must make the same types of equipment decisions as TL carriers along with deciding where to deploy this equipment. Similar to an airline equipment decision, LTL carriers need to position certain types of equipment at certain terminals. For example, city delivery vehicles and tractor–trailer combinations (either 28-foot or 40-foot trailers) will be positioned at PUD terminals, whereas line-haul trailers (usually 45, 48, or 53 feet) and line-haul tractors (single or twin axle) will be assigned to break-bulks. Compounding the LTL decision is the inclusion of 28-foot trailers (also called *pups, twins,* or *double bottoms*) in the equipment decision. Having the right mix of power and trailers at a particular terminal location determines the ability to efficiently serve customers.

Types of Vehicles

Motor carrier vehicles are either line-haul or city vehicles. Line-haul vehicles are used to haul freight long distances between cities. City straight trucks are used within a city to provide pickup and delivery service. On occasion, line-haul vehicles also will operate within a city, but the line-haul vehicle is normally not very efficient when operated this way.

Line-Haul Vehicles The line-haul vehicle is usually a tractor–trailer combination of three or more axles (see Figure 5-4). The cargo-carrying capacity of these vehicles depends on the size (length) and the federal/state maximum weight limits. A tractor–trailer combination with five axles (tandem-axle tractor and trailer) is permitted on the interstate system to haul a maximum of 80,000 pounds gross vehicle weight (20,000 pounds on a single axle or 34,000 pounds on a tandem axle). States can have different maximum weights on their highway systems. For example, Michigan allows a maximum gross vehicle weight of 164,000 pounds on their state highways (which can only be achieved by the use of 11 properly spaced axles). Motor carriers can haul freights that are heavier than these maximums by obtaining special permits from states and/or by operating long-combination vehicles (LCVs—see Figure 5-4).

FIGURE 5-4 Equipment Types

Source: *American Trucking Trends, 2016*, American Trucking Associations, p. 60.

The net carrying capacity of line-haul vehicles is also affected by the density of the freight. As an example, consider a 53-foot × 102-inch × 110-inch trailer that has 3,500 cubic feet of space and a payload limit of 45,000 pounds. If commodity A has a density of 10 pounds per cubic foot, then the maximum payload of commodity A for the vehicle is 35,000 lbs (3,500 ft^3 × 10 lb/ft^3), because in this case the volume capacity would be reached before the weight capacity would (meaning that the weight capacity is underutilized). If, in contrast, commodity B has a density of 20 pounds per cubic feet, then the maximum payload of this commodity for the vehicle is 45,000 lbs (2,250 ft^3 × 20 lb/ft^3), because in this case the weight capacity would be reached before the volume capacity would (meaning that the volume capacity is underutilized). Note that, by mixing multiple commodities or products in a shipment, better capacity utilizations (in both volume and weight) and more efficient loading can be accomplished. In the above example, if we mix the two commodities such that a shipment is comprised of 2,500 pounds of commodity A and 1,000 pounds of commodity B (which results in volume requirement of 2,500 ft^3 + 1000 ft^3 = 3,500 ft^3 and weight requirement of 2,500 ft^3 × 10 lb/ft^3 + 1,000 ft^3 × 20 lb/ft^3 = 45,000 lbs), then the capacity utilization, in both volume and weight, would be 100 percent. This can reduce the total number of shipments needed to transport commodities A and B in combination. Some smart shippers are collaborating to build such efficient loads.[13]

City Straight Trucks City vehicles, or "straight trucks," are normally smaller than line-haul vehicles and are single units (see Figure 5-4). The city truck has the cargo and power unit combined in one vehicle. The typical city truck is approximately 20 to 25 feet long with a cargo unit 15 to 20 feet long. However, there is growing use of small trailers (28 feet) to pick up and deliver freight in the city. Since these trailers can also be used for line-haul, this practice can increase the efficiency (shipments can be "loaded to ride," meaning they will not require handling at the origin terminal).

Special Vehicles In addition to the line-haul and city vehicle classifications, the following special vehicles are designed to meet special shipper needs:

- Dry van: Standard trailer or straight truck with all sides enclosed
- Open top: Trailer top is open to permit loading of odd-sized freight through the top
- Flatbed: Trailer has no top or sides; used extensively to haul steel
- Tank trailer: Used to haul liquids such as petroleum products
- Refrigerated vehicles: Cargo unit has controlled temperature
- High cube: Cargo unit has drop-frame design or is higher than normal to increase cubic capacity
- Special: Vehicle has a unique design to haul a special commodity, such as liquefied gas or automobiles

The Department of Transportation's Federal Motor Carrier Safety Administration has established many rules and regulations governing the specifications of motor carrier vehicles. These regulations cover such areas as the number of lights on the vehicle, the type of brakes used, tire specifications, and other operating parts.[14] The overall allowable length, weight, and height of the vehicle are prescribed in the various states.[15]

Terminals

Some motor carrier operations, namely TL operations, might not require terminals for the movement of freight. The carrier uses the shipper's plant for loading and the consignee's plant for unloading. Typically, TL terminals normally provide dispatching, fuel, and maintenance services. Some carriers, such as Schneider National, are expanding the services offered by their terminal facilities to include restaurant and hotel offerings to give their drivers alternatives to truck stops. These terminals are designed primarily to accommodate drivers and equipment, but not freight.

All LTL operations, on the other hand, require terminals, and they use terminals for different purposes (such as loading and consolidation) than TL operations. Some of the large LTL carriers, such as YRC Freight, have more than 250 terminals (YRC Freight once had over 500 terminals). A driver will leave a terminal to make deliveries throughout the country, but will always return to his or her domicile (a driver's domicile is the terminal that the driver originally left). Since the terminal is a key facility in the operation of an LTL hub-and-spoke system, we will present an expanded discussion of the types and roles of the terminals in the following paragraphs. The terminals used by motor carriers can be classified as pickup/delivery, break-bulk, and relay (or any combination thereof).

Pickup and Delivery Terminals (PUD) The most common type of terminal found in the LTL system is the PUD terminal. These are also called *satellite* or **end-of-the-line (EOL) terminals**. The PUD terminal serves a local area and provides direct contact with both shippers and receivers. The basic transportation service provided at this terminal is the pickup and/or delivery of freight on peddle runs. A **peddle run** (sometimes called milk run) is a route that is driven daily out of the PUD terminal for the purpose of collecting freight for outbound moves or delivering freight from inbound moves. A PUD terminal will have several peddle runs in its customer operating area. Figure 5-5 gives an example of how a peddle run is designed. The PUD terminal is located in Altoona, Pennsylvania. Attached to it are four peddle runs, one each to Tyrone, State College, Lewistown, and Huntington. Every Monday through Friday morning, a driver will depart the Altoona terminal and deliver freight to customers located on that driver's assigned peddle. During and after the deliveries, freight will be picked up from customers and returned with the driver to the Altoona terminal at the end of the day. When all the drivers return at the end of their shifts, the Altoona terminal will have freight to be consolidated and moved outbound from customers in Tyrone, State College, Lewistown, and Huntington to customers in other areas of the country.

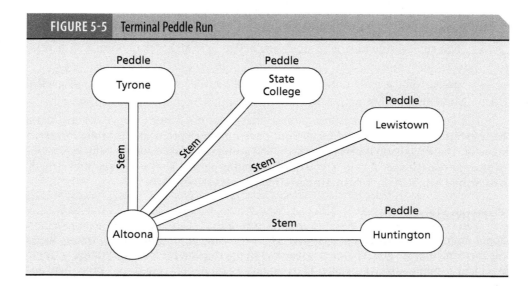

FIGURE 5-5 Terminal Peddle Run

Note that there are two elements of a peddle run, one called **stem time** and the other called *peddle time*. Stem time is the time that elapses from when the driver leaves the terminal until the driver makes the first pickup or delivery; it is also the time that elapses from when the driver makes the last pickup or delivery until returning to the terminal. This is nonrevenue-producing time because no shipments are handled. A carrier would want to locate PUD terminals in such a way that this nonrevenue-producing travel time is minimized. (This aspect of LTL service will be discussed later in this chapter.) The other type of time is peddle time. This is the time during which the driver is actively involved in the pickup and delivery of freight. This is revenue-producing time because it occurs when shipments are handled. Obviously, carriers want to maximize the amount of time a driver would spend performing these activities.

The basic terminal services performed at these facilities are consolidation and dispersion. For example, freight moving inbound to Altoona from other terminals (passing through a break-bulk) will be broken into individual deliveries by peddle run to be handled by the driver during that particular shift. Freight that is brought back by the peddle drivers for movement outbound from Altoona will be consolidated into line-haul trailers for subsequent movement to the appropriate break-bulk. This is a basic cross-dock type of operation with a direction of freight flow across the dock that changes depending on whether the move is inbound or outbound.

The dispatch operation provided at the PUD terminal is critical to the operating efficiency of the peddle runs. Freight can be picked up on peddle runs in one of two ways. First, a customer on a peddle run might have a standing order for a pickup every day at 10 a.m. The PUD driver is aware of this, so the customer has no need to notify the carrier in advance for the pickup. Second, a customer might call or email the local PUD terminal to order service for a pickup. This is where the local dispatcher becomes involved. The dispatcher records the nature of the shipment and required time of pickup and assigns that shipment to the driver on the appropriate peddle run. The PUD driver will periodically call in to or receive a satellite message from the dispatcher to determine the order and frequencies of new pickup requests. Obviously, the dispatcher needs to be familiar with the geography of the peddle runs and the capacity of the PUD drivers and trailers to efficiently route freight with the appropriate vehicle (today there are multiple software products, which are often called vehicle-routing software, that can help the dispatchers plan their peddle runs in the optimal, or near optimal, manner).

Other services that are provided at the PUD terminal might include tracing, rating and billing, sales, and claims. However, some carriers are beginning to centralize these functions at break-bulks or other locations by taking advantage of telecommunications technology. For example, many LTL carriers use the Internet for tracing purposes. When the customer accesses the carrier's website, the shipper keys in the pro number or waybill number (also called a tracking number) and the system provides the current status of the shipment.

Break-Bulk Terminals Another type of terminal found in an LTL hub-and-spoke system is called a **break-bulk**. This facility performs both consolidation and dispersion (or break-bulk) services. Customers will rarely have contact with the operations at the break-bulk facility. The main purpose of this terminal is to provide an intermediate point where freight with common destinations from the PUD terminals is combined in a single trailer for movement to the delivering PUD terminal. This can be seen in Figure 5-6. Break-bulks will have many PUD terminals assigned to them as primary loading points. For example, assume that a shipper in Toledo, Ohio, wanted to send an LTL shipment to a customer in Pottstown, Pennsylvania. The Toledo PUD terminal is attached to the Cleveland, Ohio, break-bulk, and the Philadelphia PUD terminal, which handles the Pottstown peddle, is attached to the Lancaster,

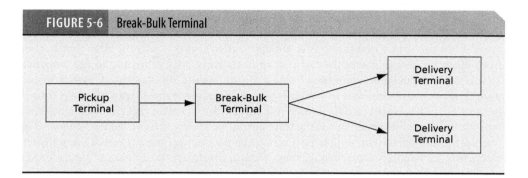

FIGURE 5-6 Break-Bulk Terminal

Pennsylvania, break-bulk. At the completion of the peddle run, the Toledo driver brings the shipment back to the Toledo PUD terminal. There it is sorted and combined with other shipments going to the Lancaster break-bulk service area. (This could include all PUD terminals covering significant portions of Pennsylvania, New York, New Jersey, and parts of Maryland.) These shipments are consolidated into one trailer that will be dispatched to the Lancaster break-bulk.

Once the trailer arrives in Lancaster, it will be unloaded, and all of the freight destined to Philadelphia and its peddle runs will be loaded into an outbound trailer. This trailer will be dispatched from the break-bulk and will arrive at the Philadelphia terminal to be unloaded in the early morning so the freight can be segregated into peddle delivery vehicles for an early morning delivery schedule.

Break-bulk facilities also serve as driver domiciles. City drivers located at a PUD terminal will always remain in their local area during their shift and will be able to return home when it is over. Line-haul drivers, however, might or might not be able to return home after a trip, depending on the length of haul they are assigned. For example, a *turn* means that a line-haul driver is assigned a load to be taken from the break-bulk (domicile) to a PUD terminal that is no more than 5.5 hours away. Because of DOT-mandated driving limits, that line-haul driver can make the trip, drop the trailer, and pick up another shipment destined back to the break-bulk within the hours of service driving limit. However, a movement that requires more than 5.5 hours driving time in one direction will require a layover; that is, when the driver reaches the destination, a 10-hour rest period is required before that driver will be able to take a return load back to the break-bulk and return to the domicile. Therefore, at the maximum, a driver facing an 11-hour run with a 10-hour layover and an 11-hour return trip will return to the domicile within 32 hours of the original departure. Sometimes, however, a return load is not immediately available, which will delay the driver's return.

Relay Terminals **Relay terminals** are different from the PUD and break-bulk terminals in that freight is never touched. The relay terminal is necessitated by the maximum hours of service regulation that is imposed on drivers. Under DOT enforcement, drivers were permitted to drive a maximum of 11 hours after 10 consecutive hours off duty. At the relay terminal, one driver substitutes for another who has accumulated the maximum hours of service. (The term **slip seat** also has been used to describe the relay terminal operation.)

As indicated in Figure 5-7, the location of the relay terminal is a maximum driving time of 11 hours from an origin. If the relay terminal is located 5.5 hours from an origin, the driver can drive to the relay terminal and return within the maximum 11 hours. (This is also called a *turn*.)

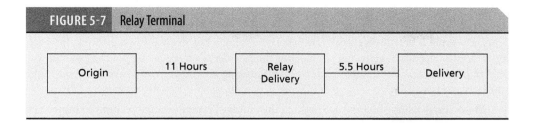

FIGURE 5-7   Relay Terminal

Using the example given in Figure 5-7, assume that the driving time is 16.5 hours between origin and destination. Without the relay terminal, the transit time is 26.5 hours. After 11 hours of driving, the driver goes off duty for 10 consecutive hours. Upon resuming duty, the driver drives 5.5 hours to the destination. The total elapsed time is 26.5 hours (11 + 10 + 5.5). With the relay terminal, however, the driver drives 11 hours to the terminal, and another driver takes over and drives the vehicle to the destination. In this instance, the relay terminal reduces the transit time by 10 hours, the mandated driver off-duty time. Note, however, that carriers might have to rethink their relay structures if the driver hours of service rule is to change in the future (U.S. Department of Transportation has been working on revising this rule for some time).

An alternative to the relay terminal is the use of a sleeper team—two drivers (this is often called team driving, too). While one driver accumulates the off-duty time in the sleeper berth of the tractor, the other driver is driving. The sleeper team has been most successful for long trips with many destinations.

Terminal Management Decisions

Many types of operating decisions need to be made when utilizing terminals in a carrier's network. Along with making these decisions, carrier management must also consider their strategic implications. This section will address a few of these types of decisions.

Number of Terminals In many modes, this is a relatively simple decision. For example, passenger airline terminals will be located close to major population centers. This decision, however, usually does not belong to the carrier but to some local government agency. Railroads must also make this decision but are limited by geography and track locations for terminal sites. Railroads will not normally have many terminals in their networks. The mode with probably the most difficult decision in this area is LTL motor carriage, primarily because of the vast numbers of terminals in these systems and the relatively small investment needed to develop a terminal site.

The obvious question for an LTL motor carrier is, "How many terminals should we have?" The obvious answer is, "It depends." First, the degree of market penetration and customer service desired by the carrier will help determine the number of terminals to establish. In theory, the more terminals closer to the customer, the better the service. This also has proven to be true in practice. Realistically, at some point additional terminals will result in no incremental increase in service and might even detract from service.

Second, the dilemma of small terminal versus long peddle must be addressed. Figure 5-8 represents this situation. In Example 1, assume that a carrier's market is the state of Pennsylvania, with one terminal located in Harrisburg with peddle runs to Erie, Scranton, Pittsburgh, and Philadelphia. This network utilizes only one terminal but has extremely long and expensive stem times for its peddle runs. The terminal must also be large to accommodate the volume of freight that will come from these four peddles. Example 2 shows a network that utilizes two terminals, each having two peddle runs with significantly shorter stem times. Each terminal in this scenario is smaller than the one terminal in Example 1. Thus, Example 2 has doubled the number of terminals but decreased stem times for customer PUD. The small-terminal versus long-peddle decision would be made based on the service implications of establishing terminals closer to customers versus the cost of adding another terminal.

Many times when shippers are making distribution system decisions, they assume that manufacturing facilities are fixed and that warehouse decisions must be made based on this fixed network. This assumption is also part of the terminal decision process for LTL motor carriers, except their "manufacturing facilities" are break-bulk terminals. Whether or not another terminal can be added to a break-bulk's operating region might simply be a question of available capacity at that break-bulk. Normally, each PUD terminal is assigned at least one door at a break-bulk. To add another PUD terminal means eliminating an existing terminal, physically adding another door to the break-bulk, or improving the productivity at the break-bulk to turn trailers in doors more than once per shift.

Locations of Terminals   Closely related to the decision of how many terminals to establish is the decision of where to establish them. As previously mentioned, for airlines and railroads, this decision can be relatively simple because of geographic, government, and demand variables. LTL carriers, however, must consider some other variables. First, the DOT limits the amount of time a driver can continuously operate a vehicle before a rest period is required. Currently, this limit is 11 hours, so optimally PUD terminals should be located no more than 11 hours away from a break-bulk. This would allow a driver to complete the run in one trip. Second, market penetration and potential will help determine terminal location. As mentioned in the decision process for determining the number of terminals, getting closer to the customer can many times improve the level of service given to that customer. Finally, accessibility to major highways and other transportation modes (airports, rail yards, etc.) must be considered to reduce unnecessary vehicle miles and to facilitate speedy intermodal freight transfers.

Recent trends in the LTL sector have seen significant reductions in the number of terminals as these carriers strive to provide overnight and second-day delivery to more and more customers. To do this, many interterminal runs have been realigned with the resultant elimination of intermediate handling. This has resulted in increased load factors and reduced transit times. Less handling has also improved the claims experience for the LTL carriers. Some long-haul LTL carriers will still favor the hub-and-spoke operation, whereas the regional carriers will still look toward fewer terminals with more direct runs.

Fuel Management

As discussed previously, motor carriers transport larger amounts of goods than any other mode of transportation in the United States, which suggests that they consume substantial amounts of fuel and emit large amounts of pollutants. In fact, it is known that the trucks emit the largest amount of pollutants within the transportation sector (Ericson et al. 2006).[16] This means that the efficient management of fuel is crucial for motor carriers for two reasons. First, since the fuel cost accounts for a significant proportion of the motor carriers' total operating cost (recall that fuel cost represents roughly 40 percent of carrier costs), reducing or minimizing fuel cost is an important issue for carriers to survive in their highly competitive market. It is worth noting that, during 2008–2009 time periods when fuel prices went up drastically, thousands of motor carriers went bankrupt simply because they could not manage fuel cost. Second, being the largest source of carbon emissions in the transportation

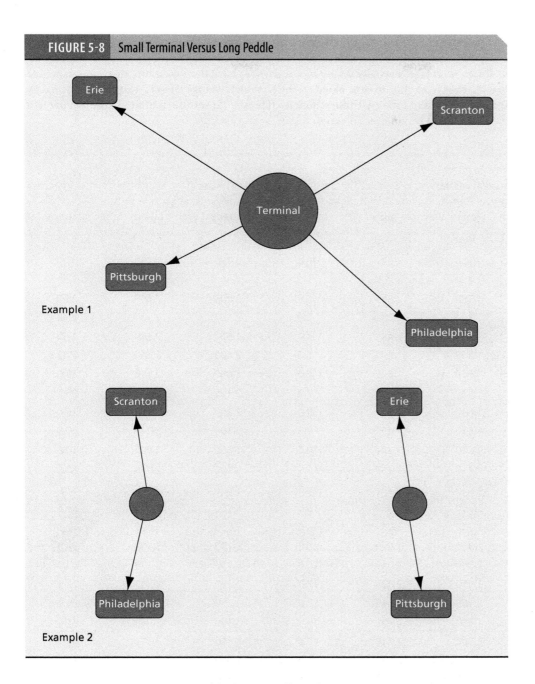

FIGURE 5-8 Small Terminal Versus Long Peddle

Example 1

Example 2

sector, motor carriers are responsible for controlling their operations to protect our environment (minimize pollutants emission). Some government agencies, such as the Environmental Protection Agency (EPA), are already working on helping carriers become greener operators. Although a comprehensive discussion of green and sustainable transportation is provided in Chapter 13, "Issue and Challenges for Global Supply Chains," this section discusses some current and future approaches used by motor carriers, especially TL carriers, to address fuel management challenges. Although we focus on discussing TL carriers (because the TL segment is considerably larger than the LTL segment), many approaches discussed here also apply to LTL carriers.

Fuel Surcharge   Fuel surcharge is commonly used by motor carriers to offset the impact of rising fuel cost on their operations. The basic idea is to pass the increased cost of fuel price to shippers, at least partially. Many motor carriers have their own fuel surcharge schedule that changes from time to time based on the National Average Diesel Fuel Price published by the Department of Energy. These schedules typically express the fuel surcharge as a percent of the line-haul revenue, as shown in the following example.

NATIONAL AVERAGE DIESEL FUEL PRICE LOWER BOUND	UPPER BOUND	% OF LH REVENUE	NATIONAL AVERAGE DIESEL FUEL PRICE LOWER BOUND	UPPER BOUND	% OF LH REVENUE
1.200	1.249	0.0	2.350	2.399	23.0
1.250	1.299	1.0	2.400	2.449	24.0
1.300	1.349	2.0	2.450	2.499	25.0
1.350	1.399	3.0	2.500	2.549	26.0
1.400	1.449	4.0	2.550	2.599	27.0
1.450	1.499	5.0	2.600	2.649	27.5
1.500	1.549	6.0	2.650	2.699	28.0
1.550	1.599	7.0	2.700	2.749	28.5
1.600	1.649	8.0	2.750	2.799	29.0
1.650	1.699	9.0	2.800	2.849	29.5
1.700	1.749	10.0	2.850	2.899	30.0
1.750	1.799	11.0	2.900	2.949	30.5
1.800	1.849	12.0	2.950	2.999	31.0
1.850	1.899	13.0	3.000	3.049	31.5
1.900	1.949	14.0	3.050	3.099	32.0
1.950	1.999	15.0	3.100	3.149	32.5
2.000	2.049	16.0	3.150	3.199	33.0
2.050	2.099	17.0	3.200	3.249	33.5
2.100	2.149	18.0	3.250	3.299	34.0
2.150	2.199	19.0	3.300	3.349	34.5
2.200	2.249	20.0	3.350	3.399	35.0
2.250	2.309	21.0	3.400	3.449	35.5
2.300	2.349	22.0	3.450	3.499	36.0

Although an effective method, fuel surcharges do not entirely protect motor carriers. It is known that motor carriers are typically able to recover only 60 to 70 percent of the increased cost of fuel through fuel surcharges, because some shippers will negotiate and play games with carriers (for example, it is hard for motor carriers to pass on the entire cost of increased fuel prices to large shippers like Walmart, because they will then say "We will go with another carrier").[17]

Off-Peak Delivery This concept is not new for fuel management, but carriers have started to seriously consider adopting this strategy only recently. Off-peak delivery simply means shifting delivery times of some customers from normal business (daytime) hours to off-peak hours (for example, nighttime delivery). There are at least two benefits of using this strategy for carriers from the standpoint of environmental sustainability. First, carriers will experience reduced fuel consumption (and thereby reduced carbon emissions) because of the favorable traffic conditions during off-peak hours (trucks will have shorter travel times and reduced idling time due to low traffic congestion).[18] Second, nighttime truck operations will result in lower pollution levels than daytime operations. Using atmospheric modeling, research in California demonstrated that the nighttime stability of the atmospheric layer is always equal to, or more stable than, daytime stability.[19] This means that the enhanced nighttime stability of the atmospheric layer can trap more pollutant particles than during the day.[20] Off-peak delivery also has several nonenvironmental advantages for motor carriers over daytime delivery, such as the enhanced vehicle utilization factor (because with off-peak delivery, trucks can deliver during both daytime and nighttime).[21]

Engine Idling Time Engine idling time reduction is another technique widely used by motor carriers to manage fuel cost. While there are certain idling times that cannot be controlled by carriers (such as those that take place during traffic congestion), there are idling times that can be reduced or eliminated by carriers. Typically, the largest amount of idling time for TL carriers comes from drivers' rest times. The U.S. Department of Transportation enforces the "hours of service" regulation for truck drivers, which requires that truck drivers do not operate vehicles beyond the maximum hours per day, and that, once reaching this maximum hours, drivers take sufficient rest (usually 10 consecutive hours) before they can start operating vehicles. This rest time usually takes place in the sleeper berth of a truck, and most drivers choose to idle engines while taking rest (because they need air conditioning during hot season or heating during cold season while sleeping). It is known that, for heavy-duty trucks (such as Class 8 trucks), engine idling consumes about 0.5–0.7 gallons of diesel fuel per hour.[22] This means that each truck spends roughly $20 per day for idling engines during rest time (assuming retail price of $3 per gallon for diesel fuel), which converts to an annual engine idling cost of tens of billions of dollars for the entire TL industry.

Several attempts have been made to reduce or eliminate such idling times. One is the use of an APU (auxiliary power unit). This is a small, economical engine attached to each truck, which is not powerful enough to move a truck but has sufficient power to run air conditioners. Many carriers are now attaching APUs to their trucks and ask drivers to use these APUs to run heaters or air conditioners during their rest time. Another is the use of electric power outlets at truck stops. Most drivers prefer to take the (overnight) rest break at the parking lot of truck stops (fueling stations that are often equipped with restaurants, shower facilities, laundry, etc.). Many truck stops now offer electric power outlets for trucks during rest time for a small charge. Trucks can use these power sources to run their air conditioners and/or heaters. This option costs considerably less money for carriers than idling large, powerful engines during rest times.

Road Speed It is known that there exists an optimal speed for each vehicle that attains the most economical fuel consumption rate, such that any deviation of speed (increase or decrease) from this level worsens the fuel economy (for heavy-duty trucks such as Class 8 trucks in the United States, the optimal speed is typically around 55–60 mph).[23] Many motor carriers are trying to control their trucks' speed during cruise at this optimal speed to achieve maximum fuel efficiency. However, it is, often difficult to do so because many truck drivers are not happy driving at 55 mph. Note that in the TL industry truck drivers are paid by miles driven, and not by the hour (strictly, they are paid by the "billed" miles, which reflects the shortest distance between origin and destination, not by the "actual" miles driven between origin and destination). This means that, given the maximum operating hours imposed by the hours-of-service regulation, drivers can maximize their income by driving at high speeds (so that they can maximize the miles driven in a given time period). As such they are reluctant to drive vehicles at slower speeds than the legal limit (usually around 70 mph on highways).

Motor carriers are using at least two approaches to slow down the average cruising speed. The first approach is to convince and/or reward drivers to drive slower. Many carriers are conducting periodical seminars for their drivers and attempting to convince them that driving at slower speeds is "safer" than driving at higher speeds. Some carriers also provide monetary rewards to those who agree to drive at slower speeds. The second approach is to mechanically control the maximum speed of trucks. Some carriers are using a device in their trucks that automatically controls the maximum speed. They work as "speed limiters" such that once the truck reaches the prespecified maximum speed (such as 65 mph), it will cut or reduce the fuel supply to the engine so that trucks cannot accelerate beyond that certain speed. You may have had an experience on a highway (with 70 mph limit) where a slow truck (65 mph) is trying to overtake another slow truck (63 mph) from the left lane, so that they are slowing down other traffic on the highway (including you). This could be because both trucks are equipped with this speed limiter.

Out-of-Route Miles As discussed above, drivers (and motor carriers) are paid by the "billed miles." This means that, for all shipments, any additional mile(s) driven beyond the shortest miles (any deviation from the shortest route between origin and destination) will result in additional cost (unpaid miles) for carriers. As such, motor carriers want to make sure that drivers strictly follow the shortest routes. Often, however, drivers do deviate from the shortest routes for personal reasons like stopping at out-of-route locations to meet with parents, girlfriends, or boyfriends, going to restaurants of their choice that are located off the route, shopping at malls and/or sightseeing. Motor carriers are using several approaches to minimize such "out-of-route miles."

First, many carriers are installing GPS devices to their vehicles, so that they can keep track of the locations of their trucks in real time. This allows carriers to not only provide timely information to their clients (shippers) regarding the present location of their shipments (the primary objective of using GPS tracking system), but also to find out if trucks are following the shortest route at all times. If a carrier finds that one of its trucks is out-of-route, it can contact the driver (via the satellite communication system or sometimes by cell phone) and ask the reason why he/she is out-of-route. Although many drivers do not like this system (many drivers do not like to be monitored once they are on the road), this gives drivers the message that they need to stay on the shortest routes. Second, some carriers that have many terminals across the nation allow drivers to go to "off-the-route" locations for personal reasons, but they ask drivers to first stop at one of their terminals near the (off-the-route) locations they wish to go to, and then use the company cars (small economical cars available at the terminals) to drive to their locations. This way the drivers can go to their locations more economically without operating heavy-duty trucks. Third, some carriers are trying to convince drivers to follow the shortest route by telling them that they can maximize their income by staying on the shortest route (minimizing the time to finish the load), because this will allow drivers to start the subsequent load quickly (which maximizes the number of loads he/she can haul in a given time period, thereby maximizing the paid miles within the time period).

Network Truck Stops Many motor carriers make contracts with a limited number of truck stop chains to reduce their fuel procurement costs. The basic approach here is to make a contract with a specific truck stop chain (for example, Flying J and Pilot), such that a carrier commits to a certain (minimum) amount of fuel purchases within a given time period from the chain, and receives a price discount in exchange. If the carrier fails to purchase the committed amount within the time period, the contract becomes void. The truck stops with which a carrier has such purchase contracts are called the carrier's "network truck stops." Typically, the network truck stops will issue fueling cards to the carrier drivers, so that when drivers buy fuel within the network, they automatically receive the price discount at the pump. Drivers are encouraged to refuel only at network truck stops (so that the carrier can meet or exceed the committed purchase quantity), unless it is absolutely necessary for them to buy fuel outside the network (for example, when fuel is low and there are no network truck stops within 100 miles). Note that drivers have incentives to refuel at network truck stops too, because if they buy fuel outside the network, they cannot use fueling cards, meaning that they may need to tentatively pay the fuel cost (which may be in excess of $500 if they top off) out of their pocket.

There are three methods of setting price discounts with truck stop chains. The first is the "retail minus" method. This method gives discount to carriers by subtracting a predetermined amount from the normal retail price (for example, "retail minus five" means that a carrier's purchase price is five cents less than the normal retail price at the pump). The second is the "cost plus" method. Under this method, the discounted price is computed by first estimating the truck stop's cost of fuel (cost of goods sold, which includes the cost of fuel per se at the nearest pipeline, called the rack price, cost of transporting fuel from pipeline to the truck stop, and other miscellaneous cost items), and then adding the profit margin of the truck stop. For example, "cost plus three" means that the discounted price is the truck stop's cost of fuel plus three cents. The third is the "best of" method, which is a hybrid of the above two methods, such that the discount price is determined by the lower of the prices given by the two methods. For example, "best of retail minus five or cost plus three" means that the price is determined by first computing the price based on the "retail minus five" and "cost plus three" methods, and then choosing the lower of the two prices. In many cases, a carrier approaches multiple truck stop chains by first providing the committed purchase quantity, and then soliciting for price quotes based on the committed purchase quantity. After obtaining responses from the chains, the carrier can either choose the chain that provided the best deal, or continue to negotiate price discounts based on the results of the responses from chains (execute the second round of bidding based on the results of the first round bidding).

Bulk Purchasing Some large motor carriers have a network of terminals across the United States. These terminals typically have fuel pumps so that their trucks can refuel at these terminals. Since these terminals refuel many trucks, they buy large amounts of fuel from fuel suppliers on a daily basis, meaning that they can receive sizable quantity discounts from suppliers. Some carriers claim that if their trucks refuel at these terminals rather than at truck stop chains, their fuel cost can become considerably lower, because this will allow them to avoid paying "profits" for truck stop chains. As such, these carriers normally encourage their drivers to refuel at these terminals whenever possible. They, however, discourage drivers to use these facilities when it requires trucks to deviate considerably, say more than 20 miles, off the shortest route between origin and destination.

Equipment Adjustments One of the most widely used approaches to enhance fuel efficiency of trucks is the adjustment of equipment (tractor or trailer). These adjustments will improve fuel consumption rates of trucks via enhancing air drags and low rolling resistance. Such adjustments include the use of trailer and cab roof fairings, trailer side skirts, aerodynamic side mirrors, and SmartWay certified tires. Some articles claim that these adjustments can give 1 percent to 6 percent savings in fuel cost.[24]

Large Fuel Tank Typically, heavy-duty trucks (such as U.S. Class 8 trucks) are equipped with fairly large fuel tanks that can carry 200 to 240 gallons. Some motor carriers, however, are installing even larger tanks to their vehicles to save fuel costs. This is because many carriers believe that having large tanks would help them reduce fuel procurement costs. The basic logic behind this approach is that, by having large fuel tanks, many trucks can possibly avoid buying fuel in regions where fuel prices are expensive. If, for example, a truck is making a round trip from a region where the fuel price is cheap (region A) to a region where the fuel price is expensive (region B), the truck may need to buy fuel before completing the round trip (possibly at or near region B) if it has a small fuel tank, whereas it may be able to finish the round trip without any refueling (avoid buying fuel at or near region B) if it has a large tank. Note, however, that there is one disadvantage associated with this approach; that is, recent studies have shown that a truck with more fuel in its tank (thus with more fuel weight) will require more fuel burns.[25] As such, the net benefit of this approach may be relatively small.

Prevent Out-of-Fuel Occasions Sometimes, trucks run out of fuel on the road for multiple reasons. Occasionally, this may be due to mechanical problems such as a fuel indicator malfunction. In most cases, however, this happens because of drivers' negligence of proper fuel indicator monitoring, or drivers' reluctance to stop for refueling (many drivers dislike making frequent fuel stops, as this tends to delay the ETA—estimated time of arrival at destination). When this happens, carriers usually have to dispatch a rescue vehicle, which supplies enough fuel to the "out-of-fuel" truck for it to move to the next available truck stop. Some carriers estimate the cost of this rescue vehicle to be around $200 per dispatch. Since this is costly, many motor carriers are creating company policies and guidelines for truck drivers that specify when they have to stop to purchase fuel. Typically these guidelines suggest that when the fuel level reaches at or below 20 percent of tank capacity (for example, 40 gallons for a truck with a 200-gallon tank) drivers must stop for refueling. Some carriers have installed "engine monitors" to their vehicles, which allow managers to monitor trucks' engine conditions, including fuel level, from the headquarters at all times.

Prevent Fuel Leakage and Theft Motor carriers lose fuel because of fuel leakage and drivers' fuel theft. It may be a surprise to some readers that some (but not the majority of) drivers steal fuel from their trucks, but this actually happens (this resembles the situation for retail stores where products are lost due to employee theft). Since the loss of fuel because of these reasons increases the cost of carriers without providing any benefit, carriers are trying to avoid such losses. They are attempting to minimize fuel leakage from tanks by performing frequent preventive maintenance of their vehicles, and minimize driver theft by performing driver education and fuel monitoring (ensuring that the fuel spent for a given trip is in agreement with the miles driven).

Fuel Optimizer Fuel optimizers are software products widely used by TL carriers to reduce the fuel procurement cost of their fleet at the point of purchase. It is well known that fuel prices vary (often substantially) from one truck stop to another, even within the same region. The basic concept of the fuel-optimizer products is to take advantage of such price variances across locations (truck stops) to reduce the cost of buying fuel. These products first download the latest price data of nearly all the truck stops in the United States and Canada (which are updated daily), and then compute the optimal fueling policy for a given origin–destination route that indicates: (1) which truck stop(s) to use, and (2) how much fuel to buy at the chosen truck stop(s).[26] The goal is to buy more gallons at truck stops where the fuel is cheap, and buy fewer gallons at truck stops where the fuel is expensive, so as to minimize the cost of refueling. These products typically work in conjunction with truck-routing software, so that users can first compute the shortest route for a given origin–destination pair, and then compute the optimal refueling policy for this route.[27] Famous product names include *ProMiles* and *Expert Fuel*. Vendors of fuel optimizers claim that, typically, cost savings achieved by the use of their products range from 4 to 11 cents per gallon of fuel, which convert to an average saving of $1,200 per truck per year.[28]

Technically, fuel optimizer is a mathematical programming (optimization) model that minimizes the cost of buying fuel for a given route by selecting the optimal fueling location (truck stops) and quantity (gallons). While optimizing, the model considers the following parameters: tank capacity (Q), trip starting fuel (SF), trip ending fuel (EF), fuel consumption rate (MPG), minimum fuel to be maintained at all times (LF) (reserve fuel, e.g., 40 gallons), minimum amount of fuel to purchase at any truck stop (MP) (to avoid frequent fuel stops, e.g., 50 gallons), and "out-of-route miles" for each truck stop (OOR) (the amount of distance a truck must deviate from the shortest route to reach the truck stop in question). The model seeks to find the solution that minimizes the cost of buying fuel along the route, while ensuring that: (1) the fuel level (fuel quantity in the tank) does not fall below LF or above Q at any point in the route, (2) the ending fuel is larger than or equal to EF, and (3) the minimum purchase quantity is MP at any truck stop.

The model allows users to incorporate certain constraints that reflect their corporate policies, so that solutions become not only "feasible," but also "practical" from the execution standpoint. One such constraint is the definition of the trucks stops to be included in the model. Specifically, model users can restrict the truck stops to be considered by the model to only those that meet certain requirements. For example, one can exclude those truck stops that are located far from the shortest route whose OOR miles are more than 3 miles. One can also exclude certain truck stops based on "driver amenities," such as the availability of shower facility, restaurant, ATM, laundry, and overnight parking. Carriers may also require the model to consider only those truck stops that are in their "networks" (recall that network truck stops are those with whom carriers have purchase contracts) to ensure that their trucks refuel only at the truck stops with price discounts (users can specify, for each specific truck stop chain, their purchase contract such as retail minus 5 or cost plus 4).

The major advantage of using the fuel-optimizer products is that motor carriers can save fuel costs at the point of purchase. Some carriers are saving reasonable amounts of fuel costs by using the model. The model, however, has at least three disadvantages. First, truck drivers generally do not like to follow fueling instructions (many drivers dislike to be told what to do once they are on the road). Thus, it is difficult for many carriers to attain high driver compliance rates, which implies that the model may give limited actual cost savings to carriers. Although some carriers have attempted to improve the compliance rates by providing monetary incentives to those who follow fueling instructions, many of these attempts have resulted in failure. Second, the use of the fuel-optimizer products can increase (worsen) the driver turnover rate. High driver turnover rate has been the major issue in the motor carrier industry for many decades—especially in the TL segment. Driver turnover rates for many large carriers are well above 100 percent, and it is estimated that the cost of replacing (recruiting) truck driver ranges between $3,000 and $12,000 per replacement[29] (we will discuss this turnover issue in more detail later in the section "Current Issues"). As such motor carriers are reluctant to do anything that can possibly increase driver turnover rates even slightly.[30] It is generally believed, however, that the use of fuel optimizers will increase the already-high driver turnover rates of TL carriers by upsetting many truck drivers (by confiscating their freedom to choose truck stops).[31] Third, the fuel-optimizer model is a static model that does not consider the dynamic movement of fuel prices (the model calculates the optimal fueling policy for each route based on the latest price data available at the time of dispatch). Thus, if multiple days are needed to complete a trip (which is common in the TL industry), the refueling policy given by the model may not be truly optimal, as the fuel price of each truck stop changes (often substantially) from day to day.

Cost Structure

Fixed Versus Variable Cost Components

The cost structure of the motor carrier industry consists of high levels of variable costs and relatively low fixed costs. Approximately 70 to 90 percent of the costs are variable, and 10 to 30 percent are fixed. The public investment in the highway system is a major factor contributing to this low fixed-cost structure because the highway is the motor carrier's "right-of-way." In addition, the motor carrier is able to increase or decrease the number of vehicles used in short periods of time and in small increments of capacity. Lastly, the carriers as a group (with the exception of the LTL carrier) do not require expensive terminals. The small investment in terminals also contributes to low fixed costs. The bulk of the motor carrier's cost then is associated with daily operating costs—the variable costs of fuel, wages, maintenance, and highway user fees (such as fuel tax and vehicle registration).

The discussion of motor carrier cost will begin with the vehicle operating costs of long-distance fleets transporting products in tractor–trailers. These data can be compared only to similar operations; that is, comparisons cannot be made to local motor carrier operations (PUD). Table 5-1 indicates that in 2015 the total cost to operate a tractor–trailer was 159.3 cents per mile. As indicated, approximately 80 percent of the cost to operate an intercity tractor–trailer is variable. The remaining 20 percent is associated with the fixed costs: vehicle depreciation and interest costs, insurance cost, and overhead (such as permits and licenses). For carriers handling LTL freight, the fixed cost is higher; that is, additional terminals, management, and overhead expenses are required to handle small-sized shipments.

The two categories with the largest share of the variable costs are labor and fuel. A discussion of each of these two variable costs will follow.

Labor The cost of drivers accounts for 40 percent of the total operating costs per vehicle mile, as shown in Table 5-1. Labor costs (wages plus fringe benefits) usually absorb about 25 to 30 percent of a carrier's revenue dollar. That is, 25 to 30 cents out of every dollar in revenue goes to labor.

The over-the-road (intercity) driver is typically paid on a mileage basis, such as 42.0 cents per mile; local drivers are paid by the hour. Over-the-road drivers are normally paid an hourly rate for operating delays resulting from loading/unloading, accidents, weather, and the like.

The DOT enforces maximum hours of service (HOS) regulation. As of 2017, the DOT's **driving time regulations** permit drivers to drive a maximum of 11 hours after being off duty for 10 consecutive hours (subject to certain rest-break constraints). A driver is permitted to be on duty a maximum of 14 hours after 10 consecutive hours off duty. In addition, no driver can drive after accumulating 60 hours on-duty in 7 consecutive days, or 70 hours in 8 consecutive days. For a more thorough discussion of the new HOS regulations, see Chapter 3.

The most pressing labor issue facing motor carriers, particularly TL carriers, is the shortage of qualified drivers. Part of the problem is that the federal government, as part of an

TABLE 5-1	Average Carrier Costs per Mile, 2015

MOTOR CARRIER COSTS	2015
Vehicle-Based	
Fuel Costs	$0.403
Truck/Trailer Lease or Purchase Payments	$0.230
Repair & Maintenance	$0.156
Truck Insurance Premiums	$0.092
Permits and Licenses	$0.019
Tires	$0.043
Tolls	$0.020
Driver-Based	
Driver Wages	$0.499
Driver Benefits	$0.131
Total	$1.593

Source: "An Analysis of the Operational Cost of Trucking: 2016 Update," *American Transportation Research Institute,* September 2016.

overall safety program, imposed stringent driver licensing requirements. Since April 1992, all operators of vehicles over 26,000 pounds gross vehicle weight must hold a commercial driver's license (CDL). Although CDLs are issued by the driver's home state, the requirements are mandated by the federal DOT. Along with the new licensing requirements, the DOT also imposed stringent rules dealing with drug and alcohol abuse. Poor driving records and inability to pass the CDL test eliminated many marginal drivers.

The hardships imposed by the very nature of long-haul motor carrier operations have also impacted the availability of drivers. Drivers are frequently away from home for long periods and often have to assist with the loading and unloading of trailers. This lifestyle is not as attractive as other career choices, so the available pool from which drivers might be drawn has declined. The motor carrier industry has undertaken several initiatives to counteract the problem of driver retention and recruitment. They have raised the per-mile and per-hour pay rates, scheduled drivers so that they can be home more frequently (for example, by focusing on short-distance shipments and dedicated loads), and worked with shippers and consignees to make freight more "driver-friendly" (that is, easier to load/unload, tarp, brace, and so on).

ON THE **LINE**

The Never-Ending Truck Driver Shortage

When it comes to the state of the never-ending truck driver shortage, the facts are out there for all of us to see.

We're consistently hearing about the projected shortfall in the difference between the actual number of drivers available and what's actually needed. We're hearing about the aging truck driver workforce as well as the fact that potential drivers don't want to be away from home for long stretches of time. And, of course, we're hearing about the Millennial effect, a group who would rather be doing something "cooler" than driving a truck for a living.

(continued)

So, unfortunately, rather than seeing things improve, the consistent themes are the ones mentioned above. Why? Because the numbers really aren't changing that much—even if the national employment outlook appears to be brightening.

According to the data that was issued by the American Trucking Associations (ATA) in the 3rd quarter of 2016, the trends remain the same. According to the report, the turnover rate at large truckload fleets with more than $30 million in annual revenue saw a 2 percent decline to 81 percent in the 3rd quarter, its lowest level going back to the 2nd quarter of 2011 and the third decline posted in 2016.

ATA chief economist Bob Costello cited various reasons for the lower turnover percentage on the truckload side, with a forecast for what may be in store for 2017.

"Ongoing softness in the freight economy has contributed to an easing of the market for drivers and a reduced turnover rate," Costello explained. "Since the end of the 3rd quarter of 2016, we've seen signs that we may be reaching the end of the poor inventory cycle that has driven a lot of the weakness in the freight economy, so we may see turnover rates rebound in the months to come."

However, Costello stressed that "despite the falling turnover rate, carriers continue to report difficulty finding well-qualified drivers, a problem that will not only persist, but which will get worse as the freight economy improves."

It's also worth mentioning that the ATA's landmark October 2015 report titled "Truck Driver Analysis 2015," whose chief findings cited how the current shortage of truck drivers stood at almost 48,000 and has the potential to go higher, noted that if current trends remain intact, the driver shortage could rise to around 175,000 by 2024.

What got me thinking about the driver situation was a recent article in the *Wall Street Journal* that mentioned people who receive training from carriers or schools affiliated with them often become independent carriers—a move that offers the promise of working for yourself. However, that move comes with the "onerous" terms of working upward of 80 hours per week to make ends meet on equipment.

So, what happens now and what needs to be done going forward? Well, increasing driver pay is a good place to start, but that's easier said than done given the typically razor-thin carrier margins. Signing bonuses can help, too, but they often lack lasting impact due to the demand-sensitive nature of trucking. In other words, drivers move around a lot due to a better offer from someone else.

Even with an increased onus on augmenting driver training, retention and compensation packages, many carriers are still struggling to fill the empty seats. In the meantime, the ongoing driver situation still serves as a major factor for tight, over-the-road capacity, which has been burdensome for shippers in that they need to pay higher rates in order to get their freight moved in a timely and efficient manner.

The entire situation is like the hamster on the wheel in many respects. Maybe the whole thing will become a memory if autonomous vehicles truly do find success; but until then, things continue to move down a highway of uncertainty when it comes to the never-ending truck driver shortage.

Source: Jeff Berman, *Logistics Management*, April 2017, p. 20. Reprinted with permission of Peerless Media, LLC.

Fuel Since 1974, the higher price of fuel has resulted in a rise in the relative proportion of fuel cost to total cost. For example, in 1976 fuel cost was 11.6 cents per mile or 19.8 percent of the total cost per mile, but in 1985 fuel cost was 24.6 cents per mile or 21.1 percent of total cost. In 2015, fuel cost was higher at 40.3 cents per mile or about 25.3 percent of total variable costs (see Table 5-1). Carriers have experienced a 251 percent increase in diesel fuel prices from 1994 to 2014—approximately $1.106 per gallon in 1994 to about $3.882 per gallon in 2014.

Included in the price of the diesel fuel is a highway user tax imposed by both the federal and state governments. The fuel tax plus other taxes for highway use are payments made by the carrier to the government for the construction, maintenance, and control of the highways. In 2014, the motor carrier industry paid $18.4 billion in federal highway-user taxes and $21.6 billion in state highway-user taxes.[32] The federal fuel tax is 24.4 cents per gallon of diesel fuel and the state fuel tax averages 27.4 cents per gallon.[33]

Economies of Scale

There do not appear to be major economies of scale for large-scale motor carrier operations. Economies of scale are realized through more extensive use of large-sized plants or indivisible inputs. However, the extensive use of indivisible inputs is not characteristic of all motor carrier operations. In addition, the large number of small firms, especially in the TL segment, suggests that small-sized operations are competitive. The concentration of the LTL business is indicative of economies of operation in this segment.

In the short run, certain economies exist in the greater use of indivisible inputs such as terminals, management specialists, and information systems. The average cost of such inputs will decrease as output (greater use) increases. Such economies of use justify the rather large-sized firms that operate transcontinentally, especially in the LTL segment. Carriers that operate over wide geographic areas require more terminals, more elaborate information systems, and more management specialists than those carriers that operate over narrow geographic areas.

For TL operations, very limited investment is required for terminals, but information systems are becoming increasingly important to efficient operations. Computers in tractors, electronic logging device (ELD), GPS systems, direct satellite communication to drivers, and bar coding with optical scanners are a few examples of the sophisticated information systems and technology that now exist in the motor carrier industry. Many of the TL carrier inputs (vehicle, labor, fuel) can be increased one at a time in response to the small increases in demand.

Operational cost trade-offs exist between large and small carriers. A large-scale operation affords savings in purchase economies of equipment and in such inputs as fuel, parts, and interest in loans. On the other hand, large LTL motor carriers might be unionized and thus pay higher labor rates, but the motor carrier industry is less unionized today than it was in 1980.

Overall, long-term economies of scale appear not to be significant in TL motor carrier transportation and are present to some degree in the LTL segment. This degree of scale economies has implications for competition and the market's capability to control such competition.

Operating Ratio A measure of operating efficiency used by motor carriers is the **operating ratio**. The operating ratio measures the percent of operating expenses to operating revenue.

Operating Ratio = (Operating expenses/Operating revenue) × 100

Operating expenses are those expenses directly associated with the transportation of freight, excluding nontransportation expenses and interest costs. Operating revenues are the total revenues generated from freight transportation services; nontransportation services are excluded. Motor carriers might use the operating ratio to support a rate increase request. The closer the operating ratio is to 100, the more indicative of the possible need to raise rates to increase total revenues. In today's market, however, a rate increase might not be a feasible solution. Carriers are more likely to seek supply chain solutions with shippers, consignees, and 3PLs to reduce operating expenses, thus increasing operating margin (for example, by coordinating multiple loads such that carriers can reduce or minimize empty miles—we will discuss how to do this in more detail in Chapter 9, "Logistics Services").

An operating ratio of 94 indicates that 94 cents of every operating revenue dollar is consumed by operating expenses, leaving 6 cents of every operating dollar to cover interest costs and a return to the owners. LTL motor carrier operating ratios usually range between 93 and 98, whereas the TL segment could see ratios in the high 80s to low 90s. The operating ratio is also a benchmark or barometer of financial viability. Obviously, if the operating ratio is equal to or greater than 100, there is no revenue available to cover fixed or overhead costs or to return a profit to owners or stockholders. Increasing revenues and/or reducing costs are viable approaches to resolving the problem of a high operating ratio.

Since the founding of the United States, the federal government has felt that it has the responsibility to provide highways to meet the national defense and commerce needs of the country. At first, the federal government was the sole financier of highways, but over the years, state and local governments have assumed a greater role. Today, the state and local governments assume the responsibility for maintaining the highways, while the federal government provides up to 90 percent of the construction cost of new highways with the designated network. The Federal Highway Administration (FHWA), part of the DOT, oversees the National Highway System (NHS). The NHS was defined in 1995 and consists of the 160,955-mile roads, including interstate highways, that are important to the U.S. economy defense, and mobility. Later, as a result of the MAP-21 (Moving Ahead for Progress in the 21st Century Act) in 2012, the "enhanced NHS" was defined and included those roads that were important but were not part of the system, which expanded NHS to about 230,000 total miles. Although the NHS includes slightly over 4 percent of the total road mileage, this network sees the transportation of more than 75 percent of intercity freight traffic.

The Intermodal Surface Transportation Efficiency Act (ISTEA) has been replaced by the Transportation Equity Act for the 21st Century (TEA-21), which has continued the role of FHWA in this area. Additional funds were added under TEA-21, which remained in place until 2004. More than $73 billion was expected to be spent on roads and related projects during this period. On June 29, 2012, the Moving Ahead for Progress in the 21st Century Act (MAP-21) was passed and allocated $105 billion to be spent on the nation's highways for the following two years.

Funding Highway users—motor carrier vehicle and automobile operators—pay for the construction, maintenance, and policing of highways through highway user taxes. The total amount of taxes paid depends on the use of the highway. The motor carrier incurs a cost for the use of the highway that is related to its amount of use. This situation contributes to the high variable cost structure of the motor carrier.

Federal and state governments assess highway user taxes. The federal highway user taxes are paid into the Federal Highway Trust Fund. From the Federal Highway Trust Fund, the federal government pays 90 percent of the construction costs for the interstate system and 50 percent of the construction costs for all other federal-aid roads. Table 5-2 indicates items taxed and the rate assessed by the Federal Highway Trust Fund.

The state also assesses highway user taxes to defray the cost of construction, mainte-nance, and policing of highways. The state taxes include fuel taxes, vehicle registration fees, ton-mile taxes, and special-use permits.

Implied in the highway user tax concept is the philosophy that the highway pre-dominantly confers benefits on specific groups and individuals. Although the general public benefits from increased mobility and the availability of a wide variety of goods and services, the motor vehicle user is presumed to be the major benefactor and there-fore is expected to pay a larger share of the costs. An analogy that illustrates this concept is the property owner who pays property taxes that include an assessment for streets (access to the property). Much debate exists as to whether motor carrier vehicles pay a fair share of the total cost of highways. In 2014, motor carriers paid $18.4 billion in federal highway-user taxes and $21.6 billion in state highway-user taxes.[34] The central issue is whether motor carriers should pay for the added construction and maintenance costs caused by their heavier weight (it is known that the road damage is an exponential function of the vehicle weight per axle, such that if the vehicle weight per axle doubles, the degree of road damage more than doubles).

Because each state must pay for the maintenance, policing, and construction of the highways within its boundaries, each state attempts to ensure receipt of taxes for using its highways. For a motor carrier operation over many states, this means buying vehicle registrations in many states and maintaining records of miles driven in a particular state so that the state will receive a fuel tax or ton-mile tax. Such record-keeping adds a cost to the carrier's operation (this task, however, is becoming less of a concern for many carriers lately with the advent of GPS systems, some of which can keep track of the miles driven in each state—before the GPS age truck drivers had to manually record the odometer miles every time they crossed state lines).

TABLE 5-2	Federal Highway Trust Fund Tax Rates
COMMODITY	**TAX**
Gasoline	18.4 cents/gallon
Diesel fuel	24.4 cents/gallon
Gasahol	18.4 cents/gallon
Special fuels	
General rate	18.4 cents/gallon
Liquefied petroleum gas	18.3 cents/gallon
Liquefied natural gas	24.3 cents/gallon
M85 (from natural gas)	9.25 cents/gallon
Compressed natural gas	18.3 cents/ 126.67 cubic feet
Tires	0 to 3,500 lb—no tax
	Over 3,500 lb—9.45 cents for each 10 lb in excess of 3,500
New truck and trailer sales	12% of manufacturer's sales price on trucks weighing more than 33,000 lb and trailers exceeding 26,000 lb
Highway vehicle use tax	For trucks weighing 55,000 lb or more, $100 + $22 for each additional 1,000 lb up to a maximum of $550

Source: FAST Act Division C; Internal Revenue Code (26 U.S.C.), 2017.

Private Trucking

What Is Private Trucking?

So far our discussion has focused on for-hire trucking operations. As discussed earlier, however, there is also another form of truck transportation called private trucking. In this section we discuss this form of trucking in detail.

Simply stated, private transportation is the movement of goods owned by a firm that also owns or leases and operates the transportation equipment for the furtherance of its primary business. A private carrier does not provide service to the general public. Rather, the private carrier serves itself by hauling its own raw materials and/or finished products. In the past the private carrier was permitted to haul goods for others (the public) only if such service was provided free of charge. Exceptions to this general prohibition against the private carrier charging a fee included the movement of exempt commodities and freight of firms that were 100-percent-owned subsidiaries. This is because, in the past, the Interstate Commerce Commission (ICC) strictly enforced the prohibition of private carriers hauling public goods for a fee. This enforcement was an extension of the control over entry for common and contract carriers, who must prove public convenience and necessity. However, the 1980 Motor Carrier Act greatly reduced controls over entry into the common and contract carrier fields, and grants of authority became easier to obtain even for an existing private motor carrier. After the abolition of the ICC in 1995, the responsibilities of regulating private transportation were transferred to the Surface Transportation Board.

Although private transportation is found in all modes of transportation, it is most prevalent in the trucking industry. ACT, a trucking research firm, says that private fleets in the United States generate $217 billion in revenue.[35] Just over half of the tons of commodities shipped domestically are hauled by private carriers.[36] Private fleets also contribute to 2.5 percent of the gross domestic product.

Prior to the dissolution of the ICC, the exact number of private fleets in operation was difficult to determine because firms were not required to report private trucking operations. However, the DOT now requires private trucking firms to register with the DOT, which provides more accurate data. The U.S. Census Bureau estimates that there are 4 million private trucks on the road, as reported by the National Private Truck Council.

It is safe to state that private trucking is an integral segment of the transportation system employed by the shipping public in the United States and most other countries because of its relatively low start-up cost and flexibility of operations. At one time or another, almost every company will study or actually operate a private truck fleet, even if the fleet consists of only one truck. For this reason, an in-depth analysis of private trucking is provided below.

Why Private Trucking? The primary reasons for a firm having a private truck fleet are improved service and/or lower costs. In either case, the private fleet operator is attempting to improve the marketability and profitability of its products. Through improved levels of service, the firm attempts to differentiate its product (lower transit time) and increase its sales and profits. Reduced costs permit the company to keep prices constant (a price reduction during inflationary times), to lower prices, or to increase profits directly. The advantages and disadvantages of private trucking are summarized in Table 5-3. This table provides a convenient reference for the discussion that follows about private truck transportation and can be a useful tool for the evaluation of the potential for private trucking in specific situations. Table 5-4 provides insight into the types of costs for private trucking.

TABLE 5-3	Advantages and Disadvantages of Private Trucking	
ADVANTAGES		**DISADVANTAGES**
Improved Service Convenience, Flexible Operation, Greater Control, Lower Transit Times, Lower Inventory Levels, Reduced Damage, Driver/Salesperson, Last Resort (special needs) **Lower Cost** Reduced Transportation Costs (Eliminates Carrier Profit), Reduced Inventory Levels, Advertising, For-Hire Authority to Backhaul, Lower Driver Turnover		**Higher Cost** Transportation Cost Higher Than For-Hire, Empty Backhaul, Lack of Managerial Talent, Added Overhead and Managerial Burden, Capital Requirements, Cargo Damage and Theft Responsibility, Liability for Accidents, Increased Paperwork, Breakdown on the Roads, Labor Union

TABLE 5-4	Private Truck Costs
FIXED COSTS	**OPERATING COSTS**
Depreciation (lease) Trucks, Trailers, Garage, Office	**Labor (drivers)** Wages, Fringe Benefits, FICA (Workers Compensation), Layover Allowances
Interest on Investment Vehicles, Garage, Office, Maintenance Equipment	**Vehicle Operating Costs** Fuel, Oil, Grease, Filters, Tires, Tubes, Maintenance (Labor and Parts), Road Service, Tolls
Management Costs Salaries, Fringe Benefits, Travel and Entertainment, FICA (Workers Compensation)	**Insurance** Liability, Collision and Comprehensive, Cargo
Office and Garage Costs Salaries, Utilities, Rent or Property Cost, Supplies, Communication	**License and Registration Fees Highway User Taxes** Fuel, Ton-Mile, Federal Use Tax

Service and Cost A private truck fleet permits a firm to have greater control and flexibility in its transportation system so it can respond to customer needs, both external (for finished goods) and internal (for raw materials). The increased responsiveness is derived from the direct control that the private carrier has over the dispatching, routing, and delivery schedules of the fleet. Such control means the private carrier can lower transit times to the customer, lower inventory levels, and possibly lower inventory stock-outs.

Because the driver is really an employee of the seller, improved relations may result from private trucking. The driver now has a vested interest in satisfying customer needs and in being courteous. In addition, the private carrier driver would probably exercise greater care in handling freight and would reduce the frequency of freight damage.

Private fleets usually have higher driver retention due to better pay, benefits, and human resource policies. While national truckload carriers often have driver turnover over 100 percent, private fleets on average have 11 percent turnover.[37]

Some firms use the private truck as a moving store, calling on many customers along a route to take orders and to deliver merchandise (a bookmobile, or mobile library, is an example of a moving store). For such merchandising operations, a for-hire carrier does not allow the firm to exercise the necessary control and direction, and private trucking is the only viable alternative.

The last-resort advantage of private trucking emanates from a lack of capable for-hire carrier service. Firms that ship products requiring special equipment (for example, cryogenics [liquid gas] require a pressurized tank trailer) may have difficulty finding for-hire carriers with such special equipment and are virtually forced into private trucking to remain in business.

Capital availability can be a problem for some firms. The money invested in truck, trailers, and maintenance facilities is money that is not available for use in the company's primary business. This capital problem can be mitigated by leasing the equipment.

As a private carrier, the firm bears the risk of loss and damage to its freight. To hedge against possible loss, the private carrier can buy cargo insurance or act as a self-insured carrier (merely absorb all losses). Customers receiving damaged goods will contact the seller (private carrier) for reimbursement, and failure (or delay) of payment is a direct indictment against the seller. When a for-hire carrier is used, the seller can "wash its hands" of the claim because the dispute is between the buyer and the carrier, assuming FOB origin terms of sale (that is, the title of a good is transferred from the seller to the buyer when the good departs the seller's facility).

The risk of public liability resulting from a vehicle accident is incurred by the private fleet. This risk can be mitigated by insurance, but the possibility of excessive court judgments is always present.

The cost of paperwork and maintenance for long-distance, multistate operations is greater than for short-distance or local operations. The clerical costs associated with accounting for mileage driven in various states, gallons of fuel purchased in different states, and vehicle licenses or permits required by different states escalate as the scope of the private carriage operation becomes multistate.

Breakdowns away from the home terminal or garage requiring emergency road service are more expensive than normal maintenance service. The possibility of such emergency service increases as the operating scope increases. Breakdowns also reduce the service levels and have an impact on customer service and eventually sales and profits.

As indicated earlier, there are disadvantages to private trucking, but the fact that there are so many private truck fleets suggests that the advantages can outweigh the disadvantages for many firms. The firm's analysis of costs and benefits of private trucking is critical at the evaluation stage as well as throughout the operation of the fleet.

Current Issues

Safety

Some members of the motor carrier industry have come to realize that improved safety can mean improved profitability. After the regulatory reform that took place in the early 1980s, motor carriers found themselves with more direct control of their economic and operating policies. Deficiencies in safety can translate into decreased profitability because of expensive claims for lost or damaged goods, increased insurance premiums, accidents, fines, and so on. These consequences are not unique to the motor carrier industry; in fact, they apply to the entire transportation industry.

The FMCSA enacted CSA 2010 to provide safety ratings for motor carrier drivers and companies with the intent of analyzing safety violations to prevent them from occurring in the future. This legislation replaced the SafeStat Program. Like its predecessor, SafeStat, CSA makes some important carrier safety information available to the general public, thereby enabling shippers and consignees to judge the safety record of their service providers. See Chapter 3 for a more thorough discussion of CSA 2010.

Many shippers seek safety fitness information as part of their selection process, so there is considerable pressure on carriers to operate safely. Many transportation contracts contain clauses that permit the shipper to cancel the contract if the carrier's safety rating is Unsatisfactory.

A major related concern is that of alcohol and drug abuse. It has been estimated that American industry pays $50 to $100 billion for the effects and results of substance abuse in the workplace every year, for either the cost of accidents or losses in productivity. In response to this problem, the motor carrier industry has begun to move toward drug screening for its employees. Drug and alcohol testing are required in the following circumstances:

- As a requirement for employment
- As a part of a regular physical exam required of current employees
- For cause, required after any accident
- On a random selection basis

Drug and alcohol rules require motor carriers to have an anti-drug program, as well as drug testing that includes random and postaccident testing. All fleets, regardless of size, are required to have a complete program, including random and postaccident testing in place. These rules apply to the owner/operator as well. Many states have drug-testing programs of their own as well with which the carrier must comply.

When proper care is taken to implement a substance abuse program, most drivers support the program because it makes their job safer. Proper care in implementing a substance abuse program involves relating substance abuse to health problems, while leaving moral judgments to the individual. Such care also includes setting consistent policies that are enforceable and apply to every employee, making policies for violations known, and providing counseling and rehabilitation services for those employees who have substance abuse problems. Support for employees with problems is critical for any substance abuse program to be successful.

Other areas of safety concerns are drivers' hours of service and fatigue issues. Before January 3, 2004, the hours of service rules dated from before World War II and did not reflect modern realities. Under a complex formula of allowed driving and required rest periods, a driver can be on duty for no more than 60 hours in 7 days or 70 hours in 8 days. As previously discussed, these rules have been altered to address today's changing environment.

Another safety issue receiving attention deals with vehicle size and weight. As shown earlier, there are a number of different sizes of vehicles, and each has its own weight-carrying regulations. Recent studies have analyzed increasing total gross vehicle weight to 94,000 pounds with the addition of a third axle to the trailer. The studies have also addressed increased use of triples. All these issues include safety concerns and will require federal legislation before any changes can be made. In addition to safety, there are significant economic issues for the motor carrier industry because these larger vehicles will improve productivity and lower cost.

Technology

The use of satellite technology has a major impact on the motor carrier industry. As discussed earlier, global positioning systems (GPS) are being used to track vehicles throughout their movement from origin to destination. The use of satellites allows the carriers to pinpoint the location of the vehicle and relay this information to the customer. The interaction between the driver, using an on-board computer, and a home-base computer allows route or arrival adjustment for poor weather or road conditions, and these adjustments can be communicated to the customers.

One area where satellite communication has had a very positive effect is in the movement of hazardous materials. For example, phosphorous pentasulfide P2S5 a very dangerous chemical if not handled properly, is shipped by Bee Line Trucking for the Monsanto Company, a corporation in the food, medicine, and health industries. The two companies have teamed up to provide safe transportation for this dangerous chemical. The satellites used in the transport allow communication between the driver and a terminal in San Diego, which forwards the information on location and status to both Bee Line and Monsanto. This tracking allows for quick reaction to any accidents or spills, and the computers can give the name of the authority in the area to call in case any emergency action needs to be taken. Satellite communication will continue to play a role in improved safety and customer service for motor carriers into the future.

The use of electronic on-board recorders (EOBRs) is becoming more prevalent today in Class 8 tractors. EOBR is an automatic on-board recording device capable of recording drivers work status information accurately as required by the Hours-of-Service rule. Many EOBRs also measure engine use, road speed, miles driven, idle time, fuel consumption, and a host of other vehicle operating data that allow carriers to be more productive and save fuel. EOBRs replace the traditional log book for drivers and monitor time on duty and off duty. Going forward, EOBRs will be, and are being, replaced with ELD with the FMCSA's ELD mandate publication in December 2015. ELD is essentially the same as EOBR, except that it meets the new technical and user standards required by the 2015 ELD mandate and HOS supporting documents final rule. ELD mandate basically says that carriers (unless exempt otherwise) have until December 2017 to comply with the ELD mandate. Some people use EOBR and ELD interchangeably.

Driver Turnover

As briefly discussed earlier, one of the challenges the trucking industry, especially the TL segment, is facing is the high driver turnover rates. The driver turnover rate of a carrier is the percentage of drivers who quit (exit) the carrier within a specified period of time (typically a year). For example, an annual turnover rate of 50 percent means that half of the drivers will leave within a year, and will eventually be replaced with new drivers. Driver replacement can be costly to carriers, as every time a driver must be replaced (a new driver has to be hired because of a driver exit) carriers will have to perform such tasks as advertising, application processing, background checks, drug screening, physical exam, road testing, orientation and training, repossession of trucks from previous drivers, and tractor cleaning and repositioning, just to name a few. Estimates of driver replacement cost (the cost incurred by a carrier every time it has to replace a driver, which includes the costs of all the tasks mentioned above plus the opportunity costs or lost revenues during the replacement period) ranges from $3,000 to $12,000. The industry (TL segment) average driver turnover rate has been over 100 percent for decades, which means that the TL carriers are collectively paying over $7 billion per year just to replace drivers (there are over 3 million truck drivers in the United States, of which roughly 1.5 million are tractor–trailer drivers).

There are two reasons why we have high driver turnover rates in the trucking industry. The first is the driver shortage. The U.S. trucking industry simply does not have enough drivers to operate vehicles. According to the study conducted by American Trucking Associations (ATA) in 2015,[38] the trucking industry was short 38,000 drivers in 2014 (this means that in 2014 there were 38,000 trucks that did nothing to generate revenue), and this figure is expected to reach 48,000 by the end of 2015. If this trend continues, ATA estimates that the industry will need to hire a total of 890,000 new drivers over the next decade. One of the main reasons why we have a shortage of drivers is the challenging working environment of drivers. Truck driving, especially over-the-road driving, requires drivers to be away from home for up to three weeks. When they leave their home, they typically do not know how long they will be gone, where they are going, and where they are staying, etc. This makes truck driving a difficult job for the people who have family. Other challenging points of truck driving include, but are not limited to, the following: (1) it is a dangerous job (truck driving is considered as having the highest fatality rate among all occupations—this is why insurance premiums are very expensive for drivers), and (2) it receives little respect from people (many drivers complain that they are not treated well by shippers and consignees because of the stereotype of truck drivers—some attorneys say that once the accident happens it is hard to protect drivers because juries view drivers as "bad guys" regardless of the cause of accidents), and (3) it is often difficult to get quality sleep (most drivers sleep in the sleeper berth of their trucks, but it is not the best place to get quality sleep, and the time they are in the sleeper berth may not necessarily be during nighttime (because of the delivery schedule requirements). Such working conditions make it difficult for the industry to retain many drivers.

The second reason is drivers' job-hop behavior; that is, they switch jobs within the same industry very often. Because of driver shortage, motor carriers are always looking for drivers to hire. This means that it is very easy for drivers to find another job (carrier) to work with at any time. If, for example, a driver finds out (perhaps by talking to another driver) that a different carrier is providing better pay, he/she will simply switch to that carrier to take advantage of the better compensation. Carriers are trying to be attractive to many drivers by providing good pay, fringe benefits, and working conditions, but once a particular carrier starts to attract many drivers, other carriers will simply match the conditions so as not to lose any more drivers. This means that increasing wages or fringe benefits may only induce more "game playing" by truck drivers. Motor carriers will need to find a better way to attract and retain drivers than providing good pay and fringe benefits (as this will only give short-term solutions to carriers), in order for the industry to reduce the cost of driver replacement in the long run. It should be noted that job-hopping and driver shortage are two different issues (although they are related). If we can stop drivers from switching jobs within the same industry (prevent job hopping), we still have the driver shortage problem, but we can at least avoid paying billions of dollars in driver replacement costs that are attributable to drivers' job-hopping behaviors.

Green and Sustainable Operations

As discussed earlier, transportation has a major impact on the greenness of our society in the form of energy consumption and carbon dioxide emissions. In particular, truck transportation plays an important role for energy consumption and pollutants emission, because most physical distribution activities involve truck transportation at some point. Trucks are also known to emit the largest amount of pollutants within the freight transportation sector. For these reasons, reducing the environmental cost (externalities) of truck transportation has been the topic of interest for both motor carriers and the general public lately. The trucking industry must work closely with relevant stakeholders, such as shippers, consignees, EPA (Environmental Protection Agency), and the U.S. Department of Transportation, to reduce or minimize the amount of greenhouse gas emissions while sustaining the level of transportation activities currently performed. Since this is an important topic, which deserves a significant amount of space, we provide detailed discussions of this issue in a separate chapter (Chapter 13 "Issues and Challenges in Global Supply Chains").

TRANSPORTATION **TECHNOLOGY**

Truckers Prepare for Era of Driverless Trucks—Coming Sooner Rather than Later

When it comes to the future of autonomous vehicles, there's a lot of work being done behind the scenes involving some of the biggest names in and out of transportation.

Mercedes has its "Future Truck 2025" already on the highways. Apple and Microsoft are working together on a project. Google is continuing to work the kinks out of some technology. Lyft and General Motors are currently combining efforts, while Tesla and its innovative CEO Elon Musk, the peripatetic business magnate, investor, engineer and inventor remains bullish.

So what's happening in trucking? Last October, a unit of Uber called Otto successfully produced a self-driving truck that hauled a load of Budweiser beer without incident on a 120-mile trek through Colorado. Otto's co-founder, Anthony Levandowski, a former self-driving car engineer for Google, said that he believes the most important thing computers will do over the next 10 years is drive cars and trucks for people.

If that does play out, it will have huge human resource ramifications for trucking, which currently has a shortage of 20,000 drivers—a number that could grow to more than 100,000 within a decade due to demographics, increased drug and alcohol testing, and tougher security screenings.

Driverless trucks would change that dynamic in a hurry. "We're going to see a wave and an acceleration in automation, and it will affect job markets," Jerry Kaplan, a Stanford lecturer and the author of *Artificial Intelligence: What Everyone Needs to Know*, recently told the *LA Times*. "Long-haul truck driving is a great example, where there isn't much judgment involved and it's a fairly controlled environment."

Preparing for such a day, the trucking industry is rapidly coming to grips with how driverless trucks may be regulated.

The Trucking Alliance board of directors, which represents eight large trucking companies that operate 68,000 trucks, 175,000 semitrailers and containers and employ more than 52,000 people, unanimously passed a resolution that "supports the development of advanced vehicle technologies that enable commercial drivers to utilize highly automated driving systems, enhancing their safety and security."

The Trucking Alliance also supports the use of these technologies to achieve safety performance levels that rival commercial airlines and support other initiatives that focus on drivers and their safety, including supporting advanced driver-assisted technologies in commercial vehicles.

Transportation Secretary Elaine Chao said recently that she's excited about the new automated technologies that have the potential to "dramatically change commercial transportation" and private travel, expanding access for millions.

"The private sector is driving these innovations, working with cities and states like yours to demonstrate the safety and efficiency of automated cars and trucks," Chao recently told a gathering of state highway officials at the annual meeting of the American State Highway and Transportation Officials.

"Automated technology, which includes autonomous or driverless vehicles, also has the potential to improve safety on our roads and highways, which is always a priority," said Chao. She noted 35,092 people died in traffic crashes in 2015, a 7 percent increase over the previous year. In the first nine months of 2016, fatalities increased again by 8 percent over the previous year. The research shows that 94 percent of crashes are due to human error.

"Automated technology has the potential to help eliminate human error and reduce crashes and fatalities," Chao added. "So there's a lot at stake in getting this technology right."

Source: John D. Schulz, *Logistics Management*, April 2017, p. 17. Reprinted with permission of Peerless Media, LLC.

There is no longer any requirement to file tariffs, and contracts can be used instead. Although carriers are still required to maintain rates, rules, and classifications, they only need be furnished to the shipper upon request. In a departure from previous regulation, rates need not be in writing to be enforceable. Shippers, however, must exercise due caution because federal oversight and enforcement is greatly diminished.

This law also reduced the time for recovery of disputed freight charges from 3 years to 18 months. If either the carrier or the shipper feels that the charges are incorrect, they must file suit no longer than 18 months from the date of the shipment. The lack of tariffs might make this more difficult unless the shippers have obtained the carrier's prices and rules in writing before tendering the shipment to the carrier.

Financial Stability

Another major concern in the motor carrier industry is financial stability. As discussed earlier, the operating ratios of many motor carriers have been in excess of 95 percent, and some companies have operating ratios of over 100. The high operating ratios are a clear indicator of the financial plight of many motor carriers and an indication of the low competitive rates.

Immediately after the initial lessening of economic regulation in 1980, a large number of motor carriers failed as the competitive environment became severe. Of the top 100 motor carriers in 1980, fewer than 10 were still in business in 1990. Only one new LTL was formed in this period that survived to the 1990s. The failures after 1990 were fewer but usually involved larger firms that could not continue to compete. In some cases, the unionized carriers were victims of labor unrest or shipper concerns about stability. In other cases, mergers and buyouts reduced the number of Class I carriers (those with annual operating revenue of $3 billion or more). Recent consolidations have also occurred in the TL sector as the larger carriers have taken over smaller firms to achieve market share. In 2015, a total of 310 motor carrier firms failed, which represents the lowest number in the last two decades, but the number is expected to rise in 2016 and onward.[39]

Overcapacity has periodically been a severe problem for the motor carrier industry, for example during the recession of 2008 and 2009. Given that there is a finite amount of freight to be transported at any one time and there is little, if anything, that carriers can do to influence this, market share changes generally occur at the expense of one carrier over another. These periods of overcapacity also lead to severe pricing pressure, which can cause weaker carriers to exit the market. Shippers often exploit these factors to lower their transportation costs.

Shippers have become increasingly cognizant of the failure rate among motor carriers, and many have introduced a financial evaluation of carriers into their overall decision framework for selecting carriers. When a carrier goes out of business, the interruption of service could have serious consequences.

SUMMARY

- Table 5-5 offers a summary of motor carrier industry characteristics.
- Motor carriers have developed rapidly during the 20th century and now represent one of the most important modes of transportation for freight movement in the 21st century. United States business and most individuals depend in whole or in part upon motor carriers for the movement of goods.
- The public provision (federal, state, and local government units) of highways has played a major role in the development of the motor carrier industry because of the ubiquitous level of accessibility provided by the comprehensive U.S. highway system.

TABLE 5-5	Summary of Motor Carrier Industry Characteristics

- Ease of entry
- Accessibility, speed, reliability, frequency, and lower loss and damage rates
- Low investments/equipment
- 90% variable costs, 10% fixed
- Monopolistic competition/oligopolistic
- Compete on price/service
- Two largest operating-cost components are driver wage and fuel cost
- High-valued products

- The private carrier is a very important part of the motor carrier industry and a viable option to large and small companies requiring special services, such as grocery or food deliveries. The need of U.S. industry for dependable and controlled service has also contributed to the development.

- For-hire motor carriers can be classified in a number of useful ways, including local versus intercity, common versus contract, regulated versus exempt, general versus specialized, and TL versus LTL.

- One of the manifestations of deregulation has been the tremendous growth in the TL segment of the motor carrier business, especially the emergence of a large number of small truckload carriers.

- The LTL segment of the motor carrier industry has experienced increased concentration; that is, the larger carriers have generated a larger share of the total tonnage, as they have aggressively expanded and marketed their services.

- The motor carrier industry plays a major role in the movement of manufactured and food products (that is, higher-valued, time-sensitive traffic) because of its generally higher quality of service compared to other modes of transportation.

- The general service characteristics of motor carriers, including accessibility, speed, reliability, frequency, and lower loss and damage rates, have given motor carriers an advantage over other modes.

- Motor carriers offer a variety of equipment for use by shippers.

- The cost structure of motor carriers is dominated by variable costs largely due to the carriers' ability to utilize a publicly provided right-of-way (highways) where payment is based upon user charges such as fuel taxes and licenses.

- Labor costs are an important element of the motor carrier industry, which tends to be much more labor intensive than other modes. Increased equipment size and more nonunion drivers have lessened, to some extent, the impact of wage costs during the 2000s.

- In contrast to railroads, motor carriers are regarded as having limited economies of scale; that is, small-scale operations are viable and competitive. The major exception would be the LTL carriers with their required investment in terminals. There is increasing evidence that there are some economies of scale among large LTL carriers.

- Public funding of highways and the level of user charges paid by motor carriers continue to be arguable issues because it is frequently maintained that motor carriers do not pay their fair share.

- A number of current issues face motor carriers, including safety, substance abuse, technology, state regulations, and green and sustainable operations.

STUDY QUESTIONS

1. The motor carrier industry is probably the most visible segment of the transportation system in the United States. The motor carrier is also the most significant element of the U.S. freight transport industry. What factors account for the motor carrier's visibility and significance?

2. The railroad industry played a significant role in the development and growth of many cities and geographic regions during the 19th century. What role, if any, have motor carriers played during the 21st century in terms of economic development?

3. Private carriage is more important in the motor carrier segment of our transportation industry than any of the other four major modal segments. What factors have contributed to private carriage becoming so prevalent in the motor carrier area?

4. The so-called local carrier is also almost unique to the motor carrier industry. Why?

5. Compare and contrast the TL segment of the motor carrier industry with the LTL segment in terms of infrastructure, cost structure, market structure, and operating characteristics.

6. What is the nature of intramodal and intermodal competition in the motor carrier industry? How have the motor carriers fared in terms of intermodal competition since 1980?

7. Describe the general service characteristics of motor carriers and explain how these service characteristics have contributed to the growth of the motor carrier industry.

8. The cost structure of the motor carrier industry is affected by its infrastructure (such as highways and terminals). Discuss the cost structure of motor carriers and how it is affected by the infrastructure. Should there be changes made in public policy with respect to the motor carriers' use of public highways?

9. Describe how fuel and labor have impacted motor carrier cost structures and how they have altered motor carrier operations.

10. What are the major issues facing motor carriers in the 21st century? How should these issues be addressed?

NOTES

1. American Trucking Associations, Inc. website. http://www.trucking.org/News_and_Information_Reports_Industry_Data.aspx. Accessed 16 May 2015.

2. Ibid.

3. Federal Motor Carrier Safety Administration, U.S. Department of Transportation website: https://ask.fmcsa.dot.gov/app/answers/detail/a_id/246. Accessed 17 May 2017.

4. Ibid.

5. Anthony D. Apostolides, *Estimation and Analysis of Multifactor Productivity in Truck Transportation: 1987–2003*, Bureau of Transportation Statistics, U.S. Department of Transportation, 2009, p. 3.

6. Ibid.

7. American Trucking Associations, Inc. website. http://www.trucking.org/News_and_Information_Reports_Industry_Data.aspx. Accessed 16 May 2015.

8. Ibid.

9. "Yellow and Roadway Get It Together," *Logistics Management*, August 2003, p. 19.

10. "Blockbuster Deal in Truckload! Knight and Swift to Merge to Create $6 Billion TL Giant," *Logistics Management*, April 2017.

11. Bureau of Transportation Statistics, *2007 Commodity Flow Survey*, Washington, DC, April 2010.

12. There are no notable exceptions to this ability to serve. Shippers located on an island are served by water or air transportation. Other unique examples exist where the motor carrier is physically unable to provide the transportation.

13. Yoshinori Suzuki and Lu Shih-Hao, "Economies of Product Diversity in Collaborative Logistics," *Journal of Business Logistics*, Vol. 38. No. 2, 2017, pp. 115–129.

14. For a complete listing of federal equipment specifications, see the U.S. Department of Transportation, Federal Highway Administration, Bureau of Motor Carrier Safety, *Federal Motor Carrier Safety Regulations*, Washington, DC: U.S. Government Printing Office, 2008.

15. Through police powers contained in the U.S. Constitution, each state has the right to establish regulations to protect the health and welfare of its citizens. Vehicle length and height laws are within these police powers, as are vehicle speed and weight laws.

16. E. Ericsson, H. Larsson, and K. Brundell-Freij, "Optimizing Route Choice for Lowest Fuel Consumption—Potential Effects of a New Driver Support Tool," *Transportation Research Part C*, Vol. 14, No. 6, 2006, pp. 369–383.

17. Joe Gardyasz, "Cost Crunch," *Des Moines Business Record*, 10 December 2007. Available: http://www.businessrecord.com/print.asp?ArticleID=5312&SectionID=4&SubSectionID=7.

18. J. McPhee, A. Paunonen, T. Ramji, and J. H. Bookbinder, "Implementing Off-peak Deliveries in the Greater Toronto Area: Cost, Benefits, Challenges," *Transportation Journal*, Vol. 54, No. 4, 2015, pp. 473–495.

19. Ibid.

20. Ibid.

21. Ibid.

22. Y. Suzuki, "A New Truck-Routing Approach for Reducing Fuel Consumption and Pollutants Emission," *Transportation Research Part D*, Vol. 16, 2011, pp. 74–77.

23. Y. Suzuki, "A Dual-Objective Metaheuristic Approach to Solve Practical Pollution Routing Problem," *International Journal of Production Economics*, Vol. 176, 2016, pp. 143–153.

24. Y. Suzuki, S. H. Lu, and F. Montabon, "DSS of Vehicle Refueling: A New Enhanced Approach with Fuel Weight Considerations," *Decision Support Systems*, Vol. 68, 2014, pp. 15–25.

25. Ibid.

26. Y. Suzuki, "A Generic Model of Motor-Carrier Fuel Optimization," *Naval Research Logistics*, Vol. 55, 2008, pp. 737–746.

27. Ibid.

28. Ibid.

29. J. Rodriguez, M. Kosir, B. Lantz, G. Griffen, and J. Glatt, "The Costs of Truckload Driver Turnover," 2000, Upper Great Plains Transportation Institute, North Dakota State University.

30. Y. Suzuki, "A Decision Support System of Dynamic Vehicle Refueling," *Decision Support Systems*, Vol. 46, 2009, pp. 522–531.

31. Ibid.

32. American Trucking Associations, retrieved from http://www.trucking.org/News_and_Information_Reports_Industry_Data.aspx. Accessed 1 June 2017.

33. Ibid.

34. Ibid.

35. John D. Schulz, "Transportation Best Practices/Trends: Private Fleets Master Their Destiny," *Logistics Management*, April 2013.

36. National Private Truck Council, "Industry Profile," 2014.

37. Deborah Lockridge and Kate Harlow, "Five Ways Private Fleets Keep Drivers Longer," Trucking Info: http://www.truckinginfo.com/channel/drivers/article/story /2014/05/five-ways-private-fleets-keep-drivers-longer.aspx. Accessed 31 July 2017.

38. American Trucking Associations (2015), "Truck Driver Shortage Analysis," available at: http://www.trucking.org/ATA%20Docs/News%20and%20Information/Reports%20Trends%20and%20Statistics/10%206%2015%20ATAs%20Driver%20Shortage%20Report%202015.pdf. Accessed 6 June 2017.

39. *Wall Street Journal* "Trucking Company Failures on the Rise," July 14, 2016. https://www.wsj.com/articles/trucking-company-failures-on-the-rise-1468486801. Accessed 5 June 2017.

CASE 5-1

Hardee Transportation

Hardee is a medium-sized, regional LTL carrier servicing the chemical industry. Because many of the shipments hauled by Hardee are hazardous in nature, its drivers need specialized training and must maintain high safety levels.

Jim O'Brien, Hardee's safety and compliance manager, takes great pride in his company's safety record as well as compliance with all local, state, and federal regulations. Being a relatively small carrier, Hardee has not yet invested in electronic on-board recorders (EOBRs) because the capital investment would put a financial strain on the company. Along with that, the average age of Hardee's drivers is 50 years, and many of these drivers are reluctant to give up their manual log books in favor of EOBRs.

Jim is concerned that if Hardee adopts the new technology, he will lose drivers. Compounding this is the driver's pool to replace these lost drivers and the new safety scoring system implemented by the passage of CSA 2010. Jim fears that even if he can find replacement drivers, their CSA scores will be too low for Hardee's standards as well as government standards for driving hazardous materials.

Although EOBRs and CSA 2010 are separate issues, they are related because both affect Hardee's drivers. Jim knows that Hardee will be required in the future to adopt EOBRs and that CSA 2010 is already in force.

CASE QUESTIONS

1. How would you advise Jim on adopting EOBRs? What would be your tactics to retain the current driver pool using the new technology?
2. If Hardee needs to replace drivers, what advice would you give Jim to make sure the drivers meet minimum CSA 2010 safety ratings and meet hazardous material driving requirements?

CASE 5-2
Cyclone Transportation

Cyclone Transportation is a medium-sized truckload carrier based in Ohio, United States. You are a procurement manager of this company, whose main responsibility is the procurement of diesel fuel for the company's fleet of Class 8 trucks.

You have been assigned to negotiate the fuel contract for the Perrysburg, Ohio market. Your assistant has collected the following per gallon information concerning the major truck stop chains (A, B, and C) around that area. You will use this information to analyze each fuel vendor's proposed contract.

	CHAIN A		
	RETAIL PRICE	RETAIL PRICE	TRUCK STOP COST
DATE	(INCL. STATE TAX)	(NO STATE TAX)	(NO STATE TAX)
10/20/17	2.822	2.568	2.514
10/21/17	2.810	2.557	2.421
10/22/17	2.938	2.674	2.460
10/23/17	2.958	2.692	2.738
10/24/17	2.927	2.664	2.570
	CHAIN B		
	Retail price	Retail price	Truck stop cost
Date	(incl. state tax)	(no state tax)	(no state tax)
10/20/17	2.972	2.705	2.475
10/21/17	2.946	2.681	2.557
10/22/17	2.922	2.659	2.606
10/23/17	2.831	2.576	2.439
10/24/17	2.846	2.590	2.550
	CHAIN C		
	Retail price	Retail price	Truck stop cost
Date	(incl. state tax)	(no state tax)	(no state tax)
10/20/17	2.956	2.690	2.618
10/21/17	2.844	2.588	2.362
10/22/17	2.794	2.543	2.466
10/23/17	2.982	2.714	2.516
10/24/17	2.802	2.550	2.353

Your company purchases approximately 100,000 gallons of diesel fuel each month in the Perrysburg market. Chains A, B, and C have each sent you a contract in hopes of winning your company's business. The contract proposals are listed below.

BIDS					
SUPPLIER	METHOD	RETAIL DISCOUNT	PUMP FEE	TRANSACTION FEE
A	Cost plus		0.02	0.25
B	Retail minus	0.03		0.00
C	Best of	0.02	0.03	0.50

As discussed in this chapter, the price of the cost-plus method is given by the truck stop cost plus pump fee, while that of the retail-minus method is given by the retail price (without state tax) minus retail discount. There is also a transaction fee associated with purchasing fuel from each of the vendors. This is a one-time cost per transaction, meaning that your trucks must pay this cost every time they buy fuel, regardless of the amount of fuel purchased. The average fuel purchase quantity of your drivers (per transaction or per refueling stop) is roughly 100 gallons.

CASE QUESTIONS

1. Given the proposed contracts, what is your company's average cost of fuel per gallon with each of the fuel vendors?
2. Which truck stop chain should you choose if your goal is to minimize fuel cost?
3. Chain B really wants your business and says they will do anything to obtain it. What should their retail discount be in order to obtain your business?

6

RAILROADS

Learning Objectives

After reading this chapter, you should be able to do the following:

> Appreciate the contributions of the railroad industry to the development of the U.S. economy

> Gain an understanding of the size and types of firms in the railroad industry

> Discuss the relevance of intermodal and intramodal competition in the railroad industry

> Know the major types of commodities hauled by the railroads

> Recognize the different types of equipment used in the railroad industry

> Discuss the nature of costs in the railroad industry and how they impact pricing decisions

> Understand the importance of intermodal carloadings on the growth of the railroad industry

> Be aware of the current issues facing the railroad industry today

TRANSPORTATION **PROFILE**

Capturing Inventory In-Transit on Rail

Shippers should be noting that rail is increasingly carrying inventory that's fueling a growing U.S. economy. According to the Association of American Railroads (AAR), intermodal rail traffic in March 2017 jumped 21 percent over February totaling almost 1.3 million units, representing a 4 percent increase over 2016 traffic and a new record in U.S. intermodal volumes.

Further, rail is making an impact on bulk shippers, as carload originations also jumped over 22 percent in March over the previous month and were 7 percent ahead of the same period in 2016. In fact, the railroads have enjoyed five years of steady growth in the carload volumes, according to the AAR.

Indeed, there's a clear need for visibility into inventory in transit as we move to shorter and shorter delivery cycles. However, rail has historically been a separate, less visible supply chain, as we could only trace at the car/container number level. In order to effectively use rail in our in-transit inventory solution, it has to be affordable, capable of being planned, predictable, visible, and flexible.

Affordable seems like a no-brainer for rail because it's so energy efficient and well-established. Unfortunately, competition for portions of the railroads' market is very limited, as consolidations have transpired over the past several decades. In fact, many markets have only one railroad serving them.

We've seen the railroads push price increases with the rationale that those industries that depend on them should share margin with them. This rationale can push shippers to painful profit levels and act as a disincentive to capital investment in rail-dependent plants.

Capable of being planned refers to the ability to generate information that can be made visible through forecasting models. With the ability to collect data at the item level inside the railcar/container and tie that to the demand in real time, shippers and their customers could rely on inventory status while in motion. In turn, this visibility will allow the substitution of virtual inventory—that which is still coming, or fixed safety stocks. This can be modeled in an inexpensive, Cloud-based network optimization tool.

Predictable is critical for in-transit inventory items, as we're literally promising usability at a given time and place for our customers. Can we predict the transit time on rail? Yes, we can. Railcar location messages with a history back to the EDI realm are linked in sophisticated systems that can statistically predict transit times. These are adjusted many times a day as rail freight passes intermediate points.

Visible refers to tracking at the item level. As noted above, with more recent systems we know where the product is on a given trailer or railcar and we can make that product and order information available to our customer through a push-based information service. Bottom line: The infrastructure of rail is in place and the software for making a dashboard for customers is still improving.

Flexibility both on an emergency route-change basis and on a sustainability, replanning basis. Flexibility has not been associated with inventory on rail in the past; however, we're seeing improved methods for tracking and a move to paperless waybills and other documentation is enabling faster response to changes by operations.

It won't be as flexible as highway, but rail is operating vastly better than it was just a decade ago. Thus, shippers can plan alternate solutions should there be a disruption in service.

Shippers can, in fact, make an impact on overall inventory levels by being able to promise delivery and allocate inventory while in motion on rail. It may be past time to integrate on-rail item level inventory into the capable-to-promise equation for customer service.

Source: Peter Moore, *Logistics Management*, June 2017, p. 17. Reprinted with permission of Peerless Media, LLC.

Introduction

The offering of scheduled common carrier freight and passenger service to the public began in the United States in 1830, with the start of operations on 13 miles of road between Baltimore and Ellicott's Mills, Maryland. At the start of the U.S. Civil War in 1861, 30,626 miles of road were in service. By then, rail transportation had proven overwhelmingly superior in both price and service quality to animal-powered road transportation, and superior in service quality to water transportation on lakes, rivers, and canals, and on the ocean between different ports within the United States.

During the first 30 years of its existence, the railroad industry evolved from a population of unconnected carriers focused on short-haul traffic to the completion of longer-distance lines located largely between the Atlantic Seaboard on the east, the Mississippi River on the west, the St. Lawrence River and Great Lakes on the north, and the Potomac and Ohio Rivers on the south. The Civil War slowed but did not stop rail construction during the 1860s. Most notable was the completion in 1869 of the first rail link between the Midwest and the Pacific Coast. Total road mileage reached 52,922 in 1870. That year marked the beginning of the greatest boom in growth of railroad mileage. By 1900, total mileage stood at 196,346, accessing all parts of the country and providing shippers and travelers with a national network of carriers that connected with one another. Movement of traffic between connecting railroads was facilitated by the industry's almost universal adoption of standard track gauge (track gauge is the distance between the inside edge of the running rails of a rail track) of 4 feet 8-1/2 in. (1,435 mm) and adherence to rolling stock design standards that permitted freight and passenger cars owned by one railroad to be run on the lines of another.

By 1900, the economic superiority of rail transportation had supplanted water transportation, on canals in particular but also on rivers, for many products and for almost all passenger traffic. Transportation of freight and passengers in horse-drawn vehicles continued, but only as short-distance feeders of traffic to and from rail terminals and from ocean, lake, and river ports. Rail transportation's cost and service quality advantages made possible the settlement and economic development, both agricultural and industrial, of landlocked areas in all parts of the United States. Many cities and towns were either founded or experienced significant growth because they stood at key points in the rail network.

The post-1870 boom in railroad network expansion was financed largely by private capital. In some locations, particularly in the East and Midwest, this led to overbuilding of the network. Some promoters of rail projects did not have profit from operation of a completed railroad as their objective. Instead, they sought profit from construction of a railroad and/or from its sale after completion to an already-existing parallel railroad that wanted to prevent erosion of its revenue base by rate competition from the new entrant. Much of this overbuilt capacity remained in operation until the 1970s and 1980s, when it was rationalized in the wake of financial failure of its owners.

Rail transportation remained the dominant, largely unchallenged, mode of intercity freight and passenger movement through the first two decades of the 20th century. However, erosion of its dominance began during the 1920s with the beginning of large-scale government-funded construction of hard-surface roads and superior service and/or cost characteristics of motor carriers and automobiles. Additional competition came from a revival of inland water transportation, which was aided by government-financed navigation improvements on rivers and by privately financed construction of oil pipelines. Air transportation emerged as a serious contender for rail passenger and mail traffic during the 1930s. Overall, the railroad industry suffered significant decline in relative importance after 1920. However, its role in freight transportation remains important in the 21st century.

The railroad industry has stabilized in relative importance during the first part of the 21st century. This trend has been well documented and can be attributed in part to the following factors: alternate transport modes with superior services and/or cost characteristics (primarily motor carriers and pipelines); a resurgence in water transportation; and the changing needs of the U.S. economy. In 2013, railroads transported only 9.4 percent of the total intercity tons transported by all modes.[1] It is important to note that, on an actual basis, rail ton-miles have continued to increase, and railroads are still the largest carrier in terms of intercity ton-miles, but not in terms of tonnage or revenues.

Starting in 1984, the railroad industry adopted a new depreciation accounting system, and **return on investment (ROI)** shot up to 5.7 percent. In 2015, ROI again showed an increase to 12.09 percent.[2] Consequently, some rail stocks have become more attractive investments.

The railroads are still vital to our transportation system and play an important role in our economy. For example, in 2016, rail revenues accounted for approximately 8.0 percent of the nation's freight expenditures.[3] Railroads in 2015 employed 169,394 people.[4] Investment is another indication of importance. In 2015, rail investment in new plant and equipment was over $181 billion. In 2015, for example, rail locomotive and freight car acquisition increased over 2014, increasing 2.5 percent and 3.4 percent, respectively.[5] These indicators have been hailed as further evidence of the success of the Staggers Rail Act of 1980.

As mentioned earlier, in 2013, he railroads shipped about 9.4 percent of all tons moved by all transport modes in the United States. This percentage of total tons has decreased since 2007. However, actual tons have, for the most part, been steadily increasing. In 1980, a total of 1,492 billion tons of domestic intercity freight were moved. In 2013, the tons moved were 1,681 billion, representing 9.4 percent of transportation's total 17,950 billion.[6]

These figures highlight the fact that, even though railroads continue to move record amounts of goods, they are capturing less of the total transportation market because other modes have been growing even faster. However, there are indications that railroads may experience a resurgence on a relative basis because of more aggressive marketing and growth in intermodal traffic. Between 2010 and 2015, intermodal traffic increased from a little over 11.2 million loadings to almost 14 million, an increase of 21.5 percent.[7] Intermodal shipments have become more attractive as fuel prices escalate and highway congestion increases.

Industry Overview

Number of Carriers

The U.S. freight railroad industry consisted of 574 different railroads in 2012. Data are not available for the 2013–2015 time period. Of them, seven were designated by the Surface Transportation Board (STB) as Class I companies, meaning that they each generated revenue of $452.7 million or more annually. In 2015, the seven Class I railroads operated over 93,628 miles of road, employed 169,394 individuals, and had a combined operating revenue of $71.7 billion. The balance of 567 non-Class I rail carriers are identified by the AAR as either "regional" or "local" lines. Regional status applies to line-haul railroads operating at least 350 route miles and/or earning annual revenue of at least $20 million but less than the Class I revenue threshold. Local status applies to line-haul railroads below the regional criteria (commonly referred to as short lines) plus railroads that provide only switching and terminal service. Some regional, short line, and switching and terminal railroads are stand-alone companies. Others are subsidiaries of holding companies such as Genesee & Wyoming, Inc. Genesee & Wyoming became one of the largest when it purchased Rail-America in 2012. In 2014, Genesee & Wyoming owned 112 subsidiary railroads operating across 11 regions over track totaling more than 15,000 miles.

Road mileage declined during the same 50-year period (see Table 6-1). Road mileage expanded rapidly during the initial construction period of 1830–1910 and reached a peak of 254,251 miles in 1916.[8] By 1929, road mileage was down to 229,530, and in 2015 it had been reduced to about 93,628 road miles.[9] This reduction is traceable largely to the abandonment of duplicate trackage that was built during the boom periods of the industry's developmental years that was no longer needed because of technology advances, market shifts, the rail merger movement, and intermodal competition.

Competition

The competitive position of the railroad industry has changed dramatically after the first two decades of the 20th century. Today, the industry is faced with intense intermodal competition, particularly from the motor carrier industry, and selective intramodal competition. Consolidations within the industry have created a situation in which only seven Class I railroads generate 94.0 percent of railroad revenue.

The industry's economic structure has developed into a fine example of differentiated oligopoly. In other words, there are a small number of very large railroads, and they serve somewhat different market areas. Their major source of competition is intermodal in nature.

Intramodal Today, only a few railroads serve a particular geographic region. This situation gives rise to an oligopolistic market structure because there are a small number of interdependent large sellers. Barriers to entry exist because of the large capital outlays and fixed costs required, and, consequently, pricing of commodity movements not easily diverted to motor carriers and water carriers can be controlled by the existing railroad firms. For this reason, economic regulations enacted by Congress and administered by the ICC before 1980 brought the geographic coverage and the rate-making procedures of the railroads under federal scrutiny and control.

TABLE 6-1	U.S. Railroad Miles and Trackage (Class I)	
YEAR	**MILES OF ROAD***	**MILES OF TRACK****
2003	99,126	169,069
2004	97,662	167,312
2005	95,830	164,291
2006	94,942	162,056
2007	94,440	161,114
2008	94,209	160,734
2009	94,048	160,781
2010	95,700	161,926
2011	95,514	162,393
2012	95,391	162,306
2013	95,235	161,980
2014	94,372	161,240
2015	93,628	160,692

* This represents the aggregate length of roadway of all line-haul railroads exclusive of yard tracks, sidings, and parallel lines.
** This includes the total miles of railroad track owned by U.S. railroads.
Source: Association of American Railroads, *Railroad Facts 2016*, Washington, DC, p. 47

With the merger trend discussed earlier, the intramodal competition has been reduced. Many cities now have only one railroad serving them. Even major rail centers such as Chicago or Kansas City have seen the number of carriers serving those areas significantly reduced. Shippers are concerned that there will not be enough effective intramodal competition to preserve railroad-to-railroad competition.

Intermodal As noted earlier, the relative market share of railroad intercity ton-miles has been steadily declining because of increased intermodal competition. Inroads into the lucrative commodity markets have been facilitated by governmental expenditures on infrastructure that have benefited competing modes. For example, the government has provided an extensive local and national highway system, especially the interstate network, for motor carrier use.

Customers look for consistent on-time performance. Railroads need to provide this level of service to stay competitive. Railroad companies usually cannot deliver freight early because the customer then has to find a place to store it.

In addition, through improvements and maintenance of the inland waterway system by the U.S. Army Corps of Engineers, the government has also provided the right-of-way for water carriers. Because of the governmental programs and the response of the railroad industry to change, railways in 2013 accounted for 9.7 percent of total revenue freight tons.

Overall, the railroads have been rate-competitive. Government expenditure programs aimed at promoting other modes, together with intermodal competition, forced the railways into making a determined effort to forestall industry decline by becoming more competitive. The Staggers Rail Act, which removed significant economic regulation, has allowed railroads to be much more price-competitive through contract rates and more tailored response to customers' service requirements.

Mergers Historically, many mergers have taken place in the railroad industry, and the size of the remaining carriers has correspondingly increased. Early rail mergers grew out of efforts to expand capacity to benefit from large-volume traffic efficiencies and economies. Later, **side-by-side** combinations were made to strengthen the financial positions of many of the railroads and eliminate duplication. More recently though, **end-to-end mergers** were created to provide more effective intermodal and intramodal competition.[10] Customer service and reliability can be improved by these mergers because the many types of operating costs, such as car switching, clerical costs, and record-keeping, can be reduced. However, such improvements, in some instances, have been slow to develop.

Previously we noted that the number of railroads and the number of miles of track (see Table 6-1) have declined. One of the major reasons for this decline in both the number of companies and the miles of track has been the significant number of mergers or unifications that have occurred in the railroad industry during the past 30 years. A total of 28 mergers have taken place during the past 30 years, and 50 unifications overall. The latter included not only mergers but also consolidations and outright purchases for control. The decade of the 1970s was very active, but the tempo of rail consolidations in the 1980s was hyperactive.

In 1920, there were 186 Class 1 railroads; by 2013, the number had declined to seven. One reason for this drop was the way in which railroads are classified by revenue; as it was adjusted for inflation, fewer roads qualified. The primary reason, however, was the accelerating trend of mergers. After the Staggers Act was passed in 1980, there was a significant increase in mergers and acquisitions so that as of 2014 the seven Class I rail lines are BNSF, Canadian National, Canadian Pacific, CSX Transportation, Kansas City Southern Railway, Norfolk Southern, and the Union Pacific Railroad.

TABLE 6-2	Railroad Intercity Ton-Miles (millions) and Tonnage (thousands)	
YEAR	REVENUE TON-MILES	PERCENT OF TOTAL
2007	1,771	1,940
2008	1,777	1,934
2009	1,532	1,668
2010	1,691	1,851
2011	1,729	1,885
2012	1,713	1,760
2013	1,741	1,758
2014	1,851	1,840
2015	1,745	1,731

Source: Association of American Railroads, *Railroad Facts 2016*, Washington, DC, pp. 30, 31.

Abandonments Recall that in 1916, at its peak, the railroad industry owned 254,037 miles of road. Today, more than half of that is gone, enough to circle the Earth three times. The early overexpansion left extensive amounts of excess trackage in many areas, and the railroads had to abandon significant portions of rail trackage to remain competitive. Parallel and overlapping routes, therefore, have been eliminated wherever possible.

Many factors led to the abandonment of track around the country. In the late 1950s, the government began the construction of the Interstate Highway System. This allowed motor carrier service to decrease transit time, which caused shippers to use these carriers. To effectively compete with motor carriers for time-sensitive traffic, railroads had to focus on efficient routes. In the 1970s and 1980s, bankruptcies forced the abandonment of portions of railroad systems such as the Rock Island, Penn Central, and Milwaukee Road. In 1980, partial deregulation gave rail companies greater freedom to buy, sell, or abandon unprofitable track. Once the railroad companies abandoned the tracks, they sold the rails and ties to scrap dealers.

GLOBAL **PERSPECTIVES**

Florida East Coast Railway to Be Acquired by Grupo Mexico

Florida East Coast Railway (FEC) and GMexico Transportes S.A. de C.V. (GMXT), the transportation unit of Mexico City-based miner Grupo Mexico, announced that they have entered into an agreement in which GMXT will acquire FEC in an all-cash transaction. Various reports said that the sale price was $2.1 billion. GMXT is comprised of 620 miles of rail across 24 states in Mexico, as well as in Texas. It connects with five points on the U.S. border and eight port terminals. FEC provides rail service along the east coast of Florida and is the exclusive provider of rail service to South Florida's ports—Port Miami, Port Everglades, and the Port of Palm Beach. FEC provides service across 351 miles of owned track and with connections to CSX and Norfolk Southern in Jacksonville, FEC is able to serve 70 percent of the U.S. population in one to four days. FEC serves a diverse mix of intermodal, aggregate, auto, chemicals, metals and lumber customers, handling approximately 550,000 loads per year.

Source: *Logistics Management*, May 2017, p. 2. Reprinted with permission of Peerless Media, LLC.

The land used for rights-of-way, abandoned by the railroads, could also be used unless the original deed required the return when the property was no longer being utilized for railroad purposes.

In some cases, all or part of the right-of-way was turned into hiking trails with some bridges left in place. The program, Rail to Trails Conservancy, has been highly successful in adding over 10,000 miles of trails to the country's recreational facilities. In other cases, the land and sometimes even the track was left in place as part of a program known as "rail-banking." The theory behind this is should the line be needed in the future, it would be much easier to restore it. In one case, a major railroad company reopened a major line after it was closed for over 10 years.

Even though the railroad industry reduced its road mileage by more than half, the lines remaining still carried a major share of the existing freight. The abandonments included both rural branches and mainlines made duplicate by mergers of parallel carriers. The ICC, and later the STB, still regulate abandonments, but changes in the law made it much easier for railroad companies to shed unprofitable lines. Not all the lines were scrapped, as discussed above, and regional and short-line operators took over some of this property.

New developments, such as unit trains carrying one commodity like coal or grain from one shipper to one consignee, helped the railroads operate more profitably. As more and more traffic was concentrated on fewer and fewer routes, overhead costs were spread over more businesses. Each time a railroad interchanged a car to another line, there was the chance for delay. As mergers reduced the number of railroads, fewer interchanges were needed.

Operating and Service Characteristics

General Service Characteristics

Commodities Hauled In the 19th century, when the railroads were the primary source of transportation, they moved almost every available type of product or raw material. Today, the railroad system has evolved into a system that primarily transports large quantities of heavyweight, low-value commodities (or bulk products).[11] However, intermodal containers and trailers, carrying high-value finished products, make up a significant portion of many railroads' movements. Motor carriers concentrate on the handling of small-volume, high-value finished goods, whereas water and pipelines carry the larger volumes of the lowest-value types of bulk commodities. The railroads therefore find themselves engaged in intense competition with these other modes for the opportunity to ship many product categories. Although railroads still handle a wide variety of commodities, more than 51 percent of total rail carloadings in 2015 involved the movement of bulk materials. Table 6-3 lists some of the products moved out of a total of 29.4 million carloadings carried by the railroads in 2015. Of the seven commodities shown in the table, only two, motor vehicles and equipment and miscellaneous and mixed shipments (intermodal), are not bulk commodities.

Coal Railroads are the primary haulers of coal, accounting for 36.9 percent of the total tonnage transported in 2015.[12] Table 6-3 indicates that 5.442 million carloadings moved in 2015, down by more than 668,000 from 2014 levels. Coal is an alternative energy source that will probably continue to be an important commodity shipped by the railroads, and this tonnage may increase if there are political challenges in the Middle East that limit the supply of petroleum and related products.

TABLE 6-3	Carloads Originated by Commodity				
COMMODITY GROUP	**CARLOADS (THOUSANDS)**		**CHANGE**		
	2015	**2014**	**CARS**	**PERCENT**	
Miscellaneous Mixed Shipments*	8,142	8,097	45	0.6	
Coal	5,442	6,110	−668	−10.9	
Chemicals and Allied Products	2,232	2,233	−2	−0.1	
Farm Products	1,574	1,604	−30	−1.9	
Motor Vehicles and Equipment	1,250	1,183	67	5.7	
Food and Kindred Products	1,587	1,614	−27	−1.7	
Nonmetallic Minerals	1,521	1,583	−62	−3.9	

* The miscellaneous mixed shipments category (STCC 46) is mostly intermodal traffic.
Source: Association of American Railroads, *Railroad Facts 2016*, Washington, DC, p. 27.

Farm Products When considered together, farm and food products constitute the fourth largest commodity group hauled by railroads. Total movement by rail amounted to about 1.574 million carloads in 2015.[13] The growth in domestic markets and the increase of exports to foreign customers have been steady for many years. For example, the exportation of grain and its related products accounted for more than 50 percent of the total grain market. Because of this growth, distribution patterns might change, but the transportation of farm products will continue to be an important rail commodity movement.

Chemicals Chemicals and allied products, a great number of which are classified as hazardous by the U.S. Department of Transportation (DOT), are transported in specially designed tank cars. A total of 2.232 million carloads of this highly rated traffic traveled by rail in 2015.[14] Railroads can safely transport chemicals in comparison with highway movements, and this safety has been steadily increasing for years. This type of long-haul bulk material is ideally suited for rail movement. Interestingly, motor carriers move more chemicals, and they compete vigorously for this traffic.

Transportation Equipment Transportation equipment carloadings, which are linked to the relative health of the domestic automobile industry, have increased to more than 5.7 percent of total carloadings in 2015, an increase of 67,000 carloads from 2014.

Although the commodities shipped by the railroad industry have changed over the years, with the emphasis placed on the movement of low-value, high-volume bulk materials, the railroads are still a possible mode of transport for many different types of goods, including both high-value merchandise and raw materials alike.

Traffic Shifts As indicated previously, the demand for freight transportation is a derived demand; that is, transportation demand is based upon the demand for products to be moved. Consequently, economic conditions have an impact upon the demand for transportation service. This is especially true for railroads because they primarily move basic raw materials and supplies (such as coal, chemicals, and so on).

There was almost universal agreement that the U.S. economy was recovering during the last three-quarters of 2003. In spite of the economic upturn, standard rail carload shipments during this period did not reflect the economic good news of 2003. However, intermodal movements by rail increased by 6.9 percent during this period. This trend toward intermodal moves could prove to be very beneficial to the railroad industry and allow them to be more competitive with the motor carriers.

Constraints

Railroads are constrained by fixed rights-of-way and therefore provide differing degrees of service completeness. For example, if both the shipper and receiver possess rail sidings, then door-to-door service can be provided. However, if no sidings are available, the movement of goods must be completed by some other mode.

The railroad system, although composed of individual companies, provides a truly nationwide network of service. Each railroad serves a specific geographic region, and freight and equipment are exchanged at interchange points. For example, a shipment between Philadelphia, Pennsylvania, and Portland, Oregon, might be handled by two or three railroads, depending on the route chosen. The through service is unique, but multiple handlings can create rate-division problems and delays in delivery.

Although on-time delivery performance and the frequency of service had deteriorated in the past, improvements have been made in recent years. The current position of the industry has been restored to competitive levels on selected movements (particularly over long distances). Railroads dominate the market for hauling 30,000 pounds or more over distances exceeding 300 miles. The industry hopes to expand its service to certain short-haul markets and selected lanes for manufactured products. Reliability and transit time, along with equipment availability, have improved to make railroads competitive in these markets.

Strengths

The large carrying capacity of rail freight cars and the economies of scale in freight train operations enable the railroads to handle large-volume movements of low-value commodities over long distances. Motor carriers, on the other hand, are constrained by volume and weight to the smaller truckload (TL) and less-than-truckload (LTL) markets. Furthermore, although pipelines compete directly with the railroads, they are restricted largely to the movements of liquid and gas (and then only in one direction).

This kind of carload capacity, along with a variety of car types, permits the railroads to handle almost any type of commodity. For the most part, the industry is not constrained to weight and volume restrictions, and customer service is available throughout the United States. In addition, railroads are able to use a variety of car types to provide a flexible service because the rolling stock consists of boxcars, tankers, gondolas, hoppers, covered hoppers, flatcars, and other special types of cars utilized in North America (see Table 6-4).

Another important service is that the **liability** for loss and damage is usually assumed by the railroads. Railroads, however, have had a comparatively high percentage of goods damaged in transit. In 2015, the total pay-out of freight claims for U.S. and Canadian railroads decreased to $80 million from $97 million in 2014.[15] Such damage occurs because rail freight often goes through a rough trip due to vibrations and shocks from steel wheels riding on steel rails. In addition, the incidence of loss is usually higher than on other modes because of the high degree of multiple handlings. Excessive loss and damage claims have tended to erode shipper confidence in the railroad's ability to provide adequate service.

To regain traffic lost to other modes and gain new traffic share, the railroads have placed an increasing amount of attention on equipment and technology. For example, to decrease damage to freight, improved suspension systems and end-of-car cushioning devices have been applied to freight cars assigned to the movement of shock-sensitive products.

TABLE 6-4	Types and Number of Freight Cars in Service in 2015 (thousands)		
TYPE	**TOTAL**	**TONS OF AGGREGATE CAPACITY**	**AVERAGE CAPACITY (TONS)**
Boxcars	109.2	9,983	91.4
Plain Box	14.1	1,167	82.9
Equipped Box	95.1	8,815	92.7
Covered Hoppers	518.5	56,175	108.3
Flatcars	196.1	20,727	105.7
Refrigerator Cars	13.8	1,141	82.8
Gondolas	224.2	25,047	111.7
Hoppers	139.8	15,597	111.6
Tank Cars	403.7	38,972	96.5
Others	3.8	429	112.3
Total	1,609.1	168,070	104.5

Source: Association of American Railroads, *Railroad Facts 2016*, Washington, DC, p. 54.

Also, the AAR has developed a quality certification program (M-1003) to ensure freight car quality and technical specifications. Finally, equipping cars with instrumentation packages to measure forces that might cause damage reduces the damage potential. One area that has received much attention has been the intermodal area, namely, **trailer-on-flatcar (TOFC)** and **container-on-flatcar (COFC)** service. Of special importance in the COFC market is the use of double-stacks, which significantly improve railroad productivity. The railroads realized the necessity of improving the TOFC and COFC services to compete effectively with motor carriers. The developments include terminal facilities for loading and unloading, as well as changes in the railcars, trailers, and containers. However, the changes have not stopped here. The railroads have invested a significant amount of money recently in improving right-of-way and structures to enhance service by preventing delays.

Microprocessors have found use in the railroad industry, particularly in communications and signaling. Computer chips are also being used in vital safety-related circuits. Fiber optics are used to improve communications, which will in turn improve service and revenues. The railroad industry hopes that these service-related improvements will increase its traffic.

Equipment

The **carload** is the basic unit of measurement of freight handling used by the railroads. A carload can vary in size and capacity depending on the type of car being used. Historically, the number of carloadings has declined since the turn of the century; there was a total of almost 37 million carloads in 1929. In 2015, the total railroad carloads equaled 29.4 million.[16] This decline has occurred primarily because of the introduction of larger cars and the increase in productivity per car type.

The increases in average carrying capacity of railroad freight cars over the past 50 years have been dramatic. In 2015, the average carrying capacity per car stood at 103.2 tons, compared to 46.3 tons in 1929.[17] Most of today's new cars have more than twice the capacity of the typical boxcar used 50 years ago. However, the carrying capacity of a new or rebuilt car could easily exceed 100 tons, and the trend of increasing average capacity will continue in the near future. A car with a 100-ton capacity probably represents the most efficient size with the present support facilities. Today's standard car gross vehicle weight is 263,000 pounds, with efforts being made to increase this to 286,000. However, bridge and track structures must be able to handle these weights.

The railroads own and maintain their own rolling stock. The characteristics of these cars have changed considerably to suit customer requirements; for example, the conventional boxcar had been de-emphasized but has seen resurgence in the past few years. Today's car fleet is highly specialized and is designed to meet the needs of the individual shipper. Following is a list of eight generalized car types:

- Boxcar (plain): Standardized roofed freight car with sliding doors on the side used for general commodities
- Boxcar (equipped): Specially modified boxcar used for specialized merchandise, such as automobile parts
- Hopper car: A freight car with the floor sloping to one or more hinged doors used for discharging bulk materials
- Covered hopper: A hopper car with a roof designed to transport bulk commodities that need protection from the elements
- Flatcar: A freight car with no top or sides used primarily for TOFC service machinery and building materials
- Refrigerator car: A freight car to which refrigeration equipment has been added for controlled temperature
- Gondola: A freight car with no top, a flat bottom, and fixed sides used primarily for hauling bulk commodities
- Tank car: Specialized car used for the transport of liquids and gases

The total number and percentage of freight cars in service in 2015 are shown in Table 6-4 and Figure 6-1. The boxcar has been surpassed in use by the covered hopper car, which is followed closely in number by the tank car. In addition, the largest increase in total new cars was in covered hopper cars. The composition of the railroad fleet has shifted from the accommodation of manufactured commodities to the movement of bulk goods. In 2015, over 90 percent of the total fleet was designed for the transport of bulk and raw materials.

To remain competitive with the other modes of transportation, the railroads have increased their capacity. The average freight train load also has increased; in 2015, more than 3,562 tons per load were carried as compared to 804 tons per load in 1929.[18] This increase in capacity is necessary if more bulk commodities are to be shipped longer distances in the future.

Service Innovations

The railroad cost structure makes it necessary to attract large and regular volumes of traffic to take advantage of scale economies and to operate efficiently. In recent years, rail management has developed or re-emphasized a number of service innovations to increase traffic volume.

The concept of piggyback service was designed by railroad management to increase service levels to intermodal customers. Piggyback traffic, which includes both TOFC and COFC services, accounted for 15.2 percent of total loadings in 1986, occupying a little less than 3 million cars and ranking second behind coal in total rail carloadings. In 2015, almost 14 million trailers and containers were loaded.[19] As can be seen in Table 6-5, intermodal

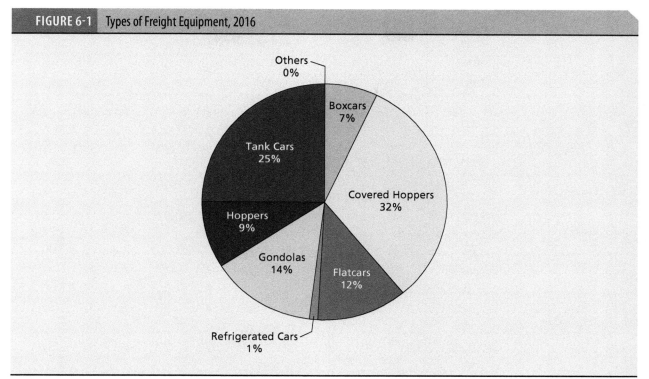

Source: Association of American Railroads, *Railroad Facts 2016*, Washington, DC, p. 54.

carloadings increased until 2000, when there was a modest decline of 2.7 percent. When discussing piggyback service, consideration must be given to the individual concepts of TOFC and COFC movements.

TOFC service transports highway trailers on railroad flatcars. It combines the line-haul efficiencies of the railroads with the flexibility of local motor carrier pickup and delivery service. On-time deliveries, regularly scheduled departures, and fuel efficiency are the major reasons for the present growth and future potential of TOFC service. For example, a 100-car train (which places two trailers on each flatcar) is more economical to run than 200 tractor–trailers over the road. Fuel is saved and railroad economies of scale are realized. Traffic congestion, road damage, and maintenance and repair costs are all reduced because of the reduction of number of tractor-trailers out on the highways.

Table 6-5 shows that the intermodal movement of trailers and containers grew rapidly during the 1980s and 1990s. This growth was stimulated by the advent of double-stack containers used in international trade. In addition, the railroads have placed new emphasis on their intermodal business after a number of years of doubting its profitability. In recent years, the railroads have largely segregated their intermodal traffic from regular freight, with most of the intermodal trains operating on a priority schedule.

One result of the new schedules has been more reliable service for shippers, which has led to increased growth in loadings. The railroads have also simplified their billing procedures and made their computers accessible to customers for service innovations.

The growing use of TOFC by motor carrier companies has also contributed to the recent growth. United Parcel Service (UPS) has been a supporter of rail intermodal service for some time and is the largest single customer of some railroads. The LTL carriers began

TABLE 6-5	Intermodal Carloadings
YEAR	**TRAILER AND CONTAINERS**
1970	2,363,200
1980	3,059,402
1990	6,206,782
2000	9,176,890
2001	8,935,444
2002	9,312,360
2003	9,955,605
2004	10,993,662
2005	11,693,512
2006	12,282,221
2007	12,026,631
2008	11,499,978
2009	9,875,967
2010	11,283,151
2012	12,267,416
2013	12,831,311
2014	13,495,876
2015	13,710,646

Source: Association of American Railroads, *Railroad Facts 2016*, Washington, DC, p. 29.

using intermodal service during the 1980s to handle their surges of traffic, and as rail service has become more reliable, they are using the rail service on a continuing basis. New labor agreements allow union motor carriers to substitute rail for over-the-road up to a certain percent of the total traffic. The biggest change came when two of the largest truckload carriers, Schneider National and J.B. Hunt, purchased equipment to use rail intermodal service on an extensive basis. This commitment by these two large carriers has had a significant influence on the growth of rail intermodal service. Figure 6-2 shows the flows of traffic in the United States.

COFC is the form of transportation for shipping containers and is equivalent to domestic TOFC for trailer movements. A container does not have wheels and must therefore be placed on a flatbed trailer for ramp-to-door delivery. The amount of handling is reduced because the container can be loaded and sealed at the origin and shipped directly to the consignee. Economies are realized because putting finished goods in containers means not only lower packaging and warehousing costs but also faster transit times because time and effort are saved in the loading, unloading, and delivery of goods. In addition, the TOFC piggyback plans can apply to COFC shipments with the substitution of the container for the trailer in the movement. Furthermore, land–bridge traffic, which substitutes railroads for ocean vessels for part of the journey, has become more widely used in international commerce because it facilitates the handling of export–import commodities.[20] The double stacking of the containers on traffic to and from West Coast ports has improved the productivity of the rail COFC service dramatically.

FIGURE 6-2 Intermodal Traffic Flows

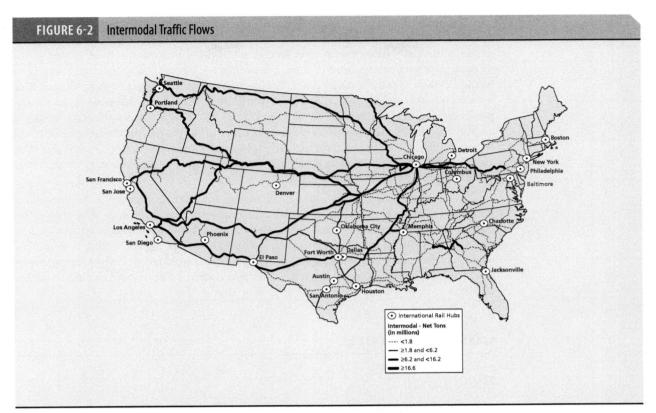

Source: U.S. Department of Transportation, Washington, DC, Federal Railroad Administration, September 2015.
Note: Line thickness corresponds to intermodal volume.

ON THE **LINE**

Schneider and CSX Ink New Rail Service Contract

Truckload carrier Schneider National and Class I railroad carrier CSX reached a new multi-year agreement last month in which CSX will continue to be one of Schneider's main rail providers, continuing to position Schneider's ability to serve the Eastern United States for intermodal services. The relationship between Schneider and CSX goes back to 2008, when CSX became Schneider's primary Eastern rail provider. In 2012, the carriers announced a multiyear agreement for CSX to continue to serve as one of Schneider's primary rail providers. Schneider officials said that because they inked that deal in 2008, they have collaborated to deliver what they call "truck-like" service for shippers. The carriers added that this pairing provides Schneider's customers with "capacity and operational interfaces that are designed to increase accessibility and efficiency of all rail moves," along with "capital investments that CSX has made in projects such as the Northwest Ohio Intermodal Terminal that have improved its infrastructure and facilitated expanded service offerings to the most Eastern origins and destinations."

Source: *Logistics Management*, April 2017, p. 3. Reprinted with permission of Peerless Media, LLC.

The **unit train**, which evolved from the rent-a-train concept for the movement of goods, specializes in the transport of only one commodity, usually coal or grain, from origin to destination. Many times the shipper owns cars, and the train is, in effect, rented to the shipper for a particular period of time. For example, a typical utility coal unit train move would involve the transportation of 10,000 tons of coal in 100 hopper or gondola cars, each with a 100-ton capacity. The movement would be directly from the mine to an electric power-generating station with no stops in transit, and loading and unloading would be accomplished while the train was moving. Because of the single commodity nature of the concept and the need to maintain regularly scheduled movements, empty backhauls occur. However, this drawback is offset by the high revenue-producing capabilities of the unit train resulting from the improved overall car utilization.

Rail management has responded by increasing the use of computers and communications to help improve discipline and maintain control over rail operations. Elaborate information and communication systems have been developed so that a railroad's progress, status, and reliability can be monitored on an online basis. Car ordering and billing is simplified, while cars are traced and located, and orders are expedited at a faster rate. Computers are not a panacea, but they do help bring about increased efficiencies without any loss in service quality.

Cost Structure

Fixed Costs

The railroad industry's cost structure in the short run (a period when both plant and capacity remain constant) consists of a large proportion of indirect fixed costs rather than variable costs.[21] This situation exists because the railroads, along with the pipelines, are the only modes that own and maintain their own network and terminals.

In addition, railroads, like other modes, operate their own rolling stock. In the past, it has been estimated by some managers that up to two-thirds of the industry's cost did not vary with volume.[22] Today, it is believed that this figure is closer to 30 percent. The investment in long-lived assets has had a major impact on the cost characteristics of the industry. Cost structures were presented in Chapter 4.

The major cost element borne by the railroad industry, and not found in the cost structure of other modes (excluding pipelines), is the operation, maintenance, and ownership of rights-of-way. **Rights-of-way** describe what a carrier's equipment uses to provide movement. For example, the railroads operate trains on tracks they own and maintain, while the motor carriers use highways. Initially, a large capital investment is required and annual maintenance costs become a substantial drain on earnings. Capital expenditures in 2015 alone amounted to $17.4 billion. [23]

Another major component of the railroad industry's high fixed costs is the extensive investment in private terminal facilities. These terminal facilities include freight yards, where trains are sorted and assembled, and terminal areas and sidings, where shippers and connecting railroads are serviced. Because of the ownership of fixed assets, the railroads as a group are not as responsive as other modes to the volume of traffic carried. Motor and water carriers, as well as the airline industry, are able to shift resources more quickly in response to changes in customer demand because of their use of "free" rights-of-way. Motor carriers, for instance, pay for their costs through user charges, tolls, and various taxes (such as fuel taxes). These charges are related and vary directly with the volume handled, thereby creating a variable rather than a fixed cost for the user. Circumstances place the railroads at a disadvantage.

The investment for equipment in rail transport, principally for locomotives, various types of rolling stock, and track, has been enormous. In 2015, more than $17.4 billion was spent on these operating necessities.[24] The Class I railroads operated 26,574 locomotives and some 1,609,052 freight cars in 2015.[25] The costs associated with equipment are both fixed and variable depending on which costs are used and what time period is being considered.

It is apparent that the railroads have a high proportion of expenses that are fixed and constant in the short run. However, they also have costs that vary substantially with volume.

Semivariable Costs

Semivariable costs, which include maintenance of rights-of-way, structures, and equipment, have accounted for more than 40 percent of railroad outlays in recent years and have amounted to more than $10 billion per year. These figures, however, are deceptive because some railroads that were in poor financial health in the 1960s and 1970s had allowed their physical plants and equipment to deteriorate at alarming rates. The Federal Railroad Administration estimated that the industry has deferred more than $4 billion in maintenance expenses in some years.[26] Railway management in financially weak railroads found it necessary to forgo maintenance to pay expenses, such as increased fuel and labor. Recently, maintenance schedules have been implemented on a regular basis so that service would not further deteriorate, and additional business would not be lost.

Variable Costs

Variable costs are one of the immediate concerns of railroad management, accounting for a large proportion of every revenue dollar spent by the railways. Labor cost is the largest single element of variable costs for railroads. Fuel and power costs are the next largest group of variable costs. Together these two categories account for a major portion of variable costs.

Labor In 2015, the cost of labor was $17.4 billion or $0.243 cents of every revenue dollar.[27] The average hourly gross earning for all employees was $35.41, with an average annual earnings of $86,321. Train and engine employees received an annual earnings of $87,093, whereas maintenance workers received about $72,269. Together, these groups accounted for 56.8 percent of all the wages paid by the railroads.[28]

Railroad labor is represented by many different unions as opposed to the motor carrier industry, the vast majority of whose unionized employees are members of one union, the Teamsters. There are three major classifications of labor unions: operating, nonoperating craft, and nonoperating industrial. Each represents a different category of employee. The large number of unions has created difficulties for railroad management because each union guards its rights. Recently, some unions have merged and have shown much more flexibility in allowing innovation.

Railroad management believes that some of the work rules for the operating unions are either out of date or inefficient. The railroad industry has been reducing the size of the standard train crew wherever possible. Many positions, such as that of fireman, a carryover from the steam engine era, are no longer needed. Changes in how crews are paid have allowed railroads to gain operating efficiencies. Furthermore, "seniority districts," or the establishment of artificial boundaries beyond which an employee is not authorized to work, is a barrier to operating efficiency. Progress has been made with these issues, but they have not been completely resolved.

The railroad industry has been addressing work rules and staffing requirements in a very aggressive manner in the past several years. Several railroads have negotiated new crew agreements that have reduced the number of personnel required for trains. Conrail started a program in 1981 to buy off unnecessary brakemen and firemen; this program eliminated more than 1,900 positions, yielding a savings of $85 million.[29]

Starting in 1982, rail management took steps to remove cabooses from freight trains. It has been estimated that the elimination of cabooses saved as much as $400 million per year. The rail unions agreed that railroads could drop cabooses by local agreement, if possible, and by arbitration, if necessary.[30] Two-person crews are now the standard, with both riding on the locomotive.

Railroad managers feel that continuing changes in modifying or eliminating work rules for rail employees must be implemented in the near future if the industry is to survive in its present form. Mutual trust and cooperation should replace impediments between labor and management that restrict productivity gains, labor-savings methods, and technological advances. Progress in other industries has indicated the productivity gains that are possible.

Fuel Fuel costs make up the second largest percentage of the revenue dollar. Fortunately, railroads have very efficient propulsion units, and productivity and fuel efficiency have increased dramatically since 1929. In the past 50 years, the railroads have more than doubled the revenue of ton-miles while reducing the locomotive units to less than one-half the 1929 level. Thus, the industry has been able to partially offset the increase in fuel costs by making locomotives more efficient. In 2015, $6.67 billion was spent on fuel, showing a decrease of $4.8 billion from the 2014 level of $11.4 billion. This is a result of using more fuel-efficient engines and other train devices, such as wind-resistance designs.[31] The railroad's efficiency in the use of fuel is an important factor in making intermodal movements more attractive for motor carriers.

Economies of Scale

As previously indicated, railroads have a high level of fixed costs as contrasted with variable costs. Fixed costs, such as property taxes, are incurred regardless of traffic volume. Variable costs, on the other hand, vary or change with the volume of traffic moved; that is, they rise with increases and fall with decreases in traffic levels.

The development of any railroad requires a very large capital investment because of the cost incurred in buying land, laying tracks, building bridges, providing terminals, and providing right-of-way facilities. In addition, equipment investment is significant. Maintenance of right-of-way structures also results in fixed costs because it is usually the weather rather than use that necessitates such expenditures. The same is also true to some extent of equipment maintenance because the equipment spends so much time in freight yards and on sidings.

All costs are generally regarded as being variable in the long run because, as traffic increases, capacity is reached and new investment is needed in plants and equipment. However, because railroads are so large and facilities are durable, the short run can be a long period of time.

The focus here is primarily on the short run. Consequently, special note should be made of the impact of the high level of fixed costs in the railroad industry. When fixed costs are present, a business will operate under conditions of increasing returns until capacity is reached. In other words, an increase in output (traffic) will not be accompanied by a proportionate increase in total costs because only the variable costs will increase. This will mean a decline in the per-unit costs because the fixed costs will be spread out over an increased number of units with subsequent unit-cost declines.

Consider several examples that illustrate the impact of fixed costs and economies of scale. Suppose that C. B. N. Railroad carries 200 million tons of freight at an average charge of $0.035 per ton. It has fixed costs of $3.5 million and variable costs of $2.5 million:

Fixed Costs	$3.5 million
Variable Costs	+ $2.5 million
Total Costs	*$6.0 million*
Revenue	$7.0 million
Profit	$1.0 million
Cost Per Ton	*$0.03*

Assume a 20-percent increase in traffic at the same average charge of $.035 per ton and no need to increase plant size:

Fixed Costs	$3.5 million
Variable Costs	$3.0 million
Total Costs	*$6.5 million*
Revenue	$8.4 million
Profit	$1.9 million
Cost Per Ton	*$0.0271*

It is obvious from the above example that, if average revenue stays the same, the economies of scale not only lower costs per unit but also increase profit.

Financial Plight

As noted previously, the railroad industry once enjoyed a virtual monopoly on the efficient and dependable transportation of passengers and freight. Railroads played a very important role in achieving various national objectives during the 19th century. Because of this, the government promoted the growth of the industry until a distinct change in public attitudes toward railroads became apparent.

The establishment in 1887 of the Interstate Commerce Commission (ICC), which was created to regulate maximum rates and to prevent discrimination to protect the rail shipper, marked the beginning of this change. In later years, the ICC's objective was to promote competition between modes of transportation while ensuring the financial health of the regulated carriers. However, this objective was never completely accomplished. Competition tended to be restrained under the regulatory environment prior to 1975.

Over the decades, competition from other modes of transportation increased dramatically. By the 1950s, more people selected buses and planes for transportation, rather than using rail transportation. The rail industry's share of the intercity freight market also declined to less than 50 percent during this time. Although competition from other modes became progressively more intense, the railroads were subject to strict regulations that frequently treated them as if they were still the dominant form of freight transportation. Government funds were used to provide rail competitors with their rights-of-way without fully charging them the cost of constructing or maintaining them as with the rail industry. Between 1946 and 1975, the federal government spent more than $81 billion on highways, $24 billion on airports and supervision of airways, $10 billion on inland waterways, and only $1.3 billion on railroads.[32]

The financial position of the railroads grew increasingly worse after World War II. During the 1970s, the railroad industry's return on investment remained near 2 percent and never exceeded 3 percent. The railroads were plagued by decreasing market shares, poor future prospects, and high debt ratios. At least 20 percent of the industry was bankrupt by 1970. These poor conditions were evident in delayed or poor maintenance, increasing claims for damages, and accidents that cost the industry many of its much-needed customers. The railroads' share of intercity freight revenues had fallen from 72 percent in 1929 to less than 18 percent in the mid-1970s.[33]

It became obvious that the railroad industry could not continue to survive under these conditions and that the main obstacle that needed to be cleared from the railroads' path to survival was probably excessive regulation that restricted their ability to compete. Poor earnings made it difficult for the railroads to earn or borrow sufficient funds to make improvements in track and rail facilities.[34]

Legislation Reform

The Rail Passenger Act of 1970 created the government-sponsored National Railroad Passenger Corporation (**Amtrak**), which relieved the railroads of their requirement to provide passenger operations that were not profitable but considered necessary for fulfillment of public benefit needs.[35]

The **Regional Rail Reorganization Act of 1973 (3R Act)** attempted to maintain rail freight service in the Northeast by creating the Consolidated Rail Corporation (Conrail), which was formed from six bankrupt northeastern railroads. The act also created the United States Railroad Association (USRA) as the government agency responsible for planning and financing the restructuring. By 1980, the federal government had granted Conrail more than $3.3 billion in federal subsidies to cover its operating expenses.[36]

Conrail proved to be very successful and was "spun off" by the sale of its stock to the investing public in 1987. Conrail's management was able to rationalize the excess track while preserving and improving service. In 1996, CSX and Conrail announced their intention to merge. This raised opposition from the Norfolk Southern (NS). This triggered a bidding war for Conrail stock between CSX and NS. Ultimately, the bidding war was settled by agreement between CSX and NS to split Conrail.

The **Railroad Revitalization and Regulatory Reform Act of 1976 (4R Act)** had two primary purposes. The first was to provide authorization for federal funding for the startup of Conrail. The second was to provide greater commercial freedom to all railroads in the United States by reducing some aspects of economic regulation that had constrained railroads to compete for freight traffic as effectively as they otherwise could have.[37]

The **Staggers Rail Act of 1980** made major reductions in the comprehensive framework of economic regulation of the railroad industry that had evolved over the years since 1887. Among the more significant changes was legalization of contract ratemaking. This enabled rail carriers to attract business with the use of confidential contracts tailored to conditions that were specific to shippers' needs. This gave railroads freedom identical to what had prevailed for many years in the motor carrier and water industries.[38] The freedoms provided by the Staggers Act aided in driving improvement of the railroad industry's financial performance and condition during the decades that have followed its enactment.

TABLE 6-6	Summary: Railroad Industry Characteristics	
• General service characteristics	• In competition with motor carriers; shippers of bulk products	
• Investments/capital outlays	• High investments/equipment, track	
• Cost structure	• High fixed costs, low variable costs	
• Ease of entry	• Low	
• Market structure	• Oligopoly/monopoly	
• Ways in which they compete	• Price (intramodal) and service (intermodal)	
• Types of commodities	• Low-value, high-volume bulk commodities	
• Number of carriers	• Small number of large carriers	
• Markets in which they compete	• High-value chemicals, long-haul but large commodities	

The **ICC Termination Act of 1995** eliminated the ICC and transferred economic rail regulation to the Surface Transportation Board (STB), which is part of the DOT. Some critics contend that the STB has been too lenient in administering the remaining modest controls over railroad rates and services it is empowered to administer. Shippers of some types of commodities contend that railroad competition for the movement of their products is insufficient to prevent them from obtaining rates and service levels that would be attainable if railroad market power were constrained by more regulation by the STB.

Improved Service to Customers

As shown in Table 6-5, intermodal traffic has expanded by 348 percent during the period of 1980–2015, while productivity measures also have shown an increase.[39] An important indicator of improved performance is the railroads' continued good safety record. Train accidents per million train-miles declined by over 77 percent from 1980 to 2015.[40] Consequently, injuries and fatalities also have fallen.

Many signs indicate that deregulation has brought improvement to the railroads (improved financial status) and to their customers. The industry has changed dramatically in many ways, including providing more tailored service and equipment and negotiating contract rates for volume movements. The railroads have worked hard to improve their operating performance times and reliability. Table 6-6 provides a comprehensive summary of railroad characteristics for review.

Current Issues

Alcohol and Drug Abuse

Alcohol and drug abuse has affected almost every workplace in the United States. Many industries, including the rail industry, are taking a close look at the problem and at possible methods of dealing with it.

The problem of substance abuse can be brought on by the very nature of railroad work. Long hours, low supervision, and nights away from home can lead to loneliness and boredom, which can then lead to substance abuse. Because of this situation, the railroads have been dealing with the problem of substance abuse for a century. Rule G, which was established in 1897, prohibits the use of narcotics and alcohol on company property. Rail employees violating this rule could be subject to dismissal; however, the severity of this punishment led to the silence of many rail workers who did not want to jeopardize the jobs of their coworkers.

To deal with this problem, the railroad industry has attempted to identify and help employees with substance abuse problems. The industry has established **employee assistance programs (EAPs)** that enable these troubled employees to be rehabilitated.

Employees can voluntarily refer themselves to EAPs before a supervisor detects the problem and disciplinary actions become necessary. However, a Rule G violation—substance abuse while on the job—usually necessitates removal of the employee from the workplace to ensure his or her safety and the safety of coworkers. Employees who are removed can still use EAPs for rehabilitation and can apply for reinstatement after they have overcome their problem.

Railroad EAPs have proven to be very effective. A recent Federal Railroad Administration report found that the rate of successful rehabilitation has risen by 70 percent. The success of these programs depends largely on support from rail workers as well as all levels of management.[41]

A current issue facing railroads is the numerous states that have legalized the medical and recreational use of marijuana. While tests have been developed to detect alcohol and drug presence in employees' blood, no such reliable test is available today for testing the presence of marijuana in the bloodstream. The transportation industry, as a whole, faces the same issue with vehicle operators. Alternative tests, like functional ability testing, might need to be employed.

Energy

The energy shortages of the 1970s made the United States increasingly aware of the need to conserve natural resources. The U.S. government, for example, decided to reduce the quantity of fuels and petroleum products that are imported into the country. Americans want to preserve and, wherever possible, clean up the environment. The railroads today are in a favorable position, especially when compared to motor carriers, because they are efficient energy consumers. For instance, a train locomotive uses less fuel than a tractor–trailer in pulling the same amount of weight. Revenue ton-miles per gallon of fuel consumed by the railroads increased by almost 101 percent from 1980 to 2015.[42] Table 6-7 shows the relative energy consumption for the various modes of transportation.

A study by the U.S. DOT concluded that railroads are more energy-efficient than motor carriers, even when measured in terms of consumption per ton-mile.[43] In addition to being

TABLE 6-7	Energy Consumed by Mode of Transportation			
	TRILLION BTU*		**PERCENT OF TOTAL BASED ON BTU'S**	
MODE	**2013**	**2014**	**2013**	**2014**
Highway	9,807	10,170	71.3%	72.0%
Air	1,565	1,602	11.4%	11.3%
Water	1,003	974	7.3%	6.9%
Pipe	859	862	6.2%	6.1%
Rail	511	511	3.7%	3.6%

*BTU British thermal units.
Source: Bureau of Transportation Statistics, Washington, DC, 2016, Table 4.6.

more energy-efficient, railroads cause less damage to the environment than do trucks. In 1980, railroad emissions (0.9 grams per net ton-mile) were 75 percent less than truck emissions.[44] Railroads, in comparison to trucks—a major competitor—are able to move large amounts of freight with less energy and less harm to the environment.

The railroads economically shipped 728.4 million tons of energy-yielding products in 2015; 87.6 percent of these loadings were coal movements.[45] Because coal, which can be converted into electricity, is an abundant substitute for oil, electric utility companies can convert their present processes to coal whenever economically possible. Because the railroads already transport approximately three-quarters of all the coal moved, they would be able to increase service to the utilities and capture more of the market using high-volume unit coal trains.

Hence, the railroads can be an important factor in the development of the nation's energy policy.

Technology

To become more efficient and consequently more competitive, the railroad industry is becoming a high-tech industry. Computers are playing a large role in every mode of transportation, and the railroads are no exception. A line of "smart" locomotives is being equipped with onboard computers that can identify mechanical problems, and the legendary red caboose was phased out by a small device weighing 30 pounds that attaches to the last car of the train. This electric device transmits important information to engineers and dispatchers alike, including information about the braking system. Other applications of computer technology are as follows:

- Advanced Train Control Systems (ATCS): A joint venture between the United States and Canada that will use computers to efficiently track the flow of trains through the entire rail system

- Rail yard control: Computer control of freight yards that is used to sort and classify as many as 2,500 railcars a day Communications and signaling: Provides quick and efficient communications between dispatchers, yard workers, field workers, and train crews

- Customer service: By calling a toll-free number, customers can receive information on the status of their shipments, correct billing errors, and plan new service schedules Radio Frequency Identification (RFID): Tags to track equipment and shipments and improve visibility

The role of high technology and computers will continue to expand and increase the ability of the railroads to provide progressively higher levels of customer service.[46]

TRANSPORTATION **TECHNOLOGY**

GAO Report Calls on Congress to Extend Positive Train Control Deadline

With most U.S.-based railroads signaling that they will miss the 2015 deadline for installing Positive Train Control (PTC), the Government Accountability Office (GAO) said in a report that it's asking that Congress consider amending the Railroad Safety Improvement ACT (RSIA) and grant the Federal Railroad Administration (FRA) the authority to extend the deadline for certain rail lines on a case-by-case basis.

The GAO added that Congress should grant provisional certification of PTC systems and approve the use of alternative safety technologies in lieu of PTC to improve safety.

The objective of PTC systems is to prevent train-to-train collisions, overspeed derailments, and incursions into roadway work limits. PTC sends and receives a continuous stream of data transmitted by wireless signals about the location, speed, and direction of trains, according to the FRA.

PTC systems, added the FRA, utilize advanced technologies including digital radio links, global positioning systems, and wayside computer control systems that aid dispatchers and train crews in safely managing train movements.

A mandate for PTC systems was included in House and Senate legislation—H.R. 2095/S. 1889, The Rail Safety and Improvement Act of 2008. The legislation was passed shortly after a September 12, 2008, collision between a freight train and a commuter train in Los Angeles. It calls for passenger and certain hazmat rail lines to take effect by 2015 and authorizes $250 million in Federal grants.

The GAO report echoes the Association of American railroads (AAR) and FRA's statements indicating they will miss the December 31, 2015, implementation deadline, coupled with most railroads saying they will as well.

Of the four major freight railroads cited in the report, GAO said just one—BNSF Railway—expects to meet the deadline, with the other three indicating that they expect to meet it by 2017 or later. The report said BNSF is on schedule to meet the deadline because of its "extensive experience working on PTC prior to RSIA, its iterative build and test approach, and the concurrent development of its PTC dispatching and back office systems."

As per the RSIA requirements, railroads are developing more than 20 major components that are in various stages of development, integrating them and installing them across the rail network, according to GAO. The AAR stated that, by the end of 2012, railroads had invested $2.8 billion on PTC and will ultimately spend $8 billion on it.

"The railroads have done everything possible to make PTC happen as quickly as possible," said Bill Rennicke, director of Oliver Wyman, a management consultancy. "The problem is that it's a hugely complex technology. In the RSIA, Congress required interoperability for all locomotives, meaning that if UP is operating on a CSX line, the traffic information needs to be built into a common technology that feeds that UP locomotive pulling trains across CSX territory with information on that train's characteristics—and that technology does not exist."

Another reason Congress should extend the deadline, said Rennicke, is that PTC is essentially an untested system, noting that PTC systems in Europe were tested for 10 years before going live.

What's more, Rennicke said that the current deadline is so tight that it does not allow for a test period, meaning that 100 percent operation is needed from the start with no system failures, which he described as unlikely.

"The railroad industry and ultimately shippers will have to pay for all of this in the form of hundreds of millions or more if Congress does not come up with a more reasonable schedule," Rennicke added.

Source: Jeff Berman, *Logistics Management* October 2013, pp. 15–16. Reprinted with permission of Peerless Media, LLC.

Future Role of Smaller Railroads

As noted, the deregulation of the railroad industry in 1980 led to a number of important changes. The consolidation among so-called Class I railroads has been noted in this chapter. The obvious outcome was a reduction in the number of carriers in this category, but interestingly, it led to an increase in the number of regional and small rail carriers. These small and regional rail carriers typically took over part of the infrastructure abandoned by the large railroads that spun off parts of their system that had low traffic levels and/or were deemed not to be needed for market success.

The small and regional carriers often have to operate at a cost disadvantage compared to the large rail system carriers who have the advantage economies of scale. However, the smaller rail companies have some advantages given that they are more flexible and adaptable in meeting the needs of their customers (shippers). They are usually not unionized, which also helps to make them more flexible. Another possible advantage is local ownership of the rail companies and the related willingness to accept lower returns and/or pay closer attention to customer needs to promote regional economic development.

It should also be noted that some local and state governments have provided financial assistance, primarily for infrastructure improvements, for the formation of short lines that have come into being in recent years. This community support is usually based upon a need to continue the rail service for the economic benefit of existing and potential new businesses. Although motor carrier transportation has often filled the need of smaller communities for transportation service, rail service may be viewed by some communities as a necessary ingredient for the economic viability of the area. Consequently, many communities have had the advantage of continuing rail service that would not have been possible otherwise.

The large Class I railroads have been frequent targets for criticism about the service they provide to their customers. The smaller lines are usually viewed in a more favorable light because of their responsiveness at the local level. However, the small and regional rail carriers are usually more vulnerable if a large shipper decides to close its operations. The future role of some of those carriers is somewhat uncertain because of these factors.

Customer Service

As suggested in this chapter, the large Class I railroads are perceived by some shippers as not being customer focused. This criticism has grown in intercity transport during the 1990s as mergers continued to occur. The new, larger companies appeared insensitive to shipper needs and concerns about equipment and service. Some of the service and equipment issues are attributable to the challenges inherent in combining relatively large organizations with unique systems and procedures, and problems always occur in spite of serious up-front planning.

The extent to which those equipment and service problems have persisted during the last several years is indicative of the legitimacy of shipper complaints. There are differences among the "majors" or Class I railroads in terms of their customer service focus, but unfortunately some shippers are inclined to lump them altogether as being unsatisfactory. Consequently, this is a major issue for railroads, and improvements need to be made to increase rail market shares of freight traffic.

Drayage for Intermodal Service

As indicated previously in this chapter, one of the constraints on rail service is the fixed nature of the rail routes and the high cost of adding rail segments to provide direct service. Consequently, the beginning and/or the end of a rail movement may depend upon motor carrier service. This is, obviously, especially true for intermodal service using trailers or containers. The pickup and delivery of trailers and containers in conjunction with a line-haul rail movement is usually referred to as *local drayage*.

When the railroads are carrying the trailers or containers of a motor carrier as a substitute for the motor carrier providing the line-haul service, local drayage is not an issue because the motor carrier will provide these links. However, when the railroad is the land carrier, it will have to arrange for local drayage for pickup and delivery. Motor carriers that are willing and able to provide this service for the railroads are becoming scarce and charging relatively high rates for the service. In some instances, the pickup and delivery time adds significantly to the total transit time. This is another area that needs attention to improve rail service.

SUMMARY

- The railroads played a significant role in the economic and social development of the United States for about 100 years (1850–1950) and continue to be the leading mode of transportation in terms of intercity ton-miles, but they no longer dominate the freight market.
- The railroad segment of the transportation industry is led by a decreasing number of large Class I carriers, but the number of small Class III carriers has been increasing in number since the deregulation of railroads in 1980.
- Intermodal competition for railroads has increased dramatically since World War II, but the level of intramodal competition has decreased as the number of Class I railroads has decreased. The increased intermodal competition has led to more rate competition.
- Mergers have been occurring among railroads for many years, but the pace has accelerated during the past 30 years, leading to rapid decrease in the number of Class I railroads.
- In recent years, the railroads have become more specialized in terms of the traffic they carry, with the emphasis being on low-value, high-density bulk products; however, there is some evidence of a resurgence of selected manufactured products such as transportation equipment.
- In recent years, railroads have been emphasizing new technologies and specialized equipment to improve their service performance and satisfy customers.
- Intermodal service (TOFC/COFC) has received renewed interest since 1980, and there has been a dramatic growth in the movement of such traffic by railroads.
- Long-distance truckload carriers and other motor carrier companies such as UPS have also begun to use rail intermodal service.
- The railroads have a high proportion of fixed costs because they provide their own right-of-way and terminal facilities. Because the large railroads are multistate operators, the amount of fixed expenditures is significant.
- The cost of labor is the single most important component of variable costs for railroads, but the railroad industry has been striving to reduce labor costs on a relative basis by eliminating work rules that were a carryover from another era.
- The high level of fixed costs helps give rise to economies of scale in the railroad industry, which can have a dramatic impact upon profits when the volume of traffic increases.
- The financial plight of the railroads has improved since deregulation in 1980 as railroads have been able to respond more quickly and aggressively to market pressures from other modes, particularly motor carriers.
- A number of important issues are facing railroads at present, including substance abuse, energy, technology, small railroads, and local drayage.

STUDY QUESTIONS

1. Railroads no longer dominate the freight transportation market, but they still lead the market in terms of freight ton-miles. What factors contribute to their leadership in this area? Why is their share of the total expenditures for freight movement so small if they lead in freight ton-miles?

2. Since the passage of the Staggers Rail Act of 1980, there has been an increase in the number of small railroads (Class III). Why has this number increased while the number of Class I railroads has decreased?

3. Explain the difference between intramodal and intermodal competition in the railroad industry. Which form of competition is most beneficial to shippers? Why?

4. One of the significant factors in rail development has been the number of mergers that have occurred, but there have been different types of mergers that have occurred over time. Discuss the major types of mergers and explain why they occurred. Will mergers continue to occur in the rail industry? Why or why not?

5. What factors have contributed to the decline in the volume of higher-value freight by the railroads? What changes, if any, could the railroads make to attract more higher-value freight from motor carriers?

6. Railroads have abandoned a significant number of miles of track (over 260,000 miles) since 1916. Why has this trend developed? Will it continue into the future? Why or why not?

7. The railroad industry has developed a number of new types of equipment to replace the standard boxcar. What is the rationale supporting the diversification of equipment?

8. The railroad industry's cost structure is different than that of the motor carrier industry. What factors contribute to this difference? What impact do these differences have for the railroads in terms of pricing, competitiveness, and investment?

9. Discuss the major current issues facing the railroad industry. Select one of these major issues and present appropriate recommendations for resolving the issue.

10. What factors have contributed to the success of intermodal rail service? What barriers exist to future expansion?

NOTES

1. *Bureau of Transportation Statistics*, Table 2.1, Washington, DC, 2017.

2. Association of American Railroads, *Railroad Facts*, Washington, DC, 2017, p. 19.

3. *28th Annual State of Logistics Report*, Council of Supply Chain Management Professionals, 2017, p. 2.

4. Association of American Railroads, *Railroad Facts*, p. 59.

5. Ibid., p. 9.

6. *Bureau of Transportation Statistics*, Table 2.1, Washington, DC, 2017.

7. Association of American Railroads, *Railroad Facts 2016*, p. 29.

8. U.S. Department of Commerce, Bureau of the Census, *Historical Statistics of the United States: Colonial Times to 1975*, Washington, DC: U.S. Government Printing Office, 1960, p. 429.

9. Association of American Railroads, *Railroad Facts 2016*, p. 47.

10. Task Force on Railroad Productivity, *Improving Railroad Productivity*, p. 161. Presented to the National Commission of Productivity, November 1973.

11. The commodity groups included here are metals and metal products; food and kindred products; stone, clay, and glass products; and grainmill products.

12. Association of American Railroads, *Railroad Facts 2016*, p. 32.

13. Ibid., p. 27.

14. Ibid., p. 27.

15. Ibid., p. 64.

16. Ibid., p. 26.

17. Ibid., p. 55.

18. Ibid., p. 40.

19. Ibid., p. 29.

20. Association of American Railroads, Press Release, Washington, DC, 1979, p. 342.

21. Fixed costs remain the same over a period of time or a range of output (such as labor costs). Semi-variable costs contain some fixed variable elements (such as setup costs on a production line).

22. R. J. Sampson and M. I. Farris, *Domestic Transportation: Practice, Theory, and Policy*, 4th ed., Boston: Houghton Mifflin, 1979, p. 59.

23. Association of American Railroads, *Railroad Facts 2016*, Washington, DC, p. 46.

24. Ibid., p. 9.

25. Ibid., pp. 49, 51.

26. U.S. Department of Transportation, *A Prospectus for Change in the Freight Railroad Industry*, Washington, DC: U.S. Government Printing Office, 1978, p. 65.

27. Association of American Railroads, *Railroad Facts 2016*, Washington, DC, p. 11.

28. Ibid., pp. 58, 59.

29. Frank Wilner, *Railroads and the Marketplace*, Washington, DC: Association of American Railroads, 1988, p. 7.

30. Ibid., p. 2.

31. Association of American Railroads, *Railroad Facts 2016*, Washington, DC, p. 63.

32. Wilner, *Railroads and the Marketplace*, p. 7.

33. Ibid., p. 9.

34. Ibid., pp. 8–12.

35. Ibid., p. 2.

36. Consolidated Rail Corporation, *Summary of Business Plan*, Philadelphia: Consolidated Rail Corporation, 1979, p. 5.

37. Wilner, *Railroads and the Marketplace*, p. 15.

38. Ibid.

39. Association of American Railroads, *Railroad Facts 2016*, Washington, DC, p. 29.

40. Ibid., p. 66.

41. Association of American Railroads, *What Are the Railroads Doing About Drug Abuse?* Washington, DC, 1986, pp. 1–4.

42. Association of American Railroads, *Railroad Facts 2016*, Washington, DC, p. 43.

43. Wilner, *Railroads and the Marketplace*, p. 15.

44. Ibid.

45. Association of American Railroads, *Railroad Facts 2016*, p. 32.

46. Association of American Railroads, *High Technology Rides the Rails*, Washington, DC, 1988, pp. 1–3.

CASE 6-1

CBN Railway Company

CEO John Spychalski is concerned about a problem that has existed at CBN railroad for almost 20 years now. The continuous problem has been that the locomotives used by the company are not very reliable. Even with prior decisions to resolve the problem, there still has not been a change in the reliability of these locomotives. Between 2015 and 2016, 155 new locomotives were purchased and one of CBN's repair shops was renovated. The renovated shop has been very inefficient. Spychalski estimated that the shop would complete 300 overhauls on a yearly basis, but instead it has only managed to complete an average of 160 overhauls per year.

The company has also been doing a poor job servicing customers (that is, providing equipment). CBN has averaged only 87–88 percent equipment availability, compared to other railroads with availability figures greater than 90 percent. Increased business in the rail industry has been a reason for trying to reduce the time used for repairing the locomotives. CBN's mean time between failure rate is low—45 days—compared to other railroads whose mean time between failure rates is higher than 75 days. This factor, Spychalski feels, has contributed to CBN's poor service record.

CBN is considering a new approach to the equipment problem: Spychalski is examining the possibility of leasing 135 locomotives from several sources. The leases would run between 90 days to 5 years. In addition, the equipment sources would maintain the repairs on 469 locomotives currently in CBN's fleet, but CBN's employees would do the actual labor on the locomotives. The lease arrangements, known as "power-by-the-mile" arrangements, call for the manufacturers doing the repair work to charge only for maintenance on the actual number of miles that a particular unit operates. The company expects the agreements to last an average of 15 years. John Thomchick, the executive vice president, estimates that CBN would save about $5 million annually because the company will not have to pay for certain parts and materials. Problems with the locomotives exist throughout CBN's whole system, and delays to customers have been known to last up to five days. Spychalski and Thomchick feel that the leasing arrangement will solve CBN's problems.

CASE QUESTIONS

1. What are potential advantages and disadvantages of entering into these "power-by-the-mile" arrangements?

2. What should be done if the problem with the locomotives continues even with the agreements?

3. Do you think that the decision to lease the locomotives was the best decision for CBN? Explain your answer.

CASE 6-2
Rail Versus Pipeline Investment

The last several years has seen a tremendous growth in rail shipments into and out of North Dakota and southern Canada. These shipments were oil outbound and water, sand, and other operating materials inbound. This growth was caused by OPEC's decision to hold steady their oil production volumes, which made U.S. fracking and oil well development in those two areas very profitable. This growth in rail shipments was also caused by the lack of oil and gas pipeline capacity outbound from those two areas to U.S. processing plants. In fact, the growth in volume was so high that the railroads serving those areas ran out of both car and track capacity.

With volumes increasing at a steady rate, the obvious solution would be for the railroads to build more track and acquire more operating equipment. However, investments in equipment and track are long-term, with equipment and track lasting decades with proper care. As such, these types of investments require a steady volume over their life.

The railroads serving these areas were faced with a difficult decision. To adequately meet demand would require billions of dollars of capital investment but, short term, could produce billions of dollars in additional revenue. However, the railroads were cautious of OPEC's influence on the price of oil. OPEC had announced that its members would be increasing the production of crude, thus driving down the world price. With the small oil and gas operators in North Dakota and Southern Canada having a much higher marginal operating cost than the OPEC countries, a declining world price for crude could force many of them to leave the industry. The negative impact of these exits could be substantial for the railroads.

CASE QUESTIONS

1. If you were president of one of these railroads, what decision would you make? Maintain current capacity and forgo additional revenue? Make the investment in additional capacity with the assumption that volume will continue to increase? Explain your answer.

2. Could there be a shorter term solution for the railroads other than acquiring more equipment and building more track that would allow them to generate revenue without making significant investments?

CHAPTER

7

AIRLINES

Learning Objectives

After reading this chapter, you should be able to do the following:

> Appreciate the importance of air transportation in the U.S. economy

> Gain knowledge of the types and number of carriers in the U.S. airline industry

> Understand the level of competition in the U.S. airline industry

> Become aware of the operating and service characteristics of airline transportation

> Be familiar with the different types of equipment used by airlines

> Appreciate the impacts of fuel and labor costs on airlines cost structures

> Understand the concepts of economies of scale and density in the airline industry

> Be aware of current issues facing airlines today

TRANSPORTATION **PROFILE**

Air: Ending on a High Note

Chuck Clowdis, managing director of transportation advisory services for HIS Global Insight, notes that air cargo activity at the end of last year exceeded all expectations—but not without raising some serious questions.

"We really don't know if we should expect to see a continuation of this growth in 2017, or if rates will accelerate despite capacity and fuel economy advances," says Clowdis.

Another question to consider is the promised investment in domestic airport improvement funding. With better infrastructure, adds Clowdis, service carriers may be more comfortable with their rate demands.

"And there's been talk of certain goods shifting manufacturing and assembly to the U.S. from overseas," says Clowdis. "Will this have a positive or negative impact on air cargo rates and volumes? It's too hard to predict at this stage."

Analysts at the International Air Transport Association (IATA) are not being as cautious in their outlook, predicting that the global airline industry will make a net profit in 2017 of $29.8 billion when cargo numbers are factored in. On forecast of total revenues of $736 billion, that represents a 4.1 percent net profit margin. This will be the third consecutive year—and the third year in the industry's history—in which airlines will make a return on invested capital (7.9 percent), which is above the weighted average cost of capital (6.9 percent).

IATA revised slightly downward its outlook for 2016 airline industry profitability to $35.6 billion (from the June projection of $39.4 billion) owing to slower global GDP growth and rising costs. This will be the highest absolute profit generated by the airline industry and the highest net profit margin (5.1 percent).

"Airlines continue to deliver strong results," says Alexandre de Juniac, IATA's director general and CEO. "This year we expect a record net profit of $35.6 billion, largely due to new cargo orders. Even though conditions in 2017 will be more difficult with rising oil prices, we see the industry earning 29.8 billion."

Source: Adapted from Patrick Burnson, "2017 Rate Outlook: Will the Pieces Fall Into Place," *Logistics Management*, January 2017, pp. 31–32. Reprinted with permission of Peerless Media, LLC.

Introduction

From the first flight, which lasted less than 1 minute, to space shuttles orbiting the earth, air transportation has come a long way in a short period of time. Wilbur and Orville Wright made their first flight in 1903 at Kitty Hawk and sold their invention to the federal government. In 1908 the development of air transportation began with the **U.S. Post Office** examining the feasibility of providing airmail service. Although airplanes were used in World War I, the use of airplanes for mail transport can be considered the beginning of the modern airline industry. Passenger transportation services developed as a by-product of the mail business and began to flourish in selected markets. Since that time, airplanes have become faster, bigger, and relatively more fuel-efficient. Although the level and degree of technological improvement have slowed in the airline industry, there is still opportunity for further innovation.

Airline travel is a common form of transportation for long-distance passenger and freight travel and the only reasonable alternative when time is of the essence. The tremendous speed of the airplane, coupled with more competitive pricing, has led to the growth of air transportation, particularly in the movement of passengers.

Industry Overview and Significance

In 2013 for-hire air carriers had total operating revenues of $199.7 billion, of which $120.6 billion (60.4 percent) came from passenger fares.[1] Between June 2013 and May 2014, air carriers transported 93.1 billion revenue ton-miles.[2] Employment in the air carrier industry totaled 589,151 people in June 2014.[3]

The airline industry is very dependent on **passenger revenues** to maintain its financial viability. However, to characterize airlines simply as movers of people presents too simplistic a view of their role in our transportation system. The airlines are a unique and important group of carriers that meet some particular needs in our society. Although their share of the freight movement on a ton-mile basis is small, the type of traffic that they carry (high-value, perishable, or emergency) makes them an important part of our total transportation system. Emphasis upon total logistics cost in a quick-response lead-time environment will continue to contribute to their growth in freight movements.

Types of Carriers

Private Carriers

Air carriers can be segmented into for-hire carriers and private carriers. A **private air carrier** is a firm that transports company personnel or freight in planes to support its primary business. The preponderance of private air transportation is used to transport company personnel, although emergency freight is sometimes carried on private airplanes as well. Rarely, however, is a private air carrier established to routinely carry freight. The private air carrier is subject to the federal safety regulations administered by the Federal Aviation Administration (FAA) of the U.S. Department of Transportation.

For-Hire Carriers

The for-hire carriers are no longer regulated on an economic basis by the federal government and cannot be easily categorized into specific types because carriers provide many types of services. For our purposes, the for-hire carriers will be discussed according to type of service offered (all-cargo, air taxi, commuter, charter, and international) and annual revenue (majors, nationals, and regionals).

A classification frequently used by U.S. air carriers is one based on annual operating revenues. The categories used to classify air carriers in terms of revenue are as follows:

Majors—annual revenues of more than $1 billion

Nationals—annual revenues of $100 million to $1 billion

Regionals—annual revenues of less than $100 million

U.S. **major carriers** have $1 billion or more in annual revenues and provide service between major population areas within the United States such as New York, Chicago, and Los Angeles. The routes served by these carriers are usually high-density corridors, and the carriers use high-capacity planes. The U.S. majors also serve medium-sized population centers such as Harrisburg, Pennsylvania. Examples of major U.S. carriers are American/US Airways, United/Continental, Delta/Northwest, and Southwest.

U.S. **national carriers** have revenues of $100 million to $1 billion and operate between less-populated areas and major population centers. These carriers operate scheduled service over relatively short routes with smaller planes. They "feed" passengers from outlying areas into airports served by the U.S. majors. Today, many of the U.S. national carriers operate over relatively large regional areas and are stiff competition for the U.S. majors on many routes. Examples of U.S. nationals include Frontier Airlines, JetBlue, and Midwest Express.

Regional carriers have annual revenues of less than $100 million and have operations similar to the nationals. The carriers operate within a particular region of the country, such as New England or the Midwest, and connect less-populated areas with larger population centers. Included in the regional category are carriers such as American Eagle Airlines, Atlantic Coast Airlines, and SkyWest Airlines.

The **all-cargo carrier**, as the name implies, primarily transports cargo. The transportation of air cargo was deregulated in 1977, permitting the all-cargo carriers to freely set rates, enter and exit markets, and use any size aircraft dictated by the market. Examples of all-cargo carriers include FedEx and UPS Airlines.

Commuter air carriers are technically regional carriers. The commuter publishes time-tables on specific routes that connect less-populated routes with major cities. As certified carriers abandon routes, usually low-density routes, the commuter enters into a working relationship with the certified carrier to continue service to the community. The commuter then connects small communities that have reduced or no air service with larger communities that have better scheduled service. The commuter's schedule is closely aligned with connecting flight schedules at a larger airport. Many commuter firms use turboprop aircraft to feed the major hubs of the major airlines. Today, however, some commuters are adding regional jets that not only continue to feed these hubs but also offer direct service to larger metropolitan areas. Many commuter operators are franchised by the majors, such as U.S. Airways Express.

The **charter carriers**, also known as air taxis, use small- to medium-size aircraft to transport people or freight. The supplemental carrier has no time schedule or designated route. The carrier charters the entire plane to transport a group of people or cargo between specified origins and destinations. Many travel tour groups use charter carriers. However, a big customer for charters is the Department of Defense; it uses charter carriers to transport personnel and supplies. For example, Operation Iraqi Freedom (OIF) relied upon charters for some of their moves of personnel and supplies. The rates charged and schedules followed are negotiated in the contract.

Many U.S. carriers are also international carriers and operate between the continental United States and foreign countries, and between the United States and its territories (such as Puerto Rico). Because service to other countries has an effect on U.S. international trade and relations, the president of the United States is involved in awarding the international routes. Examples of international carriers include United and American. Many foreign carriers, such as British Air and Air France, provide services between the United States and their country.

Market Structure

Number of Carriers

A small number of major airlines account for a majority of passenger and freight activity in the United States. Table 7-1 shows that the top 10 carriers account for approximately 96 percent of total operating revenue and approximately 96 percent of revenue passenger miles in 2016.

Private air transportation has been estimated to include approximately 60,000 company-owned planes, with over 500 U.S. corporations operating private air fleets. In addition, thousands of planes are used for personal, recreational, and instructional purposes.

TABLE 7-1	Top 10 Airlines by Various Rankings—2016		
PASSENGERS (MILLIONS)		**REVENUE PASSENGER MILES (MILLIONS)**	
1. **Southwest**	151,740	1. **American**	198,832
2. **American**	144,190	2. Delta	189,707
3. Delta	142,286	3. **United**	185,187
4. **United**	99,770	4. **Southwest**	124,801
5. **JetBlue**	38,241	5. **JetBlue**	45,627
6. SkyWest	31,205	6. **Alaska**	32,804
7. **Alaska**	24,370	7. Spirit Airlines	21,582
8. Expressjet	22,184	8. SkyWest	17,548
9. Spirit Airlines	20,998	9. Frontier	15,876
10. Frontier Airlines	14,773	10. **Hawaiian Air**	15,465

Bolded airlines = Airlines for America members.

FREIGHT TON-MILES (MILLIONS)		**TOTAL OPERATING REVENUES ($MILLIONS)**	
1. **FedEx**	10,791	1. **UPS**	60,906
2. **UPS**	7,741	2. **FedEx**	50,365
3. **Atlas**	3,516	3. **American**	40,422
4. **United**	2,805	4. Delta	39,850
5. Polar Air Cargo	2,680	5. **United**	36,556
6. **American**	2,430	6. **Southwest**	20,425
7. Delta	1,980	7. **JetBlue**	6,632
8. Kalitta Air	1,557	8. **Alaska**	5,828
9. Southern Air	1,058	9. **Hawaiian Air**	2,442
10. ABX	674	10. Spirit Airlines	2,322

Source: *Bureau of Transportation Statistics 2016.*

Deregulation in 1978 was expected to result in a larger number of airlines competing for passengers and freight traffic. The number of major airlines did increase initially, but the number of airlines has remained steady over the last several years with several consolidations taking place. Available seat miles for 2013 increased by 1.7 percent from 2012 as some carriers are increasing the size of their aircraft.[4] The number of flights decreased from 9.3 million in 2012 to 9.1 million in 2013. However, the percent of on-time departures decreased to 79.19 percent in 2013 from 82.4 percent in 2012.[5]

Competition

Intermodal

Due to their unique service, air carriers face **limited competition** from other modes for both passengers and freight. Air carriers have an advantage in providing time-sensitive, long-distance movement of people or freight. Airlines compete to some extent with motor carriers for the movement of higher-valued manufactured goods; they face competition from automobiles for the movement of passengers and, to a limited extent, from trains and buses. For short distances (under 800 miles), the access time and terminal time offsets the speed of the airline for the line-haul.

Intramodal

Competition in rates and service among the air carriers is very intense, even though the number of carriers is small. As noted, passenger air carrier regulation was significantly reduced in 1978, and new carriers entered selected routes (markets), thereby increasing the amount of competition (see Chapter 4 for a discussion of the Theory of Contestable Markets). Also, existing carriers expanded their market coverage, which significantly increased intramodal competition in certain markets. Carriers may also have **excess capacity** (too many flights and seat miles on a route) and attempt to attract passengers by selectively lowering fares to fill the empty seats. Between the fourth quarter of 2015 and the fourth quarter of 2016, average passenger airfares decreased from $369 to $347.[6]

New entrants to the airline market initially caused overcapacity to exist on many routes. To counter this and add passengers to their aircraft, carriers reduced prices and fare wars began. This caused financially weaker carriers to exit the market. This was especially true of carriers with high operating costs (many times due to high-cost union labor contracts), high cost of debt, or high levels of fixed costs. (Many of these maintained high fixed investments in hub-and-spoke terminal operations.) The remaining carriers began to enjoy economies of density (discussed later in this chapter), and the cost per passenger mile decreased and margins increased, even in the existence of relatively low fares. So, even with the discounted prices in today's airline market, many carriers have been able to remain profitable.

Service Competition

Competition in airline service takes many forms, but the primary service competition is the **frequency and timing** of flights on a route. Carriers attempt to provide flights at the time of day when passengers want to fly. Flight departures are most frequent in the early morning (7:00 a.m. to 10:00 a.m.) and late afternoon (4:00 p.m. to 6:00 p.m.).

In addition to the frequency and timing of flights, air carriers attempt to differentiate their service through the **advertising** of passenger amenities. Carriers promote such things as on-time arrival and friendly employees to convince travelers that they have the desired quality of service. JetBlue Airways was the first airline in the world that offered live satellite television free of charge on every seat in its fleet.[7] Frequent flyer programs and special services for high-mileage customers are popular examples of other services to attract loyal customers.

A post-deregulation development in service competition was **no-frills service**. The no-frills air carrier (for example, Southwest Airlines) charges fares that are lower than that of a full-service air carrier. However, passengers receive limited snacks and drinks (coffee, tea, or soft drinks). Southwest offers passengers an opportunity to purchase a boxed meal at the gate before they enter the aircraft. Another hallmark of such carriers is that they only provide one class of service. Also, the passengers provide their own magazines or other reading materials. Overall, there are fewer airline employees involved in no-frills services operations, which contribute to lower costs. The no-frills carriers have had a significant impact on fares where their service is available.

Cargo Competition

For cargo service, competition has become intense. As a result of the complete deregulation of air cargo in 1977, air carriers have published competitive rates, but these rates are still higher than those available via surface carriers. Freight schedules have been published that emphasize low transit times between given points. To overcome accessibility problems, some carriers provide door-to-door service through contracts with motor carriers. Major airline freight companies (such as FedEx and UPS Airlines) have their own fleets of surface delivery vehicles to perform the ground portion of this door-to-door service.

Although the number of major and national carriers is small, the competition among carriers is great. An interesting development has been the number of surface carriers that have added air cargo service, such as UPS. Competition for nonpassenger business will become even greater as more carriers attempt to eliminate excess capacity resulting from currently reduced passenger travel patterns. Another interesting dimension has been the growth in volume of express carrier traffic, which is an important reason for the attraction of surface carriers into this segment of the business.

Operating and Service Characteristics

General

As indicated earlier, the major revenue source for air carriers is passenger transportation. From June 2016 to May 2017, approximately 99.2 percent of total operating revenue miles were derived from passenger transportation. This revenue was generated from about 836.5 million passenger enplanements during the same period.[8] Air transportation dominates the for-hire, long-distance passenger transportation market.

By the end of the second quarter of 2017, approximately 0.8 percent of the total operating **revenue-miles** were generated from **freight** transportation.[9] The majority of freight using air service is high-value and/or emergency shipments. The high cost of air transportation is usually prohibitive for shipping low-value routine commodities unless there is an emergency.

GLOBAL **PERSPECTIVES**

Air Cargo Link to Trade Growth

The International Air Transport Association (IATA) released a study identifying a quantitative link between a country's air cargo connectivity and its participation in global trade. The study found that a 1 percent increase in air cargo connectivity was associated with a 6.3 percent increase in a country's total trade. "Air cargo is key in supporting the current global trading system," says Brian Pearce, chief economist at IATA. In 2016, airlines transported 52.2 million tons of goods, representing about 35 percent of global trade by value. That is equivalent to $5.6 trillion worth of goods annually, or $15.3 billion worth of goods every day. "We now have quantitative evidence of the important link between air cargo connectivity and trade competitiveness," said Pearce. "It's in the economic interest for governments to promote and implement policies for the efficient facilitation of air cargo."

Source: *Logistics Management*, January 2017, p. 1. Reprinted with permission of Peerless Media, LLC.

For **emergency shipments**, the cost of air transportation is often inconsequential compared to the cost of delaying the goods. For example, an urgently needed part for an assembly line might have a $20 value, but if the air-freighted part arrives on time to prevent the assembly line from stopping, the opportunity value of the part might become hundreds of thousands of dollars. Thus, the $20 part might have an emergency value of $200,000, and the air freight cost is a small portion of this emergency value.

Examples of **commodities** that move via air carriers include mail, clothing, communication products and parts, photography equipment, mushrooms, fresh flowers, industrial machines, high-priced livestock, racehorses, expensive automobiles, and jewelry. Normally, basic raw materials such as coal, lumber, iron ore, or steel are not moved by air carriage. The high value of the products that are shipped by air provides a cost-savings trade-off, usually but not always from inventory, that offsets the higher cost of air service. The old adage "Time is money" is quite appropriate here.

Speed of Service

Undoubtedly, the major service advantage of air transportation is speed. The terminal-to-terminal time for a given trip is lower via air transportation than via any of the other modes. Commercial jets are capable of routinely flying at speeds of 500 to 600 miles per hour, thus making a New York to California trip, approximately 3,000 miles, a mere six-hour journey.

This advantage of high terminal-to-terminal speed has been dampened somewhat by reduced frequency of flights and congestion at airports. As a result of deregulation, the air traffic controllers' strike of 1981, and lower carrier demand, the number of flights offered to and from low-density communities has been reduced to increase the utilization of a given plane. As previously noted, commuter airlines have been substituted on some routes where major and national lines find the traffic volume to be too low to justify using large planes. The use of commuters requires transfer and rehandling of freight or passengers because the commuter service does not cover long distances.

Air carriers have been concentrating their service on the **high-density routes** like New York to Chicago, for example. In addition, most carriers have adopted the hub-and-spoke terminal approach, in which most flights go through a hub terminal; Atlanta (Delta) and Chicago (United) are examples. These two factors have aggravated the air traffic congestion and ground congestion at major airports and have increased total transit time while decreasing its reliability. Also, some carriers have been unable to expand because of limited "slots" at major airports. At hub airports, these slots are controlled by the dominant carrier, making it difficult for new carriers to offer service at that hub.

The shippers that use air carriers to transport freight are primarily interested in the speed and reliability of the service and the resultant benefits, such as reduced inventory levels and inventory carrying costs. Acceptable or improved service levels can be achieved by using air carriers to deliver orders in short time periods. Stock-outs can be controlled, reduced, or eliminated by responding to shortages via air carriers.

Length of Haul and Capacity

For passenger travel, air carriers dominate the long-distance moves. In 2014 the average length of haul for passenger travel was 898 miles for U.S. air carriers.[10] The capacity of an airplane is dependent on its type. A wide-body, four-engine jet has a **seating capacity** of about 370 people and an all-cargo carrying capacity of 16.6 tons. Table 7-2 provides capacity and operating statistics for some of the more commonly used aircraft in both domestic and international markets. Comparable data to update this table is not available. But Table 7-2 provides a summary of the different operating characteristics of many aircraft still in service today.

Normally, small shipments that are time-sensitive are moved by air carriers. Rates have been established for weights as low as 10 pounds, and rate discounts are available for shipments weighing a few hundred pounds. Adding freight to the baggage compartment on

TABLE 7-2	Aircraft Operating Characteristics—2007					OPERATING COST	
MODEL	SEATS	CARGO PAYLOAD (TONS)	SPEED AIRBORNE (MPH)	FLIGHT LENGTH (MILES)	FUEL (GALLONS PER HOUR)	$ PER HOUR	$0.01 PER SEAT MILE
B747-200/300*	370	16.60	520	3,148	3,625	9,153	5.11
B747-400	367	8.06	534	3,960	3,411	8,443	4.6
B747-100*	–	46.34	503	2,022	1,762	3,852	–
B747-F*	–	72.58	506	2,512	3,593	7,138	–
L-1011	325	0.00	494	2,023	1,981	8,042	5067
DC-10*	286	24.87	497	1,637	2,405	7,374	5.11
B767-400	265	6.26	495	1,682	1,711	3,124	2.71
B-777	263	9.43	525	3,515	2,165	5,105	3.98
A330	261	11.12	509	3,559	1,407	3,076	2.51
MD-11*	261	45.07	515	2,485	2,473	7,695	4.75
A300-600*	235	19.12	460	947	1,638	6,518	5.93
B757-300	235	0.30	472	1,309	985	2,345	2.44
B767-300ER*	207	7.89	497	2,122	1,579	4,217	4.38
B757-200*	181	1.41	464	1,175	1,045	3,312	4.47
B767-300ER	175	3.72	487	1,987	1,404	3,873	5.08
A321	169	0.44	454	1,094	673	1,347	2.05
B737-800/900	151	0.37	454	1,035	770	2,248	3.88
MD-90	150	0.25	446	886	825	2,716	4.93
B727-200*	148	6.46	430	644	1,289	4,075	6.61
B727-100*	–	11.12	417	468	989	13,667	–
A320	146	0.31	454	1,065	767	2,359	4.14
B737-400	141	0.25	409	646	703	2,595	5.48
MD-80	134	0.19	432	791	953	2,718	5.72
B737-700LR	132	0.28	441	879	740	1,692	3.28
B737-300/700	132	0.22	403	542	723	2,388	5.49
A319	122	0.27	442	904	666	1,913	4.22
A310-200*	–	25.05	455	847	1,561	8,066	–
DC-8*	–	22.22	437	686	1,712	8,065	–
B737-100/200	119	0.11	396	465	824	2,377	6.08
B717-200	112	0.22	339	175	573	3,355	12.89
B737-500	110	0.19	407	576	756	2,347	6.49
DC-9	101	0.15	387	496	826	2,071	6.86
F-100	87	0.05	398	587	662	2,303	8.46
B737-200C	55	2.75	387	313	924	3,421	19.89
ERJ-145	50	0.00	360	343	280	1,142	8.63
CRJ-145	49	0.01	397	486	369	1,433	9.45

(continued)

TABLE 7-2	Continued							
							OPERATING COST	
MODEL	**SEATS**	**CARGO PAYLOAD (TONS)**	**SPEED AIRBORNE (MPH)**	**FLIGHT LENGTH (MILES)**	**FUEL (GALLONS PER HOUR)**		**$ PER HOUR**	**$0.01 PER SEAT MILE**
ERJ-135	37	0.00	357	382	267		969	9.83
SD 340B	33	0.00	230	202	84		644	11.6

* Data includes cargo operations.

Source: Air Transport Association, *2008 Annual Report*.

passenger flights necessitates rather small-size shipments and thus supports rate-making practices for these shipments.

In addition to small shipment sizes, the packaging required for freight shipped by air transportation is usually less than other modes. It is not uncommon in air transportation to find a palletized shipment that is shrink-wrapped instead of banded. The relatively smooth ride through the air and the automated ground-handling systems contribute to lower damage and thus reduce packaging needs.

Accessibility and Dependability

Except in adverse conditions such as fog or snow, air carriers are capable of providing **reliable** service. The carriers might not always be on time to the exact minute, but the variations in transit time are small. Sophisticated navigational instrumentation permits operation during most weather conditions. On-time departures and arrivals are within 15 minutes of scheduled times. Departure time is defined as the time the aircraft door is closed and, in the case of passenger aircraft, the vehicle is pushed away from the gate. Arrival time is defined as the time when the aircraft wheels touch down on the runway.

Poor **accessibility** is one disadvantage of air carriers. Passengers and freight must be transported to an airport for air service to be rendered. This accessibility problem is reduced when smaller planes and helicopters are used to transport freight to and from airports, and most passengers use automobiles. Limited accessibility adds time and cost to the air service provided. Even with the accessibility problem, air transportation remains a fast method of movement and the only logical mode when distance is great and time is restricted. The cost of this fast freight service is high, about three times greater than motor carrier and 10 times greater than rail. Nevertheless, the high speed and cost make air carriage a premium mode of transportation.

Equipment
Types of Vehicles

As previously mentioned, there are several different sizes of airplanes in use, from small commuter planes to huge, wide-body, four-engine planes used by the nationals. These various-sized planes all have different costs associated with using them; these costs will be addressed later in the section titled "Cost Structure." Table 7-2 compares some of the major aircraft types in terms of seats, cargo payload, speed, fuel consumption, and operating cost per hour. Airlines have many options to select from when purchasing equipment.

Terminals

The air carriers' **terminals** (airports) are financed by a government entity. The carriers pay for the use of the airport through landing fees, rent and lease payments for space, taxes on fuel, and aircraft registration taxes. In addition, users pay a tax on airline tickets and air freight charges. Terminal charges are becoming increasingly more commonplace for passenger traffic. Table 7-3 summarizes the various types of taxes paid by carriers, shippers, and passengers in the airline industry.

ON THE **LINE**

USPS and FedEx Express Re-up on Air Transportation Partnership

FedEx subsidiary FedEx Express and the USPS said last month that they've extended their air transportation contract, which was originally executed on April 23, 2013, through September 29, 2024. FedEx officials said that the modified contract is expected to generate revenue of approximately $1.5 billion per year for FedEx Express. Through this partnership, FedEx Express provides airport-to-airport transportation of USPS Priority Mail Express and Priority Mail within the United States. "We're pleased to be able to extend this agreement and to continue the outstanding service that FedEx Express has provided to the USPS for more than 16 years," said David Bronczek, president and chief operating officer of FedEx. "This contract provides USPS with the operational reliability and flexibility they have come to expect from FedEx."

Source: *Logistics Management*, March 2017, p. 1. Reprinted with permission of Peerless Media, LLC.

The growth and development of air transportation is dependent upon adequate airport facilities. Therefore, to ensure the viability of air transportation, the federal government has the responsibility of financially assisting the states in the construction of airport facilities. The various state and local governments assume the responsibility for operating and maintaining the airports.

At the airport, the carriers perform passenger, cargo, and aircraft servicing. Passengers are ticketed, loaded, and unloaded, and their luggage is collected and dispersed. Cargo is routed to specific planes for shipment to the destination airport or to delivery vehicles. Aircraft servicing includes refueling; loading of passengers, cargo, luggage, and supplies (food); and maintenance. Major aircraft maintenance is done at specific airports.

As carrier operations become more complex, certain airports in the carriers' scope of operation become **hubs**. Flights from outlying, less-populated areas are fed into the hub airport, where connecting flights are available to other areas of the region or country.

For example, Chicago, Denver, and Washington-Dulles are major hub airports for United Airlines. Flights from cities such as Toledo and Kansas City go to Chicago, where connecting flights are available to New York, Los Angeles, and Dallas. Delta Airlines uses the Atlanta and Cincinnati airports in the same way. By using the hub airport approach, the carriers are able to assign aircraft to feed passengers into the hub over low-density routes and to assign larger planes to the higher-density routes between the hub and an airport serving a major metropolitan area. In essence, the hub airport is similar to the motor carrier's break-bulk terminal.

Airport terminals also provide services to passengers, such as restaurants, banking centers, souvenir and gift shops, and snack bars. The Denver airport also includes some major general-purpose attractions similar to a shopping mall. The success of the Atlanta

TABLE 7-3 Federally Approved Taxes and Fees: 1992–2017			
	1992	**2003**	**2014**
FEE	**AIRPORT AND AIRWAY TRUST FUND (FAA)**		
Passenger Ticket Tax[1a]	10.0%	7.5%	7.5%
Flight Segment Tax[1a]	–	$3.60	$4.10
Frequent Flyer Tax[2]	–	7.5%	7.5%
International Departure Tax[3]	$6.00	$16.10	$18.00
International Arrival Tax[3]	–	$16.10	$18.00
Cargo Waybill Tax[1b] (domestic)	6.25%	6.25%	6.25%
Commercial Jet Fuel Tax	–	$0.043	$0.043
Noncommercial Jet Fuel Tax	$0.175	$0.218	$0.218
Noncommercial AvGas Tax	$0.15	$0.193	$0.193
	ENVIRONMENTAL PROTECTION AGENCY (EPA)		
LUST Fuel Tax[4] (domestic)	$0.001	$0.001	$0.001
	LOCAL AIRPORT PROJECTS		
Passenger Facility Charge	–	up to $3	up to $4.50
	DEPARTMENT OF HOMELAND SECURITY (DHS)		
September 11th Fee[5]	–	$2.50	$5.60
Aviation Security Infrastructure Fee[6]	–	–	Varies
APHIS Passenger Fee[7]	$2.00	$5.00	$3.96
APHIS Aircraft Fee[7]	$76.75	$70.50	$225.00
Customs User Fee[8]	$5.00	$5.50	$5.50
Immigration User Fee[9]	$5.00	$7.00	$7.00

[1a] Applies only to domestic transport or to journeys to Canada or Mexico within 225 miles of the U.S. border.
[1b] Applies only to flights within the 50 states.
[2] Applies to the sale, to third parties, of the right to award frequent flyer miles.
[3] Does not apply to those transiting the United States between two foreign airports; $8.70 on flights between the mainland United States and Alaska/Hawaii.
[4] Congress created the Leaking Underground Storage Tank (LUST) trust fund in 1986.
[5] Funds TSA at up to $5.60 per enplanement up to $11.20 per round trip (from 2/1/02 through 7/20/14) was $2.50 per enplanement up to $5.00 per one-way trip.
[6] Funds TSA since 2/18/02; suspended 6/1/03–9/30/03.
[7] Since 5/13/91 (passenger fee) and 2/9/92 (aircraft fee), funds agricultural quarantine and inspection services conducted by CBP per 7 CFR 354.
[8] Since 7/7/86, funds inspections by U.S. Customs and Border Protection; passengers arriving from U.S. territories and possessions are exempt.
[9] Since 12/1/86, the majority of the collections fund inspections by U.S. Customs and Border Protection and a smaller portion of the collections fund certain activities performed by U.S. Immigration and Customs Enforcement that are related to air and sea passenger inspections.

Source: Airlines for America, 2017.

airport has resulted in other airports expanding restaurants to include many popular chains (McDonald's, TGI Friday's, Pizza Hut, and so forth) and popular shops for clothing, accessories, books, and other items.

Cost Structure

Fixed- Versus Variable-Cost Components

Like the motor carriers, the air carriers' cost structure consists of high variable and low fixed costs. Approximately 80 percent of total operating costs are variable and 20 percent are fixed. The relatively low fixed-cost structure is attributable to government (state and local) investment and operations of airports and airways. The carriers pay for the use of these facilities through landing fees, which are variable in nature.

By the end of 2016, 15.1 percent of airline operating costs were incurred for fuel and amounted to $21.6 billion. The next major category of expense is labor, which totaled $46.7 billion and about 32.6 percent of total operating costs. Both of these expenses are variable costs. Depreciation accounted for about 6.8 percent of total operating expenses.[11]

Table 7-4 provides a comparison of airline cost indices for 2005, 2009, and 2016 (year 2000 = 100). Transportation related expenses decreased from 2005 to 2016, as did total fuel expense. From 2005 to 2016, labor, aircraft ownership, professional services, landing fees, and other operating expenses all increased.

The increased price competition in the airline industry has caused airlines to try to operate more efficiently by cutting costs where possible. There has been much effort put forth to decrease labor costs because the airline industry tends to be labor–intensive compared to other modes, such as railroads and pipelines. The airlines have negotiated significant labor cost reductions with many of the unions represented in the industry.

Fuel

Escalating **fuel costs** have caused problems in the past for the airlines. The average price per gallon of fuel for domestic operations was about 89 cents in 1983 compared to 57 cents in 1979 and 30 cents in 1978. It dropped to under 60 cents in 1986 but rose again in 1990

TABLE 7-4	Airline Cost Indexes		
YEAR	2005	2009	2016
Composite Index	177.9	197.3	156.5
Labor Costs	117.3	127.4	186.7
Fuel	206.6	234.9	173.7
Aircraft ownership	99.1	93.0	103.1
Nonaircraft ownership	106.1	114.8	110.2
Professional Services	105.5	118.5	128.7
Food and beverage	61.3	59.7	67.2
Landing fees	130.7	158.9	191.8
Maintenance material	59.1	83.3	91.4
Aircraft insurance	157.1	150.8	55.4
Nonaircraft insurance	319.9	184.4	52.5
Passenger commisions	31.6	26.7	19.9
Communication	73.3	77.1	59.1
Advertising and promotion	75.5	61.7	77.8
Utilities and office supplies	87.6	99.8	121.5
Transportation-related expenses	475.0	524.9	182.9
Other operating expenses	108.6	123.8	179.9
Interest	120.6	118.7	72.2

Source: U.S. Census Bureau, Statistical Abstract of the United States: 2012, Table 1074. Note: 2016 data is from Airlines for America, 2016.

to above the 1983 level. It decreased again by 1998 to about 55 cents per gallon. In 2016, the price per gallon of aviation fuel was $1.45 per gallon.[12]

The impact that such fuel increases have had can be shown by analyzing fuel consumption for certain aircraft that are commonly used today. The Air Transportation Association's annual report shows that the number of gallons of fuel consumed per hour for the following planes is as follows (see Table 7-2):

367-seat 747	3,411 gallons/hour
286-seat DC-10	2,405 gallons/hour
148-seat 727	1,289 gallons/hour
101-seat DC-9	826 gallons/hour

Using a cost of $1.45 per gallon, the fuel cost per hour is $4,945.95 for a 747, $3,487.25 for a DC-10, $1,869.05 for a 727, and $1,197.70 for a DC-9.

When fuel costs change, carriers scrutinize planes in the fleet as well as routes served. More **fuel-efficient** planes have been developed and added to carrier fleets. In the short run, carriers are substituting smaller planes on low-density (low demand) routes and eliminating service completely on other routes. Commuter lines have provided substitute service on the routes abandoned by major and national carriers. The average cost per gallon of fuel decreased from $1.84 to $1.45 from 2015 to 2016 and fuel consumption increased by 315.1 million gallons (1.9 percent increase) from 2015 to 2016, resulting in a reduced fuel expense of $6.14 billion.[13]

Labor

In 2016, average salaries and wages increased by 5.4 percent over 2015. In 2016 carriers employed 374,573 people at an average annual compensation of $87,175.[14]

Airlines employ people with a variety of different skills. To operate the planes, the carrier must employ pilots, copilots, and flight engineers. The plane crew also includes the flight attendants who serve the passengers. Communications personnel are required to tie together the different geographic locations. Mechanics and ground crews for aircraft and traffic service provide the necessary maintenance and servicing of the planes. The final component of airline employment consists of the office personnel and management. Overall employment has decreased as airlines have moved aggressively to reduce costs to improve their competitiveness and lower prices in selected markets.

Strict safety regulations are administered by the FAA. Acceptable flight operations, as well as hours of service, are specified for pilots. Both mechanics and pilots are subject to examinations on safety regulations and prescribed operations. FAA regulations also dictate appropriate procedures for flight attendants to follow during takeoff and landing.

The wages paid to a pilot usually vary according to the pilot's equipment rating. A pilot who is technically capable (has passed a flight examination for a given type of aircraft) of flying a jumbo jet will receive a higher compensation than one who flies a single-engine, six-passenger plane. Table 7-5 shows the average pilot compensation for the major airlines in the United States for narrowbody aircraft. United averages the highest pilot hourly wages, whereas Alaska Airlines has the lowest. Pilot and copilot wages have increased by 8.3 percent from 2015 to 2016.[15]

Equipment

As mentioned earlier, the cost of operating airplanes varies. Larger planes are more costly to operate per hour than smaller planes, but the cost per seat mile is lower for larger planes. That is, the larger plane has the capacity to carry more passengers; thus, the higher cost is spread out over a large number of output units.

TABLE 7-5	Average U.S. Airline Pilot Hourly Wages—2016	
AIRLINE	**LOWEST PAY**	**HIGHEST PAY**
United	$232.00	$328.00
Delta	$152.00	$321.00
American	$145.00	$302.00
Southwest	$221.00	$251.00
JetBlue	$141.00	$218.00
Allegiant	$152.00	$216.00
Alaska	$181.00	$213.00

Source: Airline Pilot Central, *2016 Airline Pilot Pay Snapshot*.

Table 7-2 shows the hourly operating costs for four aircraft used by major carriers in 2007. The cost per block hour was $8,443 for the 367-seat 747 and $2,071 for the 101-seat DC-9. However, the cost per seat mile was $0.0046 for the 747 and $0.00686 for the DC-9. This reduced operating cost per seat mile for the larger planes indicates that economies of scale exist in aircraft.

Economies of Scale/Economies of Density

Large-scale air carrier operations do have some **economies of scale**, which result from more extensive use of large-size planes or indivisible units. Of the small number of major and national carriers, approximately 10 transport over 90 percent of the passengers, indicating that large-scale operations exist.

The information contained in Table 7-2 suggests the existence of economies of scale with large-size planes. Market conditions (sufficient demand) must exist to permit the efficient utilization of larger planes (that is, if the planes are flown near capacity, the seat mile costs will obviously decrease). Contributing to the existence of economies of scale for aircraft is the inability to inventory an unused seat. For example, a 367-seat 747 is about to close its doors with 10 seats empty. If the plane takes off with the empty seats, the seats are "lost" for that flight because the airline cannot inventory the excess capacity for another flight that might be overbooked. On the other hand, the marginal cost of filling those 10 empty seats right before the doors on the aircraft are closed are negligible. This is the same concept of economies of scale as found in the railroad industry. The marginal cost of adding one more railcar to a train right before departure is negligible.

Another factor indicating large-scale operations for air carriers is the integrated **communication network** required for activities such as operating controls and passenger reservations. Small local or regional carriers find the investment required for such a communication system rather staggering, but without the communication system, the emerging carrier cannot effectively operate (provide connecting service with other carriers and ticketing to passengers). Such carriers have purchased passenger reservation systems from large carriers to be competitive.

The air carrier industry overall has a cost structure that closely resembles that of motor carriers. Long-run economies of scale, as compared to short-run economies of plane size and utilization, are not significant in the air carrier industry. Industries characterized by high variable-cost ratios (airlines and motor carriers) can relatively easily add equipment to a given market. As such, the ability to decrease fully allocated cost per mile by adding aircraft does not exist. On the other hand, when high fixed-cost industries (pipeline and rail) add fixed capacity, they can decrease fully allocated cost per mile by adding volume to the fixed capacity. In high fixed-cost industries, however, capacity is not easily added in small increments.

Economies of density exist when a carrier has significant volume between an origin–destination pair to fully utilize capacity on forward-haul movements as well as utilize significant capacity on backhaul movements. This concept can exist across all modes of transportation. Southwest Airlines uses this concept aggressively when deciding which markets to enter, choosing those city pairs that offer high volumes of potential passengers to fill outbound aircraft. Table 7-6 shows the top 25 passenger markets in the world. Of these, 7 are located in the United States. Economies of density, then, are important for all airlines servicing these airports to fully utilize capacity in their origin and destination markets. History has shown that this has been a successful strategy for new entrants to the airline passenger market.

TABLE 7-6	Top 25 Global Airports—2015[1]		
	ANNUAL PASSENGERS (THOUSANDS)		
1.	Atlanta	United States	101,489
2.	Beijing	China	89,939
3.	Dubai	UAE	78,010
4.	Chicago O'Hare	United States	76,942
5.	Tokyo	Japan	75,317
6.	London Heathrow	England	74,990
7.	Los Angeles	United States	74,704
8.	Hong Kong	Hong Kong	68,343
9.	Charles De Gaulle	France	65,771
10.	Dallas/Ft. Worth	United States	64,072
11.	Ataturk	Turkey	61,837
12.	Frankfurt	Germany	61,032
13.	Shanghai	China	60,053
14.	Amsterdam	Netherlands	58,285
15.	JFK/New York	United States	56,845
16.	Singapore	Singapore	55,449
17.	Guangzhou	China	55,202
18.	Soe Karno-Hatta	Indonesia	54,054
19.	Denver	United States	54,015
20.	Bangkok	Thailand	52,808
21.	San Francisco	United States	50,058
22.	Incheon	South Korea	49,413
23.	Kuala Lumpur	Malaysia	48,934
24.	Madrid	Spain	46,815
25.	New Delhi	India	45,982

[1] Includes all commercial airports in a metropolitan area.

Source: Airport Codes, *2017 Economic Report*.

Over the years the federal government has provided direct operating **subsidies** (that is, public service revenues) to air carriers. The subsidies have been provided to ensure air carrier service over particular routes where operating expenses exceed operating incomes. The subsidies enable regional carriers to provide service to less-populated areas that otherwise would probably not have air service.

Rates

Pricing

Airline pricing for passenger service is characterized by the **discounts** from full fare. Seats on the same plane can have substantially different prices depending on restrictions attached to the purchase, such as having to stay over a weekend or having to purchase the ticket in advance. Businesspeople generally pay more for their airline travel due to the more rigid schedules they are on and the fact that they usually depart and return during the high-demand times. JetBlue, Southwest, and AirTran have aggressively discounted prices in major passenger markets. However, inflation-adjusted airfares decreased by 9.5 percent from 2015 to 2016 and declined by 25.6 percent between 2000 and 2016.[16] The price of seats on different flights and the price of the same seat on a particular flight can vary due to competition with other airlines, the time and day of departure and return, the level of service (first class versus coach or no-frills service), and advance ticket purchase. Discount pricing has continued throughout the 2000s as airlines have attempted to increase their "payload." Industry load factors in 2016 were 82.43 percent, slightly down from 82.68 percent in 2015.[17] This is a result of aggressive pricing as well as more systematic allocation of capacity to markets.

Cargo pricing is dependent mainly on weight and/or cubic dimensions. Some shipments that have a very low density can be assessed an over-dimensional charge, usually based on 8 pounds per cubic foot. This over-dimensional charge is used to gain more appropriate revenue from shipments that take up a lot of space but do not weigh much. An exaggerated example of a shipment to which this rule would apply is a shipment of inflated beach balls. Other factors affecting the price paid to ship freight via air transportation include completeness of service and special services, such as providing armed guards.

Operating Efficiency

An important measure of operating efficiency used by air carriers is the **operating ratio.** The operating ratio measures the portion of operating revenue that goes to operating expenses:

Operating Ratio = (Operating Expense/Operating Revenue) × 100

Only revenue and expenses generated from passenger and freight transportation are considered. Like the motor carrier industry, the air carrier industry's operating ratio was in the low to mid-90s between 1994 and 2000, ranging from 96.9 in 1994 to 94.7 in 2000. The operating ratio for the industry in the first quarter of 2017 was 91.7.[18] The overall profit margin is small, and a loss is incurred when the operating ratio exceeds 100.

Another widely used measure of operating efficiency is the load factor (previously discussed). The load factor measures the percentage of a plane's capacity that is utilized.

Load Factor = (Number of Passengers/Total Number of Seats) × 100

Airlines have raised plane load factors to the low 80 percent range. The particular route and type of plane (capacity) directly affect the load factor, as does price, service level, and competition.

Again, referring to Table 7-2, the relationship among load factor, cost, plane size, and profitability can be seen. Assume that a route requires one hour to traverse and has a load factor of 65 percent; the average operating cost per passenger for a 747 is $35.39 ($8,443 per hour/367 [capacity] = 0.65 [load factor]). If the demand drops to 80 passengers on the route, the load factor for the 747 would be 21.8 percent (80/367), and the hourly operating cost per passenger would be $105.54 ($8,443/80). At this level of demand, the carrier would substitute a smaller capacity plane, such as a 727 or DC-9. With 80 passengers, the load factor for the DC-9 would be 79.2 percent (80/101) and the average operating cost would be $25.89 ($2,071/80). The small aircraft would be more economical to operate over this lower-density route, and the carrier would substitute this more efficient plane (DC-9) on this hypothetical route.

Equipment substitution, however, might not be possible, and substitution might result in excess capacity. The jumbo planes have large carrying capacities that might not be utilized in low-demand routes. Thus, large-capacity planes are used on high-demand routes such as New York–Chicago and New York–Los Angeles, and smaller capacity planes are used on low-demand routes such as Toledo–Chicago and Pittsburgh–Memphis.

Current Issues

Safety

The issue of **airline safety** is of great importance to the airline industry. Any incident involving airplanes receives a great deal of publicity from the media because of the large number of people affected at one time. (Accidents involving motor vehicles affect only a few people in each incident but affect a greater number of people than do airline accidents in the long run.)

Several factors affect airline safety. First, airport security has come under close scrutiny over the past several years. On September 11, 2001, four aircraft were hijacked and two were flown into the Twin Towers in New York City, killing and injuring thousands of people. As a result, airport security has reached an all-time high, causing more delays at airport terminals. The U.S. government created the Office of Homeland Security to be the agency that monitors and manages the security of the U.S. borders.

Air travel is more popular than ever, as indicated previously, but there is still great concern about safety. The 1990s had some significant air disasters among major carriers, including TWA, American, U.S. Airways, Swissair, and the ValuJet crash in the Florida Everglades. In addition, the frequent reportings of near collisions, minor accidents, and airplane recalls have heightened public awareness of the air safety problem. However, air travel is still the safest way to travel. Table 7-7 shows the trend of aircraft accidents from 2005 through 2015. Table 7-8 shows that even though there is a significant loss of life in an airline tragedy, air travel is still the safest mode for passenger travel based on total miles traveled, with automobiles being the most dangerous. In Table 7-7, air fatalities represent those that incurred in U.S. trunk lines (e.g., United). Air fatalities in Table 7-8 include U.S. trunk lines, commuter, on-demand air taxi, and general aviation.

Finally, as with other transportation modes, the issue of substance abuse concerning pilots and ground crews has become important. Strict drug-testing policies and alcohol consumption guidelines are in effect for pilots and other aircraft personnel. In spite of these concerns, airline travel is still a very safe form of transportation; however, these issues are currently being addressed by the airlines to ensure that airline transportation remains safe.

TABLE 7-7	U.S. Air Carriers Operating Under 14 CFR 121—Scheduled Service				
YEAR	DEPARTURES (000ₛ)	TOTAL ACCIDENTS	FATAL ACCIDENTS	FATAL ACCIDENT RATES[1]	FATALITIES
2005	28,077	34	3	0.027	22
2006	28,776	26	2	0.019	50
2007	29,869	26	0	0	0
2008	29,907	20	2	0	0
2009	29,364	26	1	0.010	49
2010	30,745	28	0	0	0
2011	31,758	29	0	0	0
2012	32,183	26	0	0	0
2013	32,573	19	0	0	0
2014	33,263	28	0	0	0
2015	34,183	27	0	0	0

[1] Fatal accidents per 100,000 departures; excludes incidents resulting from illegal acts.

Source: Airlines for America, *2016 Economic Report.*

TABLE 7-8	U.S. Passenger Fatalities			
YEAR	AUTOS	BUSES	RAILROADS	AIRLINES
2006	42,708	27	180	774
2007	41,259	36	216	540
2008	37,423	67	229	568
2009	33,883	26	214	548
2010	32,999	44	215	477
2011	32,479	55	189	499
2012	33,782	39	199	450
2013	32,894	54	195	430
2014	32,744	44	216	444
2015	35,092	49	247	404
10-Yr. Avg.	35,526.3	44.1	210.0	513.4

Source: Bureau of Transportation Statistics, *Department of Transportation 2016.*

Security

The aftermath of the tragic air fatalities of 9/11 gave rise to the establishment of the Department of Homeland Security as well as the Transportation Security Administration (TSA). Both of these agencies are responsible for the safety of passengers while in airports and in flight. New screening procedures have been established at airports for passengers and new guidelines developed for carry-on luggage. Another area of security concern is for freight loaded onto passenger-carrying aircraft. This freight, most times arranged for movement by air freight forwarders, has not been subject to a high level of security screening in the past. However, new legislation passed in the United States is calling for 100 percent screening of all freight loaded onto passenger-carrying aircraft. The intent of this legislation is to prevent unnecessarily dangerous freight from threatening the lives of passengers in an aircraft. Aircraft security is, and will continue to be, an important issue in defending the United States from terrorist acts.

Technology

Because the airline industry must offer quick and efficient service to attract business, it constantly needs more sophisticated equipment. With other modes such as railroads and water carriers, travel times are measured in days; however, air carriers measure travel time in hours.

For this reason, the airline industry has developed automated information-processing programs like the Air Cargo Fast Flow Program, which was designed by the Port Authority of New York/New Jersey. The Fast Flow Program is a paperless system that speeds the processing of air freight cargo through customs processing, which was found to take 106 out of 126 hours of processing time for international shipments. The system allows the air freight community to tie into customs-clearing systems and thus reduce paperwork and time requirements dramatically. The system also will provide better tracking of shipments and better communication between connecting carriers. These improvements will allow customers to receive their inbound shipments faster than ever before.

The FAA and the federal government are proposing an entire overhaul to the current air traffic control system that would rely on the use of GPS navigational aids. This would increase the capacity for aircraft in operating space as well as reduce travel times between origin–destination pairs. However, this change would also require new technology on current and new aircraft. The plan will cost billions of dollars and take years to develop, but will offer airlines an opportunity to reduce operating costs and increase service.

SUMMARY

- The airline industry began its development in the early part of the 20th century, and its growth was influenced to a great extent initially by government interest and policy.
- The airline industry is dominated by revenue from passenger service, but air freight revenue is growing in importance.
- Both private and for-hire carriers operate as part of the airline industry, but private carrier service is predominantly passenger movement.
- For-hire carriers can be classified based on service offered (all-cargo, air taxi, charter, and so on) or annual operating revenue (majors, nationals, or regionals).
- All-cargo carriers and commuter operators have grown in importance in recent years and play a more important role in the total airline industry.
- A relatively large number of airline companies exist, but a small number (10) account for more than 96 percent of the total revenue.
- Deregulation of airlines was rationalized to some extent with the argument that an increase in the number of carriers would increase competition. Initially, there was an increase followed by a decrease; today the number is lower.
- Airlines are unique in that they face limited intermodal competition, but intramodal competition is very keen in terms of pricing and service and has been exacerbated by unused capacity.
- Airline service competition is usually in terms of frequency and timing of flights, but special passenger services and programs are important.

- The express portion of air freight has grown dramatically. A growing number of commodities use air freight service, and increased growth is expected.
- Speed is the major advantage of airlines for both passengers and freight, but the airlines' speed of service has been offset recently by congestion and fewer flights.
- The higher cost of airline service can be a trade-off against lower inventory and warehousing costs, as well as other logistics-related savings.
- Airline carriers are essentially long-haul service providers for passengers and freight because the cost of takeoffs and landings makes short hauls relatively uneconomical.
- Airlines usually provide service for small shipments where value is high and/or the product may be perishable.
- Airlines offer a generally reliable and consistent service, but their accessibility is limited.
- Airlines use different types of equipment that limits their carrying capacity, but their overall equipment variety is also limited.
- Airlines use publicly provided airways and terminals, but pay user charges on both, which helps make their cost structure highly variable.
- Major and national airlines use a hub approach to their service, which contributes to operating efficiency but often adds travel time.
- Fuel and labor costs are important expense categories for airlines and have received much managerial attention. The low fuel cost of the late 1990s helped the airlines improve their profitability; today, fuel prices have stabilized and are lower than they were five years ago.
- Economies of scale and economies of density exist in the airline industry, making larger-scale carriers usually more efficient, based on equipment, markets, and communications.
- In the era of deregulation, discount pricing has become very popular, and it has made the rate schedules of airlines for passenger services complex.
- Airline safety is an important issue, but overall airlines have a very good record.
- Traditionally, airlines have capitalized on new equipment technology to improve their operating efficiency and to expand capacity. In recent years, technology improvements have come in a variety of other areas.

STUDY QUESTIONS

1. Discuss the ways in which air carriers compete with each other. How have regulatory changes affected this competition?

2. What is the major advantage of air carriers? How does this advantage impact the inventory levels of those firms using air transportation? Explain how this advantage relates to the choice of modes when choosing between air carriage and other modes of freight and passengers transport.

3. Discuss the length of haul and carrying capacity of the air carriers. Explain how they both favor and hinder air carriers from a competitive standpoint.

4. What is the role of government in air transportation? Include both economic and safety regulations in your answer.

5. How does fuel cost and efficiency affect both air carrier costs and pricing?

6. What is the current situation of labor within the air industry? Are unions a major factor? How does skill level vary within the industry? Do you think this situation is similar to other modes? If so, which one(s)? Explain why.

7. Do air carriers have economies of scale at any level? Economies of density? Discuss and support your answer with examples.

8. How do air carriers price their services? Is the weight or density of the shipment a factor? Explain this factor as part of your answer. How does air carrier pricing relate to the value of the goods being transported?

9. What are the current issues facing the air industry? Discuss how each impacts the industry, its customers and employees.

10. What is the cost structure of the air industry? How does it compare with other modes? How does this affect pricing, particularly for passengers? Be sure your answer includes examples from either advertising or the Internet.

NOTES

1. Bureau of Transportation Statistics, *U.S. Department of Transportation*, Washington, DC, 2014.

2. Ibid.

3. Ibid.

4. Ibid.

5. Ibid.

6. Ibid.

7. Hoover's Online, June 7, 2004, from http://www.jetblue.com/learnmore/factsheet.html.

8. Bureau of Transportation Statistics, *U.S. Department of Transportation 2016*.

9. Ibid.

10. Ibid.

11. Airlines for America, *2014 Economic Report*.

12. Bureau of Transportation Statistics, *U.S. Department of Transportation 2016*.

13. Ibid.

14. MIT Global Airline Industry Program, *Airline Data Project*, MIT, 2016.

15. Ibid.

16. Bureau of Transportation Statistics, *U.S. Department of Transportation 2016*.

17. Ibid.

18. MIT Global Airline Industry Project, *Airline Data Project*, 2017.

CASE 7-1

NextGen Technology

The United States air traffic control system, managed by the Federal Aviation Administration (FAA), provides the necessary guidance for aircraft to fly safely between and origin–destination pair. The current system utilizes a series of radar towers throughout the United States that communicate navigational assistance to pilots while in the air. These towers are placed strategically in the United States so aircraft can fly in a relatively straight line from Point A to Point B. Aircraft must fly within a certain distance of these towers to remain in constant contact. This is a disadvantage since it allows basically one route between two points, allowing for only one type of aircraft to utilize that route. However, within the route, multiple aircraft can operate but at different altitudes.

The FAA is implementing the NextGen Technology to replace the aging radar system. It will be fully implemented by January 1, 2020. NextGen utilizes GPS satellite technology to allow multiple routes and elevations between two points for an aircraft.

CASE QUESTIONS

1. In your opinion, what impact could NextGen have on airspace congestion, especially in the Northeast Corridor?
2. Would NextGen have a positive or negative impact on passenger safety?
3. What impacts might NextGen have on aircraft efficiency and fuel consumption?
4. Are there any negative impacts from the implementation of NextGen Technology?

CASE 7-2
Airline Consolidations

According to Airlines for America, there have been approximately 51 airline mergers/ acquisitions since 1930. Although this is not necessarily a verifiable number, it does show the magnitude of the consolidations that have taken place in the passenger airline industry. Probably the most significant combinations of carriers began in 2009 with Delta and Northwest, followed by United and Continental in 2010, Southwest and Airtran in 2011, and American and U.S. Airways in 2013. These four "mega-carriers" account for approximately 80 percent of all domestic airline passengers today.

The Airline Deregulation Act of 1978 was intended to open the passenger market to new entrants to increase the level of competition. Since then, however, there have been no new entrants into the traditional hub-and-spoke airline market. While there have been a few successful entrants into the market (for example, Southwest), they were point-to-point airlines that did not compete against the legacy hub-and-spoke carriers (for example, United).

CASE QUESTIONS

1. Based on publicly available data, compare the four mega-carriers across the following characteristics:
   a. Number of aircraft by type;
   b. Number of employees;
   c. Departures;
   d. Revenue passengers;
   e. Revenue passenger miles;
   f. Available seat miles;
   g. Operating revenue (total);
   h. Operating revenue per seat mile;
   i. Operating profit.
2. Knowing the intent of the Airline Deregulation Act of 1978, explain why the number of passenger airlines in the industry has actually decreased. Be sure to include a discussion of barriers to entry in your explanation.
3. With the total U.S. market being oligopolistic in nature and at some hubs monopolistic, should the federal government take steps to impose economic regulation on the passenger airlines again? Explain your opinion.
4. In your opinion, why did the Justice Department allow such consolidations to take place?

8

WATER CARRIERS AND PIPELINES

Learning Objectives

After reading this chapter, you should be able to do the following:

> Understand the importance of domestic and global waterways to the development of the global economy as well as the economy of the United States

> Appreciate the role and significance of the water carrier industry to the global economy and to the United States, and how the water carrier industry complements the other basic modes of transportation

> Discuss the various types of water carriers and their roles in the overall water carrier system

> Understand the competitive environment for water carriers on an intramodal as well as an intermodal basis

> Discuss the service and operating characteristics of water carriers as well as their cost structure and equipment challenges

> Understand the challenges and issues faced by the water carrier industry in the 21st century

> Appreciate the development and current position of the pipeline industry globally as well as in the U.S. economy

> Discuss the various types of pipeline companies and their importance in the global transportation system

> Understand the nature of the operating and service characteristics of pipeline carriers and what makes them unique in the transportation system

> Discuss the cost structure and rates of pipelines and understand how it impacts their rates and services

Introduction

Water carriers and pipelines are frequently overlooked by the general public. Most people are aware of trucks, planes, and trains, but they have limited appreciation of the role and contribution of water and pipeline carriers to businesses and our economy. These two modes of transportation are a very important part of the global transportation system and overall infrastructure, particularly for certain types of products. For example, it has been estimated that the cargo operations for the West Coast ports of Seattle and Tacoma supported more than 48,000 jobs in 2014 and generated about $75.2 billion in global trade in 2016. The combination of the global activity and the port infrastructure was the basis of this good news and is indicative of the growing importance of appropriate transportation infrastructure to economic development and employment growth.

In this chapter, we will explore the growing role and importance of water carriers and pipelines to a modern transportation system to gain an understanding and appreciation of their significance and potential impact in the global economy. One would expect that the general public will become more interested in these two modes of transportation in the future as they become more appreciative of how they contribute to global economic development and employment opportunities.

Brief History of Water Transportation

The inland or domestic waterways (canals, rivers, lakes, and oceans) have provided an important link for freight and people movement for centuries. Waterways can be a natural highway and even provide some motive power (currents and wind). Water transportation has, of course, been improved by modern technology and federal investment to enhance motive power, vessel carrying capacity, and even the waterways by building dams, locks, and canals and dredging to increase the potential of water transportation for economic development. Today, there are over 40,000 navigable kilometers of waterways in the United States.

In Europe and other countries, rivers have also been important and efficient channels connecting cities and countries for commerce and passenger transportation. The Danube and the Rhine in Europe, the Amazon (longest river) in South America, the Nile in Egypt, the Yangtze in China, and the Ganges in India are additional examples of natural waterways that have helped to promote commerce and development in their respective regions or countries. Each has a story to tell of their historical importance for economic, political, and social impact that rivals that of the Mississippi River System in the United States.

Water transportation played an important role in the early development of the United States, providing the settlers with a link to markets in England and Europe. In addition, many of our major cities, Boston, New York City, Philadelphia, Baltimore, and so on, developed along the Atlantic coast and still thrive in those locations. As the internal sections of the country developed, water transportation along the rivers and the Great Lakes linked the settlements in the "wilderness" with the coastal cities and also gave rise to interior cities such as Pittsburgh, Cincinnati, and Memphis. Buffalo became a major entryway to the Great Lakes with the opening of the Erie Canal in 1825. New York City was a major beneficiary with its access to the Great Lakes via the Canal, and also the cities on the Lakes such as Toledo and Chicago. New Orleans on the Gulf Coast was the beneficiary of the traffic on the Mississippi River, as were other cities along that waterway route. The subsequent economic growth of New York City spurred interest in other East Coast cities to establish an efficient link to the Great Lakes. For example, Pennsylvania developed a canal system (canal and tram) to connect Philadelphia to Pittsburgh and the Ohio River and the Great Lakes.

The waterways were the most important and efficient form of transportation available until the railroads were developed in the mid-18th century, especially for the United States, and were a prime determinant of population centers, as well as industrial and commercial concentration at port cities along the rivers and Great Lakes. Early private and public sector construction projects in transportation included the Erie, C&O, and other canals to provide inexpensive and efficient water transportation. On a global basis, the oceans of the world provided an economical avenue of commerce to connect continents and countries and their respective ports of entry.

The Panama and Suez canals have been the most important manmade waterways for global commerce, but both have challenges with the new, larger ships. As noted previously, the Panama Canal is being expanded for larger vessels and increased speed through the channel. In addition, the Saint Lawrence Seaway provides access from the Great Lakes to the Saint Lawrence River onto the Atlantic Ocean, but has serious challenges because its locks limit the size of vessels and the ice in the winter months is another hindrance to efficient movement. One of the oldest, but perhaps the most spectacular, canals is the Corinth Canal in Greece. Because of its limitations, it is used mostly for local traffic and tourist vessels. There are additional potential sites for manmade waterways throughout the world that would connect and/or provide access for geographic areas. However, the cost combined with military and political issues has been a deterrent to their construction in spite of the potential economic benefits.

This chapter focuses on the basic economic and operating characteristics of water and pipeline transportation. An overview of each mode is provided first, followed by a discussion and overview of the types of carriers, market structure, operating and service characteristics, equipment cost structure, and current issues for both modes. Given the global scope of this edition, the tables and figures will refer to both domestic and foreign commerce.

Water Transport Industry Overview

Significance of Water Transport

In spite of some recent declines in domestic traffic, water transportation remains a very viable mode of transportation for the movement of products, especially for basic raw materials. Domestic water carriers compete with railroads for the movement of bulk commodities (such as grains, coal, ores, and chemicals) and with pipelines for the movement of bulk petroleum, petroleum products, natural gas, and chemicals. Globally, water carriers are usually the primary means of transportation between countries for a large variety of finished products, especially for those moved in containers on large ships as well as bulk commodities that can be moved in the holds of large ships. Container movements are also quite common on some inland waterways such as the Great Lakes and for coastal shipments. The significance and importance of water transportation will be examined from the perspectives of ton-miles, market share, and shipper-freight expenditures.

In 2015, for-hire transportation accounted for $542.5 billion of U.S. gross domestic product (GDP), approximately 3.01 percent of the total, which was an increase from 2014 of $32.3 billion. Water carriers accounted for about 3.5 percent of the total expenditures of for-hire transportation included in GDP. Motor carrier expenditures dominated the market with 26.9 percent of the total for-hire expenditures included in GDP.

The distribution of domestic intercity freight as measured in ton-miles changed since the advent of transportation deregulation in 1980. Motor carriers were the biggest beneficiary, as noted previously. From 2012 to 2015, internal domestic water traffic increased by about 75 million tons. Projections for 2045 show water volume increasing 217 million tons, a 29.8 percent increase over 2015 levels (see Table 8-1). The increase in domestic water transportation is evidence that many manufacturers and suppliers would experience serious problems in maintaining their competitive position without the availability of low-cost water transportation. The increase in water transportation shipments is attributable in part to the growth of U.S. exports.

An interesting dimension of the freight traffic carried by water carriers is the impact of global commerce. Table 8-2 shows foreign and domestic waterborne commerce from 1990 to 2014 as well as the total commerce for the years indicated. The table indicates that total commerce increased over the 15-year period from 1990 to 2005 and then declined slightly over the next seven years. The biggest decline was in the volume of domestic traffic between 1990 and 2014, which was the result of less basic manufacturing and more effective intermodal

TABLE 8-1	Freight Carried on Major U.S. Waterways 2012–2045		
	2012	2015	2045
Total U.S. Tons of Freight (millions)	16,953	18,056	25,345
Air	7	7	24
Truck	10,871	11,513	16,543
Railroad	1,820	1,788	2,295
Domestic Water Transportation	654	729	946
Pipeline	2,932	3,315	4,563

Source: U.S. Department of Transportation, Bureau of Transportation Statistics, *Pocket Guide to Transportation*, Washington, DC, 2017.

TABLE 8-2	Total Waterborne Commerce of the United States—Metric Tons					
	1990	2000	2005	2010	2013	2014
Total	2,163,854,373	2,424,588,877	2,527,622,229	2,334,398,600	2,274,777,616	2,345,765,093
Foreign	1,041,555,740	1,354,790,984	1,498,711,806	1,440,937,396	1,383,625,910	1,408,702,424
Domestic	1,122,298,633	1,069,804,693	1,028,910,423	893,461,204	891,151,706	937,062,669

Source: U.S. Army Corps of Engineers, *Waterborne Commerce of the United States* (Washington, DC: Author, Annual Issues).

TABLE 8-3	Trade Within U.S. Waterways (Millions of Short Tons)						
RIVER SYSTEM		**1995**	**2000**	**2005**	**2010**	**2013**	**2014**
Great Lakes	Foreign	52.4	66.8	61.6	40.9	36.0	36.8
	Domestic	125.3	120.7	107.8	88.6	91.7	95.5
	Total	177.7	187.5	169.4	129.5	127.6	132.3
Gulf Intracoastal	Foreign	-	-	-	-	-	-
	Domestic	118	113.8	116.1	116.2	115.4	126.1
	Total	118	113.8	116.1	116.2	115.4	126.1
Mississippi River System	Foreign	197.3	188.2	165.5	187.2	194.0	209.5
	Domestic	510	527.2	512.6	474.3	476.0	509.1
	Total	707.3	715.4	678.1	661.5	670.0	718.6
Columbia River	Foreign	39.5	33.2	33.9	41.5	40.2	45.5
	Domestic	17.6	22	17.5	13.3	15.1	16.2
	Total	57.1	55.2	51.4	54.8	55.3	61.7
Snake River	Total	6.8	6.7	5.2	3.3	3.7	4.4

Source: U.S. Army Corps of Engineers, *Waterborne Commerce of the United States* (Washington, DC: Author, Annual Issues).

competition. However, it is interesting to note that the volume of foreign commerce on the waterways has increased, which mitigated the overall decline in the total waterborne commerce. A somewhat similar pattern is seen in the data (see Table 8-3) for the river system of the United States. Domestic commerce has declined, and foreign commerce has increased on some river systems. As one would expect, the inbound flow of foreign commerce has increased more than the outbound flow reflecting the level of imports versus exports on our balance of payments.

Another interesting comparison is the principal commodities moving in waterborne commerce. Table 8-3 lists the commerce for 2013 and 2014 indicating the totals, as well as the splits between foreign and domestic commerce. Examining the data for total commerce, there is a 7 percent increase between 2013 and 2014. The largest increases among the commodities moved were 18.3 percent for food and farm products and 15.5 percent for primary manufactured goods—both changes were attributable to intermodal competition and structural changes in the industry.

It is interesting to note the importance of petroleum and chemicals for both foreign and domestic commerce (38.6 percent and 7.7 percent of total commerce, respectively). It will be interesting to see the future impact of the new oil wells in the United States based upon fracking technology. The new oil fields will make the United States less dependent upon imports of crude oil and most likely will mean an increase in exports. The impact upon the waterways remains to be seen because of the location of the oil sources and the increase in rail and pipeline infrastructure.

Types of Carriers

Like motor carriers, the first major distinction for the domestic water carrier industry is classification of for-hire and private carriers. A private carrier transports freight for the company that owns or leases the vessel. Private water carriers are permitted to transport, for a fee, exempt commodities; when they are hauling such exempt goods, they are technically exempt for-hire carriers. Bona fide private water carriers (transporting company-owned freight and exempt commodities) are excluded from federal economic regulation, as are water carrier shipments of three or fewer commodities within the same barge unit. The water carrier industry, as previously noted, has less stringent requirements than the motor carrier industry to meet the exemption qualifications.

The for-hire water carriers consist of regulated and exempt carriers that charge a fee for their services. Exempt carriers, as indicated earlier, are excluded from the federal economic regulations administered by the Surface Transportation Board (STB). When authority was transferred to the STB under the ICC Termination Act of 1995, the STB's authority was expanded over domestic water traffic. In addition to inland river traffic, the STB has jurisdiction over port-to-port traffic when both ports are in the United States as well as transportation between the United States and its territories. Water carriers are exempt from economic regulation when transporting bulk commodities, both dry and liquid. Because the majority of freight transported by domestic water carriers consists of bulk commodities, exempt carriers dominate the for-hire segment of the industry.

Regulated water carriers are classified as either common or contract carriers. Economic regulation, similar to that controlling motor carriers, is administered by the STB. Although the majority of water traffic is exempt from regulation, a small number of regulated common and contract carriers does exist.

The domestic water carrier industry is most commonly classified by the waterway used. Carriers that operate over the inland navigable waterways are classified as internal water carriers. Internal water carriers use barges and towboats and operate over the principal U.S. rivers—the Mississippi, Ohio, Tennessee, Columbia, and Hudson—plus smaller arteries. Internal water carriers dominate the north–south traffic through the central portion of the United States via the Mississippi, Missouri, and Ohio rivers. The volume of freight moved on the major inland waterways is listed in Table 8-3 from 1995 to 2014. As indicated previously, the Mississippi River System is clearly the most important with over 718.6 million short tons in 2014.

The Great Lakes carriers operate along the northeastern portion of the United States and provide service between ports on the five Great Lakes that border the states of New York, Pennsylvania, Ohio, Michigan, Indiana, Illinois, Wisconsin, and Minnesota. The lake ships normally remain on the lakes, but access to Atlantic and Gulf ports is possible via the Saint Lawrence Seaway. This Great Lakes-to-Atlantic traffic is classified as a coastal operation.

TRANSPORTATION **TECHNOLOGY**

Federal Maritime Commission Hosts Blockchain Discussion

The Federal Maritime Commission recently hosted an informal discussion where the topic of blockchain technology and its applicability to supply chain management and increasing efficiency in international trade was explored. Blockchain is a relatively new technological protocol for managing and tracking information and is most commonly related to financial transactions. However, there's an increasing interest in the international ocean shipping industry in applying blockchain technology to improve transparency, accountability, and accuracy of the processes involved in transporting a container over the seas. Additionally, the United States and other governments are now considering the applicability of the technology for meeting their data management needs and omission requirements. Four individuals from three different organizations participated in the event: Gerard Dache of the Government Blockchain Association; Henrik De Gyor, a consultant and the co-author of *Blockchain Billions*; and Mark Tierney and Annette Mueller, both of Maersk Line.

Source: *Logistics Management*, August 2017, p. 2. Reprinted with permission of Peerless Media, LLC.

As indicated previously, coastal carriers operate along the coasts serving ports on the Atlantic or Pacific oceans or the Gulf of Mexico. Intercoastal carriers transport freight between East Coast and West Coast ports via the Panama Canal. Coastal and intercoastal carriers use oceangoing vessels, but some operators use oceangoing barges (18,000-ton capacity). Currently, large quantities of petroleum, crude and refined, are moved between points on the Atlantic and Gulf of Mexico. Likewise, oil from Alaska moves via coastal carriers to refineries along the Pacific coast.

Table 8-3 indicates foreign, domestic, and total short-ton movements on the important inland waterways. Some highlights to be noted are that the Mississippi River is the most important component of the inland waterway system with 718.6 million short tons in 2014, which is about 55.7 percent of the total tonnage moved that year and is a clear indication of the overall importance of the Mississippi and why the initial profile about the "Big Muddy" is of special interest. Domestic traffic was clearly more important than foreign on the inland river system by a ratio of 2.43 to 1. However, on the Columbia River, foreign commerce was 2.8 times that of domestic, which is indicative of Canadian movements into the United States. The peak year for the period 1995 to 2014 was 2000, which supports the observation made previously about the decrease in waterway traffic in recent years reflecting structural changes in the economy and intermodal competition.

Number and Categories of Carriers

The domestic for-hire water carrier industry consists of a limited number of relatively small firms. The latest numbers available from the Bureau of Transportation Statistics are for 2011, when it was reported that there were 584 vessel operators in service, and that number had decreased from 1,114 in 2000.

Excluding support activities such as port and harbor operations and navigation services, total employment for water transportation was 62,000 in 2014. In 2012, vessels on the Mississippi and Gulf intracoastal water accounted for 77.5 percent of U.S. vessels, and Great Lakes vessels represented 1.4 percent; the remainder of the vessels navigated the coastal areas, including the Atlantic, Pacific, and Gulf of Mexico. Based upon operating revenues for hauling domestic freight, the inland waterways (rivers and canals) were the most important, followed by the coastal waterways and then the Great Lakes carriers. Operating revenues on the inland waterways have remained relatively constant over the last decade, whereas revenue on the Great Lakes has increased about 23 percent because of an increase in higher-valued freight movements. Freight revenue on the coastal waterways declined about 40 percent during the 1990s as explained below. Water carriers have experienced increased competitive pressure, but the intensity has varied from segment to segment, with carriers operating along the coastal waterways experiencing the greatest impact of the competition, especially from railroads and pipeline carriers.

Competition

Water carriers vigorously compete for traffic with other modes and, to a limited degree, with other water carriers. The relatively small number of water carriers results in a limited degree of competition. Because the number of carriers on a given waterway is limited, there is little incentive for the water carriers to compete with one another by lowering rates because they realize that the rate decrease will most likely be matched.

The major water carrier competition is with two other modes, namely rail and pipelines. Water carriers compete with railroads for the movement of dry bulk commodities such as grain, coal, and ores. For example, the movement of grains from the Midwest to New Orleans (for export traffic) is possible by rail as well as by water carrier. The water carriers can use the Mississippi and Missouri river systems to connect the Great Plains states with New Orleans. Both modes move sizable amounts of grain along this traffic corridor.

Rail and water carriers compete heavily to move coal out of the coal-producing states of Pennsylvania, West Virginia, and Kentucky. The water carriers are capable of transporting coal via the Ohio and Mississippi rivers to southern domestic consuming points (utilities), as well as to export markets.

On the Great Lakes, water carriers compete with railroads for the movement of coal, ores, and grain. Iron ore and grain originating in Minnesota, Michigan, and Wisconsin are moved across the Great Lakes to other Great Lakes ports, or out of the Great Lakes region via the Saint Lawrence Seaway to Atlantic and Gulf ports or to export markets. As will be explicated below, the development of the technology for fracking oil and gas from new geographic areas in the United States and Canada has resulted in renewed competition between railroads and pipelines for moving these products, particularly oil. It has also caused rail equipment shortages for shippers of grain in the upper Midwest of the United States. In fact, fracking capability is causing transportation challenges in other areas discussed below. These "new" oil fields are in some ways a mixed blessing, at least in the short run, as adjustments are made for substantial flows of traffic in new directions. Our ability to develop the so-called shale fields has outpaced the development of additional transport equipment and infrastructure for domestic and global movements. The example of the Port of Toledo discussed below is another indication of the criticality of infrastructure.

The Port of Toledo became an important interchange point between rail and water carriers for the transport of coal. Railroads haul coal out of the coal-producing states to Toledo, where the coal is loaded onto lake ships for movement to northern Great Lakes ports. In essence, the railroads helped to overcome the water carrier accessibility problem by moving coal from the mines to Toledo, which suggests that the modes are partners rather than competitors. Because the cost of the water–rail combination is lower than the all-rail route, shippers continue to request the combined water–rail service. Again, the infrastructure of the port and its facilities is an important ingredient for the efficiency and effectiveness of the total movement.

Water carriers and pipelines are vigorous competitors for the movement of bulk liquids as indicated earlier. Bulk liquids (petroleum, petroleum products, and chemicals) account for about one-third of the total tonnage transported by domestic water carriers. Bulk liquids are important commodities to both modes, and vigorous competition exists for moving bulk liquids along the Gulf, Atlantic, and Pacific coasts, as well as the Mississippi River System.

To a very limited degree, water carriers compete with trucks. However, trucks are usually used to overcome the accessibility constraints of water carriers because trucks tie inland areas to the waterways for pickup and/or delivery. Shipment quantities are usually prohibitive for an all-motor carrier movement for long hauls because one barge can transport the equivalent of 58 tractor–trailers or more.

Operating and Service Characteristics

Commodities Hauled and Related Characteristics

Figure 8-1 indicates the relative importance of the major commodities moved on the U.S. waterway system in terms of their annual volume. In 2014, water carriers hauled 906 million short tons of petroleum, which represents 38.6 percent of the total short tons hauled that year.

Crude materials were the second most important commodity with about 354.3 million short tons or 15.1 percent of the total. Food and farm products were a close third with over 319.4 million short tons.

FIGURE 8-1	National Internal Commodities Shipped by Waterborne Traffic of 2012 (Millions of Short Tons)

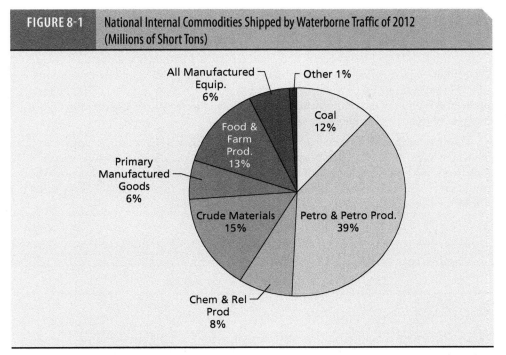

Source: U.S. Army Corps of Engineers, *Waterborne Commerce of the United States* (Washington, DC: Author, Annual Issues).

It is obvious that water carriers are important for low-value, bulk movements of liquid and dry materials. The low rates of water carriers are attractive to the shippers of such commodities, and the service requirements are not as stringent for these products.

Water carriers are considered to be medium- to long-haul carriers. Their carrying capacity is relatively large, which makes short hauls with frequent stops uneconomical. However, the length of haul varies by segment from about 400 miles for inland water carriers to over 1,500 miles for coastal carriers. As noted, the carrying capacity is large. Barges are capable of carrying 1,500 to 3,000 tons, and lake carrier vessels can carry about 20,000 tons. A 1,500-ton load represents the typical carrying capacity of 15 railcars or about 50 trucks. The long hauls and the large carrying capacity combined with fuel efficiency allow water carriers to offer low-cost service—about 72 cents per ton-mile on average.

The low cost of the water carrier comes with some service disadvantages that need to be considered by shippers. Water carriers are relatively slow, with average speeds on inland rivers, for example, of 5.5 to 9 miles per hour. The limited accessibility of the water carrier usually necessitates pickup or delivery by another mode of transportation to bridge the accessibility gap. The transfer between modes will obviously add to the total cost.

Service can also be disrupted by weather. Rivers and lakes freeze during the winter months in the northern states, which can interrupt service for several months. Drought conditions can lower water levels and restrict traffic flow. Conversely, heavy rains can cause flooding, which is also disruptive to service. The waterways are a natural highway, but Mother Nature can also constrain the flow of traffic.

Overall, water carriers are an attractive alternative for low-value traffic, where transportation rates are a significant part of the total delivered cost and price of the good. However, the poor service characteristics may add costs for the user, which have to be traded off against the low rate to calculate the true total cost.

Equipment

Types of Vehicles Because most domestic water carriers transport bulk materials, they use ships with very large hold capacity and openings to facilitate easy loading and unloading. Watertight walls dividing the holds allow a ship to carry more than one commodity at a time. However, most carriers will only carry a limited variety of products. The importance of the major types of equipment utilized on the inland waterways is indicated in Figure 8-2 in terms of their percentage of the total fleet.

The largest ship in the domestic water carriage industry is the tanker. A tanker can carry anywhere from 18,000 to 500,000 tons of liquid, generally petroleum or petroleum products. Due to oil spill problems, the use of double-hulled tankers has become preferable to the use of the more conventional single-hulled tankers. However, the building of these ships has diminished greatly since 1991.

FIGURE 8-2	U.S. Flag Vessels by Type

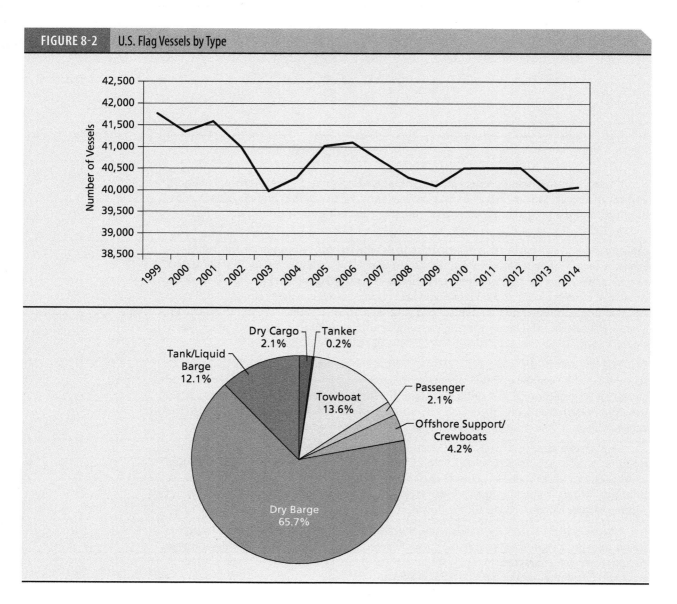

FIGURE 8-2 U.S. Flag Vessels by Type (*Continued*)

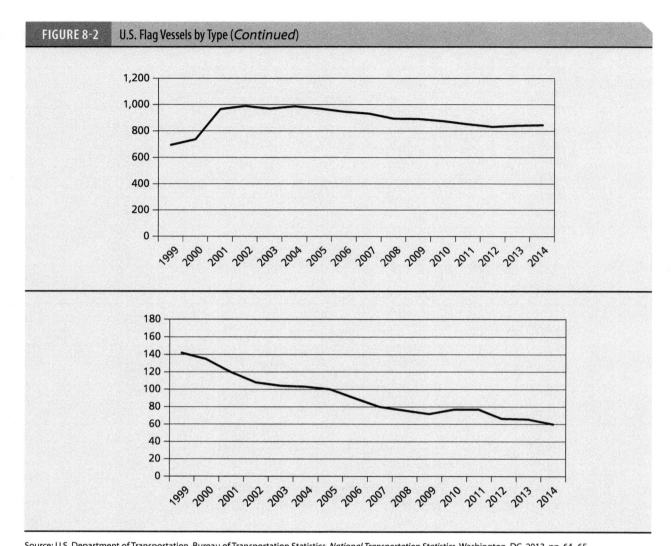

FIGURE 8-2   U.S. Flag Vessels by Type (*Continued*)

Source: U.S. Department of Transportation, Bureau of Transportation Statistics, *National Transportation Statistics*, Washington, DC, 2013, pp. 64–65.

Original Source: U.S. Army Corps of Engineers, *Waterborne Transportation Lines of the United States: Volume 1, National Summaries* (New Orleans, LA: Author, Annual Issues), Table 13, available at http://www.navigationdatacenter.us/wcsc/wcsc.htm as of Nov. 19, 2013.

Another type of vessel is the barge, a powerless vessel towed by a tugboat. Barges are most commonly used by internal waterway carriers. Additional barges can be added to a tow at very little additional cost. Consequently, barge transportation offers capacity flexibility comparable to railroads, at lower rates. Dry barge movements are the most popular.

Fuel   As seen in Figure 8-3, the majority of fuel used by water transportation is residual fuel oil, also known as heavy fuel oil. This is the remainder, or residue, of fuel after crude oil is distilled. Diesel, also typically extracted from crude oil, makes up about a quarter of fuel consumption in water transportation.

Terminals   Water carrier terminals are often provided by the public. Most ports are operated by local government agencies, and many ports have publicly operated storage facilities. It has been recognized for a long time that water transportation is a catalyst to economic activity in the community, and it is this belief that has spurred public investment in the operation of ports.

Some volume users of transportation invest in and operate port facilities or shipper terminals. Individual firms that handle such commodities as grain, coal, and oil commonly build docks, terminals, and commodity-handling facilities to meet their unique needs. The water carriers have the opportunity to use these private facilities owned by shippers.

Over the past few decades, major port improvements have centered on the mechanization of materials-handling systems, especially for internal waterway ports. Efficient handling of larger volumes of bulk commodities has been a prerequisite for ports that desire to remain economically competitive with other ports along the waterway and for water carriers that seek to be competitive with other modes.

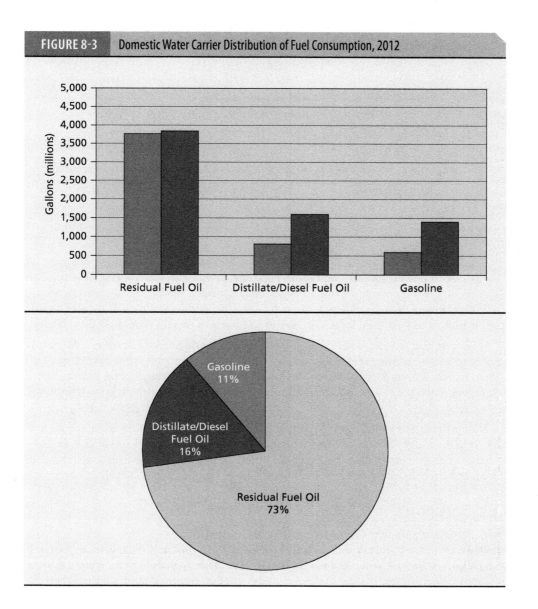

FIGURE 8-3 Domestic Water Carrier Distribution of Fuel Consumption, 2012

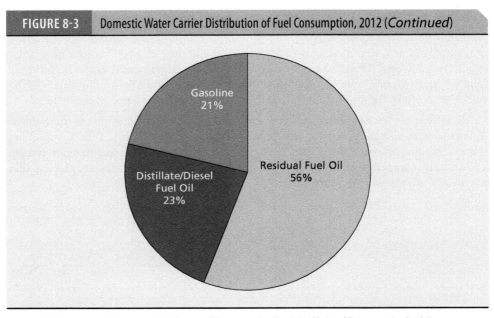

| FIGURE 8-3 | Domestic Water Carrier Distribution of Fuel Consumption, 2012 (*Continued*) |

Source: U.S. Department of Transportation, Bureau of Transportation Statistics, *National Transportation Statistics*, Washington, DC, 2013, p. 247.
Original Source: Residual and Distillate/Diesel Fuel Oil:
1960–1980: American Petroleum Institute, *Basic Petroleum Data Book* (Washington, DC: Author, Annual Issues), Tables 10, 10a, 12, and 12a.
1985–2011: U.S. Department of Energy, *Energy Information Administration, Fuel Oil and Kerosene Sales* (Washington, DC: Author, Annual Issues), available at http://www.eia.doe.gov/oil_gas/petroleum/data_publications/fuel_oil_and_kerosene_sales/foks.html as of March 9, 2012.
Gasoline:
1970–2011: U.S. Department of Transportation, *Federal Highway Administration, Highway Statistics* (Washington, DC), Table MF-24 and similar tables in earlier editions, available at http://www.fhwa.dot.gov/policy/ohpi/hss/hsspubs.cfm as of May 8, 2013.

The port facilitates ship loading and unloading, which means that the port must be equipped with cranes, forklifts, and other handling equipment. Certain commodities like oil, grain, and coal require more technically advanced loading equipment, such as pneumatic loaders and railcar dumping equipment. Such materials-handling equipment reduces unproductive port delays and enables water carriers and ports to remain economically viable.

The port also facilitates the transfer of freight from one mode to another. The port is usually served by railroads and motor carriers. Terminals at the port will have railroad sidings to handle inbound and outbound rail freight as well as parking lots for motor carrier equipment. Ports play a key role in promoting the efficiency of intermodal transportation.

Because barges and ships carry larger loads than rail or motor carrier vehicles, storage facilities are necessary at the port. The storage areas receive cargo from many trucks and railcars. This freight is held until sufficient volume is obtained to be handled effectively by barge or ship. Conversely, when a loaded vessel arrives at port, the freight is unloaded, stored, and then dispatched in hundreds of railcars or trucks at some later date.

Cost Structure

Fixed- Versus Variable-Cost Components The basic cost structure of water carriers consists of relatively high variable costs and low fixed costs. Like motor carriers and air carriers, water carriers do not provide their own highways (rights-of-way). The waterways are provided by nature (except canals) and are maintained, improved, and controlled by the government. The carriers pay user charges—lock fees, dock fees, and fuel taxes—for the use of government-provided facilities. These user charges are directly related to the volume of business and therefore are considered variable costs.

The operating costs for water carriers are approximately 85 percent variable and 15 percent fixed. Fixed costs include depreciation and amortization and general expenses. The major variable expenses are line-operating costs, operating rents, and maintenance. Line-operating costs are those expenses associated with renting operating equipment and facilities.

Infrastructure   As indicated earlier, the domestic water carriers' low fixed costs can be attributed in part to public aid in the area of infrastructure. For water carriers, the major public aid is the construction and maintenance of waterways. The construction of canals with public funding opens new markets and sources of revenue for water carriers. The construction of locks and dams on rivers makes the waterways navigable for domestic water carriers. The dredging of the Mississippi River, for example, is performed by the Army Corps of Engineers to maintain channel depth and width. Port facilities are maintained by federal and local monies.

An example of a major public aid for domestic water carriers is the Tennessee–Tombigbee (Tenn-Tom) project. Opened in 1985, the project connects the Tennessee River and the Warrior River via the Tombigbee River. Another example of public aid was when, in 1986, the federal government built two 1,200-foot locks and a new dam at Lock and Dam Number 26 on the Mississippi River System.

Critics of waterway projects like Tenn-Tom often refer to them as "pork barrel projects," suggesting that they are funded by government funds for the benefit of only a small number of the legislators' constituents. Critics question their value to society and maintain that these projects probably would not have been constructed if the actual users or local taxpayers had to assume the full burden of the costs. The U.S. Army Corps of Engineers has been responsible for conducting benefit/cost analysis to determine if such projects deserve to be funded by federal dollars, but critics question whether the Corps' analyses are realistic and whether the projects' expected benefits will ever be realized.

Labor   Water transportation is not labor-intensive. The Bureau of Labor Statistics calculates a multifactor productivity index (MFP) which is outputs divided by labor hours, fuel, equipment, and materials. In 2013, the MFP for domestic water transportation was 103.869. This compares to an MFP of 103.589 for rail, 104.929 for motor, and 108.486 for pipeline.

Labor is required at the terminal to load and unload general commodities. The freight is moved from the dock onto the ship and into the appropriate hold for the voyage (and vice versa for unloading). In addition, labor is required to handle the loading of freight from connecting modes, such as truck and rail, and to store the freight waiting to be loaded onto the ship or connection carriers.

Domestic water carriers usually do not require much labor at the terminal, because the carriers primarily transport bulk commodities that can be loaded mechanically. Great Lakes carrier companies have developed ships that are equipped with automatic unloading devices that reduce the amount of labor required to unload the ships. Even the container vessels operated on the Great Lakes are designed for expedited loading and unloading with appropriate cranes and other material handling equipment. Sometimes the biggest obstacle to efficiency is labor related.

Current Issues

Drug and Alcohol Abuse   The grounding of the Exxon tanker *Valdez* off the shores of Alaska in March 1989 exemplifies the need for strong measures against drug and alcohol abuse in the water transportation industry. The captain of the *Valdez* was found to be intoxicated at the time the ship ran aground and spilled 10 million gallons of oil off Alaska's shores. The full impact of this disaster may not be known for many years to come; however, it is known that the environmental damage resulted in the deaths of hundreds of sea life, including some endangered species, and the loss of income and jobs for many of Alaska's citizens (such as fishermen, for example).

In recognition of the problem of substance abuse, the U.S. Coast Guard now tests American seamen for drug abuse before they are issued a seaman's license and before they can be employed. Seamen are also tested randomly during their employment.

Port Development Because of today's environmental concerns, ports are having trouble keeping pace with the accelerated developments in global trade. They now have to balance competitive economic concerns with the concerns of the public, which, rightly or wrongly, often view ports as a main source of air, water, and noise pollution.

An example of the struggle would be the problems the Port of Oakland, California, faced in trying to get permission to dredge its harbors to a lower depth in order to berth new, larger vessels. Without the dredging, Oakland's competitiveness would decrease. But proposals for dumping the spoil from the dredging were denied at every turn. Soon, another problem developed. The city's mayor decided to siphon port revenues into the city's coffers to alleviate budget problems. After local and international businesspeople united in support of the port's autonomy, the mayor backed down. Months later, thanks to the concerted efforts of two U.S. representatives and California's governor, the port got approval to dredge and dump the spoil in a cost-effective spot in the bay. Now, California is considering a bill that would allow the state to take revenue from the ports to replenish the state's depleted treasury.

Another current issue facing North American ports is the growth of multicarrier alliances, leading to the expansion of the already gargantuan ships. An increase from 10,000 to 18,000 TEUs per ship has many ports worried for the future. The larger the ships are, the deeper their draft, meaning that many of the smaller ports will need to begin the dredging process as soon as possible to be able to compete in the future. The dredging process would allow ports to make their waterways deeper and wider in order to accommodate these new, larger ships and allow them to stay competitive. However, as indicated earlier, the approval process for the dredging is sometimes problematic.

Brief History of Pipelines

Pipelines have played an important role in the transportation industry in the post–World War II era. Originally, pipelines were used to feed other modes of transportation, such as railroads or water carriers. The Pennsylvania Railroad initiated the development of pipelines in the oil fields of Pennsylvania in the 19th century and then sold out to the Standard Oil Company, establishing the precedent of pipelines being owned by the oil companies. Early in the 20th century, the oil companies operated the pipelines as integrated subsidiaries and often used them to control the oil industry by not providing needed transportation service to new producers. Consequently, after World War II, in a decision rendered by the U.S. Supreme Court, known as the Champlin Oil Case, pipelines were required to operate as common carriers if there was a demand by shippers of oil for their services. This decision was coupled with the growth in demand for gasoline after World War II and the need to move oil and oil products from the oil fields in Texas and Oklahoma to the markets in the northeastern states. The subsequent development of large-diameter pipelines, which were seamless for longer distance shipments, also spurred development and increased the efficiency of the pipeline industry.

Pipeline Industry Overview

The pipeline industry is unique in a number of important aspects, including the type of commodity hauled, ownership, and visibility. The industry is relatively unknown to the general public, which has little appreciation of the role and importance of pipelines. Pipelines are limited in the markets they serve and very limited in the commodities they can haul. Furthermore, pipelines are the only mode with no backhaul; that is, they are unidirectional with products that only move in one direction through the line.

Significance of Pipelines

As seen in Table 8-4, pipelines accounted for about 27 percent of total ton-miles in 1980, but their share of the total has declined in recent years and was 19 percent in 2015. However, their total ton-miles rose to a peak in 2008 of almost 954 billion ton-miles before declining through 2014. In 2015, pipelines generated 967.1 billion ton-miles. Their share of total ton-miles moved in the United States is comparable to the share carried by water carriers. Few people in the United States would guess that pipelines are compared to other transport modes in terms of traffic volume. Pipelines are virtually unknown to the general public, but represent a key component in our transportation system. Oil and oil products represent two-thirds of the ton-miles transported by pipeline, and natural gas makes up the other third.

As shown in Table 8-5, the oil pipeline network grew steadily until about 1980, which allowed pipelines to move an increased amount of tonnage. However, this does not adequately reflect the increase in total capacity because it does not show the diameter of pipelines. As we will discuss later, pipeline diameters have increased in recent years, and the larger diameters have increased capacity significantly because of the increased volume that can move through the pipeline. The larger diameter has also allowed the total oil network to decrease since the early 1980s to about 161,000 miles in 2014. Interestingly, natural gas pipelines (includes transmission and distribution lines) had almost 10 times the mileage of oil pipelines, 1,586,000 miles, in 2014. The distribution network of natural gas pipelines is the reason for the difference because it is the means of delivery to the ultimate user in most cases as opposed to truck deliveries for oil and oil products. The operating revenue of gas pipelines is more than six times greater than the operating revenue of oil.

TABLE 8-4	Pipeline Share of U.S. Ton-Miles of Freight		
YEAR	TON-MILES FROM PIPELINE (IN BILLIONS)	TOTAL U.S. TON-MILES (IN BILLIONS)	PERCENTAGE SHARE OF PIPELINE
2006	906.7	4,630.8	20
2007	904.1	4,609.1	20
2008	953.8	4,647.6	21
2009	909.7	4,302.3	21
2012	820.8	4,861.6	17
2013	891.8	4,954.5	18
2014	929.0	5,092.5	18
2015	967.1	5,118.6	19

Source: U.S. Department of Transportation, Research and Innovative Technology Administration (RITA), Bureau of Transportation Statistics (BTS), special tabulation.

TABLE 8-5	Pipeline Network (Thousands of Miles)	
YEAR	**OIL PIPELINE**	**NATURAL GAS PIPELINE**
1960	191	631
1970	219	913
1980	218	1,052
1990	209	1,189
1995	182	1,278
2000	177	1,340
2005	131	1,489
2010	148	1,545
2013	152	1,576
2014	161	1,586

Sources:
2000 and before:
U.S. Department of Transportation, Bureau of Transportation Statistics, *National Transportation Statistics*, Washington, DC, 2008, p. 28.

After 2000:
U.S. Department of Transportation, Bureau of Transportation Statistics, *National Transportation Statistics*, Washington, DC, 2016, Table 1-10.

The tonnage comparison shown in Table 8-4 is a sharp contrast to the IR revenue picture indicated in Table 8-6. Here the low rates of the pipeline, which are discussed later in this chapter, are reflected in the very low percentage of the total intercity revenue paid to oil pipeline carriers. The pipelines account for approximately 5.7 percent of the total transportation revenues that contribute to GDP, compared to motor carriers, for example, which account for more than 43.8 percent of the total revenue.

Types of Carriers

As noted earlier, due to the decision rendered by the U.S. Supreme Court in the Champlin Oil Case, many pipelines operate as common carriers. Hence, although some private carriers exist today, the for-hire carriers dominate the industry. Common carriers account for approximately 90 percent of all pipeline carriers.

Ownership

With some exceptions, oil companies have been the owners of the oil pipelines—beginning with Standard Oil Company purchasing the pipelines operated by the Pennsylvania Railroad. Subsequently the oil companies developed pipelines more extensively to control the industry and enhance its market dominance. Oil companies became the principal owners of pipelines, but there has been some shift more recently with an increased number of pipeline companies operating as transport carriers.

The federal government entered the pipeline business briefly during World War II when it developed two pipelines to bring crude oil and oil products from the oil fields of the Southwest to the Northeast to ensure an uninterrupted flow of oil. These two pipelines, known as the Big Inch and the Little Inch, were sold to private companies after the war.

Some pipelines are joint ventures among two or more pipeline companies because of the high capital investment necessary for large-diameter pipelines. Individual, vertically

TABLE 8-6	Total Operating Revenue of Pipelines ($ in Millions)			
	OIL PIPELINE		**GAS PIPELINE**	
YEAR	**OPERATING REVENUE**	**NET INCOME**	**OPERATING REVENUE**	**NET INCOME**
2008	19,798	5,105	9,244	3,932
2009	18,953	4,657	9,987	4,131
2010	19,790	5,210	11,219	1,582
2011	20,546	4,888	12,562	6,109
2012	20,970	4,765	14,007	6,423
2013	21,273	4,302	15,734	6,981
2014	24,514	4,776	19,281	9,573
2015	24,093	5,418	22,019	6,689

Source: U.S. FERC Annual Reports (Forms 2, 2A, and 6) by Regulated Interstate Natural Gas and Oil Companies.

integrated oil companies control the largest share of the pipeline revenues, followed by jointly owned pipeline companies. Railroads, independent oil companies, and other industrial companies control the remaining percentage.

Number of Carriers

Like the railroad industry, the pipeline industry has a small number of very large carriers that dominate the industry. In 2015, there were approximately 2,644 total pipeline operators. The oligopolistic nature of the industry is demonstrated by the fact that 20 major integrated oil companies control about two-thirds of the crude oil pipeline mileage.

There are a number of reasons for the limited number of pipeline companies. First, startup costs (capital costs) are high. Second, like railroads and public utilities, the economies of scale are such that duplication or parallel competing lines would be uneconomic. Large-size operations are more economical because capacity rises more than proportionately with increases in the diameter of the pipeline and investment per mile decreases, as do operating cost per barrel. For example, a 12-inch pipeline operating at capacity can transport three times as much oil as an 8-inch pipeline.

The procedural requirements for entry and the associated legal costs also contribute to the limited number of companies. An additional factor is the industry itself, which has been dominated by the large oil companies that joined together in the post–World War II era to develop pipelines from major fields and entry ports.

Oil Carriers The pipeline industry experienced rapid growth after World War II, but the rate of growth (percentage increase) has since decreased dramatically. Freight ton-miles increased to about 939 billion in 2005 but declined through 2014 and then increased to 967.1 in 2015. There were corresponding changes in other data, including the number of employees, which also decreased. Overall, however, oil pipelines play a major role in our transportation network because, as previously mentioned, they transport about 19 percent of the total freight ton-miles in the United States.

Natural Gas Carriers Another part of the pipeline industry is involved with the transportation of natural gas, which, like oil, is an important source of energy. The movement data for natural gas are recorded in cubic feet, rather than ton-miles. The industry is comparable in size to the oil pipeline industry in terms of the number of companies and, as in the oil pipeline industry, there has been a growth in the number of companies since 1975. It should be noted that there has been a reclassification of some companies since 1975, so the growth numbers are not exactly comparable. Natural gas pipelines represent about 7 percent of domestic ton-miles of freight. Finally, operating revenues have increased by about 26.2 percent between 2000 and 2009.

Operating and Service Characteristics

Commodities Hauled Pipelines are specialized carriers in that they transport a very limited variety of products. The four main commodities hauled by pipeline are oil and oil products, natural gas, coal, and chemicals.

Oil and Oil Products The majority of pipeline movements are crude oil and oil products. In 2014, pipelines moved about 14 billion barrels of crude oil and petroleum products. Pipelines in total (including natural gas) experienced a 3.1 percent increase in freight ton-miles shipped from 2007 to 2013.

The total volume of petroleum transported domestically in the United States declined slightly during the 1990s. However, the split by modes between pipeline and water carrier has changed for several reasons. A pipeline was built across Panama during the 1980s, virtually eliminating long movements of Alaskan crude oil tankers around South America. The Alaskan crude oil is now transshipped via the pipeline to Atlanta tankers for Gulf and Atlantic Coast deliveries to refineries. Also, another large crude oil pipeline has been built, providing service from the West Coast to Midwest refineries and reducing the need for tanker movements even further.

The length of haul in the oil pipeline industry is medium in length compared to other modes. Crude oil movements average about 800 miles per shipment, and product lines average about 400 miles per movement. The average shipment size for these movements is very large. (This will be discussed later in the section titled "Equipment.")

Natural Gas Natural gas pipelines are an important part of our total pipeline network. The natural gas pipeline companies produce about 10 percent of the gas they transport. Independent gas companies produce the remaining 90 percent and transport it via the pipelines. Similar to oil pipelines, the natural gas pipelines operate as public carriers.

Coal Coal pipelines are frequently called slurry lines because the coal is moved in a pulverized form in water (one-to-one ratio by weight). Once the coal has reached its destination, the water is removed and the coal is ready for use. Coal pipelines are primarily used for transporting coal to utility companies for generating electricity. The large slurry pipeline that operates between Arizona and Nevada covers 273 miles and moves 5 million tons of coal per year. Coal pipelines use enormous quantities of water, which causes concern in several western states where their installation has been proposed, because there is a scarcity of water and the water is not reusable (as there is no backhaul).

Chemicals Chemical lines are another type of product line, although only a limited number of different types of chemicals are carried by pipelines. The three major chemicals are anhydrous ammonia, which is used in fertilizer; propylene, which is used for manufacturing detergents; and ethylene, which is used for making antifreeze.

Relative Advantages

A major advantage offered by the pipeline industry is low rates. Pipeline transportation can be extremely efficient with large-diameter pipelines operating near capacity. Average revenues for pipeline companies are below one-half of a cent per ton-mile, which is indicative of their low-cost service.

Two additional user cost advantages complement the low rates. First, pipelines have a very good loss and damage record (L and D). This record is attributed in part to the types of products transported, but it is also related to the nature of the pipeline service, which provides underground and completely encased movement.

The second important cost advantage is that pipelines can provide a warehousing function because their service is slow. In other words, if the product is not needed immediately, the slow pipeline service can be regarded as a form of free warehousing storage. (Products move through pipelines at an average of 3 to 5 miles per hour.)

Another positive service advantage of pipelines is their dependability. They are virtually unaffected by weather conditions, and they very rarely have mechanical failures. Although the service time is slow, scheduled deliveries can be forecasted very accurately, diminishing the need for safety stock. The risk of terrorism is reduced when the pipelines are buried in the ground.

Relative Disadvantages

Although the pipelines' slow speed can be considered an advantage due to its use as a free form of warehousing, in some instances, the pipelines' slow speed can be considered a disadvantage. For example, if a company's demand is uncertain or erratic, it will have to hold higher levels of inventory to compensate for possible shortages because the pipeline will not be able to deliver an extra amount of the product in a short period of time.

Pipelines are also at a disadvantage when it comes to completeness of service because they offer a fixed route of service that cannot be easily extended to complete door-to-door service. That is, they have limited geographic flexibility or accessibility. However, because the source of the pipelines and the location of the refineries are known and are fixed for a long period of time, the fixed-route service factor may not be a critical problem. Frequently, pipelines depend on railroads and motor carriers to complete delivery, which adds to user costs.

The use of pipelines is limited to a rather select number of products: crude oil, oil products, natural gas, coal, and a limited number of chemicals. There is interest in using pipelines for other products because of their cost advantage, but the technology for such use has not yet been fully developed. Capsule and pneumatic pipelines can carry and extend the low-cost, high-volume, reliable service to other bulk products. Frequency of service (the number of times a mode can pick up and deliver during a particular period) is a characteristic of interest to some users. On one hand, the large tenders (shipment size requirements) and slow speed of pipelines reduces the frequency. On the other hand, service is offered 24 hours a day, seven days a week.

Pipelines are generally regarded as somewhat inflexible because they serve limited geographic areas and limited points within that area. Also, they carry limited types of commodities and only offer one-way service. Finally, the operations technology precludes small shipment sizes.

In summary, pipelines offer a very good set of services for particular types of products, but they have some serious limitations for many other products.

Competition

Intramodal   Intramodal competition in the pipeline industry is limited by a number of factors. First, there are a small number of companies—slightly more than 100. The industry, as noted previously, is oligopolistic in market structure, which generally leads to limited price competition. Second, the economies of scale and high fixed costs have led to joint ownership of large-diameter pipelines because the construction of smaller parallel lines is not very efficient. Finally, the high capital costs preclude duplication of facilities to a large extent.

Intermodal The serious threats to the pipeline industry are in terms of traffic diversion to other modes of transportation. Technically, pipelines compete with railroads, water carriers, and motor carriers for traffic. However, even with these forms of transportation, the level of competition is limited. The most serious competition is water tanker operations, because their rates are competitive with pipelines. However, the limited coverage of water carrier service also limits its effective competitiveness. Trucks have increased the number of products they carry that can also be carried by pipelines. However, truck service complements rather than competes with the pipeline because trucks often perform a distribution function (delivery) for pipelines.

Once a pipeline has been constructed between two points, it is difficult for other modes to compete. Pipeline costs are extremely low, dependability is quite high, and there is limited risk of damage to the product being transported. The major exception is coal slurry pipelines because the need to move the pulverized coal in water can make the costs comparable to rail movements. Water carriers come closest to matching pipeline costs and rates as indicated.

Equipment

The U.S. Department of Transportation estimates that the total pipeline investment is in excess of $21 billion, based on historical costs. Also, the department estimates it would cost about $70 billion to replace the system at today's costs. This great investment in the equipment is necessary to finance the complex operation of getting oil from the well to the market. From 1980 to 2014, oil pipeline infrastructure (in standard miles) dropped 26.1 percent, while the natural gas infrastructure rose 50.8 percent.

Pipelines can be grouped into other categories in addition to for-hire or private carriers. For instance, they are frequently classified as gathering lines or trunk lines, particularly in reference to the movement of oil. The trunk lines are further classified or subdivided into two types: crude and product lines. The gathering lines are used to bring the oil from the fields to storage areas before the oil is processed into refined products or transmitted as crude oil over the trunk lines to distant refineries. Trunk lines are used for long-distance movement of crude oil or other products, such as jet fuel, kerosene, chemicals, or coal.

Early in the history of the oil industry, the refineries were located primarily in the eastern part of the United States, and thus the long-distance movement of oil was basically the movement of crude oil. The state of technology in the industry also made it much easier to control leakage with crude oil than with refined oil products such as gasoline or kerosene. After World War II, however, refineries were developed at other locations, especially in the Southwest, when better technology (limited seams and welding techniques) made the long-distance movement of oil products easy to accomplish.

When comparing gathering lines and trunk lines, there are several important differences to note. First, gathering lines are smaller in diameter, usually not exceeding 8 inches, whereas trunk lines are usually 30 to 50 inches in diameter. Gathering lines are frequently laid on the surface of the ground to ensure ease of relocation when a well or field runs dry. Trunk lines, on the other hand, are usually seen as permanent and are laid underground.

The term *trunk line* is often used in conjunction with oil movements and can refer to crude oil trunk lines or oil product lines. Oil trunk lines move oil to tank farms or refineries in distant locations, whereas oil product lines move the gasoline, jet fuel, and home heating oil from refineries to market areas. Technically, however, any long-distance movement via a large-diameter, permanent pipeline implies a trunk-line movement. Therefore, when coal, natural gas, or chemicals move via pipelines, such movement is usually classified as trunk-line movement.

Commodity Movement

Gathering lines bring oil from the fields to a gathering station, where the oil is stored in sufficient quantity to ship by trunk line to a refinery. After the oil is refined, the various products are stored at a tank farm before they are shipped via product line to another tank farm with a market-oriented location. A motor carrier most frequently makes the last segment of the trip, from the market-oriented tank farm to the distributor or ultimate customer.

Trunk lines, as indicated previously, are usually more than 30 inches in diameter and are the major component of the pipeline system. Stations that provide the power to push the commodities through the pipeline are interspersed along the trunk line. For oil movements, pumps are located at the stations, which vary in distance from 20 to 100 miles, depending on the viscosity of the oil and the terrain. Figures 8-4 and 8-5, the latest data available, illustrate the major interstate and intrastate pipelines in the United States.

The pumping stations for large-diameter pipelines can provide 3,000 to 6,000 horsepower. Compressors are used for the movement of natural gas, and pumps are used for the liquid items that move through the pipelines.

Computers at the pumping stations continually monitor the flow and pressure of the oil system. Any change indicating a leak is easily detected. Routine visual checks and searches

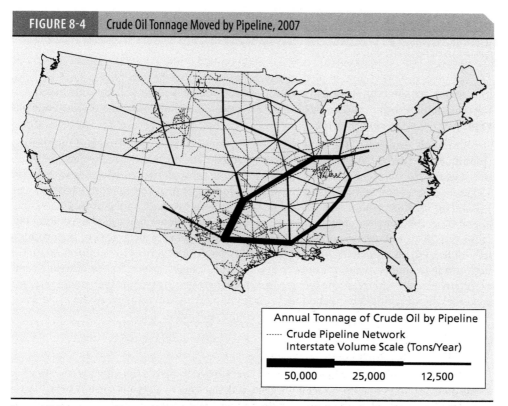

FIGURE 8-4 Crude Oil Tonnage Moved by Pipeline, 2007

Source: U.S. Department of Transportation, *Federal Highway Administration*, Office of Freight Management and Operations, Freight Analysis Framework, Version 3.4, 2012.

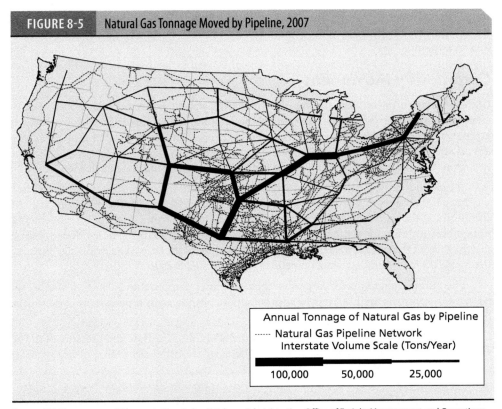

FIGURE 8-5   Natural Gas Tonnage Moved by Pipeline, 2007

Annual Tonnage of Natural Gas by Pipeline
----- Natural Gas Pipeline Network
Interstate Volume Scale (Tons/Year)

| 100,000 | 50,000 | 25,000 |

Source: U.S. Department of Transportation, *Federal Highway Administration*, Office of Freight Management and Operations, Freight Analysis Framework, Version 3.4, 2012.

by airplane are sometimes used to locate leaks. Great care is rendered, not only because of the potential losses but also because of the lawsuits that could ensue as a result of damage to property and the environment.

In the oil segment of the pipeline industry, sophisticated operating and monitoring techniques are used because of the different petroleum products moving through the product lines and the different grades of crude oil moving through the crude oil lines. There are 15 grades of crude oil and a range of products including jet fuel, kerosene, and aviation fuel. When two or more grades of crude oil or two or more products move through a system at one time, the "batches" may need to be separated by a rubber ball called a batching pig. However, this is not always necessary because the different specific grades of the products help to keep them separated. Any mixing (slop) that does occur is only minor amounts of high-grade products mixed into lower-grade items. Usually, products are scheduled one month in advance with kerosene moving first, then high-grade gasoline, then medium-grade gasoline, then various other products, with home heating oil last. Before the cycle starts again, the pipeline is usually scoured to prevent mixing problems.

Cost Structure

Fixed- Versus Variable-Cost Components   Like the railroad industry, the pipeline industry has a high proportion of fixed costs with low capital turnover. The pipeline owners have to provide their own right-of-way by purchasing or leasing land and constructing the pipeline and pumping stations along the right-of-way. The property taxes, amortizations of depreciation, return to investors, and preventative maintenance all contribute to the high ratio of fixed to variable expenses.

In addition to the right-of-way costs, the terminal facilities of pipelines contribute to the high level of fixed costs. The same types of expenses associated with the right-of-way, such as depreciation and property taxes, are incurred by the pipeline terminals.

As stated previously, the pipeline industry has significant economies of scale. The high fixed costs and the economies of scale help to explain the joint ownership and investment in large-diameter pipelines. Pipelines do not operate vehicles like other modes of transportation because the carrying capacity is the pipe itself, which is best regarded as part of the right-of-way. This unique element of the pipeline operation helps to explain the low variable costs because vehicles are frequently a major source of variable expense.

Labor costs are very low in the pipeline industry because of the high level of automation. One example is the Trans-Alaska Pipeline System, built at a cost of $9.2 billion and operated by 450 employees. In 2014, pipelines employed about 47,000 people compared to about 1.4 million in the motor carrier industry. Another variable cost is the cost of fuel for the power system.

Rates Pricing in the pipeline industry is unique compared to its major modal competitors. First of all, pipelines do not use the freight classification system that underlies the class rates of railroads and motor carriers. The limited number and specialization of commodities make such a practice unnecessary. A crude oil pipeline or natural gas pipeline has little need for an elaborate classification system.

Even though pipelines have high fixed costs, the differential pricing practices common in the railroad industry are virtually nonexistent among pipelines. The nature of operation (one-way movement, limited geographic coverage of points, limited products, and so forth) provides little opportunity to provide differential pricing practices. Pipelines quote rates on a per-barrel basis (one barrel equals 42 gallons). Quotes for rates are typically point-to-point or zone-to-zone. Also, minimum shipment sizes, usually called tenders, are required; these range from 500 to 10,000 barrels.

ON THE LINE

OPEC's Production Cuts Are Greatly Overrated

The fundamentals of supply and demand are inexorable. In a world in which futures traders set the price of oil, temporary sentiment can push prices above or below the market equilibrium. But eventually the lights are turned on, the market is left bare, and traders see whom they've been rooming with.

Before jumping into the fundamentals, we need to recognize that the current market is out of balance. According to OPEC's analysis, world oil production outstripped world consumption by an average of 1.1 million barrels per day through the first three quarters of 2016. This oversupply has pushed prices down to levels that reflect the marginal oil producer that today is drilling in one of the domestic shale plays.

Because the market is oversupplied, the volume of oil in storage has been increasing at a rapid clip, and a significant portion of this volume has been flowing into China's strategic petroleum reserves (SPR). This is important because these volumes may not reflect what we may call "real demand," that is demand that is associated with harnessing the potential energy that makes crude oil so valuable.

It has been estimated that China's stockpiles have been growing at a rate between 350,000 and 400,000 barrels per day—or between one and two tanker deliveries per week. While it's not possible to know if this will continue in 2017, it's very possible that the rate of growth is sensitive to price. If it's price sensitive, rising price will quickly eat into "demand."

Global economic growth over the coming year is going to be less driven by China and the developing world economies than has been the case over the last decade. Moreover, interest rates are most likely going to continue to rise over the coming quarters, and as a result, the value of the dollar should increase. And as it does so, developing countries will see more of their export earnings going to debt servicing, leaving less for other activities that generate oil demand.

In addition to suppressing oil prices in the United States (where incomes are earned in dollars), developing countries will find oil and all other imports becoming increasingly expensive. This will have the effect of further suppressing oil consumption.

For the reasons stated above, it's reasonable to assume that oil demand could fall short of most expectations.

Source: Adapted from Derek Andreoli, *Logistics Management*, January 2017, p. 24. Reprinted with permission of Peerless Media, LLC.

Pipeline rates are very low, which is reflected in the fact that they carry about 20 percent of the total intercity ton-miles and receive only about 4 percent of the total revenues.

SUMMARY

- Water carriers played a key role in the development of many cities and regions both globally and domestically.

- The water carrier system is still a viable part of the total transportation system and competes with the railroad system and pipelines for the movement of bulk, low-value commodities.

- The domestic water carrier system can be classified in terms of inland carriers (rivers, canals, and Great Lakes) and coastal/intercoastal carriers. Both types are important components of the water carrier system.

- Intramodal competition among water carriers is not as important as intermodal competition with railroads and pipelines. All three of these modes compete for long-distance movements of bulk commodities.

- Water carriers offer low-cost services, but their transit time is slow and can be interrupted by weather conditions. Accessibility and potential product damage are also service disadvantages.

- Water carriers have relatively low fixed costs because they use a right-of-way provided by the government for which they pay user charges, like motor carriers and airlines.

- Water carriers are not labor-intensive for their movement operations but may require more labor in terminal areas for certain types of freight.

- The development of pipelines began in the 19th century in Pennsylvania by the Pennsylvania Railroad, but subsequently the ownership and development were taken over by the oil companies, who operated them as integrated subsidiaries.

- Ownership of pipelines by oil companies has continued to the present, but some oil pipelines are now owned by nonoil companies. Also, joint ownership by several companies has become common because of the large investment of capital necessary for construction.

- The pipeline industry is a large component of our transportation industry (more than 20 percent of intercity ton-miles), but it is largely invisible to many people.

- Because of market-control tactics used by some oil companies, an important U.S. Supreme Court ruling after World War II required pipelines to operate as common carriers even if owned by an oil company.

- Pipelines are very specialized in terms of the commodities that they carry. Most of the traffic is oil and oil products, but they also carry natural gas, chemicals, and coal.

- Only a small number of pipeline companies operate in the United States (about 100), and they have limited intramodal competition.

- Pipelines are low-cost carriers when operated near capacity, but they have high levels of fixed cost because of the heavy investment necessary in infrastructure. They need volume to lower unit costs.

- Pipeline service is relatively slow and has limited accessibility, but it is very reliable in terms of delivery with little or no loss and damage.

- Intercity pipeline service is provided by large-diameter (30–50 inches) pipelines called trunk lines. Small-diameter pipelines, called gathering lines, are used to bring the oil from the producing area to the terminals for storage before processing and/or transporting.

- Pipelines are a highly automated, efficient form of transportation. Oil moves in one direction in large volumes at a steady, slow speed.

- Although there is always concern about safety and the environment, pipelines have been a relatively safe mode of transportation.

STUDY QUESTIONS

1. The integrated ownership of pipelines was initially used by some oil companies to gain control of oil-producing areas. How did they use their transportation network to gain market control? What other reasons can be offered for integrated ownership? Are these reasons valid in today's business environment?

2. The pipeline industry has approximately 100 companies, as compared to the motor carrier industry with more than 50,000. What are the underlying economic causes for this difference, given the fact that they both carry approximately the same volume of intercity ton-miles?

3. The typical pipeline company has high fixed costs. What economic factors account for this situation? What advantages and disadvantages does their cost structure present?

4. Pipelines account for more than 20 percent of the intercity ton-miles but less than 5 percent of the revenue paid by shippers to transportation companies. What factors account for this contrast? Is this situation likely to change? Why or why not?

5. The economic and market position of the pipelines has been described as mature and stable with little likelihood of significant growth in the near future. Do you agree? Why or why not?

6. Water carriers played a dominant role in the transportation system of the United States in the 18th and 19th centuries. Why has their relative position declined during the 20th century? Are they still an important component of the total transportation system? Why or why not?

7. What would be the impact of higher fuel charges on the water carrier industry? Provide a rationale for raising their user charges.

8. Technology often offers the potential of improving efficiency and effectiveness of transportation companies, but water carriers do not appear to have applied much new technology to improve their service. What impediments slow technological progress in the water carrier industry?

9. Intermodal competition is more intense than intramodal competition for water carriers. Why?

10. Why are pipelines unknown to many individuals? Do you think the pipelines should advertise to change this?

CASE 8-1

Great Lakes Carriers: A Sequel

During the summer of 2014, Ben Heuer, president and chief operating officer of Great Lakes Carriers (GLC), and E. Kate Weber, vice president of business development, revisited the port directors of every major port on the Great Lakes. Their objective was to seek additional business for GLC's bulk cargo division with a related objective of exploring potential demand for increased containership operations on the Great Lakes.

GLC was founded in 1940 by Ben's grandfather with one ship hauling coal and iron ore from the mines along the Great Lakes to the steel mills in Indiana, Ohio, and surrounding areas. Today the company has a fleet of 12 bulk vessels that move grain from the upper Great Lakes area to Chicago, Buffalo, and Erie. There is also some continued demand for bulk coal and iron ore movements. The demand for the movement of such commodities has decreased in the 21st century because of increased foreign steel production, and the railroads have increased their share of the grain movement with new, larger, hopper cars, which provide more dependable movement.

GLC has developed some containership service on the Great Lakes, but the volume has been disappointing. Container traffic between the United States and the European Union can move via railroad to the port of Montreal, where it is transloaded to an oceangoing containership. Substantial NAFTA container traffic (USA–Canada) moves via either railroad or truck to major cities adjacent to the Great Lakes. Lastly, the area surrounding the Great Lakes is a major manufacturing region with large volumes of traffic moving among the major port cities and to inland locations. Radio Frequency Identification (RFID) technology is providing GLC with some competitive advantage for higher-value container traffic where visibility could help improve supply chain efficiency and effectiveness. Kate also believed that they could charge higher rates with RFID tags and explore the possibility of diversifying even further into logistics-related services.

Ben and Kate discussed the type of vessel that would be needed to move containers and concluded that current GLC vessels could not be retrofitted for container operations. Furthermore, the new ship would have a maximum carrying capacity of about 1,000 containers because of the size limitations imposed by the locks on the Saint Lawrence Seaway. The typical oceangoing containership has a minimum carrying capacity of 2,500 containers.

The proposed operation would consist of weekly sailing schedules beginning in Duluth and stopping at Chicago, Detroit, Toledo, Cleveland, Buffalo, and Montreal. Containers would be picked up and delivered at each port along the route. The transit time from Duluth to Montreal was estimated to be five to seven days, compared to four to five days by rail and two days by truck. For intermediate origin–destination pairs, such as Chicago to Cleveland, the transit time was estimated to be three days, which compared favorably with railroad service; however, the truck transit time was one day. The rate for the container service was estimated to be 40 percent of the current truck rate and 75 percent of the current rail rate, but the RFID program may allow higher rates because it would be a premium service and differentiate GLC from the rail and motor carriers.

The meetings with the port directors confirmed that the volume of grain and iron ore being handled by Great Lakes carriers was on the decline and the predictions for the next five years were for a continued decline. The lack of adequate containership service on the Great Lakes was also confirmed and the port directors were enthusiastic about the possibility of

GLC initiating such service. They were also interested in the advantages of the RFID technology even though it would require some additional investment for them.

Ben and Kate decided to delay the decision to invest in the new equipment and technology because of the economic forecasts for the Great Lakes region and related potential cash flow problems. Also, the development of new oil fields more recently with the development of fracking technology in New York, Ohio, and Pennsylvania were changing the economic landscape of the Great Lakes region. Now they were reconsidering their alternatives before moving ahead, with their plans for investment in new technology and equipment.

CASE QUESTIONS

1. What is the overall impact of the new sources of energy in the Great Lakes area? What is the likely impact on commodity flows in that area? What will be the likely impact on GLC?

2. What are some of the logistics supply chain issues that GLC should consider?

3. What recommendation would you make to the GLC board of directors regarding a containership operation and the possibility of new bulk shipments of oil and possibly chemicals?

CASE 8-2

The Keystone Pipeline

Oil production in the Bakken Region of the United States and southern Canada has increased rapidly over the last few years because of the world price for oil. In North Dakota alone, from July 2012 to July 2017, barrels per day rose 54.9 percent from 20,969,942 to 32,473,306. During the same time period, the number of wells producing rose 86.7 percent from 7,309 to 13,648.

This rising production required increases in transportation capacity to move the oil to markets. While pipeline is the traditional mode of choice to move oil, its infrastructure was inadequate to move the product to markets on the East Coast of the United States and to refineries in Texas and Louisiana. To fill this transportation need, rail carriers, such as the Canadian National, Canadian Pacific, and the BNSF, increased railcar movements of oil to both the East Coast and Southwest. Because of the volatile nature of the oil being produced in the Bakken Region, rail movements can pose a safety hazard during transit and several derailments of these cars caused severe damage and environmental concerns.

The Keystone XL Pipeline was proposed by TransCanada to increase capacity to move oil from southern Canada and the Dakotas. Starting in Alberta, Canada, the Keystone would travel 1,179 miles south to the junction of Steele City, Nebraska. From there, oil could be moved east to the Wood River Refinery in Roxana, Illinois, and south to refineries in Port Arthur and Houston, Texas.

The State Department raised concerns about the construction because of its possible negative effects on the fragile ecosystem in the Sandhills Region of Nebraska. Environmentalists raised concerns over the increased energy needed to extract the oil from the tar sands, which would add to global warming and the possible chemical leakage into groundwater. However, environmentalists are also concerned with the negative impact to public safety of transporting the oil by rail.

The U.S. government has vowed to invest $1 trillion over the next 10 years in U.S. infrastructure. Although this investment is typically made in public projects (such as highways and bridges), there is an opportunity to also subsidize the construction of pipelines and rail trackage, which are privately owned. With the growing production of domestic oil and natural gas, the need for increased capacity in transportation infrastructure is evident.

CASE QUESTIONS

1. Given the importance of domestically produced oil to the U.S. economy, should the U.S. government promote and subsidize the construction of pipeline and/or rail infrastructure? Explain your answer.

2. Discuss the advantages and disadvantages of increasing capacity to move this oil by pipeline and by rail. Be sure to include in your discussion environmental, safety, and economic impacts of using each mode.

3. If you had the authority as a U.S. government official, which mode would you choose and why?

Suggested Readings

Chapter 5   Motor Carriers

Bernstein, Mark, "Wireless Takes to the Road," *World Trade* (April 2008): 26.

Burnson, Patrick, "Parcel Express Roundtable: Slugfest," *Logistics Management* (January 2009): 33–36.

Cantor, David E., Thomas M. Corsi, and Curtis M. Grimm, "Safety Technology Adoption Patterns in the U.S. Motor Carrier Industry," *Transportation Journal*, Vol. 45, No. 3 (Summer 2006): 20–45.

"Critical Issues in the Trucking Industry," *The American Transportation Research Institute* (October 2008).

Donath, Max, "Homeland Security and the Trucking Industry," *The American Transportation Research Institute* (July 2005).

Schulz, John D., "Only the Strong Will Survive," *Logistics Management* (April 2009): 46S–54S.

Schulz, John, "Cutting LTL Costs: Going to the Bench," *Logistics Management* (February 2009): 35.

Zuckerman, Amy, "Transportation Management Systems Give Shippers Power to Make Smarter Trucking Choices," *World Trade* (January 2008): 34.

Chapter 6   Railroads

Berman, Jeff, "Senate Committee Endorses Railroad Antitrust Legislation," *Logistics Management* (April 2009): 15–16.

Berman, Jeff, "2008 Annual Report—Railroads: Volume Is Down, but Business Is Up," *Logistics Management* (July 2008): 38.

Berman, Jeff, "Study Says Railroad Fuel Surcharges Exceeded $6.5 Billion," *Logistics Management* (October 2007): 19.

Boyd, John D., "Carloads in Reverse," *Traffic World* (January 5, 2009): 26.

McCue, Dan, "The Changing Landscape of U.S. Railroads," *World Trade* (January 2009): 30.

Sheys, Kevin, "Rail Safety Is No Paper Chase," *Traffic World* (January 5, 2009): 7.

Chapter 7   Airlines

Abeyratne, Ruwantissa, "Competition in Air Transport—The Need for a Shift in Focus," *Transportation Law Journal*, Vol. 33, No. 2 (2005–2006): 29.

Cheng, Yung-Hsiang, and Chian-Yu Yeh, "Core Competencies and Sustainable Competitive Advantage in Air Cargo Forwarding: Evidence from Taiwan," *Transportation Journal*, Vol. 46, No. 3 (Summer 2007): 5–21.

Sowinski, Lara, "Air Cargo Flies a New Heading," *World Trade* (August 2008): 34.

Theurmer, Karen E., "Air Cargo: Flying Low," *Logistics Management* (May 2009): 31.

Theurmer, Karen E., "2007 State of Logistics Report/Air Cargo: Nowhere to Go but Up," *Logistics Management* (July 2007): 42.

Wong, Jehn-Yih, and Pi-Heng Chung, "Retaining Passenger Loyalty Through Data Mining: A Case Study of Taiwanese Airlines," *Transportation Journal*, Vol. 47, No. 1 (Winter 2008): 17–29.

Chapter 8   Water Carriers and Pipelines

"Discussion of Effects of Long-Term Gas Commodity & Transportation Contracts on the Development of Natural Gas Infrastructure," *Interstate Natural Gas Association of America* (2005).

Farris, M. Theodore, "Are You Prepared for a Devastating Port Strike in 2008?" *Transportation Journal*, Vol. 47, No. 1 (Winter 2008): 43.

Higginson, James K., and Tudorita Dumitrascu, "Great Lakes Short Sea Shipping and the Domestic Cargo-Carrying Fleet," *Transportation Journal*, Vol. 46, No. 1 (Winter 2007): 38.

Ives, Buddy, "Pipeline Activity May Slow but Won't Be at Crawling," *Pipeline and Gas Journal*, Vol. 236 (March 2009): 64.

Jewell, Michael T., "The Evolving Pipeline Regulations: Historical Perspectives and a New Model for Pipeline Safety in the Arctic National Wildlife Refuge," *Transportation Law Journal*, Vol. 34 (2007): 173–189.

Shister, Neil, "Ocean Transport Adjusts to New Realities," *World Trade*, Vol. 21 (June 2008): 48.

Warner, Bruce E., and Mark S. Shaffer, "Carbon Capture and Sequestration (CSS): A Pipedream or a Real Business Opportunity for Gas Pipeline Developers?" *Pipeline and Gas Journal*, Vol. 236 (May 2009): 5.

PART III

The first eight chapters of the textbook provide a solid foundation of transportation knowledge. The topics have focused on key issues regarding the role of transportation and the modal options available to freight shippers. We now turn to the strategic activities and challenges involved in the flow of goods through complex, global supply chains. The five chapters in Part III focus on critical transportation management issues.

Chapter 9 explains the roles and industry composition of third part logistics (3PL) providers. Given the financial and service impact of transportation on supply chain success, many companies are turning to external experts to assist with their freight flows. This chapter discusses the structure of the 3PL industry and highlights the current perspectives of 3PL users. Specific issues related to establishing and managing 3PL relationships are addressed, along with a discussion of current and future 3PL issues.

Chapter 10 examines the topic of transportation risk management. Companies must proactively work to understand and mitigate the potential freight flow disruptions that exist across the supply chain. Following a general overview of key concepts and the risk management process, the chapter focuses on transportation risk reduction strategies, methods, and outcomes. Special attention is given to the increasingly important topic of supply chain security.

Chapter 11 has combined chapters 10 and 11 from the previous edition of this text. This chapter focuses on the extensive set of planning activities related to the timely flow of freight between countries. Proper management of trade terms, insurance, and documentation set the stage for successful global flows. As companies shift their sourcing in the pursuit of lower landed cost and greater flexibility, they need to review and revise the mode, carrier, and route selection options that facilitate effective global freight flows. The execution activities related to these flows are also discussed in this chapter. International freight must be properly packed, transported, and cleared through Customs. This chapter discusses the key intermodal options for moving freight by appropriate combinations of land, sea, and air. Also highlighted are the key service providers who streamline the freight flows and minimize border crossing complications.

Chapter 12 provides an overview and examines the development and role of government regulation and public policy directed at transportation service, particularly in the United States. Local, state, and federal regulation of private transportation companies has been in existence since the 19th century in the United States. These controls are on one level a recognition of the importance of transportation to the development and ongoing vitality of an economy. In many countries of the world, important parts of the transportation system are provided by the government. This is especially true of railroad and air carrier service.

There have been major changes in the regulatory structure in the United States and elsewhere, but regulations, particularly in the area of safety, continue to play a role that needs to be understood.

Transportation is a dynamic field that must constantly adapt to the world it serves. As supply chain requirements expand, economic conditions change, and technological innovations emerge, transportation professionals must respond accordingly. **Chapter 13** tackles the major issues of transportation infrastructure, talent management, sustainability, and fuel cost and consumption, as well as other challenges. Emerging transportation strategies and technologies for improving transportation capabilities are also discussed in this forward-looking wrap up.

9

THIRD PARTY LOGISTICS

Learning Objectives

After reading this chapter, you should be able to do the following:

> Understand the concept of third party logistics and its role in the movement of goods

> Identify the different types of third party logistics service providers

> Describe the four types of transportation activities that are outsourced

> Discuss the reasons why companies seek integrated third party logistics services

> Understand the size and scope of the third party logistics market

> Evaluate the reasons for outsourcing and the results achieved

> Summarize the process for outsourcing transportation and logistics activities

> Appreciate the current challenges and competitive issues in the third party logistics industry

> Recognize the importance of information technology in managing outsourced activities

TRANSPORTATION **PROFILE**

Key Criteria for Evaluating Potential 3PL Providers

Selection of a third party logistics service provider (3PL) should not be a quick decision. You must take the time to evaluate and choose a partner that is capable of providing excellent service, driving innovation, and creating value for your supply chains. A weak selection process runs the risk of establishing a relationship with an ineffective, inconsistent 3PL service provider.

You must properly vet each potential service provider's cost, capacity, coverage, and capabilities to ensure that they can consistently meet your requirements. This vetting process includes a number of important considerations and related questions:

1. Expertise. Does the 3PL have a deep talent pool with industry-specific supply chain knowledge?
2. Integrated services. Does the provider offer multiple logistics capabilities–fulfillment, inventory management, multimodal delivery, and so on?
3. Global coverage. Does the 3PL conduct operations in your worldwide markets?
4. Performance excellence. Does the 3PL have an established and verifiable track record of highly effective and efficient service?
5. Scalability. Does the 3PL have the flexibility to handle your seasonal demand patterns, geographic expansion, and new fulfillment channels?
6. Technological innovation. Does the 3PL deploy integrated planning and execution tools that meet your needs for shipment visibility, process optimization, and remote data access?
7. Financial stability. Does the 3PL conduct its business in a profitable manner and maintain a reasonable debt load?

This level of due diligence in the 3PL evaluation and selection process is essential for achieving long-range success. A well-chosen 3PL service provider will provide tangible and readily measurable benefits of transportation cost reductions, inventory cost reductions, and logistics fixed asset reductions, as well as improvements in order fill rate, accuracy, and timeliness. Given these impacts you cannot afford to make poor 3PL selection decisions.

Sources: C. John Langley and Capgemini, *2015 Third Party Logistics Study: The State of Logistics Outsourcing*, retrieved 24 November 2014, from http://www.3plstudy.com/; and Jamie Wyatt, "Evaluating Potential 3PL Logistics Providers and What You Should Be Looking For," *Supply Chain 24/7*, May 19, 2013, retrieved 24 November 2014, from http://www.supplychain247.com/article/evaluating_potential_3pl_logistics_providers_and_what_you_should_be_looking.

Introduction

Outsourcing continues to grow in the second decade of the 21st century. Reliance on external experts for noncore services and capabilities is commonplace as few organizations can afford to manage all business activities in-house. Hence, it is common, for example, to shift information technology (IT) processes to an external service provider that manages the systems, software, and equipment. This allows the company to focus on using the technology to operate the business rather than having to manage all the technical issues and challenges. Similarly, external experts are frequently used for accounting, payroll and tax preparation, advertising, human resources benefits administration, and numerous other activities. Some companies outsource their production to contract manufacturers located around the world.

Transportation is another activity that is widely outsourced to external experts. Global companies like COSCO (China Ocean Shipping Company), Deutsche Post (owner of Exel and DHL), FedEx, C.H. Robinson, and UPS provide a wide variety of transportation and logistics services to individuals and companies around the world. These third party logistics service providers (3PLs) are experts in the management and flow of freight, allowing customers to focus their resources on other activities. Some of these larger organizations provide a one-stop shopping solution where customers can purchase all their transportation service needs, regardless of mode or geographic requirements.

Given the financial and service impact of transportation on a company's success, developing an effective transportation outsourcing strategy is critical. As the Transportation Profile suggests, you should not just hire the first 3PL that comes to the door. It is imperative to find a 3PL with a track record of providing quality transportation management and services that support execution excellence. How to accomplish this is the goal of this chapter. We will discuss the general structure of the 3PL industry, customer characteristics, and relationship options. Specific issues related to establishing and managing 3PL relationships will be addressed, followed by a discussion of current and future 3PL industry issues. Throughout the chapter, you will gain an understanding of the key benefits and challenges of outsourcing transportation requirements.

Industry Overview

If you were to conduct an Internet search for a definition of *third party logistics* or *3PL*, the responses would be numerous and varied. These explanations range from simple and arbitrary to extensive and specific. Here are a few examples:

Wikipedia: a company's use of third-party businesses to outsource elements of the company's distribution and fulfillment services.[1]

EFT (eyefortransport): an organization that manages and executes a particular logistics function, using its own assets and resources, on behalf of another company.[2]

BusinessDictionary.com: arrangement in which a firm with long and varied supply chains outsources its logistical operations to one or more specialist firms, the third party logistics providers.[3]

Council of Supply Chain Management Professionals: outsourcing all or much of a company's logistics operations to a specialized company. The term *3PL* was first used in the early 1970s to identify **intermodal marketing companies** (IMCs) in transportation contracts. Up to that point, contracts for transportation had featured only two parties, the shipper and the carrier. When IMCs entered the picture—as **intermediaries** that accepted shipments from the shippers and tendered them to the rail carriers—they became the third party to the contract, the 3PL. Definitions have broadened to the point where these days, every company that offers some kind of logistics service for hire calls itself a 3PL. Preferably, these services are integrated, or "bundled," together by the provider. Services they provide are transportation, warehousing, cross-docking, inventory management, packaging, and freight forwarding. In 2008, legislation passed declaring that the legal definition of a 3PL is "A person who solely receives, holds, or otherwise transports a consumer product in the ordinary course of business but who does not take title to the product."[4]

Pulling the key points from these definitions, a 3PL firm may be defined as "an external supplier that performs or manages the performance of all or part of a company's logistics functions."[5] This definition is purposely broad and is intended to encompass suppliers of services such as inventory management, warehousing, distribution, financial services, and

TABLE 9-1	Role of Outsourced Logistics Providers
ROLE	**DESCRIPTION**
1PL	Shipper or consignee
2PL	Individual, asset-based provider of logistics services
3PL	Firm that manages and/or provides multiple logistics services for use by customers
4PL	Firm that provides broader scope of services to help manage elements of supply chain
5PL	Broader range of companies that aggregate demands of 3PLs into bulk volumes to negotiate better rates with airlines and shipping companies
LSP	Logistics Service Provider—actually can refer to any or all of the above

Source: Based on C. John Langley Jr., Ph.D., Penn State University.

transportation. This chapter will focus on the transportation aspects of the 3PL industry, though it is important to remember that transportation services provided by a 3PL must be well integrated with the customer's other logistical activities. The transportation-focused 3PLs must also provide solutions to logistics challenges and supply chain problems.

Table 9-1 highlights the terminology related to the use and provision of logistics services. As you can see, while the term 1PL relates to the shipper or consignee, 2PL relates to the asset-based provider of logistics services. Then, 3PL includes those provider organizations that manage or provide multiple logistics services for use by customers. The term 4PL broadens the perspective to reflect the provision of a broader scope of services (for example, managing multiple 3PLs; advanced IT services; strategic consultancies; and "control tower"), and 5PL suggests the concept of further aggregating demand for logistics services in the interest of creating cost efficiencies. Note, however, that the definitions of outsourced logistics providers do vary across individuals and companies, so that the definitions provided in Table 9-1 may not be the most widely accepted ones. In this chapter, we often use 3PL and LSP interchangeably, to indicate that 3PLs are general service providers who can perform any logistics function for their clients.

Types of 3PL Providers

Just as there are many ways to define third party logistics, there are many ways to categorize the service providers. Figure 9-1 identifies the prominent types of logistics service providers and shows how they differ in terms of service offerings, asset intensity, and geographic diversity. For example, while asset-intensive ocean liners and railroads have more limited service offerings and geographic diversity, many 3PLs are significantly less asset intensive, more geographically diverse, and provide a broader range of service offerings. Also, identified on the right side of this figure are several competitive threats that are faced to some extent by these various types of providers.

One very fundamental distinguishing feature of logistics service providers is the resources that they use to fulfill customer requirements. 3PLs with tangible equipment and facilities are called **asset-based providers**. In contrast, 3PLs that leverage the resources of other companies are called **nonasset-based providers**. A few details on each of these types are included below.

Asset-Based Providers When a 3PL owns many or all of the assets necessary to run its customers' transportation and logistics activities, it is known as an asset-based provider. This

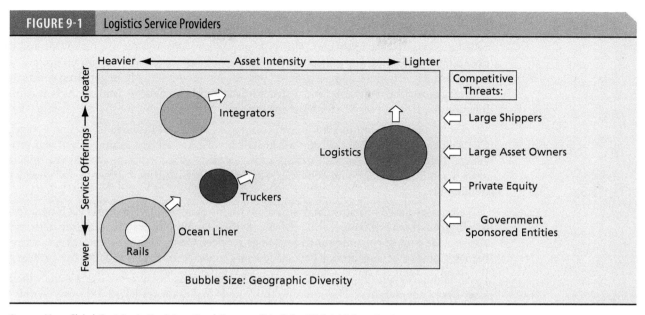

| FIGURE 9-1 | Logistics Service Providers |

Sources: MergeGlobal, Containerization International, Company Data, Robert W. Baird & Co. estimates.

category includes companies that own truck fleets, ocean vessels, aircraft, terminals and warehouses, material handling equipment, technology systems, and/or other resources. An asset-based provider typically has its own labor force to perform the customers' work and a management team to oversee the day-to-day operations. Having these internal resources allows the 3PL to leverage internal strengths and infrastructures to provide direct, immediate solutions.

This type of 3PL includes widely known companies such as UPS, J.B. Hunt, Exel, Ryder, and FedEx. We are familiar with them because we see their vehicles on the road and pass by their facilities. FedEx Corporation, for example, has a network of company-owned facilities that are linked by FedEx vehicles and aircraft. Their various operating divisions—FedEx Express, FedEx Freight, FedEx Custom Critical, and so forth—are capable of moving shipments ranging from single packages to full truckloads, as well as managing customers' inventory and order fulfillment needs from FedEx-owned distribution centers.

Many customers choose to work with asset-based providers because they have readily available **capacity**, permanent employees, and direct control of the customers' freight. They prefer to work with a single 3PL that will take total responsibility for the outsourced activity and assume accountability if problems occur. Customers can also maintain greater visibility of outsourced activities and inventory if they are handled by a technology savvy asset-based provider who performs all activities internally rather than handing them off to other companies.

The primary concern with asset-based providers is the potential for bias toward use of their internal resources. The argument is that these companies have made significant investments in physical assets and are tethered to those assets when developing solutions for customers (for example, even if there is a TL carrier that gives lower rates for a particular client, the provider that owns trucks may be tempted to use their own trucks for this client to improve their equipment utilization rates). This internal focus may not always generate the most flexible solutions or produce the most cost-efficient transportation and logistics services for the customers.

Nonasset-Based Providers When a 3PL contracts with other firms to provide transportation and logistics services rather than owning the required equipment and facilities, it is called a nonasset-based provider. This type of provider acts as a service integrator and is not restricted to using any particular warehouse or transportation company in providing services to its customers. Nonasset-based providers offer expertise in negotiating contracts with transportation companies and distribution centers in an effort to achieve the best combination of price and service for their customers.

From a transportation standpoint, companies like C.H. Robinson, Kuehne + Nagel, CEVA Logistics, and XPO Logistics are heavily involved in **freight management** and brokerage, helping customers with freight activities such as securing capacity at reasonable costs, scheduling pickups and deliveries, **routing and scheduling** shipments, and auditing freight bills.

Nonasset-based providers may also focus on international freight flows via freight forwarding, **customs brokerage**, and related activities. Finally, nonasset-based providers may also provide strategic planning and technology services. Consulting firms such as Accenture, Bain & Company, Capgemini, KPMG, and some software firms may fall into this category.

Customers typically view nonasset-based providers as being more flexible than their asset-based counterparts. The common thinking is that nonasset-based 3PLs can be unbiased in their decision making as they are not limited to an internal infrastructure of assets. Because they are not restricted to using any particular transportation company or set of facilities to serve customers, they are free to objectively choose the best set of service providers and create innovative solutions for customers. This can lead to tailored services and lower overall costs for the customer.

There are also concerns with nonasset-based providers. First, these companies do not have significant internal capability to handle customers' requirements. This can be a problem during times of economic expansion when there may be limited availability of purchased transportation alternatives. Also, there are more moving parts and relationships to manage when a nonasset-based provider uses external service providers on behalf of their customers, and nonasset-based providers need to make sure that their cost of purchased transportation services may align with how they price their services to their clients and customers. Last, it is imperative to have strong IT capabilities to maintain control and visibility of customers' freight that is dispersed among a variety of transportation and warehousing companies.

Another method for distinguishing 3PLs is by the primary services provided. While many 3PLs promote themselves as **integrated service providers** with a comprehensive range of logistical capabilities, most have their origins and greatest level of expertise in a specific logistics activity. Hence, the easiest way to categorize these service providers is on the basis of their foundation service offerings. 3PLs are typically categorized as being transportation-, distribution-, forwarder-, financial-, or information-based firms. Each of these is discussed briefly in the following paragraphs.

Transportation Based These 3PLs trace their origins to freight movement via truck, rail, air, or other modes of transportation. As customer requirements expanded, these transportation companies developed 3PL subsidiaries or major divisions to provide a broader set of capabilities to serve the marketplace. Not only do these organizations move freight, they may also manage transportation operations on behalf of customers, provide **dedicated contract carriage**, operate fulfillment centers, and develop logistics solutions, among other services.

Transportation company-based 3PL services include UPS Supply Chain Solutions, FedEx Trade Networks, Schneider Logistics Services, Damco (Maersk Group), and BNSF Logistics. Some of the services provided by these 3PLs leverage the transportation assets of their parent companies, while others rely upon the assets of other companies. In all instances, these firms extend beyond the transportation activity to provide a more comprehensive set of logistics offerings.

Distribution Based   These 3PL suppliers originated from the public or contract warehousing business and have expanded into a broader range of logistics services. Based on their traditional orientation, these types of organizations are heavily involved in logistics activities such as inventory management, warehousing, and order fulfillment. Some have added transportation services to assist customers with the coordination, optimization, and execution of shipments via all modes. The combination of distribution and transportation capabilities creates a one-stop integrated logistics service offering so that customers have the option of working with a single 3PL.

Distribution-based 3PLs range from single facility operators to global organizations with strategically located operations centers. Major players include Exel (DHL Supply Chain), DSC Logistics, Saddle Creek Logistics, and DSV. This category also includes a number of 3PL firms that have emerged from larger corporate logistics organizations. For example, Neovia Logistics Services was developed by Caterpillar Inc. and Intral Corporation was created when The Gillette Company spun off its in-house import/export logistics department in an effort to focus on core competencies, increase efficiencies and recognize bottom-line savings.

These providers have significant experience in managing the logistics operations of the parent firm and, as a result, prove to be very capable providers of such services to external customers. Though it has not technically spun off its logistics expertise into a stand-alone organization, Amazon.com is rapidly developing a variety of 3PL-like fulfillment and transportation services.

Forwarder Based   This group of 3PLs includes **freight forwarders**, brokers, and agents that primary facilitate the flow of goods on behalf of customers. Though these companies do not own equipment, they arrange transportation services for LTL (less-than-truckload) shipments, air cargo, and ocean freight, as well as providing other transportation-related services. Many are engaged in the support of international freight movement, booking cargo space with carriers, arranging freight movement to and from carrier facilities, preparing and processing documentation, and performing related activities.

Some of these brokerage-based organizations, such as C.H. Robinson Worldwide Inc., Hub Group Inc., and Kuehne+Nagel Inc. have extended their primary roles into a broader range of 3PL services. Others are focusing on consolidating assets in the highly fragmented freight brokerage space. This merger and acquisition activity is driven by the goal of increasing profitability through economies of scale. For example, XPO Logistics made 13 acquisitions between 2011 and 2014. The company expects to spend $2.75 billion on acquisitions over the next several years.[6]

Financial Based   This category of 3PL providers helps customers with monetary issues and financial flows in the supply chain. Their traditional roles include **freight rating**, freight payment, **freight bill auditing**, and accounting services. Some of the financial-based 3PLs have added information system tools to provide freight visibility (such as **tracking** and **tracing** capabilities) and assist customers with electronic payment, carrier compliance reporting, and freight claims management.

Primary players among this category include Cass Information Systems, Inc.; CT Logistics; U.S. Bank (Syncada); enVista; and TranzAct Technologies. In addition, companies like GE Capital (General Electric) and CIT Transportation Finance provide transportation equipment financing, leasing services, and asset tracking.

Information Based The Internet has provided an excellent platform for the growth of information-based 3PLs. These companies have digitized many activities that were previously performed manually or required the use of licensed software. Today, these information-based 3PLs provide online freight brokerage services as well as cargo planning, routing, and scheduling. They also offer companies access to **transportation management systems (TMS)**, warehouse management systems, and performance management tools via the Internet on a per use basis. This software as a service capability allows customers to avoid the high cost of licensed software implementation, instead paying for access on a variable cost basis.

Though many information-based 3PLs have come and gone during the Internet era, a few strong players have emerged. Companies like Descartes Systems Group, Transplace, and MercuryGate are among the leaders in creating robust information tools and online capabilities for the coordination, optimization, and control of transportation and logistics activities. Another interesting move is that Uber recently made official entrance into the trucking market using its app (see the On the Line box). The emerging generation of transportation management systems from information-based 3PLs will empower shippers and 3PLs that want to better manage the transportation process—perhaps even blending their own private or dedicated fleets with third-party assets—to reduce costs and gain significantly greater supply chain visibility.[7]

ON THE **LINE**

Uber Freight Makes Official Entrance into Trucking Market

While anticipated for some time, ubiquitous ride-sharing service Uber said last month it has officially entered the freight transportation arena, specifically truckload brokerage, with the introduction of Uber Freight. In a blog posting, Eric Berdinis, Uber Freight product manager, wrote that Uber Freight is an app that matches trucking companies with loads to haul—taking the guesswork out of finding and booking freight, a stressor for drivers.

"What used to take several hours and multiple phone calls can now be achieved with the touch of a button," Berdinis explained. Vetted users download the Uber Freight app, search for a load and tap to book it. Rate confirmation comes within seconds, eliminating the common anxiety about confirmation. And, Berdinis said that rather than the common practice of a trucker waiting 30 days or more to get paid, Uber Freight is "committed to paying within a few days, fee-free, for every single load," and "when things don't go as planned or drivers have to wait longer than expected, we pay for that, too," with accessorial rates published on the Uber Freight blog and website.

Uber has had its sights on the truckload brokerage market for some time, with a September 2016 Reuters report noting that it was keen on becoming a freight hauler through its acquisition of Otto, a self-driving truck startup for $680 million in August 2016, and a technology partner for trucking. Uber is now pitching its services to shippers, truck fleets and independent drivers, not just to outfit trucks with self-driving technology, but also to be a player in the highly competitive $700-billion truckload brokerage arena—which is replete with major players such as C.H. Robinson Worldwide, XPO Logistics, and Echo Global Logistics among others.

Uber's Berdinis said in an interview that the company has been testing its freight platform for several months. "We firmly believe we can make a significant impact in the future of trucking with a new way of booking freight and a new way of connecting small fleets and owner–operators with the large tail of capacity out there to the community of shippers that don't traditionally have the resources to go out and find capacity," he said.

Prior to this launch, Uber had been piloting a program with a handful of United States-based shippers as well as a number of small carriers based in the triangle between Dallas, Houston, and San Antonio.

Going forward, Berdinis said that Uber Freight will focus on independent drivers and small fleets, noting that owner–operators may be viewed as a dying breed these days due to the challenges in finding consistent freight.

Uber Freight's initial focus is on the two most common freight types in the United States, dry van and refrigerated (reefer), which offers a lot of space to route and optimize movements of these small fleets using the app. "Going into this space and doubling down on small fleets and creating a top-quality service for a shipper base offers room for growth," he said.

According to Morgan Stanley analyst Ravi Shanker, the move marks an escalation in the truck brokerage disruption wars. "Thus far, we've seen several startups vying to be the 'Uber of freight' achieve scale in the past two years, but Uber's launch marks the entry of the first tech giant into this space ahead of Amazon's impending launch this summer."

In the long-term, Shanker says his firm is seeing secular margin compression at all of the 3PLs. "This is due to the threat of increased competition from startups vying to crowd-source freight, and they continue to raise meaningful amounts of private capital; insourcing at e-commerce and other logistics giants; and vertical integration into the asset-light business by asset-heavy players including, eventually, OEMs."

Source: *Logistics Management*, June 2017, p. 12.

3PL Services and Integration

As the preceding discussion indicates, there are many types of 3PL service providers offering a vast array of capabilities. Name any type of transportation or logistics requirement that a customer may have and there is a 3PL able to support it. These customer requirements range from strategic supply chain design to daily operations. Within the transportation function, 3PLs provide four primary types of services: freight movement, freight management, intermediary services, and specialty services. Figure 9-2 highlights key capabilities within each service type.

Most of the service offerings related to freight movement and freight management are discussed in detail in other chapters. However, you may not be familiar with some of the intermediary and special services offered by 3PLs to their customers. Each service option is briefly described below.

Surface Freight Forwarding Surface freight forwarders pick up, assemble, and consolidate shipments and then hire carriers to transport and deliver the consolidated shipments to the final destination. They match demand with capacity and help customers obtain economic rates for the consolidated shipments. From the perspective of the customer, freight forwarders act as the carrier, and, therefore, are liable to shippers for loss and damage to freight that occurs during transit.

Air Freight Forwarding Air freight forwarders consolidate small shipments for long-haul movement and distribution. They primarily use the services of major passenger and freight airlines for long-haul service. The air freight forwarder serves the shipping public with pickup service, a single bill of lading and freight bill, one-firm tracing, and delivery service.

FIGURE 9-2	3PL Primary Transportation Offerings
FREIGHT MOVEMENT	**FREIGHT MANAGEMENT**
• For-hire carriage	• Carrier selection, routing, and scheduling
• Contract carriage	• Contract compliance
• Expedited service	• Performance analysis
• Time definite service	• Freight bill auditing and payment
• Intermodal service	• Transportation management systems
INTERMEDIARY SERVICES	**SPECIALTY SERVICES**
• Surface forwarding	• Dedicated contract carriage
• Air forwarding	• Drayage
• Freight brokerage	• Pool distribution
• Intermodal marketing	• Merge in transit
• Shippers associations	• Household good movement

Freight Brokerage Brokers function as middlemen between the shipper and the carrier much the same as a real estate broker does in the sale of property. A broker is an independent contractor paid to arrange transportation. The broker normally represents the carrier and seeks freight on their behalf to avoid moving empty equipment. They may also represent shippers seeking capacity on the spot market.

Intermodal Marketing Companies IMCs are intermediaries between shippers and railroads and are also known as consolidators or agents. They are facilitators or arrangers of rail transportation service. They assume little or no legal liability; the legal shipping arrangement is between the shipper and the railroad, not the agent. Freight charge payment usually is made to the IMC who, in turn, pays the long-haul carrier.

Shippers Associations These nonprofit transportation membership cooperatives arrange for the domestic or international shipment of members' cargo with motor carriers, railroads, ocean carriers, air carriers, and others. The association aggregates cargo and ships the collective membership cargo at favorable volume rates.[8]

Dedicated Contract Carriage 3PLs offering this hybrid private/for-hire arrangement serve as a customer's private fleet with a customized turnkey solution. Dedicated contract carriage includes the management of drivers, vehicles, maintenance services, route design, delivery, and administrative support for a fixed price. Companies gain the advantages of a private fleet without the direct responsibility of capitalizing and operating it.

Drayage These companies provide local transportation of containerized cargo. Drayage companies specialize in short-haul movement of intermodal containers from origin to ocean ports and rail yards and from these facilities to their ultimate destination. They are typically contracted by the rail or ocean carrier to provide these pickup and delivery services.

Pool Distribution As an alternative to direct LTL service, a 3PL may move a large quantity of product in bulk to a specific market or regional terminal. From there, the pooled freight is offloaded, sorted by customer, and then reloaded onto local delivery trucks for distribution to final destinations. Pool distribution can reduce transit times, maintain shipment integrity, reduce claim potential due to less handling, and generate cost discounts versus LTL rates.[9]

Merge-in-Transit A merge-in-transit system unites shipments from multiple suppliers at a specified merge point located close to the end customer. It avoids the need for traditional warehousing, in which orders are assembled from inventory in stock for shipment. Merge-in-transit provides a number of customer benefits, including the delivery of a single, consolidated shipment, reduced order cycle time, and lower transportation costs with less inventory in the system.

Last Mile Delivery The final leg of the transportation journey can be very expensive, accounting for up to 28 percent of total delivery costs.[10] It has become a significant challenge with the growth of e-commerce delivery of goods that consumers would normally purchase in-store and carry home. While UPS, FedEx, and postal services handle the bulk of these deliveries, they do not typically provide same-day delivery or handle large shipments like appliances and furniture. In response, a new breed of last mile service providers has emerged to cover the final dock-to-door or store-to-door delivery and provide value-added services such as inside delivery, product assembly, installation, and testing, and packaging removal. These last mile service providers represent the final opportunity to impress customers and provide a high-quality delivery experience. Retailers like Macy's, eBay, and Amazon provide a wide array of last mile services including same-day delivery in an attempt to differentiate themselves from the competition.

While many 3PLs have expertise in different areas, leading 3PLs are pursuing two additional capabilities. First, they are developing integrated service offerings to accommodate customer desires for one-stop shopping with a single service provider. Second, they are expanding service territories to meet the requirements of increasingly global customers.

These two customer-driven moves go hand in hand. As customers embrace global sourcing and distribution, their supply chains become more complex and challenging. In turn, they need the assistance of highly capable 3PLs to develop integrated, cross-functional global supply chains. Transportation expertise is not enough to capture the attention of these increasingly sophisticated customers. 3PLs must play an essential architect role in the

TABLE 9-2	FedEx Capability Expansion Timeline
YEAR	**EVENT**
1998	• Acquires Caliber System Inc. comprised of small-package carrier RPS, LTL carrier Viking Freight, Caliber Logistics, Caliber Technology, and Roberts Express.
1999	• Acquires air freight forwarder Caribbean Transportation Services.
2000	• Company is renamed FedEx Corporation.
	• Expanded service capabilities are divided into operating companies: FedEx Express, FedEx Ground, FedEx Global Logistics, FedEx Custom Critical, and FedEx Services.
	• FedEx Trade Networks is created with the acquisitions of Tower Group International and WorldTariff.
	• FedEx Supply Chain Services became part of FedEx Services.

(continued)

TABLE 9-2	Continued
YEAR	**EVENT**
2001	• Acquires LTL carrier American Freightways.
2002	• FedEx Freight is created with rebranding of Viking Freight and American Freightways.
2004	• Acquires Kinko's printing company.
2006	• Acquires LTL carrier Watkins Motor Lines.
2007	• Acquires international firms to enhance global capabilities: express company ANC (United Kingdom), Flying-Cargo Hungary Kft (Hungary), Prakash Air Freight Pvt. Ltd. (India), and DTW Group's 50 percent share of the FedEx-DTW International Priority express joint venture (China).
2011	• Acquires the logistics, distribution and express businesses of AFL Pvt. Ltd. and its affiliate, Unifreight India Pvt. Ltd. to generate more robust domestic transportation and added capabilities in India.
	• Acquires the distribution, transportation, and retail operations of MultiPack (Mexico).
2012	• Acquires the Polish courier company Opek Sp.z o.o.
	• Acquires TATEX, a leading French business-to-business express transportation company.
	• Acquires Rapidão Cometa, one of the largest transportation and logistics companies in Brazil.
2014	• Acquires Bongo International, a leader in cross-border enablement technologies and solutions.
2015	• Acquires GENCO, one of North America's largest third-party logistic providers.
2016	• Acquires TNT Express, significantly enhancing the FedEx network worldwide.

Source: FedEx Timeline, available at http://about.van.fedex.com/our-story/history-timeline/timeline/. Used with permission.

design and execution of interconnected supply chain networks.[11] This requires strong IT tools, multimodal capabilities, and the ability to manage and streamline the flow of goods through the supply chain.

In response to the demand for integrated services, larger 3PLs (such as Deutsche Post, UPS, and FedEx) have embarked on an aggressive plan to expand and integrate their capabilities. Table 9-2 provides an example of this expansion, revealing how FedEx has acquired numerous companies since 1998. The company has leveraged the strength of its express delivery service to create a more diversified portfolio of global transportation, e-commerce, and business services. For example, FedEx SupplyChain executes solutions that leverage the FedEx shipping and information networks in commercial markets around the world. The division provides integrated services for customers with high-value products or complex supply chain requirements.

FedEx is not alone in the pursuit of integrated capabilities and global reach. Customers' increasing activity in global sourcing and distribution has driven 3PLs like Exel, CEVA Logistics, and GEODIS to bolster their international resources through the creation of internal divisions, acquisition of smaller 3PLs, or the development of partner relationships with other 3PLs. They are building logistics expertise and well-developed transportation networks to accommodate the growing volume of trade between key regions of the world.

Another option to address customers' global service requirements is to invest in strategically located transportation and distribution facilities. These assets can help an organization establish critical hubs, streamline flows, and support customer fulfillment needs. UPS has been very active in this regard, establishing a physical presence in Asia, Europe, and Latin America that allows the company to serve more than 200 countries and territories. However, investments in these facilities alone may not always streamline flows. The Global Perspective feature highlights the challenges the shippers and 3PLs face in global supply chain operations.

GLOBAL **PERSPECTIVES**

Global 3PL Management: Factors to Keep at Top of Mind

Global third party logistics providers (3PLs) are not a dime a dozen; in fact, there are only a few truly global supply chain managers—and they are a part of large, diverse global transportation networks. Most of the major players, such as UPS, FedEx, DHL, and DB Schenker, all have IT platforms interfacing with their customers to provide global visibility from origins to destinations; they're experts at Customs clearance around the globe; and they're active in all transportation modes and regularly adjust between ocean, air, trucking, and same-day delivery to best accommodate individual orders.

However, global shippers need to keep in mind that supply chain management capabilities—even those managed by the most expansive global 3PLs—vary greatly between countries. The biggest challenge is often managing expectations within a region's physical limitations.

Advanced economies generally have better highways, ports and railways as well as better communication systems and technology. Political changes can especially complicate matters, but those issues are normally limited to emerging market and developing economy countries.

As a general rule, logistics costs as a percent of GDP are lower in advanced economies and higher in emerging market/developing countries. Not surprisingly, the countries with the largest economies dominate infrastructure statistics.

The United States has the most miles of highways, railways, and pipelines. Meanwhile, China, with the second largest economy, has the third largest amount of highways and railways. India is second in the total miles of roadways; however, only 2 percent to 3 percent of India's roadways are modern highways. Even some of these, like Highway 9 from Mumbai to Pune, have uneven surfaces and transportation obstacles.

These persistent infrastructure challenges create opportunities for modern, sophisticated 3PLs. Global shippers who seek to succeed in today's landscape should remember the following: Even when a global supply chain is managed by an experienced and expansive global 3PL, many regions and countries have limitations such as infrastructure, technology, and carrier service levels. It's important to manage expectations based on your areas of operation and seek out "true" global 3PLs that know the lay of the land.

Source: *Logistics Management*, June 2017, pp. 63S–64S.

3PL User Overview

In the previous section, you were introduced to different types of 3PLs and specific service providers, as well as brief references to 3PL customers. In this section, we dig into the customer aspects of 3PL. The key issues include who these customers are, why they outsource transportation and logistics activities to 3PLs, and what services they require. As you will learn, outsourcing has become a way of life for shippers, who rely heavily on 3PLs to help plan, execute, and control their supply chains.

Table 9-3 provides an overview of global logistics expenditures for 2015, as reported by Armstrong & Associates in their annual study of service trends, 3PL market segment sizes, and growth rates.[12] As you can see, the steady growth and expansion of the global 3PL industry produced 3PL revenues in 2015 of $788.4 billion. Looking at this figure, the 3PL industry in North America accounted for $195.5 billion, or 25 percent of the global total.

Looking more closely at the United States, Figure 9-3 provides annual data on 3PL revenues from 2000 to 2017 (estimated). Over this time frame, these revenues have increased from $56.6 billion in 2000 to $156.8 billion in 2016 and an estimated $172.5 billion in 2017. With the exception of the U.S. revenues in 2009 (global economic recession), there has been steady growth in these revenue figures for almost the past 20 years.[13]

This spending, in both the domestic and international markets, is driven by large companies. The 2017 Armstrong study found that 90 percent of the Fortune 500 companies outsourced some or all of their logistics and supply chain functions with technology, automotive, and retailing industries as leading users.[14] Major 3PL users include companies such as General Motors, Procter & Gamble, and Walmart with each using 50 or more 3PLs to help manage and operate their extensive supply chains. While many 3PLs rely upon these Fortune 500 clients for current revenues, future growth opportunities also lie with small and midsize companies.

Reasons for Outsourcing

The most logical reason for using 3PL services is a lack of internal capabilities. Companies with little transportation and logistics expertise would be wise to outsource rather than attempting to build internal operations. They can leverage the knowledge, skills, networks, and resources of experienced 3PLs.

You may be surprised to find that Procter & Gamble and Walmart, companies with premier supply chain capabilities, make extensive use of 3PL services. They, like other companies, use 3PLs when it is appropriate to reduce costs, increase resource capacity, and fill

TABLE 9-3	Global Logistics Costs and Third-Party Logistics Revenues (US$ Billions)				
REGION	2013 GDP	LOGISTICS (% OF GDP)	2013 LOGISTIC COST	3PL REVENUE (%)	2013 3PL REVENUE
North America	21209.6	8.6%	1825.6	10.7%	195.5
Europe	17487.3	9.5%	1657.5	10.4%	171.6
Asia Pacific	24161.4	12.8%	3082.5	9.5%	292.1
South America	3641.5	12.0%	438.6	8.6%	37.9
Remaining Regions/Countries	7697.1	14.7%	1130.3	8.1%	91.3
Total	74196.9	11.0%	8134.5	9.7%	788.4

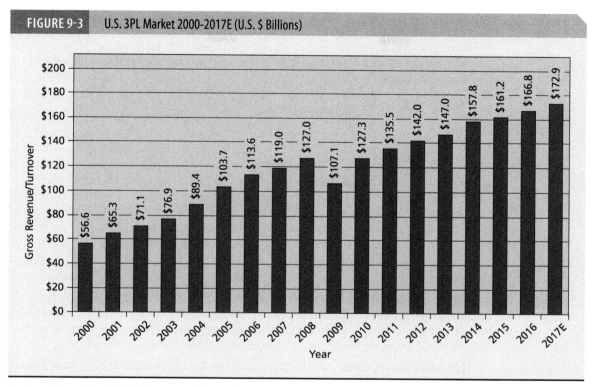

FIGURE 9-3 U.S. 3PL Market 2000-2017E (U.S. $ Billions)

gaps in expertise. For example, Walmart contracts with Exel to handle distribution of automotive tires to its U.S. stores. Walmart avoids the cost of building a dedicated tire warehouse, leverages Exel's inventory management capabilities, and reduces the need to expend energy on a product line that is not sold in all stores.

Numerous studies have identified why companies outsource or do not outsource their transportation and logistics requirements. Table 9-4 provides lists from two studies that

TABLE 9-4 Reasons for and Against 3PL Use

REASONS FOR USING 3PL SERVICES	REASONS AGAINST USING 3PL SERVICES
Opportunity for cost reductions	Logistics is a core competency of company
Ability to focus on core competencies	Cost reductions would not be experienced
Opportunity to improve customer service	Control over outsourced function would diminish
Improve return on assets	Service level commitments would not be realized
Increase in inventory turns	Company has more expertise than 3PL providers
Productivity improvement opportunities	Logistics is too important to consider outsourcing
Generate logistics process flexibility	Outsourcing is not a corporate philosophy
Access to emerging technology	Global capabilities of 3PL need improvement
Expansion to unfamiliar markets	Inability of 3PLs to form meaningful relationships
Ability to divert capital investments	Issues related to security of shipments

Sources: B. S. Sahay and Ramneesh Mohan, "3PL Practices: An Indian Perspective, *International Journal of Physical Distribution & Logistics Management*, Vol. 36, No. 9, 2006; and Georgia Tech and Capgemini LLC, *Eleventh Annual 3PL Study*, 2006.

highlight these factors. Note that there is some conflict between the results, as a reason for outsourcing may also be listed as a reason for not outsourcing. Clearly, outsourcing transportation and logistics is not for every organization. Before choosing to use 3PL services, an organization should spend time developing clear transportation objectives and then analyze if and how 3PLs can provide key support.

Primary Activities Outsourced

While the use of 3PLs has grown significantly, customer engagement patterns have not changed dramatically from year to year. Organizations predominantly use 3PL service providers for approximately three different services, led by transportation management as the most frequently used service, according to Armstrong and Associates. Their recent study of nearly 6,400 shipper–3PL relationships revealed that 81 percent remain "tactical" in nature, meaning 3PLs are mostly used for specific tasks such as transportation or warehousing. Only 19 percent of the relationships are classified as "strategic," where a 3PL manages a customer's entire logistics and supply chain operation on an integrated basis.[15]

Table 9-5 provides information pertaining to logistics activities outsourced from the annual Penn State–Capgemini, KornFerry International, and Penske study of 3PL customers and 3PLs.[16]

As you can see in Table 9-5, domestic and international transportation are the top two logistics activities outsourced, with 86 percent and 66 percent of global shippers, respectively, indicating they outsource at least some of these two activities. Also among the more widely outsourced activities are warehousing, customs brokerage, and freight forwarding.

The heavy use of tactical transportation activities does not mean that 3PLs should abandon their drive toward integrated global service capabilities. Over three-quarters of the

TABLE 9-5 Activities Outsourced to 3PLs	
OUTSOURCED LOGISTICS SERVICES	**PERCENTAGES OF 3PL USERS**
Domestic Transportation	86%
Warehousing	66%
International Transportation	60%
Freight Forwarding	44%
Customs Brokerage	42%
Transportation Management and Planning	36%
Cross-docking	34%
Freight Bill Auditing and Payment	32%
Inventory Management	24%
Order Management and Fulfillment	24%
Reverse Logistics (defective, repair, return)	23%
Product Labeling, Packaging, Assembly, Kitting	22%
Supply Chain Consultancy Services Provided by 3PLs	19%
Information Technology (IT) Services	17%
Fleet Management	15%
Service Parts Logistics	12%
Lead Logistics Provider/4PL Services	10%
Customer Service	9%

Source: 2017 21st Annual Third Party Logistics Study, C. John Langley Jr., Ph.D., Penn State University and Capgemini LLC.

participants in the Penn State–Capgemini study look to their 3PLs for needed integration, rather than trying to accomplish it internally. 3PL customers, particularly those with mature and complex supply chains, prefer to work with strategic service providers that can integrate processes, people, and services. It is not surprising that these customers view IT as exceptionally critical to this integration capability.[17]

Results Achieved

3PL users are satisfied with their outsourcing results, according to results of the Penn State–Capgemini annual studies. The 2014 study participants, from across industries and around the globe place a high value on their relationships with 3PL service providers. A distinct majority of users (90 percent) and 3PL service providers (97 percent) state that their relationships are successful. In addition, 55 percent of the users indicate that their use of 3PL services has led to year-over-year incremental benefits in order fill rates and accuracy.[18]

These positive evaluations are not surprising, given the financial results achieved on a year-to-year basis. For the most recent year of the Annual 3PL Study, study participants report logistics cost reductions of 11 percent, inventory cost reduction of 6 percent, and fixed logistics asset reductions of 23 percent.[19]

Establishing and Managing 3PL Relationships[20]

The development of a 3PL relationship should not happen by chance. A purchaser should carefully evaluate potential 3PL service providers and select the one whose capabilities, commitment level, and price match the buyer's requirements. This can be a time-consuming process but it will greatly increase the likelihood of a mutually beneficial relationship.

Figure 9-4 outlines the steps involved in establishing and sustaining 3PL relationships. For purposes of illustration, let us assume that the model is being applied from the

FIGURE 9-4	3PL Relationship Development Process

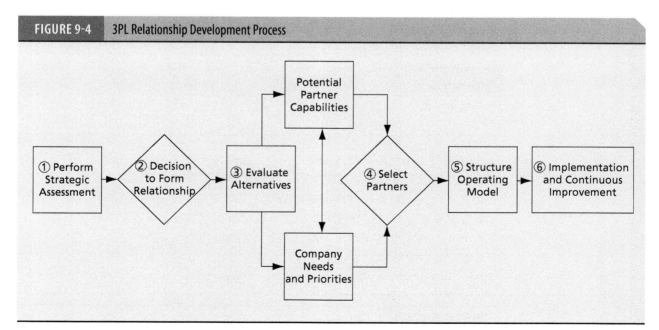

perspective of a manufacturing firm, as it considers the possibility of forming a relationship with a 3PL service provider.

Step 1: Perform Strategic Assessment This first step focuses on the company becoming fully aware of its transportation and logistics needs and the overall strategies that will guide its operations. An audit provides a perspective on the firm's transportation and logistics activities, as well as generating useful information for assessing 3PL relationship options. Information derived from this audit includes:

- Overall role of transportation and logistics in supporting business goals and objectives
- Needs assessment to include requirements of customers, suppliers, and key logistics providers
- Identification and analysis of strategic environmental factors and industry trends
- Profile of current logistics network and the firm's positioning in respective supply chains
- Benchmark, or target, values for logistics costs and key performance measurements
- Identification of gaps between current and desired measures of logistics performance (qualitative and quantitative)

Given the significance of most transportation and logistics relationship decisions, and the potential complexity of the overall process, time taken at the outset to gain an understanding of one's needs is well spent.

Step 2: Decision to Form Relationship When contemplating a 3PL relationship, it is necessary to identify needed capabilities. A suggested approach is to make a careful assessment of the areas in which the company appears to have **core competency**. As Figure 9-5 indicates, for a firm to have core competency in transportation and logistics, it is necessary to have expertise, strategic fit, and ability to invest. The absence of any one or more of these may suggest that the use of 3PL services is appropriate.

Determining whether a partnership is warranted and, if so, what kind of partnership should be considered has been the subject of much research. One such study created a partnership model that incorporates the identification of "drivers" and "facilitators" of a

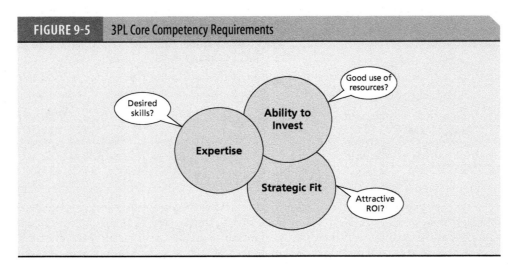

| FIGURE 9-5 | 3PL Core Competency Requirements |

Source: C. John Langley Jr., Penn State University.

relationship; it indicates that for a relationship to have a high likelihood of success, the right drivers and facilitators should be present.[21]

Drivers are defined as "compelling reasons to partner." Drivers are strategic factors that may result in a competitive advantage and may help to determine the appropriate type of business relationship. The primary drivers include:

- Asset/Cost efficiency
- Customer service
- Marketing advantage
- Profit stability/Growth

For a relationship to be successful, the participants must believe that they will receive significant benefits for one or more of these drivers and that these benefits would not be possible without a partnership. **Facilitators** are defined as "supportive corporate environmental factors that enhance partnership growth and development." When present, these factors promote success in the relationship. The main types of facilitators include:

- Corporate compatibility
- Management philosophy and techniques
- Mutuality of commitment to relationship formation
- Symmetry on key factors such as relative size, financial strength, and so on

A number of additional factors have been identified as keys to successful 3PL relationships. Included are factors such as: exclusivity, shared competitors, physical proximity, prior history of the potential partner, previous experience with the partner, and a shared high-value end user.

Step 3: Evaluate Alternatives These drivers and facilitators can be used to identify the most appropriate type of 3PL relationship. If neither the drivers nor the facilitators are present, then the relationship should be more transactional or "arm's length" in nature. Alternatively, when all parties to the relationship share common drivers, and when the facilitating factors are present, then a more structured, formal relationship is justified.

It is also important to conduct a thorough assessment of the company's needs and priorities in comparison with the capabilities of each potential partner. This task should include critical measurements of past performance, interviews of key personnel, and site visits.

Transportation and logistics executives have the primary roles in the decision to form 3PL relationships. However, it can be advantageous to bring managers from other functions such as finance and production into the evaluation process. Their valuable perspectives will contribute to the analysis and promote a strong decision. Thus, it is important to promote broad representation from across the company in this step of the partnership formation process.

Step 4: Select Partners While this stage is of critical concern to the customer, the selection of a transportation or logistics partner should be made only after very close consideration of the credentials of the top candidate 3PLs. Also, it is highly advisable to interact with the final candidates on a professionally intimate basis.

It is important to achieve consensus on the final selection from the executives involved in the evaluation process. This will create a significant degree of buy-in and agreement among those involved. Due to the strategic significance of a 3PL relationship, everyone must have a consistent understanding of the final selection and what is expected of the chosen service provider.

Step 5: Structure Operating Model The process does not end with the selection of a service provider. The companies must also develop working agreements and contracts that clarify the activities, processes, and priorities that will drive day-to-day operations. A well-designed operating model will clarify each party's responsibilities and will help to sustain the relationship. A suggested list of operating model elements includes:

- Planning
- Joint operating controls
- Communication
- Risk/Reward sharing
- Trust and commitment
- Contract style
- Scope of the relationship
- Financial investment[22]

Step 6: Implementation and Continuous Improvement With commencement of 3PL service operations, the most challenging step in the relationship process begins. Depending on the complexity of the new relationship, the overall implementation process may be relatively short or it may be extended over a longer period of time. If the situation involves significant restructuring of the company's transportation or logistics network, then full implementation may take longer to accomplish. In a situation where the degree of change is modest, the time needed for successful implementation may be abbreviated.

Finally, the future success of the relationship will be a direct function of the ability of the involved organizations to achieve both continuous and breakthrough improvement. As indicated in Figure 9-6, there are a number of steps that should be considered in the continuous improvement process. In addition, efforts should be made to create breakthrough improvements that drive the relationship to new levels of competitive advantage.

FIGURE 9-6 **3PL Continuous Improvement Process**

Source: Adapted from Ray A. Mundy, C. John Langley Jr., and Brian J. Gibson, Continuous Improvement in Third Party Logistics, 2001. Used with permission.

The ultimate goal of this six-step process is to develop productive relationships between companies and 3PL service providers that create outstanding customer service and cost-efficient operations. Like any relationship, both organizations must invest time and energy into its development and sustainment. Both parties must share information, trust their counterparts, and be open to new ideas and methods. The most successful long-term 3PL relationships occur when the organizations collaborate on a regular basis, adopt a team approach to problem solving, and leverage each other's capabilities.

Strategic Needs of 3PL Users

As discussed earlier, results from the Penn State–Capgemini 19th annual study indicates that 3PL users are satisfied with their outsourcing activities. However, the continuous change taking place in supply chains and the ongoing need for improved service and relationships means that 3PLs cannot be complacent. Figure 9-7 highlights the capabilities needed by 3PLs to keep pace with the strategic needs of their customers.[23] Although the 3PLs bear primary responsibility for providing these capabilities, the customers must take a collaborative role in achieving maximum success. Among the most important needs of 3PL users are strategic innovation, technological strength, capacity access, talent availability, omni-channel agility, and sustainability expertise. Each issue is discussed briefly below.

Strategic Innovation The 3PL community has long been lauded for their execution prowess and performance consistency. They are viewed as fast and reliable but not particularly innovative. This is a problem for customers whose supply chains are changing quite rapidly due to the explosion in omni-channel activity, the growth of nearshoring initiatives, and the

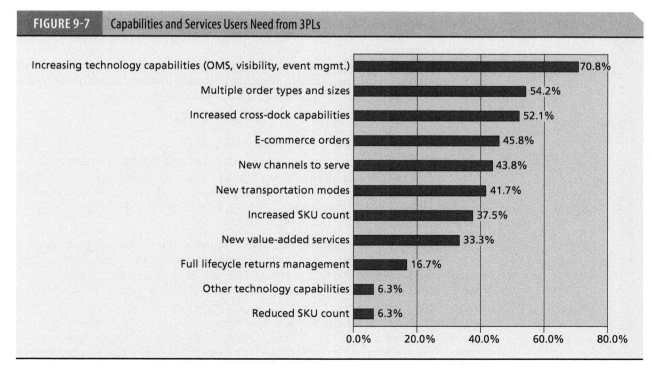

FIGURE 9-7   Capabilities and Services Users Need from 3PLs

Source: 2014 Tompkins Supply Chain Consortium.

increasing level of transportation regulation. Traditional fulfillment channels and delivery methods may not effectively serve user requirements in these scenarios.

To provide maximum value to the customer base, 3PLs must be innovative and collaborative in solutions development. Information sharing on changing requirements is essential for the two parties to understand the dynamics of the situation at hand. Then, the 3PL must have the willingness and capability to develop novel solutions. They also need to be more proactive in suggesting strategic solutions.

To encourage innovation, the customer must remain patient as breakthrough improvements are not developed overnight. They need to realize that a pure cost savings focus with related financial metrics do not encourage innovation. There is risk and cost involved in creating solutions. Thus, customers must collaborate with 3PLs on risk mitigation and create incentives to maximize innovative thinking.[24]

Technological Strength As Figure 9-7 indicates, a top need of 3PL users is upgraded technology capabilities. Customers view technology as a critical capability of 3PL service providers to improve order management, cross-chain communication, enhance shipment visibility and **event management**, and manage day-to-day transportation operations. This need for strong, integrated technology capabilities from their service providers is essential for proactive control of freight as it moves across global supply chains.

The good news is that most large 3PLs have integrated systems platforms to support global transportation and warehouse management operations. These platforms offer the much-desired Internet-based shipment tracking and process visibility, exception resolution capability, and transportation management systems functionality. This allows customers to effectively manage orders, control inventory, and optimize thousands of shipments across large geographical areas.[25] Additional benefits of working with 3PLs having these types of IT capabilities are highlighted in the Transportation Technology feature.

Of course, not every 3PL uses cutting-edge technology to manage customer activity. This is evidenced by the IT gap revealed in the Penn State–Capgemini annual study. It highlights a 36 percent gap between the users who indicate that IT capabilities are a necessary element of 3PL expertise (96 percent of respondents) and the percentage who are satisfied with 3PL IT capabilities (60 percent of respondents).[26] With technology rapidly evolving and customer needs changing, it will be challenging for 3PLs to narrow this gap. However, those that do will become valued service providers.

Capacity Access When domestic and global economies are strong; the market for transportation services becomes very competitive. This makes it difficult for companies to maintain access to adequate transportation capacity. This is particularly true for companies that do not have adequate freight volume to create purchasing clout with trucking companies, railroads, and other modes. This can lead to higher costs, shipment delays, and service inconsistency.

A solution to the capacity dilemma is to work with 3PL service providers such as freight forwarders and brokers that have ongoing relationships with multiple carriers. The combined volume of the 3PL's customer base can be leveraged for consistent access to much needed capacity at competitive rates. Integrated 3PLs also have their own transportation equipment and labor that can be exclusively assigned to their customer base through dedicated contract carriage and other agreements. To make the situation workable, 3PL users must accurately plan their capacity needs and effectively collaborate with the service providers on their volume growth, geographic delivery patterns, and service requirements.

TRANSPORTATION **TECHNOLOGY**

The Payoffs of 3PL Investment in IT Capabilities

When a 3PL makes effective investments in integrated IT tools that contain both planning and execution capabilities, both the customers and the 3PL will reap valuable results.

Choosing a technology savvy 3PL will help a customer gain relatively rapid access to valuable resources without a significant out-of-pocket investment. This will generate the following benefits:

- **Lower IT costs.** The shipper can leverage the 3PL's software for its outsourced transportation and logistics activities. The key is to clarify the IT commitments in the contractual agreement.

- **Higher levels of service.** Use of transportation management systems (TMS) helps the 3PL better plan, execute, and manage product flows for customers. This will promote in-transit visibility and delivery optimization that improve customer satisfaction.

- **Stronger communication.** Deployment of event management tools generate early warning signals of delivery problems so that the 3PL can rapidly resolve the issue. This will avoid the surprises and long delays that dissatisfy customers.

Fortunately, IT benefits are not one-sided. The 3PL can also gain value from their technology spending. The service provider payoffs include:

- **Increased customer satisfaction.** Technology drives the dissemination of timely and accurate transportation information to customers. This supports operational control and informed decision making, both of which boost customer satisfaction.

- **Better data for planning.** Access to a data warehouse of customer transaction information (delivery lanes, volume, spending, and so forth), will help the 3PL better plan its operations. This will ensure capacity is available when and where it is needed at the right price.

- **Lower costs.** 3PLs can use technology to optimize performance across multiple customers' transportation activities. The 3PL can use TMS tools to create better routes and utilize capacity more effectively to reduce the cost of serving customers.

Given these dual benefits, IT capabilities have become an essential component of the 3PL-customer relationships. When the technology helps the 3PL improve its capabilities and performance, customer satisfaction will increase and future revenue growth will be achieved.

Sources: Adapted from Chris Norek and C. John Langley Jr., "IT in the 3PL Industry: Trends and Expectations," *Logistics Quarterly*, Fall/Winter 2013/14. Used with permission.

Talent Availability At a time when SCM is gaining stature as a strategic driver of success, many organizations face a critical supply chain talent void due to years of headcount reduction, training budget cuts, and the retirement of highly skilled individuals. Supply chain leaders must address this talent gap by assembling a team of talented professionals with skills that are core to the organization's SCM mission.[27]

One way to address the talent crisis is to hire a 3PL with strong and stable talent. Top 3PLs have the strategic foresight to invest in training, development, and retention programs that help them maintain a strong pipeline of leaders who can diagnose customer needs, develop effective solutions, and manage the implementation process. These people investments boost morale, increase productivity, and reduce turnover, which are essential for relationship continuity and customer satisfaction. In turn, strategic workforce spending translates to revenue and profitability growth for the 3PL.[28]

Omni-Channel Agility The emergence of new distribution channels has created a much more complex working environment for transportation and logistics managers, particularly for retailers. No longer are they merely managing deliveries to the back door of retail outlets. Today, they are supporting home delivery, manufacturer direct delivery, alternate site delivery, and variations of buy online and pickup in stores. On top of this, companies like Amazon.com, eBay, and Macy's offer same-day delivery in some markets.

Collectively, this makes for huge omni-channel transportation and logistics challenges that many companies are not equipped to handle with their existing processes, talent, and IT resources. As highlighted in Figure 9-7, these customers desire to work with 3PLs that can effectively handle a growing inventory base and e-commerce orders that vary in type, size, and delivery location. These 3PLs must offer flexible solutions for rapidly moving inventory through these networks to customer and managing returns from customers.

Sustainability Expertise The execution of supply chain processes has a significant impact on the environment—delivery processes require heavy use refined oil products, generate carbon emissions, and contribute to congestion. Transportation managers are under increased pressure to deploy delivery methods that have lower environmental impacts—without raising the cost or reducing the quality of service. This is a difficult task, given the scope of global transportation networks and the growth of e-commerce home delivery, but one that has important societal and financial implications.

3PL users need to work with service providers that are committed to sustainable supply chain practices and have developed expertise over time. While many 3PLs have adopted TMS tools to help them minimize resource use through the optimization of routes and the reduction of empty miles, a much smaller group has invested in alternative fuel equipment and LEED (Leadership in Energy and Environmental Design) certified facilities. For example, Saddle Creek has established a fleet of more than 200 trucks that run on compressed natural gas, one of the cleanest burning alternative fuel options available with near-zero emissions. The equipment reduces carbon footprint and noise levels, leverages the domestic U.S. fuel supply, and minimizes fuel cost fluctuations.[29] This investment is a win for the company, its customers, and the environment.

Future Requirement 3PL industry revenues have increased from $30.8 billion in 1996 to $161 billion in 2015 (estimates).[30] This is due to the 3PL service providers' collective ability to provide high quality, competitively priced services in increasingly complex supply chains. As customers shift their global activities, expand their omni-channel activities, and pursue new innovations, the level of supply chain complexity will also grow. In turn, their service requirements will evolve. 3PLs, especially those developing far-reaching physical networks, integrated logistics capabilities, and effective IT tools, will be well positioned to serve the emerging transportation and logistics needs of their customers.

To maintain pace with customers' future requirements, 3PLs will need to effectively expand their capabilities through internal growth, mergers, and strategic acquisition of competitors. As customers shift production from faraway locations to nearby emerging markets where the cost of labor, shipping, and land is less expensive, 3PLs will need to establish a presence in these new regions. 3PLs will also need to enhance their breadth of capabilities and strategic services to serve customer desires for one-stop shopping and lead logistics provider skills. Finally, 3PLs will need to be a driving force of transportation and logistics innovation to ensure that they can meet the cost-efficiency and service quality requirements of customers.

3PL Versus Private Carrier

So far our discussions in this chapter have focused on the use of 3PLs. While it is certainly a viable option for companies to outsource their transportation activities to 3PLs, many companies choose to insource their transportation activities; that is, to manage transportation by using their own fleet (private carrier). In a sense, private carriage is on the opposite side of using 3PLs, because private carriage does not rely on anyone outside (3PLs or for-hire carriers) to meet the transportation needs. While many companies are attracted by the idea of a private carrier—"Avoid paying 'profits' to carriers and 3PLs by having a private fleet"—to many companies, managing a private carrier is a challenging task. Although many companies are enjoying success by using private fleet, many others have tried but given up using private fleet because they were not getting the results they expected; such as reduced cost and improved customer service. In order to benefit from the use of private carrier, companies (shippers) must be able to manage their own fleet effectively and efficiently, which requires a certain level of knowledge in carrier management. Since a company's decision on whether to use 3PLs or not should be made only after carefully examining all available options, which include managing private fleet, this section discusses issues on how to manage private fleet. Companies that can manage the issues discussed below quite well should consider using private fleet, but those that cannot do so should consider using 3PLs. Since private truck fleet is the most widely used type of private carriage, the discussions that follow will focus on covering private motor carriage.

Operating Cost

A fundamental requirement for an economical private truck fleet is knowing the costs. Once the costs are known and analyzed, effective decisions can be made. In general, the two most important cost items for carriers (for-hire or private) are driver cost and fuel cost, as they constitute the largest costs. As such the discussions that follow will focus on how to manage these two costs.

Fleet operators should carefully manage their fleet operations so as to minimize the cost of drivers. Usually driver cost is the largest cost for carriers. If the fleet is managed poorly, fleet operators will face increased amounts of total mileage and driver time. Since the operating cost of private fleet is a direct function of these two metrics, namely mileage and driver time, it is important that fleet operators monitor these metrics carefully. The following paragraphs describe how drivers are paid.

Over-the-road drivers are usually paid on the basis of the miles driven. City drivers are paid on an hourly basis. Table 9-6 provides an example (typical case) of a union contract covering drivers in the Midwest. As indicated in the table, over-the-road drivers are paid 42.0 cents per mile; this rate of pay is the same whether the tractor–trailer is loaded or empty. The rate is 43.0 cents per mile for driving a tractor pulling double trailers or twins. However, the over-the-road driver is paid $17.10 per hour for delays such as breakdowns. If we assume an over-the-road driver drives 125,000 miles per year (2,500 miles per week × 50 weeks), the fringe benefit cost equals 15.0 cents per mile ($18,803.70/125,000).

The city (pickup and delivery) driver is paid $17.36 per hour. To this hourly rate for city drivers (and over-the-road drivers) the cost of fringe benefits must be added, which amount to $9.79 per hour. The total driver costs, then, is $27.15 per hour ($17.36 hourly rate plus $9.79 fringe benefits per hour). Fringe benefits represent roughly 36.1 percent of the total city driver cost.

In addition to managing driver costs, fleet operators should also try hard to improve fuel mileage of their vehicles because the savings potential is great. For example, assume the fleet

TABLE 9-6	Example of Driver Costs		
DRIVER WAGES			
OVER-THE-ROAD			**CITY**
0.42 cents/mile (five axle combination) 0.43 cents/mile (double trailer) $17.10/hour (waiting)			$17.36/hour
FRINGE BENEFITS			
BENEFIT		**TOTAL COST**	**COST/HOUR (1920 HRS/YR)***
Hospitalization ($112.70/week)		$5,860.40	$3.05
Pension ($88.00/week)		4,576.00	2.38
Holidays (10 days @ $138.88/day)		1,388.80	0.72
Vacation (2.0 weeks @ $781.20/week)**		1,562.40	0.81
FICA (7.65%)		2,775.60	1.45
Federal Unemployment		64.00	0.03
State Unemployment ***		762.38	0.40
Worker's Compensation ***		1,814.12	0.95
Total Fringe Costs		**$18,803.70**	**$9.79**

*Total hours possible = 52 weeks × 40 hours/week
  Less: Vacation (80 hours), Holidays (80 hours) Hours worked/year 2,080 hours – 160 = 1,920
**Vacation is an average; Actual is based on years of service
***Varies by state (5 percent rate used)

can increase vehicle mileage per gallon by 10 percent, from 5 miles per gallon to 5.5 miles per gallon. The total fuel cost savings for 140,000 miles per year would amount to $2,800 per truck or 9.1 percent. Such potential savings are usually sufficient justification for purchasing certain equipment parts to enhance fuel efficiency, such as trailer and cab roof fairings, trailer side skirts, aerodynamic side mirrors, and SmartWay certified tires. Fleet operators should also be familiar with, and be willing to adopt, other methods of reducing fuel consumption or costs that are discussed in Chapter 5 (Motor Carriers) Fuel Management section, which includes the use of network truck stops, fuel optimizers, and bulk purchasing strategy.

Equipment   The private trucking manager is concerned with two basic equipment questions: What type of equipment should be selected, and should this equipment be purchased or leased? Each of these questions is discussed below.

Choosing the type, size, make, model, type of engine, and so on of the vehicle used in private trucking seems to be an overwhelming challenge. However, the equipment used is determined by the firm's transportation requirements. The size of the shipment, product density, length of haul, terrain, city versus intercity operation, and special equipment needs are the equipment determinants to be examined. Table 9-7 provides a summary of the equipment selection factors and implications.

The size of the shipment and product density determine the carrying capacity desired in the vehicle. Shipments averaging 45,000 pounds will require five-axle tractor–trailer combinations. However, a low-density commodity such as fiberglass insulation requires a large carrying capacity, even though the weight of the shipment is low (only 10,000 pounds of fiberglass insulation can be carried in a trailer 40 feet long).

TABLE 9-7   Equipment Selection Factors and Implications

SELECTION FACTOR/CHARACTERISTICS	EQUIPMENT IMPLICATION
Shipment Size Large Size Shipment (> 35,000 lbs) Small Size Shipment (< 10,000 lbs)	Vehicles That Can Haul 80,000 lbs Vehicles That Can Haul 30,000 lbs
Product Density • Low Density (< 15 lbs/feet cubed) • High Density (> 15 lbs/feet cubed)	High Cube Capacity Vehicles (Trailers That Are 110 Inches High, 102 Inches Wide, and 57 Feet Long) Normal Cube Capacity
Length of Haul • < 75,000 Miles Annually • > 75,000 Miles Annually • Trips > 1,000 One-Way Miles	Gasoline Powered Diesel Powered Diesel Powered with Sleep Cells
City Operations	Gasoline Powered
Intercity Operations	Diesel Powered
Terrain • Mountainous • Level	Higher-Powered Engines Lower-Powered Engines
Special Needs • Controlled Temperature • Customer Required Unloading	Refrigerated Trailers Power Tailgate

Long-distance operations, 300 miles or more one way and 75,000 or more miles per year, usually indicate the use of diesel-powered equipment. Diesel engines have a longer life and get better mileage than gasoline engines, but diesel engines have a higher initial cost. Some recent developments in diesel engine design have produced an economical, short-range, city diesel engine.

The terrain over which the vehicle travels affects the selection of certain equipment component parts such as the engine and drive train. For mountainous operations, the truck will require a high-powered engine and a low-geared drive train. For level, interstate highway operations, a lower-powered engine with a high-geared drive train is in order. Vehicles designed for mountainous operations usually are restricted to the mountainous regions because it makes sense to use different powered units in different regions.

Another transportation factor to be considered is the need for special equipment—refrigeration, power tailgates, high cube capacity, and so on. The nature of the product and customer requirements will dictate the type of special equipment to be considered.

A final consideration is the use of sleeper cabs for tractors. The sleeper cab adds several thousand dollars to the initial price of the vehicle and is usually only considered when the trips are more than 1,000 miles one way. The sleeper permits the use of two drivers: One can accumulate the required off-duty time in the sleeper bed while the other driver continues to drive. The two-driver team produces lower transit time and better service. However, lower transit time also can be accomplished by substituting drivers at appropriate intervals.

The sleeper cab also can eliminate the cost of lodging for a one-driver operation. Instead of paying for a room, the driver accumulates the required 10 hours off duty in the sleeping bed. However, there is a fuel cost to run the engine to produce heat or cooling for the driver in the sleeper. This fuel consumption per hour for a diesel engine can range from 0.5 to 4 gallons depending on several factors such as the vehicle make, type, and age, as well as the situations in which the idling occurs (this fuel consumption translates into the fuel cost of between $1.10 and $8.80 per hour at $2.20 per gallon). The sleeper cost per 8-hour rest could be up to $88.80, which is comparable to current daily lodging costs. An increased focus on reducing idling time, reducing both fuel costs and emissions, is a trend that many firms are embracing. As discussed in Chapter 5, using auxiliary power units (APUs) to provide secondary power to sleeper cabs can reduce fuel costs during non-driving hours.

Leasing One of the disadvantages of private trucking is the capital requirement for the equipment. Many firms are finding it difficult to buy money to use in the primary business; they cannot afford to buy a fleet of trucks as well. Leasing the equipment for a private truck operation reduces demands on company funds and enables existing capital to be used in the primary business of the company.

There are two basic types of lease arrangements available: the full-service lease and the finance lease. Both types are available with a lease–buy option that gives the lessee the option to buy the equipment, at book value, at the end of the lease.

The full-service lease includes the leased vehicle plus a variety of operating support services. The more services requested by the lessee, the greater the lease fee. The full-service leasing fee consists of a weekly or monthly fixed fee per vehicle, plus a mileage fee.

In addition, the cost of fuel purchased from the lessor will be charged to the lessee. The full-service lease is a popular method of leasing trucks and tractors that require maintenance, repair, and other services.

The finance lease is only a means of financing equipment. Under the finance lease, the lessee pays a monthly fee that covers the purchase cost of the equipment and the lessor's finance charge. No services are provided by the lessor: All maintenance is the responsibility of the lessee. The finance lease is a common method of leasing trailers that require little maintenance.

The economic test of buying versus leasing is a comparison of the net present cost of buying versus leasing. The net present cost is a flow discounted cash approach that considers the cost and savings of both buying and leasing as well as the tax adjustments. Private fleet operators should perform this type of test before deciding whether to lease or buy equipment.

Organizing the Private Fleet Once the fleet is in operation, intra-organizational conflicts may arise. These conflicts center on the incompatibility of departmental (user) demands and the private fleet goals.

To avoid this conflict, the goal of the private fleet should normally be a cost-constrained service goal. That is, the goal is to provide good service at a given level of cost (rather than to minimize operating cost). The fleet manager can then provide the best service that a given level of cost will permit.

Another organizational problem is the user's concept that private trucking is free transportation.

One organizational approach to eliminate the idea of free transportation is to establish the private fleet as a profit center. The income generated by the fleet is a paper or internal budget fee assessed to the using departments. The real costs are subtracted from the paper income to generate a paper profit. The manager's performance is evaluated on this paper profit. To guard against the idea that the private fleet must make a profit at any cost to the user, the departments must be given the option of using the private fleet or for-hire carriers (competition).

By establishing the fleet as a profit center, the fleet is operated as a separate business entity with management responsible for profitability and asset utilization. The establishment of a separate corporate entity for the fleet that has secured operating authority permits the fleet to solicit business from other shippers, thereby increasing the fleet utilization, eliminating the empty backhaul, and possibly generating a profit for the parent firm. Sometimes private fleet operators use 3PL services to find businesses from other shippers to reduce empty hauls.

The question of where to position the fleet in the organization (in which department) is another important question. Usually a profit-center fleet is set up as a separate department reporting to the chief executive officer of the parent company.

Many private fleets are centrally organized because that permits the fleet manager to provide service to different departments and divisions in the organization, thus increasing fleet utilization. A decentralized operation usually is found where separate divisions have different operating and vehicle requirements and have sufficient volume to make the separation economical.

Controlling the Private Fleet A key element to an effective and efficient private truck fleet is control over cost and performances. Table 9-8 is a list of cost and performance criteria for effective private truck fleet control.

Costs by function must be collected at the source. Fuel costs (and gallons) should be noted for each vehicle. This notation of functional costs at the cost source permits analysis of individual cost centers for the actual costs incurred. It is very difficult to analyze the fuel efficiency of individual vehicles in a fleet when fuel costs are aggregated for the entire fleet.

Furthermore, the collection of functional costs by driver, vehicle, plant, and so on will permit analysis of problem areas within the fleet. The use of fleet averages only may conceal inefficient operations at particular markets or plants. However, functional costs by vehicle, plant, and driver can be compared to fleet-wide averages, and a management-by-exception approach can be practiced. That is, if the specific costs (fuel cost/given driver) are within acceptable limits, nothing is done. Management action is taken when the specific costs are out of line with the desired level.

The performance criteria to be considered are miles operated (loaded and empty), human resource hours expended, vehicle operating hours, number of trips made, tonnage hauled, and the number of stops made. By collecting the above performance data, the fleet manager

TABLE 9-8	Private Cost and Performance Control Criteria
COST	**PERFORMANCE**
By function Fuel (and gallons), Driver, Maintenance, Interest, Depreciation, Tires, Parts, Management, Overhead, License and Registration	Miles Operated By Vehicle, By Driver Empty Miles Total, By Location Human Resource Hours Total, Driving, Loading and Unloading, Breakdown
Functional Cost By Vehicle, Driver, Plant, Market, Warehouse, Customer	Vehicle Operating Hours By Vehicle Number of Trips By Vehicle/Time Period Tonnage By Vehicle Number of Stops (Deliveries) By Driver

is able to measure the fleet's utilization and the drivers' productivity. Control measures such as overall cost per mile, per hour, and per trip can be computed and used in determining unacceptable performance areas in the fleet. Such information also is valuable to marketing and purchasing departments that determine the landed cost of goods sold or purchased.

Likewise, performance measures must be collected and identified at the source. Total fleet mileage and total fleet fuel consumption (gallons) will permit determination of overall fleet fuel efficiency. However, collection of fuel consumption and mileage per individual vehicle will provide the information necessary for purchasing fuel-efficient vehicles as replacements or additions to the fleet.

The performance criteria enable the fleet manager to analyze the productivity of drivers. The number of miles driven per day, the number of stops (deliveries) made per day, or the number of hours per run or trip, are driver productivity measures that can be collected for each driver. From this productivity data, individual drivers who drive fewer miles per day, make fewer stops per day, or take a longer time to make a run than the standards (fleet average, for example) are singled out for further investigation and corrective action.

Regulations As stated earlier, bona fide private trucking is exempt from federal economic regulations in the United States. The private carrier need not secure authorization (certificate of public convenience and necessity) to transport the firm's products. Because private coverage is not for-hire service, no tariffs are published.

A common problem many private fleets face is how to eliminate the empty backhaul. Miles traveled without a load add cost to the company, including the time consumed. In Figure 9-8, the cost of filling that backhaul can be calculated in comparison to leaving those miles empty.

Fleets with for-hire authority must publish rates and charges with the government, which is a shift from the lack of reporting requirements under exclusive private transportation.[31]

One option that eliminates the requirement for for-hire authority is trip leasing. The lease agreement is between a private carrier and another firm, for a single trip, and cannot last more than 30 days. The private carrier is responsible for licensing and recordkeeping, and a copy of the trip lease agreement must be carried in the vehicle during the trip.[32] The private carrier also may trip lease to another private carrier and charge a fee for the service provided.

FIGURE 9-8	Backhaul Cost Analysis Form

Total trip miles including backhaul	=	_____ miles (A)
Normal deliver round-trip miles	=	_____ miles (B)
Difference (excess miles)	=	_____ miles (C)
Multiplied by cost per mile	=	$ _____ (D)
Additional labor expended		
____ (hr) × $____ (avg wage + benefits)	=	$ _____ (E)
Total cost (D + E)	=	$ _____ (F)
Gross backhaul revenue	=	$ _____
Less total cost (Line F)	=	$ _____
Profit (or loss)	=	$ _____

Source: National Private Truck Council, "Filling Backhaul Miles for Private Fleets," 2006.

Another solution to eliminating empty backhaul is the transportation of exempt commodities. Exempt commodities may be hauled without economic regulations. Some examples of exempt commodities are ordinary livestock, agricultural products (grain, fruits, vegetables), horticultural goods (Christmas trees), newspapers, freight incidental air transportation (to and from airports), used shipping containers, and fish.

Private trucking is subjected to all federal safety requirements in the areas of:

- driver qualifications
- driving practices
- vehicle parts and accessories
- accident reporting
- driver hours of service
- vehicle inspection and maintenance
- hazardous materials transportation
- vehicle weight and dimensions

These safety regulations are enforced by the U.S. Department of Transportation (DOT), Bureau of Motor Carrier Safety, and the private carrier must register with the U.S. DOT.

In addition, the private fleet must comply with the state safety regulations governing speed, weight, and vehicle length, height, and width. Such state regulations fall within the purview of the constitutionally granted police powers that permit states to enact laws to protect the health and welfare of their citizens. Because the safety regulations are not uniform among the states, the fleet management must be aware of specific regulations in each of the states in which the fleet operates.

Driver hours-of-service (HOS) regulations establish the maximum number of hours (minimum safety level) a driver may operate a vehicle in interstate commerce, and consequently they affect the utilization of drivers. Federal Motor Carrier Safety Administration is requiring all carriers, including private fleets, to operate in full compliance with their ELD (Electronic Logging Device, which is designed to record a driver's hours of service log automatically) mandate by the end of year 2017, so private fleet operators must be prepared to adopt this technology and be able to use it soon, if they have not done so yet.

SUMMARY

- A third party logistics (3PL) service provider is defined as an "external supplier that performs all or part of a company's logistics functions." It is desirable that these suppliers provide multiple services and that these services are integrated in the way they are managed and delivered.

- The several types of 3PLs are transportation-based, distribution-based, forwarder-based, financial-based, and information-based suppliers.

- Asset-based providers serve customers with tangible equipment and facilities, while nonasset-based providers leverage the resources of other companies.

- 3PLs provide a variety of transportation services, including freight movement, freight management, intermediary services, and specialty services.

- Customer demands for integration of 3PL services have led to significant expansion and acquisition activities among major service providers.

- The 3PL industry is a growing and substantial force in logistics, with more than $788 billion spent globally on 3PL services in 2015.
- When outsourcing labor-intensive logistics operations, companies seek cost reduction, the ability to focus on core competencies, and service improvement.
- According to an annual study of 3PL users, customers are satisfied with their 3PL relationships and credit 3PLs with helping them attain goals related to reduction of operating costs, fixed asset investment, and order cycle time.
- There are six steps involved in the development and implementation of a successful 3PL relationship. The ultimate goal of the process is to develop outstanding customer service capabilities and cost-efficient operations.
- Although the industry is poised for future growth, 3PLs must support customers' needs through strategic innovation, technological strength, capacity access, talent availability, omni-channel agility, and sustainability expertise.
- Customers can use private carriage instead of 3PLs, but they must be able to manage their own fleet in a cost-efficient manner.

STUDY QUESTIONS

1. Define the concepts of outsourcing and third party logistics. What role does transportation play in 3PL?

2. What are the basic types of 3PL firms? How do they facilitate the planning and execution of freight transportation?

3. Why would a company use an asset-based 3PL service provider versus a nonasset-based provider?

4. Discuss the four primary types of transportation services offered by 3PL service providers.

5. Why is service integration an important issue to the 3PL industry? What companies are developing these capabilities?

6. What are some of the more frequently outsourced logistics activities? Less frequently outsourced?

7. To what extent are clients/customers satisfied with 3PL services? What can 3PLs do to improve customer satisfaction?

8. Describe the six steps involved in establishing and managing 3PL relationships. Which step(s) do you feel is (are) most critical?

9. If you were given the task of outsourcing your company's transportation operations, what types of capabilities and core competencies would you seek in a 3PL service provider?

10. After implementing a 3PL relationship, how should transportation managers promote continuous improvement of performance and achieve supply chain value?

11. Discuss the strategic needs and challenges that transportation managers face. How can 3PL service providers help them improve performance and reduce costs?

12. Why is information technology an important issue to customers when outsourcing transportation and logistics activities?

13. What are the six issues customers must deal with if they choose to use private carriage, instead of 3PLs?

NOTES

1. Retrieved 14 July 2017, from https://en.wikipedia.org/wiki/Third-party_logistics.

2. "eyefortransport Transportation Glossary," retrieved 14 July 2017, from http://events.eyefortransport.com/glossary/ab.shtml.

3. "Third party logistics (3PL) definition," retrieved 14 July 2017, from http://www.businessdictionary.com/definition/third-party-logistics-3PL.html.

4. Council of Supply Chain Management Professionals, *Supply Chain Management Terms and Glossary*, 2013, retrieved 14 July 2017, from http://cscmp.org/sites/default/files/user_uploads/resources/downloads/glossary-2013.pdf.

5. John J. Coyle, C. John Langley Jr., Robert A. Novack, and Brian J. Gibson, *Supply Chain Management: A Logistics Perspective*, 9th ed., Mason, OH: Cengage Learning, 2013, Chap. 4.

6. Gillian Tan, "XPO Logistics Gets $700 Million Investment to Fund Acquisition," *Wall Street Journal*, 11 September 2014.

7. Scott Vanselous, "The Next Generation of TMS Helping More Carriers Become Comprehensive Logistics Service Providers," *Logistics Viewpoints*, 25 November 2014, retrieved 25 November 2014, from http://logisticsviewpoints.com/2014/11/25/the-next-generation-of-tms-helping-more-carriers-become-comprehensive-logistics-service-providers/,

8. Export.gov, "What Is a Shippers Association?" 14 October 2012, retrieved 25 November 2014, from http://www.export.gov/logistics/eg_main_023294.asp.

9. "Consolidation & Pool Distribution," retrieved 28 July 2017, from http://www.dohrn.com/logistics-consolidation-pool-distribution.html.

10. Jean-Paul Rodrigue, Claude Comtois, and Brian Slack, *The Geography of Transport System*, 2nd ed., New York: Routledge, 2009.

11. François Fulconis, Virginie Hiesse, and Gilles Paché, "Catalyst of Coopetitive Strategies—An Exploratory Study," *Supply Chain Forum: An International Journal*, Vol. 12, No. 2, 2011.

12. Retrieved 28 July 2017, from http://www.3plogistics.com/3pl-market-info-resources/3pl-market-information/global-3pl-market-size-estimates/.

13. Ibid.

14. Armstrong & Associates, Inc., "3PL Customers Report Identifies Service Trends, 3PL Market Segment Sizes, and Growth Rates," 18 May 2017, retrieved 28 July 2017, from http://www.3plogistics.com/3pl-customers-report-identifies-service-trends-3pl-market-segment-sizes-growth-rates/.

15. Ibid.

16. Retrieved 28 July 2017, from http://www.3plstudy.com/media/downloads/2016/10/2017-report_new.pdf.

17. Ibid.

18. Ibid.

19. Ibid.

20. Unless otherwise noted, information in this section is adapted from John J. Coyle, C. John Langley Jr., Robert A. Novack, and Brian J. Gibson, "Supply Chain Management: A Logistics Perspective," 9th ed., Mason, OH: Cengage Learning, 2013, Chap. 4.

21. Douglas M. Lambert, Margaret A. Emmelhainz, and John T. Gardner, "Developing and Implementing Supply Chain Partnerships," *International Journal of Logistics Management*, Vol. 7, No. 2, 1996: pp. 1–17.

22. Ibid.

23. Bruce Tompkins and Chris Ferrell, *Reinventing the 3PL Model: Trends, Challenges, and Opportunities*, September 2014, retrieved 28 November 2014, from http://www.tompkinsinc.com/reinventing-3pl-model-trends-challenges-opportunities-3/.

24. Patrick Burnson, "Optimizing 3PL Relationships: How to Avoid Commoditization," *Logistics Management*, October 2014.

25. Richard Armstrong, "Where the 3PL Action Is: A Scan of Logistics Providers & Services Worldwide," *SupplyChainBrain*, March/April 2014.

26. Penn State and Capgemini, *The State of Logistics Outsourcing*, 19th Annual 3PL Study, 2015.

27. Brian J. Gibson, Sean P. Goffnett, Zachary Williams, and Robert L. Cook, *SCM Talent Development Module 1: The Acquire Process*, Oak Brook, IL: Council of Supply Chain Management Professionals, 2013.

28. Penn State and Capgemini, *The State of Logistics Outsourcing*, 19th Annual 3PL Study, 2015.

29. "More Clean Energy CNG for Saddle Creek," *Fleets & Fuels*, 11 July 2014, retrieved 30 November 2014, from http://www.fleetsandfuels.com/fuels/cng/2014/07/more-clean-energy-cng-for-saddle-creek/.

30. Armstrong & Associates, Inc., "Global 3PL Market Size." Retrieved 25 July 2017, from http://www.3plogistics.com/3pl-market-info-resources/3pl-market-information/global-3pl-market-size-estimates/.

31. National Private Truck Council, "Filling Backhaul Miles for Private Fleets," 2006.

32. Ibid.

33. C. Caplice and Y. Sheffi, "Optimization-Based Procurement for Transportation Services." *Journal of Business Logistics*, Vol. 34, No. 2, 2003, pp. 109–128.

34. Kevin McCarthy, Chris Brady, Steve Raetz, Bobby Martens, and Yoshinori Suzuki, "Stale Rates Research: Benefits of Frequent Transportation Bids," C.H. Robinson Worldwide White Paper, Prairie, MN, 2012.

35. Ibid.

36. Ibid.

37. Ibid.

38. Ibid.

CASE 9-1

Closet Concepts Ltd.

Closet Concepts Ltd. (CCL) is a rapidly growing provider of home storage and organization products. They manufacture a wide range of products ranging from wire closet organizers to wood shelving systems. Basic CCL product lines are sold through home improvement retailers and the premier product line is sold through designers and custom homebuilders.

The CCL leadership team has been pondering an e-commerce strategy and worries that it may lose sales to competitors if a CCL.com online shopping option is not soon established. Fortunately, the CCL website is fairly robust and it would not be difficult to add shopping capabilities to it. All that was really needed was the approval to begin the project.

The approval came during a quarterly executive retreat. During her opening speech, the CEO stated: "Increasingly, do-it-yourself customers have expressed a desire to order product directly from CCL. The customers claim to have difficulty in getting unique items and parts from the CCL product line because the retailers don't carry them in stock. This can delay project completion and create customer dissatisfaction. By the end of this retreat, I want a high-level plan that establishes our e-commerce strategy and our plan for managing customer orders. I want us to have excellent omni-channel fulfillment and delivery capabilities, but we cannot compromise our service quality to existing retailers, designers, and builders. Now, break into teams and do some brainstorming."

A fulfillment analysis team was hastily assembled. It consisted of Riley Sheahan, the chief customer relations officer; Jim Howard, the vice president of logistics; and Tomas Tatar, the senior director of transportation. All agreed that it would be a challenge to quickly add omni-channel fulfillment capabilities and each had contrasting ideas about how to proceed.

Sheahan suggested that CCL handle all fulfillment activities in-house and to use its private fleet to move customer orders to major markets for pool distribution by local delivery firms. "This will give us the greatest control over our processes to ensure a superior customer experience," she explained.

"I'm not so sure about that strategy," replied Tatar. "Our fleet is small and we use it to deliver high margin custom orders to 30 key distributors. You're talking about a tenfold increase in the number of delivery points." He also noted that total demand for online orders was unknown and nobody had any idea about average order size.

Howard noted that CCL's distribution centers were geared toward massive orders from home improvement retailers that moved in cost-efficient truckload quantities. "We already have difficulty handling the smaller orders from designers and builders. Besides, Tomas will tell you that our products can be odd-shaped and low density, attributes that lead to high less-than-truckload delivery rates."

Sheahan replied: "I don't want some second rate trucking company trying to fill our orders or damaging our product just because Tomas is looking to save a few transportation dollars. We must maintain exceptional control over these direct customer engagements. This e-commerce initiative is just too important for us to cut corners."

"I agree that we want it done correctly, but we don't have the resources or expertise to do this in-house," stated Howard. "We need to find a high quality 3PL that knows how to handle Internet orders."

"Good point," noted Tatar. "Partnering with the right provider could be the ideal solution. They can serve CCL customers effectively without busting our budget."

"I need to know more about these so-called 3PL experts," replied Sheahan. "Gather some information and bring it to our late afternoon session." With that statement, she got up and left the meeting.

CASE QUESTIONS

1. What roles can 3PL play in the CCL e-commerce initiative? Is it a viable alternative to Sheahan's private fleet/pool distribution strategy?
2. What type of 3PL service provider is best suited to serve the CCL e-commerce customers? Why?
3. Should Howard and Tatar consider the use of an integrated 3PL? Why or why not?
4. If CCL decided to add installation services to its e-commerce initiatives, what types of 3PL service provider should be used? Why?

CASE 9-2

C.H. Robinson Worldwide, Inc.

C.H. Robinson, headquartered in Eden Prairie, Minnesota, is one of the largest nonasset-based 3PLs in North America and the world. The firm has extended its service from its historical brokerage service to virtually every aspect of transportation and logistics service, which ranges from truckload/ocean/air shipping to TMS platform services and supply chain consulting. Today the company delivers supply chain solutions to more than 113,000 customers across the world, and works with 107,000 contract carriers of all modes and suppliers through an integrated network of 280 offices and more than 14,000 employees.

You, an undergraduate junior student majoring in supply chain management at a major state university, were just hired by C.H. Robinson as a summer intern at any one of C.H. Robinson's global offices. Your role will most certainly involve engaging shippers and/or carriers in the process of managing freight transportation services through the use of C.H. Robinson's Transportation Management System (TMS). TMS is a technology that connects C.H. Robinson with its customers, as well as with its contract carriers, to meet the transportation needs of customers in a cost efficient manner. Basically, customers use TMS to find the best carrier, or the best combination of carriers (which may involve multiple transportation modes), to ship freights in a timely manner while satisfying the delivery time window of consignees at minimal shipping costs. Customers also use TMS to check shipment status, manage invoices, and gather transportation data. C.H. Robinson provides two types of TMS to its customers, each of which has different features and price.

Navisphere®

The first TMS is called *Navisphere®*. This TMS is a comprehensive system that provides flexible, efficient, and integrated technology solutions to customers that bring all aspects of supply chain together. The system is capable of managing all transportation needs of customers (all modes and customs clearance globally), and allows customers to enhance supply chain visibility, optimize their business processes, connect with service providers and consignees, and obtain strategic data and reporting to help drive decisions.

Customers access Navisphere® via the Internet; no installation of software is required. They can request quotes and send freight tenders at any time with detailed freight specifications (when it needs to be shipped, when it needs to be delivered, what kind of equipment is required, etc.), and the system can provide the solutions that meet the customer's requirements with minimal cost. Tenders, shipment specifics, and facility profiles can be pre-established and can include defined business processes that ensure consistent data capture and timing of order lifecycle events. Communication between the shipper and C.H. Robinson can be either manual or fully automated. Once the freight tender is provided, C.H. Robinson will optimize the best way to ship the freight, so customers do not need to contact each individual carrier or negotiate rates with them. Navisphere® also allows customers to obtain near real-time updates on the status of freight. Navisphere® is connected with contract carriers' freight tracking systems, which usually take advantage of GPS systems (either the one installed in vehicles or the GPS-capable cell phones used by vehicle operators), so that customers can monitor the progress of freight in Navisphere®. In the event that a shipment will be delivered late, the system notifies the customer about this incident in a timely manner, and provides a new estimate of the expected arrival time. Navisphere®

can be integrated with a customer's ERP (Enterprise Resource Planning) system, so that it automates workflows between transportation and other business operations, which gives customers greater control over their supply chain activities, and allows customers to easily access transportation data for various analytics.

Navisphere® is also used by C.H. Robinson's contract carriers, which allows them to access to shipper freight they might not otherwise have access to due to the size of their business or technical limitations. The system used by carriers is called Navisphere® Carrier. It is used by trucking companies, and can be used by both dispatchers and drivers (the system used by drivers is called Navisphere® Driver). Each driver can install Navisphere® Driver in his/her cell phone. The system then works as a communication tool between the driver and his/her manager (dispatcher) and C.H. Robinson. Drivers using the Navisphere® Driver app have access to assigned load information and maps directly on their smartphones, so that they know the location of the next load promptly without contacting their dispatcher. Navisphere® Driver also allows drivers to update freight status automatically. The system uses cell phones GPS capability to automatically send location information to C.H. Robinson on a regular basis, so that drivers can focus on driving without being bothered by phone calls or messages asking for the current location. Drivers can start the automatic tracking by selecting "on way to pick-up" button in the app. Once tracking begins, the system receives timely location updates. Automatic stop updates are received when drivers cross a predetermined geo-fence at stop locations. After delivering a load, drivers can also use the app to submit load documents (e.g., delivery confirmation with consignee signature), which can speed up the payment process. Shippers and dispatchers can monitor all payment statuses through Navisphere® too. Dispatchers can use Navisphere® Carrier to manage loads for their drivers. It allows dispatchers to send load information to assigned drivers, monitor the status of all freights with hourly updates, check billing status, and find loads.

Freightview®

The second TMS is called *Freightview®*. This TMS is a tool for small- and medium-sized shippers that may not have other enterprise planning and operations tools to adopt a comprehensive TMS. Freightview® focuses on shipping freight by trucks, including both TL and LTL. Freightview® uses an online platform, meaning that customers can use this TMS via standard Internet Web browsers without installing any program in their PCs. Freightview® is designed to help shippers cut the time and money they spend on managing their shipping needs, and it seeks to provide streamlined quoting, booking, tracking, reporting, and visibility of shipments. It is a tool that can find efficient and cost-effective ways of shipping freight for customers with low implementation effort and low fee-based costing model.

Small- to medium-sized shippers, that normally ship less than truckload (LTL), typically must obtain quotes from multiple LTL carriers and choose the one that provides the best rates (subject to the condition that the arrival time of a freight to consignee is within the specified time window). This requires shippers to log in to multiple LTL carrier websites, and provide necessary information for getting quotes multiple times, which is quite time consuming. Often times, these shippers must also contact multiple TL carries to obtain quotes and compare them with the LTL quotes, because when they are shipping freight that is LTL but fairly large, the use of TL service can sometimes save freight costs (as we discussed in Chapter 4—Costing and Pricing for Transportation). Hence, these shippers are very often spending much time and effort to find the best available rates, TL or LTL, for a given freight shipment, or a set of freight shipments. Freightview® can help these shippers save time and effort.

Freightview® works as follows. A customer first identifies the set of its preferred carriers from the marketplace of trucking companies including both LTL and TL carriers. Once this carrier set is identified, Freightview® automatically obtains tariffs of LTL carriers that are included in this set. This means that after the initial set up is completed, the customer will only need to provide the freight information just once to Freightview®, and it will automatically obtain quotes from all the LTL carries in the set of preferred carriers by using the latest tariffs. Hence, the customer no longer has to log in to multiple carrier Web sites, or enter freight information multiple times, which will save customers time. Freightview® can also obtain TL quotes based on the freight information already entered (for LTL or TL quotes) in a timely manner, so that the customer can compare the best LTL rate with the best TL rate to find out if using TL service makes sense for a specific shipment.

Freightview® also allows customers to track shipments in the manner similar to Navisphere®, so that customers can obtain freight status information at any time online. Freightview® may be used to generate reports as well. With Freightview®, customers have access to the data such as on-time delivery statistics (average, standard deviation, etc.), which are not generally available to many small shippers. Freightview® charges customers based on the volume of usage (how many freight shipments they shipped per month), so that small shippers do not need to pay large costs to use this TMS.

CASE QUESTIONS

1. What are advantages and disadvantages of using *Navisphere*®? Make sure that you discuss this from the viewpoint of both customers and contract carriers.

2. What are advantages and disadvantages of using *Freightview*®? Make sure that you discuss this from the viewpoint of both customers and contract carriers.

3. What type of companies are good targets (potential users) for *Navisphere*®? Make sure that you discuss specific characteristics of target customers such as size, industries to which they belong, technological capabilities, and geographic locations.

4. What type of companies are good targets (potential users) for *Freightview*®? Make sure that you discuss specific characteristics of target customers such as size, industries to which they belong, technological capabilities, and geographic locations.

5. As you learned in Chapter 5, the trucking industry is highly fragmented (that is, there are many small carriers and few large carriers). Does this fact affect your answers to the above questions; that is, does this fact affect your strategy of customer segmentation?

6. Do you think it is a good idea for C.H. Robinson to approach companies (shippers) that have their own fleet (private carrier)? Why or why not? How can the TMS of C.H. Robinson help these firms?

APPENDIX 9A
Third Party Logistics and TL Auction

As discussed in Chapter 5, motor carriers, especially TL carriers, transport larger amounts of goods than any other mode of transportation in the United States. For many shippers, however, procuring TL services can be challenging because shippers often have complex transportation networks consisting of many origin-destination lanes, and securing transportation services from TL carriers that provide good customer service, reliability, and rate in each of these many lanes can be time consuming and difficult. Many shippers, especially those with respectable shipment volume, very often choose to conduct TL auctions on a regular basis (for example, once a year) to procure TL services. In each TL auction, a shipper first communicates with participating carriers the detailed information about their transportation needs within their network, and then solicits bids from carriers, selects the set of carriers that meets their needs, and determines the lanes to be assigned to the chosen carriers. This allows shippers to update the list of preferred (primary) carriers and adjust their rates to market equilibrium on a regular basis. Third-party logistics companies (3PLs) can help shippers perform this auction (also called "procurement exercise" by some 3PLs). This appendix describes this TL auction process, and explains how 3PLs can help shippers manage their TL needs in a cost-effective manner. The appendix also discusses how the auction process has evolved over time and where it may be going in the future. Most of the discussions provided in this appendix are based on the articles by Caplice and Sheffi[33] and McCarthy et al.[34]

TL Auction: The Traditional Procedure

Historically, the TL auction has been done in a way such that the cost of transportation in each lane would be minimized by selecting the carrier that provided the best (lowest) bid for the lane. This lane-by-lane optimization is often subject to the constraint that the carrier chosen for the lane must meet the minimum requirements on service quality, such as reliability (or on-time delivery rate), and on other conditions such as financial stability and satisfactory safety records in recent years.

The auction consists of three steps: bid preparation, bid execution, and bid analysis phases.[35] In the bid preparation phase, shippers determine what to bid out, which carriers to invite to auction, and how to communicate with potential participants. In the bid execution phase, shippers communicate their transportation needs to the participants (TL carriers) and solicit their bids for each lane included in the auction. This phase can involve multiple rounds of bids. Multiple rounds of bids can be conducted in such a way that, after each round, the shipper communicates to carriers the best bid received for each lane during the round, and solicits another round of bids in order to give carriers the chance to beat the best bid received in the previous round (this process can be repeated iteratively until no carrier is willing to provide bids that beat the best existing bids). In the bid analysis phase, shippers analyze carrier responses (bids), determine the set of carriers to choose, and assign lanes to the chosen carriers.

The traditional auction process of "lane-by-lane" optimization is not complex, because all shippers must simply (1) create the list of acceptable carriers that do not violate the minimum requirements (reliability, financial stability, etc.), (2) solicit bids from these acceptable carriers, and (3) for each lane find the carrier that offered the lowest rate (best bid). However, actually conducting this process may not be easy, since it can be time consuming. The bid preparation phase requires shippers to collect such information as on-time performance, safety records, and financial stability, for all the potential participants, and the bid execution and analysis phases require a significant amount of human time and cost for data analyses. The 3PLs, especially those that are "transportation based" can help shippers fulfill all of these requirements. Since they manage transportation activities for many clients, they have rich data on their clients' carriers, including on-time delivery rates and financial stability. This means that 3PLs can efficiently gather the needed information for shippers. They can also execute the bids on behalf of their clients (shippers), and perform bid analyses for them. Since 3PLs are usually viewed as "large customers" by carriers (because they procure transportation needs of many clients), shippers often have better chances of getting attractive bids from carriers by performing auctions through 3PLs, rather than executing the auctions themselves. Furthermore, if using 3PLs for auctions, a shipper can update the contract rates used in its TMS (Transportation Management System) with little, if any, effort after the auction, because 3PLs are usually in a better position to manipulate TMS parameters (when shippers use 3PLs to outsource their transportation functions, they normally use the TMS provided by 3PLs, which are often developed by 3PLs themselves).

Limitation with Traditional Procedure

Historically, shippers believed that the aforementioned traditional auction procedure could minimize their TL transportation costs. This makes intuitive sense, because what the traditional procedure does is to optimize (minimize) the rate in each lane (that is, it performs a lane-by-lane optimization). Recently, however, studies have shown that this procedure does not actually minimize the transportation cost of shippers. This is because the traditional procedure tends to encourage "price hedging" by participating carriers. Price hedging refers to the act of carriers where they tend to increase their rates at the time of bidding to compensate for the uncertainties they must face. To illustrate this point, consider the following TL auction example.

You are a sales manager of a TL carrier based in Chicago, Illinois, which was invited to participate in an auction by Shipper X. Shipper X provided the list of lanes in which they have shipping needs, along with the expected shipping volume for each lane. You are considering submitting a bid for the lane from Chicago to St. Louis, but because your company does not have much business in the St. Louis area, you are concerned that you may not always be able to find backhaul customers that would be willing to ship loads from St. Louis back to Chicago (or connection customers that would be shipping loads from St. Louis to somewhere else). This means that, in this lane, you must face uncertainties (or risk) associated with backhaul, meaning that your trucks must sometimes return to Chicago with an empty load. In this case, how do you come up with the rate for this lane if you want to make profits? Typically you would include the cost of backhaul (empty haul), which you must incur whenever you cannot find backhaul customers, in the headhaul cost (rate). If, for example, your cost of moving a truck from Chicago to St. Louis is $1,000 (forward or backward) and your profit margin is 5 percent, then you may want to include, in addition to $1,050 (the rate you would charge in situations where you are 100 percent certain that you can always find backhaul customers in St. Louis), the partial cost of backhaul in the headhaul rate to compensate for the risks associated with finding backhaul customers. In this case the headhaul cost may be computed as $1,050 + (1 - P^{back})$ $\times$ $1,000, where P^{back} is the probability that your company can find the backhaul customer in St. Louis. The second part of this formula. i.e., $(1 - P^{back}) \times $1,000$, represents that part of the rate that you charge because of the uncertainties you must face in the lane, and is often called "hedging." Note that you need not hedge if $P^{back} = 1$ (100 percent certain that you can find a backhaul customer), but your hedging can be as large as \$1,000 if $P^{back} = 0$ (no chance that you can find a backhaul customer in St. Louis).

The above example shows that the lane-by-lane auction, while seemingly optimal, does not necessarily minimize the shippers' cost of transportation in each lane because this procedure involves price hedging by carriers. If shippers can find a way to eliminate the uncertainties that the carriers will face in auction, they will be able to reduce their shipping costs. The traditional lane-by-lane procedure, however, cannot eliminate such uncertainties because when a carrier is bidding on a particular lane the carrier does not know which other lanes the carrier will win (i.e., the carrier does not know at the time of bidding the lane if it will win either the backhaul or connection lanes), so the carrier has no choice but to hedge. Another issue with the traditional auction procedure is that it does not allow shippers to control the number of carriers with which to have contracts. Often, shippers do not want to have too many contract carriers (bid winners) because this can result in the loss of leverage (if a shipper has too many carriers, the shipper may be giving limited business volume to each carrier, so that many carriers may treat the shipper as a "small customer"). The shippers, on the other hand, may not want to have too few carriers either, because in this case the shippers are relying on a very limited number of carriers, which implies that carriers may have leverage on shippers rather than shippers having leverage on carriers (that is, carriers may start behaving in the manner that is consistent with the argument "If we don't do our jobs, you are going to be in trouble, so you ought to treat me well").

A New Recent Approach

A new TL auction approach, which resolves the limitations mentioned above, was developed by two academicians Caplice and Sheffi.[36] The basic approach is to take advantage of the economies of scope that can be realized by allowing participating TL carriers to submit the "package" bids, rather than providing a bid on each lane. The package can include bids for more than one lane, and each carrier can ask the shipper to choose or reject the package as a whole; that is, if the package is chosen, all the lanes contained in the package will have to be offered to the carrier. This auction process is called by several names including, conditional bids, package bids, combinatorial bids, and so on. There are multiple advantages associated with using this new approach from both the shippers' and carriers' perspectives.

Perhaps the largest advantage is that this approach can eliminate "hedging" by carriers, and thus can lower the shippers' transportation cost. Notice that if carriers are allowed to submit package bids, they can create their packages in such a way that there are little or no uncertainties (risks associated with finding backhaul or connection-load customers) on their side. For example, the carrier mentioned in the above example, that is about to submit a bid for the Chicago–St. Louis lane, can now submit a package such that it contains both the Chicago–St. Louis lane and St. Louis–Chicago lane. Thus, the carrier will either get both of these lanes (both headhaul and backhaul as a package), or they will not get either lane. This means that when submitting this package, the carrier no longer faces the backhaul uncertainties that they had to face under the traditional approach (lane-by-lane bidding), so the carrier no longer needs to hedge when it submits bids. There are many other ways to create attractive packages. For example, if a carrier is already serving the Kansas City–Chicago lane for a shipper that is different from Shipper X, the carrier may submit a package to Shipper X that contains Chicago–St. Louis and St. Louis–Kansas City lanes, so that it can create a network in which empty moves of trucks can be minimized (provided that both Chicago–St. Louis and St. Louis–Kansas City lanes are available for bids by Shipper X and the expected shipping volume of these two lanes are similar to that of the existing Kansas City–Chicago lane). In this way, participating carriers can create their own package that is attractive from the standpoint of their own existing network. Notice that this new auction approach gives benefits to both shippers and carriers; that is, shippers benefit from reduced shipping cost, and carriers benefit from reduced backhaul uncertainties (that is, the approach creates a win–win situation for both parties).

Note that the new approach will make the bid-analysis phase of the auction more complex than before, because shippers must now choose the set of packages in such a way that every lane in the shipper's network is covered by exactly one carrier (this may not always be the case) that has sufficient capacity to meet the shipper's shipping needs in the lane, while ensuring that the total cost of the entire network is minimized. This is a much more complex problem to solve than that required in the traditional approach, where shippers only needed to choose the best (lowest bid) carrier in each lane. Fortunately, Caplice and Sheffi[37] showed that this complex package-bid problem can be formulated as a mixed-integer linear program, so that the optimal solution can be obtained easily by using "off the shelf" commercial optimization software products, such as CPLEX (or even by a spreadsheet optimizer if the number of participating carriers is not large). Some 3PLs can use sophisticated computer software to implement this new approach.

Another advantage associated with the new approach is that shippers can impose certain constraints on problem solutions. For example, with this new approach, shippers can now control the number of carriers to offer businesses (which was not possible under the traditional approach, as discussed earlier). Since the new approach finds the solution (which carriers to use) by solving an optimization problem (linear program), shippers can easily control both the lower bound and upper bound of the number of winning carriers by imposing constraints on the linear program. Shippers can also impose other constraints, such as the minimum shipping volume (combined volume across lanes) to give to each winning carrier (to maintain a minimum threshold leverage on each carrier), which was also impossible under the traditional approach.

Future Direction

Although the new approach discussed above has many advantages over the traditional approach, it has some disadvantages, too. One disadvantage is that, because it attempts to remove hedging by allowing carriers to create attractive packages that work well with their (carriers') existing networks, the package may suddenly become unattractive if their network changes (which can be caused by the loss of clients or addition of new clients). Consider the example we discussed earlier where a carrier is already serving the Kansas City–Chicago lane for an existing client (shipper), so that the carrier is interested in submitting a package that contains Chicago–St. Louis and St. Louis–Kansas City lanes in an auction conducted by Shipper X. If this carrier wins the package above, the carrier will be able to create the network in which there are few empty moves of trucks. However, in the event that this carrier loses the shipper that moves freights in Kansas City–Chicago lane, the package above suddenly becomes unattractive to the carrier, because the carrier now has to face the risks associated with finding backhaul or connection loads for the trucks that serve the St. Louis–Kansas City lane.

When network changes like this happen, the carrier in question typically takes one of the following two actions. First, it can stop accepting load tenders from the shipper. If a tender is rejected by the carrier, the shipper will have to look for another carrier that can take the loads. This rejection process is sometimes called "routing guide bleed" by shippers, because every time a load tender is rejected by the primary carrier, the tender will have to be given to the secondary carrier (or tertiary carrier if it is rejected by the secondary carrier), whose rate is generally more expensive than that of the primary carrier. If the carrier continues to reject load tenders, the shipper eventually will have to change the carrier's designation from "primary carrier" to "secondary" or "tertiary" carrier. Second, the carrier can change the rate. The carrier can adjust its rate so that the rate now includes "hedging" in order to compensate for the increased uncertainties (in many TMSs this rate change can be initiated from the carrier side at any time). This means that, while the new approach is able to reduce the cost of transportation for shippers considerably, the benefit of this approach may not last for long (in some cases a carrier can stop honoring the contract rates as quickly as just a few days after the auction). This, in turn, suggests that the new approach may force shippers to execute the bids (auction) more frequently than the traditional approach, if shippers wish to keep their rates low (close to market equilibrium). This is unattractive from the shippers' perspective, since there are fixed costs associated with executing a TL auction.

The study by McCarthy et al. (2012)[38] showed that the benefit of performing an auction under the new approach may completely evaporate in less than one year from the time of auction. This finding, however, merely indicates that the rate of evaporation (duration of time it takes for the rates to become "stale") is, on average, less than one year. It is likely that the rate of evaporation would vary significantly across shippers depending on many factors, such as the size of a shipper and the stability of a shipper's network. In the future more studies will be needed that investigate the optimal timing (or frequency) of executing an auction for each individual shipper which considers both the cost and merit of executing an auction.

CHAPTER 10

TRANSPORTATION RISK MANAGEMENT

Learning Objectives

After reading this chapter, you should be able to do the following:

> Understand the nature of transportation risk and disruptions

> Explain the concept of risk management

> Identify the primary categories and types of transportation risk

> Describe the general process for managing transportation risk

> Understand the key factors in risk assessment

> Discuss the four techniques for managing transportation risks

> Appreciate the importance of an ongoing risk monitoring process

TRANSPORTATION **PROFILE**

The New Transportation Risk

What's the top of mind concern of transportation executives? You may think that it is cargo theft and damage, poor weather, capacity shortages, or some other physical threat to timely and safe freight flows. These issues haven't disappeared but they have given way to another risk that warrants significant attention—cyber vulnerability.

Recent surveys reveal that the growing dependence of transportation on technology is not a risk-free proposition. Cyber risk was listed as a top five concern in the World Economic Forum's Global Risk 2015 report. Likewise, cyber vulnerability was the highest ranked concern in the Willis Tower Watson Transportation Risk Index, which analyzes the severity of impact and ease of management of the top 50 risks facing the transportation industry.

Why are transportation executives so concerned about technology security breaches, information theft, and other data disruption problems? Their transportation equipment, networks, and processes are increasingly digital and dependent upon continuous information flows. With a growing reliance on cloud technology, more Internet of Things devices in use, and greater amounts of data sharing between carriers and customers, the potential for disruptive cyber breaches also grows.

At times, the potential becomes reality. Documented cyberattacks include the ransomware virus attacks on transportation providers' systems, theft of customer data from a rail carrier's reservation system, and a breach of an airline's ground computer system that led to flight cancellations. Such events can disrupt the company's operations, damage its reputation, and threaten its profits.

These risks will become more acute as cyber criminals increasingly target the transportation industry. Carriers must develop proactive, ongoing strategies to identify and mitigate their growing level of cyber risk. They must enhance network resiliency by building security best practices into systems, continuously monitoring potential threats, establishing incident response capabilities, and collaborating with supply chain partners.

Attention to detail and cross-chain focus are essential, according to a cybersecurity expert. "All it takes is one weak link in the security chain for hackers to access and corrupt a product feature, an entire supply chain, or a critical piece of infrastructure," he notes. "The stakes are too high for complacency or inattention."

Sources: Raphael Satter and Frank Bajak, "New Cyberattack Wallops Europe; Spreads More Slowly in US," *Associated Press*, June 28, 2017, retrieved June 30, 2017 from https://apnews.com/57bb0af7145e4aefbe050b33636a15cf; Reynolds Hutchins, "Cyber Security Tops List of Transport Industry Threats, Survey Says," *JOC.com*, September 6, 2016, retrieved June 30, 2017 from http://www.joc.com/international-logistics/logistics-technology/cyber-security-tops-list-transport-industry-threats-survey-says_20160906.html; "Top 25 Risk Factors for Manufacturing Supply Chain," *Supply Chain 24/7*, July 26, 2016, retrieved June 30, 2017 from http://www.supplychain247.com/article/top_25_risk_factors_for_manufacturing_supply_chains/; *Marsh Insights: Cyber Risk in the Transportation Industry*, 2015, retrieved June 30, 2017, from https://www.marsh.com/uk/insights/research/cyber-risk-in-the-transportation-industry.html.

Introduction

Petya and WannaCry are not fictitious hackers from the latest spy movie. They are malware programs that disabled computer systems in 2017, causing significant information disruptions and financial losses for affected companies. Criminals use these programs to hijack computers and lock all files until a ransom is paid to restore them. As the Transportation Profile highlights, transportation companies have been the victims of these attacks, as well as a variety of other malicious efforts to steal, delete, or corrupt vital data about shipments, customers, and operations. It is a major problem worldwide, with ransomware attacks rising 6,000 percent in 2016 at a cost that is approaching \$1 billion.[1]

Cyberattacks are just one type of threat that organizations face when moving goods around the globe. Major incidents—hurricanes, pandemics, labor unrest, and terrorism—create societal problems and significant business challenges. From a transportation standpoint, they are disruptive events that result in supply chain disorder and discontinuity. The outcomes can vary dramatically from minor inconveniences and delivery delays to tremendous problems that threaten a company's image and financial outlook.

Companies cannot idly stand by and hope for the best when they move freight. They must actively work to limit exposure to legitimate hazards. This chapter focuses on the management of transportation risk and service disruptions. We will discuss the general concepts of disruption, risk, and business continuity, as well as the risk management process. Specific issues related to transportation risk management strategies will be addressed, followed by a discussion of expected outcomes. Throughout the chapter, you will gain an understanding of the true challenges involved in the global movement of goods as well as the methods available to mitigate transportation risk.

Risk Concepts

Risk is an everyday part of life. Whenever we get behind the wheel of our cars, the potential exists for us to be involved in an accident, to be delayed due to congestion, or to get lost. Although the likelihood of anything bad happening may be remote, each of these risks poses an unpleasant consequence for us—costs, missed appointments, stress, and so on.

The same issues arise when companies put freight in a container, railcar, or trailer. The freight could be stolen, damaged, lost, or delayed. Problems can occur when the freight is in motion or at rest in a port, trucking terminal, rail yard, or other intermediate facility. There are many disruption risks from the time freight leaves the origin location until it reaches its final destination.

So what exactly are disruptions and risks? A review of dictionary entries and magazine article descriptions reveals a dizzying variety of definitions. For the purpose of this chapter, we will use the following characterizations as the foundation of our discussion:

> **Disruption**—disturbance or problems that interrupt an event, activity, or process.[2]
>
> **Transportation Disruption**—any significant delay, interruption, or stoppage in the flow of trade caused by a natural disaster, heightened threat level, an act of terrorism, or any transportation security incident.[3]
>
> **Risk**—expose (someone or something valued) to danger, harm, or loss.[4]
>
> **Transportation Risk**—a future freight movement event with a probability of occurrence and the potential for impacting supply chain performance.

Problems arise when the threat of transportation disruptions and hazards become reality and the global supply chain is negatively affected.

At minimum, these disruptions are nuisances, creating extra work and delays. Recovery efforts hurt productivity, involve expensive expediting efforts, and require premium freight services. At worst, disruptions inflict long-term damage to a company's image, profitability, and stock price. A Zurich Insurance Ltd. study revealed that 74 percent of businesses around the world experience supply chain disruptions. Nearly 14 percent of the disruptions have a financial cost in excess of $1.1 million.[5]

These eye-opening numbers, along with high-impact events like the 2016 bankruptcy filing and 2017 liquidation order of Hanjin Shipping Co., the world's seventh largest container carrier,[6] have prompted transportation managers to pay more attention to risks like permanent loss of freight capacity. These managers are actively engaged in efforts to reduce the probability of disruptions through a process called risk management:

> **Risk Management**—the identification, analysis, assessment, control, and avoidance, minimization, or elimination of unacceptable risks.[7]

How does risk management work? Going back to the driving example, it is possible for you to plan a car trip so that the likelihood of getting delayed or lost is minimized. By studying traffic patterns, mapping out a route, and printing step-by-step directions (or using a GPS navigation system), you can develop a plan to greatly reduce the risk of a trip disruption. This proactive planning initiative will minimize your potential for getting caught in rush hour traffic, being forced into construction detours, or becoming lost. Of course, your risk management plan isn't totally foolproof because unpredictable events such as accidents may still occur.

A key aspect of managing transportation risk is to prepare for the inevitable freight-related problems. Developing planned responses to deal with high-probability risks—like hazardous winter weather in Minnesota—is far more effective than waiting until a blizzard occurs to formulate solutions. This process of proactive planning for fast recovery from disruptions is called business continuity planning:

> **Business Continuity Planning**—task of identifying, developing, acquiring, documenting, and testing procedures and resources that will ensure continuity of a firm's key operations in the event of an accident, disaster, emergency, and/or threat.[8]

Business continuity planning efforts focus on developing and testing your ability to deal with a crisis situation. In transportation management, this involves having readiness plans to reestablish full functionality of delivery processes as swiftly and smoothly as possible when a disruption occurs. Poor advanced planning will produce ineffective, slow recovery and a protracted interruption of freight flows.

As you might expect, risk management and business continuity planning are not simple tasks. They demand significant time and expertise, involve financial investment, and require frequent revision. Hence, risk management activities must be driven by the top management of companies across a supply chain if global transportation disruption risks are to be minimized. Company leaders must view risk management as a critical tool for protecting profitability and implement detailed, cyclical processes to control risk. A four-step risk management methodology is discussed later in the chapter.

Transportation Risks

Every time freight is handled, a shipment is moved, or ownership transfer takes place, there is a risk that a transportation disruption will occur. Trouble can occur with the product being displaced, critical information being hacked, payments being delayed, or any number of other problems. In short, transportation is a risk-laden activity. Supply chain professionals on both the shipper and carrier sides of the transaction must develop a comprehensive understanding of their challenges to moving freight safely, quickly, and securely.

Given the wide array of problems that can occur as freight flows from one supply chain partner to another, it would be very challenging to discuss every potential risk in this chapter. Instead, we target six major risk categories related to freight transportation: product loss, product damage, product contamination, delivery delay, supply chain interruption, and security breach. While specific risk issues within a category will vary by company type, primary mode used, and region of the world, common headaches are addressed below.

Product Loss

Everyone knows that cargo gets stolen, but the magnitude of the problem is staggering. BSI Group estimated global cargo theft would reach $24 billion in 2016.[9] However, the economic loss to firms goes far beyond the value of the stolen goods. Indirect costs of cargo theft include lost sales, expedited delivery of replacement goods, disrupted customer service, and damaged brand value. Other indirect costs include claims processing expenses and higher insurance rates.

Product loss is not limited to criminals stealing entire shipments. Product loss includes any type of action or negligence that leads to product not reaching the intended buyer. This includes:

- **Product Pilferage**—the theft of individual items from a shipping package by freight handlers, equipment operators, and managers is problematic. It is a particular challenge with smartphones, pharmaceutical products, designer clothes, and other high-value goods that can be easily concealed and later sold for cash.

- **Shipment Jettison**—in the movement of freight via water, it may be necessary to cast all or part of a ship's cargo overboard to save the ship, crew, and other cargo from perils such as catastrophic weather, running aground, or fire. The master of the ship has the absolute right to jettison cargo when he reasonably believes it to be necessary, and the owners of the ship incur no liability. If the ship is carrying goods of more than one shipper, the rule of **general average** provides for apportioning the loss among all the shippers because all have benefited by the master's action.

- **Piracy and Hijacking**—these product and equipment loss risks are a continuing challenge with 191 reported incidents in 2016.[10] Not only do these crimes create financial losses for companies but they often put ship crews and truck drivers at risk of being kidnapped, injured, or killed.

- **Product Damage**—damage is a potential peril that arises every time a shipment is handled. Employee inattention, negligence, and poor training all contribute to this very costly problem. Damaged product may need to be repaired or salvaged to recoup some value, or discarded, incurring a total loss. The cost of freight claims processing and product replacement add to the financial impact of damage incidents.

Product Damage

Product damage can result from a wide array of actions or inactions on the part of equipment operators and freight handlers. Damage risks include:

- **Equipment Accidents**—415,000 U.S. commercial trucks were involved in crashes during 2015. The economic impact of the resulting cargo damage, vehicle damage, injuries, fatalities, and related costs exceeds $100 billion each year.[11] Accidents involving other modes incur similar types of expenses.

- **Poor Freight Handling**—a failure to use caution when moving product in/out of equipment can increase the risk of damage. In particular, fragile goods are susceptible to damage from impact, vibration, and rough handling hazards when not carefully handled.
- **Improper Equipment Loading**—the long distance movement of freight may involve a rough ride, especially for rail and ocean transportation. Freight damage risks from falling, shifting, or compression are high if the load is not properly secured and stacked.

Product Contamination

A particular risk to food, pharmaceutical goods, and other consumables is the possibility that product becomes contaminated while en route from origin to destination. Customers may reject a delivery of goods if there is evidence of possible adulteration. They do not want to assume the risk of product loss, customer liability, or the responsibility for disposal.

Product contamination risk increases along with trip distance and time in transit. The longer the goods are out of your control, the more opportunity exists for natural or manmade contamination issues to arise. Primary **freight contamination** risks include:

- **Climate Control Failure**—environmentally sensitive goods such as fruit, vegetables, electronics, biomedical samples, and chemicals often require transportation within a strict temperature or humidity range. Failure to provide a stable climate inside the container during transit will result in product degradation, spoilage, or contamination.
- **Product Tampering**—the deliberate contamination of goods after they have been manufactured is a remote but potentially devastating risk. Given the threat of lawsuits and brand damage, the mere hint of tampering may require a costly effort to clear product from store shelves, restock the supply chain, and rebuild consumer confidence.
- **Exposure to Contaminants**—the risk of freight coming in contact with potentially undesirable substance (physical, chemical, or biological) occurs when different types of freight are commingled. Contamination issues also arise if transportation equipment is used to move different commodities on consecutive trips (for instance, filling a railroad tank car with food-grade oil after it was used to transport an industrial solvent).

Delivery Delay

There are few things more frustrating than late delivery of a time-sensitive shipment like concert tickets. If they arrive the day after the concert, the tickets are rendered worthless and you missed a great event. Companies who rely upon **just-in-time delivery** of inventory to keep their production lines running may experience the same frustration, only to a much higher level of financial pain. If a critical shipment is delayed even a few hours, there is a chance of production lines stopping. The lost productivity cost may be tens of thousands of dollars.

There are numerous **delivery delay** risks. Some transportation perils result from strategic decisions such as sourcing goods from low-cost manufacturers in the Far East. This strategy significantly increases supply chain complexity and distance, boosting the possibility of late deliveries. Other risks are out of the company's control, though it is important to recognize their potential impact. Common delivery schedule disruptors include:

- **Congestion**—overburdened roadways, railways, and port facilities impede product flows and create bottlenecks in the supply chain. As equipment sits idly in traffic and average speeds drop, slower-than-anticipated transit times are achieved, fuel is wasted, and delivery windows are missed. Congestion on U.S. highways costs the trucking industry over $63 billion in operating expenses a year and includes over 996 million hours of lost productivity.[12] Seaports also struggle with congestion created by larger containerships, peak season activity, and late ship arrivals.[13]

- **Poor Weather**—as environmental conditions deteriorate, it becomes more challenging to maintain an accurate delivery schedule. Companies located in or delivering to customers in dangerous climate zones—hurricanes, blizzards, heat waves, ice, and so on—must factor these uncontrollable issues into freight movement planning and delivery commitments.

- **Equipment Malfunction**—mechanical breakdowns of delivery vehicles can cause product to get stranded en route. Likewise, problems with freight handling equipment at ports (such as container cranes) and other freight transfer facilities can delay shipments beyond their scheduled delivery times.

Supply Chain Interruption

Many transportation risks are created by poor execution of day-to-day operations. Ineffective decision making, employee errors, and technology glitches may slow freight flows. Such risks pale in comparison to the devastating effects of border disputes and port strikes that bring transportation operations to a grinding halt. The cost of such disruptions is high and recovery time is prolonged.

Although they don't occur frequently, these problems often fall outside the control of the company. Recent examples of transportation-altering **supply chain interruptions** include:

- **Industry Consolidation**—in times of excess capacity and low rates, financially unstable transportation companies are unable to compete. Such is the case in the global container shipping industry where carriers have merged or joined operations alliances to survive.[14] The changing market structure can cause capacity and cost challenges for customers due to fewer scheduled routes.

- **Labor Disruptions**—many transportation companies and facilities rely upon unionized labor for freight handling and movement. When work-related disputes occur or labor contracts expire, a labor strike risk arises. Some strikes can be predicted in advance, though others are sudden "wild cat" strikes that occur with little warning and create havoc. The cost of these supply chain interruptions can be severe.

- **Capacity Shortages**—during peak seasonal demand, transportation capacity is stretched to the point that carriers are often unable to provide enough equipment and operators to service all customers. Transportation companies are able to increase rates or apply peak season surcharges to freight. At the same time, there is a risk of service quality failures due to facility congestion, equipment shortages, and operator inexperience.

Security Breach

Terrorist attacks, organized crime activity, and illegal immigration have driven a worldwide effort to secure freight. Global transportation companies must refine their policies and procedures to protect in-transit freight. A failure to do so leaves the company, its customers, and the general public vulnerable to security threats. Repeated failures drive government demand for time-consuming freight inspections and costly countermeasures.

There is no shortage of security challenges facing organizations, especially with shrewd criminals scheming to exploit system flaws and security vulnerabilities. Common points of exposure are:

- **Lax Security Processes**—supply chain security and **resiliency** are not optional; they must be built into global transportation operations. Companies must think about their potential security vulnerabilities and develop appropriate defenses.
- **Unprotected Transfer Facilities**—some transportation companies fail to do the simple things like lock doors, fence in facilities, and require security badges to limit access to freight and transportation equipment. Ease of facility entry and access promotes product theft, deliberate contamination, or catastrophic disruptions (such as hiding a bomb in a freight container).
- **Shipment Control Failures**—freight **visibility** and access control are the keys to protecting in-transit goods from harm. When freight is not properly controlled, security risks and disruption opportunities increase. For example, unsupervised or unlocked freight containers provide hiding spots for stowaways attempting to illegally enter a country. Stowaways may contaminate the container's contents and cause legal headaches for authorities.

Although we have identified six categories of risk and discussed 18 specific risks, the list is not by any means comprehensive. The perils of transportation are many and varied. Hazardous materials dangers, corrosive saltwater, border crossing issues, military conflicts, and other issues constantly threaten to disrupt transportation operations. Managers must remain vigilant to possible threats and constantly analyze transportation risk, both natural and manmade.

Transportation Risk Management Process

Risk management is an integral part of effective transportation management. It is an iterative process that enables continuous performance improvement. Risk management is the process of identifying risk, its causes and effects, and its ownership with a goal of increasing overall understanding in order to manage, reduce, transfer, or eliminate threats to supply chain success.

The objectives of **risk management** include the following:

- Develop a common understanding of risk across functions and business units.
- Manage risk cost-effectively on an enterprise-wide basis.
- Build and improve capabilities to respond effectively to low-probability, catastrophic risks.
- Achieve a better understanding of risk for competitive advantage.
- Build safeguards against earnings-related surprises.
- Achieve cost savings through better management of internal resources.
- Allocate capital more efficiently.

It is important to align these risk management objectives with the organization's strategies and goals. These strategies and desired outcomes provide the context for risk management.[15]

Risk management objectives are addressed through implementation of the four-step process outlined in Figure 10-1. Each step is described below.

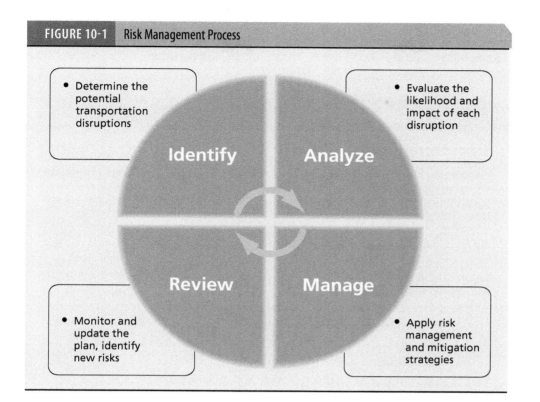

FIGURE 10-1 | Risk Management Process

- Determine the potential transportation disruptions

Identify

- Evaluate the likelihood and impact of each disruption

Analyze

Review

- Monitor and update the plan, identify new risks

Manage

- Apply risk management and mitigation strategies

Step 1—Risk Identification

Accurate and detailed **risk identification** is vital for effective risk management. Thus, the first step in developing an effective transportation risk management program is to discover, define, describe, document, and communicate risks before they become problems and adversely affect freight flows.

The goal of risk identification is to recognize as many transportation disruption risks as possible. During this process, all possible transportation risks that can occur along the global and domestic segments of the transportation network should be recorded. Both inbound and outbound delivery processes should be studied as well. And, both natural and manmade risks need to monitored as highlighted in the Global Perspectives feature.

There are various techniques that can be used for risk identification. Useful techniques include:

- **Brainstorming** is a common risk identification technique used to ascertain high-level risks. Knowledgeable participants—both management and hourly personnel—engage in an open-ended dialogue to collaboratively develop a comprehensive list of threats, concerns, and possible issues.

- Interviews and surveys can be used to capture transportation risk information. The goal is to quickly and efficiently capture their lessons learned from first-hand experience with disruptions.

- Analysis of transportation records for disruption information (frequency, service impact, and recovery costs) provides a data-driven risk knowledge base.

Brainstorming efforts will produce a long list of potential disruptions. Rather than trying to assess each one independently, it is beneficial to organize the disruptions into broad risk categories. This will streamline the risk management process and limit duplication of efforts.

GLOBAL **PERSPECTIVES**

Transportation Risk—Who or What Is to Blame?

If a company is to effectively manage risk, it needs to understand the sources of transportation headaches and disruptions. As operations expand from local, to national, to international networks, the array of potential problems will grow exponentially. Also, the ability to directly control the risks diminishes.

Particularly difficult to predict and manage are the risks created by Mother Nature. While a company can develop a robust understanding of regional weather patterns and climate risks, it is not so easy to do on a worldwide scale. A quick review of the five largest supply chain disruptions in 2016, reveals that these events can happen anywhere, anytime, with limited advanced warning:

1. 6.4 Magnitude Earthquake in Taiwan, February
2. Series of earthquakes in Japan, April
3. Typhoon Haima, which hit Taiwan, China, and the Philippines, October
4. Typhoon Napartak, which hit China and Taiwan, July
5. Typhoon Megi, which affected Taiwan and China, September

Fully returning a transportation network to normal operations in the wake of such catastrophes can be a weeks-long, if not months-long challenge. Hence, most companies have learned to not be totally reliant on a single factory, port, or carrier.

Man and management strategy are also sources of transportation risk. Sometimes we make poor decisions or engage in risky behaviors that manifest in transportation disruptions. Dispatching a load at the last minute can miss a scheduled voyage or international flight, delaying delivery by days or weeks. Other times, we deploy plans that have unintended consequences. Such is the case with ultra-large containerships.

Developed with the idea that bigger ships create greater efficiency, vessels with the ability to carry 18,000 TEU (20-foot equivalent) or more have been built. The idea is to have fewer, larger, more fuel-efficient vessels plying major shipping lanes of the world to reduce operating costs. However, the strategy does create risks:

- Carrying many thousands of containers with a collective value potentially exceeding $1 billion creates an inviting target for cyberattacks and terrorism
- Offloading these vessels requires extensive time and special equipment, which leads to congestion in the harbor and onshore, as well as greater landside expense
- Few world ports have the available space to support quarter-mile-long ships that require about 100 acres of terminal space for efficient operations

These Mother Nature and manmade risks reveal an important truth for transportation professionals. It is imperative for them to think through the potential consequences of expansion plans and transportation strategies before taking action.

Sources: MH&L Staff, "Five Important Supply Chain Events of 2016," *Material Handling & Logistics* , February 14, 2017, retrieved July 10, 2017, from http://mhlnews.com/global-supply-chain/five-important-supply-chain-events-2016; Adam Minter, "Ships Have Gotten Too Big," *Bloomberg View* , June 14, 2016, retrieved July 10, 2017, from https://www.bloomberg.com/view/articles/2016-06-14/ships-have-gotten-too-big ; and, Sri Laxmana, "Mega Ships: A Look at the Effect of Larger Ocean Vessels at Port," *Talking Logistics* , May 17, 2016, retrieved July 10, 2017, from https://talkinglogistics.com/2016/05/17/mega-ships-look-effect-larger-ocean-vessels-port/.

Step 2—Risk Assessment

Evaluating transportation risks is a challenging proposition because they do not affect organizations equally. Risks and their potential impact are influenced by supply chain strategy, modes used, and operational capabilities. For example, if a company focuses on international sourcing of materials for their assembly plant, delivery delays from distant suppliers pose a high risk of shutting down the production line. In contrast, late deliveries are not a major issue for a company that locally procures raw materials. Thus, managers must determine which risks are of direct relevance to their organization.

The objective of risk assessment is to evaluate the seriousness of each risk identified during Step 1 (Risk Identification). In making this determination, an organization should evaluate three parameters:

- **Probability**—the likelihood of the risk occurring
- **Impact**—the consequences if the risk does occur
- **Proximity**—the anticipated timing of the risk

Impact can be assessed in terms of the transportation risk's effect on time, cost, and/or quality. Proximity focuses on the temporal aspect of disruptive events, such as hurricanes or blizzards. Understanding their seasonality considerations and preparing appropriate strategies will help organization proactively manage these events. Risk assessment can be qualitative or quantitative in nature. **Qualitative risk analysis** provides a baseline evaluation of risks in a rapid and cost-effective manner. Knowledgeable individuals classify each risk in terms of its probability and impact (see Figure 10-2). For example, a border crossing delay

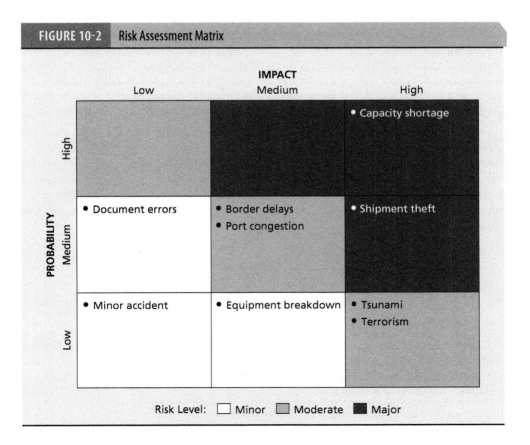

| FIGURE 10-2 | Risk Assessment Matrix |

Risk Level: ☐ Minor ▨ Moderate ■ Major

may be a medium-impact, medium-probability risk for freight moving from Mexico City to Dallas. In contrast, border crossing delays would be a low-impact, low-probability risk for freight moving between Paris and Amsterdam and other EU cities.

An issue landing in the "Major Risk" category is deemed unacceptable. The organization must actively seek to mitigate the probability and impact of these potential disruptions. The organization should also address issues in the "Moderate Risk" and "Minor Risk" categories through contingency planning. The required level of management attention is tempered by the reduced risk potential.

Quantitative risk analysis often builds upon the foundation created by qualitative analysis. Those risks falling into the "Major" risk level category may warrant detailed assessment of available data to evaluate their relative danger levels. Quantitative analysis incorporates numerical estimates of frequency or probability and consequence. This data can be expensive to acquire or may not be available.

Risk assessment is a time-consuming task. To be of value, this activity needs to generate useful information for the organization. Based on the Risk Identification (Step 1) results, transportation managers should diagnose the risks to analyze what could happen if the hazard occurs.

Risk assessment is an invaluable activity for identifying global transportation challenges and primary disruption concerns. This effort ensures that organizations focus their scarce resources on relevant risk management and mitigation strategies.

Step 3—Risk Management Strategy Development

Using the output from the risk assessment, the next step is to create a coherent strategy for managing and mitigating transportation risks in a cost-effective manner. The mitigation strategy identifies specific efforts, actions, and procedural changes that must be taken by management to reduce high priority risks. The goal is to lower the probability of risk occurrence and/or minimize the negative impact if the risk occurs. A risk can never be totally eliminated, but its frequency and effects can be reduced if properly addressed.

Mitigation strategies must not be haphazardly applied to disruption risks. First, the strategies must be in sync with the overall supply chain strategy and corporate strategy. Second, mitigation strategies and actions must focus on high priority issues. Third, the mitigation action must be reasonable in terms of cost and time to implement versus the likelihood of success. Otherwise, money and effort will be wasted on low priority risks or ineffective risk remedies. Finally, a standardized process should be used to mitigate disruptions.

Each **risk mitigation** strategy should produce an action plan that identifies:

- roles and responsibilities for developing, implementing, and monitoring the strategy
- resources required to carry out the planned actions
- timelines
- conditions present in order for risk level to be acceptable

A well-developed plan plays an important role in decreasing the risk of transportation disruptions as well as their effect on the supply chain and company performance. These plans typically focus on one of four techniques to manage and mitigate risk: avoidance, reduction, transfer, or retention.[16]

Risk Avoidance The simplest way to eliminate a risk is to not perform an activity that carries risk. For example, a company could avoid transportation hazards by refusing to accept a customer's high-value freight. No freight needs to be shipped, meaning that the risk of in-transit freight loss or damage is eliminated. However, the company also misses the revenue and profit opportunities for moving the goods.

An alternative to this conservative pure avoidance strategy is to take steps to remove the risk. When possible, the ideal solution is to keep the risk from happening. Tools like root cause analysis can be used to pinpoint the reasons why a disruption occurs. Processes can be revised to eliminate the disruption's causes and greatly minimize the risk. For example, if an investigation revealed that all thefts occurred at a specific international port, the simple solution would be to never flow product through that port again. Hence, that particular theft risk would be removed.

Another avoidance strategy would be to sidestep the specific exposure. In the case of freight loss or damage risk, the seller could choose to work only on an Ex Works (EXW) basis. Under these International Commercial Terms—discussed in full detail in Chapter 11—the seller fulfills his or her obligations by having the goods available for the buyer to pick up at a named place such as the factory or warehouse. The buyer bears all risk, costs, and responsibilities after picking up the products at the seller's location. In contrast, a buyer may want to minimize his or her risk by purchasing goods on a Delivered Duty Paid (DDP) basis. In that scenario the seller bears all transportation risk, cost, and responsibility.

Risk Reduction Given that many risks cannot be completely avoided, it is important for companies to proactively mitigate or limit risk. This involves adopting risk management strategies that reduce the likelihood of a disruption and/or limit the severity of financial loss. For example, a company could attempt to reduce the risk of theft or hijacking by hiring armed guards to travel with high-value freight. This strategy could be effective at reducing risk to a more acceptable level, but it may be expensive and/or raise other risks.

There are numerous types of strategies to pursue the goal of risk reduction. Some companies will use a **hedging strategy** to offset or balance out the risks presented by a single option. This diversification avoids the inflated risk of having "all your eggs in one basket." In transportation, companies can disperse their freight among multiple carriers to reduce the financial risk of a sole sourced carrier bankruptcy or service interruption. Hedging can also be used to protect against the risks of rising expenses as discussed in the On the Line feature.

A **postponement strategy** seeks to limit risk by delaying a commitment of resources. Trucking companies could reduce the risk of productivity losses by delaying the dispatch of drivers until after a customer has loaded a trailer and submitted proper documentation. This will reduce driver wait time and maximize the use of available service hours for transporting freight.

A **buffering strategy** provides additional resources to reduce risks related to capacity shortages or performance problems. An air cargo company may have extra jets available to reduce the impact of equipment failures. They may also have a few pilots on call each day to be prepared for volume spikes. Both buffering actions will reduce the likelihood of freight delays.

ON THE **LINE**

Hedging Those Transportation Bets

Hedging is a risk management strategy used to limit or offset the probability of loss from fluctuations in the prices of commodities, currencies, or securities. Hedging fundamentally involves taking equal and opposite positions in two different markets such as the cash market and futures market. The hedge investment attempts to reduce the risk of adverse price movements in the asset.

A futures contract is a hedging tool that obligates the buyer of the contract to buy the commodity at the price stated in the contract. It also obligates the seller of the contract to sell the commodity at the price stated in the contract. The buyer is essentially betting that the commodity price will rise and attempts to lock down a low price for future purchases. The seller is forecasting that the price will drop, the contract will expire unused, and keep the premium payment.

In freight transportation, hedging has long been by transportation companies to protect against rising fuel prices. Whether the need is bunker fuel, diesel fuel, jet fuel, or gasoline, carriers across all modes have been known to hedge their fuel purchases. Why is this the case? Fuel is one of their highest expenses and the price for this commodity can be volatile.

Airlines have used hedging strategies due to the extreme cost of jet fuel and the vast volume of fuel consumed each day. Of course, fuel hedging is not always guaranteed to save money. When airlines pay a contract premium to lock in future rates at current day prices and the price decreases over time, the airline will lose money on those contracts.

Such is the case with Southwest Airlines. After years of successfully hedging 60 percent to 70 percent of its fuel purchases to slash its fuel expenses in an era of rising jet fuel prices, 2015 and 2016 were not so kind to the airline. With fuel prices dropping, Southwest's hedging contract rates through 2018 represent a loss of $1.8 billion when compared to much lower January 2016 open market rates. To eliminate some of this risk, the company is now only hedging 30 percent to 35 percent of its expected fuel purchases. Other airlines are reassessing their hedging strategies to avoid similar issues.

Hedging is also used in ocean transportation to manage freight rates. Bulk shippers and carriers routinely buy and sell futures contracts called freight forward agreements based on the Baltic Dry Index of bulk rates. The contracts are used to hedge against the risk that a rise or fall in the spot rate might cut into the expected profit from the voyage.

In a new twist on that concept, a trucking industry veteran is working to create a truck pricing futures exchange. The intention is to help transportation buyers shield their companies from rising truck rates when capacity is thin. Rates can be very volatile in the short run and buyers currently have few options to mitigate the risk of rising rates. A side benefit of the exchange will be pricing transparency and real-time visibility of the direction that freight costs are headed, according to the exchange creator.

Will these hedging tools protect carriers from rising fuel costs and freight buyers from higher freight rates in the future? The potential for overall savings exist. However, just as a gambler doesn't win every hand of poker, savings on every futures contract is not possible.

Sources: Business Dictionary, "Hedging," retrieved July 9, 2017, from: http://www.businessdictionary.com/definition/hedging.html ; William B. Cassidy, "TransFX Wants to Help Shippers Hedge Against Truck Rate Hikes," JOC.com, April 19, 2017, retrieved July 9, 2017, from http://www.joc.com/trucking-logistics/truckload-freight/transfx-wants-help-shippers-hedge-against-truck-rate-hikes_20170419.html ; Mercatus Energy Advisors, "A Beginner's Guide to Fuel Hedging—Futures," December 6, 2016, retrieved, July 9, 2017, from: https://www.mercatusenergy.com/blog/bid/81549/a-beginners-guide-to-fuel-hedging-futures ; and, Jeffrey Dastin, "US Airlines Tried to Save Money on Fuel, and Now They're Regretting It," *Business Insider*, January 22, 2016, retrieved July 9, 2017, from: http://www.businessinsider.com/r-us-airlines-rethink-hedges-as-oil-plunges-2016-1.

Given the vast array of transportation risks, it is impossible to discuss in detail the reduction strategies that have been developed. Table 10-1 highlights a variety of risk reduction strategies that align well with the six risk categories and 18 specific risks discussed earlier.

Risk reduction requires that companies be proactive in establishing plans to deal with the high-probability/high-impact risks that emerge from the identification and analysis processes. The strategies discussed briefly below will help companies reduce a variety of common transportation risks that affect all modes around the world.

- Develop and maintain relationships with quality carriers—effective service providers are reliable, reasonably priced, and protect freight. Transportation buyers must make a concerted effort to balance service dependability, cost efficiency, and safety when selecting carriers. Hiring financially stable carriers, actively monitoring their performance, and pursuing continuous improvement will reduce the risk of delays and damage.

TABLE 10-1   Transportation Risk Reduction Strategies

RISK CATEGORY	SPECIFIC RISKS	REDUCTION STRATEGIES	ANTICIPATED OUTCOMES
Product Loss	Theft and pilferage Piracy and hijacking Cargo jettison	Use generic packaging and descriptions Avoid crime hot spots Strategic routing	Mitigate risk of financial loss, reduce customer delivery delays, and avoid replacement shipment expenses.
Product Damage	Operator accident Poor freight handling methods Improper equipment loading	Use protective packaging Establish training programs Monitor carrier performance	Enhance freight safety, reduce freight claims administration, and profit margin protection.
Product Contamination	Temperature control failure Product tampering Exposure to hazardous materials	Secure freight/lock containers Isolate dangerous freight Leverage IoT monitoring tools	Safeguard brand equity, decrease potential for product liability lawsuits, and trim product recalls and inventory replacement costs.
Delivery Delay	Congestion Poor weather Equipment malfunction	Use event management software Employ dynamic re-routing tools Avoid ill-equipped and congested ports	Proactive response to problems resulting in less wait time, greater delivery reliability, and improved customer satisfaction.
Supply Chain Interruption	Capacity shortage Carrier bankruptcy Labor disruptions and strikes	Contract with quality carriers Monitor carrier finances Secure backup capacity Identify alternate ports and service providers	Avoid major disruptions of product flows that can impact supply chain productivity, and product availability.
Security Breach	Shipment control breakdown Unprotected transfer facilities Lax security processes	Employ cargo tracking technology Screen and evaluate vulnerabilities Participate in government-sponsored programs	Greater protection against terrorist activity, fewer government inspections, and streamlined border clearance.

- Use protective product packaging—freight is often handled by forklifts, conveyors, cranes, and multiple transportation vehicles on the way to its final destination. To minimize the risk of concealed product damage or contamination, protective materials like cardboard, bubble wrap, foam packing forms, plastic bags, and other materials should be used inside shipping cartons. Insufficient packaging increases the risk of product damage and limits carrier liability in freight claim situations.

- Properly secure freight inside containers—assuming that the ride will be rough encourages companies to safeguard their in-transit inventory. Loads should be secured and protected as needed by using blocking and cleats nailed to the floor, braces, straps, load bars, or air bags and other void fill materials. In addition, the use of stretch wrap, shrink wrap, banding, and edge protectors will stabilize and protect unitized freight.

- Require the use of reliable equipment—allowing carriers to use defective or poorly maintained equipment to move your freight produces transportation risk. Poor vehicle maintenance raises the potential for delivery delays due to equipment breakdowns and inspection failures. Equipment malfunctions increase the likelihood of product damage due to accidents, poor ride quality, leaks, and other problems. To avoid these problems, work only with carriers that perform preventative maintenance, regularly upgrade their fleets, and have a strong track record of equipment safety compliance.

- Leverage freight visibility technology to monitor in-transit freight not only provides peace of mind, it helps managers avoid potential problems and respond rapidly to disruptions. Visibility tools provide a seamless flow of timely information across the supply chain. Accurate knowledge of in-transit freight allows managers to be proactive in routing and scheduling to meet delivery windows. Exception management tools detect performance problems and alert the affected organization. Corrective action can be taken to resolve the situation before the supply chain is adversely impacted. The Transportation Technology box highlights the growing role of IoT—the Internet of Things—for maintaining freight visibility and control to reduce risk.

Risk Transfer Through risk analysis, an organization may identify potential problems that are too problematic to internally manage or mitigate. In these situations, the organization may seek outside assistance in controlling those risks. This risk transfer strategy provides a means to place liability on a third party should the risk occur. Of course, the third party doesn't freely accept the risk. They are paid by the customer to assume or share the risk.

Insurance is a common method of risk transfer. Individuals can purchase medical, life, and property insurance. Transportation companies and their customers can also do the same to reduce their risks. For example, the financial risks stemming from commercial vehicle accidents and related lawsuits are very high. Rather than setting aside a large pool of money to self-insure against these possible problems, most transportation companies purchase coverage from insurance companies. They are using the strategy of risk transfer as the means to place financial liability on a third party (the insurance company) should the risk (a vehicle accident) occur.

TRANSPORTATION **TECHNOLOGY**

Those Things Can Reduce Your Risk

Properly deployed, technology like GPS tracking supports freight visibility and control. This real-time knowledge of shipment location and condition can help an organization identify problems and develop appropriate responses to minimize the risk of product loss, damage, or delay. That is especially important when dealing with temperature-sensitive products, high-value goods, and high-risk freight.

Advanced sense-and-respond capabilities are emerging thanks to the Internet of Things (IoT). IoT focuses on the ability to connect any device with an on/off switch to the Internet (and/or to each other). This networked connectivity enables transportation companies to capture vast data and intelligence about freight, equipment assets, and operators as freight moves across the supply chain. When a potential problem is detected, those on/off switches can be automatically flipped or adjusted to mitigate the risk. Operational efficiencies can also be improved.

IoT can be implemented in numerous transportation applications to reduce risk. Examples include:

- **Product Climate Control**. Just as IoT devices like Nest thermostats can be used to monitor and adjust temperatures, the conditions inside a trailer, container, or railcar can be remotely managed via IoT. Temperature, humidity, and light can be readily detected using IoT sensors. System adjustments are made as needed to maintain maximum product freshness and safety.

- **Equipment Status**. IoT technology in trucks can be used to monitor equipment temperature, emission levels, and fuel efficiency. Readings outside accepted ranges would trigger diagnostic tests to find the problem and make adjustments such as an automatic inflation system resolving a low tire pressure problem. IoT sensor-equipped trucks can also tell maintenance crews when it's time to bring a truck in for servicing brakes, engines, and other critical systems.

- **Driver Safety**. IoT telematics tools can be used to monitor equipment operator activities and report on problems with driver behavior. Issues of speeding, unsafe maneuvers, heavy braking, and related safety problems can be detected during the trip. Automated messages can be sent to the driver and reports can be generated for managerial counseling with the goal of reducing the risk of accidents.

It is important to note that IoT use can open the door to unpleasant side effects. As discussed in the opening pages of the chapter, any time technology is used to connect the supply chain, there is a chance of cybercrime, malicious hacking, and system failure. Companies must be vigilant and take steps to identify, evaluate, and mitigate their cyber risks. That will reduce the potential for disruptions.

The future potential for IoT in transportation and logistics is staggering. Experts predict that there will be over 50 billion connected devices by 2020. More importantly, they expect IoT in transportation and logistics to generate over $1.9 trillion in value. Transportation providers that do not adopt IoT are missing a great opportunity to transform their businesses, achieve operational efficiency, and reduce risk.

Sources: Willis Tower Watson, "The Internet of Things: Driving Transformation in Trucking and Logistics," retrieved July 10, 2017, from http://blog.willis.com/2017/02/the-internet-of-things-driving-transformation-in-trucking-and-logistics/; Gary Wollenhaupt, "How the Internet of Things Transforms Trucking," *Supply Chain 247*, December 30, 2015, retrieved July 9, 2017, from http://www.supplychain247.com/article/how_the_internet_of_things_transforms_trucking . C. John Langley, Jr. "The Internet of What? Of Things, Of Course," *NASSTRAC NewsLink*, Edition 6, 2015.

Freight owners often purchase insurance as a means to transfer their risk of in-transit freight loss, damage, and delay. This is a prudent move because carriers across all modes assume very limited liability for these types of problems. For example, FedEx and UPS limit their risk to $100 per package. Imagine buying a case of six Apple MacBook Air computers valued at $999 each on a F.O.B. Origin basis. Without insurance, you are taking a $5,894 gamble ($999 × 6 − $100) that the carrier will deliver your goods loss- and damage-free. Instead, purchasing an adequate amount of insurance from the transportation company, a cargo insurance broker, or an insurance underwriter will minimize your risk and help you sleep better at night.

It is also possible to transfer risk to **third party logistics** service providers (3PLs). These experts—the focus of Chapter 9—are external suppliers that perform all or part of an organization's logistics services. Companies contract with 3PLs because these service providers have the knowledge, capacity, technologies, and capability to mitigate some risk factors. 3PLs provide a diverse array of transportation services, administrative support, and strategic planning. Some 3PLs cover the full spectrum of global freight management issues while other companies assist with specific risks like asset protection, cargo loss control, or hazardous materials movement.

Regardless of a 3PL company's role and the risk transfer provisions in 3PL contracts and insurance policies, organizations are not absolved of their responsibilities. They must remain vigilant of potential risks and continually strive to reduce their exposures. After all, they own the freight and must protect it along with their customer relationships.

Risk Retention Risk is inevitable, but not all risk is created equal. Organizations must evaluate risk and make a judgment and determine what, if anything, they will do about it. Those issues falling in the minor risk categories of Figure 10-2, particularly the low-probability, low-impact issues, warrant little attention. These risks have limited potential to negatively affect the supply chain. They present an acceptable level and the organization will retain the risks.

In other situations, the cost of mitigating a risk may outweigh the benefits realized. For example, the potential savings from a low deductible insurance policy may not be enough to offset the additional policy cost. A transportation company may have a $2,500 deductible on their collision insurance. They will retain all financial risks related to small accidents and the deductible portion of larger incidents.

Finally, some risks are so large or catastrophic that they either cannot be reasonably mitigated or insured against. Examples include war, terrorism, and natural perils like the 2016 earthquake that occurred near an electronics manufacturing hub in southern Taiwan. Though the impact to semiconductor production facilities was limited, deliveries of some customer orders were delayed 10 to 50 days causing problems in their downstream supply chains.[17]

Regardless of the reason for retaining a risk, it cannot be ignored. Retained risks must be monitored to ensure that any escalation is captured and appropriate strategies are then implemented.

Collectively, these four types of risk management strategies help organizations adhere to the Boy Scout motto: "Be Prepared." When organizations conscientiously evaluate risks, determine the best course of action (avoid, reduce, transfer, or retain), and establish business continuity plans for major and moderate risks, the negative consequences and duration of incidents will be reduced. Furthermore, the organization will likely improve performance on all transportation fronts—cost, safety, product protection, and delivery reliability.

Step 4—Risk Review and Monitoring

Risk management planning is not a static, one-time process. Organizations cannot analyze risks, develop plans, and simply assume that the plans can be perfectly implemented as needed. Instead, a testing and review process must be instituted to ensure that existing risk mitigation efforts and disruption recovery processes work as intended. Thus, risk management requires ongoing effort by the organization. As Figure 10-1 suggests, it is a cyclical or continuous process.

Conducting tests of risk management action plans is the only way to know that they will actually work when a true disruption occurs. These testing initiatives should demonstrate and measure the effectiveness of risk mitigation activities. The central concern at this stage is to validate the process and its ability to reduce or eliminate unacceptable risks.

A thorough testing program simulates disruptions and defines benchmarks for recovery processes. Separate test plans should be developed by the organization for each disruption scenario. It is important to accurately simulate each disruption's impact on inventory, physical plant, people, and external parties. These stress tests help the organization understand its sources of disruptions, develop recovery responses, and evaluate how these responses affect cost efficiency.[18]

Organizations must also periodically review and update risk management plans. Risks are not static, making it imperative for organizations to regularly reassess the likelihood and expected impact of risks. This will help the organization evaluate whether its previously selected plans are still applicable and effective. Also, the organization must be cognizant of emerging challenges that change risk profiles and introduce new risks. As economic conditions change, competitive threats arise, new regulations are enacted, and customer expectations grow, the organization must respond to these new and diverse risks.

Realize that risk management and mitigation plans are not perfect. Testing, experience, and actual disruptions will necessitate action plan changes and improvements to better deal with the risks being faced. The goal of the risk review stage is to establish a repeatable, measurable, verifiable validation process that can be run from time to time to continually verify the organization's ability to manage risk.

In summary, the risk management process described in this section outlines the steps that organizations must take to identify, monitor, and control transportation risk. The purpose of the process is to effectively address, prevent, and reduce risks that prevent the organization from meeting its goals. It must always be remembered that the key to risk management is active engagement. The process will fail if organizational commitment and contribution are lacking and risks are not efficiently identified, assessed, and pursued to their conclusion.

SUMMARY

- Transportation risks are potentially disruptive events that produce supply chain disorder. Uncontrolled risk can produce negative outcomes ranging from minor delivery delays to major product losses that affect financial performance.

- Organizations can reduce threats to the continuing efficiency and effectiveness of their transportation operations through a process of risk management.

- Despite best efforts to reduce risks, most cannot be totally eliminated and disruptions may occur. Business continuity planning focuses on dealing with and recovering quickly from these disruption episodes.

- Risk management is the process of identifying risk, its causes and effects, and its ownership with a goal of increasing overall understanding in order to manage, reduce, transfer, or eliminate threats to supply chain success.

- The perils of transportation are many and varied. Managers must remain vigilant to all types of risk and work to discover, define, document, and communicate risks before they adversely affect freight flows. There are six common risk categories related to freight transportation: product loss, product damage, product contamination, delivery delay, supply chain interruption, and security breach.

- It is not enough to identify risks. Managers must work to understand how serious each risk is to the organization. They must assess both the likelihood of a disruption risk occurring and the consequences of a disruption incident.

- Transportation managers must be proactive in developing specific action plans and procedural changes to address supply chain risks. Risk mitigation options include risk avoidance, reduction, transfer, or retention.

- Risk is a never-ending challenge. Organizations must establish a repetitive, measurable, verifiable risk monitoring process to remain focused on existing and emerging transportation disruptions.

STUDY QUESTIONS

1. Describe the concepts of disruptions and risks as they apply to transportation. Why are they important from financial and service standpoints?

2. Risk management consists of a series of steps that should be followed to reduce the consequences of disruptions. Briefly discuss these steps.

3. Is risk a natural phenomenon or a manmade problem in transportation? Briefly defend your perspective.

4. Six different categories of transportation risk were discussed in the chapter. Identify these categories, describe them, and give transportation examples for each risk categories.

5. How can transportation professionals identify the specific risks facing their companies? Briefly describe these methods.

6. Risk analysis is a critical component of risk management. When conducting this activity, what are the two components of risk that must be analyzed? Why are they important?

7. What are the key outputs of a risk assessment process? What should be done with these outputs?

8. Describe the three types of strategies that a company can deploy to proactively limit its transportation risks.

9. Discuss how companies can use the Internet of Things and other technologies to understand and respond to transportation risk.

10. What is the role of insurance in transportation risk management?
11. Why is risk management considered to be a continuous loop process?

NOTES

1. Harriet Taylor, "Ransomware Spiked 6,000% in 2016 and Most Victims Paid the Hackers, IBM Finds," CNBC (December 14, 2016), retrieved June 30, 2017, from http://www.cnbc.com/2016/12/13/ransomware-spiked-6000-in-2016-and-most-victims-paid-the-hackers-ibm-finds.html.

2. Google Dictionary, retrieved July 3, 2017, from https://www.google.com/search?q=definition%3A+disruption&ie=utf-8&oe=utf-8#q=define+disruption.

3. US Legal, Inc., *Transportation Disruption*, retrieved July 3, 2017, from http://definitions.uslegal.com/t/transportation-disruption/.

4. Google Dictionary, retrieved July 3, 2017, from https://www.google.com/search?q=definition%3A+disruption&ie=utf-8&oe=utf-8#q=define+risk.

5. UPS, "Preparing Your Business for a Supply Chain Disruption," retrieved July 3, 2017, from https://solvers.ups.com/preparing-your-business-for-a-supply-chain-disruption/.

6. In-Soo Nam, "Hanjin Shipping Is Declared Bankrupt," *The Wall Street Journal*, February 16, 2017.

7. BusinessDictionary.com, retrieved July 2, 2017, from http://www.businessdictionary.com/definition/risk-management.html.

8. BusinessDictionary.com, retrieved July 3, 2017 from http://www.businessdictionary.com/definition/business-continuity-planning-BCP.html.

9. Kaitlyn McAvoy, "Report: Companies Lose Billions Each Year to Cargo Theft," *Spend Matters*, March 31, 2016, retrieved July 5, 2017, from http://spendmatters.com/2016/03/31/report-companies-lose-billions-each-year-to-cargo-thieves/.

10. IMB Piracy Reporting Centre, "Piracy and Armed Robbery Facts & Figures," retrieved July 3, 2017, from https://icc-ccs.org/index.php/piracy-reporting-centre/piracynewsafigures.

11. U.S. Department of Transportation, *Pocket Guide to Large Truck and Bus Statistics*, 2017, retrieved July 5, 2017, from https://www.fmcsa.dot.gov/safety/data-and-statistics/commercial-motor-vehicle-facts.

12. Clarissa Hawes, "Traffic Congestion Costs Trucking Industry $63 Billion Annually," *Trucks.com*, May 17, 2017, retrieved July 5, 2017, from https://www.trucks.com/2017/05/17/traffic-congestion-costs-trucking-industry-63-billion-annually/.

13. Turloch Mooney, "Shippers Partly to Blame for Port Congestion, Report Argues," *JOC.com*, May 8, 2017, retrieved August July 5, 2017, from http://www.joc.com/regulation-policy/transportation-regulations/international-transportation-regulations/paper-blames-end-carrier-conferences-industry-woes_20170508.html.

14. Alan Zarach, "The Changing Shape of Ocean Alliances," April 27, 2017, retrieved July 5, 2017, from http://www.intlfreight.net/2017/04/27/ocean-alliances/.

15. Lark Scheieman, "How to Define Risk Management Goals and Objectives in Your Organization," *KnowledgeLeader Blog*, February 13, 2017, retrieved July 3, 2017, from http://info.knowledgeleader.com/bid/164011/how-to-define-risk-management-goals-and-objectives-in-your-organization.

16. Mark S. Dorfman and David Cather, *Introduction to Risk Management and Insurance*, 10th Edition, Englewood Cliffs, NJ: Prentice Hall, 2012.

17. Jonathan Webb, "The Taiwanese Earthquake That Nearly Flattened the Apple iPhone 7," *Forbes*, February 29, 2016, retrieved July 5, 2017, from: https://www.forbes.com/sites/jwebb/2016/02/29/the-taiwanese-earthquake-that-nearly-cancelled-the-apple-iphone-7/#32a0fbff4da7.

18. Sunil Chopra and ManMohan S. Sodhi, "Reducing the Risk of Supply Chain Disruptions," *MIT Sloan Management Review*, March 18, 2014, retrieved July 5, 2017, from http://sloanreview.mit.edu/article/reducing-the-risk-of-supply-chain-disruptions/.

CASE 10-1

Young Again Pharmaceuticals

Joe Hannibal, senior director of transportation for Young Again Pharmaceuticals (YAP), is gearing up for his company's most critical product rollout in more than a decade. YAP has developed a breakthrough liquid suspension that reverses the aging process for anyone over 35 years of age. Available only by prescription, the new product has been dubbed "Twenty-something in a Bottle" by the media. Demand is expected to be very high despite the out-landish price tag of $395 for a month's supply.

The product is being manufactured in YAP's Dublin, Ireland, laboratory and will be dis-tributed to major retail pharmacies in the United States and Canada. Hannibal is responsible for selecting the mode and contracting with carriers to deliver the product. He is concerned about the safe and timely delivery of the initial product shipments in April to the retailers' distribution centers. The product is high value, somewhat fragile, and susceptible to theft. Some product, stolen from the laboratory, has already appeared on auction websites.

In an effort to make effective transportation decisions and minimize YAP's risks, Hannibal decided to hold a brainstorming session with his logistics team before signing any carrier contracts. The discussion of key risks produced the following list of concerns:

- "If shipments are late or incomplete, retailers will penalize us with vendor charge-backs. You know they will hit us with small fines for delivery mistakes."

- "I'm worried about shipment delays or freight loss from hurricanes in the Atlantic Ocean."

- "You've got to consider temperature sensitivity issues. If the product freezes, we won't be able to sell it."

- "I've been reading about all the piracy problems experienced by ocean carriers. You know, a 20-foot container of our product has a retail value of nearly $875,000."

- "I worry about theft of individual cases at ports and while the product is on the road."

- "We're looking at border delays and Customs fines if we don't properly document and mark our freight."

- "Our brand image will take major damage if the product gets into unauthorized distribution channels due to theft or misdirected deliveries."

- "The company sustainability push has led to reduced packaging and biodegradable packing materials. If the cartons get wet or bounced around, we're going to end up with a lot of damaged, unsellable product."

- "The major U.S. East Coast ports can get very congested during peak shipping season. That will cause delays."

By the time the meeting was over, Hannibal realized that he needed to spend some time looking into these issues. While he was pretty sure that some problems were remote, Hannibal thought that it would be wise to evaluate each one. His new concern became how to conduct an effective risk assessment.

CASE QUESTIONS

1. Assess the risks identified in the brainstorming session. Create and populate a table similar to Figure 10-2.

2. Based on your answer to Question 1, what are the three primary risks that you believe YAP must address? Why?

3. What do you recommend that YAP do to mitigate each of the three risks identified in Question 2?

4. What should YAP focus on after attempting to mitigate these transportation risks?

CASE 10-2

RIoT Athletic

Glenda Litchee, chief technology officer for RIoT Athletic has developed a revolutionary running shoe that uses Internet of Things (IoT) technology. Sensors in the sole, heel, and tongue of the shoe monitor temperature, pressure, and moisture. Automatic adjustments are made to the shoe's venting and sole density in response to the readings. The goal is to reduce foot stress and improve comfort for long-distance runners.

Litchee has a patent on the shoes but fears that cheap, copycat models will arise as soon as her $200 RIoT Runners® hit the stores. Thus far, news of these revolutionary shoes has not leaked out and that has prevented the major shoe companies from responding. She needs rapid market entry with precise, stealthy delivery to fend off competition, acquire shelf space in retail stores, and gain a foothold in the running community.

Production is on schedule and two large North American retailers have quietly committed to participate in a star-studded product launch, similar to what happens when a new iPhone is released. The last issue to resolve is directly delivering 5–10 cases of shoes to each of the retailers' stores.

Litchee has hired Rick Rasgen, a transportation expert, to analyze delivery options. After conducting a thorough analysis of 12 different transportation providers, Rasgen has narrowed the list to three potential carriers:

- Arrow Speed is an integrated package carrier with a national network of terminals, company-owned planes, and delivery trucks. The company has experience with domestic operations but RIoT must find other carriers to handle deliveries to Canada and Mexico. Arrow is a popular carrier, often used by RIoT Athletics' competitors, and its capacity is often stretched thin. The delivery quote from Arrow averages out to $100 per case with three-day transit time to U.S. locations.

- Bravo Freight is a freight forwarder. Bravo is a non-asset-based logistics service provider that contracts with air cargo companies and regional trucking companies to move freight from origin to destination. The company has international experience and has a network of partners in Canada and Mexico. The delivery quote from Bravo averages out to $150 per case with next-day delivery service to U.S. locations and two-day service to Canada and Mexico.

- Clipper Transport is a less-than-truckload carrier. Clipper has recently been created through the merger of three regional U.S. carriers. Solid alliances are in place with a Canadian carrier but two different freight forwarders are used to serve Mexico. There are some reports about problems with the integration of Clipper's three different operations. The delivery quote from Clipper averages out to $60 per case with five-day transit time.

Rasgen presented his analysis to Litchee for a final decision. However, Litchee was concerned that each option presented some risk. Was she just being overly anxious or were her concerns valid? Litchee needed some time to think it over and to talk through the options with one more expert—you!

CASE QUESTIONS

1. What issues should Litchee take into consideration in her assessment of transportation risks for RIoT Runners?

2. Analyze each carrier option that Rasgen presented. What specific risks does each carrier present?

3. Which carrier would you recommend that Litchee choose to best balance company goals with transportation and supply chain risks?

4. How can Litchee minimize the potential for in-transit product theft?

11

GLOBAL TRANSPORTATION MANAGEMENT

Learning Objectives

After reading this chapter, you should be able to do the following:

> Discuss the relationship between international trade and global transportation

> Identify the three critical transportation processes in global supply chains

> Recognize the roles of Incoterms, insurance, and terms of payment in managing global transportation risks and costs

> Analyze the key issues in effective international transportation mode selection

> Understand the unique capabilities of ocean, air, and intermodal transportation in moving freight globally

> Evaluate the critical factors in carrier selection and route design for international shipments

> Describe the need for proper packaging, ancillary service providers, and effective ports in delivery execution

> Appreciate the value of timely, accurate global freight documentation and visibility tools

> Articulate the customs clearance process for import goods

TRANSPORTATION **PROFILE**

F⁴—Fast Flowing Fast-Fashion

The term "fast fashion" refers to a phenomenon in the fashion industry whereby production processes are expedited in order to get trendy clothing to the market as quickly and cheaply as possible. As a result, the tradition of introducing new fashion lines on a seasonal basis is being challenged. Retailers like Zara, H&M, and Forever 21 introduce new products multiple times each week.

While rapid production is critical, timely, and efficient distribution to global markets is equally important to a fast-fashion retailer like Zara. With 2,200 stores in 93 countries, Zara needs an extensive supply chain network to develop a new product and stock it in stores within two weeks. This high-velocity supply chain helps the $17.2 billion retailer stay ahead of the competition, particularly traditional retailers whose design-to-delivery cycle is six months.

Rapid speed to market is only possible with timely, delay-free global transportation. From its factories in Zaragoza, Spain, finished goods are delivered throughout Europe by truck and worldwide via air freight. Opting for air cargo versus ocean shipping shaves six weeks off the delivery schedule. Garments arrive to stores worldwide in just a few days: China—48 hrs; Japan—72 hrs; United States—48 hrs.

By using air cargo, fast-fashion retailers encounter high costs. Goods arriving at U.S. airports must be transported to centralized distribution centers where they are broken down and delivered to stores. The added movement and product handling adds time and expense.

To counter delays, some fast-fashion retailers are using direct shipping from source to stores. However, direct delivery of small orders further increases transportation costs, cutting into profit margins. Proponents of fast-fashion counter that the combination of small inventories and rapid transportation lead to lower inventory carrying costs and less in-store discounting.

There's certainly some truth to both perspectives. To succeed in fast-fashion, global transportation speed and cost must be balanced against other supply chain savings and the benefits of being first to market. Sometimes that means spending more on transportation to have the right inventory available when the customer is ready to make a purchase.

Sources: Cyndi Fulk Lago, "How Fast Fashion Exposes Retailers to Supply Chain Compliance Risks," *Apparel*, 29 March 2017, retrieved 6 August 2017, from https://apparelmag.com/how-fast-fashion-exposes-retailers-supply-chain-compliance-risks; "The World's Most Valuable Brands," *Forbes*, 23 May 2017, retrieved 6 August 2017, from https://www.forbes.com/companies/zara/; Investopedia, *Fast Fashion*, retrieved 6 August 2017, from http://www.investopedia.com/terms/f/fast-fashion.asp#ixzz4ozkQ5fPG; Walter Loeb, "Who Are the Fast Fashion Leaders and Why Does It Matter?" *Forbes*, 23 October 2015, retrieved 6 August 2017, from https://www.forbes.com/sites/walterloeb/2015/10/23/who-are-the-fast-fashion-leaders-and-why-does-it-matter/#2a18890d1555.

Introduction

Global trade is big business with world merchandise exports of $15.5 trillion in 2016, according to the World Trade Organization. Moving these goods requires a freight spend of $427 billion. The largest proportion of these global transport exports involves seaborne cargo, with a 60 percent share of international freight exports or $269 billion.[1]

With these levels of freight moving across oceans and country borders, transportation complexity is ever present for exporters and importers. Compared to domestic freight movement, there is longer and more variable transit time, risk of in-transit product damage or theft, higher delivery and accessorial service expenses, and greater in-transit inventory

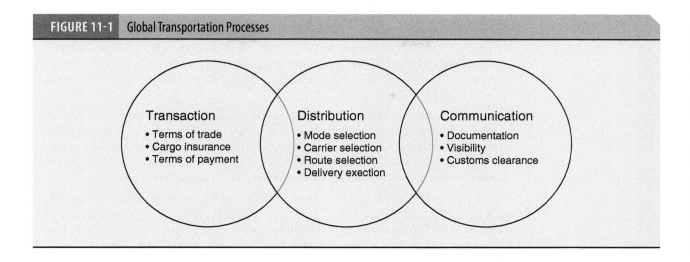

FIGURE 11-1 Global Transportation Processes

Transaction
• Terms of trade
• Cargo insurance
• Terms of payment

Distribution
• Mode selection
• Carrier selection
• Route selection
• Delivery exection

Communication
• Documentation
• Visibility
• Customs clearance

carrying costs. These heightened challenges must be accurately weighed against the relative costs and benefits of domestic or nearshore sourcing.

Transportation managers must also be cognizant of broader issues that impact global transportation performance. Savvy global transportation managers take the time to monitor business trends, government activity, and consumer demand. A failure to understand and respond to changes in these macrolevel issues creates unnecessary costs, capacity challenges, and competitive disadvantage.

Overcoming these issues to fully exploit global commerce opportunities requires a multipronged approach to freight planning and movement as demonstrated by the Transportation Profile. Using the channel conceptualization created by Wood et al. (2002), global transportation can be clustered into three major processes.[2] Transaction processes and control decisions precede the flow of goods from the exporters. Next, distribution processes and selection decisions generate freight movement activities across borders. Lastly, communication processes and information sharing enable timely freight arrival. Throughout the chapter, you will gain greater insights into the global transportation processes outlined in Figure 11-1.

Transaction Processes

When purchasing goods, paying for them, and preparing for their movement, the buyer (importer) must take steps to protect its financial interests and reduce risk. The importer must effectively negotiate details with the seller (exporter) that go beyond the basics of product quality, price, and quantity. In global transactions, it is also important to clarify the location and point in time at which legal title for the goods transfers from the exporter to the importer.

Why is this so important? **Transfer of ownership** is linked to a host of transportation risks and responsibilities. Ownership also determines which party will make decisions regarding mode and carrier selection, routing, and delivery execution. These flow-related decisions are discussed later in the chapter.

Terms of Trade

When a company purchases goods from an international supplier, it is critical to include terms of trade in the purchase contract. These terms clarify which transportation-related responsibilities are handled by the exporter and which are managed by the importer.

Importantly, they show precisely where the exporter's responsibilities end and where the importer's responsibilities begin. They govern decision-making authority for movement of the product, establish when the ownership and title of the goods pass from the exporter to the importer, and identify which organization incurs delivery-related costs. Clearly established terms of trade avoid the types of challenges and disputes that impede international commerce and the flow of goods.

If each country established its own terms of trade, there would be a confusing array of rules and processes. Fortunately, a harmonized set of selling terms has been established by the **International Chamber of Commerce (ICC)** to largely avoid freight movement complexity. Widely known as **Incoterms**, these *In*ternational *C*ommercial *Terms* make international trade easier and facilitate the flow of goods between different countries.

As described by the ICC, Incoterms are an internationally recognized standard and are used worldwide in international and domestic contracts for the sale of goods. First published in 1936, Incoterms rules provide internationally accepted definitions and rules of interpretation for most common commercial terms. They help traders avoid costly misunderstanding by clarifying the tasks, costs, and risks involved in the delivery of goods from sellers to buyers.[3]

Incoterms have been revised and refined six times since the original set was put into effect. The most recent set of trade rules, known as Incoterms 2010, includes 11 options that are organized into modal categories as described below. The 2010 terms also spell out rules regarding the use of electronic procedures; detail information on security-related clearances for shipments; and offer advice with respect to domestic trade.[4]

Four of the Incoterms apply only to sea and inland waterway transport. The remaining seven Incoterms apply to any mode or intermodal transportation. Figure 11-2 indicates the proper usage of each Incoterm by mode. Also, Incoterms are typically expressed as three-letter acronyms with a named location and the Incoterms version to avoid confusion. For example, a properly completed Incoterm description on a document would read: "DAP, Mobile, Alabama, USA, Incoterms 2010" to indicate that the exporter is responsible for the goods from the point of origin until they are unloaded at the Port of Mobile.

FIGURE 11-2 Incoterms Applicability by Mode

Mode	EXW	FCA	FAS	FOB	CFR	CIF	CPT	CIP	DAT	DAP	DDP
🚢	✓	✓	✓	✓	✓	✓	✓	✓	✓	✓	✓
🚂	✓	✓					✓	✓	✓	✓	✓
🚚	✓	✓					✓	✓	✓	✓	✓
✈	✓	✓					✓	✓	✓	✓	✓

Incoterms fall into four primary groups. The E term is used when the importer takes full responsibility from the point of departure; F terms are used when the main carriage is not paid by the exporter; C terms are used when the main carrier is paid by the exporter; and D terms are employed when the exporter takes full responsibility to the point of arrival. Each group is discussed in more detail below.

E Terms The lone E term, **Ex Works (EXW)**, is a departure contract that maximizes the importer's responsibility. The exporter's sole role is to make the shipment available at its facility. The importer agrees to take possession of the shipment at the point of origin and to bear all of the cost and risk of transporting the goods to the destination. Table 11-1 identifies additional responsibilities of the E term.

F Terms Three F terms obligate the exporter to incur the cost of delivering the shipment cleared for export to the carrier designated by the importer. The importer selects and incurs the cost of main transportation, insurance, and customs clearance.

Free Carrier (FCA) can be used with any mode of transportation. Risk of damage is transferred to the importer when the exporter delivers the goods to the international carrier named by the importer.

Free Alongside Ship (FAS) is used for water transportation shipments only. The risk of damage is transferred to the importer when the goods are delivered alongside the ship. The importer must pay the cost of "lifting" the cargo or container onboard the vessel.

Free On Board (FOB) is used for water transportation shipments only. The risk of damage is transferred to the importer when the shipment crosses the ship's rail (when the goods are actually loaded on the vessel). The exporter pays for loading. See Table 11-1 for additional responsibilities of the F Terms.

C Terms Four C terms create shipment contracts that obligate the exporter to obtain and pay for the main carriage and in some cases, cargo insurance.

Cost and Freight (CFR) is used for water transportation only. The exporter incurs all costs to the port of destination. The importer assumes all risks once the goods are onboard

EVENT	EXW	FCA	FAS	FOB	CFR	CIF	CPT	CIP	DAT	DAP	DDP
Packaging	E	E	E	E	E	E	E	E	E	E	E
Loading Charges	I	E	E	E	E	E	E	E	E	E	E
Origin to Port Delivery	I	E	E	E	E	E	E	E	E	E	E
Export Duties and Taxes	I	E	E	E	E	E	E	E	E	E	E
Origin Terminal Charges	I	I	E	E	E	E	E	E	E	E	E
Loading	I	I	I	E	E	E	E	E	E	E	E
Port to Port Delivery	I	I	I	I	E	E	E	E	E	E	E
Insurance						E		E			
Destination Terminal Charges	I	I	I	I	I	I	E	E	E	E	E
Port to Destination Delivery	I	I	I	I	I	I	I	I	I	E	E
Import Duty and Taxes	I	I	I	I	I	I	I	I	I	I	E

TABLE 11-1 Incoterms Importer/Exporter Responsibility

Key: E = Exporter, I = Importer, Blank = Not specifically assigned, may be negotiated the vessel and is responsible for all activities and costs after the ship arrives at the destination port.

Cost, Insurance, Freight (CIF) is used for water transportation only. The exporter bears the cost of freight and insurance to the destination port. The importer is responsible for all activities and costs after the ship arrives at the destination port.

Carriage Paid To (CPT) can be used with any mode of transportation. The exporter incurs the cost of freight to a named place of destination, but is not responsible for insurance. The importer assumes all risks during the delivery process and is responsible for all activities and costs after the goods arrive at the named place.

Carriage and Insurance Paid To (CIP) can be used with any mode of transportation. The exporter incurs the cost of freight to a named place of destination and is responsible for procuring insurance coverage to the named place. The importer is responsible for all activities and costs after the goods arrive at the named place. See Table 11-1 for additional responsibilities of the C terms.

D Terms Three D terms obligate the exporter to incur all costs related to delivery of the shipment to the foreign destination. Each D term requires the exporter to incur all costs and the risk of damage up to a named delivery location. These terms can be applied to any mode of transportation.

Delivered At Terminal (DAT) means the exporter is responsible for transportation and incurs the risk of damage until goods are delivered to a named terminal in the destination country. The importer is responsible for import clearance and any further in-country carriage.

Delivered At Place (DAP) requires the exporter to pay for the main carriage and to deliver goods to the importer's facility or another named location (other than a terminal) in the destination country. The importer is responsible for import clearance and any further in-country carriage.

Delivered Duty Paid (DDP) requires the exporter to assume responsibility for all costs involved in delivering the goods to a named place of destination and for clearing customs in the country of import. The exporter provides door-to-door delivery, bearing the entire risk of loss until goods are delivered to the importer's premises. See Table 11-1 for additional responsibilities of the D terms.

Proper Incoterm choice effectively balances the responsibilities for international transportation between the exporter and the importer. Key determinants of Incoterm selection include the relative expertise of each firm as well as their willingness to perform the required tasks. Other relevant factors include the type of product being sold, the mode of transportation being used, the level of trust between the firms, and the relative exposure to risk being assumed.

Finally, it is important to realize that Incoterms do not cover every aspect of an international delivery. Incoterms do not constitute a contract between the exporter and importer. They don't provide specific delivery details. And, they don't protect a party from risk of loss. That is the role of cargo insurance.

Cargo Insurance

With the exception of CIF and CIP terms, Incoterms place no obligation on the seller or buyer to provide insurance. However, depending upon the actual term used for each shipment, the seller or buyer bears responsibility for loss or damage to the goods at some point during transit. Prudence would dictate that this exposure to financial loss be insured against.[5]

When an exporter or importer takes responsibility for insuring the freight, they will encounter one of the most complex issues in global transportation. Cargo insurance is challenging because of the unique terminology, centuries-old traditions, and confusing regulations that limit carrier liability.

Regardless of the challenges, cargo insurance is critical. Importers and exporters are exposed to countless perils and financial risks when their freight moves through the global supply chain. They must determine their insurable interests and how to most effectively manage risk. These insurance-related issues are introduced below and in Chapter 10.

Financial Risks Trying to recover financial losses from international carriers for freight damage or loss is difficult and time consuming. Regulations like the Carriage of Goods by Sea Act limit an ocean carrier's liability to $500 U.S. per customary shipping unit. However, this liability is limited in 17 defensible situations. The regulation states that neither the carrier nor the ship shall be responsible for loss or damage arising or resulting from fire, perils of the sea, acts of God, acts of war, labor stoppage, and 10 other circumstances.[6]

Similarly, an air carrier's liability is minimal versus the actual value of most air cargo. Liability is limited in special cases of inherent defect, cargo quality or vice, defective packaging, acts of war, or an act of public authority carried out in connection with the entry, exit, or transit of the cargo. In 2010, the International Air Transport Association helped standardize the cargo liability limits from the Montreal Protocol No. 4 to 19 Special Drawing Rights (SDR) per kilogram.[7] At a $1.40 U.S. rate per SDR, this is $26.60 per kilogram.[8] Often, this amount will not adequately offset the value of product loss or damage.

In both modes, the burden of proof is on the importer or exporter to prove that the carrier was at fault. With all the liability limitations provided in the regulations, substantiating carrier responsibility can be very difficult. If they cannot prove fault, importers and exporters have little legal recourse against international carriers.

Transportation Perils International cargo is subject to the six risk categories identified in Chapter 10, but at a heightened level versus domestic freight. This is due to the extended origin-to-destination distance, number of transfers between carriers, and varying climatic conditions. Theft is an ever-present threat as revealed in the On the Line feature. In particular, ocean freight faces considerable obstacles to incident-free delivery. In addition to vessel hijacking, sinking, or collision, freight damage and loss risks include:

- **Cargo Movement**—ocean freight is subject to a harsh ride with the ship moving in six different directions (heave, pitch, roll, surge, sway, and yaw) during a voyage
- **Water Damage**—water from storms and waves can infiltrate cargo
- **Overboard Losses**—cargo containers can be lost overboard during storms
- **Jettison**—cargo may be purposely dumped overboard to save the ship or prevent further cargo losses
- **Fire**—most dangerous cargo (chemicals, ammunition, and so forth) moves via ocean transport, creating fire and explosion risk
- **Stranding**—mechanical breakdowns, storms, groundings, and other problems can lead to damaged or delayed freight
- **General Average**—loss or damage to another customer's freight is shared by all parties involved in the voyage
- **Other Risks**—freight contamination, government delays, and port strikes[9]

International freight moving via air also face perils, though they are minimal compared to ocean freight. Air cargo is a very safe mode with limited risk of loss due to crashes or accidents. Movement risk exists as cargo can shift during takeoff or landing and turbulence can occur during transit. Cold temperatures can also be a problem for sensitive freight. Finally, theft is an ongoing challenge, particularly when freight sits idle at air forwarder and freight terminal facilities.

ON THE **LINE**

Cargo Theft—A Global Epidemic

Cargo theft is a critical concern for the global transportation manager. A review of transportation industry surveys and tracking reports reveals that cargo theft, along with terrorism, is a major supply chain risk. And, this risk is not limited to a single region. While war-torn countries like Syria, Libya, and Southern Sudan have severe theft problems, cargo can just as easily be stolen in industrialized nations. A snapshot of recent statistics indicates that theft is a global problem.

The Americas: BSI reports that cargo theft is a main concern for the Americas. Brazil has major problems. Rio de Janeiro reported a total of 9,870 cargo theft incidents in 2016, 36 percent more than in 2015. Year-over-year increase in cargo theft incidents in both Rio de Janeiro and São Paulo, combined with minimal efforts to curb the rate of theft, suggests that Brazil could see another year of increased cargo theft in 2017.

Europe, Middle East, and Africa (EMEA): The Transported Asset Protection Association reports that a 92 percent increase in cargo-related crimes occurred during the first six months of 2016. The United Kingdom had the most cargo crimes with 415 reported thefts. Across the region, there were 50 major crimes with losses exceeding $110,000 each, including a theft of a truck containing $4.5 million worth of gold in Arezzo, Italy.

United States and Canada: A CargoNet report indicates that there were 838 recorded cargo thefts in 2016. With an average loss of $206,837 per shipment, the 838 cargo thefts in 2016 totaled nearly $172.9 million. California, Texas, and New Jersey had the most reported thefts.

Theft typically focuses on high-value, finished goods that can be quickly resold. Food products, electronics, fuel and prescription drugs are the items most sought by criminal groups.

To combat these problems, transport companies report spending up to 13 percent of their revenues on security measures. Operational solutions include ensuring that freight is never left unattended, conducting background checks on drivers, vetting carrier security performance, and using armed escorts. Technology solutions include using containers equipped with security features including satellite tracking, Navalock, geo-fencing, and electronic door monitoring. Purchasing extra insurance is also a wise move when transporting goods to/from high-risk countries.

Sources: Lisa Alves, "Brazil Has 6th Highest Cargo Transport Risk Rate in World," *The Rio Times*, 14 March 2017; Fwd News, *Cargo Thefts Soar in First Half of 2016*, 28 September 2016, retrieved 3 August 2017, from https://www.fwd.news/cargo-thefts-soar-first-half-2016/; "Cargo Theft, Terrorism Top Global Supply Chain Risks in 2016" *Security Magazine*, 23 May 2017, retrieved 3 August 2017, from http://www.securitymagazine.com/articles/88037-cargo-theft-terrorism-top-global-supply-chain-risks-in-2016; Road Scholar Transportation Blog, *2016 Theft Statistics*, retrieved 3 August 2017, from http://www.roadscholar.com/2016-cargo-theft-statistics/.

Managing Risks Financial threats and transportation perils for international cargo must be actively managed. At risk are the owner of the goods in transit and anyone who would suffer a loss if the cargo were damaged or destroyed or who would benefit from the safe arrival of the cargo. This is known as an insurable interest. With insurance, the goal is to transfer some of all risk of loss versus retaining the risk.

Risk transfer means that a company shifts its potential problems to an insurance company through cargo insurance. There are a wide variety of policies available to the customer to cover both freight loss and general average liability in ocean shipping. Insurance can be obtained through carriers, freight forwarders, or directly from an insurance company. Insurance makes sense when a company's perceived risks are too high, the product is fragile or a theft risk, or operations would be severely disrupted.

A mixed approach combines risk retention and risk transfer to a third party. Just as an individual may reduce his or her insurance policy costs through a higher deductible in the event of a loss, exporters and importers can use deductibles to reduce insurance costs. The company must negotiate a contract with an insurance provider for the amount above the maximum financial exposure that it is willing to risk.[10]

Terms of Payment

The transfer of ownership and physical goods create another set of risks. Exporters are concerned about nonpayment for goods that are sold internationally. They may not have personal experience with the importer, creditworthiness of the importer may be unknown, and there is limited legal recourse if the importer fails to pay for the goods. Also, the cost of litigation or mediation in the country of import is high. Hence, exporters must be cautious about extending credit to global customers.

Importers may also have concerns regarding payment timing and methods. When dealing with an unfamiliar supplier, an importer will not want to pay for goods before knowing that product quality, quantity, price, and delivery are consistent with the contract terms.

Balancing the parties' respective risks is challenging. Exporters would reduce their risk of nonpayment by demanding **cash-in-advance**. This would ensure that payment is received before the goods are shipped. However, doing so creates a risk of losing business to a more aggressive competitor. Importers would reduce their risk of product problems by purchasing goods on **open account**. However, demanding this option may cause potentially excellent suppliers to walk away from the business. Between these two extremes are two payment term options that facilitate trade without placing all financial risk on one party.

A **letter of credit** (LC) protects both the importer and exporter by introducing a middleman. The LC is a commitment by a bank on behalf of the importer that payment will be made to the exporter, provided that the terms and conditions stated in the LC have been met, as verified through the presentation of all required documents. The importer establishes credit and pays his or her bank to render this service. An LC is useful when reliable credit information about a foreign buyer is difficult to obtain, but the exporter is satisfied with the creditworthiness of the buyer's foreign bank. Depending on the seller's terms, the LC could also protect the importer since no payment obligation arises until the goods have been shipped as promised.[11]

Used primarily for ocean shipments, a **documentary collection** (DC) is a payment mechanism whereby the exporter entrusts the collection of the payment for a sale to its bank (remitting bank), which sends the documents to the importer's bank (collecting bank), with instructions to release the documents to the buyer for payment. Funds received from the importer are remitted to the exporter through the banks involved in the collection in exchange for those documents.

DCs involve using a draft that requires the importer to pay the face amount either at sight (document against payment) or on a specified date (document against acceptance). The collection letter gives instructions that specify the documents required for the transfer of title to the goods. Although banks act as facilitators, DCs offer no verification process and limited recourse in the event of nonpayment. DCs are generally less expensive than LCs.[12]

Without question, global transportation management begins long before the freight is loaded and transported to its destination. Key strategies must be developed, decisions made, and requirements completed. These transaction processes—choosing appropriate terms of trade, securing freight insurance, and agreeing upon the terms of payment—clarify the respective responsibilities of each party and protect their respective financial interests. Ultimately, these efforts facilitate problem-free global movement of goods.

Distribution Processes

Problem-free global distribution of goods is not easily accomplished. The scope of the global transportation network increases the potential for disruptions due to the extended travel distances, freight handling at multiple facilities, and involvement of numerous intermediaries. Also, transportation infrastructure, regulations, and service options vary from country to country, adding complexity to the situation. As a result, global freight is at greater risk of erratic and extended transit times, freight stoppages, visibility problems, and loss of control than domestic freight.

To overcome these challenges, global transportation managers must actively manage a variety of distribution processes. These managers must make effective decisions regarding mode selection, carrier selection, route design, and delivery execution to ensure efficient and effective movement of international freight to its final destination. Doing so promotes supply chain excellence and future growth of global trade for the organization.

Mode Selection

When the Incoterms dictate that an organization has control over international transportation, mode selection becomes a key decision point. Mode selection focuses on determining which mode or combination of modes best suits the requirements of the global transportation buyer.

Mode selection is very important because it affects how quickly and efficiently products will flow across the supply chain. Although, all five modes of transportation—truck, rail, water, air, and pipeline—provide the same basic service of moving freight from point to point in the supply chain, the realistic options available for global transportation are often limited. Issues such as modal capabilities, modal costs, and shipment characteristics must be considered.

You learned in Chapters 5–8 that each mode has unique attributes and capabilities that affect its ability to fulfill customer requirements. According to numerous research studies, a global transportation manager must consider each mode's accessibility, capacity, transit time, reliability, and product safety. Each is discussed below and typical modal capabilities are highlighted in Table 11-2.

Accessibility Freight buyers must consider a mode's ability to reach origin and destination facilities and provide service over the specified route. The geographic limits of a mode's infrastructure or network and the operating scope authorized by governmental regulatory agencies also affect accessibility. For example, moving cargo from Valparaiso, Chile, to Brisbane, Australia, is limited to air or ocean transport. Intermodal transportation can be used to overcome accessibility problems.

Capacity The amount of product being moved can render a mode infeasible or impractical. Transportation managers must match the capacity of a mode to the size and nature of the product being moved. Some modes are well-suited to handling a large volume of goods in an economical fashion while others are better suited to smaller shipments.

Transit Time Time is a key consideration in mode selection as transportation impacts inventory availability, stock out costs, and customer satisfaction. Transit time is the total elapsed time that it takes to move goods from the point of origin to their final destination. This includes the time required for pickup activities, terminal handling, line-haul movement, and customer delivery. Modal speed can greatly affect transit time.

Reliability The consistency of the transit time provided by a transportation mode is called reliability. It is easier to forecast inventory needs, schedule production, and determine safety stock levels if goods arrive with some certainty. Thus, many companies feel that transit time reliability is more important than speed in mode selection. Internationally, reliability is impacted by distance, port congestion issues, security requirements, and border crossings—especially when the two countries do not have a proactive trade agreement.

Safety Goods must arrive at the destination in the same condition they were in when tendered for shipment at the origin. Precautions must be taken to choose a mode with the ability to protect freight from damage due to poor freight handling techniques, inferior ride quality, and accidents. Fragile products must be shipped via modes with the best ride quality. Temperature-sensitive goods must move on modes with equipment that provides consistent atmospheric conditions. Perishable goods require modes with the fastest transit times.

Transportation cost is another critical consideration in mode selection. Expenses include the rate for moving freight from origin to destination plus any accessorial and terminal fees for additional services provided.

The cost analysis must also address product value. If a company spends too much on transportation relative to the value of a product, the product cannot be sold at a competitive price. Thus, water, rail, and pipeline are suitable for low-value commodities, while truck and air costs can be more readily absorbed by higher value finished goods.

Mode selection is also influenced by the goods being moved. The nature of a product—size, durability, and value—may eliminate some modes from consideration as they cannot physically, legally, and/or safely handle the goods. Also, shipment characteristics—size, route, and required speed—are important considerations. Modal capacities must be matched to the total weight and dimensions of shipments, while modal capabilities must be matched to customer service requirements.

Finally, geography is a critical consideration. Goods moving between adjacent countries can leverage all five modes in a similar fashion to domestic transportation. Goods moving across oceans and seas present accessibility challenges that limit a global transportation manager's options to international air, ocean, and intermodal transportation. These intercontinental modal options are briefly discussed below to supplement the content in Chapters 5–8.

Ocean Shipping Ocean shipping is an essential resource in global supply chains. The majority of containerized finished goods, as well as bulk materials moving across oceans, travel via this mode. Ocean shipping is a very diverse industry with a variety of service options, equipment types, service providers, pricing alternatives, and key issues that must be addressed. Regardless of the commodity, freight volume, and geographic requirements involved, there is an ocean carrier with the capability and capacity to move the cargo.

TABLE 11-2	Comparison of Modal Capabilities			
MODE	**STRENGTHS**	**LIMITATIONS**	**PRIMARY GLOBAL ROLE**	**TYPICAL FREIGHT CHARACTERISTICS**
Water	• High capacity • Low cost • Commodity flexibility	• Slow line-haul transit • In-country accessibility	• Move goods between international seaports	• Low-value raw materials and bulk commodities • Containerized goods
Air	• Speed • Freight protection • Flexibility	• Accessibility beyond airports • High cost • Low capacity	• Move urgent shipments between international airports	• High-value, time-sensitive goods • Small shipments
Truck	• Accessibility • Fast and versatile • Customer service	• Limited capacity • High cost	• Move goods to/from international seaports and airports • Move goods from exporter to importer in adjacent countries	• High-value goods • Small shipments
Rail	• High capacity • Low cost • Intermodal support	• Accessibility beyond rail yards • Inconsistent service • Damage rates	• Move goods to/from international seaports • Move goods from exporter to importer in adjacent countries	• Low-value raw materials • Containerized finished goods
Pipeline	• In-transit storage • Efficiency • Low cost	• Slow • Limited network	• Move commodities between storage facilities in adjacent countries	• Low-value liquid commodities • Not time sensitive

Service Options Ocean transportation service providers can be segmented into three different categories—liner service, charter service, and private service.

Liner service is provided by ships that travel on regularly scheduled voyages, following fixed routes with predetermined ports of call, similar to a bus route. Typically, a liner ship will serve a particular trade area, such as the trans-Pacific lanes between Asia and North America, trans-Atlantic lanes between Europe and North America, or Asia–Europe lanes. Some liner ships travel the globe on "round the world" schedules, passing through the Panama Canal and the Suez Canal.

Charter service is similar to hiring an Uber vehicle for direct point-to-point service. The ship owner essentially leases the vessel to a **charterer** (the customer) who uses the ship to move its own cargo. Some charterers move cargo for other companies with the goal of making money on the difference between leasing costs and the prices charged to other customers. Ship owners offer voyage charters for specific origin to destination trips or time charters for a specific period of time. A demise charter is a special time charter involving a long period lease of a vessel.

Private service is similar to operating a personal vehicle or private truck fleet. Private ships are owned or leased on a long-term basis by the exporter or importer. For example, Chiquita Brands International uses a private fleet of refrigerated ships called the Great White Fleet to move bananas and other fruits from Central American plantations to world markets.[13] The return trip carries specialized shipping cartons and other supplies to the plantations. Oil and lumber products are also moved via private service.

Equipment Types According to the 2015 Equasis database, there were 49,948 cargo ships in the world fleet.[14] Most ships fly a **flag of convenience**, with the owners registering their ships in countries that offer advantageous fees and regulations rather than in their home country. Popular countries for ship registration include Panama, Liberia, Marshall Islands, and Malta. These countries register ships of all types and sizes ranging from private yachts to oil **supertankers**.

Individual ships are designed for specific roles and can be unique. However, there are five general groups of ship types relevant to international trade.

Containerships are built for the specific purpose of moving standardized 20-foot and 40-foot oceangoing containers. In general, these "box ships" hold up to 19,000 20-foot equivalent units (TEUs) with containers stored under deck in specific slots created by vertical guides. After the hatch covers are put in place, additional containers are loaded above or on deck by stacking them on top of each other. The containers are secured via metal bars and twistlocks. Some newer ships extend the vertical guides, eliminating the hatch covers and decks, to increase the speed of loading and unloading at ports. The top container lines in the world, which control 75 percent of global TEU capacity, are presented in Table 11-3.

The combination of loading/unloading speed, intermodal transferability, and freight protection makes container shipping very popular. While a break-bulk ship might require many days to unload and load its cargo by small crane and manpower, a container ship can enter, unload, load, and clear a port in less than 12 hours using the huge portside container cranes. Such speed has brought about labor savings to both the shipper and the ocean carrier, as well as increased ship (and capital) utilization. Because a ship is only earning revenue at sea, it is easy to see why containers have become a dominant form of packaged-goods international shipping.

Break-bulk ships are multipurpose vessels that transport shipments of unusual sizes, unitized on pallets, in bags, or in crates. The ships tend to be smaller and have onboard cranes, giving them the flexibility to serve nearly any port. Many of these ships are engaged in specialized trades or serve specific trading lanes. The problem with break-bulk shipping

TABLE 11-3   Top 10 Container Lines

COMPANY	COUNTRY	TEUs	SHIPS	SHIPS ON ORDER
A.P. Moeller-Maersk	Denmark	3,520,751	655	22
Mediterranean Shipping Co.	Switzerland	3,057,506	504	15
CMA CGM Group	France	2,450,347	484	15
COSCO Container Lines	China	1,804,594	325	30
Hapag-Lloyd	Germany	1,514,958	216	1
Evergreen Line	Taiwan	1,031,713	192	33
OOCL	Hong Kong	655,746	100	5
Yang Ming Marine Transport	Taiwan	587,815	98	5
Hamburg Sud Group	Germany	555,943	102	8
NYK Line	Japan	538,101	95	9
Total of Top 10 Carriers		**15,717,414**	**2,771**	**143**

Source: Adapted from Alphaliner, *Alphaliner–Top 100*, retrieved 7 August 2017, from http://www.alphaliner.com/top100/.

is the labor-intensive loading, unloading, and load securing processes. Because each unitized piece of the shipment must be handled separately, port dwell times are longer, which is costly and time consuming. Hence, break-bulk shipping's share of international trade is decreasing.

Roll-on/roll-off (RORO) ships were created to move wheeled vehicles such as cars, trucks, farm equipment, and construction equipment that can be driven on and off the vessel. Since it would be costly, slow, and dangerous to use a crane to load this type of freight, the RORO ship has a ramp that drops down to the wharf, allowing vehicles to be quickly loaded or unloaded. The interior of the ship has many decks to store the cargo, similar to a parking garage. In some ships, the height of the decks can be adjusted to accommodate different sizes of rolling cargo.

Bulk carriers constitute a catch-all category for ships that are dedicated to the transport of a specific bulk commodity on a voyage basis. **Crude carriers** move petroleum products in massive quantities. The size and draft of these ships severely limits the routes available, as they need deep-water ports. **Dry-bulk carriers** have several holds in their hulls in which loose cargo like grains, coal, ore, and other commodities are loaded. These ships are generally small enough to move through the Panama Canal and serve smaller ports. **Gas carriers** move compressed gases like liquefied natural gas and liquefied petroleum gas in specialized tanks. These unique ships are employed on long-term time charters and travel a stable schedule similar to liner ships.

Combination ships are multipurpose vessels that can handle different types of commodities and load types. A typical ship design has under-deck holds for bulk or break-bulk cargoes, a tween deck to hold vehicles or break-bulk cargo, and a main deck, which carries containers. These vessels are likely to have their own cranes and other equipment for loading and unloading cargo. The cargo flexibility, smaller size, and handling equipment help combination ships thrive in smaller markets and developing countries.

Rate Structure Ocean shipping rates are impacted by carrier cost structure, commodity, freight volume, origin and destination points, and ancillary services required. The type of service provided—liner or charter—has a major influence on rate structures.

Historically, the majority of liner rates were determined collectively by a group of carriers serving specific trade routes and ports. These shipping **conferences** were essentially legal cartels in which the carriers agreed not to compete on price by publishing standardized rate **tariffs**. The conferences were allowed to exist with antitrust immunity by governments because of the high fixed-cost structure of the industry. Contract rates and independent rates were not widely available.

The **Ocean Shipping Reform Act** (OSRA) altered the balance of ratemaking power in the liner industry. OSRA expanded the ability of shippers to negotiate private, confidential service contracts with liner companies. A service contract is an agreement in which the shipper commits to provide a certain minimum quantity of cargo over a fixed period of time and the ocean carrier commits to a certain rate or rate schedule and a defined level of service. Today, the vast majority of liner cargo moves under independently negotiated service contracts.

The total price for service under these service contracts will typically contain three components: a basic rate, mandatory surcharges, and extra services. The basic rate focuses on the cost of moving cargo. It is determined by cargo type, origin–destination route, and other factors. Mandatory surcharges are included to cover pass-through charges or charges beyond the ocean transport service. Frequently, these include a fuel surcharge called a bunker adjustment factor, terminal handling charges, and documentation charges. Special requests such as container cleaning or use of controlled atmosphere containers are additional costs.[15]

Charter rates are individually negotiated based on the type of charter (voyage or time) and services required. The market for ship chartering is a fluid supply-and-demand situation. At any given time, the charter rate situation can be one of feast or famine for shipowners. In the short run, the demand for a ship and charter rates at a single port area will depend on shipper movement needs and available ship supply within a time span as short as a month. Over longer periods, a market can be considered glutted or tight, depending on the number and types of ships that are available in the world during the span of a year.

A successful negotiation will result in a charter party, a contract in which the shipowner agrees to place their ship, or part of it, at the disposal of the charterer for the carriage of goods for a voyage or time period for a specified rate. The charter party states in written form the agreement between a shipowner and a charterer, and factually records the agreement and the terms and conditions that have been negotiated.

International Air

Air cargo is a $70-billion business that transports 35 percent of the value of world trade by value of goods. Air carriers transport small quantities of high-value, low-weight, semi-finished, and finished goods. Primary commodities moved globally as air cargo include technology products, precision instruments, electronics, pharmaceuticals, perishable foods, and apparel. Global transportation managers with pressing needs opt for speedy air cargo services.

Service Options   International air transportation is available in virtually every market of the world. Wherever passenger service is available, you can also find air cargo service. Two primary carrier types dominate this mode.

Combination carriers move freight and passengers, with cargo loaded in the belly of the aircraft. As demand has grown, some of the larger international carriers have created separate divisions or companies to focus on air cargo movement and provide scheduled service to meet the needs of global commerce. Seven of the top 10 air cargo carriers (freight ton-kilometers carried), led by Emirates, Cathay Pacific Airways, and Qatar Airways, are combination carriers. Table 11-4 provides a list of the top air cargo carriers.

Table 11-4	Top 10 Air Cargo Carriers—2016	
COMPANY	**COUNTRY**	**FREIGHT TONNES KM CARRIED (BILLIONS)**
Federal Express	USA	15,712
Emirates	United Arab Emirates	12,270
UPS	USA	11,264
Cathay Pacific Airways	Hong Kong	9,947
Qatar Airways	Qatar	9,221
Korean Air	South Korea	7,666
Lufthansa	Germany	7,384
Cargolux	Luxembourg	6,878
Singapore Airlines	Singapore	6,345
Air China	China	6,089

Source: Adapted from "Top 25 Cargo Airlines: FedEx Maintains Top Spot but ABC and Qatar on the Up," *Air Cargo News*, 13 July 2017.

Air cargo carriers focus exclusively on the movement of freight, packages, letters, and envelopes. Like ocean carriers, customers have the option of using scheduled service or on-demand charter service. The majority of large air carriers provide regularly scheduled service through a highly coordinated network of operations and equipment.

Some air cargo carriers offer door-to-door service. **Integrated carriers** like FedEx and UPS have this capability because they own ground delivery equipment as well as aircraft. They can offer a consistent schedule of pickup and delivery windows and standard expedited service through their hub-and-spoke networks. Thanks to their well-controlled processes, they are key players in the global delivery of expedited movement of letters, packages, and small shipments.

In contrast, **nonintegrated carriers** like Cargolux and AirBridgeCargo Airlines provide transport service from airport to airport. They rely on air freight forwarders or the customer to provide delivery service to and from the airport. Some nonintegrated carriers provide on-demand (charter) service for customers whose requirements dictate rapid, direct movement of goods. Given the high cost of on-demand service from these carriers, it is reserved for emergency shipments, unique products, and unusual route requirements.

Equipment Types   While there are many sizes of aircraft used for moving international cargo, the primary difference between equipment type focuses on the internal configuration of the plane. Some equipment is set up to carry freight only while others carry a combination of passengers and cargo. Each type is discussed below.

Air freighters are aircraft dedicated solely to the movement of freight. They range in size from the Cessna Caravan that FedEx uses for small market pickup and delivery (capacity of 4,000 pounds) to the Anatov AN-124, a huge plane capable of handling over-sized payloads (capacity of nearly 265,000 pounds). The main deck of an air freighter has no amenities and is set up to quickly move freight on and off the plane using a roller deck. A **roller deck** is a main deck equipped with rollers on the floor that allows palletized or containerized cargo to be pushed into position. In the air freight industry, these specially designed containers that fit properly inside the rounded fuselage are called **unit load devices** (ULDs). The pallets and ULDs are then secured to the aircraft floor using hooks and slings.

Cargo also travels on **passenger airplanes**. The passengers travel on the main deck or cabin of the plane while luggage and some cargo are loaded into the lower deck or belly of the aircraft. The cargo is commonly restricted to smaller individual shipments of cargo rather than full pallets or ULDs, due to the weight limitations of the aircraft, the capacity of the hold, and the exterior door size. Also, certain items considered hazardous or a fire threat (such as nonrechargeable lithium-ion batteries) are no longer allowed to be carried by passenger aircraft. A benefit of using passenger airplanes for cargo is the frequency of service and ability to move critical shipments on the next flight out.

Whatever the international shipment requirement may be, an aircraft with an appropriate combination of payload, range, and speed is likely available.

Rate Structure   Air cargo rates are based on the **value of service** or the **cost of service**. Value of service rates are demand based and consider the sensitivity of the cargo being shipped to freight rates. The less sensitive cargo is to rates, the higher the rate will be. On traffic lanes where demand is strong and plane capacity is limited, the air rates will be high and vice versa for traffic lanes where supply exceeds demand. Also, products with high prices or emergency conditions surrounding the move will be charged high rates because the freight rate is a small portion of the landed selling price.

Cost of service factors also enter into air carrier pricing of cargo. Given the limited cargo-carrying capacity of a plane, space is at a premium. The utilization of this space is related to the **density** of the cargo, with low-density cargo requiring more space per weight unit than high-density cargo.

Air carriers calculate the **dimensional weight** (dim weight) of a shipment to evaluate the weight versus space issue. Freight carriers use the greater of the actual weight or dimensional weight to calculate shipping charges. Carriers calculate international air shipments as (Length × Width × Height)/(Dimensional Factor). The common dimensional factor for international freight by FedEx and UPS is 139 for shipments measured in inches and 5,000 for shipments measured in centimeters.

For example, an international shipment weighing 1,500 pounds with 100 cartons measuring 16 inches by 12 inches by 18 inches has a dim weight of 24.86 pounds per case (16 × 12 × 18)/139 and a total dim weight of 2,486 pounds. Thus, the air carrier will charge the customer based on the higher dim weight of 2,486 pounds instead of the actual weight of 1,500 pounds.

Dimensional weight favors shippers of dense objects and penalizes those who ship lightweight cartons. For example, a carton of unpopped corn kernels will likely be charged by gross weight while a carton of popcorn will probably be charged by its dimensional weight. This is because the large box of popcorn takes up excess space but does not fill up a plane's capacity in terms of weight, making it an inefficient use of cubic capacity.

Major carriers tend to develop their own rates based on the commodity and market competition. Airlines and air freight forwarders use the Air Cargo Tariff (TACT) as a reference for pricing. TACT is a set of guidelines that contains comprehensive information regarding air cargo rules, regulations, rates, and charges. TACT contains information regarding 5 million rates for 350,000 city pairs with information contributed by more than 100 airlines.[16]

Container rates are also available for cargo shipped in a container. The rate is cost based, rather than value of service or commodity based. The rate applies to a minimum weight in the container. Some carriers offer a container rate discount per container shipped over any route of the individual carrier. The discount is deducted from the tariff rate applicable to the commodity being moved in non containerized form, and a charge is assessed for returning the empty container.

Intermodal Transportation

Intermodal transportation involves the use of two or more modes of transportation in moving a shipment from origin to destination. It is often said that international transportation is intermodal transportation because so many goods moving from one country to another involve the use of multiple modes.

Shifting freight between modes may seem inefficient and time consuming, but the improved reach and combined service advantages of intermodal transportation offsets these issues. The primary benefits of intermodalism include the following:

- *Intermodal transportation facilitates global trade.* The capacity and efficiency of ocean transportation allows large-volume shipments to be transported between continents at relatively low per unit costs. The rapid speed of air transportation allows perishable goods to flow quickly between countries. The final domestic leg of the delivery can take place via truck. The ocean-truck combination makes products competitive across global markets by keeping the landed cost in check. The air-truck combination facilitates expedited flows of high-value goods and rapid replenishment of fast selling products like fast-fashion.

- *Greater accessibility is created by linking the individual modes.* The road infrastructure allows trucks to reach locations that are inaccessible to other modes. For example, air transportation can only move freight between airport facilities. Trucks provide the flow between the origin and departure airport as well as the arrival airport and the customer destination. Railroads can facilitate the use of international ocean transportation. Getting low-sulfur coal from a Wyoming mine to a utility company in Japan would be best accomplished through a combination of rail and water transportation.

- *Overall cost efficiency can be achieved without sacrificing service quality or accessibility.* In other words, intermodal transportation allows supply chains to utilize the inherent capabilities of multiple modes to control cost and fulfill customer requirements. If a U.S. furniture manufacturer needed to move 10 containers of furniture from North Carolina to California for export, a combination of truck and rail transportation would improve upon truck-only service. The speed and accessibility of trucks would be used for the initial pickup and delivery to the rail yard, a cost-efficient railroad would provide cross-country transportation to the Port of Oakland, and a containership would provide ocean transport.

Service Options It can be argued that flexibility is another valuable trait of intermodal transportation. Companies can use any combination of the five transportation modes that best suits their freight and trip requirements. In a global scenario, this is essential because transportation options may be limited at origin points and/or destination points.

Figure 11-3 highlights the most prevalent intermodal combinations for global transportation. The accessibility of truck transportation makes it ideally suited for short-distance pickup and delivery of containerized international freight, while rail works well for long-distance moves of containers to and from ports. Rail and barge transportation are

FIGURE 11-3   Common Intermodal Combinations

suitable for moving export-bound raw materials and other bulk commodities to port facilities. The long-distance, cross-ocean moves are handled by air and ocean carriers.

Large carriers, including Canadian National Railway, A.P. Moeller-Maersk, and DHL, offer multimodal capabilities. These allow the carriers to utilize the most efficient and economical combination of intermodal transportation for their international customers. In the majority of cases, the carrier determines the modal combination to be used based on capacity, route, cost efficiency, and delivery deadline. After all, when customers drop overnight packages in an express delivery box, they are not concerned about the combination of modes used as long as their shipments arrive safely and on time!

Freight and Equipment Types Another valuable aspect of intermodalism is its ability to handle multiple types of freight. Whether the goods are commodities, component parts, or finished products, they can be transported by intermodal methods. The key is to have the right transportation equipment, freight handling capabilities, and transfer methods to effectively move goods between modes. The primary freight types are bulk, break-bulk, and containerized freight.

Bulk freight includes raw materials and other loose cargo that must be transferred between transportation equipment by means of pumps, vacuums, scoops, or conveyors. Given the massive weight and volume of these commodities, water, rail, and pipeline are the primary intermodal option for bulk freight. For example, orange juice concentrate may be picked up using a rail tank car, pumped into the hold of a cargo ship for the line-haul move, and then pumped into a tank truck for final delivery to the bottling facility.

While bulk freight efficiently uses the capacity of a cargo ship or railcar, there are significant challenges. The items are loose, meaning that product is susceptible to contamination, spillage, or theft. Also, significant investments in loading/unloading equipment must be made to facilitate quick transloading of the freight between modes. Finally, not all ports and transfer facilities are equipped with modern handling tools to facilitate rapid, cost-efficient transfers.

Break-bulk freight includes a wide array of products that must be moved individually between transportation equipment and modes. Palletized machinery, bagged cement, strapped steel coils, or drummed liquids fall into this category. Cranes, forklifts, and other industrial equipment are needed to transfer the goods between modes. For example, steel coils may be rolled and strapped at the foundry, sent to the port on a flatbed truck, and moved via break-bulk ship to its destination port where it is delivered to a customer via rail.

Break-bulk freight shares a primary challenge with bulk freight—costly and slow loading/unloading. One option for speeding the process and overcoming the lack of port equipment is to use geared break-bulk ships. These ships have their own cargo loading equipment such as onboard cranes. This creates the flexibility to operate from any berth or terminal, regardless of landside equipment availability.

Containerized freight is loaded into or onto storage equipment (a container or pallet) at the origin and delivered to the destination in or on that same piece of equipment with no additional handling. For example, if a load of smart speakers needed to be shipped from the factory to the market, they would be loaded into a 40-foot container at the factory in Taiwan, transferred to the port via truck, and loaded on a containership bound for Savannah, Georgia. Upon arrival, the container would be moved from the ship onto another truck and delivered to the retailer's distribution center.

The development of freight containers has made intermodal transportation of finished goods very economical. A standardized dry box container looks much like a truck trailer without the chassis. It can be lifted, stacked, and moved from one piece of equipment to another. Specialized freight containers are available for handling temperature-sensitive goods (refrigerated containers), liquids (tank containers), commodities (dry bulk cargo containers), and other unique cargoes.

A critical step in the growth of containerization and intermodalism was the development of container standards in the late 1960s. By building containers to consistent dimensional height and width specifications, containerships, railroads, and trucking companies can readily move containers owned by any company. As a result, approximately 60 percent of world trade (in value) is containerized.[17]

There are five common standard lengths, 20 feet (6.1 m), 40 feet (12.2 m), 45 feet (13.7 m), 48 feet (14.6 m), and 53 feet (16.2 m). Container capacity is often expressed in **TEU** which is one standard 20-foot (length) × 8-foot (width) container. It has a payload weight of 48,000 to 62,000 pounds and 1,172 cubic feet of capacity. A 40-foot container is the equivalent of two TEUs with twice as much cubic capacity, but the payload weight range is not significantly larger at 58,000 to 63,000 pounds.

Other factors have contributed to the growth of containerized intermodal transportation. They include improvements in information systems to track containers as they move through the supply chain and the development of intermodal terminals to facilitate efficient container transfers between modes. In addition, new generations of larger ocean vessels have greatly expanded TEU capacity. Figure 11-4 highlights the evolution of containerships and the Global Perspective feature highlights the benefits and challenges of today's mega containerships.

FIGURE 11-4 Evolution of Containerships

Source: Based on Vessel Tracking, Biggest Container Ships – Industry Overview. Available from http://www.vesseltracking.net/article/biggest-container-ship

GLOBAL **PERSPECTIVES**

Are Bigger Ships Better?

The bigger is better mentality has been adopted by ocean carriers, with increasingly larger container ships being built. The most recently launched behemoth is the *Madrid Maersk*, a ship that is 400 meters long, 58 meters wide, and capable of carrying 20,568 TEUs. It is the latest in a series of ultra-large container ships (ULCS) that is now traversing the Asia to Europe trade lane.

On the plus side, *Maersk* has redesigned the ship so that it can handle 2,000 more TEUs than the previous generation without significantly increasing ship size. That increased capacity, along with appropriate sailing speeds, lowers energy usage and costs per container carried. *Maersk* estimates that efficiency gains are 7 percent versus its earlier ULCS and 35 percent greater than the average vessel on the Asia to Europe trade lane.

However, bigger ships do create challenges. As new ships enter the market, an oversupply of capacity is created unless demand is high. In 2016, the idle container ship fleet stood at 1.6 million TEUs and a shipper could pay less than $800 for a 40-foot container shipped from Shanghai to the west coast of North America. Further industry consolidation and old ship retirements are needed to ensure that the ULCS are fully loaded and generating maximum efficiency. However, consolidation may ultimately reduce competition on certain trade lanes, allowing oligopolistic market structures to emerge.

Also, ULCS benefits may not be equally distributed. While ULCS reduce unit costs for carriers; ports, onward transport providers, and insurance companies incur higher expenses to serve them. The overall system costs may rise and the size benefits are lost.

These mega-ships strain every aspect of port operations. The arrival of an ULCS at a port creates a surge of container loading/unloading activity and a slowdown for all other traffic. ULCS also require more access channel depth and width, longer docks, larger ship-to-shore crane systems, more landside storage capacity, and greater road, rail, and barge access. Without significant expansion, ULCS will be limited to a few world ports and routes.

If ports, railroads, and trucking companies adapt to growing vessel sizes, landside costs will stabilize. In the meantime, the pressure on maritime freight rates will continue, and the resulting low trade costs may help the global economy recover.

These concerns beg the question: Are bigger ships better? It is likely in the long run but the transition will create growing pains.

Sources: John Churchill, *Ships for the Long (and Short) Haul*, 1 May 2017, retrieved 2 August 2017, from http://www.maersk.com/en/hardware/2017/05/ships-for-the-long-and-short-haul; Transvoyant, *New "Megamax" Container Ships Create New Risks for Global Supply Chains*, 14 April 2017, retrieved 2 August 2017, from https://www.transvoyant.com/new-megamax-container-ships-create-new-risks-global-supply-chains/; *Review of Maritime Transportation 2016*, United Nations Conference on Trade and Development, Geneva, Switzerland, 2016.

Carrier Selection

After selecting the appropriate mode or intermodal combination, the global transportation manager must focus on carrier selection. Like the modal decision, selection of carriers is based on a variety of shipment criteria and carrier capabilities: transit time average and reliability, equipment availability and capacity, geographic coverage, product protection, and freight rates.

A major difference between modal and carrier selection is the number of options. Modal selection involves few realistic options, but the number of carriers can vary greatly. In some remote locations only a single carrier within a mode is available. In major markets like Shanghai or Rotterdam, dozens of carrier options exist. Time and effort must be spent to compare carriers' capability, service quality, and price.

Another difference is that carrier selection requires more active and frequent engagement of the transportation buyer than does modal selection. After choosing a carrier, the buyer must remain vigilant. Given the challenges of international transportation, it is critical to monitor a carrier's service level and freight rates. Should performance deteriorate, it may be necessary to hire a different carrier.

The type of service provided within a mode affects carrier selection. Direct service between adjacent countries provides point-to-point flows of goods, generating the advantages of speed and safety because freight is handled less and moves straight to the destination. Indirect service such as cross-ocean intermodal transportation requires interim stops and transfers between equipment. This reduces transit speed and subjects the freight to additional handling, but offers lower cost because carriers consolidate the freight for more efficient transportation.

Because the cost structures are essentially the same for carriers in a given mode, their rates tend to be aligned for a given move. Thus, service performance is often the key determinant in carrier selection. Carrier selection research suggests that reliability of on-time delivery and on-time pickup, technical capabilities, carrier response to emergencies, information sharing, freight damage experience, carrier financial stability, and total transit time are among the most important criteria to transportation service buyers.[18]

To maintain greater control and to leverage volume for lower rates, global transportation managers concentrate their freight with a limited number of quality carriers. Using these core carriers also allows the organization to focus its attention on other supply chain issues. Stronger relationships with the carriers emerge to enhance mutual understanding of requirements, coordination of processes, and quality of service. Being a carrier-friendly shipper of choice can also give a company priority access to the carriers' limited capacity.

Route Selection

Route selection and delivery scheduling activities are not trivial topics—they affect costs, impact customer service, and can cause major headaches if not properly managed. Conceptually, they are not difficult problems to understand, but they can be challenging to solve, particularly with the long distances and unique challenges of global transportation.

It would be easy to assume that route planning simply is a carrier responsibility. Global transportation managers should take active involvement because effective routing impacts supply chain performance and organizational success. Transit time and on-time performance depend heavily on proper scheduling and sequencing of stops. Effective routing also helps avoid poorly equipped ports and congested border crossing points that may drastically delay cargo flows.

Efficiency is another major issue, given the sheer amount of money spent on transportation. Carriers must develop more efficient routes that maximize equipment capacity utilization. They also need to use routes that minimize tolls, port costs, and route-related surcharges.

Product safety is the third concern when developing routes, particularly for surface transportation. Major trouble spots for hijacking and product theft, such as the Gulf of Aden and the South China Sea, should be factored into route planning. Land routes with poor-quality roads and inferior freight handling capabilities also pose problems. Sometimes a more expensive indirect or circuitous route is used to mitigate these safety risks.

Intermodal transportation brings about unique routing considerations. The land–bridge concept involves a combination of ocean-rail-ocean intermodal transport. Land–bridges serve as alternatives to all-water routes through the Panama Canal, the Magellan Straits, and other canals around the world, reducing total transit time. Also, vessel size limitations are avoided, allowing the use of larger, more efficient ships.

Using the land–bridge strategy, a container could be routed from Tokyo to Seattle via ocean vessel, from Seattle to New York via train, and onward to Rotterdam via ocean vessel. Compared to the all-water option through the Suez Canal, this routing option reduces transit time by two weeks.

It is important to note that routing decisions should not be made independently of other global transportation processes. Routing decisions must be integrated into a larger transportation strategy that supports global supply chain excellence. Thus, global transportation managers must coordinate mode selection, carrier selection, and route planning with delivery execution to achieve success.

Delivery Execution

The actual flow of goods across global transportation networks can be a weeks-long journey with high potential for disruptions and challenges. To mitigate risks and facilitate timely flows, global transportation managers must take numerous precautions and seek assistance when needed. Properly packing the freight, selecting appropriate ports, and deploying ancillary services will avoid chaos.

Freight Protection Exporters must pay attention to the stress that global transportation puts on packaged goods, particularly goods moving via ocean. Four potential in-transit problems should be kept in mind when choosing packaging materials: breakage, moisture, pilferage, and excess weight. While shipping containers provide some protection from these issues, it is critical to protect products as they are packed in shipping cartons and to protect the cartons when they are packed in the shipping container. To provide proper balance in the container, the weight must be evenly distributed.

There is a great deal of container handling and transfers during an indirect international move. Containers can get dropped or can collide with each other during the loading/unloading processes. Hence it is important to use protective packaging around each product. Also, it is important to secure the cartons within the container by packing the shipping cartons as tightly as possible. Gaps and empty spaces should be filled with dunnage, paper, or air bags to eliminate in-transit load shifting.

Moisture is a constant concern because condensation can accumulate inside the container. Another aspect of this problem is that cargo may also be unloaded in precipitation or the foreign port may not have covered storage facilities. It is important to use packages and packing filler made of moisture-resistant material. Plastic can be used inside cartons to protect freight and shrink–wrap can be used around palletized or unitized product to create a moisture barrier.

Theft and pilferage are added risks. To avoid pilferage, avoid writing contents or brand names on exterior cartons. Other safeguards include using straps, seals, and shrink–wrapping. The goal is to limit awareness of the contents of the cartons and eliminate the opportunity for undetected access to the shipment.

Finally, because transportation costs are determined by volume and weight, specially reinforced and lightweight packing materials have been developed for global transportation. Packing goods to minimize volume and weight while reinforcing them may save money, as well as ensuring that the goods are properly packed. It is recommended that a professional firm be hired to pack the products if the seller is not equipped to do so. This service is usually provided at a moderate cost.

Normally, air shipments require less packing than ocean shipments, though they should still be adequately protected, especially if they are fragile and/or of interest to thieves. In many instances, standard domestic packing is acceptable, especially if the product is durable and there is no concern for display packaging. In other instances, high-test (at least 250 pounds per square inch) cardboard or tri-wall construction boxes are more than adequate.

While advertising and logos on cartons are not desirable, certain carton markings are essential. The information provided on the outside of the cartons must comply with customs regulations of the country of destination, enable freight handlers and receivers to correctly identify shipments, facilitate proper handling of shipments, and adhere to environmental and safety regulations for hazardous materials. At minimum, each carton should prominently display the following information:

- Customer and destination information—business name, ship-to address
- Seller and origin information—business name, ship-from address, and country of origin
- Cargo information—weight in pounds and kilograms, size in inches and centimeters, cautionary and handling markings using international pictorial symbols, handling instructions, and package number (for example, "2 of 14")
- Hazardous materials markings should also be used as needed. These markings should follow the United Nations harmonized standards and use internationally recognized symbols.

Port Selection Most exporters and importers are not located directly on a waterway, rail line, or airport runway. Hence, they need freight handling and transfer services between carriers and modes at borders. Ports provide the infrastructure, equipment, and labor needed to load, unload, and transfer freight between carriers. Without efficient port operations, it would be extremely difficult to facilitate high-volume container flows.

Intercontinental trade moves primarily through airports and seaports, while intracontinental trade moves directly from origin to destination through international gateways or indirectly through intermodal transfer terminals and **inland ports**. Airports and seaports can be privately owned, though the vast majority of major international seaports and airports are government owned. The facilities are managed by a **port authority**, a governmental or quasigovernmental public agency charged with creating and supporting economic development in the port area. Table 11-5 identifies the top global seaports and airports for freight movement.

Seaports play a critical role in global trade, given that the vast majority of intercontinental cargo moves via ocean carriers. A seaport is an area of land and water with related equipment to permit the reception of ships, their loading and unloading, and the receipt, storage, and delivery of their goods. There are thousands of seaports around the world, though the vast majority of international trade flows through a small group of major, deep draft commercial seaports.

When determining which ports to use, an exporter or importer must consider dockside infrastructure, water depth, and landside operations. It is critical to match freight with port capacity and cargo handling capabilities as some ports focus on containerized freight while others focus on bulk, break-bulk, or rolling freight. Adequate landside operations and space are necessary for efficient freight transfer between modes. And, strong port

RANK	SEAPORT – TOTAL CARGO	TONS (,000)	SEAPORT – CONTAINER TRAFFIC	TEUs (,000)	AIRPORT – INTERNATIONAL AIR FREIGHT	METRIC TONS (,000)
					TABLE 11-5 Top World Ports	
1	Shanghai, China	646,514	Shanghai, China	36,516	Hong Kong, China	4,380
2	Singapore, Singapore	575,846	Singapore, Singapore	30,922	Dubai, U.A.E.	2,506
3	Qingdao, China	476,216	Shenzhen, China	24,142	Incheon, South Korea	2,490
4	Guangzhou, China	475,481	Ningbo, China	20,636	Shanghai, China	2,379
5	Rotterdam, Netherlands	466,363	Hong Kong, China	20,073	Tokyo, Japan	2,036
6	Port Hedland, Australia	452,940	Busan, South Korea	19,469	Taipei, Taiwan	2,005
7	Ningbo, China	448,828	Qingdao, China	17,323	Anchorage, Alaska, USA	1,957
8	Tianjin, China	440,430	Guangzhou, China	17,097	Frankfurt, Germany	1,951
9	Busan, South Korea	347,713	Dubai Ports, U.A.E.	15,585	Paris, France	1,861
10	Dalian, China	320,658	Tianjin, China	13,881	Singapore, Singapore	1,853
11	Kwangyang, South Korea	272,007	Rotterdam, Netherlands	12,235	Miami, Florida, USA	1,738
12	Hong Kong, China	256,488	Port Kelang, Malaysia	11,887	Amsterdam, Netherlands	1,621
13	Qinhuangdao, China	246,550	Kaohsiung, Taiwan, China	10,264	London, Great Britain	1,495
14	South Louisiana, U.S.A.	235,058	Antwerp, Belgium	9,654	Doha, Qatar	1,444
15	Port Kelang, Malaysia	219,786	Dalian, China	9,591	Bangkok, Thailand	1,189

Source: Adapted from AAPA, *World Port Rankings 2015*, retrieved 7 August 2017, from http://aapa.files.cms-plus.com/Statistics/WORLD%20PORT%20RANKINGS%202015.xlsx; and, Airports Council International, *Preliminary World Airport Traffic and Rankings*, April 4, 2016, retrieved 7 August 2017, from http://www.aci.aero/News/Releases/Most-Recent/2016/04/04/ACI-releases-preliminary-world-airport-traffic-rankings-.

information technology and security systems to maintain visibility, control, and safety of the freight.

Airports provide rapid transfers of freight between airlines and landside carriers. Dual-purpose **cargo service airports** handle both passenger planes and cargo-only aircraft. **Cargo-only airports** such as Alliance Airport in Fort Worth, Texas, and Montreal Mirabel International Airport in Canada provide alternative landing locations to congested dual-purpose airports and reduce operating costs.

When determining which airports to use, air carriers, exporters, and importers must consider geographic access to key markets. The number and size of airport runways must be matched to aircraft requirements and suitability for use. Only when these hurdles have been cleared do air cargo companies consider landing fees, weather factors, and infrastructure issues such as runway length, terminal facilities, and ramp access for ease of freight transfer.[19]

Airports must also have the necessary equipment to efficiently handle cargo. Terminals are needed to facilitate fast intermodal transfers of freight, while warehouses are needed to protect and store cargo. Finally, hours of operation are critical because air freighters tend to fly at night and use airports during off-hours to avoid congestion with passenger flights. It is imperative that noise regulations not restrict an air carrier's ability to land or takeoff.

Ancillary Services Deployment   The complexity of international transportation makes it difficult for importers and exporters to independently manage global freight flows. Fortunately, they can leverage the expertise of third party logistics (3PL) service providers. 3PLs facilitate the international movement of goods by developing exceptional capabilities in one or more steps in the global freight flow process.

International freight forwarders (IFFs) are often seen as the travel agents of international freight transportation. These service providers identify and book the best routes, modes of transport, and specific carriers based on the needs of importers and exporters. Many IFFs specialize in particular service areas, modes of transport, or markets.

IFFs can consolidate freight going to a single destination. This allows the IFF to negotiate lower transportation rates than many individual customers could achieve on their own. In addition to cost savings, companies should consider using an IFF when the scale and complexity of freight transportation is high or when there is limited internal expertise to manage the process.

IFFs often offer a wide range of other trade-related services that help customers avoid common errors and pitfalls of cross-border trade. These include completion of freight documentation, customs clearance services, insurance services, inventory management, and other value-added logistics services. Additionally, IFFs are valuable sources of trade information.

Non Vessel-Operating Common Carriers When an organization wishes to move a small volume of containers and less-than-container load (LCL) quantities, an effective service provider is a nonvessel-operating common carrier (NVOCC). These cargo consolidators do not own ships but act as carriers legally by accepting required responsibilities of a carrier that issues a bill of lading.

NVOCCs book container berths on ships on a regular basis, allowing them to gain advantageous rates from the ocean carriers. They are able to resell the space to customers in smaller increments at favorable rates. For LCL quantities, the NVOCC combines the goods from multiple customers into a single load to fill a container. The container is then loaded on an ocean carrier for movement to the destination port. Upon arrival, the NVOCC receives the container and delivers the contents to each final destination.

Export Packers Given the challenges of properly packing, marking, and loading shipments, many companies seek the assistance of export packing companies. These service providers work to ensure that products arrive safely. Export packers also help save money by using economical packing materials, improving space utilization inside cartons and containers, and taking steps to prevent theft. Finally, export packers also ensure that all packing regulations and marking requirements are met across the channel.

The largest global freight companies like DHL, FedEx, and UPS provide multiple ancillary services as well as the logistics capabilities discussed in Chapter 09.

In sum, global transportation managers must engage in a wide variety of distribution processes to achieve delivery excellence. They must match freight to the most appropriate international mode(s), select reputable transportation service providers, pick optimal routes, and execute seamless delivery. These efforts ensure that shipments move safely and quickly across the global distribution network.

Communication Processes

One of the major challenges in global transportation is maintaining control and visibility of freight as it moves across borders and is handed off between carriers and intermediaries. Proper freight documentation ensures compliance with government regulations and facilitates the uninterrupted flow of goods. Timely information sharing and the use of technology can vastly improve shipment visibility and speed goods through border crossings and ports.

Freight Documentation   Freight documents facilitate the flow of cargo on its journey from the exporter's factory to the importer's distribution center. Missing or incorrect paperwork can cause loading delays, customs clearance deferrals, additional inspection, and improper application of duty rates. Hence, proper and accurate documentation is critically important to global trade.

Documentation requirements are governed by the customs regulations of the exporting and importing nations. Because these regulations differ, the number and types of documents required may vary widely, depending on the origin and destination of the shipment. Experts suggest enlisting the assistance of specialists in this communication channel process like freight forwarders and customs brokers.

In general, international cargo travels with four types of documents: invoices, export documents, import documents, and transportation documents. Each is briefly discussed below, with an emphasis on the transportation paperwork category.

Invoices are requests for payment from the exporter to the importer for the purchased goods. That sounds straightforward, but international invoice requirements are complex. Invoice types include the **commercial invoice**, **pro forma invoice**, and **consular invoice**.

The widely used commercial invoice accompanies the shipment unless the terms of payment dictate that the commercial invoice is sent directly to the importer or a bank involved in the transaction. Precision is critical as commercial invoices are often used by governments to determine the true value of goods when assessing customs duties. Governments that use the commercial invoice to control imports will often specify its form, content, number of copies, language to be used, and other characteristics.

As the sample commercial invoice in Figure 11-5 indicates, a commercial invoice must contain a precise description of the product, quantities, and value, as well as the country of origin. These factors are critical as they affect the duty rates applied to the shipment. Other important information includes the Incoterms used in the transaction, delivery-related charges paid by the exporter, and details regarding the companies engaged in the transaction (buyer, seller, shipping origin, and shipping destination). Payment terms and currency in which the payment is to be made should also be clearly stated.

Export documents are required by countries to report information on goods being sold internationally to generate accurate trade statistics and to control the outflow of strategic materials (such as military items, telecommunications equipment, computer technology, and so forth) and national treasures. Sometimes, a government may prevent exporters from selling these products abroad or require authorization to export these goods. An **export license** is the government document that authorizes the export of specific goods in specific quantities to a particular destination.

The **Shipper's Export Declaration** (SED) is used to control exports and act as a source document for official U.S. export statistics. SEDs, or their electronic equivalent, are required for shipments of commodities whose value exceeds $2,500. Regardless of value, SEDs must be prepared and submitted for all shipments that require an export license or are destined for countries restricted by the Export Administration Regulations.[20]

A **Certificate of End Use** is a document intended to assure authorities in the exporting country that the product will be used for legitimate purposes. For example, enriched uranium will be used to operate a nuclear power plant rather than in nuclear weapons. End-use certificates are provided by the importing country's government. Other export documents facilitate government collection of export taxes and control of export quotas.

Import documents are required by the governments of importing countries. The documents seek to protect its citizens from inferior quality products, properly classify products

| FIGURE 11-5 | Sample Commercial Invoice |

COMMERCIAL INVOICE

DATE OF EXPORT	TERMS OF SALE	REFERENCE	CURRENCY
11/21/2014	FAS - Qingdao, China	LL-01-23-1962	US DOLLAR

SHIPPER / EXPORTER	CONSIGNEE
Jinto Exports Intl. 2390 Xinhua East Hohhot, Niemongol, 00010 86-471-6607777	Moberg Enterprises 5549 Bobcat Ave. Athens, Ohio, US 45700 (740) 559-1000

COUNTRY OF ULTIMATE DESTINATION	IMPORTER (IF DIFFERENT THAN CONSIGNEE)
UNITED STATES	

COUNTRY OF MANUFACTURE
China

OCEAN BILL OF LADING NUMBER
95G630587-X1

FULL DESCRIPTION OF GOODS	WEIGHT (LBS.)	QUANTITY	UNIT VALUE	TOTAL VALUE
TC0085 TOOL CART	10,230.00	220	58.00	12,760.00
CJ01 ROLLING RACK	17,500.00	500	35.00	17,500.00
			0.00	0.00
SUB-TOTAL	27,730.00	720		30,260.00

TOTAL NO. OF PACKAGES	Shipped via Maersk AVON From Quingdao, China to New York, USA Container No: CIU32587440	
720	FREIGHT COSTS	3,593.00
	INSURANCE COSTS	490.00
	ADDITIONAL COSTS	0.00

TOTAL INVOICE VALUE $ 34,343.00

I hearby certify that this invoice shows the actual price of goods described, that no other invoice has been issued, and that all particulars are true and correct.

SIGNATURE OF SHIPPER / EXPORTER

Sen Yiaboi

PRINT NAME HERE

for collection of duties, and limit the importation of products that the government finds inappropriate. Some onerous import documents create artificial trade barriers to protect certain industries from foreign competition.

The **Certificate of Origin** is an international trade document attesting to the origin of specified goods. It is often required by the customs authorities of a country as part of the entry process. The document is completed by the exporter or its agent and certified by an organization in the country of the exporter, such as a chamber of commerce, trade organization, or consular office.

A **Certificate of Inspection** attests to the authenticity and accuracy of the goods. An independent company inspects the goods and confirms that they conform to the description contained in the commercial invoice. This document is used in situations where the payment terms involve a letter of credit or documentary collection.

The Importer Security Filing (ISF) applies to import cargo arriving to the United States by vessel. The information submitted in the ISF improves U.S. Customs and Border Protection's (CBP) ability to identify high-risk shipments in order to prevent smuggling and ensure cargo safety and security. Within the ISF, importers, or their agent, must provide eight data elements, no later than 24 hours before the cargo is laden aboard a vessel destined to the United States. Those data elements include:

- Seller
- Buyer
- Importer of record number/FTZ applicant identification number
- Consignee number(s)
- Manufacturer or supplier
- Ship to party
- Country of origin
- Commodity Harmonized Tariff Schedule of the United States number

Two additional data elements must be submitted as early as possible, but no later than 24 hours prior to the ship's arrival at a U.S. port. These data elements are:

- Container stuffing location
- Consolidator

Failure to comply with the ISF rule may result in monetary penalties, increased inspections, and delay of cargo unloading.

Transportation Documents The disruption-free flow of goods also depends upon the availability of key transportation documents. Typically, freight carriers will only accept cargo if it is accompanied by thorough and accurate paperwork. Otherwise, it will be difficult to create an accurate **manifest**. This internal carrier document lists the exact makeup of the cargo, its ownership, ports of origin and ports of destination, handling instructions, and other key information.

A distinction is made between a cargo manifest, a freight manifest, and a manifest of hazardous goods. The cargo manifest solely lists the details of the goods (nature, quantity, types and numbers, sender, destination, and so on) and service for customs declaration of the goods. In addition to that, the freight manifest lists details of the seaborne freight and serves to collect the sea freights payable at destination and as basis for certain commission calculations. A hazardous goods manifest solely lists hazardous goods onboard the vessel.[21]

For security purposes, many countries require that manifest information for import shipments be provided electronically to its customs agencies 24 hours prior to containerized freight being loaded onto an ocean vessel. The United States initiated their Advance Cargo Manifest Declaration Rule in 2002, followed by Canada and China. The European Union adopted a similar program called the Entry Summary Declaration for its 27 member counties, effective January 1, 2011. In comparison, road, rail, and air manifest information must be submitted between one and four hours prior to arrival.[22]

Another primary transportation document is the **bill of lading**. When signed, the carrier acknowledges that it has received the cargo in good condition in the right quantity. The bill of lading acts as a contract of carriage between the transportation company and the cargo owner—either the exporter or importer, depending on the Incoterm used. It specifies the price and instructions for moving the freight.

Various international bill of lading types exist. An **ocean bill of lading** is used for water transport and an **air waybill** is used for air carrier shipments. Figure 11-6 provides a sample ocean bill of lading. A **through bill of lading** allows the carrier to move cargo via several different modes of transportation and/or several different distribution centers. Each carrier has liability for its phase of the journey. In contrast, a **multimodal bill of lading** tasks the principal carrier or freight forwarder for liability across the entire journey.

FIGURE 11-6 Sample Bill of Lading

Additional documents facilitate the transport of international cargo. A **packing list** is a detailed inventory of the contents of a shipment. It lists the seller, buyer, shipper, invoice number, date of shipment, mode of transport, carrier, and itemizes quantity, description, the type and quantity of packages, net and gross weight (in kilograms), package marks, and dimensions, if appropriate.[23] A **shipper's letter of instructions** is a document that spells out the requirements for handling in-transit goods. It is an important document when the cargo is susceptible to damage or requires special attention (such as live animals and plants, temperature-sensitive goods, and so forth). Special documentation is also required for dangerous or hazardous goods.

The transportation industry is slowly working toward a paperless environment with electronic documentation. The **International Air Transport Association (IATA)** estimates that the average air freight shipment generates 20 different paper documents. These paper-based processes are inefficient, error-prone, and can cause unnecessary freight delays.[24] Similar challenges exist in the ocean transport industry. The Transportation Technology feature highlights industry efforts to convert paper shipping documents to electronic formats.

TRANSPORTATION **TECHNOLOGY**

Paperless Global Transportation—Slow but Steady Progress

Paper documents traveling with international freight are relics of the 20th century. In this age of Internet-based procurement, blockchain technology, and scanning tools, a paperless environment seems logical. Despite its many benefits, moving to electronic documentation has proven to be a difficult task with slower than planned uptake. Industry associations and government carriers are adopting various approaches to paperless transportation flows.

The IATA is working on an initiative called Simplifying the Business to make air cargo easier, smarter, and faster. The initiative began in 2006 as *e-freight* to replace the most widely used paper documents for air cargo (packing lists, invoices, certificates of origin, and others) with electronic messages. Later, efforts focused on replacing paper air waybills with electronic air waybills.

Achieving a paperless air cargo supply chain is a multifaceted challenge. The engagement of multiple participants, creation of standardized business processes like an electronic customs environment, and compatible platforms for the exchange of electronic data are required. Despite many years of work, the global electronic air waybill penetration was just 51 percent as of August 2016. The IATA target is 62 percent by 2017.

IATA is not backing down from its pursuit of electronic communication processes. The association is moving forward with its Digital Cargo project, which will deploy smart data-sharing principles. The goal is to replace documents and peer-to-peer messaging with a single master Digital Shipment Record. IATA also aims to use intelligent systems in its Interactive Cargo project to develop real-time cargo monitoring and alerting by customers.

Government agencies are also developing technology-based systems to remedy the paper chase. Substantial improvements have been made to computerize various documents and processes, but these automation improvements have not been made in all countries. Canada has a computerized system called the Pre-Arrival Review System to speed the release or referral for examination of imports by the Border Service Agency. Taiwan uses a three-stage automated customs system to clear cargo.

The U.S. Customs and Border Patrol (CBP) is using technology to track imports and exports. The Automated Commercial System is used by CBP to track, control, and process all imported goods. The Automated Brokers Interface allows qualified brokers, importers, carriers, port authorities, and independent service centers to electronically file required import data with Customs. Eventually, the CBP will transition cargo processing to the Automated Commercial Environment. It will become the primary, modernized system through which the U.S. government will track, control, and process all imported and exported goods.

Sources: Canada Border Services Agency, *Other Service Options*, retrieved 27 July 2017, from http://www.cbsa-asfc. gc.ca/import/services-eng.html#opt_01; International Air Transport Association, *e-AWB*, retrieved 27 July 2017, from http://www.iata.org/whatwedo/cargo/e/eawb/Pages/index.aspx; International Air Transport Association, *StB Cargo*, retrieved 27 July 2017, from http://www.iata.org/whatwedo/cargo/Pages/stb-cargo.aspx; and, U.S. Customs and Border Protection, *Automated Commercial System and the Automated Broker Interface*, retrieved 27 July 2017, from https://www.cbp.gov/trade/acs#.

Shipment Visibility Most intercontinental shipments involve three distinct moves—from origin to port of export, from port of export to port of import, and from port of import to destination. Multiple carriers and ancillary service providers are involved in the freight flows, making it difficult to maintain oversight and capture important data. Historically, this meant that global transportation managers could only estimate where their freight was located at any given time.

Fortunately, there are fewer blind spots in the international supply chain thanks to technology. It is becoming easier to track freight, accurately estimate when it will arrive, and proactively manage exceptions. There are also efforts underway to analyze historical and real-time data for greater business intelligence of freight costs and key performance indicators. Most of these technological innovations are discussed in Chapter 3, so our coverage here will be brief.

Global positioning satellite tags can be attached to freight containers for one-off tracking of shipment flows. Regular updates are provided to the customer at preprogrammed intervals on the movement and location of the container. The location messages are sent via satellite service to an Internet-connected server for viewing on a Web map. Advanced tracking devices can alert customers to changes in temperature, humidity, and light as well as the container being opened. This provides security as well as visibility.

Newer visibility tools are attempting to eliminate the cost and hassle of placing tracking devices on individual containers. Instead, they regularly feed shipment and vessel information to Web-based applications and platforms. Global transportation managers can use these big data tools to enhance visibility, boost control, and reduce costs.[25]

Both governments and industry are taking an active role in improving global freight visibility and control. The United States Federal Maritime Commission has convened a Supply Chain Innovation Team of industry experts who understand the challenges of importing and exporting goods. Their task is to identify the actionable information needed by all players for improved supply chain system visibility, reliability, and resilience.[26]

On the industry side, Maersk recently announced that it is partnering with Microsoft on technology solutions to simplify and enhance visibility through a seamless end-to-end digital experience for customers.[27] It builds upon the Maersk-Ericsson initiative to create a Connected Vessel program that provides live fleet monitoring during voyages. Using industrial Internet of Things solutions and mobile networks, Connected Vessel gives the company a higher degree of control over the entire shipping process and the ability to keep customers apprised of their freight location.[28]

Given the ongoing advances in technology, real-time global freight visibility will be widely available. The issue will become how much data is needed and how frequently updates are required to provide effective communication and decision support. Too much information can become distracting and just as much of a problem as not enough information. A healthy balance will need to be achieved.

Customs Clearance[29] When cargo reaches its destination country, it must be cleared through customs. Each country's regulations and process may be unique, so it is important to fully understand the process. Depending on the product, country of origin, and other relevant issues, the customs entry and clearance process can be complex. Figure 11-7 and the accompanying discussion provide a brief overview of the U.S. clearance process.

In the United States, the importer of record will file entry documents for the goods with the port director at the goods' port of entry. Imported goods do not legally enter the country until after the shipment has arrived within the port of entry, delivery of the merchandise has been authorized by U.S. Customs, and estimated duties have been paid. It is the importer of record's responsibility to arrange for examination and release of the goods.

Entry Filing Entering merchandise is a two-part process consisting of (1) filing the documents necessary to determine whether merchandise may be released from CBP custody, and (2) filing the documents that contain information for duty assessment and statistical purposes. To streamline the process, key documents should be filed 7 to 10 days prior to the physical arrival of the goods. These documents include the CBP entry summary, commercial invoice or pro forma invoice, packing lists, shipping documents, and related forms.

The entry must be accompanied by evidence that a bond has been posted with CBP. The customs bond is a form of insurance required by CBP to protect the Treasury in case an importer defaults on debts related to duties, taxes, and penalties that may accrue. Bonds may be posted in cash, secured through a surety company, or provided by a Customs broker.

Arrival As the goods arrive at the seaport or airport, CBP is notified of arrival and unloading. Carriers can apply for release of the goods upon arrival. If the application is approved, the shipment will be released expeditiously after it arrives at the port. This process is useful for time-sensitive products, perishable goods, and tariff quota merchandise.

Examination Following presentation of the entry documents and arrival of the shipment, it may be examined by CBP or the examination may be waived. Reasons for examining the goods and documents include determining the value of the goods for customs purposes and their dutiable status, whether the goods are properly labeled with their country of origin or other required markings, whether the shipment contains prohibited articles or illegal

FIGURE 11-7   Customs Clearance Process

Entry Filing → Arrival → Examination → Classification → Taxation → Release contraband, and whether the goods match the invoice. If no legal or regulatory violations have occurred, the clearance process continues. If problems are found, the shipment can be held pending correction, exported, or destroyed.

Classification   All goods imported into the United States are subject to duty or duty-free entry in accordance with their classification in the Harmonized Tariff Schedule (HTS) of the United States. This classification is based on the name, use, and/or the material used in the construction of a good. Related duty rates are based on product classification, quantity, and country of origin. Access to the most current HTS is available from the U.S. International Trade Commission website (hts.usitc.gov).

Taxation   A **duty** is the tax that an importer must pay in order to bring goods into the country. When goods are dutiable, ad valorem, specific, or compound, tax rates may be assessed. An ad valorem rate, the type of rate most often applied, is a percentage of the value of the merchandise. For example, a 5 percent ad valorem duty on a $50,000 shipment is $2,500.

Import duties vary by product and are driven by the commodity being imported, its declared value, its country of origin, and other factors like antidumping legislation and quota controls. Import duty values can be as low as zero for favored trading partner countries like Canada and Mexico or as high as 100 percent (or more) of the product's declared value.

Release   After the clearance requirements are completed and CBP has accepted the rate and amount of duty ascertained, the entry is considered to be liquidated. The goods can be released to the importer for onward domestic delivery of the goods.

In some situations, the importer may wish to postpone release of the goods. The goods are placed in a CBP **bonded warehouse** under a warehouse entry. The goods may remain in the bonded warehouse up to five years from the date of importation. There, under CBP supervision, the goods may be cleaned, sorted, repacked, or improved (though no manufacturing can take place). At any time during this five-year period, warehoused goods may be re-exported without paying duty, or they may be withdrawn for consumption upon paying duty at the duty rate in effect on the date of withdrawal. Perishable goods, explosive substances, or prohibited importations may not be placed in a bonded warehouse.

Another option for postponing release of goods is through the use of a **Foreign Trade Zone (FTZ)**. FTZs are sites within the United States (in or near a U.S. Customs port of entry) where foreign and domestic goods are held without time limit until they are ready to be released into international commerce. Merchandise may enter an FTZ without a formal CBP entry or the payment of customs duties or government excise taxes. If the final product is imported, duties are not paid until the goods are released into the U.S. market. Items that are processed in FTZs and then re-exported are charged no duties. While in the FTZ, goods may be assembled, repaired, tested, repackaged, cleaned, or combined with other products.

Careful consideration of these communication processes, in concert with the transaction and distribution processes, drives global transportation success.

Global transportation managers must focus on the ownership transfer, freight control, and payment issues in the transaction processes. They must also overcome the extended distance and time challenges in the distribution process activities of mode, carrier, route, and port selection. Finally, managers must negotiate communication processes to complete required documentation, create cross-chain visibility, and streamline the customs entry process. Coordinating decisions across the three major processes and making conscientious trade-offs between activities will ensure safe and timely passage of goods between countries.

SUMMARY

- Moving goods globally adds layers of complexity to transportation decision making. Extensive planning and execution efforts are needed to overcome longer and more variable transit time, risk of in-transit product damage or loss, higher delivery expenses, and greater in-transit inventory carrying costs.

- Three primary transaction processes must be addressed before moving cargo: choosing the terms of trade, securing freight insurance, and agreeing upon the terms of payment.

- Proper choice from among the 11 Incoterms should be based on the relative expertise of the exporter and importer to effectively manage transportation responsibilities, control, and risk.

- Importers and exporters are exposed to unique financial risks and countless perils when their freight moves through the global supply chain. Hence, cargo insurance is an essential risk mitigation tool.

- Letters of credit and other payment tools can be used to balance the exporter's risk of nonpayment with the importer's risk of product problems and fraud.

- Global mode selection involves the analysis of accessibility, capacity, transit time, reliability, safety, and cost. Often, only one or two of the five modes are realistic options, given the product and shipment characteristics.

- Ocean carriers have a huge role in global transport, moving both containerized finished goods and bulk materials.

- International air cargo transportation is a critical mode for time-sensitive, high-value freight.

- Intermodal transportation—the use of two or more modes of transportation in moving a shipment from origin to destination—is widely used to improve accessibility and cost efficiency of global transport.

- Carrier selection is based on a variety of shipment criteria and carrier capabilities: geographic coverage, transit time average and reliability, equipment availability and capacity, product protection, and freight rates.

- Route planning for global shipments is important as it affects transportation cost, product availability, and cargo security.

- Global transportation may subject freight to a variety of damage risks. It is critical to protect products as they are packed in shipping cartons and to protect the cartons when they are loaded in the shipping container.

- Seaports and airports are critical links in the global supply chain, providing the infrastructure, equipment, and labor needed to efficiently load, unload, and transfer freight.

- A variety of ancillary service providers—international freight forwarders, NVOCCs, and export packers—help exporters and importers move international freight quickly and efficiently.

- Four types of documentation are used to control global cargo and comply with government requirements: invoices, export documents, import documents, and transportation documents.

- When cargo reaches the destination country, it must receive government approval to enter the country and travel to the final destination. Customs clearance involves entry, arrival, examination, classification, taxation, and release.

STUDY QUESTIONS

1. Why is global transportation such an important issue in supply chain success?
2. What is the role of trade terms in global transportation? Briefly describe the four groups of Incoterms.
3. What risks and perils are present in global transportation? Discuss how exporters and importers can manage these risks.
4. What payment options are available for international transactions? How does each option protect the interests of the exporter and the importer?
5. What factors impact mode selection for global transportation?
6. Why would companies use ocean transportation versus air freight service to move international freight?
7. How are air cargo rates calculated? Calculate the cost of international air transportation for the following shipment: 200 cartons of fine jewelry weighing a total of 2,500 pounds. The carton dimensions are 18 inches by 12 inches by 12 inches (L × W × H). The freight rate is $10.25 per pound.
8. What are the benefits and drawbacks of intermodal transportation for international freight?
9. What combination of intermodal services would be most beneficial for the following products?
   a. Lumber moving from British Columbia, Canada, to London, England
   b. Seedless grapes moving from Valparaiso, Chile, to Phoenix, Arizona
   c. iPhones moving from Zhengzhou, China, to Johannesburg, South Africa
10. When developing transportation routes for global freight, what considerations should influence the decision maker?
11. If you need to move two TEUs of Adidas footwear from the factory in Vung Tau, Vietnam to the European distribution center in Antwerp, Belgium, what route options should be considered? Which would you choose?
12. What value do ancillary service providers bring to global transportation execution? Discuss the roles of
    a. International freight forwarders
    b. NVOCCs
    c. Export packers
13. Why is documentation important to global transportation? Briefly describe the primary documents used to facilitate global cargo flows.
14. Identify and briefly describe the six steps involved in the CBP customs clearance process. What can individual companies do to streamline this process?

NOTES

1. World Trade Organization, *World Trade Statistics Review 2017*, 15 May 2017, retrieved 1 August 2017, from https://www.wto.org/english/res_e/statis_e/wts2017_e/wts17_toc_e.htm.

2. Donald. F. Wood, Anthony Barone, Paul Murphy, and Daniel Wardlow, *International Logistics*, 2nd ed., New York, NY: AMACOM, 2002.

3. International Chamber of Commerce, *Incoterms Rules*, retrieved 25 July 2017, from https://iccwbo.org/resources-for-business/incoterms-rules/.

4. Export.Gov, *What Are Incoterms?* retrieved 25 July 2017, from https://www.export.gov/article?id=What-are-Incoterms.

5. Chubb, *Ocean Cargo Incoterms and Insurance*, retrieved 8 August 2017, from https://www2.chubb.com/us-en/business-insurance/ocean-cargo-incoterms-insurance.aspx.

6. Legal Information Institute, *Chapter 28-Carriage of Goods by Sea: Rights and Immunities of Carrier and Ship*, retrieved 25 July 2017, from https://www.law.cornell.edu/uscode/html/uscode46a/usc_sec_46a_00001304----000-.html.

7. International Air Transport Association, *News Brief: Cargo Liability Limited Standardized—Major Step Forward to Simplify Air Cargo*, retrieved 25 July 2017, from http://www.iata.org/pressroom/pr/pages/2010-07-14-01.aspx.

8. International Monetary Fund, *SDR Valuation*, retrieved 25 July 2017, from http://www.imf.org/external/np/fin/data/rms_sdrv.aspx.

9. Pierre David, *International Logistics: The Management of International Trade Operations*, 4e, Berea, OH: Cicero Books LLC, 2013.

10. A detailed discussion of international freight insurance can be found in Pierre David, *International Logistics: The Management of International Trade Operations*, 4e, Berea, OH: Cicero Books LLC, 2013.

11. Export.Gov, *1-Methods of Payment*, retrieved 25 July 2017, from https://www.export.gov/article?id=How-to-Get-Paid.

12. Ibid.

13. Chiquita Brands International, *The Great White Fleet Story*, retrieved 26 July 2017, from http://www.greatwhitefleet.com/#/Page/201.

14. Equasis Statistics, *The World Fleet 2015*, retrieved 26 July 2017, from http://www.equasis.org/EquasisWeb/public/PublicStatistic?fs=HomePage.

15. Maersk Line, "Freight Shipping Rates and Container Costs," retrieved 10 December 2014, from http://www.maerskline.com/en-ug/shipping-services/rates-and-pricing.

16. International Air Transport Association, *TACT*, retrieved 26 July 2017, from http://www.iata.org/publications/Pages/air-cargo-tariff.aspx.

17. World Shipping Council, About the Industry, 2017, retrieved 27 July 2017 from http://www.worldshipping.org/about-the-industry.

18. Mary J. Meixell and Mario Norbis, "A Review of the Transportation Mode Choice and Carrier Selection Literature," *International Journal of Logistics Management*, Vol. 19, No. 2, 2008: pp. 183–211.

19. John Gardiner, Ian Humphreys, and Stephen Ison, "Freight Operators Choice of Airports: A Three-Stage Process," *Transport Reviews*, Vol. 25, No. 1, January 2005: pp. 85–102.

20. U.S. Census Bureau, *The Correct Way to Complete the SED*, retrieved 27 July 2017, from https://www.census.gov/foreign-trade/schedules/b/2011/correctwayforb.pdf.

21. Logistics Glossary, *Manifest*, retrieved 27 July 2017, from http://www.logisticsglossary.com/term/manifest/.

22. European Union, *The Entry Summary Declaration*, retrieved 27 July 2017, from http://ec.europa.eu/ecip/documents/procedures/entry_summary_declaration_en.pdf.

23. Export.gov, *Common Export Documents*, retrieved 27 July 2017, from http://2016.export.gov/logistics/eg_main_018121.asp.

24. International Air Transport Association, *e-freight Fundamentals*, retrieved 27 July 2017, from http://www.iata.org/whatwedo/cargo/e/efreight/Documents/e-freight-fundamentals.pdf.

25. Will Waters, "DHL Launches New Sea Freight Visibility Tool," Lloyd's Loading List, 12 June 2017, retrieved 6 August 2017, from http://www.lloydsloadinglist.com/freight-directory/news/DHL-launches-new-sea-freight-visibility-tool/69518.htm#.WYcz06JWLHE.

26. Patrick Burnson, "Export Phase of Supply Chain System Information Initiative Launched by FMC," *Logistics Management*, 12 July 2017, retrieved 6 August 2017, from http://www.logisticsmgmt.com/article/export_phase_of_supply_chain_system_information_initiative_launched_by_fmc.

27. Patrick Burnson, "Maersk Deal with Microsoft Brings More Digitization to Global Supply Chain," *Logistics Management*, 1 May 2017, retrieved 6 August 2017, from http://www.logisticsmgmt.com/article/maersk_deal_with_microsoft_brings_more_digitization_to_global_supply_chain/transportation.

28. Phillip Tracy, "Ericsson and Maersk Create Floating Networks," *RCR Wireless News*, 27 July 2016, retrieved 6 August 2017, from http://www.rcrwireless.com/20160727/internet-of-things/ericsson-maersk-industrial-internet-of-things-tag31-tag99.

29. This section is based upon materials U.S. Customs and Border Protection, *Importing into the United States*, retrieved 27 July 2017, from https://www.cbp.gov/document/publications/importing-united-states.

CASE 11-1

3D Printers for the Masses

Bobby Cook is trying to capture the attention of Black Friday shoppers for OptiShop, a discount chain with 1,500 stores in Canada and the United States. Bobby wants to offer a tabletop 3D printer at a price point of $299 that rivals more expensive options from Dell and Flashforge. He believes that it will be possible to sell 150,000 units during the holiday season and 15,000 units per month over the subsequent 12 months.

After much effort to ensure feasibility of the initiative, evaluate product quality, and compare supplier capabilities, Bobby has narrowed his focus to three options. Each supplier offers a reasonably priced, high-quality home 3D printer that meets OptiShop specifications. However, each supplier is in a different country, which gives Bobby some concerns about delivery costs, risks, and foreign exchange rate exposure. Highlights of each proposal are provided below.

Option 1—purchase printers from Takena Electronics in Nagano, Japan, a longtime supplier of products to OptiShop. Takena works on an open account basis and promises to make shipments of 2,500 units in 40-foot containers under terms Incoterm DAP, Port of Long Beach. The price offered per unit is 19,000 JPY (Japanese Yen).

Option 2—purchase the printers from TriTex Industries, a Kuala Lumpur, Malaysia-based manufacturer. TriTex has a solid reputation and Bobby nearly purchased virtual reality goggles from them last year. Their offer is based on 1,300 units shipments in 20-foot containers under Incoterm FOB, Port of Tanjung Pelepas. The price offered is 727 MYR (Malaysian Ringgit) using Letter of Credit payments.

Option 3—purchase the printers from Luca Enterprises, an electronics distributor in Bucharest, Romania. Luca sources printers from contract manufacturers in Eastern Europe. Their offer is based on OptiShop taking control of the product at the Luca distribution center under Incoterm EXW. The price offered is 625 RON (Romanian Leu), cash in advance.

As Bobby considered his options, he consulted an online currency converter to evaluate the quotes. He found the following exchange rates:
1 USD = 110.20 JPY 1 USD = 64.12 MYR 1 USD = 3.86 RON

CASE QUESTIONS

1. What is the price per 3D printer in USD for the Takena Electronics offer? What costs, responsibilities, and risks does OptiShop assume under DAP, Port of Long Beach?
2. What is the price per 3D printer in USD for the TriTex Industries offer? What costs, responsibilities, and risks does OptiShop assume under FOB, Port of Tanjung Pelepas?
3. What is the price per 3D printer in USD for the Luca Enterprises offer? What costs, responsibilities, and risks does OptiShop assume under EXW, Bucharest?
4. What other issues and transportation costs must Bobby consider to make an effective supplier selection?
5. Which of the three options would you recommend? Why?

CASE 11-2

As the Blade Turns

Revolving Wings (RW) is a Kalamazoo, Michigan, manufacturer of equipment for the renewable energy sector. The company has a strong domestic market for their fiberglass composite wind turbine blades. Still, RW has some excess plant capacity and is investigating opportunities to enter the export market. Demand for turbine blades is strong in India, where there is a strong commitment to renewable energy, but a shortage of critical parts to meet the growing need for power generating capacity.

During its annual executive retreat, exporting is a major topic of discussion. After a presentation by the business development team and a similar evaluation by an industry analyst, RW's CEO sees the light. He quickly becomes a strong proponent of selling wind turbine blades to a power company near Bangalore, India. "Now all we have to do is figure out how to get the blades there quickly and without damage," says the CEO. "Thomas, get your team on this one. I want some solid answers."

Thomas Shelby, RW's transportation director, knows this is a big opportunity for the company but it comes with tremendous challenges. Picking the right mode, finding ports that can handle the blades safely, and routing the freight are just a few of the issues that keep Shelby awake the night after the CEO tagged him to lead the "export to India" project.

At his next staff meeting, Shelby reminds his team: "These blades can be up to 68 feet long and weigh 6 tons. We have to first get them from the plant to the point of export. That's not easy, since we need to plan routes to avoid urban rush hours, sharp curves, narrow roads, and weight-limited bridges."

"On top of those usual challenges, we have to find a high-quality international carrier to get the blades to India," Shelby adds. "And don't forget the port challenges and final delivery to Bangalore."

Turning to you, Shelby says: "We need a plan of action for the CEO by Friday. Don't mess this up, our company's fortunes are riding on this export program."

CASE QUESTIONS

1. What are the major problems and pitfalls that RW faces as it tries to go global with its product line?
2. What mode(s) of transportation would you recommend to Shelby as most appropriate for moving the turbine blades domestically and internationally?
3. How would you route shipments of turbine blades from Kalamazoo to Bangalore? Why?
4. What role will ports play in the flow of turbine blades from the United States to India?

12

GOVERNMENTAL ROLES IN TRANSPORTATION

Learning Objectives

After reading this chapter, you should be able to do the following:

> Recognize the links among national transportation policy, transportation regulation, and public promotion of transportation

> Understand the role and importance of national transportation policy

> Articulate the basis for the regulation of transportation in the United States

> Appreciate the regulatory roles of federal and state agencies and the courts

> Discuss the different types of transportation regulation

> Obtain a knowledge of past and current regulations affecting transportation

> Identify and assess the roles of public promotion in transportation

> Appreciate the role of user charges in funding transportation initiatives

TRANSPORTATION **PROFILE**

Late Push to Extend ELD Implementation Date Nixed by House Vote

A late push for a legislative delay for implementing the electronic logging device (ELD) mandate for motor carriers, which is set to take effect on December 18, was turned down by the U.S. House of Representatives this week.

This stemmed from a proposal by Rep. Brian Babin (R-Texas) that was part of a Fiscal Year 2018 funding bill and called for more time for motor carriers to be in compliance with the ELD mandate. Specifically, Babin requested that no funds issued to the DOT would be used to implement or enforce the ELD mandate until September 30, 2018.

The **Federal Motor Carrier Safety Administration** (FMCSA) formally announced in late 2016 that the federal mandate for electronic logging devices (ELD) for commercial motor carriers was official and would take effect in December 2017, basically confirming the inevitable in some ways within the freight transportation and logistics sectors. The objective of the rule, according to FMCSA, is to strengthen commercial truck and bus drivers' compliance with hours-of-service (HOS) regulations that combat fatigue. The rule will take full effect on December 10, 2017, two years after the date of the final rule being issued. ELDs automatically record driving time and monitor engine hours, vehicle movement, miles driven, and location information.

Many trucking observers maintain that the need for ELDs is obvious, with most explaining that the industry has been reliant on paper logs for far too long. And there could likely be economic benefits through ELD usage, as observers say it could likely reduce the effective number of miles a driver could log, further tightening trucking capacity at a time of ongoing limited truck driver supply, rising pay, and higher overall fleet costs.

Earlier this summer, Rep. Babin, who is a member of the House Transportation and Infrastructure Committee and the Highways and Transit Subcommittee, proposed legislation calling for the ELD implementation to be delayed for two more years, as opposed to the scheduled 2017 ELD mandate that takes effect on December 18.

"While technology like ELD's have great promise, I didn't come to Washington to force those ideas on small businesses—and neither did President Trump,' said Rep. Babin in late July. "If trucking companies want to continue implementing and using ELD's, they should go right ahead. But for those who don't want the burden, expense and uncertainty of putting one of these devices into every truck they own by the end of the year, we can and should offer relief."

Babin added at the time that even though the ELD mandate was crafted with the good intention of modernizing America's freight truck network, as well as helping truckers comply with Hours-of-Service and other regulations, it is "abundantly clear" more time is needed, especially for small trucking companies and independent drivers that will be affected by the cost of compliance with the ELD mandate.

The American Trucking Associations (ATA) applauded the House's 246–173 vote to not move forward with an ELD implementation date being delayed.

"ATA has supported, and will support, this important regulation," said ATA President and CEO Chris Spear. "Congress has now voted a fourth time to move forward with electronic logging of the existing hours of service information required for decades. Make no mistake, the time for debate about electronic logging is over, and we're pleased that Congress has rejected this ill-conceived effort to delay their implementation. For a decade, the Federal Motor Carrier Safety Administration has repeatedly spoken, the Courts have spoken, law enforcement has spoken, the industry has spoken' and Congress has spoken in favor of the benefits of electronic logging devices," he said, "all the while, opponents of electronic logging have delayed, dissembled and deceived about this technology. Tonight's vote should end what is left of this debate so our industry can carry on with the business of complying with this regulation."

And FMCSA Deputy Administrator Daphne Jefferson wrote in a letter to Bill Sullivan, Executive Vice President Advocacy, FMCSA supports the ATA's support of the ELD mandate.

Jefferson added that based on FMCSA research, it is estimated that ELDs will eliminate 1,844 crashes and save 26 lives and 562 injuries annually, coupled with an estimated $2.4 billion in paperwork savings through ELD usage. "ELDs will improve the accuracy of HOS logs, improve compliance, reduce falsification that occurs with paper log books, and reduce crashes," wrote Jefferson. "Any delay in implementation will diminish rather than enhance highway safety."

Stifel analyst John Larkin said that the House vote makes ELDs that much more of a certainty in the trucking sector, adding that it will have the semblance of a net capacity reduction somewhere between 2% and 5%, if not more.

"A lot of it depends on the extent to which the rule is enforced by the police, insurance companies, shippers or brokers," he said. "There is a lot of cheating that goes on to the extent that if drivers caught cheating are eliminated by this mandate it will have a net effect of reducing capacity."

Source: Jeff Berman, *Logistics Management*, September 7, 2017, http://www.logisticsmgmt.com/article/late_push_to_extend_eld_implementation_date_nixed_by_house_vote. Reprinted with permission of Peerless Media, LLC.

Introduction

Transportation has long been a critical component of world economies. From the development of the Egyptian empire because of the Nile River to the expansion of the U.S. economy because of the Interstate Highway System, transportation has allowed civilizations to expand through domestic and global trade. Because of its impact on a nation's economy, many countries have developed policies and regulations for transportation to assure a safe, reliable, and fair transportation network for their citizens.

When the United States was an agricultural society, it relied on wagons and railroads to move products from points of surplus to points of demand. As the United States evolved into a manufacturing economy, it utilized railroads, motor carriers, water carriers, pipelines, and air carriers to create time and place utilities. While the United States has evolved into a service-based society, it continues to rely heavily on transportation to add product value and accessibility.

Throughout history, the United States has attempted to create policies and establish regulations, at both the state and federal levels, to ensure that the transportation activities are conducted in a sound manner. The Transportation Profile highlights a regulatory effort to ensure the safety of the traveling public and compliance with existing hours of service regulations. As the Profile reveals, there are many stakeholders in the regulatory development process who may not always share the same goals. That often leads to extensive debate and enforcement delays.

Despite these challenges, the boundary-spanning nature of transportation and its multiple constituents demand that the U.S. government and its regulatory agencies develop a fair and equitable transportation network for all parties. This is an ongoing challenge for the transportation agencies that must balance the interests of freight carriers, shippers, industry groups, and citizens.

This chapter will examine the ongoing involvement of government in freight transportation. The vital role of transportation policy is discussed, followed by the key aspects of transportation regulation, and the need for public promotion. Figure 12-1 highlights the important links between these elements. Throughout the chapter, you will learn that governmental oversight and investment are necessary facilitators of a vibrant transportation network and a strong economy.

Transportation Policy

Policy is defined as the declared objectives that a government or party seeks to achieve and preserve in the interest of national community.[1] Given the major effects that transportation has on the nation's collective interests—economic development, public safety, mobility, and national defense—federal and state governments cannot take a hands-off approach. They must develop policies that mold the transportation system into an efficient and effective network. These policies must also strive to protect and promote the different modes of transportation to create a fair and competitive marketplace for freight services.

Currently, there is no single, unified federal transportation policy statement that can be downloaded from a government website. Various attempts have been made to establish an explicit statement of national transportation policy, but the last significant efforts occurred more than 20 years ago. In 1990, Secretary of Transportation Samuel Skinner and the **Department of Transportation** (DOT), produced a national transportation policy that focused on creating a system to meet the needs of the 21st century. The document states:

> To ensure the continued vitality of our Nation, we all must participate in making the investments today that will spur productivity and allow transportation to be an engine of tomorrow's growth and prosperity. We need to focus our investment dollars on the areas with highest payback, and we need to take full advantage of new and emerging transportation technologies. At the same time, we must ensure that transportation supports the interests of safety, national security, conservation of energy, and environmental quality.

FIGURE 12-1	Government Engagement in Transportation

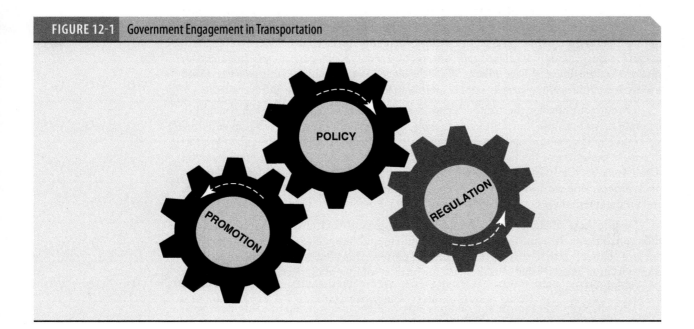

"The directions for national transportation policy are captured under six major themes:

- Maintain and expand the Nation's transportation system

- Foster a sound financial base for transportation

- Keep the transportation industry strong and competitive

- Ensure that the transportation system supports public safety and national security

- Protect the environment and the quality of life

- Advance U.S. transportation technology and expertise."[2]

Five years later, the **Interstate Commerce Commission Termination Act** (ICCTA) of 1995 included statements of national transportation policy. Congress made these statements to provide direction to the newly created Surface Transportation Board (STB) in administering transportation regulation over railroads, motor carriers, water carriers, and pipelines. It focused on issues of preserving the inherent advantages of each mode, promoting safe and efficient transportation, keeping rates reasonable, encouraging fair wages and working conditions in the transportation industry, and fostering federal–state cooperation in transportation matters.[3]

In reality, much of the national transportation policy is implicit. It exists through various federal and state laws, regulatory agency rulings, and funding programs. Key policy developments and financial support are generated by the executive branch and Congress. Additionally, federal agencies and congressional committees shape transportation policy. Independent regulatory agencies interpret transportation law, establish operating rules, and set policy. Lastly, the Justice Department interprets statutes involving transportation and reconciles differences between carriers, shippers, and the public.

This section examines how national transportation policy, both explicit and implicit, shapes the U.S. transportation system. Although the objectives and plans are constantly evolving, there are major underpinnings upon which a national transportation policy is built.

Why Do We Need a Transportation Policy?

A good starting point of a national transportation policy review is the consideration of our need for such a policy. The answer lies in the significance of transportation to the very life of the country. Transportation permeates every aspect of a community and touches the life of every citizen. The transportation system ties together spatially separated communities of a country, making possible the movement of people, goods, and services. These physical connections also build societal cohesion.

In addition, transportation is fundamental to U.S. economic activity. Transportation supports the exchange of goods that are mass-produced in one location to locations deficient in these goods. The secondary benefits of economic activity—jobs, improved goods and services, and so on—would not be enjoyed by citizens without a sufficient transportation system that is built upon a logical set of policies.

An efficient transportation system is also fundamental to national defense. In times of emergencies, people and materials must be deployed quickly to various trouble spots within the United States or throughout the world to protect American interests. This rapid responsiveness reduces the amount of military equipment that must be staged around the world and consumes fewer resources.

Many of our transportation facilities could not be developed by private enterprise. For example, the capital required to build a transcontinental highway is beyond the resources of the private sector. Efficient rail and highway routes require government assistance in securing land from private owners; if the government did not assert its power of eminent domain, routes would be quite circuitous and inefficient. Furthermore, public ownership, operation, and maintenance of transportation infrastructure, such as highways or waterways, are necessary to ensure access to all who desire to use the system.

Another purpose of transportation policy is to direct resources toward specific needs. Transportation policy provides guidelines to the many agencies that exercise transportation decision-making powers and to Congress, the president, and the courts that make and interpret the laws affecting transportation. Thus, transportation policy provides the framework for the allocation of resources.

In sum, establishing and executing a national transportation policy is a necessary and important responsibility. Given the need to address diverse stakeholder interests and balance environmental, energy, economic, and social requirements, national transportation policy is also challenging and ever evolving.

Who Establishes Policy?

National transportation policies are developed at various levels of government and by many different agencies. The specifics of a particular policy might reflect the persuasion of a group of individuals (for example, a consumer group) or of a single individual (for example, an elected official). The purpose of this section is to examine the basic institutional framework that aids in the development of national transportation policy.

Executive Branch Many departments within the executive branch of government drive transportation policy. Leading these departments is the office of the president. The president has authority over international air transportation and foreign air carriers operating in the United States. The president also appoints individuals to lead the various agencies that influence transportation and to lead two independent federal agencies—the STB and the Federal Maritime Commission (FMC).

The Department of State is directly involved in developing policy regarding international transportation by air and water. The policies and programs designed to encourage foreign visitors to the United States are implemented by the U.S. Travel Service. The Maritime Administration (MARAD) is involved with ocean (international) transportation policy. It determines ship requirements, service, and routes essential to foreign commerce. In addition, international transportation policies and programs are shaped by the U.S. Transportation Command—the single manager of America's global defense transportation system.

At the domestic level, the U.S. Postal Service (USPS) contracts with carriers for transportation of the mail; such contracts have been used to promote air transportation as well as motor and rail transportation. The Army Corps of Engineers is responsible for constructing and maintaining rivers, harbors, locks, and dams for the protection of navigable waterways. The Department of Energy (DOE) develops policies regarding energy availability and distribution.

The DOT, however, is the most pervasive influencer of transportation policy at the domestic level. The centralization of federal transportation activities under the auspices of this department in the executive branch highlights the critical nature of transportation in the economy. The DOT was established in 1966 by an act of Congress. Its mission is to: "Serve the United States by ensuring a fast, safe, efficient, accessible and convenient transportation system that meets our vital national interests and enhances the quality of life of the American people, today and into the future."[4]

As indicated in Figure 12-2, the DOT consists of 10 operating administrations whose activities and programs are mode focused. A description of each operating administration's roles is found at www.transportation.gov/administrations. The DOT also operates the Bureau of Transportation Statistics and the Research and Innovative Technology Administration.

The Secretary of Transportation is responsible for the overall planning, direction, and control of DOT activities but does not exercise direct operating control over the administrations. Rather, the secretary's office is concerned with policy development, resource allocation, program evaluation, agency coordination, and intermodal matters. The secretary also serves as the principal advisor to the president on matters relating to federal transportation.

Congressional Committees   The laws formulated by Congress are the formal method by which Congress influences national transportation. The congressional committee structure is the forum in which Congress develops policies, programs, and funding for transportation.

Within the Senate, two committees influence transportation. The Committee on Commerce, Science, and Transportation deals with surface and air transportation issues through two subcommittees. The Subcommittee on Surface Transportation and Merchant

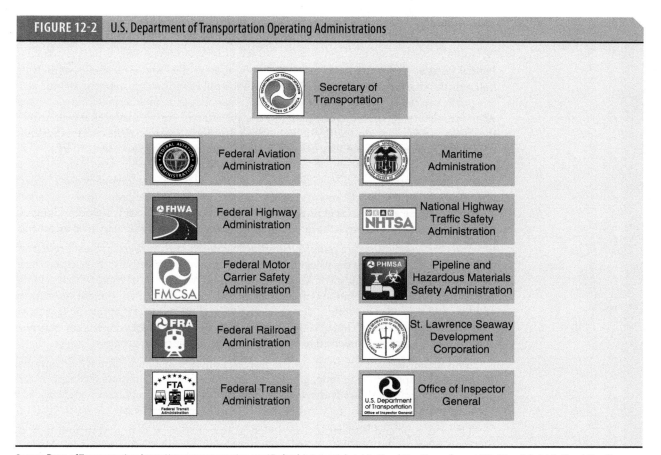

FIGURE 12-2   U.S. Department of Transportation Operating Administrations

Source: Dept. of Transportation: https://www.transportation.gov/ Federal Aviation Administration: https://www.faa.gov/ Maritime Administration: https://www.marad.dot.gov/ Federal Highway Administration: https://www.fhwa.dot.gov/ National Highway Traffic Safety Administration: https://www.nhtsa.gov/ Federal Motor Carrier Safety Administration: https://www.fmcsa.dot.gov/ Pipeline and Hazardous Materials Safety Administration: https://www.phmsa.dot.gov/ Federal Railroad Administration: https://www.fra.dot.gov/ Saint Lawrence Seaway Development Corporation: https://www.seaway.dot.gov/ Federal Transit Administration: https://www.transit.dot.gov/ Office of Inspector General: https://oig.hhs.gov/

Marine Infrastructure, Safety, and Security handles motor carrier, rail, marine, and bus issues. The Aviation Operations, Safety, and Security Subcommittee focuses on air traffic congestion, aviation safety, the Federal Aviation Administration (FAA), and the National Transportation Safety Board (NTSB). The Senate's Committee on Environment and Public Works deals with internal waterway and harbor projects, highway construction and maintenance projects, and air and water pollution regulations.

The House of Representatives has restructured its committees regarding transportation into two groups. The Transportation and Infrastructure Committee is concerned with the FAA, rail infrastructure projects, the STB, pipeline safety, hazardous material transportation, the NTSB, and the U.S. Coast Guard (USCG). The Energy and Commerce Committee has primary responsibility for interstate and foreign commerce.

In addition to the above committees, numerous other congressional committees have an impact on transportation. Federal funding can be decided in the Appropriations Committee, Senate Banking Committee, Housing and Urban Affairs Committee, House Ways and Means Committee, or the Senate Finance Committee.

Regulatory Agencies The STB and FMC are independent agencies charged with implementing the laws regulating transportation. The agencies have quasi-judicial, quasi-executive, and quasi-legislative powers. They can establish policy when they interpret law, can decide on cases (such as the reasonableness of rates), and can enforce their decisions with the help of the court system.

Judicial System The courts have been called upon to interpret laws or reconcile conflicts. In doing so, the courts have an impact on transportation policies. Carriers, shippers, and the general public can call upon the courts to change existing policy through interpretation of statutes. As the regulatory agencies exercise their powers, the affected parties may seek recourse from the courts to determine the legality of the agency's decisions. The role of the courts is basically to interpret the meaning of policy as stated in laws, regulations, and executive orders.

Industry Associations An often-overlooked facet of national transportation policy development is the role of industry associations in shaping national, state, and local promotion, regulation, and policy. These associations exist in most industries and their focus is to lobby Congress and other influential groups in the government to take actions that will help their members.

Industry associations are nonprofit entities that derive their powers and resources from member firms. They act on the priorities given to them by their members. In transportation, the railroads in the Association of American Railroads (AAR) and the motor carriers in the American Trucking Associations often meet to resolve matters of equipment uniformity and loss and damage prevention. On the policy side, these associations pursue legislative and administrative ruling concepts that favor their collective memberships. They may also oppose policies that are perceived to be harmful to their respective groups.

Two major associations exist for the interests of large shippers. One is the National Industrial Transportation League, and the other is the National Shippers Strategic Transportation Council. Both are active before congressional bodies, regulatory agencies, and carrier groups.

Other groups and associations are involved in transportation policy, including non-transportation special-interest groups such as labor unions and safety coalitions. Various government agencies, including the Department of Agriculture and the Department of Defense, influence existing and proposed transportation legislation on their behalf, or on the behalf of their stakeholders.

The ongoing fight over the proposed use of twin 33-foot truck trailers nationwide is a notable transportation policy battle between multiple industry stakeholders. This policy saga is discussed in the On the Line feature.

ON THE **LINE**

The Fight Over Five Feet

For years, a transportation policy debate over five feet has raged on. The issue? Allowing trucking companies to change their fleets from twin 28-foot trailers to twin 33-foot trailers.

Proponents of twin 33s contend that the change will lead to greater productivity, greater safety, less highway congestion, less wear and tear on the nation's aging infrastructure, and carrier cost savings. The lobbying group Americans for Modern Transportation (AMT), strongly supports twin 33s. Key members of AMT include: Amazon, the National Shippers Strategic Transportation Council (NASSTRAC), and less-than-truckload carriers FedEx, UPS, and YRC.

Gail Rutkowski, NASSTRAC's executive director, notes that allowing advanced trucking equipment like twin 33s is a straightforward way to reduce the industry's impact on the environment and society. According to data from the Coalition for Efficient and Responsible Transportation (CERT), full deployment of twin 33s on the national highway network will result in 6.6 million fewer truck trips and 1.3 billion miles traveled. Expected outcomes of such reductions include: lowering carbon emissions by 4.4 billion pounds and saving 204 million gallons of fuel each year.

Adding five feet to each trailer will not compromise the condition or safety of our nation's highways, according to twin 33s proponents. AMT and CERT estimate that twin 33s will eliminate 912 crashes over the course of a year.

"There was an argument on the other side last time that twin 33s are unsafe, that is a myth," said UPS Freight President Rich McArdle during an industry conference. "We have run them millions of miles in the state of Florida and did not have a single recorded accident so we believe them to be safer."

Given these outcomes, who would oppose twin 33s? The answer is those who will not benefit from twin 33s. Unlike less-than-truckload carriers and small packages carriers, truckload carriers typically use 53-foot single trailers and have no operational need for twin 33s. Without any obvious financial benefits to glean, the truckload carriers view the lobbying effort for twin 33s to be a waste of valuable political capital.

Truck size and weight is also a volatile transportation policy issue. Any proposed change in truck configurations generates opposition from safety groups that oppose longer combination vehicles and from railroads that have built intermodal railcars to handle 28- and 53-foot trailers. The railroads and their allies argue that they will be forced to develop new equipment to handle 33-foot trailers. Hence, a change would disrupt existing standards and force undue costs on intermodal transport for minimal gains.

How will the fight over five feet end? With powerful interests taking both sides on this ongoing transportation policy debate, only time will tell if we eventually will see twin 33s on U.S. highways.

Sources: Jeff Berman, "FTR Report Makes the Case for Twin 33-Foot Trailers in the LTL Sector," *Logistics Management*, June 22, 2017. Retrieved September 15, 2017, from http://www.logisticsmgmt.com/article/ftr_report_makes_the_case_for_twin_33_foot_trailers_in_the_ltl_sector; John Schulz, "Fedex"s Smith Again Leads Push for Twin 33s, Truckload Carriers Again Push Back," *Logistics Management*, February 20, 2017. Retrieved September 15, 2017, from http://www.logisticsmgmt.com/article/fedexs_smith_again_leads_push_for_twin_33s_truckload_carriers_again_push_ba; Gail Rutkowski, "A New Effort to Modernize America"s Transportation System," *NASSTRAC Fast Lane*, November 30, 2016. Retrieved September 15, 2017, from http://www.nasstrac.org/blogpost/1307595/263457/A-New-Effort-to-Modernize-America-s-Transportation-System.

In sum, national transportation policy is very important, though it is neither definitive nor easy to coordinate. Many policy declarations are vague, providing only general guidance about the issues and factors that should be considered in transportation decision making. Also, policy statements created at various times by different authorities reflect inconsistent goals and contain conflicting provisions. Finally, stakeholder groups often attempt to steer policy toward their vested interests rather than the common good.

Given these challenges, it is easy to see how transportation policy conflicts and confusion can occur. To rectify these problems and carry out transportation policies, regulatory action may be necessary.

Transportation Regulation

Regulations, by definition, are rules or directives made and maintained by an authority.[5] Laws are rules based on and meant to carry out a specific piece of legislation and typically enforced by a regulatory agency.[6] As transportation is a complex industry that is vital to the economic and social well-being of the United States, the government uses regulations and laws to ensure that transportation activities are conducted in a sound manner. Their intention is to promote transportation competition, safety, security, trust, and environmental protection.

Regulation may seem inconsistent with the U.S. free-market economy that relies on competition and private enterprise. However, the existence of pure competition and free markets involves several conditions that might not exist in reality. Products are justified only by the market's willingness to buy them. A product should not be sold at a price below the marginal cost of making the last unit. The free-market theory also assumes that producers and consumers can readily assess whether or not a given economic act will provide them with a positive return.

Although pure competition conceptually provides a marketplace that is desirable to consumers, a monopoly does not. In a monopoly, only one seller exists and can control the price of each individual unit of output. Consumers have no opportunity to switch suppliers.

If market structures took the form of either pure competition or monopoly, the case for regulation would be obvious. A valid case can be made for little to no regulation in an economy characterized by pure competition. In contrast, heavy regulation of a monopolistic economy could be justified. However, reality is not that clear cut. Market structures usually fall between the extremes of pure competition and monopoly.

The imperfections in the marketplace in a free-enterprise economy provide the rationale for government intervention. The controls exercised by the government can take one of several forms. One form is that of maintaining or enforcing competition—for example, the transportation antitrust laws set forth by the government. Second, the government can substitute economic regulation for competition, as it has historically done in the transportation industry. Third, the government can assume ownership and direct control, as it has done with the U.S. Post Office.

The basic challenge of regulation in our society is to create and maintain conditions that allow economical use of resources by private enterprise. Regulators should pursue a competitive framework that relies on competitive forces whenever possible. This section addresses the key facets of U.S. transportation regulation—the basis of regulation, the parties responsible for regulation, the focus of regulation, and a concise historical timeline.

Basis of Regulation

The legal system in the United States is based upon a combination of common law and civil or statutory law. Each law has played a critical role in the development of national and state transportation regulation.

Common law is a primary basis of regulation in most English-speaking countries because it was developed in England. Common law relies on judicial precedent or principles of law developed from former court decisions. When a court decision establishes a rule for a situation, then that rule becomes part of the law. As conditions change, the law sometimes needs further interpretation. Therefore, an important feature of the common law system is that it changes and evolves as society changes.[7]

The common law approach fits well with a free-market economy because the individual is the focus of attention and can engage in any business that is not prohibited. Each individual is regarded as possessing equal power and responsibility before the law.[8]

The early regulation of transportation developed under common law. The obvious connection is with the concept of *common carriage*, in which transportation providers were required to serve all shippers and charge reasonable rates without discrimination.

Statutory law or civil law is based upon the Roman legal system and is characteristic of continental Europe and the parts of the world colonized by European countries. Statutory law is enacted by legislative bodies, but it is a specific enactment. A large part of the laws pertaining to business in general and to transportation are based upon statutory law. However, two points are important to note in this regard. First, common law rules are still very important in the transportation industry because many statutes were, in effect, copied from common law principles. Second, statutes are usually general in nature and need to be interpreted by the courts. Thus, in the United States, there is a very close relationship between common law and statutory law.

Transportation regulation in the United States began at the state level under the common law system when many important regulations, as well as the basic issue of whether a business could even be regulated at all, were developed. In the latter regard, a concept of "business affected with the public interest" was developed under common law. There is clearly a public interest in transportation that serves as the foundation for its regulation.

State regulation included the use of charters for some of the early turnpike companies and canal operations. The development of the railroad industry necessitated a move to statutory regulation, which was in effect by 1870 with the passage of **granger laws** in several states. Granger laws were the product of the granger movement, which began about 1867 in states such as Illinois, Iowa, Minnesota, and Wisconsin. Granges were organizations formed by farmers in various states and functioned as political action groups where farmers could discuss problems. Farmers joined the granger movement because of their dissatisfaction with railroad rates and service. The creation of state laws, and later federal laws, necessitated the delegation of responsibility for transportation regulation development, oversight, and enforcement to various government entities.

Responsibility for Regulation

Many of the parties involved in setting transportation policy are also tasked with developing the framework for regulation and enforcing it. This may seem contradictory, but recall that policy often influences the expansion, contraction, and focus of transportation regulation. These regulatory powers are distributed among the three branches of federal and state governments, independent regulatory commissions, and the 10 DOT operating administrations.

Executive and Legislative Branch Responsibilities[9] Both the president and Congress play important roles in transportation regulation. In simple terms, the primary role of Congress is to make laws while a key role of the executive branch is to carry out and enforce the laws.

The executive branch plays a substantial role in transportation rulemaking. The president, as chief executive, supervises department and agency work through his appointed cabinet, secretaries, and department heads. The Secretary of Transportation serves at the pleasure of the president and is a cabinet member. Much of the executive branch's rulemaking work falls to the White House Office of Management and Budget (OMB). It helps set the president's budget and settling the administration's priorities. OMB's Office of Information and Regulatory Affairs plays a significant role in rulemaking by conducting reviews of agency regulatory policy.

Congress creates federal agencies to ensure that its legislation is properly implemented and its policies are carried out. All departments and agencies obtain their rulemaking authority from Congress. Congress "delegates" its Article I authority "to make all laws" to departments and agencies. This is done by either broad grants of authority that are part of the mandate that is given to the department when it was established or through periodic "reorganizations" or by specific statutes that direct departments and agencies to regulate certain issues.

Congress reserves the right to intervene in the process when it is unhappy with an action that a department or agency has taken and often acts to make its opinion known. It wields this influence through its authority to approve presidential appointees such as the Secretary of Transportation, to conduct investigations, and to provide oversight by congressional committee to examine how agencies are implementing laws.

Importantly, Congress is responsible for the appropriations process and uses the "power of the purse" to influence department and agency actions. Their budgets are funded annually by Congress, providing effective leverage for Congress to make its opinion known. Congress can also add appropriations provisions called riders to funding bills that prohibit or restrict spending on the development, finalization, implementation, or enforcement of particular rules.

Independent Regulatory Commission Responsibilities Our regulatory laws are often stated in vague terms, such as *reasonable rates*, *inherent advantages*, and *unjust discrimination*. The roles of the regulatory commissions are to interpret the meaning of these terms as they are stated in the law and to develop regulations that define their intent. These regulations, then, are codified and serve as the basis for decisions made by the regulatory commissions.

The independent regulatory commissions are administrative bodies created by legislative authority operating within the framework of the U.S. Constitution. The members of these commissions are appointed by the president and approved by the Senate for a fixed term in office.

The **Interstate Commerce Commission (ICC)** was the first federal independent regulatory commission established in the United States. The ICC served as an expert body, providing continuity to regulation that neither the courts nor the legislature could provide. The ICC exercised legislative, judicial, and executive powers. As a result, it was often labeled a quasi-legislative, quasi-judicial, and quasi-executive body. When the ICC enforced statutes, it served in its executive capacity. When it ruled upon the reasonableness of a rate, it served in its judicial capacity. When it expanded legislation by promulgating rules or prescribing rules or rates, it exercised its legislative powers. Hence, regulatory agencies can be regarded as a fourth branch of the government.

On December 31, 1995, the ICC was abolished. The ICCTA ended the 108-year-old ICC and replaced it with another independent agency, the STB. The agency is charged by Congress with resolving railroad rate and service disputes and reviewing proposed railroad mergers. The STB also has limited jurisdiction over rate matters in other modes. The STB wields far less power than the ICC did in its heyday. Congress intends for the marketplace, not the STB, to be the primary control mechanism for rates and service.

The FMC was created in 1961 to administer the regulations imposed on international water carriers. The FMC exercises control over the rates, practices, agreements, and services of common carriers operating in international trade and domestic trade to points beyond the continental United States. The Ocean Shipping Reform Act of 1998 relaxed some of the economic powers of the FMC by allowing shippers and ocean carriers to enter into confidential contracts. This is discussed more in Chapter 8.

The **Federal Energy Regulatory Commission** (FERC) was created to administer the regulations governing rates and practices of oil and natural gas pipelines. Today, this independent agency regulates the interstate transmission of electricity and the transportation of natural gas and oil by pipeline. FERC also reviews proposals to build liquefied natural gas terminals and interstate natural gas pipelines as well as licensing hydropower projects. FERC is organized as part of the DOE.

The **Civil Aeronautics Board** (CAB) was established by the Civil Aeronautics Authority Act of 1938 to administer the economic regulations imposed upon airlines. The CAB was abolished in 1985 by the CAB Sunset Act and the remaining regulatory jurisdiction over air safety was transferred to the DOT.

Department of Transportation Responsibilities In addition to its role in national transportation policy development, the DOT is a cabinet-level agency. It has an important role in advising the president on transportation subjects. Also, each of the 10 DOT operating administrations have statutory responsibility for a wide range of regulations.

Agencies like the DOT engage in rulemaking when Congress creates a statutory mandate; when the agency identifies a problem or a need to modify an existing rule; when the public petitions for an agency to issue, modify, or rescind a rule; or when another governing body develops recommended rules. DOT then will evaluate possible alternatives before making a new rule. Economic analysis is used by the agency to determine the best alternative and whether the benefits of the rule would justify its costs.[10]

Safety is a major DOT priority. The DOT regulates safety in the aviation, motor carrier, railroad, mass transit, motor vehicle, maritime, commercial space, and pipeline transportation areas. The agency also regulates aviation consumer and economic issues and maintains governmental control over the construction and operation of bridges over navigable waters, the prevention of oil pollution, and the security of commercial aviation and passenger vessels.[11]

Judicial Branch Responsibilities Although the regulatory commissions and DOT operating administrations play key roles in regulating transportation, they are still subject to judicial review. The courts are the sole determinants of the intent of the law, and only court decisions can serve as legal precedent under common law. The courts make the final ruling on the constitutionality of regulatory statutes and the interpretation of the regulation. The review of the courts act as a check on arbitrary or capricious actions, on actions that do not conform to statutory standards or authority, or on actions that are not in accordance with fair procedure or substantial evidence. The parties involved in a commission decision have the right, therefore, to appeal the decision to the courts.

Over the years, the courts came to recognize the ICC as an expert body on policy and the authority on matters of fact. This recognition has now been given to the STB. The courts limited their restrictions on ICC and STB authority. The courts would not substitute their judgment for that of the ICC or STB on matters such as what constitutes a reasonable rate or whether discrimination is unjust because such judgments would usurp the administrative function of the commission.

States' Responsibilities The states establish various transportation safety regulations to protect the health and welfare of their citizens. In addition, the states exercise limited economic regulations over the transportation of commodities and passengers wholly within the state. These powers were given to the states by the Commerce Clause of the U.S. Constitution. The states' powers were greatly limited under various federal laws. States generally cannot impose stricter regulation than imposed on a given mode at the federal level. States can still regulate safety, provided these regulations do not impose an undue burden on **interstate commerce**. This type of transportation is known as **intrastate commerce**, and most states had a regulatory commission that was charged with enforcing these intrastate controls. These agencies might still exist to regulate utilities, such as telephone or electric companies.

Intrastate economic regulations vary from state to state, but they are generally patterned after federal economic regulations. The federal government eliminated the intrastate economic regulation of air carriers and motor carriers in Section 601 of the Airport Improvement Act of 1994. State and local authorities are prohibited from enacting or enforcing any law, rule, or regulation relating to the price, route, or service of any air carrier, carriers affiliated with a direct air carrier, and any other motor carrier or private motor carrier with respect to the transportation of property. Section 601 neither restricts nor expands the authority of states to regulate such traditional areas relating to safety, vehicle size and weight, insurance, or hazardous materials routing.[12]

The determination as to what constitutes commerce subject to state economic regulations is generally based on whether the shipment crosses a state boundary. If the shipment has an origin in one state and a destination in another state, it is an interstate shipment and is subject to federal regulations, if any exist. However, for shipments that are moved into a distribution center from a point outside the state and then moved from the distribution center to a destination in the same state, the distinction is not fully clear. The move within the state from the distribution center to the final destination may be considered interstate commerce and subject to federal regulations.

Focus of Regulation

Given the importance and widespread impact of transportation on the economy and society, the U.S. government uses regulation to protect key interests. Economic regulation is needed to promote healthy competition. Antitrust regulation is needed to avoid illegal trade and pricing inequities. Safety regulation is necessary to protect the health and welfare of citizens. And, security regulation is needed to combat terrorism. Each is discussed briefly in general terms along with highlights of key regulations.

Economic Regulation Transportation does not operate in a completely free-market environment. The U.S. government has controlled the economic operations of transportation since the 1860s because it is essential to the development of the country. Another key reason for regulation was the inherent monopolistic nature of the railroad industry.

The role of economic regulation is to transform a monopolistic industry into a competitive one. Under economic regulation, the government can (1) determine if a firm can enter an industry; (2) determine which market(s) a firm can serve in that industry; and (3) determine the prices that a firm can charge customers in the markets it serves. By enforcing these three regulatory practices, the government can provide the basis for competition in a monopolistic industry.

Federal economic regulation was established through the Act to Regulate Commerce of 1887. This Act gave the ICC the power to regulate the U.S. railroad industry. Originally, the ICC had limited powers, partially because of the inexperience of the U.S. government in regulating an entire industry. However, over several years, many additional pieces of legislation were passed to strengthen the powers of the ICC over the railroad industry. The Motor Carrier Act of 1935, the Transportation Act of 1940, and the Freight Forwarder Act of 1942 gave similar economic powers to the ICC over the motor carrier, domestic water carrier, and freight forwarding industries, respectively.

In our modern era, most modes operate free from economic regulation. Air cargo and passenger rates are no longer controlled by the government. Domestic air carriers are permitted to serve any market as long as the carrier meets safety regulation and landing slots are available. Because most water carrier operations are exempt from economic regulation, domestic water carrier economic regulation is a moot issue. And, the majority of the economic regulation of pipelines has been transferred to FERC.

The ICCTA abolished the ICC, and with it, significant power to economically regulate the transportation industry. The exception to this trend is the economic regulation of railroads, which was basically unchanged by the ICCTA. As discussed earlier, the STB replaced the ICC and administers the remaining economic regulations in transportation. The STB focuses mainly on railroads as follows:

- The STB has jurisdiction over rates, classifications, rules, practices, routes, services, facilities, acquisitions, and abandonments.
- Railroads continue to be subject to the common carrier obligations (to serve, not discriminate, charge reasonable rates, and deliver).
- Rail tariff filing is eliminated; railroads must provide 20 days advance notice before changing a rate.
- Rail contract filing is eliminated except for agricultural products.

The Surface Transportation Board Reauthorization Act of 1999 continued this economic deregulation theme, removing most of the remaining regulations imposed by the STB on motor carriers. The STB would no longer consider competitive issues and would eliminate references to federal regulatory approval requirements for collective motor carrier activities submitted to it for approval. The STB would no longer be able to grant antitrust immunity for motor carriers for collective activities such as rate bureaus and national freight classification. The motor carrier industry would be subject to competitive regulations as in other industries.

In practice, the ICCTA and subsequent rulings brought the economic regulation of transportation back to its beginning in 1887 by retaining regulatory powers over the railroads. Because of the decreasing cost nature of the railroad industry and its tendency toward monopoly, the STB maintains comprehensive guidelines to assure that railroads operate without discrimination or undue or unjust prejudice toward shippers. The other modes largely operate in a free-market economy. Still, they are subject to antitrust and other regulations that govern all industries.

Antitrust Regulation The deregulatory movement has exposed many practices to be in violation of antitrust laws. Antitrust regulations were first established in 1890 with passage of the **Sherman Anti-Trust Act**. The key points of this Act are as follows:

Section 1: Trusts, etc., in restraint of trade illegal; penalty.

Every contract, combination in the form of trust or otherwise, or conspiracy, in restraint of trade or commerce among the several States, or with foreign nations, is declared to be illegal. Every person who shall make any contract or engage in any combination or conspiracy declared by Section 1 to 7 of this title to be illegal shall be deemed guilty of a felony, and, on conviction thereof, shall be punished by fine not exceeding one million dollars if a corporation, or if any other person, one hundred thousand dollars, or by imprisonment not exceeding three years, or both said punishments, in the discretion of the court.

Section 2: Monopolizing trade a felony; penalty.

Every person who shall monopolize, or attempt to monopolize, or combine or conspire with any other person or persons, to monopolize any part of the trade or commerce among the several States, or with foreign nations, shall be deemed guilty of a felony. . . .[13]

The thrust of the Sherman Act was intended to outlaw price fixing among competing firms, eliminate business practices that tended toward monopolization, and prevent any firm or combination of firms from refusing to sell or deal with certain firms or avoiding geographic market allocations.

The law was strengthened in 1914 by the **Clayton Act**. This Act specifically described some other practices that would be interpreted as attempts to monopolize, or as actual monopolization. These practices include exclusive dealing arrangements whereby a buyer and/or seller agree to deal only with the other party for a period of time. Another prohibited practice is a tying contract. This is where a seller agrees to sell goods to a buyer only if the buyer also buys another product from the seller.

Also in 1914, the **Federal Trade Commission** (FTC) was created. This agency was the primary overseer and enforcement agency in antitrust situations.

Collective rate making by transportation carriers was made exempt from antitrust laws by the passage of the **Reed-Bulwinkle Act of 1948**, which empowered the ICC to oversee carrier rate making. As such, it limited traditional jurisdiction by the FTC and the Department of Justice in this area.

The **Motor Carrier Act of 1980** and the **Staggers Act of 1980** eliminated many of the exemptions from antitrust laws for motor carriers and railroads, respectively. The ICCTA confirmed the role of antitrust laws in transportation and further limited exemptions from these laws.

Another major law that is relevant to transportation deregulation is the **Robinson-Patman Act of 1936**. This law prohibits sellers from practicing price discrimination among buyers unless the difference in price can be justified by true differences in the costs of servicing these buyers. Defenses against such a practice are (1) differences in cost, (2) the need to meet competition, and (3) changing market conditions. Although this law was created for application to the buying and selling of goods, it may be applicable to contracts for transportation services. Whether this law applies in carrier pricing is only determined by the courts as suspected violations occur.

In the selling and purchase of transportation services, two types of antitrust violations can occur. The first is called a **per se violation**. This type of violation is illegal regardless of whether any economic harm is done to competitors or other parties. Types of per se violations include price fixing, division of markets, boycotts, and tying agreements. If economic harm has been caused to any party because of this violation, the damages are tripled as compensation to the harmed parties.

The second type of antitrust violation is called **rule of reason**. In this type of violation, economic harm must be shown to have been caused to competitors or other parties because these activities can be undertaken by firms with no antitrust implications. Rule of reason violations include exclusive deals, requirements contracts, joint bargaining, and joint action among affiliates. Recently, the FMC rejected the proposed merger of three Japanese ocean liners for this type of antitrust issue. It is described briefly in the Global Perspectives feature.

Carriers, in the selling of transportation services, are normally thought to be the party to which antitrust regulations apply. However, in buying these services, shippers are also subject to the same laws and are at an equal risk of committing an antitrust violation. Some of the transportation applications of these rules have yet to be fully tested in the courts.

GLOBAL **PERSPECTIVES**

State of Ocean Cargo: Carriers Cope with Regulatory Restrictions

The ocean carrier industry was handed another setback by a major regulatory agency last month as the U.S. Federal Maritime Commission (FMC) rejected the proposed merger of three Japanese liners.

The unanimous decision to nix the Tripartite Agreement, comprising Kawasaki Kisen Kaisha, Ltd. (K Line), Mitsui O.S.K. Lines Ltd. (MOL), and Nippon Yusen Kaisha (NYK) represents a fresh challenge to the "3-J" alliance for the time being. Furthermore, delays in Japanese antitrust approval mean that the carrier's contract deadline for next month will be missed.

Much of what the Tripartite parties were asking for, says FMC commissioner William Doyle, revolved around premerger or preconsolidation "coordination." For example, the parties were seeking authority to share information and conduct joint negotiations with third party businesses in the United States for as much as a year in advance of any potential merger.

"These provisions would violate 'gun jumping' laws that forbid the sharing of competitively sensitive information or the premature combining of the parties," adds Doyle. "In order to receive the benefits of a merger, one needs to first merge."

Chris Rogers, an analyst with the global trade consultancy Panjiva, is not particularly alarmed by FMC's decision, which he describes as "technical in nature." More of a worry, however, is the ongoing Department of Justice (DoJ) investigation of the container liner industry and what Rogers describes as "Congressional concerns" about alliances more broadly.

In an advisory letter written by DoJ assistant district attorney general Renata Hesse, the FMC was called upon to forbid the creation of the Ocean Alliance, or to at least have the carriers rewrite the agreement to ensure competition. "The DoJ has long taken the position that the general antitrust exemption for international ocean shipping carrier agreements is no longer justified," she says.

For the time being, however, both the Ocean Alliance and The Alliance still control 45% of the global business by sharing vessels and operating joint services.

Source: Patrick Burnson, "State of Ocean Cargo: Carriers Cope with Regulatory Restrictions," *Logistics Management*, June 1, 2017. Retrieved September 12, 2017 , from http://www.logisticsmgmt.com/article/state_of_ocean_cargo_carriers_cope_with_regulatory_restrictions. Reprinted with permission of Peerless Media, LLC.

Safety Regulation Large vehicles, trains, airplanes, and ships, particularly those carrying dangerous goods, create hazards for the traveling public and the environment. Federal and state governments enact transportation safety regulations to alleviate some of these risks and hazards within our transportation systems. The primary objective of safety regulations is to establish a **minimum level of safety** for transportation providers to maintain. Many transportation companies establish higher safety levels than those required by law, and these companies have their own enforcement personnel to ensure compliance.

Since **economic deregulation**, greater attention has been given to the establishment and enforcement of safety regulation to alleviate concerns that carriers would pursue productivity and profit at the expense of safety. Safety regulation is intended to ensure that transportation providers do not defer required vehicle and operating safety requirements in lieu of corporate goals.

Safety regulations cover a wide array of activities regarding operations, personnel qualifications, vehicles, equipment, hours of service for vehicle operators, and so forth. Two of the most prominent operations-focused safety regulations in recent memory are the **Compliance, Safety, and Accountability Act of 2010 (CSA 2010)** and the **Hours of Service of Drivers Final Rule** in 2011 for the trucking industry. Their current provisions are highlighted in Table 12-1.

Labor safety regulations establish minimum qualifications for operating personnel, including such factors as age, health, training, licensing, and experience. Minimum age requirements were established for driving a tractor–trailer in interstate commerce, and a nationwide commercial driver-licensing program was initiated in 1988. Airline pilots are required to pass a physical exam, to have training and experience on specific types of aircraft,

TABLE 12-1	Highlights of Current Motor Carrier Safety Regulations	
	COMPLIANCE, SAFETY, ACCOUNTABILITY PROGRAM	**HOURS OF SERVICE RULES**
Purpose	Safety compliance and enforcement program of the FMCSA that holds motor carriers and drivers accountable for their role in transportation safety.	DOT regulations limit daily and weekly driving time to ensure commercial truck drivers are properly rested, safe, and not a threat to others on the road.
Summary of Provisions	CSA 2010 has three main areas of focus: • Measurement: CSA uses inspections and crash results to measure safety performance; • Evaluation: CSA addresses these behaviors using the Safety Measurement System (SMS); and • Intervention: Investigators are equipped with a variety of interventions to contact and work with motor carriers that have safety performance and compliance problems. The SMS assesses motor carrier on-road performance and compliance by organizing data into seven Behavior Analysis and Safety Improvement Categories (BASICs): Unsafe Driving, Crash Indicator, Hours-of-Service Compliance, Vehicle Maintenance, Controlled Substances/Alcohol, Hazardous Materials Compliance, and Driver Fitness. In each BASIC, the SMS quantifiably measures a motor carrier's performance.	HOS regulation has multiple elements: • Drivers may drive up to 11 hours but are limited to 14 hours in a duty period. • Drivers must take a mandatory 30-minute break by their eighth hour of coming on duty. • The 14-hour duty period may not be extended with off-duty time for breaks, meal and fuel stops, etc. • Drivers may work no more than 60/70 hours on-duty in 7/8 consecutive days. • Drivers can restart the 7/8 consecutive day after taking at least 34 consecutive hours off duty. • Drivers using the sleeper berth provision must take at least 8 consecutive hours in the sleeper berth, plus a separate 2 consecutive hours either in the sleeper berth, off duty, or any combination of the two.

(continued)

TABLE 12-1	Continued	
	COMPLIANCE, SAFETY, ACCOUNTABILITY PROGRAM	**HOURS OF SERVICE RULES**
Enforcement	Using the SMS data and a Safety Fitness Determination rating system, FMCSA investigators assess the safety fitness of carriers with the following ratings: Satisfactory—safety controls are sufficient to ensure compliance with the safety fitness standard. Conditional—safety controls are inadequate but have not yet resulted in violations of the safety fitness standard. Unsatisfactory—safety controls are inadequate and have resulted in violations of the safety fitness standard. A motor carrier with a final rating of Unsatisfactory is prohibited from operating a commercial motor vehicle in interstate commerce.	• Drivers may be forced to stop working until enough off-duty time has been accumulated to be in compliance. • State and local law enforcement officials may assess fines. • FMCSA may levy civil penalties on a driver or carrier, ranging from $1,000 to $11,0000 per violation. The carrier's safety rating can be downgraded for a pattern of violations. • Federal criminal penalties can be brought against carriers who knowingly and willfully allow or require HOS violations; or against drivers who knowingly and willfully violate the HOS regulations.
For more information	www.csa.fmcsa.dot.gov	www.fmcsa.dot.gov/regulations/hours-of-service

and to be certified for various types of flying conditions. Similar regulations govern rail engineers and ship captains.

Transportation equipment standards are also stipulated in safety regulations. These standards range from design specifications for aircraft to required safety equipment for automobiles. Vehicle manufacturers must adhere to these safety specifications, and the vehicle operator is required to maintain the vehicle and equipment in good operating condition and to use the safety equipment. For example, the automobile manufacturer must equip each vehicle with seat belts, a minimum number of headlights and taillights, a horn, and so forth. The auto owner then is required by state law to use the seat belts and to ensure proper functioning of the lights, horn, and other features.

The movement of hazardous materials and hazardous wastes are subjected to considerable regulations due to their threat to public safety and the environment. A hazardous material is a substance that poses more than a reasonable risk to the health and safety of individuals and includes products such as explosives, flammables, corrosives, oxidizers, and radioactive materials. Regulations govern loading and unloading practices, packaging, routing, commodity identification, and documentation. Transportation personnel must be trained to properly handle hazardous cargoes and to respond to emergencies.

Regulations regarding domestic transportation of hazardous materials are published in the Code of Federal Regulations, Title 49. Safety regulations governing domestic movement of hazardous wastes are found in the Code of Federal Regulations, Title 40. Technical requirements for transporting hazardous materials internationally by air and sea are managed by the International Civil Aviation Organization and the International Maritime Dangerous Goods Code.

These regulations overlap somewhat because of the overlapping jurisdiction of the regulatory agencies originating and enforcing the rules. For example, the DOT promulgates and enforces hazardous materials regulation, while the Environmental Protection Agency regulates the movement of hazardous wastes. In addition, the various states and municipalities within the states establish laws affecting the movement of hazardous commodities through their jurisdiction.

Transportation safety regulation extends to environmental safety. Emission standards are designed to protect air quality; flight takeoff procedures and patterns are designed to reduce noise levels for the citizens living near airports; and tanker loading and unloading procedures for petroleum products are designed to protect animals, sea life, and the landscape from the devastating effects from an oil spill.

Safety regulation is not free. The safety regulations imposed by government usually add a direct cost to a transportation operation, making its service costlier to consumers. However, when the indirect social costs are considered, society feels that the benefits of safety regulations, including fewer deaths and injuries and a cleaner environment, more than offset the direct cost. In the future, the number and scope of safety regulations will increase as government expands its safety regulating authority into additional transportation areas.

Safety regulations can be enacted into law by Congress or developed by key agencies. The DOT plays a prominent safety role through its administrations:

- The FAA enforces and promulgates safety regulations governing the operations of air carriers and airports.
- The FMCSA administers motor carrier safety regulations.
- The **National Highway Traffic Safety Administration (NHTSA)** has jurisdiction over safety features and the performance of motor vehicles and motor vehicle equipment.
- The **Federal Railroad Administration** (FRA) has authority over railroad safety regulations.
- The **Pipeline and Hazardous Material Safety Administration** (PHMSA) seeks to protect people and the environment by advancing the safe transportation of energy and other hazardous materials that are essential to our daily lives through the establishment and enforcement of standards for oil and natural gas pipelines. Its Hazardous Materials Safety Office manages hazardous materials regulations for all other modes of transportation.

Outside the DOT's purview, multiple federal agencies and departments support transportation safety regulation. For example, USCG is responsible for marine safety standards for vessels and ports. And, the NTSB is charged with determining the probable cause of every civil aviation accident the United States and significant accidents in other modes of transportation.

State governments, through the **police powers** contained in the Constitution, also regulate transportation safety. State agencies exercise various controls over the safe operation of vehicles. These safety regulations set standards for speed, vehicle size, operating practices, operator licensing, and so forth. The purpose of the state safety regulations is to protect the health and welfare of the citizens of that state.

At times, federal and state safety regulations conflict. For example, the federal government restricted the automobile speed limit to 55 miles per hour on the highway system during the energy crisis of the 1970s. Some states did not agree with the mandate but followed the requirement to qualify for federal money to construct and maintain the highway system. In 1982, the Surface Transportation Act established federal standards for vehicle weight and length of tractor–trailers operating on the interstate highway system. The states complied with the standards for the interstate highways but many maintained different standards for state highways.

Security Regulation   After the September 11, 2001, terrorist attack on the United States, transportation security has taken on a new dimension. Securing the nations transportation system from terrorism became a major governmental focus because of the massive geographic expanse of the U.S. border and the millions of tons of freight and millions of passengers entering and leaving the United States.

The Department of Homeland Security (DHS) was established in 2002 with the goal of mobilizing and organizing the nation to secure the homeland from terrorist attacks. Its mission is to lead a unified national effort to secure America; to prevent and deter terrorist attacks and protect against and respond to threats and hazards to the nation; and to ensure and secure borders, welcome lawful immigrants and visitors, and promote the free flow of commerce.

DHS is charged with protecting the security of the transportation system. DHS transportation security programs and regulations are administered through the USCG, Transportation Security Administration (TSA), and Customs and Border Protection (CBP). Transportation security is a never-ending task. For example, a typical CBP day includes screening nearly one million international travelers and more than 67,000 cargo containers arriving at U.S. borders. Annually, CBP facilitates an average of more than $3 trillion in legitimate trade while enforcing U.S. trade laws.[14]

These DHS operational components have been given key roles in security legislation. The following initiatives seek to protect transportation in the 21st century:

- **Aviation and Transportation Security Act of 2001** (ATSA) established the TSA. One of TSA's primary roles is to screen all passengers and property that will be carried aboard an aircraft. For flights and flight segments originating in the United States, the screening takes place before boarding and is carried out by uniformed federal TSA personnel.

- **Maritime Transportation Security Act of 2002** (MTSA) seeks to protect U.S. ports and waterways from a terrorist attack. The key MTSA provisions include: conducting vulnerability assessments for port facilities and vessels; developing security plans to mitigate identified risks for the national maritime system, ports, port facilities, and vessels; developing the Transportation Worker Identification Credential, a biometric identification card to help restrict access to secure areas to only authorized personnel; and, establishing a process to assess foreign ports, from which vessels depart on voyages to the United States.

- **Security and Accountability for Every Port Act of 2006** (SAFE) is a comprehensive port security law designed to keep nuclear, chemical, and biological weapons out of freight containers traveling to U.S. ports. This act requires that all containers entering high-volume U.S. ports be scanned for radiation sources and codified the Container Security Initiative (CSI) and the Customs-Trade Partnership Against Terrorism (C-TPAT), two programs administered by CBP to help reduce threats associated with cargo shipped in containers.

Additionally, President Bush signed into law the Implementing Recommendations of the 9/11 Commission Act of 2007 (public law 110-53). This law has four major sections: (1) transportation security planning and information sharing; (2) transportation security enhancements; (3) public transportation security; and (4) surface transportation security. The goal is to thwart terrorists and criminals who relentlessly pursue opportunities to exploit transportation system security weaknesses.

These transportation-based security acts aim to balance the protection of people with the need for unencumbered global trade. Hence, security regulations and programs must constantly be scrutinized and improved to deal with new threats while keeping compliance costs reasonable and transit delays to a minimum. Government-industry collaboration is critical in the security effort.

Transportation regulation extends beyond economic, antitrust, safety, and security issues. Issues related to the transportation's role in environmental protection, transit safety, military support, and other issues are also the subject of regulation. An extended discussion of these topics is beyond the scope of this chapter. Effective resources are available via the Transportation Environmental Resource Center website (www.tercenter.org) and the Federal Transit Administration website (www.transit.dot.gov).

A Concise Chronology of Transportation Regulation

The transportation industry has been subject to regulatory mandates for nearly 140 years. Table 12-2 provides an abbreviated chronology of significant transportation regulation from the 1880s through the present.

The history of transportation regulation can be broken down into four eras. First, the Initiation Era from 1887 to 1920 saw the establishment of federal transportation regulation and the ICC. Second, the Era of Positive Regulation from 1920 to 1935 was oriented toward promoting transportation. Third, the Intermodal Era from 1935 to 1976 witnessed the expansion of regulation to motor carriers, air carriers, water carriers, and freight forwarders. Finally, the New Economic Era from 1976 to the present was the period of gradual lessening and eventual elimination of much economic regulation, culminating in the abolishment of the ICC. This era also has been marked by the development and strengthening of transportation safety and security regulations.

TABLE 12-2	Chronology of Major Transportation Regulation	
DATE	**ACT**	**NATURE OF REGULATION**
Initiation Era		
1887	Act to Regulate Commerce	Regulated railroads and established ICC; required rates to be reasonable; discrimination prohibited
1903	Elkins Act	Prohibited rebates and filed rate doctrine
1096	Hepburn Act	Established maximum and joint rate controls
1910	Mann-Elkins Act	Gave shipper right to route shipment
1912	Panama Canal Act	Prohibited railroads from owning water carriers
Positive Era		
1920	Transportation Act of 1920	Established a rule of rate-making; pooling and joint use of terminals permitted; began recapture clause
1933	Emergency Transportation Act	Granted financial assistance to railroads
Intermodal Era		
1935	Motor Carrier Act	Federal regulation of trucking, similar to rail
1938	Civil Aeronautics Act	Federal regulation of air carriers; established Civil Aeronautics Board (CAB)
1940	Transportation Act	Provided for federal regulation of water carriers; declaration of national transportation policy
1942	Freight Forwarder Act	Federal reregulation of surface freight forwarders
1948	Reed-Bulwinkle Act	Established antitrust immunity for joint rate making
1958	Transportation Act	Eliminated umbrella (protective) rate making and provided financial aid to railroads

(continued)

DATE	ACT	NATURE OF REGULATION
TABLE 12-2 Continued		
1966	Department of Transportation Act	Established the U.S. Department of Transportation
1970	Rail Passenger Service Act	Established Amtrak
1973	Regional Rail Reorganization Act	Established Consolidation Rail Corporation (Conrail)
New Economic Era		
1976	Railroad Revitalization and Regulatory Reform Act	Granted rate freedom; allowed ICC to exempt rail operations; began abandonment and merger controls
1977	Airline Deregulation Act	Deregulated air transportation, sunset CAB (1985)
1980	Motor Carrier Act	Eased entry restrictions and permitted rate negotiation
1980	Rail Staggers Act	Permitted railroads to negotiate contracts, allowed rate flexibility, and defined maximum rates
1993	Negotiated Rate Act	Provided for settlement options for motor carrier undercharges
1994	Trucking Industry Regulatory Reform Act	Eliminated motor carrier filing of individual tariffs; ICC given power to deregulate categories of traffic
1994	FAA Reauthorization Act	Prohibited states from regulating (economic) intrastate trucking
1995	ICC Termination Act	Abolished ICC; established STB; eliminated most truck economic regulation
1996	Maritime Security Act	Authorized a program to assist an active, privately owned U.S.-flagged and U.S.-crewed merchant shipping fleet
1998	Transportation Equity Act for the 21st Century	Allocated $216+ billion for the maintenance and safety of surface transportation
1999	STB Reauthorization Act	Removed economic regulations on motor carriers
2001	Aviation and Transportation Security Act	Established the Transportation Security Administration
2002	Homeland Security Act	Moved Coast Guard and TSA into Department of Homeland Security
2010	Compliance, Safety, and Accountability Act	Created scoring system for motor carrier companies and drivers to help promote safer operations
2011	Hours of Service	Places stricter rules on a driver's restart options: maintains 11-hour daily driving limit and 14-hour workday
2012	Motor Vehicle Safety Enhancement Act	Set forth a series of trucking safety provisions, including electronic logging devices, and harsher penalties for DOT regulation noncompliance

Transportation Planning, Promotion, and Programs

Planning determines future transportation needs and then establishes policies or programs to bring about certain goals through the public or private sector. Promotion connotes encouragement or provision of aid or assistance so transportation can grow or survive. Programs involve actual public cash investments into or funding for transportation activities both privately and publicly owned. All three activities benefit transportation and cause it to grow or survive in instances in which pure market forces could not have done so. These three Ps of transportation are discussed in this section.

Transportation Planning and the Public Sector

Transportation project planning is the process whereby federal, state, or local groups review the movement needs or demands of a region or population segment, develop transportation alternatives, and usually propose and implement an alternative. This process enables the development of new movement processes or allows existing ones to continue in an environment of change.

Transportation project planning is a public activity; purely financial returns and other concerns are not the overriding benefits sought. The government does this for several reasons. First, public transportation processes can facilitate trade or movement where private actions have not or would not have been enticed to do so for financial gain alone. Second, various cultural and political benefits often come from public transportation projects and programs. Third, transportation planning may lower the cost of living or reduces the social costs of delay, congestion, or pollution. Finally, transportation planning provides services that are not financially rewarding but are deemed socially necessary or desirable. Such is the case with the Port of Oakland's $60 million investment in a shore power program that greatly reduces ship diesel emissions. It is discussed in the Transportation Technology feature.

TRANSPORTATION **TECHNOLOGY**

A Unique and Clean Approach to Shore Power

When five ocean carrier members of the World Shipping Council (WSC) convened in the San Francisco Bay Area recently, their technical experts requested a visit to the Port of Oakland to evaluate the port's unique approach to shore power.

Port of Oakland Executive Director Chris Lytle was only too happy to oblige, meeting with them for an hour before conducting a tour of Oakland's largest marine terminal for a live demonstration.

"If there are ways to strengthen our port electrical infrastructure to promote more use of electrical power from our grid, we will do it," said Lytle. "We will collaborate with shipping lines and the marine terminal operators here in Oakland to build on the progress we've already made."

Ports spokesman, Mike Zampa, adds that it's regarded as "a shared responsibility."

The Bay Area is arguably the most "environmentally aware" region in all of the United States, as demonstrated by a host of high-tech shippers and manufacturers based here.

Meanwhile, California's third largest ocean cargo gateway promises to intensify efforts to curb diesel emissions by plugging more vessels into shore power. Known as cold-ironing in industry vernacular, it's the practice of plugging ships into landside power grids. Using shore power, vessels can switch off their diesel engines at berth.

The port said it spent $60 million building the infrastructure to plug in ships with financial assistance from federal, state, and local partners. Ship owners spend about $1 million per vessel for shipboard equipment that allows them to plug in at California ports.

"Our goal is to plug in every vessel," the Executive Director said.

Lytle said shore power has helped Oakland reduce diesel emissions by 75 percent in the past decade. The Executive Director told his audience of shipping experts that he wants to up the ante.

"We've reduced truck diesel emissions by 98 percent," Lytle said. "So the real opportunity now is on the vessel side."

According to port data, more than 70 percent of all ships visiting Oakland rely on shore power. That's in line with existing rules governing California seaports. But state regulators indicate they may increase the requirement in the coming decade. To prepare, Lytle said Oakland is taking inventory of roadblocks to shore power use. The challenges can range from ill-equipped ships to not enough electrical vaults at the dock. "We're trying to identify why every single vessel that comes here can't plug in," Lytle said.

The Executive Director said Oakland is considering a number of enhancements to increase shore power use. Among them:

- Additional landside electrical vaults;
- More substations to increase the power supply; and
- Standardized procedures to ease the plug-in process for vessel crews.

Oakland's shore power program began in 2012.

Source: Patrick Burnson, "Port of Oakland Wants Ocean Carriers to Invest More in Shore Power," *Logistics Management*, September 8, 2017, Retrieved September 12, 2017, from http://www.logisticsmgmt.com/article/port_of_oakland_wants_ocean_carriers_to_invest_in_more_shore_power. Reprinted with permission of Peerless Media, LLC.

Transportation planning is critical because private firms have withdrawn from many areas of transportation investment. Many forms of transportation today are no longer economically profitable or compensatory. Urban bus systems, commuter railroads, rail and urban research and development, and many rail services would not exist without public sector involvement.

Transportation requires large capital investments that discourage or prohibit private investment. Port dredging and development, as well as airport and highway construction, are examples of capital items that are not affordable by the carriers using them. Instead, the ability of a public authority to attract capital enables the asset to be built; cost is recovered through user charges.

Public planning of transportation is generally found in situations where environmental or social needs override financial ones. A major argument used in modern subway construction is that, although the system might not recover its full costs from passenger fares, the city will benefit from increasing citizens' access to existing downtown facilities, including buildings, offices, stores, and water utility systems. Constructing other facilities in developing suburban areas will not be necessary. Also, commuters save time and money because the subway reduces road congestion, eliminates the need for long driving times, reduces fuel consumption, avoids costly parking, and so on. Public planning of transportation involves a different viewpoint and set of objectives than does capital investment analysis in private firms.

An Approach to Public Project Planning Analysis

While a private firm seeks a financial return to the firm itself, public planning agencies compare the initial costs of a project to the financial, environmental, and measurable social benefits to everyone affected by the project. Thus, it compares total societal cost to total societal benefits, whether they be monetary or nonmonetary in nature.

The specific analytical tool typically used in public planning is the **benefit/cost ratio** (BCR). In essence, the BCR is a measure of total measurable benefits to society divided by the initial capital cost. The formula in its basic form is as follows:

$$\text{BCR} = \frac{\text{Sum of yearly benefits to society}}{\text{Sum of costs to agencies and those in society initially impacted}}$$

$$= \frac{\text{Sum of benefits}}{\text{Sum of initial costs}} = \frac{\text{Year 1 benefit} + \text{Year 2 benefit} + \dots}{\text{Sum of all initial costs}}$$

If the resulting answer is greater than one, the project is said to produce a "profit" for society. A BCR of one indicates the break-even point; less than one indicates that the agency will spend more on the project than society will reap in long-term benefits.

The major costs of a project include expenditures for planning, engineering, construction, and financing. Other costs include delay or congestion measured in terms of dollars per hour and in terms of everyone in society who will be inconvenienced during the construction phase of a transportation project. Project costs can also include a cost of lost sales to businesses; for example, stores are more difficult to access during several years of subway construction. The costs of bond financing incurred to construct the system are also pertinent. All costs are measured or translated into monetary terms and listed according to the year in which they will occur. Typically, the major expenses arise in the initial years of construction; financing is a major cost carried through the project's life.

The benefits of a project include any measurable benefit to the agency, other agencies, and the public. Benefits include increased employment, decreased prices for products, lowered costs of commuting or freight transport, reduced maintenance, improved health due to lessened pollution, and so on. Many benefits are easily quantified, though others pose analytical difficulties in the form of forecasting volumes and cost relationships in future periods.

The timing and **time value of funds** are important parts of any capital project analysis. Political controversy exists about the choice of the specific discount rate and its application. Several analytical points can be examined that will shed light on this task. First, the discount rate should reflect the interest cost and impact to the public agency that borrows the initial funds. Second, the rate should rise in later years to reflect increasing risk, inflation, uncertainty, and forecasting difficulties. This is a conservative practice of private project financial managers, and the logic of it can be applied soundly in a public setting. Third, the counting of benefits should cease in some future period, even though the project might last longer. This is another practice that is an implicit way of conservatively considering only those benefits within the intermediate term, unless a logical case can be made for an extended period of time. These points are made as to ensure that benefit overcounting is minimized.

An example of a benefit/cost ratio application to a proposed subway line will show how public planning processes are employed. Costs include those of organization development, design, engineering, initial financing, land purchases, relocation, and disruption to the public. Costs projected into the future include operations, lost property taxes, interest costs, and any other costs directly tied to the project. Benefits to the agencies include lowered operational costs of city buses; alternative application of funds released from the bus operation (reduced street and highway requirements); decreased need to expand highways or downtown parking; increased property, sales, and wage taxes from higher economic activity downtown; avoidance of federal penalties for not reducing citywide auto emissions; and many others. Benefits to society include the income multiplier effect from the initial project investment in the form of employment and flow of dollars from the construction itself. The system will improve society in the form of time savings, lower pollution levels, and reduced commuting stress. The subway will generally cause the downtown to become more fully utilized, resulting in a steady or increasing tax base.

Public planning involves many of the basic concepts inherent in private planning, but the application is different. The public agency is concerned about costs and benefits to all parties affected by the project. Thus, costs, benefits, and "profits" are measured for society as a whole in tangible and intangible ways.

Modal Promotion Activities

Nearly every mode of freight and passenger transportation benefits from government project planning and programs that create and maintain infrastructure, provide subsidies, and conduct research.

Air The domestic air system benefits from several government programs. Foremost is the FAA **air traffic control system**. This system provides navigation and safety for every aircraft in flight within the United States. The system assesses no direct fee to the airlines for its use and captures its operating expenses from airlines and passengers through user charges.

Another direct airline benefit is the subsidy program. These subsidies generally apply to short and medium nonjet flights to cities that are unable to support high traffic volumes. The subsidy has been a significant support mechanism for regional airlines. In recent years, the growth of commuter airlines has enabled regional airlines to discontinue service to small cities. The Air Deregulation Act of 1978 accelerated this trend, which resulted in a lessened need for regional airline subsidies.

The USPS also provides substantial support to airlines. The prime source of income for airlines during their early years came from this subsidy program. In recent years, mail income has not been as significant, but this subsidy remains a valuable revenue source for the industry.

State and local agencies help promote the airline industry through air terminal development and construction. Terminals represent substantial capital investments and would be difficult for the industry to finance and construct. State and local agencies raise the necessary construction funds at reasonable municipal bond interest rates, often backed by the taxing power of the community. The airlines then rent terminal and hangar facilities and pay landing fees for each flight.

The federal government handles many aircraft safety matters. The FAA provides aircraft construction and safety rules as well as pilot certification. In another capacity, the NTSB investigates accidents so that others might be avoided or reduced through improvement of aircraft specifications or flight procedures.

Another indirect form of promotion to the airline industry comes from the military. Defense contracts for military aircraft development often provide direct benefits to commercial aviation in the form of mechanical or navigational aircraft improvements. Without military-related research and development activity, advancements in this area would take place at a slower pace and at a higher cost to the private sector.

A last form of airline promotion, which is not found in the U.S. system, is direct government ownership, operation, or subsidy of air service. This is common with foreign airlines that serve the United States. In these instances, airlines are subsidized so the countries can have some degree of control over traffic to and from their nations and gain balance-of-payment benefits and hard currencies through ticket revenues.

A related form of such **home-flag airline** promotion exists in the United States and in most foreign nations. In the United States, there is a requirement that only United States flag carriers with domestically owned aircraft and domestic crews may originate and terminate domestic passengers and freight. Many foreign lines serve both New York and Los Angeles, for example, with a flight originating abroad, but these flights are limited to international passengers. The only way in which a foreign line can originate and terminate a passenger in two U.S. cities is when that passenger is exercising stopover privileges as part of a tour or through movement. This home-flag requirement serves to protect U.S. airlines.

Several forms of **user charges** are designed, in whole or part, to have the modes pay for many of the public benefits they receive. Landing fees are charged to repay investments or generate revenue for specific airports. A major user charge is levied against passenger movements through ticket taxes. An international per-head tax is also part of this user tax, as are some aircraft registration fees. Many of these funds go into the **Airport and Airway Trust Fund**, which is used for airport facility projects on a shared basis with local agencies.

Motor and Highway   With regard to public promotion, the highway system and motor carrier firms have a joint relationship. There is no direct promotion to the motor carriers themselves, but indirect benefit comes to the industry through **highway development** because most highway projects are completed with government funds.

The Federal Highway Administration (FHWA) branch of the DOT is responsible for federal highway construction and safety. A predecessor agency, the Bureau of Public Roads, carried out the mandate to build the Interstate Highway System, which was paid for on a 90 percent/10 percent federal/state cost-sharing basis. Today the FHWA is largely devoted to highway research, development, and safety. It also is charged with certain repair projects on critical parts of the federal and interstate highway system. Motor carriers benefit from the increased access, speed, and safety of this system because without it they would have to travel more congested routes, presenting safety hazards.

NHTSA is responsible for highway and auto safety. It also conducts major research into vehicle safety, accidents, and highway design related to safety. This agency provides administrative regulations for certain minimum automobile safety features.

The FMCSA is a noneconomic regulatory body whose main purpose is motor carrier vehicle safety. Though this agency imposes strict standards on motor carrier vehicle safety, the long-term benefit is increased safety for everyone on the highways.

Highway development also comes from states and various regional planning commissions. One example is the Appalachian Regional Commission, which is charged with improving the infrastructure and economy of that region. Many highway and improvement projects are funded by this agency.

User charges are present in the highway systems in several forms. A major form is the fuel tax. States look to this per-gallon tax as a major revenue source for highway construction and maintenance. The federal government's fuel taxes go to the **Federal Highway Trust Fund**, which is the financing source for the Interstate Highway System. Some states have switched from a per-gallon to a percent of sales price method of fuel-based taxation because, in recent years, the number of gallons of fuel sold has decreased, leaving state agencies with less revenue in times that demand greater highway maintenance. The percent of sales price approach can avoid much of this decline. Another public revenue source is the federal excise tax on vehicle tires. States also obtain revenues through vehicle registration fees. These mostly are assessed on a vehicle weight basis so as to recoup, somewhat, a proportionate share of construction costs related to heavier versus lighter vehicles. Further, some states (such as Oregon) assess a ton-mile tax. Finally, tolls are a form of user taxes on turnpikes and many bridges.

Two major controversies are taking place with regard to highway user charges. One concerns the Federal Highway Trust Fund. The tax money that goes into this fund is collected primarily for interstate highway construction. Approximately 96 percent of the interstate system has been built, but doubt exists over whether the remaining portions, mostly very costly urban sections, will ever be built. Meanwhile, the fuel tax continues to be collected and accumulated in the fund.

A second problem with user taxes is on the state level. Most states collecting vehicle fees and vehicle taxes only return a portion of them for highway purposes. Some states have earmarked some of these funds for education and other uses. In addition, industry groups continue to seek a greater share of these funds for highway development and improvement.

Rail The railroads receive direct assistance from the Regional Railroad Reorganization Act of 1973, the Railroad Revitalization and Regulatory Reform Act of 1976, and the Staggers Rail Act of 1980. Most of the assistance is in the form of track repair and motive power acquisition financing. These provisions are attempts to overcome the problem of poor equipment and facilities, which lead to ineffective service and severe financial conditions.

Another form of funding has been available as a subsidy to lines that are abandoned by railroads but that states and other groups continue to operate. This assistance was designed to make rail line abandonment easier for railroads while still allowing service to continue.

The Consolidated Rail Corporation (Conrail) had been the subject of special federal funding and promotion. It had received special appropriations for operations capital improvements, mainly through provisions of the Regional Railroad Reorganization Act of 1973 to ensure railroad service in the east after six major northeastern railroads went bankrupt in a six-year period. After a successful reorganization and transformation, Conrail was purchased by the Norfolk Southern and CSX railroads. Conrail's routes were integrated into these two companies.

Research and development in this mode essentially disappeared in the late 1950s. Financial problems in most railroads caused reductions in the research and development area, thereby stagnating the technology. In response to this situation, the FRA was created as part of the DOT in 1966. The FRA is a major source of gains in railroad technology as well as in safety. A test facility located near Pueblo, Colorado, originally owned by the FRA, is used to test improvements in existing motive power and rolling equipment and to develop advanced high-speed rail technologies for the future. This facility, now known as the Transportation Technology Center, has been privatized and is managed by the AAR.

Another form of assistance to the railroad industry is **Amtrak**. In 1969, the industry's intercity passenger deficit reached more than $500 million. Because the ICC, the DOT, and the public deemed many passenger services essential to the public need, the railroads could only discontinue them slowly after major procedural steps were taken. Amtrak was created to relieve this burden from the railroads, while at the same time providing some of the needed services to the public. Thus, much of the passenger train deficit was shifted from the railroads and their customers and stockholders to the federal taxpayer. The annual federal appropriation to Amtrak was nearly $1.4 billion in 2016.

Domestic Waterway Operations The inland barge industry receives two major forms of federal promotion. The first is from the **Army Corps of Engineers**, which is responsible for river and port channel dredging and clearances, as well as lock and dam construction. Operation and maintenance of these facilities rest with the Corps as well. The second form of federal promotion is provided by the USCG, which is responsible for navigation aids and systems on the inland waterway system.

Historically, the barge industry paid no user charges except what could be interpreted as a very indirect form through general income taxes. A major controversy over a critical lock and dam on the upper Mississippi River in Alton, Illinois, brought the free-use issue to a decision. The competing railroad industry lobbied to prevent this lock from being improved and enlarged. The resulting legislation and appropriation provided for improvement of that lock and initiated a fuel tax user charge for the barge industry.

International Water Carriage   The American flag overseas steamship industry receives major assistance from the federal government through MARAD. The Merchant Marine Act of 1936 was designed to prevent economic decline of the U.S. steamship industry. One major portion of this Act is construction differential subsidies (CDS). These are paid by MARAD to U.S. steamship yards that are constructing subsidized lines' ships. A ship that might only cost $20 million to build in Asia might cost $30 million to build in a U.S. yard. A CDS of $10 million is given to the U.S. shipyard so it can charge the U.S. steamship company $20 million, rather than $30 million, to build its ship. Without CDS, U.S. lines would build their ships abroad and American ship-building capacity would cease to exist. The survival of the U.S. shipyard is also viewed as essential to U.S. military capability. The Merchant Marine Act of 1936 also provides for operating differential subsidies (ODS), which cover the higher cost increment resulting from having higher-paid American crews on ships, rather than less costly foreign labor.

Several **indirect forms of promotion** exist in this industry as well. The U.S. cabotage laws state that freight or passengers originating or terminating in two U.S. points can only be transported in ships constructed in the United States and owned and managed by U.S. citizens. The United States also has a **cargo preference** law that assists the U.S. fleet. Enacted in 1954, it stipulates that at least 50 percent of the gross tonnage of certain U.S. government-owned and -sponsored cargoes must be carried by U.S. flagships. This law extends to Department of Defense military goods, foreign aid by the State Department, surplus food movements by the Department of Agriculture, and products whose financing is sponsored by the Export–Import Bank. To be granted a U.S. flag registry, all of a ship's officers and pilots, as well as 75 percent of its other onboard personnel, must be U.S. citizens or residents. The ship must also be owned by U.S. citizens and constructed in a U.S. shipyard.

Several planning and facilitating promotional efforts also assist the American flag ocean fleet. MARAD continually studies and develops plans for port improvements and ways in which export–import movements can be made more efficient. The Department of Commerce has a subagency (the International Trade Administration) whose prime purpose is to stimulate export sales that also benefit the U.S. fleet.

Two points should be mentioned with regard to the major funding and support roles played by MARAD. One deals with the control MARAD has over the lines it subsidizes. The agency exercises decision powers over the design and construction of each ship. It also plays a major role in the routes taken by each one. In this manner, the agency makes certain decisions that are normally within the discretion of carrier managements. This form of control is unique to the transportation industry in the United States.

The other point relates to the rationale for such extensive assistance to this one industry. A strong U.S. shipping fleet is a vital part of national defense sealift capacity in the event of war. Also, existence of the fleet tends to exert some influence on services and rates on various trade routes to the benefit of the United States and its interests.

The **Shipping Act of 1984** (replaced by the Foreign Shipping Practices Act of 1998) is a further example of the U.S. policy toward supporting a strong U.S. ocean fleet. The Act was designed with the following goals:

- Establishing a nondiscriminatory regulatory process for common ocean carriers with a minimum of government intervention and regulatory costs;
- Providing an efficient and economic transportation system in the ocean commerce of the United States that is in harmony and responsive to international shipping practices; and
- Encouraging the development of an economically sound and efficient U.S. flag fleet capable of meeting national security needs.

The St. Lawrence Seaway Development Corporation within the DOT functions as the U.S. financing and operating arm of the joint United States/Canada venture to upgrade the Great Lakes waterway and lock system to accommodate oceangoing ships. This waterway opened a fourth seacoast for the United States, enabling oceangoing ships to call at Buffalo, Cleveland, Toledo, Chicago, Duluth, and other inland ports.

A final, and major, positive role in the water carrier industry is played by various port authorities. These agencies provide financing, major construction, and leasing of facilities in much the same way that the airport authorities provides facilities to the air industry.

Pipeline The pipeline industry receives no public financial support, but it has benefited in a legal sense from the right of eminent domain permitted to oil, gas, and petroleum product lines. Typically, a pipeline will negotiate for land acquisition or rental. If the landowner will not negotiate at all or in good faith, the law of eminent domain will uphold the use of the land for a pipeline right-of-way in a court of law.

Miscellaneous Forms of Promotion Various activities directly or indirectly benefit the transportation industry. The DOT conducts planning and research activities in several ways. First, the Office of Assistant Secretary for Policy and International Affairs is involved with improving international goods flow and conducting studies about the transportation system and data coordination. Second, research and development studies of benefit to transportation are conducted by the Transportation Research Board and the National Science Foundation. Third, the Department of Agriculture conducts ongoing research and analysis of agriculture transportation, packaging, and logistics to support efficient movement of food. Finally, the Department of Defense continually examines methods to improve transportation, and many improvements carry over to the commercial sector.

Paying for Transportation Programs

Two major concepts override the entire topic of transportation promotion: user charges and nationalization. User charges often are created and assessed to pay for some or all services used by the carrier or mode. Nationalization represents an extreme form of public assistance or provision of transportation.

User Charges User charges are assessments or fees charged by public bodies against carriers. They are created for a variety of reasons. One is to compensate the public for assistance during modal conception and encouragement. Some user charges are assessed to finance construction. The federal fuel tax on gasoline and diesel is an example, as is the barge fuel tax. Coverage of operating costs is often a reason for the origin of user charges. Examples here are airport landing fees, road tolls, and state fuel tax when it is applied to road maintenance. In addition, a user charge can also serve to equalize intermodal competitive conditions. The barge fuel tax, while paying for some lock construction, also makes barge operators bear some of the cost of providing their service. This lessens, to a degree, some of the advantage that existed when right-of-way costs were borne by the public and not by the barge firm.

User charges are present in three basic forms. The first is an **existence charge**, a charge related to the existence of some tangible item. This is similar to driver's license and auto registration fees. A charge is made against the person or unit regardless of the extent of use made of the services.

A second user charge is a **unit charge**. This is a fee assessed for use of a facility or resource. This fee is variable according to use, but it does not distinguish between passengers or freight within each unit. Tolls and fuel mileage taxes are examples. Thus, a bus with two passengers pays the same as does a bus with 40 passengers. An empty tractor–trailer or one that is full is charged the same. This form of fee assessment does not take into account the economic value of the service being performed.

A third user fee is based upon **relative use**. This form assesses fees according to the investment of cost incurred by the agency to provide the service. An increased vehicle registration fee for heavier tractor–trailers is an example. Deeper road bases are required for heavier vehicles. Road and bridge wear and damage are believed to be experienced on the basis of vehicle weight. Another example of relative use charge is a commuter route bridge toll. In the San Francisco area, bridge tolls are assessed for each vehicle. However, cars and vans having more than four passengers can cross the bridge toll-free. In this instance, the user charge becomes a behavior inducement. *Nonuser fees* have also arisen. Atlanta and San Francisco and area counties are partially paying for their shares of rapid transit development through a one-cent additional sales tax on all retail transactions within those areas. Here, many persons do not, or might not, ever use the rapid transit system, but they do bear some of its costs. A major rationale behind this nonuser charge is that all persons in a community benefit at least indirectly from the improved infrastructure provided by the system.

Nationalization Nationalization is an extreme form of public promotion that involves public ownership, financing, and operation of a business entity. No true forms of nationalization exist in the U.S. transportation system except the Alaska Railroad, which was owned by the DOT and is now owned by the state of Alaska. Nationalization is a method of providing transportation service where financing, ownership, or operations are not possible by private sources. Railroads and airlines in foreign countries are examples of nationalization, but some countries have privatized their railroads.

The often-cited advantage of nationalization is that services can be provided that would not exist under private ownership, and that capital can be attracted at favorable rates. But nationalized organizations have been criticized as being slow to innovate, unresponsive to the general public, dependent on large management staffs, and subject to political influence.

SUMMARY

- Transportation influences society, commerce, and the environment. Governments cannot afford to take a hands-off approach to the management of this vital industry.
- Policy molds the transportation system into an efficient and effective network, protects the different modes of transportation, and promotes a fair and competitive marketplace for freight services.
- National transportation policy is developed by federal and state governments with input from the three branches, various agencies, industry groups, and companies.
- U.S. transportation policy is somewhat fluid and not explicitly defined in a single unifying document.

- The imperfections in the marketplace in a free-enterprise economy provide the rationale for government intervention and regulation.

- The basis of U.S. transportation regulation is a combination of common law, statutory law, and state regulation. Focal points of regulation include: economic, antitrust, safety, and security.

- Potential monopolistic abuses in transportation motivated the federal government to create the Interstate Commerce Commission (ICC) to economically regulate the transportation industry. The Surface Transportation Board (STB) replaced the ICC.

- In today's transportation environment, the federal government is a proponent of less economic regulation, preferring to allow market forces to regulate carrier prices and availability of supply.

- All modes are subject to safety regulations administered by both federal and state agencies.

- Increasing regulations for safety and security are placing a higher burden on carriers but lessening the risk to the public at large.

- Transportation regulation has progressed through four phases: Initiation Era, Positive Era, Intermodal Era, and the New Economic Era.

- Government planning and funding of transportation needs are needed to ensure that the transportation system is viable and supports the efficient movement of freight and passengers.

- Every mode of transportation benefits from government programs that develop infrastructure, operate networks, conduct research, and/or protect domestic industries.

- Transportation programs and promotion are funded through user fees and direct government investment.

STUDY QUESTIONS

1. Why are transportation policy, regulation, and planning important? How do they feed off each other?
2. What are the primary themes or goals of U.S. national transportation policy?
3. What groups play a role in the development of national transportation policy? What roles does each group take?
4. How has common law provided a basis for the government's regulation of transportation in the United States?
5. Why is the judicial system involved in transportation policy and regulation?
6. What roles do individual states play in transportation regulation?
7. Identify the four primary types of transportation regulation. Describe the purpose or rationale for each type.
8. Discuss the advantages and disadvantages of increasing transportation safety and security regulations. Be sure to include both transportation providers and transportation users in your discussion.
9. Identify and describe the four major eras of transportation regulation.
10. What is the rationale for the public promotion of transportation?
11. Which mode of transportation has received the greatest level of government promotional support? Defend your answer.
12. What are transportation user charges? What is the purpose of such charges?

NOTES

1. BusinessDictionary, *Policy*, retrieved September 10, 2017, from http://www.businessdictionary.com/definition/policy.html.

2. U.S. Department of Transportation, *Moving America: New Directions, New Opportunities*, Washington, DC, February 1990, p. vii. Retrieved September 12, 2017, from https://ntl.bts.gov/lib/56000/56400/56470/movingamericanew00unse_0.pdf.

3. 104th Congress, *Public Law 104-88 Chapter 131—General Provisions*, December 29, 1995, p. 853. Retrieved September 12, 2017, from https://www.congress.gov/104/plaws/publ88/PLAW-104publ88.pdf.

4. U.S. Transportation, *About DOT*, June 17, 2016. Retrieved September 13, 2017, from https://www.transportation.gov/about.

5. *English Oxford Living Dictionaries*, s.v. "Regulation." Retrieved September 15, 2017, from https://en.oxforddictionaries.com/definition/us/regulation.

6. *BusinessDictionary*, s.v. "Regulation." Retrieved September 15, 2017, from http://www.businessdictionary.com/definition/regulation.html.

7. Dudley F. Pegrum, *Public Regulation of Business*, Homewood, IL: Richard D. Irwin, 1959, pp. 21–24.

8. Ibid.

9. This section is based on Thomas J. Spulak, "The Role of Congress in the Federal Regulatory Process," March 17, 2010. Retrieved September 16, 2017, from https://www2.gwu.edu/~clai/recent_events/2010/Spring_Regulatory_Program/Speaker%20Presentations/The_Role_of_Congress_in_the_Federal_Regulatory_Process_2010.pdf.

10. U.S. Department of Transportation, *Rulemaking Process*, May 23, 2016. Retrieved September 16, 2017, from https://www.transportation.gov/regulations/rulemaking-process

11. *FindLaw*, s.v. "General Description of the Department of Transportation's Regulatory Responsibilities." Retrieved September 15, 2017, from http://corporate.findlaw.com/litigation-disputes/general-description-of-the-department-of-transportation-s.html.

12. Thomson Reuters, "Congress Acts to Preempt Regulation of Intrastate Transportation of Property," *FindLaw*. Retrieved September 18, 2017, from http://corporate.findlaw.com/law-library/congress-acts-to-preempt-regulation-of-intrastate-transportation.html.

13. Sherman Anti-Trust Act of 1890, Sections 1 and 2.

14. U.S. Customs and Border Protection, *About CBP*, November 21, 2016. Retrieved September 17, 2017, from https://www.cbp.gov/about.

CASE 12-1

Who Pays the Price?

Over the last 10 years the federal government has dramatically increased the number of regulations pertaining to transportation safety and security. Two such regulations are presented below. Review them and answer the case questions.

Transportation Safety—December 18, 2017, is set as the implementation day for electronic logging devices (ELD) in trucks. ELDs will replace paper logbooks for truck drivers to provide better control over their compliance with Hours of Service regulations that are designed to combat driver fatigue. It is believed that paper logbooks are subject to fraud and allow drivers to exceed 11 hours of driving time per day and more than 60 hours in a seven-day period. On the other hand, drivers will not be able to easily exceed the limits as ELDs are not easily manipulated. The cost of ELD purchase, installation, and operation is the responsibility of the trucking company or the independent truck driver.

ELD critics believe that, at a cost of up to $2,500 per unit, the expense of ELD adoption is excessive for small companies and independent truckers. They also project productivity decreases of 15 percent fewer miles traveled per day and nominal rate increases of 5 to 10 percent for loads booked on the spot market. Proponents indicate that ELDs will improve the accuracy of HOS logs, improve Hours of Service compliance, reduce falsification that occurs with paper logbooks, and reduce crashes by over 1,800 annually.

Transportation Security—After the terrorist attack on the United States on September 11, 2001, the Transportation Security Administration (TSA) was established and tasked with implementing regulations to protect the safety of passengers using the U.S. airline industry. TSA manages Secure Flight, a risk-based prescreening program to identify high-risk passengers; conducts passenger screening for illegal items before they enter the secure area of airports; and screens checked bags for explosives and other dangerous items. TSA has implemented congressionally mandated security fees to help finance the increased cost of securing the nation's aviation transportation system. This passenger paid fee was increased to $11.20 per round trip ticket in 2014.

Critics of TSA screening programs complain that these policies increase travel time, invade privacy, are of limited effectiveness, and increase costs for passengers and airlines. Proponents of these policies argue that the safety of air passengers is more important than delays or increased costs.

CASE QUESTIONS

1. In each of the scenarios presented in the case, opponents and proponents have divergent views of government regulations. One view is on the public benefit, the other is on the cost to individuals and/or private industry. How can you decide which view to accept?

2. In each of the scenarios earlier, identify the benefits versus the costs for both viewpoints.

3. Should the government intervene in setting regulations to increase transportation safety and security? Or should private industry take on this role? Discuss.

CASE 12-2

Federal Highway Infrastructure Funding

The Federal Highway Trust Fund (HTF) was designed and passed by Congress to set tax rates per gallon of gasoline and diesel consumed by vehicles using the federal interstate system. The HTF is then used to maintain the thousands of miles of interstate highway in the United States.

This program has worked successfully up until the last several years when stricter EPA rules on fuel consumption have been implemented along with the introduction of hybrid and electric vehicles. Total miles driven and fuel consumed have decreased and, as such, have resulted in a decrease in taxes coming into the fund. The federal per-gallon tax rates of 18.4 cents for gasoline and 24.4 cents for diesel fuel have not changed since 1993. As a result, HTF is spending more money annually than it is taking in and faces a funding gap of $107 billion, according to the Congressional Budget Office. Critics complain that lawmakers have failed to provide an adequate, sustainable funding source.

With the U.S. interstate highway system in need of major repairs, the Trump administration is proposing a $1 trillion investment in improving the quality of the nation's roads and highways. However, what is not yet agreed upon is where the additional funding will come from. Three main ideas have surfaced to generate these funds: (1) the Trump administration is proposing a public–private partnership plan in which $200 million of federal spending will spur $800 million in private investment by companies that will operate the roads and collect road tolls. (2) a gradual increase in the per-gallon fuel taxes over several years; (3) converting major portions of the interstate system into toll roads. There has been much debate about these approaches and many interest groups have voiced their opinions. As of yet, no decision has been made about this intended infrastructure investment program, funding level, or its sources of fees.

CASE QUESTIONS

1. Which of the three funding approaches make the best economic sense? Which one makes the best political sense?

2. What are the pros and cons of each funding approach? Be sure to include in your discussion the views of personal vehicles versus commercial vehicles.

3. Is there another funding alternative not yet introduced? What would it be and how would it be implemented?

13
ISSUES AND CHALLENGES FOR GLOBAL SUPPLY CHAINS

Learning Objectives

After reading this chapter, you should be able to do the following:

> Appreciate the serious challenges and major issues faced by the current transportation system for continued domestic and global economic growth

> Understand why and what factors contributed to the growth and prosperity that was experienced in recent years

> Discuss the economic and competitive challenges being caused by the decaying U.S. infrastructure and the threat to the economic viability of the major modes of transportation in the United States

> Gain a perspective on the critical role of government leadership and policy to resolve the crisis that exists for our global economy without capital funding for the U.S. transportation system

> Appreciate the crisis in the gap for supply chain talent, its causes, and solutions

> Understand why sustainability has become a major objective for businesses and especially for transportation and the potential positive benefits of proactive sustainability strategies

> Appreciate the impact of new energy sources for the global economy

> Discuss the role and objectives of the SmartWay Transport Partnership sponsored by the U.S. Environmental Protection Agency

> Develop insights into the special challenges that transport companies will face in the 21st century with increased competition and changes in energy sources

> Understand the opportunities that transportation carriers will have to improve overall supply chain performance through proactive collaboration and appropriate use of new technology

> Discuss how supply chain technology can help transport carriers to improve efficiency and effectiveness for their operations and for their customer's costs and service

TRANSPORTATION **PROFILE**

It's "Beyond Time" to Modernize U.S. Infrastructure, U.S. Chamber of Commerce Urges

The general message sent during the recently held "Infrastructure Week" was loud and clear: The lack of U.S. infrastructure modernization is increasingly causing expensive bottlenecks at ports and around our cities that are responsible for expensive delays in an ever-complex worldwide market.

"I've been playing around with supply chain issues since I was a young man—which is a long time ago," said Thomas Donohue, former head of the American Trucking Associations (ATA) and for the past 20 years the president and CEO of the U.S. Chamber of Commerce. "Today's supply chain is not what I grew up with, and change is inevitable in this business."

Donohue and others spoke during "Infrastructure Week" at the U.S. Chamber's fifth annual Global Supply Chain Summit in May 2017. He added that this is a "once in a generation" opportunity to modernize the U.S. infrastructure to the tune of $1 trillion in investment.

The quest, as always, is how to pay for it. Fuel tax increases are apparently back on the table in Congress, and that was music to the ears for some in attendance. Ed Mortimer, executive director of the U.S. Chamber's transportation initiative, has backed the Chamber's call for a gradual increase in the federal fuels tax—currently 18.4 cents a gallon on gasoline, 24.4 cents on diesel, unchanged since 1993.

"It's not just time to fix it," Mortimer said, "it's time to modernize it and improve it, and that not only includes roads and bridges." He added that intermodal access to ports around the country is clogged due to the increase in foreign trade and water advocates don't want to be left out in any building boom.

Molly Campbell, a director at the Port Authority of New York and New Jersey, added that "infrastructure is our bread and butter." She said that their port is undergoing a major dredging program to help accommodate larger, deeper ships. "We would love to have infrastructure spending that's more flexible, but the government needs to invest in projects that make the most economic sense, not just merely on political will," she said.

As always, truckers are in the vanguard of those calling for increased spending on infrastructure. FedEx and other truckers have openly called for an increase in the fuel tax to pay for improvements to alleviate bottlenecks.

Bill Sullivan, executive vice president of advocacy at the ATA, said that big investments are needed for the trucking industry, adding that ATA officials recently met face-to-face with President Trump and Vice President Mike Pence to lobby for more spending on highways.

Sullivan reiterated ATA's call for an increase in the fuel tax—which, notably, he called a "user fee." Trucking interests are vigorously opposed to tolling of existing highways, although Sullivan left the door open for tolls on newer highways.

"The highway is our office," Sullivan said. "And we believe that there has to be a suitable funding mechanism to find dedicated funding for highway investment," adding that a recent freight bottleneck survey showed that congestion costs U.S. shippers $63 billion a year in delays—an embarrassingly high figure for a country with the biggest economy in the world.

Source: Adapted from John D. Schultz, *Logistics Management*, June 2017, p. 13. Reprinted with permission of Peerless Media, LLC.

Introduction

Chapters 1 and 2 discussed the role and importance of transportation in the firm and in the economy. The economic, political, and social contributions and significance of transportation were examined. Transportation was described as the "glue" that holds supply chains together and the "lifeblood" of economies, regions, and cities. Our modern civilization and the developments, which have occurred in many countries, would not have been possible without an efficient and effective transportation system. It was also noted that transportation has been a critical part of economic, political, and social development for hundreds of years. In fact, transportation may be the most important business for a developed economy.

During the 1980s, 1990s, and the early part of the 21st century, transportation became relatively less expensive for a given level of service, which contributed significantly to enhanced productivity and economic growth. This phenomenon was attributable to two major factors, namely, relatively inexpensive fuel and competition, particularly in the motor carrier sector of the transportation industry. In fact, one could argue that we were "spoiled" by these two conditions that fostered economic prosperity. However, times have changed, with increased fuel prices and a reduction in available capacity in the motor carrier sector, due to driver hour restrictions and other factors discussed in Chapter 5. The other modes of transportation, especially air carriers, have faced similar challenges. This change has occurred at a crucial time in global development. The concern is that fuel charges, competitive market forces, and other factors could cause the cost of moving goods to increase in the years ahead. There are a number of factors, including congestion, the environment, and the transport infrastructure, that may affect the long global, and frequently, vulnerable supply chains with their movements of high-value, time-sensitive commodities. If these challenges are not mitigated, the cost of moving freight will thwart economic progress in developed as well as underdeveloped economies. Figure 13-1 clearly indicates the long-run potential for the U.S. transportation system when all three flows for the system are considered. The flows associated with imports into the country are particularly noteworthy. It is imperative to the economic health of the United States and its citizens that the challenges indicated above and discussed in this chapter be addressed in an objective manner.

Since the transportation industry will have to address these challenges and issues in the future, we will discuss major issues in detail and examine their impact on the important sectors of the transportation industry. The initial issue will be the transportation infrastructure, followed by energy, talent management, and sustainability.

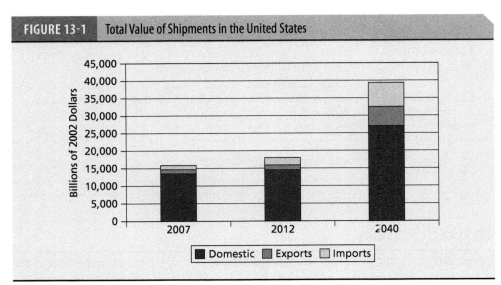

FIGURE 13-1 Total Value of Shipments in the United States

Source: Federal Highway Administration, U.S. Department of Transportation, Freight Facts and Figures 2013, Table 2-2: Value of Shipments by Transportation Mode: 2007, 2012, and 2040.

Transportation Infrastructure

Everyone has probably experienced the frustration associated with congestion, usually when riding in an automobile on the highway; or perhaps it was on an airplane trying to take off or land at an airport. Some individuals experience congestion on a regular, daily basis if they live in or near a city and have to commute to and from work. However, we seldom consider the total or real cost of congestion. For individuals, the cost of extra fuel is the most obvious cost of congestion, but there is also the cost of the personal time lost, which could reduce personal earnings. If the congestion does not cause an obvious economic loss, it usually has an impact in the area of what an economist would call a social cost—reduced opportunity for leisure, reduced time with family, inconvenience for friends and family, and so on. The social cost is difficult to calibrate, but nevertheless, it is a societal cost that needs to be included in the analytical equation for congestion.

For many businesses, however, the cost of congestion is real and important. Consider the fact that Nike estimates that it has to spend an additional $4 million per week to carry an extra 7 to 14 days of inventory to compensate for congestion delays. One day of delay requires American President Lines' eastbound trans-Pacific services to increase its use of containers and chassis by 1,300 units, which adds $4 million of additional cost per year. The bottleneck delays of trucks on the U.S. highways cause over 250 million hours of delay to truckers throughout the United States. A conservative estimate of the cost of these delays is about $7 billion per year. When fuel costs and/or labor costs increase, the costs are compounded.[1]

Changes in costs to carriers are eventually reflected in their transportation rates for shippers. Between 2013 and 2016, rates decreased 0.99 percent for truck transportation, 4.39 percent for rail transportation, 4.27 percent for scheduled air freight, 2.66 percent for water transportation, increased 7.41 percent for port and harbor operations, increased 7.74 percent for marine cargo handling, increased 12.27 percent for pipeline transportation of crude oil, and increased 13.98 percent for refined oil products.[2] Obviously, these increases reflect a combination of cost and demand factors, but the cost factors are the most important.

Highway Traffic and Infrastructure

It is estimated that congestion on highways will spread from large urban areas and some intercity routes to large stretches of intercity highways in both urban and rural areas. Without operational improvements, it is estimated that by 2035 recurring peak-period congestion will slow traffic on 20,000 miles of the National Highway System and create stop-and-go conditions on an additional 45,000 miles. The top 10 highway interchange bottlenecks cause an average of 1.5 million annual truck hours of delay. The (conservative) estimated delay costs are about $30/hour to the trucking companies, but the cost to the shippers would usually be higher.[3]

Figure 13-2 indicates the funding challenges faced by our highway system. The revenue inflow is below the "need to maintain" level required to keep the current highway system operating effectively. The delay costs indicated above will also need funds to improve the current system. The graph shows the projections for the 50 states and federal-level needs for what are considered to be required improvements. The combined total shows a staggering gap for the future. Revenues will have to be increased or the demand for highway usage decreased. Evidence of the problem is evident in almost every state and certainly on most parts of the interstate system. While national defense and societal needs are important, the highway infrastructure is the lifeblood of the economy's engine. The lack of federal and state investment is very shortsighted for the U.S. economy's future staying power.

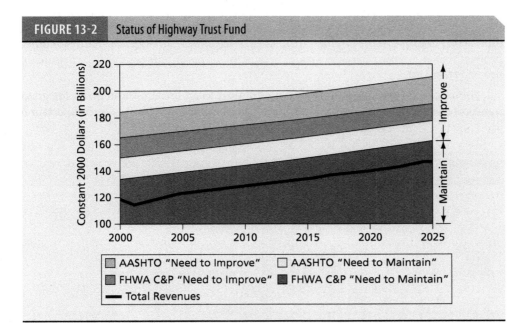

FIGURE 13-2   Status of Highway Trust Fund

Source: An Initial Assessment of Freight Bottlenecks on Highways, White Paper, October 2005. Prepared for Federal Highway Administration, Office of Transportation Policy Studies. Prepared by Cambridge Systematics, Inc. in association with Battelle Memorial Institute. Accessible online at http://www.fhwa.dot.gov/policy/otps/bottlenecks/index.htm.

Railroad Traffic and Infrastructure

The large interregional freight railroads have experienced a significant increase in demand, especially for trailer-on-flatcar (TOFC) and container-on-flatcar (COFC) movements. TOFC and COFC, once a relatively small market segment, is now a major source of revenue and traffic. These relatively high-speed intermodal trains compete for network space with the bulk traffic trains. The congestion is frequently exacerbated by seasonal surges in freight demand and disruptions that add to the congestion as volumes reach capacity on the reduced mainline rail network (reduced 50 percent between 1960 and 1980).

Congestion on the mainline railroad network is forecast to spread significantly by 2035. The American Association of Railroads reports that congestion will increase to almost 16,000 miles on the main lines of the railroads (30 percent of the network) if current capacity is not increased. Rail routes that have moderate to very limited capacity to accommodate maintenance without servicing delays and disruption will almost double by 2035, which will affect about 25 percent of the network. A potential solution to the rail congestion problem is the construction and return of double tracks to accommodate two-way traffic simultaneously, which was common on the main lines of most large railroads prior to World War II. The Union Pacific Railroad has already initiated a doubletrack program in some areas. The addition of another track can be accomplished more quickly and usually at less cost than adding lanes to an interstate highway, but there is still a major investment cost that railroads are reluctant to accommodate on a private basis; that is, they want a government subsidy to underwrite the cost in whole or in part, similar to the other modes of transportation. Figure 13-3 clearly indicates the magnitude of the budget funding gap.[4]

The challenge for the railroads since 2010 has been the increased volumes of additional traffic associated with the development of fracking technology for exploiting gas and oil in the new reserves in various areas of the United States especially in the Upper Midwest, the Great Lakes region, and eastern states like Pennsylvania and New York. There were no pipelines in place, as previously noted, which placed the burden on motor carriers and railroads to transport these products that has caused a critical shortage of capacity for other products (such as grain) and safety issues because of the hazardous nature of the petroleum products from the Upper Midwest.

A bumper harvest of grain in 2014 contributed to an increase in demand for grain transportation by rail of 15 percent. There was also an increase in demand for transportation

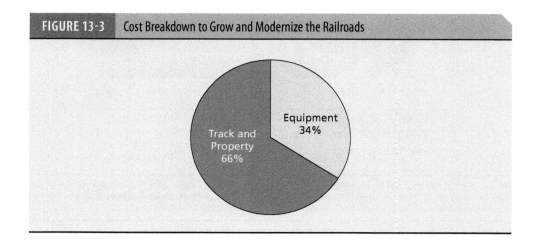

FIGURE 13-3   Cost Breakdown to Grow and Modernize the Railroads

of oil/petroleum products of over 13 percent. There is tremendous pressure building on railroads like the BSNF Railway to speed delivery on its congested tracks of critical products (like coal) for the winter. The BSNF Railway organization has invested $5.5 billion in its infrastructure to fix the problem and had added 500 locomotives and 5,000 railcars and hired 6,000 new employees to solve their delivery challenges. If the problem is not fixed, the utility customers will have to pay much higher rates for electricity and other energy-related products. This situation illustrates again the critical and important role of transportation for the economic viability of the United States and other economies of the world.[5]

Waterway Traffic and Infrastructure

On inland waterways, aging infrastructure and locks frequently cause bottlenecks. For example, of the 510,000 commercial vessel passages through federal and state locks, 31 percent experienced delays. Average delays for barge tows were one hour and 32 minutes. The average processing time was about 30 minutes. The challenge is that inland waterways are especially susceptible to weather delays, including problems caused by flooding, draughts, ice, and other storm-related disruptions.

Deep-draft ports on the three major coastlines have capacity challenges, which will be explored in the next section. The inland ports have capacity issues also, but most of them are not as problematic as the ocean ports. As indicated previously, the congestion problem at the ports is a significant challenge, especially since these ports are the gateways for imports and exports, and the long-run projection for growth in global trade (imports and exports based upon weight) in the United States is 77 percent. The West Coast ports are particularly vulnerable because of the growth in trade with Asian countries and the new mega containerships.[6]

The concentration of vessels bringing container freight through the West Coast ports is evident in Figure 13-4. However, the Gulf and East coasts dominate the movement of non-containership calls. To what extent the expansion of the Suez and Panama canals will

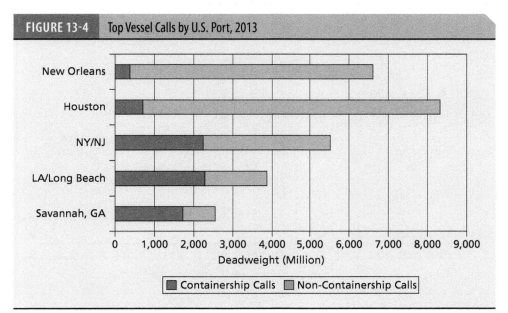

FIGURE 13-4   Top Vessel Calls by U.S. Port, 2013

Source: Vessel Calls Snapshot, 2011, U.S. Department of Transportation Maritime Administration.

shift some of the container traffic to East Coast ports remains to be seen. However, it is quite evident that even with a shift to some East Coast ports the port infrastructure on both the West Coast and East Coast is insufficient to support the needs of the global flows of traffic for global economic progress. New Orleans had the most activity, but the majority of the vessels are non containerships that are usually smaller vessels moving oil and oil products and dry bulk that do not cause the same level of activity in the port area, which means less congestion.

The port congestion problems are manifested in several areas. A growing share of water-borne commerce, especially imports, moves in very large containerships, the largest of which can carry more than 18,000 containers. These large ships can take five to seven days to unload, compared to two to three days for most containerships. Only a few ports can accommodate these ships because of the draft requirements in the channels leading into the port areas. They also require more berths for unloading, special cranes for unloading and loading, and more dock space and transportation-related equipment for moving the containers from the dock area to local terminals or distribution centers. In addition, the congestion problem is exacerbated by the fact that trans loading of the containers is frequently required since domestic containers can usually hold 50 to 60 percent more freight than the ISO international containers. In fact, this has caused an imbalance and shortage of the international ISO containers. Another related problem is that many port areas are constrained by the scarcity of land nearby and/or the high cost of such land for the development of marine terminals and related facilities.

The growth in containerships relative to regular vessels is clearly indicated in Figure 13-5, which shows percentage growth in deadweight capacity from 2004 to 2016. There are only four years (2010 to 2013) where the percentage growth of deadweight capacity for containerships is lower. Currently, the port congestion challenges are being partially addressed by improved

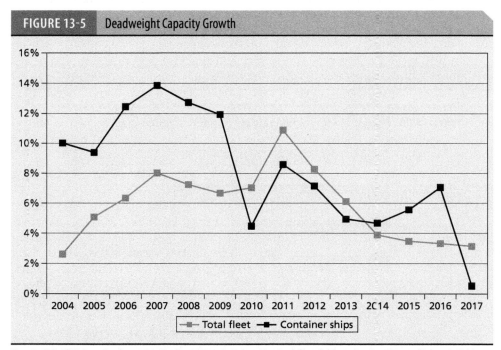

FIGURE 13-5 Deadweight Capacity Growth

Legend: Total fleet — Container ships

Source: United Nations Conference on Trade and Development, Merchant Fleet by flag of registration and by type of ship, annual, 1980–2014.

port access (for example, with dredging); investment in technology and equipment by carriers and port operators; and longer operating hours. These strategies are aimed at reducing the dwell time of ships and containers in port areas and relieving some of the pressure for expansion. The trade-off costs associated with improving access routes and round-the-clock operations, which often include overtime payments, need to be evaluated. The situation is also exacerbated by the public's hue and cry about the disruption around the port areas when vessels are loading and unloading. There are also environmental challenges in the port area with the discharge of various fluids (intentionally or unintentionally); the garbage, trash, and other debris that may be thrown overboard; and other ecological damage. Some port areas are notorious for their insensitivity to the ecology of the marine environment. Major efforts are underway to improve the environmental impact of port area.[7]

On a related note, the larger containerships have also caused some capacity and congestion problems on certain key waterways. A case in point is the Panama Canal, with locks that were built over a hundred years ago when ships were much smaller. Most of these larger ships have had to take the longer route around South America, which adds about 9,000 miles to the journey. Cognizant of this problem, the Panama Canal authority has undertaken a $5.25 billion construction project to add a third lane to the ocean-linking canal waterway, add two new locks (one on the east side of the canal and the other on the west side), and to dredge the existing waterway, which will double the canal's capacity and allow the canal to accommodate the supersize containerships. The third lane is open today, and should have a major impact on global trade routes as the large containerships are using the canal.

Talent Management

People are the most important asset of any organization. They provide the leadership, management, and innovation required to make any organization successful. As such, managing talent, through acquisition and retention, must be a key strategic strength of any company. This is especially true for supply chain talent in today's environment. According to the Bureau of Labor Statistics, jobs for logistics professionals are predicted to grow 26 percent between 2010 and 2020.[8] However, a severe supply chain talent gap exists today. According to a DHL Supply Chain research project, there are six supply chain job openings for every supply chain graduate.[9] The shortage of over-the-road truck drivers is another example. According to the American Trucking Association (ATA), the driver turnover rate in the third quarter of 2016 for carriers with revenue exceeding $30 million was 81 percent. Along with this, the ATA estimates that the driver shortage in 2015 stood at 48,000 and could rise to 175,000 by 2024.[10]

There are several reasons behind the supply chain talent gap. First, approximately 1.3 percent of all business students in the United States are supply chain majors.[11] Because of this, many undergraduates are not aware of supply chain as a professional career. In addition, since supply chain activities are "hidden" from the average consumer, many do not know what the profession entails. Second, there can be a perceived lack of opportunity for growth in a supply chain role.[12] In many organizations, individuals in functional roles other than supply chain, like finance and marketing, are perceived to be on the path to fill the roles at the top executive levels. As such, when young professionals are making the decision on their academic majors, supply chain is not a top priority. Third, for the over-the-road trucking industry, millennials perceive the aging workforce (baby boomers), long hours on the road, relatively low pay, and time away from home as negative aspects of this profession.

A key aspect for companies to attract young supply chain talent is to recognize that millennials (born between 1985 and 2004) have different perspectives of the ideal job versus baby boomers (born between 1946 and 1964). A recent study conducted by Supply Chain Insights found that the top five most important aspects of a job for all age groups are: (1) competitive salary; (2) challenging work; (3) work–life balance; (4) working with a talented team; and (5) appreciation for your work. These results can be seen in Figure 13-6. However, Figure 13-7 shows that there is a difference in these preferences between millennials and baby boomers. Millennials prefer work–life balance, career path, and training/professional development as key aspects of a job while baby boomers preferences are a belief in work, challenging work, and leaders you admire. Firms that recognize these differences are more likely to be able to attract young professionals into a supply chain career.

Retaining supply chain talent is another key strategy for successful companies. Figure 13.8 shows the results of the Supply Chain Insights research on what current employees feel is important about their jobs. As can be seen, all age groups agree that challenging work and competitive salary are the most important aspects of their current jobs. Table 13-1 shows the differences between millennials and baby boomers. While baby boomers consider challenging work to be the most important, millennials consider it to be the top priority.

There are several strategies firms can use to acquire and retain supply chain talent. First, establish recruiting relationships with universities that have a well-developed supply chain curriculum. Second, change the perception of supply chain management as being a profession with a progression path. Third, develop supply chain management internally through training and professional development. Fourth, some long-haul truckload carriers are regionalizing their operations to be able to give their drivers more "home" time. In addition, they are establishing dedicated routes to guarantee their drivers a steady and

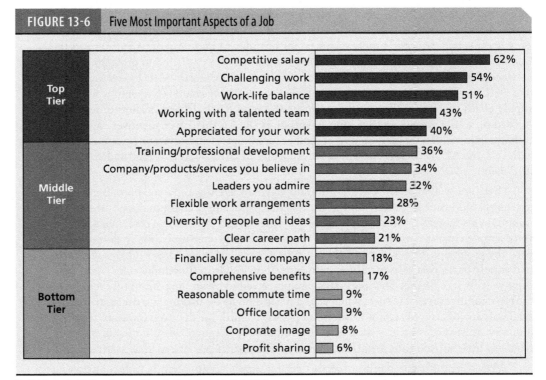

FIGURE 13-6   Five Most Important Aspects of a Job

Redistributed with Permission of Supply Chain Insights LLC, 2017.

| FIGURE 13-7 | Five Most Important Aspects of a Job: Baby Boomer vs. Millennial |

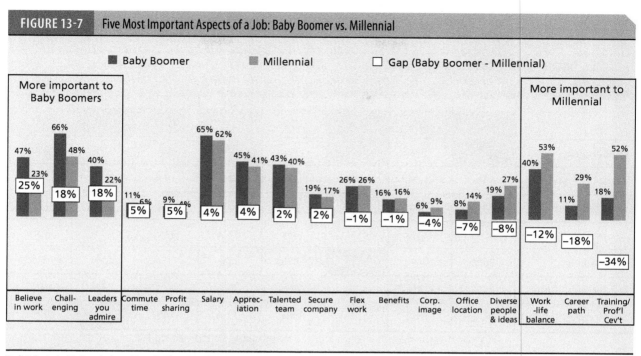

Redistributed with Permission of Supply Chain Insights LLC, 2017.

| FIGURE 13-8 | Five Best Aspects About Current/Recent Job |

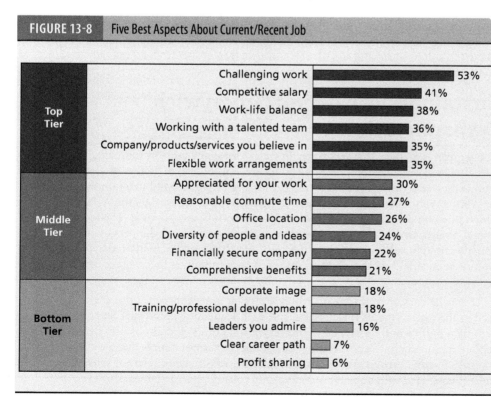

Redistributed with Permission of Supply Chain Insights LLC, 2017.

TABLE 13-1	Most Important vs. Best Aspects of Job: by Generation							
	TOTAL		**GENERATION**					
			Baby Boomer		**Generation X**		**Millennial**	
	Important	Impt. vs. Best	Important	Impt. vs. Best	Important	Impt. vs. Best	Important	Impt. vs. Best
Base:	426	426	89	90	246	246	90	90
Salary	64%	-23%	65%	-20%	63%	-20%	67%	-34%
Challenging	56%	-3%	66%	-7%	53%	-3%	51%	2%
Work-life balance	49%	-12%	40%	0%	52%	-13%	50%	-19%
Talented team	44%	-8%	43%	4%	45%	-9%	42%	-17%
Appreciated	40%	-10%	45%	-8%	37%	-11%	42%	-10%
Believe in it	36%	0%	47%	-3%	36%	-1%	23%	6%
Leaders you admire	34%	-18%	40%	-20%	36%	-22%	22%	-4%
Training/Prof'l Dev't	34%	-15%	18%	-8%	33%	-14%	52%	-27%

Top 2 Important   **Top 2 Performance Gaps**

Source: Redistributed with Permission of Supply Chain Insights LLC, 2017.

predictable income. Finally, recognize the differences between millennials and baby boomers. Utilizing these strategies will allow companies to develop a supply chain talent pipeline that will result in successful acquisition and retention of supply chain talent.

Sustainability: Going Green with Transportation

Going green is a slogan that was given lip service for many years by individuals and organizations. There was an assumption that going green would mean increased cost to the enterprise, which was viewed as unacceptable. Pressure began to build in a number of quarters for green supply chains, which meant that both shippers and carriers would have to initiate efforts to eliminate pollutants, reduce carbon footprints, and so forth. The local, state, and federal governments also began to exert pressure on carriers and shippers to improve. Interestingly enough, some organizations found that they could actually reduce their carbon footprint and still lower their costs, along with their initiatives to lower the negative impact on the environment.

Some discussion of the term **carbon footprint** is appropriate at this point. It is widely used by the various media (print, radio, and TV), academics, politicians, and others and has become a part of our vernacular. However, in spite of its ubiquitous use, definitions vary and are frequently not very specific. The common interpretation is that a carbon footprint is equated with a certain amount of gaseous emissions that are relevant to climate change and are associated with human production and consumption activities. However, there does not appear to be any consensus on how to measure or quantify the carbon footprint. The spectrum of definitions ranges from direct CO_2 definitions to full life-cycle greenhouse gas emissions. There is an emphasis, however, on measuring CO_2 emissions directly and indirectly caused by an activity, which is the preference of the authors.

There is no doubt that the higher fuel prices in 2008 helped spur interest among carriers and shippers to reduce fuel consumption. This effort to improve fuel efficiency also reduced the carbon footprint of commercial transportation, but it is only one of several reasons that is motivating business to drive their sustainability agenda. The other reasons include corporate responsibility, a desire to increase or maintain brand reputation, competitive pressures, and internal and external stakeholder pressure, or expectations as well as potential regulatory action by the federal and state regulatory agencies.

The unexpected happened in the second decade of the 21st century with developments discussed above, namely, new technology (fracking), that made the drilling and production of oil economically feasible in additional areas in the United States and other countries such as Canada. The impact began to be felt in 2014 with significant reductions in gasoline prices at the retail level below $3.00 per gallon. These price levels were much lower than what experts deemed possible again. The lower cost of so-called fossil fuels made some alternate energy sources economically impractical and provided an economic growth engine for parts of the United States and Canada. There is some concern that these lower prices will lessen the impetus for sustainability initiatives of the previous decade. However, it is important to note that the green supply chain initiatives had important economic benefits that will likely continue and will be supported by government pressure. It is worth noting that the government as well as private pressures are stronger in European (and some other) countries than those in the United States. For example, United Kingdom and France plan to ban sales of new petrol and diesel cars by year 2040, and Norway by 2025. The EU predicts that electric cars will account for all new vehicles sales in Europe by 2035.

It should also be noted that in addition to fuel efficiency, there are a number of other sustainability issues that are impacted by supply chains. These areas include packaging, facilities, and waste disposal. The important point is that there are many opportunities for transportation and logistics service companies to improve in areas related to sustainability and to reduce their negative impact on the environment. The internal and external stakeholder pressures have provided impetus for such change, but in the long run, the recognition that going green has economic advantages impacting profitability will be the most important driving force.

It is important to understand that there is an interrelationship or systems impact in play among logistics-related factors impacting the green supply chain. There are several time-proven axioms from transportation economics that are important to consider, such as "don't ship air" and "don't ship water." The first one recognizes that empty space in a motor carrier trailer or railcar from empty backhauls or less-than-capacity dispatches is wasted and never recovered. Transportation companies do not have the luxury of accumulating inventory. As noted in Chapters 1 and 2, they provide capacity to transport between two or more points, which is instantly perishable if not used. For this reason, several attempts are being made to reduce or minimize the amount of empty space in transportation equipment. They include load-matching operations by Uber Freight, which can reduce empty miles of trucks, and shipper-to-shipper collaboration that will match shippers of different product densities to maximize the capacity utilization of trucks. The concept of the former attempt is to quickly match the available capacity (including empty haul) with freight demands by using cell-phone apps that can match shippers and carriers in the way similar to standard Uber rides. The concept of the latter attempt is to fill a truck with different types of goods such that the truck's capacity utilizations in both volume (cubic feet) and weight (pounds) are maximized simultaneously. For example, we can match the shippers of potato chips and water bottles. Note that, if large amounts of potato chips are shipped as a full TL shipment, a truck will reach the volume capacity well before it reaches the weight capacity, whereas if large amounts of water bottles are shipped as a full TL shipment, a truck will reach the weight capacity well before it reaches the volume capacity. But if these shippers collaborate such that they always jointly ship the loads by mixing their goods (say 50 percent potato chips and 50 percent water bottles in each load), it can be shown that the capacity utilization of a truck for each shipment would be close to 100 percent in both volume and weight.[13] This means that the overall number of TLs that the two shippers must ship will decrease (thereby saving freight miles and fuel consumption).

Transportation companies and shippers put an emphasis on consolidation to fill equipment to capacity or near capacity. Such a strategy has the potential to significantly reduce network miles, especially in the motor carrier sector. The reduction in network miles will improve fuel efficiency and reduce the carbon footprint. During the era of low-cost fuel and with pressure to have lean, demand-driven supply chains, transportation equipment was frequently dispatched without enough consideration for capacity utilization in an effort to improve customer service and lower inventory costs. Higher fuel charges along with sustainability-related costs have changed the system dynamics and more emphasis is being given to "don't ship air," for the reasons cited above. While consolidation efforts may have an impact on shipment time, the reductions in fuel and carbon levels mitigate it. In addition, when necessary, shipments can be expedited.

It should be noted that in addition to consolidation, packaging has an impact on wasted transportation capacity. Marketers have often followed one of their axioms from the theory of consumer behavior, namely, "perception is reality." Consequently, if consumers perceive that they are getting more for their money, it is "reality." One approach to influencing value perception is through packaging—using larger packages. For example, the paper-based rolls inside plastic wrap and aluminum foil were larger than they needed to be, which resulted in an overall larger package. The larger package filled transportation equipment, warehouse space, and retailer shelves more quickly than necessary. The net result was a lot of "air" and wasted space. The trade-off was more sales revenue (hopefully). The current economic and social environment has led companies like Wal-mart to request change, and it has happened. The smaller rolls have led to smaller packages and improved capacity utilization in transport equipment, warehouses, and retail stores. This is only one example of many possibilities. Hopefully, the impetus for improving sustainability will lead to other packaging changes. Excess packaging is prevalent in our economy, and it usually ends up in landfills and, of course, increases logistics cost. The caveat on packaging is that it is also used to reduce damage, which can be a big issue for carriers. Obviously, this issue requires consideration, but there are many instances of too much packaging and wasted space inside packages—there is room for improvement.

The other old axiom noted above was "don't ship water," and it has a relationship to the "don't ship air" axiom. This axiom is based upon the premise that water is ubiquitous; that is, it is found almost everywhere. Early location theory and transport economics concluded that water should be added as close as possible to the point of consumption to reduce cost and especially to reduce transportation cost. The classic examples are beer and soda, which are about 90 percent water in terms of finished product weight. The conventional wisdom was that breweries and soda bottling plants should have market-oriented locations, where the water was added, to reduce total transportation costs by moving the water relatively short distances. The growing popularity of so-called "craft beers" from smaller, more localized breweries is a positive impact for sustainability.

Over the course of the last several decades, an increasing number of consumer products that were sold in a liquid form had water added, which gave the appearance of "getting more for your money." This was especially true of liquid detergents. Wal-mart and other retailers put pressure upon their suppliers, to eliminate about half the water. The result was a smaller plastic bottle that had the same washing power. However, the total supply chain (manufacturer, warehouse, transporter, and retailer) benefited because the final product weighed less and occupied about 50 percent of the original space. It was an important outcome for sustainability. The cost of transportation and warehousing was significantly reduced while improving the shelf space challenge of retailers—a classic win–win–win! It also reduced the cost of packaging and improved capacity utilization. It was clearly a "home run" in spite of some initial resistance by consumers. There are many other possibilities for removing water and/or reducing the size of consumer packages. Consider, for example, the possibility of manufacturing a detergent tablet, and all the water being added in the washing machine (this concept is not new, but it received consumer resistance when previously tried).

The examples of green initiatives discussed are cascading through supply chains and encouraging initiatives by other suppliers and transportation companies. The transport sector is being pushed in this direction by customers, the government, and increased operating costs. As indicated above, most of the steps taken by the trucking industry to become greener are focused upon cost reductions related to fuel efficiency. However, fleet managers are investigating "clean" fuels and hybrid tractors and joining with shippers to examine reducing network miles, consolidating loads, and even changing the type of lightbulbs used in terminals. Some of these changes, such as load consolidation and network mileage optimization, can be made in the short run for immediate impact, while others, such as alternative fuels and hybrid tractors, are longer-run changes that need evaluation. Again, the reduction in fuel prices has raised a red flag and concern that companies will lack the impetus to continue their sustainability efforts.

The sustainability initiatives were frequently enhanced by government programs such as the SmartWay Transport Partnership. This is a federal program initiated by the Environmental Protection Agency (EPA) in 2004 to target selected carriers to reach out to shippers. The goals of the program are a cleaner environment, more efficiency, and less costly transportation options through collaborative efforts. The program has doubled in size each year since 2004 and attained 3,500 members in 2017. The EPA expects the program to continue its growth. The members include motor carriers, railroads, ocean carriers, logistics service providers, and large shippers—including Best Buy, Target, Coca Cola, Johnson & Johnson, Procter and Gamble, and Wal-mart. Even nonprofit groups, such as the American Trucking Association, are participating in these programs. SmartWay offers several tools and recommends a number of fuel-saving strategies. According to the EPA, motor carriers can save several thousand dollars per truck per year by implementing some or all of the recommended measures. Collectively, SmartWay participants have saved 196.5 million barrels of oil and lowered fuel costs by about $27.8 billion since 2004. Furthermore, they have reduced emissions of harmful air pollutants, such as carbon dioxide, by 94 million tons.

Sustainability and an emphasis on "green supply chains" have gained momentum among major shippers and the various transportation modes. The recognition of the environmental and economic benefits for carriers and shippers along with government policy and public pressure has given these efforts much momentum. However, transportation companies still have many opportunities to improve. For example, have any trucks passed you lately on the highway when you were driving at the maximum posted speed (hopefully)?

Wal-mart's "Project Gigaton" Focuses on Major Supply Chain Greenhouse Gas Emissions Reduction Effort

Taking steps to cut greenhouse gas emissions (GHG) from its supply chain, retail giant Wal-mart recently announced that it has rolled out an initiative entitled "Project Gigaton" that's geared toward helping the company achieve its goal of eliminating 1 gigaton—or 1 billion tons—of emissions from its supply chain by 2030.

This follows a November 2016 announcement Wal-mart made in which it rolled out goals specific for their own operations and fleets and focused on an 18 percent reduction in GHG emissions between 2015–2015.

According to Wal-mart, a key component of the project focuses on working with suppliers to achieve the reduction stemming from its operations and supply chains, with the help of what it calls a "sustainability platform."

This platform functions as a toolkit for a broad network of Wal-mart suppliers, with a focus on manufacturing, materials, and use of products by 2030, which Wal-mart said is the equivalent of taking more than 211 million passenger vehicles off U.S. roads and highways for a year.

The retailer added that it has banded together with nongovernmental organizations, including World Wildlife Fund and Environmental Defense Fund (EDF), among others, in creating the emissions reduction toolkit, which makes the business case for why shippers should consider becoming part of the Project Gigaton project.

"Through the years, we've seen that integrating sustainable practices into our operations improves business performance, spurs technological innovation, inspires brand loyalty, and boosts employee engagement," said Laura Phillips, senior vice president of sustainability for Wal-mart. "Our suppliers recognize the opportunity to realize those same benefits in their businesses. By working together on such an ambitious goal, we can accelerate progress within our respective companies and deep in our shared supply chains."

One of the main drivers for Project Gigaton runs in tandem with an analysis from the EDF on the relative impact of supply-chain-based emissions compared to direct emissions—with a major takeaway being that 80 percent of the emissions associated with U.S. retail and consumer goods industry is in the supply chain.

"The vast majority of the impact is in the supply chain, which is why what Wal-mart is doing is so important," said Jason Mathers, senior manager of supply chain logistics at the EDF. "This is on par with the ambition we see true leaders do these days."

Source: Jeff Berman, *Logistics Management*, Vol. 56, No. 7, July 2017, pp. 16–17. Reprinted with permission of Peerless Media, LLC.

Fuel Cost and Consumption

Fuel price volatility, including frequent price changes, has been an issue for transportation carriers and shippers since the mid-1970s. Overall, it can be argued that this is the result of changes in the global demand and the supply of crude oil. The demand for oil as a source of energy to power transport equipment and for private use has been growing steady. The new technology discussed above and the opportunity to recover oil and natural gas from important new sources in the United States and elsewhere has alleviated the situation and resulted in lower fuel costs. However, the historic volatility of energy prices, particularly oil and natural gas, requires caution and careful management by individuals and organizations as well as effective government policies. The reduction in price also has important economic

FIGURE 13-9   WTI Crude Oil Prices

Sources: FRED Graph Observations, Federal Reserve Economic Data, Economic Research Division and Federal Reserve Bank of St. Louis.

implications for counties and regions that have been supplying oil for many developed countries. In other words, it is good news and bad news, depending on whether the country is a net importer or exporter of oil.

As illustrated in Figure 13-9, the pattern of price changes and volatility have been a special challenge and issue in the first decade of the 21st century. World crude oil prices increased 113 percent between 2005 and mid-2008, when they reached a peak of $137.11 per barrel in July 2008. The prices abated significantly in 2009 because of the economic recession that triggered a global decrease in demand for oil and other energy related minerals. The price of a barrel of oil dipped to $75 in 2009 but rose again in 2010 with the economic recovery in major countries like the United States. The economic recovery resulted in increased demand, but the impact has been mitigated by the exploitation of new sources of fossil fuels mentioned above. The price of oil slipped to $65 per barrel in December 2014 and continues to stay at relatively low levels (as of the time this book was written). Gasoline was reported to be selling at prices as low as $2.00 per gallon in some states, which was about 50 percent of the previous high for gasoline at retail pumps. However, with the recent disasters occurring in Texas and other parts of the United States, including hurricanes Harvey and Irma, which damaged oil refineries in oil-producing states, the price of fuel may rise, at least in the short run.

The challenge, then, for carriers and shippers will be to deal with the uncertainty and volatility of fuel prices, and the expectation that the price will be increasing over time. The impact of fuel prices will vary among the modes of transportation because some are more fuel efficient than others, as noted in Chapters 5 through 8. In addition, there is interest in low-sulfur diesel fuel, which is cleaner for the environment.

Some discussion of the future impact of fuel prices on the various modes of transportation is appropriate at this point. As one would expect, the impact of fuel price will differ among the modes not only because of their fuel efficiency differences, but also due to their different operating and market conditions.

Motor Carriers

As previously noted, the motor carrier industry is highly fuel intensive and therefore very sensitive to price increases and associated volatility. Motor carriers consume over 54 billion gallons of fuel per year.[14] The annual cost for fuel escalated over 70 percent over the course of 2004–2008. To put this in perspective, the 2008 diesel expenses for the motor carrier industry were more than three times higher than the annual fuel bill for airlines, which is the most fuel-intensive mode of transportation. Fuel approached the annual labor cost in 2008, which is usually the largest expense for the motor carrier industry. Fuel surcharges helped the industry cope during that period to some extent, but it was still challenging and some companies did not survive (as discussed in Chapter 5, fuel surcharges recover only about 60 to 70 percent of increased cost of fuel for motor carriers). In fact, almost 3,000 motor carrier companies went bankrupt in 2008, reducing truck capacity by about 130,000 trucks. This was the largest number of carrier failures since 2001. The truckload carriers had the biggest challenges in passing off the increased fuel charges.

The lower fuel prices reached in late 2014 helped the motor carriers to be more competitive with the railroads in certain market situations, particularly for long-haul truckload traffic. When oil prices are in the $50 to $60 per barrel range, over-the-road motor carriers can be more competitive with TOFC movements. However, infrastructure-related congestion can mitigate the impact of lower fuel charges.

Air Carriers

As indicated previously, airlines are the most intensive users of fuel Similar to motor carriers, fuel costs have grown to be the largest expense for airlines. Fuel was normally 12 to 15 percent of the operating costs of airlines, but it grew to over 30 percent by 2008. The airlines have also used fuel surcharges for freight movements, but with limited success, and the surcharges inhibited air cargo growth because their rates were already relatively high. The increased gap between air cargo rates and ground transportation rates has shifted traffic away from airlines for distances up to 1,500 miles. The new, lower fuel costs could decrease the aforementioned gap and bring more freight traffic back to the airlines.

The high fuel charges were also challenging for passenger movements. Airlines have responded to this challenge by decreasing aircraft size and seat size as well as eliminating some flights in order to improve the revenue per passenger (as seat supply decreases the price can be increased without reducing demand) and passenger load factor. This, however, has resulted in a negative impact on air freight volume. Airlines have also responded by eliminating fuel-inefficient aircrafts from their fleet (such as the four-engine Boeing 747s) and adopting newer, more fuel-efficient aircrafts (such as Boeing 777 and 787, which have only two engines). Nonetheless, bankruptcy filings among some of the largest airlines have been an outcome of the higher fuel prices. The fuel price reductions of 2009 and 2014 provided some relief. The airlines are the most sensitive mode to increased fuel charges. Like motor carriers, oil prices in the $50 to $60 per barrel range would have a positive impact on airline efficiency and the expected lowering of air fares could generate more traffic.

Water Carriers

While water carriers are very fuel efficient, they are not insensitive to fuel price increases. This is particularly true for the global container shipping lines. Annual marine bunker fuel costs nearly doubled between 2005 and mid-2008. Fuel cost became the biggest challenge, reaching 50 to 60 percent of ship operating costs, depending on the type of ship. In addition, the marine carriers pay surcharges to the motor carriers and railroads that provide their intermodal moves for through service to and from inland points. To the extent that these surcharges cannot be passed on to shippers, they are additional cost pressures on the carriers. Consequently, the shipping lines became more aggressive about collecting bunker fuel surcharges, but they were not as successful as trucking companies in implementing an explicit set of charges related to the price of bunker fuel. Lower fuel costs would be expected to have a positive impact on global traffic flows.

Rail Carriers

With the advantages of fuel efficiency and constrained capacity, the railroad sector has not experienced the same level of cost pressure as the other modes of transportation. In fact, railroad profits increased by double digits in 2008 even with some decrease in traffic levels. The improved profit levels were attributable to a number of factors, including rate increases, fuel surcharges, and added efficiency. The latter was the result of faster line-haul time and faster terminal turnarounds.

Domestic rail service benefited from the higher fuel costs, since more shippers were interested in switching to rail intermodal service for long-haul freight. This is true for both trailers (TOFC) and containers (COFC) moving on an intermodal basis. Even with the decline in fuel prices in 2009, the demand for rail intermodal service remained high. This phenomenon is probably attributable to a belief that the fuel price reduction will be a short-run event; that even with lower fuel prices, rail intermodal service is more economical; and to the improved service times of the rail carriers. A sustained lowering of fuel costs would not be as beneficial to the railroads as it would be to motor and air carriers since it makes the latter carriers more competitive for certain types of traffic when fuel prices are high.

Pipeline Carriers

As indicated previously, during the period 2003–2006, pipeline rates for moving crude oil increased 22 percent, and for refined oil products, they increased 8 percent, which is an indication of higher operating costs. Some of this cost increase was attributable to the increase in pipelines' energy cost, but it is also a reflection of other cost increases related to security along the pipelines. As noted, pipelines operate very efficiently compared to other modes, which allowed them to price their services competitively as fuel prices escalated between 2006 and 2008. Also, some shippers are "tied" to the pipelines because of their location and limited alternatives for service. The net result was that pipeline traffic did not vary much in volume with the changes in fuel costs.

Carriers' Responses

Fuel surcharges have become the major component of the strategy of carriers to increase revenues for fuel cost recovery measures. Carrier contracts have become more sophisticated, with new surcharge formulas and new contract clauses to be more transparent and to correlate more closely with the fuel fluctuations. Surcharges have become a common practice for all modes in recent years and have become a centerpiece for carrier–shipper negotiations. However, there is no standard surcharge policy or formula for the transportation industry. The biggest challenge appears to be in the ocean shipping area because of the multiplicity of fuels, indexes, and carriers.

A second response, suggested above, has been service capacity and network rationalization. Some TL carriers have focused upon shorter routes or traffic lanes. One relatively simple response that impacts service capacity is to reduce cruise speed (it is knowledge known among carrier managers that the most economical cruise speed for heavy-duty trucks is around 55 mph, which is lower than the speed limit on most highways). Both the trucking companies and the ocean liners have implemented this approach with mixed results. There are definite fuel savings, but the reduced speed impacts customer service, which has been a contentious point with some shippers. Reduced speed can also have negative impacts on carriers' driver retention rates, as many truck drivers do not like to cruise at low speeds (in the TL industry, drivers are typically paid by the miles driven, so that slow speeds can reduce their daily income, given that there is a limit on the number of hours they can drive trucks per day based on the hours of service regulation). Network rationalization usually means cutting or reducing service on unprofitable routes.

The important point for the future is that fuel prices will continue to have a major impact on transport carriers in terms of cost and service, which in turn will impact shippers. Some shippers are responding by implementing regionalized distribution centers with the expectation that with fuel price volatility and price increases, change will continue.

A third response to the fuel issues is to improve the operational efficiency of carriers. This can be done through fleet replacement and equipment modernization in terminal areas. As part of the fleet replacement program, carriers—especially motor carrier companies—can consider the option to buy equipment that utilizes alternate fuels.

The future will bring technology improvements that hopefully will make feasible alternatives available, such as electric hybrids. Also, lighter-weight equipment can be utilized. Additionally, there are many ongoing studies that investigate how carriers can minimize the fuel consumption of their transportation activities from the operations–research perspective (such as the development of new vehicle-routing algorithms that minimize the fuel consumption or carbon emissions of a fleet of vehicles). Some carriers are also exploring the use of night-delivery strategies to reduce fuel consumption and cost.[15] Again, there will be continuing pressure, because of fuel costs and the environment, to investigate opportunities to improve operating efficiency through equipment, fleet management, and network change.

A fourth response both to the fuel issue and sustainability is the use of technology to manage and control equipment effectively. With large and/or widely dispersed fleets, this usually requires technology to provide visibility of the assets and related information to improve operations. Large motor carrier companies in particular are investing in relatively expensive technology that allows them to track-and-trace equipment on a real-time basis. It is useful for security purposes but is also enabling them to reduce their fleet size, because it does not get "lost." In addition, the improved visibility can provide exception reporting when there is a problem, such as a breakdown, and corrective action can be taken.[16]

The visibility feature can also allow carriers to share information with their shippers/customers. This can lead to shared information about shipment needs to help carriers plan in advance to meet demand. Such collaborative efforts offer much promise for a win–win environment for improving equipment efficiency.

SUMMARY

- Demand for transportation service has increased significantly during the last 10 years with the expansion of global trade, but the investment in transportation-related infrastructure has not kept pace with the growth in traffic on a domestic basis or on a global basis. The declining fuel costs will present an opportunity for the state and federal governments to increase fuel taxes to alleviate the infrastructure problem.

- Congestion has become a major issue for the U.S. transportation system, causing delays and inconvenience to ordinary citizens and increased cost in operations for carriers and shippers. Shippers have also experienced increased inventory carrying cost and stockouts because of the delays.

- Highway congestion has some significant costs associated with it for carriers. It is estimated that the top interchange bottlenecks cause an average of 1.5 million annual truck hours of delay.

- Rail and water carriers also are challenged by congestion and infrastructure problems. The projected growth in demand by 2035 will strain an already busy system of highways, railways, and waterways unless improvements are made.

- The supply chain talent gap is facing the profession today. However, companies can employ several strategies that will allow them to successfully acquire and retain talent.

- Sustainability will become even more important in the future, and transportation and related supply chain services will continue to be a focus for reducing carbon footprints to improve the environment, but there are opportunities to also reduce cost.

- The green supply chain focus of many companies has led them back to some old axioms for transportation efficiency, namely, "don't ship air" and "don't ship water." The former refers to unused space or capacity in transportation equipment. The latter refers to the extra weight of water in products, which could be added in near the point of sale. Both axioms have an impact on sustainability and also on cost.

- The federal government's SmartWay Transport Partnership, initiated by the EPA, has solicited carriers to reach out to their customers in an effort to collaborate and to develop less costly transport options that are more environmentally friendly. SmartWay offers strategies to save fuel and help reduce carbon footprints.

- The volatility in fuel prices has been a challenge for carriers in terms of their costs and profits. This situation has led carriers to insert fuel surcharges into their price structure to protect their financial viability when fuel prices increase.

- Fuel cost was the first or second highest cost for motor carriers, airlines, and even some water carriers, but the declining prices beginning in 2014 will change the competitive rate making in various market areas and will result in traffic shifts among modes of transportation during a shakeout period.

- Rail carriers fared well during the era of higher fuel changes since they are very fuel efficient; their intermodal service has become more attractive to shippers and other carriers, especially motor carriers, during high-fuel-price periods. The lower fuel prices will change some of these patterns in the future.

- Transportation and logistics organizations have an opportunity to provide leadership and promote more efficient and effective supply chains through collaborative strategies and technology applications.

STUDY QUESTIONS

1. There have been an increasing number of editorials in newspapers and magazines about concerns over transport capacity and infrastructure. What is the nature of this issue? Why is it such a problem? How can it be resolved?

2. While we have concerns about transportation service currently, there did not appear to be any special challenges or big problems during the 1980s and 1990s. Why were these two decades so different as far as transportation is concerned?

3. We have all experienced highway congestion and "bumper-to-bumper" traffic, but congestion is a bigger issue for supply chains and transport service providers. Why?

4. The supply chain industry is facing a severe talent gap. What are the causes of this gap? What can companies do to acquire and retain supply chain talent?

5. Sustainability and the environment have captured the attention of ordinary citizens and also of shippers and carriers. What is the nature of the concern? How can shippers and carriers mitigate their impact on the environment?

6. "Don't ship air" and "don't ship water" are the bases of some important supply chain strategies. What do these statements really mean? What are the related strategies? How do these strategies help?

7. The U.S. Environmental Protection Agency has implemented the SmartWay Transport Partnership. Discuss the nature and role of the program. Do you think it will be effective? Why or why not?

8. Fuel prices have been very volatile during the last five years. What factors have contributed to this volatility? What impact will lower fuel prices have on transportation?

9. What is collaboration? How can transportation companies and shippers use collaboration to reduce fuel consumption and cost?

10. What is your view of the use of technology to enhance sustainability in transportation systems in the future?

11. Are you optimistic or pessimistic about transportation services for shippers in the 21st century? Why?

NOTES

1. "An Economic Analysis of Transportation Infrastructure Investment," National Economic Council and the President's Council of Economic Advisors, The White House, July 2014, pp. 3–6.

2. Bureau of Transportation Statistics, *Freight Facts 2016*, Figure 4.3.

3. FHWA, "The Economic Cost of Freight Transportation," Freight Management and Operations, U.S. DOT, Washington, DC, May 2009, pp. 1–5.

4. Association of American Railroads, *Fact Sheet*, 2016.

5. "Surge in Rail Shipments of Oil Side Tracks Other Industries," *Wall Street Journal*, March 13, 2014.

6. "Rail," *CSCMP Supply Chain Quarterly*, Vol. 8, Special Issue, 2014, pp. 25–26.

7. Ibid.

8. "The Supply Chain Talent Shortage: From Gap to Crisis," DHL Supply Chain, 2016.

9. Ibid.

10. Jeff Berman, "The Never-Ending Truck Driver Shortage," *Logistics Management*, April 2017, p. 20.

11. "Millennials and the Supply Chain Talent Gap", *Supply Chain*, 2017, p. 4.

12. DHL Supply Chain, 2016, op.cit.

13. Yoshinori Suzuki, and Shih-Hao Lu, "Economies of Product Diversity in Collaborative Logistics," *Journal of Business Logistics*, Vol. 38, No. 2, 2017, pp. 115–129.

14. American Trucking Association. Retrieved September 15, 2017, from http://www.trucking.org/News_and_Information_Reports_Energy.aspx.

15. Jessica McPhee, Ari Paunonen, Taufiq Ramji, and James H. Bookbinder, "Implementing Off-Peak Deliveries in the Greater Toronto Area: Costs, Benefits, and Challenges." *Transportation Journal*, Vol. 54, No. 4, pp. 473–495.

16. "Sustainability: The 'Embracers' Seize the Advantage," *Sloan Management Review*, Research Report, Winter 2011.

17. Some contents of this case are adopted from Jessica McPhee, Ari Paunonen, Taufiq Ramji, and James H. Bookbinder, "Implementing Off-Peak Deliveries in the Greater Toronto Area: Costs, Benefits, and Challenges," *Transportation Journal*, Vol. 54, No. 4, pp. 473–495.

CASE 13-1

Sustainability and Night Delivery[17]

Eric Paulsen is a manager of Cyclone Ice Cream LTD., a manufacturer of several ice cream products, based in a suburban city near Chicago, IL. One of the largest customers for Eric is ABC Mart, which is a grocery chain store with about 30 stores in the Chicago metropolitan area and its surrounding regions. Cyclone delivers its ice cream products to ABC Mart every day by using several delivery trucks that Cyclone owns. These trucks normally make deliveries in the morning and early afternoon to ABC Mart stores.

One day, Eric was talking to Frank Smith, the VP of purchasing at ABC Mart. During that meeting Frank mentioned to Eric that ABC Mart is initiating a sustainability project, and would like Eric to participate in this project. Frank told Eric that the objective of this project is to reduce the amount of carbon emissions resulting from the activities performed by ABC Mart. Frank asked Eric to come up with a strategy to reduce the amount of carbon emissions that results from Cyclone's delivery operations to ABC Mart. Frank wants to see an idea and the estimates of carbon or fuel reduction that may be expected from the use of Eric's strategy. Eric was thinking about this project on the way back to his office, and remembered that he recently read an article about off-peak deliveries and fuel savings resulting from this strategy. As he recalled this article, he remembered that there are both advantages and disadvantages associated with off-peak, or more specifically nighttime, deliveries.

The main advantages include the following: First, lower truck emissions are expected due to favorable nighttime traffic conditions (higher speed and reduced idling time). Second, it can avoid making deliveries to stores during the peak sale times, which will reduce disturbances for shop owners. Third, it can improve vehicle utilization rates and thus reduce the fleet size needed to meet customer demands. This is because Cyclone makes deliveries to other retailers during daytime, so that trucks can be used during both daytime and nighttime. Fourth, it can reduce the parking fines for Cyclone. Because many ABC Mart stores are located in Chicago metropolitan areas, Cyclone trucks often have to park illegally on streets during deliveries, which results in parking fines. During nighttime, however, roadside parking is legal in many store locations. Fifth, research has shown that the enhanced nighttime stability of the atmospheric layer could trap more pollutant particles than during the day, so that nighttime driving results in reduced carbon emissions relative to the same-distance daytime driving.

The main disadvantages include the following: First, it requires the stores to have trained staff who can accept deliveries during the nighttime, which may cost the stores (for increased shifts and training). Similarly, the stores may have to incur higher heating and lighting costs due to additional operating hours. Eric is concerned that this additional store cost will eventually be passed on to Cyclone. Second, it results in increased noise during nighttime. In many city areas, there are "quiet times" during nighttime, which forbids certain loading and unloading operations that generate large noise. This may require Cyclone to purchase quieter vehicles and equipment. Third, it can cause driver fatigue. With night deliveries, some drivers are asked to drive both daytime and nighttime, which can result in higher driver fatigue and possibly higher accident rates. Fourth, it may result in higher risk for theft during delivery. It is known that theft can happen with higher probability during nighttime than during daytime, so that delivery trucks may face higher risks of theft with night deliveries. This may require Cyclone to provide extra securities for their vehicles and drivers.

CASE QUESTIONS

1. Create a list of benefits for adopting night deliveries, including (but not limited to) those that are mentioned above.

2. Create a list of disadvantages associated with night deliveries, including (but not limited to) these that are mentioned above.

3. After considering both advantages and disadvantages, do you recommend that Cyclone adopt nighttime delivery? Why or why not? Should your recommendation be based only on costs?

CASE 13-2

Bald Eagle Valley Trucking

SCOR is a local nonprofit organization that provides advice and direction to new and/or small companies. The volunteers for the SCOR organization are all retired executives and/or entrepreneurs. At their weekly meeting, Herb Graves and Ned Book were discussing a proposal that they had received from a local trucking company that had been founded about two years ago. The company, Bald Eagle Valley Trucking (BEV), had enjoyed some success and had been able to secure a loan enabling it to expand to 10 tractor and trailer units. Its success had been based largely upon a water bottling plant, owned by the Coca Cola Company, that had been increasing the volume it shipped. BEV felt that there was an opportunity to expand its business with Coca Cola into the Philadelphia, New York, and Washington, DC, areas, but it needed additional capital to buy more equipment. BEV had requested help from SCOR to assist it with developing a strategic plan and supporting its request for a loan from a Pittsburgh-based bank.

Herb and Ned were very experienced executives but they had no direct experience in the transportation and supply chain business. So they contacted a nearby state university with a large and well-known Supply Chain and Logistics department. The department had a program whereby its students could be assigned a business-related project for course credit, and it would be supervised by a faculty member.

CASE QUESTIONS

1. You have been chosen to work on the BEV project, which will require you to answer the following questions:
   a. What are the major opportunities and issues trucking companies face presently?
   b. What insights can you provide to help BEV mitigate some or all of the issues?
2. Herb and Ned both feel that BEV can be a successful company with appropriate planning and direction. What major points do you think that they should consider in their strategic plan for the future? Indicate at least five such points of emphasis and why you think that they are important.

Suggested Readings

Chapter 10   Transportation Risk Management

Manuj, Ila, and John T. Mentzer, "Global Supply Chain Risk Management," *Journal of Business Logistics*, Vol. 29, No. 1 (2008): 133–156.

Murphy, Sean, "Stepping Up Security: An Interview with James Williams," *Supply Chain Management Review*, Vol. 12 (November 2008): 40.

"Ocean Supply Chain Security," United States Government Accountability Office (April 2008): GAO-08-240.

Sarathy, Ravi, "Security and the Global Supply Chain," *Transportation Journal*, Vol. 45, No. 4 (Fall 2006): 28–51.

Voss, M. Douglas, Judith M. Whipple, and David J. Closs, "The Role of Strategic Security: Internal and External Security Measures with Security Performance Implications," *Transportation Journal*, Vol. 48, No. 2 (Spring 2009): 5–23.

Chapter 11   Global Transportation Management

Bichou, Khalid, Kee-Hung Lai, Y. H. Venus Lun, and T.C.E. Cheng, "A Quality Management Framework for Liner Shipping Companies to Implement the 24-Hour Advance Vessel Manifest Rule," *Transportation Journal*, Vol. 46, No. 1 (Winter 2007): 5–21.

Burnson, Patrick, "Ocean Shipping Strategies: Risk Versus Reward," *Logistics Management* (September 2007): 35.

Miller, Tan and Renato de Matta, "A Global Supply Chain Profit Maximization and Transfer Pricing Model," *Journal of Business Logistics*, Vol. 29, No. 1 (2008): 175–200.

Schulz, John D., "Global Transportation: The Big Picture," *Supply Chain Management Review*, Vol. 11 (March 2007): 20.

Wagner, Stephan M., "Innovation Management in the German Transportation Industry," *Journal of Business Logistics*, Vol. 29, No. 2 (2008): 215–232.

"America's Container Ports: Delivering the Goods," *Bureau of Transportation Statistics* (2007).

Burson, Patrick, "Ocean Shipping Strategies," *Logistics Management* (November 2008): 33–36.

Burson, Patrick, "U.S. Seaport Update: Location Matters," *Logistics Management* (September 2008).

Burson, Patrick, "Top U.S. Seaports: Slower Trade Means Time to Rebuild," *Logistics Management* (February 2009).

Carmichael, Gil, "Intermodal a 'No Brainer' for Energy Efficiency," *Logistics Management* (May 2007): 16.

Paul Bergant, Interview, "Soaring Fuel Prices Are Driving Shippers to Embrace the Intermodal Option," *Global Logistics & Supply Chain Strategies* (August 2008).

Quinn, John Paul, "U.S. Ports Expand Keeping Pace with Import Growth," *Supply Chain Management Review*, Vol. 11 (April 2007): 57.

Theurmer, Karen E., "Intermodal Grows Up," *World Trade* (January 2009): 36.

Chapter 12   Governmental Roles in Transportation

Cassidy, William B., "Safety First," *Journal of Commerce* (March 31, 2014): 16–18.

Fuetsch, Michele, "States Slow Highway Projects as U.S. Funding Crisis Looms," *Transport Topics* (June 23, 2014): 1.

O'Reilly, Joseph, "U.S. Creates a 'Single-Window' for Import/Export Data Transmission," *Inbound Logistics* (April 2014): 25–28.

Terry, Lisa, "Protecting High-Value Cargo: A Sense of Security," *Inbound Logistics* (April 2014): 89–93.

Chapter 13   Issues and Challenges for Global Supply Chains

Berman, Jeff, "Shippers Say Wall Street Crisis to Hinder Transportation Operations," *Logistics Management* (November 2008): 21.

Bowen, Douglas John, "Pacific Harbor Line Goes Green," *Railway Age* (April 2009): 23.

Bowman, Robert J., "Ships and Ports Find Many Ways to Go Green," *Global Logistics & Supply Chain Strategies* (September 2008).

Burnson, Patrick and Jeff Berman, "Panama Canal Development Project on Pace for Completion," *Logistics Management* (January 2009): 20–21.

Burnson, Patrick, "Update on Vietnam and India Logistics: Strained," *Logistics Management* (May 2009): 36–38.

Hong, Junjie and Binglian Liu, "Logistics Development in China: A Provider Perspective," *Transportation Journal*, Vol. 46, No. 2 (Spring 2007): 55–65.

Lu, Chin-Shan and Ching-Chiao Yang, "Comparison of Investment Preferences for International Logistics Zones in Kaohsiung, Hong Kong, and Shanghai Ports from a Taiwanese Manufacturer's Perspective," *Transportation Journal*, Vol. 45, No. 1 (Winter 2006): 30–51.

Quinn, Paul John, "The Greening of America's Ports," *Logistics Management* (September 2007): 62S.

Glossary

A

accessibility The ability of the carrier to provide service between the origin and the destination. It also refers to the carrier's ability to serve the shipper or consignee's place of business. For example, in order to ship and receive a railcar, both the origin and the destination must have a side track.

advanced shipment notices (ASNs) Electronic notification of pending deliveries; an electronic packing list.

advertising The public promotion of some product or service.

air cargo carriers Carriers that focus exclusively on the movement of freight, packages, letters, and envelopes.

air carriers A transportation firm that operates aircraft for the transportation of passengers or freight as a "common carrier."

air freighters Aircraft dedicated solely to the movement of freight.

air traffic control system The method by which aircraft traffic is controlled in the air so that planes are separated by altitude and distance for safety. This system is administered by the Federal Aviation Administration.

air waybill A contract for transportation between a shipper and an air carrier, which also evidences receipt of the cargo by the carrier.

airline safety The theory, investigation, and categorization of flight failures and the prevention of such failures through regulation, education, and training.

Airport and Airway Trust Fund A federal fund that collects passenger ticket taxes and disburses those funds for airport facilities.

airports

all-cargo carrier An air carrier that transports cargo only.

Amtrak A quasi-governmental agency that provides interstate rail passenger service.

Army Corps of Engineers A federal agency and major military command whose mission is to provide military and public works services to the United States by providing vital engineering services and capabilities, as a public service, across the full spectrum of operations—from peace to war—in support of national interests.

asset-based providers 3PLs that fulfill customer requirements via tangible equipment and facilities they own.

average cost Production cost per unit of output, computed by dividing the total of fixed costs and variable costs by the number of total units produced (total output); also known as "unit cost."

B

backhaul The return trip made, as by a truck or cargo ship, after delivering a load to a specified destination.

bareboat charter A long-term lease or charter where the lessee provides the crew, fuel, and supplies and operates the ship. The lessor provides only the ship.

benefit/cost ratio An analysis of the cost effectiveness of different alternatives in order to see whether the benefits outweigh the costs.

bill of lading A transportation document that is the contract of carriage between the shipper and the carrier; it provides a receipt for the goods tendered to the carrier, the "terms and conditions of sale" between the carrier and shipper, and the evidence of who has title to the goods while in transit.

bonded warehouse Building in which goods, on which the duties are unpaid, are stored under bond and in the joint custody of the importer or his agent and the customs officers.

brainstorming An informal group problem solving technique in which members spontaneously share ideas and solutions.

break-bulk Ocean cargo that is not containerized but must be handled manually into and out of a ship.

break-bulk freight

break-bulk ships They are multipurpose vessels that are capable of transporting shipments of unusual sizes, unitized on pallets, in bags, or in crates.

buffering strategy Method of reducing risk related to capacity shortages or performance problems by providing additional resources.

bulk carriers Catchall category for ships that are dedicated to the transport of a specific bulk commodity on a voyage basis.

bulk freight

bull whip effect Businesses that must forecast demand to properly position inventory will often carry an inventory buffer to anticipate spikes in demand, which varies in size depending on the participant's place in the supply chain. It has been observed that variations are amplified as one moves upstream in the supply chain, not unlike the cracking of a whip.

business logistics The process of planning, implementing, and controlling the efficient, effective flow and storage of goods, services, and related information from the point of origin to the point of consumption for the purpose of conforming to customer requirements. Note that this definition includes inbound, outbound, internal, and external movements.

C

capability The ability of a carrier to provide service or multiple services to the shipper to meet the specific requirements of that customer.

capacity The ability to bear people or things.

carbon footprint The total set of greenhouse gas emissions caused by an organization, event, or product, often expressed as an amount of carbon dioxide.

cargo inspection Critical appraisal involving examination, measurement, testing, gauging, and comparison of materials or items to determine if the material or item is in proper quantity and condition.

cargo preference A federal law requiring that at least 50 percent of certain U.S. government-owned or -sponsored cargo move on U.S. flag-registered vessels.

cargo service airports Airports that, in addition to any other air transportation services that may be available, are served by aircraft providing air transportation of cargo only, with a total annual landed weight of more than 100 million pounds.

carload A full weight or size shipment placed into or on a railcar. This term also refers to rates that apply to a specific minimum weight for railcar shipments.

Carriage and Insurance Paid To (CIP)

Carriage Paid To (CPT)

carrying capacity The capability of a transport vehicle to carry or transport shipments of a particular weight or size in relation to the shipper's requirements. As an example, a 53-foot trailer could carry 48,000 pounds or a shipment of 3,392 cubic feet.

car-supply charge In a rail contract rate, a fee imposed that depends on the specific type of car supplied for loading and shipment.

Cash-in-Advance

Certificate of End Use Document that attests that the product will be used for legitimate or approved purposes.

Certificate of Inspection A legal document that attests to the authenticity and accuracy of the goods.

Certificate of Origin A legal document that verifies the country where a particular product originated. This certificate must often accompany the shipment so the importing country can determine if it complies with that country's laws.

chandlers Dealers in sails and ropes and other supplies for sailing ships; retail dealers in provisions and supplies.

channel members Other parts of a transportation system delivering similar services or utilizing similar or different modes.

charging what the traffic will bear Setting the highest price you can sell your goods at in the market you are in.

charter carriers An exempt for-hire air carrier that will fly anywhere on demand; air taxis are restricted to a maximum payload and passenger capacity per plane.

charter party Standard charter contract used to record the exact rate, duration, and terms agreed between the ship owner and the charterer.

charter service In ocean shipping, ships that are hired for a specific voyage or amount of time.

charterer The customer who hires a ship for charter service.

Civil Aeronautics Board Federal agency, created in 1940, that focused on safety rulemaking, accident investigation, and economic regulation of the airlines.

class rate A rate constructed from a classification and a uniform distance system. A class rate is available for any product between any two points.

Clayton Act A law that strengthened the Sherman Anti-Trust Act and specifically described some business practices as violations of the law. This was done to counter some practices that were used to avoid the Sherman Anti-Trust Act.

Coast Guard A military unit attached to the Department of Transportation. The Coast Guard is charged with certain law enforcement tasks related to protecting the shores of the United States and the usage of waters both domestically and along the coasts. The Coast Guard is also tasked with safety standards for commercial users, search and rescue missions on inland and coastal waters, and small boat safety programs.

combi airplane Hybrid type of aircraft with the flexibility to move passengers and/or cargo on the main deck of the aircraft, depending on temporary configuration via movable partitions.

combination carriers   They are carriers that move freight and passengers, with cargo loaded in the belly of the aircraft.

combination ships   Multipurpose vessels that can handle different types of commodities and load types.

commercial invoice   A specifically prepared invoice for the merchandise contained in a shipment. The document is often required for international shipments.

commercial service airport   A publicly owned airport that has scheduled passenger service with at least 2,500 passenger boardings each calendar year.

commodities   Some good for which there is demand but which is supplied without qualitative differentiation across a market; that is, it is the same no matter who produces it.

commodity rates   A rate for a specific commodity and its origin–destination.

common carrier   A transportation company that provides freight and/or passenger service to any who seek its services.

common costs   A cost that a company cannot directly assign to particular segments of the business; a cost that the company incurs for the business as a whole.

common law   A legal system based on court decisions and precedents that recognizes past decisions when deciding current legal questions. The legal system of the United States is based on common law along with civil or statutory law.

communication network   Infrastructure and devices linked together so that messages may be passed from one part of the network to another over multiple links and through various nodes.

commuter air carriers   An exempt for-hire air carrier that publishes a time schedule on specific routes; a special type of air taxi.

"Compliance, Safety, and Accountability Act of 2010 (CSA 2010)"   The act initiated by the federal government in 2010 with a goal of reducing accidents by identifying and addressing areas of concern.

conferences   Groups of carriers that serve specific trade routes and ports and cooperate as legal cartels when setting prices for certain routes, agreeing not to compete on price and publishing standardized rate tariffs.

consular invoice   A specifically prepared invoice that is prescribed by the importing country for the merchandise contained in a shipment. The invoice will be written in the language of the importing country and may be required to be signed by an employee of the government of the nation to which the shipment is destined.

container rates   A rate that applies only when the shipment is placed into a container prior to tendering the shipment to the carrier. This rate recognizes that the shipment is much more easily handled by the carrier.

containerized freight   Freight that is loaded into or onto storage equipment (a container or pallet) at the origin and delivered to the destination in or on that same piece of equipment without additional handling.

container-on-flatcar (COFC)   A type of rail shipment where only the container or "box" is loaded on the flatcar. The chassis with the wheels and landing gear is only used to carry the container to and from the railroad.

containerships   Ships built for the specific purpose of moving standardized 20-foot and 40-foot oceangoing containers.

core competency   The set of skills, technologies, and processes that provide the basics for what a company does well.

Cost and Freight (CFR)

Cost, Insurance, Freight (CIF)

cost of service   A method used by carriers when they seek to only cover the actual expense of providing that specific service. Such pricing does not usually cover shared or overhead costs.

cost-of-service pricing   A method used by carriers when they seek to only cover the actual expense of providing that specific service. Such pricing does not usually cover shared or overhead costs.

crude carriers   Ships that move petroleum products (crude oil, gasoline, diesel fuel, and so forth) in massive quantities.

customs brokerage   Company that clears goods through customs barriers for importers and exporters (usually businesses).

customs brokers   A firm that represents importers/exporters in dealings with customs. Normally responsible for obtaining and submitting all documents for clearing merchandise through customs, arranging inland transport, and paying all charges related to these functions.

D

decreasing cost industries   The relation between market price and the quantity supplied by all firms in a perfectly competitive industry after the industry has completed its long-run adjustment; an increase in the quantity produced leads to a decrease in the price per unit.

dedicated contract carriage   A third-party service that dictates equipment (vehicles) and drivers to a single customer for its exclusive use on a contractual basis.

Delivered At Place (DAP)

Delivered At Terminal (DAT)

Delivered Duty Paid (DDP)

delivery delay   Failure to make a scheduled delivery.

demand elasticity   The amount that the demand for a product or service will change by the changes in price and the availability of substitutes.

demise charter   The hiring of a ship and crew that shifts the control and possession of the vessel; the charterer takes full control of the vessel along with the legal and financial responsibility for it.

density   A physical characteristic measuring a commodity's mass per unit volume or pounds per cubic foot; it is an important factor in rate making because density affects the utilization of a carrier's vehicle.

Department of Transportation

derived demand   The demand for a product's transportation is derived from the product's demand at some location.

differential   A distinction between individuals or classes.

dimensional weight   Unit of measurement used by air carriers to calculate rates for carrying cargo, based on measuring volume taken as well as cargo weight.

direct service   Movement of a shipment straight from its origin to its destination without transshipment.

discounts   Reductions made from the gross amount or value of something.

documentary collection (DC)

draft   A type of bank transaction that insures payment for goods. It is a written order for a sum of money to be paid by the buyer to the seller upon presentation of the document to the buyer's bank.

drivers   In the context of forming a partnership, compelling reasons to partner.

driving time regulations   U.S. Department of Transportation rules that limit the maximum time a driver may drive in interstate commerce; the rules prescribe both daily and weekly maximums.

dry-bulk carriers   Ships with several holds in their hulls in which loose cargo such as grains, coal, ore, and other commodities are loaded.

duty   A tax on imports.

E

economic deregulation   The removal of governmentally enforced price and entry controls in the transportation industry. The "free market" will provide the necessary competition to ensure competitive prices and services.

economies of density   Savings realized wherein unit costs are lower in relation to population density. The higher the population density, the lower the likely costs of infrastructure required to provide a service.

economies of scale   As production of a good increases, the cost of producing each additional unit falls.

emergency shipments   Expedited, as-soon-as possible delivery of items.

employee assistance programs (EAPs)   Employer-sponsored programs provided to their employees suffering from substance-abuse problems.

end-of-the-line (EOL) terminal   Terminal that serves a local area, providing direct contact with both shippers and receivers. The basic transportation service provided at this terminal is the pickup and/or delivery of freight.

end-to-end mergers   Type of railroad company merger that aims to result in more effective intermodal and intramodal competition, usually by combining firms from different but complementary territories.

equipment substitution   Advantageous replacement of a carrier's mode of transportation in order to maximize return; for example, changing a flight to a smaller plane in response to a shortfall in reservations.

Erie Canal   Man-made waterway extending 363 miles from Albany to Buffalo, New York, linking the Atlantic seacoast to the Great Lakes; in the years after its completion in 1825, the cost of transporting goods between the Midwest and New York City fell precipitously, in some cases by 95 percent.

event management   An aspect of shipment visibility that incorporates when things happen into its reporting system.

Ex Works (EXW)   The price that the seller quotes applies only at the point of origin. The buyer takes possession of the shipment at the point of origin and bears all costs and risks associated with transporting the goods to the final destination.

exception rates   A deviation from the class rate; changes (exceptions) made to the classification.

excess capacity   Underused or unused facilities and/or infrastructure; for example, an empty seat on an air carrier's flight.

exempt carriers   A for-hire carrier that is exempt from economic regulations.

existence charge   A shipping charge related to the existence of some tangible item that is made against the person or unit regardless of the extent of use made of the services.

export documents

export license   A document indicating that a government has granted a licensee the right to export specified goods to specified countries.

exporter   One who sells to merchants or industrial consumers in foreign countries.

extended enterprise   A way of looking at a process that extends beyond the bounds of a single firm to span the related activities of several participating or affected firms; a supply chain is an example of an extended enterprise that crosses the boundaries of the individual firms.

F

facilitators   In the context of forming a partnership, supportive corporate environmental factors that enhance partnership growth and development.

fair wage   A wage fairly and reasonably commensurate with the value of a particular service or class of service rendered.

FAK rates   They are rates expressed in cents per hundredweight or total cost per shipment.

Federal Aviation Administration   The federal agency within the Department of Transportation that is responsible for regulating air safety, promoting development of air commerce, and controlling navigable air space.

Federal Energy Regulatory Commission   The federal agency that oversees rates and practices of pipeline operators and is part of the Department of Energy.

Federal Highway Trust Fund   A fund that receives federally collected fuel taxes used for highway construction and upkeep.

Federal Maritime Commission   The federal agency that regulates international rates, practices, agreements, and services of common carrier water carriers.

Federal Motor Carrier Safety Administration   Federal agency, created in 2000, whose primary mission is to reduce crashes, injuries, fatalities, and property loss involving large trucks and buses by regulating the workers involved.

Federal Railroad Administration   The federal agency that oversees railroad safety by establishing and enforcing rules and regulations. This agency is part of the Department of Transportation.

Federal Trade Commission   The federal agency that administers the Sherman Anti-Trust Act and the Clayton Act. This agency does not have direct control over transportation.

fixed costs per unit

flag of convenience   A ship registered in a foreign country for purposes of reducing operating costs or avoiding government regulations or taxes.

Foreign Trade Zone (FTZ)   An area or zone set aside at or near a port or airport, under the control of the U.S. Customs Service, for the holding of goods duty-free, pending customs clearance.

for-hire   A carrier that provides transportation service to the public on a fee basis.

Free Alongside Ship (FAS)

Free Carrier (FCA)

free cash flow   In corporate finance, describes the fiscal condition of companies with negative working capital who must collect from their customers before they can pay their vendors or suppliers.

Free On Board (FOB)

free trade agreements   Treaties between nations that agree to eliminate tariffs, quotas, and preferences on many goods and services traded between them.

freight   Goods to be shipped; cargo.

freight bill auditing   A thorough examination of carrier's invoice for a freight shipment's transportation charges.

freight contamination   To make goods unfit for use by the introduction of unwholesome or undesirable elements.

freight damage   Injury or destruction of cargo.

freight forwarders   A carrier that collects small shipments from shippers, consolidates the small shipments, and uses a basic mode to transport these consolidated shipments to a consignee destination.

freight management   A strategic system to optimize the efficiency of freight and commercial transport.

freight rating   Performing the calculations appropriate to calculate freight costs based on contract and tariff terms.

frequency and timing   How often and at what time a group of scheduled events occurs.

fuel costs   Amounts paid for materials used to power the engines driving a carrier's machines.

fuel-efficient   Operable using comparatively less fuel.

G

gas carriers   Ships that transport compressed gases such as liquefied natural gas and liquefied petroleum gas in specialized tanks.

general average   The legal principle of maritime law according to which all parties in a sea venture proportionally share any losses resulting from a voluntary sacrifice of part of the ship or cargo to save the whole in an emergency.

Global Positioning System (GPS)   Signals that enable companies to accurately pinpoint the exact location of equipment and materials.

granger laws   A series of laws passed in the western United States after the Civil War to regulate grain elevator and railroad freight rates and rebates and to address long- and short-haul discrimination and other railroad abuses against farmers.

green supply chains   Supply chain management with an emphasis on energy efficiency and environmental friendliness.

H

hazardous materials   Materials that the Department of Transportation has determined to be a risk to health, safety, and property; includes items such as explosives, flammable liquids, poisons, corrosive liquids, and radioactive material.

headhaul   The first half of a round-trip move from origin to destination. The opposite is "backhaul," which is the return of the equipment to its origin point.

hedging strategy   Method of reducing risk by diversifying the risks presented by a single option.

high-density routes   Transportation route with the greatest number of users or carrying the highest amount of cargo.

highway development   Planning and construction of high-speed roadways.

home-flag airline   An airline owned or sponsored by the government of the country in which the carrier is based. Typically, only home-flag airlines are allowed to operate between airports within that country. This prevents foreign carriers from serving domestic locations.

Hours of Service (HOS)   A piece of legislation under Compliance, Safety, and Accountability Act with a new requirement of stricter rules effective from 2013 on a driver's restart options with the intent to improve safety.

Hours of Service of Drivers Final Rule

hubs   A central location to which traffic from many cities is directed and from which traffic is fed to other areas.

I

ICC Termination Act of 1995   Federal statute that eliminated the Interstate Commerce Commission and transferred economic rail regulation to the Surface Transportation Board.

import documents

importer   One who brings goods or merchandise from other countries into this one.

incentive rates   A rate that induces the shipper to ship heavier volumes per shipment.

Incoterms   International terms of sale developed by the International Chamber of Commerce to define sellers' and buyers' responsibilities.

indirect forms of promotion   Subsidies and incentives intended to preserve the domestic ship-building industry.

indirect service   Movement of a shipment from its origin to its destination, making interim stops and/or transfer of freight between equipment.

inelastic   In the context of economic supply and demand, elasticity refers to the sensitivity of customers to changes in price; if customers are not sensitive to price, then demand is considered inelastic.

information flow   The flow or movement of information or data between trading partners or companies that facilitates commerce or business.

inland ports   A specialized facility that executes some functions traditionally carried out at a seaport, made possible by the use of container shipping.

insurance   Coverage by contract whereby one party promises to guarantee another against loss by a specified contingency or peril.

integrated carriers   Air carrier companies that have the capability to provide door-to-door service because they own ground delivery equipment as well as aircraft.

integrated logistics management   The management of all activities involved in physically acquiring, moving, and storing raw materials, in-process inventory, and finished goods inventory from the point of origin to the point of consumption.

integrated service providers   For-hire firms that perform a variety of logistics service activities such as warehousing, transportation, and other functional activities as a package service.

intermediaries   Those being or occurring at the middle place or stage, such as brokers between ocean shippers and rail carriers.

intermodal marketing companies   Intermediary that sells intermodal services to shippers.

International Air Transport Association (IATA)   An international industry trade group of airlines that represents the airline industry.

International Chamber of Commerce (ICC)   An international organization established to reduce some of the confusion and complexity involving international shipments.

international freight forwarders (IFFs)

interstate commerce

Interstate Commerce Commission (ICC)   A former independent federal agency that supervised and set rates for carriers that transported goods and people between states.

Interstate Commerce Commission Termination Act

intrastate commerce   The transportation of persons or property between points within a state. A shipment between two points within a state may be interstate if the shipment had a prior or subsequent move outside of the state and the shipper intended an interstate shipment at the time of shipment.

invoices

J

joint costs

just-in-time delivery Component of an inventory strategy that strives to improve a business's return on investment by reducing in-process inventory and associated carrying costs.

K

Known Shipper Program A security system put in place following the attacks of 9/11 that essentially eliminates the anonymous shipment of all documents, parcels, counter-to-counter packages, and freight on both passenger and cargo-only flights originating within the United States.

L

landed cost The cost of the product at the source combined with the cost of transportation to the destination.

Lardner's Law A finding by transportation economist Dionysius Lardner that when transportation cost is reduced, the area where the producer can compete is increased in a directly proportional basis.

Law of Squares An increase in the distance over which a given amount will cover the transport of goods will increase the market area of the product in an even greater ratio; also known as Lardner's Law.

less-than-truckload (LTL) A less-than-truckload shipment, one weighing less than the minimum weight a company needs to use the lower truckload rate.

letter of credit (LC) A document issued by the buyer's bank that guarantees payment to the seller if certain terms and conditions are met.

liability Any legal responsibility, duty, or obligation.

limited competition A condition in which the competition is limited among the sellers.

line-haul A part of the trip where the shipments are loaded into 28-foot, 48-foot, or 53-foot trailers depending on the state's trailer configuration permitted over the route of travel.

liner service International water carriers that ply fixed routes on published schedules.

longshoremen Persons employed in loading or unloading cargo from ships.

M

major carriers For-hire air carriers with annual revenues of more than $1 billion.

make or buy decision A situation in which organizations have the option of providing items or services themselves internally or buying them from another source.

manifest A list of all cargoes that pertain to a specific shipment, grouping of shipments, or piece of equipment. Ocean carriers will prepare a manifest for each container.

maquiladora The name for a manufacturing facility established inside Mexico within close distance of the U.S. border. Materials are shipped from the United States, processed in the maquiladora plant, and returned to the United States. No customs duties or fees are accessed.

marginal cost The cost to produce one additional unit of output; the change in total variable cost resulting from a one-unit change in output.

Maritime Administration (MARAD) A U.S. Department of Transportation agency that aids and advances the use of water transportation.

market share pricing In an industry whose revenues are stagnant or declining, a firm will try to take market share from competitors through the use of lower prices.

marketing mix This consists of the four basic elements of marketing: product, price, place, and promotion. This is also known as the "four P's" of marketing.

mileage rate A rate or price based on the total mileage between the origin and the destination including stop-offs, if any.

minimum level of safety A base requirement for all aspects of safe operation by a transportation firm, as prescribed by a government agency.

modal split The relative use that companies make of transportation modes; the statistics include ton-miles, passenger-miles, and revenue.

monopolistic The ability of very few suppliers to set a price well above cost by restricting supply or by limiting competition.

monopolistic competition A condition in which there are many small sellers but there is some differentiation of products.

monopoly A market segment where there is only one supplier, such as public utilities.

Motor Carrier Act of 1980 An act by the federal agency which defines a zone of rate freedom for motor or railroad carrier policies in which a rate change of 10 percent either up or down in one year is presumed to be reasonable.

multimodal bill of lading A transportation document that tasks the principal carrier or freight forwarder for liability across the entire journey.

N

national carriers   A for-hire certificated air carrier that has annual operating revenues of $100 million to $1 billion; the carrier usually operates between major population centers and areas of lesser population.

national defense   A primary function of a sovereign state is its ability to defend its territory, national waters, and air space against internal and external threats.

National Highway Traffic Safety Administration (NHTSA)   This branch of the U.S. Department of Transportation is responsible for motor vehicle safety. In this role, NHTSA oversees design features, sets performance-related safety standards, and oversees governmental fuel economy standards.

National Transportation Safety Board   This agency is responsible for investigating transportation-related accidents, regardless of whether or not the incident involved the private sector or a public carrier. They are responsible for recommending preventative measures to avoid future accidents.

nationalization   Public ownership, financing, and operation of a business entity.

no-frills service   Any service or product for which the nonessential features have been removed to keep the price low.

non-asset-based providers   3PLs that fulfill customer requirements via the resources of other companies.

nonintegrated carriers   Air carrier companies that only provide service from airport to airport.

nonjoint common costs

O

ocean bill of lading   A contract for transportation between a shipper and an ocean carrier, which also evidences receipt of the cargo by the carrier.

Ocean Shipping Reform Act   Federal law passed in 1998 that effected significant deregulation of the ocean carrier industry.

oligopoly   A shared monopoly where there are few suppliers and, in the case of transportation, entry barriers and cost are significant. Examples would be railroads and airlines.

open account   A credit account extended by a business to a customer or another business.

operating ratio   A measure of operating efficiency defined as operating expenses/operating revenues $\times$ 100.

out-of-pocket costs

outsourcing   Purchasing a logistics service from an outside firm, as opposed to performing it in-house.

P

packing list   A detailed inventory of the contents of a shipment.

passenger airplanes   Aircraft designed to carry people.

passenger revenues   Fares paid by passengers for traveling on transportation routes.

passenger transportation   The means and equipment necessary for the movement of persons, as opposed to freight.

passenger-mile   A measure of output for passenger transportation that reflects the number of passengers transported and the distance traveled; a multiplication of passengers hauled and distance traveled.

peddle run   A truck operation where many pickups or deliveries are made while the vehicle travels over a preset route.

penetration price   A pricing strategy that sets a price designed to allow the supplier to enter a market where there is already established competition by slightly underpricing the existing firms.

per se violation   A violation of the law that is, on its own, deemed to be harmful, regardless of its effect on the market or competitors.

physical distribution management   The management and control of the activities involved in the storage, handling, and movement of goods within an organization and in their shipment to customers.

pickup and delivery (PUD)   The act of collecting freight from shippers or delivering freight to consignees.

Pipeline and Hazardous Material Safety Administration   Federal agency, created in 2004, whose primary focus is pipeline safety and hazardous materials transportation safety operations.

place utility   The usefulness or value of a good or service as a function of the location at which it is made available; For example, snow shovels have greater place utility in Boston than in El Paso.

place value   The usefulness or value of a good or service as a function of the location at which it is made available; For example, snow shovels have greater place utility in Boston than in El Paso.

police powers   The United States constitutionally granted right for the states to establish regulations to protect their citizens' health and welfare; truck weight and speed, length, and height laws are examples.

port authority A state or local government that owns, operates, or otherwise provides wharf, dock, and other terminal investments at ports.

postponement strategy Method of reducing risk by delaying a commitment of resources.

private air carrier Air carrier that only transports company personnel or freight for the company that owns or leases the planes in support of the company's primary business.

private carrier A carrier that provides transportation service to the firm that owns or leases the vehicles and does not charge a fee. Private motor carriers may haul at a fee for wholly owned subsidiaries.

private service Charter service where the ships are owned or leased on a long-term basis by the company moving the goods.

product density The mass of a product that directly impacts the use of the carrier's vehicle and the cost per hundredweight.

profit maximization The process by which a firm determines the price and output level that returns the greatest profit.

pro-forma invoice A document issued by the seller to acquaint the importer/buyer and the importing country's government authorities with the details of the shipment.

pure competition A condition in which there are a large number of sellers, the product or service is standardized and interchangeable, and no one seller can control the price or output. An example would be the LTL sector.

Q

qualitative risk analysis A baseline evaluation of risks.

quantitative risk analysis

quantity utility The usefulness or value of a good or service as a function of timely delivery and undamaged condition.

R

Radio Frequency Identification (RFID) Signal that can tag a container, trailer, or car to track the progress of the shipment.

Railroad Revitalization and Regulatory Reform Act of 1976 (4R Act) Federal statute that provided federal funding for the startup of Conrail.

rate base point The major shipping point in a local area; carriers consider all points in the local area to be the rate basis point.

rate basis number This number is an expression of the relative distance between an origin and a destination. The number may be given in miles or another factor and will form one of the required inputs to develop a rate between the two points.

Reed-Bulwinkle Act of 1948 Federal law permitting motor carriers to fix rates in concert with each other, thus exempting such carriers from antitrust laws.

regional carriers A for-hire air carrier, usually certificated, that has annual operating revenues of less than $100 million; the carrier usually operates within a particular region of the country.

Regional Rail Reorganization Act of 1973 (3R Act) A law passed by Congress in response to the bankruptcies of the Penn Central and other railroads. Conrail, which has since been purchased by the Norfolk Southern Railroad and CSX, was created from this law to operate the lines of six northeastern U.S. railroads.

relative use A fee placed on the users of a service or facility to cover the cost of providing that service or facility.

relay terminals A motor carrier terminal that facilitates the substitution of one driver for another who has driven the maximum hours permitted.

reliability A carrier selection criterion that considers the carrier transit time variation; the consistency of the transit time the carrier provides.

reliable Suitable or fit to be relied upon; dependable.

resiliency The ability to recover from or adjust easily to misfortune or change.

return on investment (ROI) The amount of money realized or generated on an investment that flows back to the lenders. This is often used to gauge the worthiness of an investment by measuring the potential profits and the source of the capital.

revenue miles

reverse flow logistics Logistical systems for the return of products that were unacceptable to the buyer for some reason (damage, maintenance, obsolescence, etc.); employed by an increasing number of organizations.

reverse logistics system

rights-of-way The privilege of someone to pass over land belonging to someone else; the right of one vehicle or vessel to take precedence over another; the passage consisting of a path or strip of land over which someone has the legal right to pass.

risk identification The effort to discover, define, describe, document, and communicate hazards before they become realized.

risk management   Systematic approach to identifying risk, its causes and effects, and its ownership with a goal of reducing or eliminating hazards.

risk mitigation   Reduction of the chance of a hazard occurring.

risk retention   Self-insurance; a company may determine that it is more economical to forgo cargo insurance for the anticipated risks and bear the loss itself.

risk transfer   Purchasing insurance to cover anticipated risks.

Robinson-Patman Act of 1936   Federal law that prohibits sales that discriminate in price on the sale of goods to equally situated distributors when the effect of such sales is to reduce competition.

roller deck   The main deck of an air freighter equipped with rollers on the floor, which allows palletized or containerized cargo to be pushed into position.

roll-on/roll-off   A type of vessel that has ramps upon which vehicles can be driven directly into the hold of the ship. This type of vessel is often used to transport buses, trucks, construction machinery on wheels, and other types of wheeled shipments.

routing   Directing to a specific direction or destination.

routing and scheduling   Directing to a specific direction or destination by a predetermined time.

Rule of reason   An alleged violation of an antitrust law where economic harm to competitors must be proved.

S

seaports

seating capacity   The maximum number of passengers that can be accommodated.

security   The actions of a carrier to protect the goods entrusted to their care from loss or damage.

separable costs

Sherman Antitrust Act   A body of law that restricts businesses' ability to dominate a market by engaging in certain practices. This includes price fixing and other free-market-constricting activities.

shipbrokers   A firm that serves as a go-between for the tramp ship owner and the chartering consignor or consignee.

Shipper's Export Declaration   A document filed by the shipper/exporter or its agent with the government of the country in which the shipper/exporter resides. This form supplies the government with information about the shipment for statistical and control purposes.

shipper's letter of instructions   Document that spells out the requirements for handling in transit goods; important when the cargo is susceptible to damage or requires special attention, such as live animals and plants.

Shipping Act of 1984   A body of law that governs the pricing and services of ocean carriers operating between the United States and foreign countries.

side-by-side   A merger of railroads whose lines operate in proximity of each other, rather than end-to-end.

sight draft   A customer's order to a financial institution holding the customer's funds to pay all or part of them to another institution in which the customer has another account.

skimming price   A price set by a provider who seeks to attract a market that is more interested in quality, uniqueness, or status and is relatively unconcerned with price.

slip seat operation   A motor carrier relay terminal operation in which a carrier substitutes one driver for another who has accumulated the maximum driving time hours.

social responsibility pricing   Lowering prices in pursuit of advancing ethical or social values apart from maximizing profitability.

Staggers Act of 1980   Federal statute that provided major deregulation of the railroad industry.

Staggers Rail Act of 1980   Federal statute that provided major deregulation of the railroad industry.

standards   Accepted or approved examples of something against which others are judged or measured.

state regulation   Laws passed on the state and federal level that restrict a company's freedom of action.

statutory law   This is based on the Roman legal system and refers to a body of law passed by legislative bodies.

stem time   The time consumed by a truck to reach its first delivery after leaving the terminal and the time consumed by the truck to return to the terminal after making its last pickup.

stevedore services   Services provided by persons employed in loading or unloading cargo from ships.

stevedores   Persons employed in loading or unloading cargo from ships.

stowability and handling   The ease or difficulty experienced in loading, handling, and unloading freight. This factor influences the carrier's cost of providing a service and will be reflected in the price charged for the shipment. These are also two of the four factors considered when classifying freight.

subsidies   Grants by a government to a private person or company to assist an enterprise or industry deemed advantageous to the public.

sunk costs

supertankers   The largest of the ships designed for the bulk transport of oil.

supply chain interruptions   Problems with a transportation channel that fall outside the control of the company.

supply chain management   The integration of the flows of products, information, and financials through the entire supply pipeline from the supplier's supplier to the customer's customer.

Surface Transportation Board   The agency created under the Interstate Commerce Commission Termination (ICC) to replace the ICC and exercise economic jurisdiction of the modes of transportation.

survival-based pricing   The use of low prices to increase cash flow and volume and to encourage the higher utilization of equipment.

sustainability   The skill or potential of a process or a thing to retain itself without interference.

T

tariffs   A publication that contains a carrier's rates, accessorial charges, and rules.

terminals   Either end of a carrier line having facilities for the handling of freight and passengers.

terms of payment   Contractual terms governing what will be given in exchange for the object of the transaction and the method of its delivery.

terms of trade   In an international transaction, terms specified in the contract that determine which shipping responsibilities are handled by the exporter (the international supplier) and which are managed by the importer (the company making the purchase).

TEU

third-degree price discrimination   A situation where a seller sets two or more different prices for separate groups of buyers of essentially the same commodity.

third-party logistics   An external supplier that performs all or part of a company's logistics functions.

through bill of lading   A single bill of lading covering receipt of the cargo at the point of origin for delivery to the ultimate consignee, using two or more modes of transportation both domestically and internationally.

time charter   A rental or long-term lease that includes both the vessel and the crew and is for a specific length of time.

time draft   A customer's order to a financial institution holding the customer's funds that is payable at a specified point in the future or under certain circumstances.

time utility   The usefulness or value of a good or service as a function of its timeliness in meeting seasonal demand; the demand for a particular commodity may exist only during certain periods of time.

time value of funds   This relates to the value of money over the lifetime of a project. As inflation reduces the value or purchasing capability of a dollar over the life of a project, this must be taken into consideration when establishing an interest or discount rate for the borrowed funds.

TL (truckload)   A shipment weighing the minimum weight or more. Carriers give a rate reduction for shipping a TL-size shipment.

ton-mile   A unit of measurement utilizing the distance that freight is hauled (measured in miles) and the weight of the cargo being hauled (measured in tons), expressed as a product (that is, multiplied by each other); thus moving one ton for one mile generates one ton-mile.

total fixed costs

total landed cost   Total cost of a product once it has arrived at the buyer's door, including the original cost of the item, all brokerage and logistics fees, complete shipping costs, customs duties, tariffs, taxes, insurance, currency conversion, crating costs, and handling fees.

tracing   Determining a shipment's location during the course of a move.

tracking   Observing, plotting, and reporting the location of cargo or a cargo item throughout the transportation channel.

Trailer-on-flatcar (TOFC)   A method where a highway trailer complete with wheels and chassis is loaded on a flatcar.

transfer of ownership   Act of conveying possession along with its benefits and responsibilities.

transit time   The total time that elapses between a shipment's pickup and its delivery.

transload freight   Freight that must be handled individually and transferred between transportation equipment multiple times.

transportation management systems (TMS)   Logistics tool used to improve management of a firm's transportation processes, both inbound and outbound. A TMS can help optimize the movements of freight into multiple facilities, assist in tracking the freight through the supply chain, and then manage the freight payment process to the user's carrier base.

twenty-foot equivalent units (TEUs)   Twenty-foot equivalent unit, a standardized intermodal container.

U

U.S. Coast Guard   A branch of the U.S. military (but operating under the Department of Homeland Security during peacetime) whose mission is maritime law enforcement.

U.S. Department of Transportation   A federal Cabinet department of the U.S. government, established in 1966, which is concerned with transportation.

U.S. Post Office   Federal agency responsible for the posting, receipt, sorting, handling, transmission, or delivery of mail.

unit charge   A shipping charge assessed for use of a facility or resource; variable according to use, but does not distinguish between passengers or freight within each unit.

unit load devices   Specialized containers used in air freighters that fit properly within the rounded fuselage of an aircraft.

unit train   An entire, uninterrupted locomotive, car, and caboose movement between an origin and a destination.

unit volume pricing   This is a technique whereby the carrier sets its prices to utilize its capacity to the fullest. Multiple pickup discounts in the LTL area and multiple car rates in the railroad sector would be two examples.

user charges   Costs or fees that the user of a service or facility must pay to the party furnishing this service or facility. An example would be the landing fee an airline pays to an airport when one of its aircraft lands or takes off.

V

value of service   The rates charged for a transportation service or a particular level of service influence the demand for the product and thus the demand to transport the product; this impact on demand can be assessed as the value of service provided to the user of the product.

Value-of-service pricing   Pricing according to the value of the product the company is transporting; third-degree price discrimination; demand-oriented pricing; charging what the traffic will bear.

variable costs

vertically integrated   It is a process in which the supply chain of the firm is self-owned.

visibility   In the context of cargo shipping, the capability to track the whereabouts of items throughout their journey through the channel.

voyage charter   A rental or term lease that includes both the vessel and the crew and is for a specific trip.

W

working conditions   The physical environment in which an employee works, including the actual space, the quality of ventilation, heat, and light, and the degree of safety.

Z

zone pricing   The constant pricing of a product at all geographic locations within a zone.

Name Index

Subject Index